D0045083

P.S.
j305.231
FRO

neighborhoods : the
science of early child
development.
03/07/2011

DATE DUE

JUN 2 7 2011	
SEP - 2 2011	
MAR 2 9 2013	
JAN 2 9 2014	

GAYLORD   PRINTED IN U.S.A.

From Neurons
to Neighborhoods

The Science of
Early Childhood
Development

Committee on Integrating the Science of
Early Childhood Development

Jack P. Shonkoff and
Deborah A. Phillips, *Editors*

Board on Children, Youth, and Families

National Research Council
and
Institute of Medicine

NATIONAL ACADEMY PRESS
Washington, D.C.

NATIONAL ACADEMY PRESS   2101 Constitution Avenue, N.W.   Washington, D.C. 20418

NOTICE: The project that is the subject of this report was approved by the Governing Board of the National Research Council, whose members are drawn from the councils of the National Academy of Sciences, the National Academy of Engineering, and the Institute of Medicine. The members of the committee responsible for the report were chosen for their special competences and with regard for appropriate balance.

The study was supported by funds provided by the National Institute of Child Health and Human Development, the National Institute of Mental Health, the Office of Maternal and Child Health Bureau of the Health Resources and Services Administration, the Substance Abuse and Mental Health Services Administration, the Centers for Disease Control and Prevention, the National Institute of Nursing Research, the U.S. Department of Health and Human Services' Office of the Assistant Secretary for Planning and Evaluation, the Administration on Children, Youth, and Families, the Administration for Children and Families, the Office of Special Education Programs in the U.S. Department of Education, The Commonwealth Fund, the Ewing Marion Kauffman Foundation, the Heinz Endowments, the Irving B. Harris Foundation, and National Academies funds. Any opinions, findings, conclusions, or recommendations expressed in this publication are those of the author(s) and do not necessarily reflect the view of the organizations or agencies that provided support for this project.

Library of Congress Cataloging-in-Publication Data

From neurons to neighborhoods : the science of early child development / Jack P. Shonkoff and Deborah A. Phillips, editors.
    p. cm.
    Includes bibliographical references and index.
    ISBN 0-309-06988-2 (hardover : alk. paper)
    1. Child development—United States. 2. Preschool children—United States. 3. Preschool children—Services for—United States. 4. Nature and nurture—United States. 5. Early childhood education—United States. I. Shonkoff, Jack P. II. Phillips, Deborah.
HQ767.9.F76 2000
301.231—dc21   00-010760

Additional copies of this report are available from National Academy Press, 2101 Constitution Avenue, N.W., Lockbox 285, Washington, D.C. 20055. Call (800) 624-6242 or (202) 334-3313 (in the Washington metropolitan area). This report is also available online at http://www.nap.edu

Printed in the United States of America

Copyright 2000 by the National Academy of Sciences. All rights reserved.

Suggested citation: National Research Council and Institute of Medicine (2000) *From Neurons to Neighborhoods: The Science of Early Childhood Development.* Committee on Integrating the Science of Early Childhood Development. Jack P. Shonkoff and Deborah A. Phillips, eds. Board on Children, Youth, and Families, Commission on Behavioral and Social Sciences and Education. Washington, D.C.: National Academy Press.

THE NATIONAL ACADEMIES

National Academy of Sciences
National Academy of Engineering
Institute of Medicine
National Research Council

The **National Academy of Sciences** is a private, nonprofit, self-perpetuating society of distinguished scholars engaged in scientific and engineering research, dedicated to the furtherance of science and technology and to their use for the general welfare. Upon the authority of the charter granted to it by the Congress in 1863, the Academy has a mandate that requires it to advise the federal government on scientific and technical matters. Dr. Bruce M. Alberts is president of the National Academy of Sciences.

The **National Academy of Engineering** was established in 1964, under the charter of the National Academy of Sciences, as a parallel organization of outstanding engineers. It is autonomous in its administration and in the selection of its members, sharing with the National Academy of Sciences the responsibility for advising the federal government. The National Academy of Engineering also sponsors engineering programs aimed at meeting national needs, encourages education and research, and recognizes the superior achievements of engineers. Dr. William A. Wulf is president of the National Academy of Engineering.

The **Institute of Medicine** was established in 1970 by the National Academy of Sciences to secure the services of eminent members of appropriate professions in the examination of policy matters pertaining to the health of the public. The Institute acts under the responsibility given to the National Academy of Sciences by its congressional charter to be an adviser to the federal government and, upon its own initiative, to identify issues of medical care, research, and education. Dr. Kenneth I. Shine is president of the Institute of Medicine.

The **National Research Council** was organized by the National Academy of Sciences in 1916 to associate the broad community of science and technology with the Academy's purposes of furthering knowledge and advising the federal government. Functioning in accordance with general policies determined by the Academy, the Council has become the principal operating agency of both the National Academy of Sciences and the National Academy of Engineering in providing services to the government, the public, and the scientific and engineering communities. The Council is administered jointly by both Academies and the Institute of Medicine. Dr. Bruce M. Alberts and Dr. William A. Wulf are chairman and vice chairman, respectively, of the National Research Council.

COMMITTEE ON INTEGRATING THE SCIENCE
OF EARLY CHILDHOOD DEVELOPMENT

JACK P. SHONKOFF (*Chair*), Heller Graduate School, Brandeis University

DEBORAH L. COATES, Department of Psychology, The City University of New York

GREG DUNCAN, Institute for Policy Research, School of Education and Social Policy, Northwestern University

FELTON J. EARLS, Department of Child Psychology, Harvard Medical School

ROBERT N. EMDE, Department of Psychiatry, University of Colorado Health Sciences Center

YOLANDA GARCIA, Children's Services, Santa Clara County Office of Education

SUSAN GELMAN, Department of Psychology, University of Michigan

SUSAN J. GOLDIN-MEADOW, Department of Psychology, University of Chicago

WILLIAM T. GREENOUGH, Departments of Psychology and Cell and Structural Biology, University of Illinois at Champaign-Urbana

RUTH T. GROSS, Department of Pediatrics (emeritus), Stanford University Medical School

MEGAN GUNNAR, Institute of Child Development, University of Minnesota

MICHAEL GURALNICK, Center on Human Development and Disability, University of Washington

ALICIA F. LIEBERMAN, Department of Psychiatry, University of California at San Francisco

BETSY LOZOFF, Center for Human Growth and Development, University of Michigan

BRIAN MacWHINNEY, Department of Psychology, Carnegie Mellon University*

RUTH MASSINGA, The Casey Family Program, Seattle, Washington

STEPHEN RAUDENBUSH, School of Education, University of Michigan

ROSS THOMPSON, Department of Psychology, University of Nebraska

CHARLES A. NELSON (*liaison from the MacArthur Foundation/ McDonnell Foundation Research Network on Early Experience and Brain Development*), Institute of Child Development, University of Minnesota

DEBORAH A. PHILLIPS, *Study Director*
NANCY GEYELIN MARGIE, *Research Assistant*
RONNÉ WINGATE, *Senior Project Assistant*

*Resigned October 1998.

BOARD ON CHILDREN, YOUTH, AND FAMILIES

JACK P. SHONKOFF *(Chair)*, Heller Graduate School, Brandeis University

EVAN CHARNEY *(Vice Chair)*, Department of Pediatrics, University of Massachusetts Medical Center

JAMES BANKS, Center for Multicultural Education, University of Washington

SHEILA BURKE, John F. Kennedy School of Government, Harvard University

DAVID CARD, Department of Economics, University of California, Berkeley

DONALD COHEN, Department of Child Psychiatry, Yale University

MINDY FULLILOVE, Department of Clinical Psychobiology, Columbia University

KEVIN GRUMBACH, Department of Family and Community Medicine, University of California, San Francisco

MAXINE HAYES, Community and Family Health, Department of Health, Olympia, Washington

MARGARET HEAGARTY, Department of Pediatrics, Harlem Hospital Center, Columbia University

RENÉE JENKINS, Department of Pediatrics and Child Health, Howard University Hospital

SHEILA KAMERMAN, School of Social Work, Columbia University

HARRIET KITZMAN, School of Nursing, University of Rochester

SANDERS KORENMAN, School of Public Affairs, Baruch College

HONORABLE CINDY LEDERMAN, Circuit Court Judge, Juvenile Division, Dade County, Florida

SARA McLANAHAN, Office of Population Research, Princeton University

VONNIE McLOYD, Department of Psychology, University of Michigan, Ann Arbor

PAUL NEWACHECK, Institute of Health Policy Studies and Department of Pediatrics, University of California, San Francisco

GARY SANDEFUR, Department of Sociology, University of Wisconsin, Madison

RUTH STEIN, Department of Pediatrics, Albert Einstein College of Medicine

PAUL WISE, Department of Pediatrics, Boston Medical Center

RUTH T. GROSS *(liaison from the Board on Health Promotion and Disease Prevention, Institute of Medicine)*, Department of Pediatrics (emeritus), Stanford University

ELEANOR MACCOBY *(liaison from the Commission on Behavioral and Social Sciences and Education, National Research Council)*, Department of Psychology (emeritus), Stanford University
WILLIAM ROPER *(liaison from the Institute of Medicine)*, School of Public Health, University of North Carolina, Chapel Hill

MICHELE D. KIPKE, *Director*
ELENA O. NIGHTINGALE, *Scholar-in-Residence*
MARY GRAHAM, *Associate Director, Dissemination and Communications*
MARY STRIGARI, *Administrative Associate*

Acknowledgments

From Neurons to Neighborhoods is the product of a two-and-a-half-year project during which 17 individuals, as a committee, evaluated and integrated the current science of early childhood development. In view of the wide range of scientific and policy considerations that fall within the scope of the committee's mandate, it is particularly significant that the funding for this project was provided by a broad diversity of public and private sponsors: Administration for Children and Families, Administration on Children, Youth, and Families, Assistant Secretary for Planning and Evaluation, Centers for Disease Control and Prevention, Maternal and Child Health Bureau of the Health Resources and Services Administration, National Institute for Child Health and Human Development, National Institute of Mental Health, National Institute of Nursing Research, and the Substance Abuse and Mental Health Services Administration, all of the U.S. Department of Health and Human Services; Office of Special Education Programs in the U.S. Department of Education; The Commonwealth Fund; Irving B. Harris Foundation; Heinz Endowments; and Ewing Marion Kauffman Foundation. The committee wishes to express particular appreciation to Duane Alexander, director of the National Institute of Child Health and Human Development, and Ann Rosewater, regional director of the U.S. Department of Health and Human Services for Region IV, who played a critical role in organizing an early meeting with potential federal sponsors and demonstrated unwavering faith in the ability of the committee to address its very ambitious charge.

Beyond the expertise and diligence of the committee, we had the extraordinary good fortune of working with a number of highly knowledgeable people who shared our enthusiasm for this project. We are deeply indebted to the intellectual insights and support that they provided.

In June 1999 the committee convened a two-day Workshop on the Science of Developmental Promotion and Early Childhood Intervention. Participants included leading researchers and practitioners from the fields of pediatric primary care and nursing, child care and early childhood education, child welfare, mental heath, public health, early intervention for children living in poverty, and early intervention for children with developmental disabilities: Kathryn Barnard, University of Washington; Barbara T. Bowman, Erikson Institute, Chicago; Jeanne Brooks-Gunn, Columbia University; Mary Beth Bruder, University of Connecticut Health Center; Mary Dozier, University of Delaware; Dale Farran, Vanderbilt University; Veronica Feeg, George Mason University; Barbara Howard, Johns Hopkins University School of Medicine; Jane Knitzer, Columbia University; Samuel Meisels, University of Michigan; Craig Ramey, University of Alabama at Birmingham; Arnold Sameroff, University of Michigan; Ruby Takanishi, Foundation for Child Development; Deborah Klein Walker, Massachusetts Department of Public Health; Mark Wolery, University of North Carolina at Chapel Hill; and Hiro Yoshikawa, New York University. All of the workshop participants, both in their prepared written comments and through their contributions during the discussion sessions, added valuable scientific input to the committee's work. Two additional workshops organized by the Board on Children, Youth, and Families, one on home visiting interventions and another on early precursors of antisocial behavior, also contributed greatly to our work. The committee and staff are grateful to everyone who participated in these meetings.

We also wish to acknowledge several consultants who contributed to the committee process: Donald Hernandez, State University of New York at Albany, who provided data and advice on the demographics of the birth to five age group; Laurence Leonard, Purdue University, who advised us on atypical language development; Joshua Brown, Columbia University, for his synthesis of the literature on the developmental consequences of community violence; Kathleen Allen-Wallner, National Institute on Child Health and Human Development, for her synthesis of research on regulation of attention and executive function in young children; and Michael Georgieff, University of Minnesota Hospital, who provided extensive information and advice on the effects of prematurity on early brain development. We would also like to thank Bonnie Keilty, a doctoral student in education and human development at George Washington University, for her assistance with the committee's review of the literature on early intervention and her staff support for the Workshop on the Science of Developmental Promotion and Early Childhood Intervention. In addition, many generous hours of expert consultation were provided by Charles A. Nelson, chair of the John D. and Catherine T. MacArthur Foundation and James S. McDonnell Foundation Research Network on Early Experience and Brain Development, who served as a formal liaison to the committee.

In addition to formal workshops, a number of individuals were invited to make presentations and participate in discussions at committee meetings. In December 1998, H. Hill Goldsmith, University of Wisconsin at Madison, Kathleen R. Merikangas, Yale University, and David Reiss, George Washington University Medical Center, participated in a panel on the genetics of early development, which informed the committee about cutting-edge research on a range of issues in this area. In July 1999, Joseph Campos, University of California at Berkeley, addressed the interplay of experience and early brain development, and Robert LeVine, Harvard University, spoke about the promise of cross-cultural research, the symbiotic development of individuals and societies, and the importance of integrating knowledge and research methods from a variety of disciplines.

A number of experts assisted the committee by responding in writing to questions about the relations among culture, early childhood development, and early interventions. We are grateful to the following individuals for their thoughtful comments on this issue: Catherine Cooper, University of California at Santa Cruz; Doris Entwisle, Johns Hopkins University; Andrew Fuligni, New York University; Harriette McAdoo, Michigan State University; Suzanne Randolph, University of Maryland at College Park; Diana Slaughter-Dafoe, University of Pennsylvania; Paul Spicer, University of Colorado Health Sciences Center; Ruby Takanishi, Foundation for Child Development; and Thomas Weisner, University of California at Los Angeles.

We would also like to thank Thomas Cook and Ken Howard, Northwestern University, for sharing their expertise in intervention methods and for helping the committee examine research and evaluation methods in depth.

Shortly after the initiation of the study process, the committee interviewed a broad cross-section of individuals involved in early childhood policy and service delivery (in contrast to research) to ensure that the final report would be responsive to the issues that practitioners and local and state government officials are dealing with every day. We are grateful to the following people for taking the time to share their expertise: Douglas Baird, Associated Day Care Services; Hedy Chang, California Tomorrow; Veronica Feeg, George Mason University; Andrea Genser, Center for Career Development in Early Care and Education, Wheelock College; Stacie Goffin, National Association for the Education of Young Children; Douglas Howard, Family Independence Agency, State of Michigan; Elizabeth Iida, SRI International; Barbara Ferguson Kamara, Office of Early Childhood Development, District of Columbia Department of Human Services; Andrew Kennedy, Los Angeles County Office of Education; Joan Lombardi, Child and Family Policy Specialist, formerly with the Child Care Bureau of the U.S. Department of Health and Human Services; Matthew Melmed, Zero to Three: National Center for Infants, Toddlers and Families; Cheryl Mitchell, Vermont Agency of Human Services; Karabelle Pizzigatti, Child Welfare League of America; Calvin Sia, Hawaii Medical Association; Jolene Smith, Santa Clara County, Social Services Agency; Valora Washington, Unitarian Universalist Service Committee; and Barry Zuckerman, Boston Medical Center.

We are grateful to the following people for reviewing our syntheses of research on a variety of topics: Geraldine Dawson, University of Washington, for reviewing the section on maternal depression; Michael Georgieff, University of Minnesota Hospital, and Sandra Jacobson, Wayne State University, for their careful reading and feedback on early versions of Chapter 8, The Developing Brain; Lawrence Hirschfeld, University of Michigan, for clarifying our representation of his work on preschoolers' conceptualization of race; Tama Leventhal, Columbia University, for her assistance with the literature on continuity of care and turbulence; Kenneth Rubin, University of Maryland, Willard Hartup, University of Minnesota, and Carollee Howes, University of California at Los Angeles, for reviewing early drafts of Chapter 7, Making Friends and Getting Along with Peers; Delia Vazquez, University of Michigan Medical School, and Seymour Levine, University of California at Davis, for reviewing the section on neuropeptides; and Steven Warren, Vanderbilt University, for reviewing a portion of Chapter 6, Communicating and Learning.

Dozens of scientists provided articles, papers, chapters, and books. We are most appreciative of the generous responses to requests for information that we received from: Lynette Aytch, University of North Carolina at Chapel Hill; John Barks, University of Michigan; Cathryn Booth, University of Washington; Mary Bowler, U.S. Bureau of Labor Statistics; Sandra Calvert, Georgetown University; Harry Chugani, Wayne State University; James Connor, Pennsylvania State University; E. Mark Cummings, University of Notre Dame; Geraldine Dawson, University of Washington; Barbara Devaney, Mathematica Policy Research, Inc.; Susan Dickstein, Brown University; JoAnn Farver, University of Southern California; Marc Fey, University of Kansas Medical Center; Daniel Goldowitz, University of Tennessee; Mari Golub, University of California at Davis; John Hewitt, University of Colorado at Boulder; Jay Hirschman and colleagues, U.S. Department of Agriculture; Myron Hofer, Columbia University; Carollee Howes, University of California at Los Angeles; Aletha Huston, University of Texas at Austin; Mark Innocenti, Utah State University; Sandra Jacobson, Wayne State University; Mark Johnson, Birkbeck College, University of London;

Jerome Kagan, Harvard University; Peter Kaplan, University of Colorado at Denver; Eric Knudsen, Stanford University; Mary Clare Lennon, Columbia University; Tama Leventhal, Columbia University; Mark Lipsey, Vanderbilt University; Bruce McEwen, The Rockefeller University; Editha Nottelman, National Institute of Mental Health; David Olds, University of Colorado at Denver; Joy Osofsky, Louisiana State University Health Sciences Center; Bruce Pennington, University of Denver; Tony Raden, Columbia University; Mabel Rice, University of Kansas; Donald Roberts, Stanford University; Robert Sapolsky, Stanford University; Mary Schneider, University of Wisconsin at Madison; Carla Shatz, University of California at Berkeley; L. Alan Sroufe, University of Minnesota; Phillip Strain, University of Colorado at Denver; Ann Streissguth, University of Washington; Douglas Teti, University of Maryland at Baltimore County; Edward Tronick, Harvard University; Delia Vazquez, University of Michigan Medical School; Peter Vietze, New York State Institute for Basic Research in Developmental Disabilities; Douglas Wahsten, University of Alberta; Joanne Weinberg, University of British Columbia; Larry Wissow, Johns Hopkins University; Fred Wulczyn, Chapin Hall Center for Children, University of Chicago; Paul Yoder, Vanderbilt University; and Charles Zeanah, Jr., Tulane University School of Medicine.

We would also like to thank Gina Adams and Jennifer Ehrle, The Urban Institute, who provided data from the 1997 National Survey of American Families; Jerry West and DeeAnn Brimhall, U.S. Department of Education, who generated multiple tables for us from the 1999 National Household Education Survey; Paul Newacheck, University of California at San Francisco, who provided data from the 1996 National Health Interview Survey; Christine Ross, Mathematica Policy Research, Inc., who provided information about infant child care in the context of welfare reform; Steve Savner and Rachel Schumacher, Center for Law and Social Policy, who provided information from the State Policy Documentation Project; and Kristen Smith, U.S. Bureau of the Census, who provided data from the Survey of Income and Program Participation.

This report has been reviewed by individuals chosen for their diverse perspectives and technical expertise, in accordance with procedures approved by the Report Review Committee of the National Research Council. The purpose of this independent review is to provide candid and critical comments that will assist the authors and the National Research Council/ Institute of Medicine in making the published report as sound as possible and to ensure that the report meets institutional standards for objectivity, evidence, and responsiveness to the study charge. The review comments and draft manuscript remain confidential to protect the integrity of the deliberative process.

We thank the following individuals for their participation in the review of this report: Thomas Cook, Institute for Policy Research, Northwestern University; Roy D'Andrade, Department of Anthropology, University of California, San Diego; William Danforth, Washington University, St. Louis; Dale D. Farran, Department of Teaching and Learning, Vanderbilt University; Nathan Glazer, Professor of Education and Sociology, Emeritus, Harvard University; Jacqueline Goodnow, Department of Psychology, Macquerie University, New South Wales, Australia; Myron A. Hofer, College of Physicians & Surgeons of Columbia University; Jerome Kagan, Department of Psychology, Harvard University; Sanders Korenman, School of Public Affairs, Baruch College, City University of New York; Eleanor Maccoby, Department of Psychology, Stanford University; Barbara Rogoff, Psychology Department, University of California, Santa Cruz; Michael Rutter, Social, Genetic, and Developmental Psychiatry Research Center, Institute of Psychiatry, London, England; and Richard Weinberg, Institute of Child Development, University of Minnesota.

Although the individuals listed above have provided many constructive comments and suggestions, responsibility for the final content of this report rests solely with the authoring committee and the National Research Council (NRC) and the Institute of Medicine (IOM).

The committee wishes to recognize the important contributions and support provided by several individuals connected to the NRC and IOM. We thank the original members of the Board on Children, Youth, and Families, under the leadership of its founding chair, Sheldon White, who believed in the importance of this study from the time it was first proposed in 1993, and supported the protracted, multiyear search for funding that culminated in its full implementation. We also thank Kenneth Shine, Susanne Stoiber, Barbara Torrey, Faith Mitchell, Michele Kipke, and Clyde Behney for their steadfast support of the project and their critical reviews of early drafts of the report. We are deeply indebted to Eugenia Grohman, associate director for reports of CBASSE, who patiently worked with us through several revisions, and Christine McShane, who provided superb editorial assistance. Mary Graham patiently proofread the entire report and has provided superb advice and assistance with report dissemination, as has Vanee Vines of the National Academies' Office of News and Public Information. We are also grateful to Katherine Magnuson at Northwestern University for her extensive assistance with research on the portions of the report having to do with family resources and neighborhoods. In addition, we wish to acknowledge the research assistance provided by Pam Gardner at the University of Michigan and Jeanette Mitchell and Mariolga Reyes at the City University of New York and the administrative support provided by Amy Belue at the Heller Graduate School at Brandeis University.

Finally, it would be impossible to overstate the extraordinary effort and critical contributions of Nancy Geyelin Margie, research assistant, and

Ronné Wingate, project assistant, who served as the primary administrative staff for the committee at the NRC. Each of these talented and highly dedicated individuals played the kind of critical role "behind the scenes" that ensures a successful project. We remain deeply grateful for their exceptional level of support.

Jack P. Shonkoff, *Chair*
Deborah A. Phillips, *Study Director*
Committee on Integrating the Science of
Early Childhood Development

Contents

From Neurons
to Neighborhoods

Executive Summary

Scientists have had a long-standing fascination with the complexities of the process of human development. Parents have always been captivated by the rapid growth and development that characterize the earliest years of their children's lives. Professional service providers continue to search for new knowledge to inform their work. Consequently, one of the distinctive features of the science of early childhood development is the extent to which it evolves under the anxious and eager eyes of millions of families, policy makers, and service providers who seek authoritative guidance as they address the challenges of promoting the health and well-being of young children.

PUTTING THE STUDY IN CONTEXT

Two profound changes over the past several decades have coincided to produce a dramatically altered landscape for early childhood policy, service delivery, and childrearing in the United States. First, an explosion of research in the neurobiological, behavioral, and social sciences has led to major advances in understanding the conditions that influence whether children get off to a promising or a worrisome start in life. These scientific gains have generated a much deeper appreciation of: (1) the importance of early life experiences, as well as the inseparable and highly interactive influences of genetics and environment, on the development of the brain and the unfolding of human behavior; (2) the central role of early relationships

1

as a source of either support and adaptation or risk and dysfunction; (3) the powerful capabilities, complex emotions, and essential social skills that develop during the earliest years of life, and (4) the capacity to increase the odds of favorable developmental outcomes through planned interventions.

Second, the capacity to use this knowledge constructively has been constrained by a number of dramatic transformations in the social and economic circumstances under which families with young children are living in the United States: (1) marked changes in the nature, schedule, and amount of work engaged in by parents of young children and greater difficulty balancing workplace and family responsibilities for parents at all income levels; (2) continuing high levels of economic hardship among families, despite overall increases in maternal education, increased rates of parent employment, and a strong economy; (3) increasing cultural diversity and the persistence of significant racial and ethnic disparities in health and developmental outcomes; 4) growing numbers of young children spending considerable time in child care settings of highly variable quality, starting in infancy; and (5) greater awareness of the negative effects of stress on young children, particularly as a result of serious family problems and adverse community conditions that are detrimental to child well-being. While any given child may be affected by only one or two of these changes, their cumulative effects on the 24 million infants, toddlers, and preschoolers who are now growing up in the United States warrant dedicated attention and thoughtful response.

This convergence of advancing knowledge and changing circumstances calls for a fundamental reexamination of the nation's responses to the needs of young children and their families, many of which were formulated several decades ago and revised only incrementally since then. It demands that scientists, policy makers, business and community leaders, practitioners, and parents work together to identify and sustain policies and practices that are effective, generate new strategies to replace those that are not achieving their objectives, and consider new approaches to address new goals as needed. It is the strong conviction of this committee that the nation has not capitalized sufficiently on the knowledge that has been gained from nearly half a century of considerable public investment in research on children from birth to age 5. In many respects, we have barely begun to use our growing research capabilities to help children and families negotiate the changing demands and possibilities of life in the 21st century.

THE COMMITTEE'S CHARGE

The Committee on Integrating the Science of Early Childhood Development was established by the Board on Children, Youth, and Families of the National Research Council and the Institute of Medicine to update scientific knowledge about the nature of early development and the role of early experiences, to disentangle such knowledge from erroneous popular beliefs or misunderstandings, and to discuss the implications of this knowledge base for early childhood policy, practice, professional development, and research.

The body of research that the committee reviewed is extensive, multi-disciplinary, and more complex than current discourse would lead one to believe. It covers the period from before birth until the first day of kindergarten. It includes efforts to understand how early experience affects all aspects of development—from the neural circuitry of the maturing brain, to the expanding network of a child's social relationships, to both the enduring and the changing cultural values of the society in which parents raise children. It includes efforts to understand the typical trajectories of early childhood, as well as the atypical developmental pathways that characterize the adaptations of children with disabilities.

The committee's review of this evidence addresses two complementary agendas. The first is focused on the future and asks: How can society use knowledge about early childhood development to maximize the nation's human capital and ensure the ongoing vitality of its democratic institutions? The second is focused on the present and asks: How can the nation use knowledge to nurture, protect, and ensure the health and well-being of all young children as an important objective in its own right, regardless of whether measurable returns can be documented in the future? The first agenda speaks to society's economic, political, and social interests. The second speaks to its ethical and moral values. The committee is clear in our responsibility to speak to both.

CORE CONCEPTS OF DEVELOPMENT

As the knowledge generated by interdisciplinary developmental science has evolved and been integrated with lessons from program evaluation and professional experience, a number of core concepts, which are elaborated in the report, have come to frame understanding of the nature of early human development.

1. Human development is shaped by a dynamic and continuous interaction between biology and experience.
2. Culture influences every aspect of human development and is reflected in childrearing beliefs and practices designed to promote healthy adaptation.
3. The growth of self-regulation is a cornerstone of early childhood development that cuts across all domains of behavior.

4. Children are active participants in their own development, reflecting the intrinsic human drive to explore and master one's environment.

5. Human relationships, and the effects of relationships on relationships, are the building blocks of healthy development.

6. The broad range of individual differences among young children often makes it difficult to distinguish normal variations and maturational delays from transient disorders and persistent impairments.

7. The development of children unfolds along individual pathways whose trajectories are characterized by continuities and discontinuities, as well as by a series of significant transitions.

8. Human development is shaped by the ongoing interplay among sources of vulnerability and sources of resilience.

9. The timing of early experiences can matter, but, more often than not, the developing child remains vulnerable to risks and open to protective influences throughout the early years of life and into adulthood.

10. The course of development can be altered in early childhood by effective interventions that change the balance between risk and protection, thereby shifting the odds in favor of more adaptive outcomes.

POLICY AND PRACTICE

The committee's conclusions and recommendations are derived from a rich and extensive knowledge base and are firmly grounded in the following four overarching themes:

- All children are born wired for feelings and ready to learn.
- Early environments matter and nurturing relationships are essential.
- Society is changing and the needs of young children are not being addressed.
- Interactions among early childhood science, policy, and practice are problematic and demand dramatic rethinking.

All Children Are Born Wired for Feelings and Ready to Learn

From the time of conception to the first day of kindergarten, development proceeds at a pace exceeding that of any subsequent stage of life. Efforts to understand this process have revealed the myriad and remarkable accomplishments of the early childhood period, as well as the serious problems that confront some young children and their families long before school entry. A fundamental paradox exists and is unavoidable: development in the early years is both highly robust and highly vulnerable. Although there have been long-standing debates about how much the early years really matter in the larger scheme of lifelong development, our conclusion is unequivocal: What happens during the first months and years of life matters a lot, not because this period of development provides an indelible blueprint for adult well-being, but because it sets either a sturdy or fragile stage for what follows.

Conclusions

• From birth to age 5, children rapidly develop foundational capabilities on which subsequent development builds. In addition to their remarkable linguistic and cognitive gains, they exhibit dramatic progress in their emotional, social, regulatory, and moral capacities. All of these critical dimensions of early development are intertwined, and each requires focused attention.

• Striking disparities in what children know and can do are evident well before they enter kindergarten. These differences are strongly associated with social and economic circumstances, and they are predictive of subsequent academic performance. Redressing these disparities is critical, both for the children whose life opportunities are at stake and for a society whose goals demand that children be prepared to begin school, achieve academic success, and ultimately sustain economic independence and engage constructively with others as adult citizens.

• Early child development can be seriously compromised by social, regulatory, and emotional impairments. Indeed, young children are capable of deep and lasting sadness, grief, and disorganization in response to trauma, loss, and early personal rejection. Given the substantial short- and long-term risks that accompany early mental health impairments, the incapacity of many early childhood programs to address these concerns and the severe shortage of early childhood professionals with mental health expertise are urgent problems.

Recommendations

• **Recommendation 1** — Resources on a par with those focused on literacy and numerical skills should be devoted to translating the knowledge base on young children's emotional, regulatory, and social development into effective strategies for fostering: (1) the development of curiosity, self-direction, and persistence in learning situations; (2) the ability to cooperate, demonstrate caring, and resolve conflict with peers; and (3) the capacity to experience the enhanced motivation associated with feeling competent and loved. Such strategies and their widespread diffusion into the early childhood field must encompass young children both with and without special needs. Successful action on this recommendation will require the long-term, collaborative investment of government, professional organizations, private philanthropy,and voluntary associations.

• **Recommendation 2** — School readiness initiatives should be judged not only on the basis of their effectiveness in improving the performance of the children they reach, but also on the extent to which they make progress in reducing the significant disparities that are observed at school entry in the skills of young children with differing backgrounds.

• **Recommendation 3** — Substantial new investments should be made to address the nation's seriously inadequate capacity for addressing young children's mental health needs. Expanded opportunities for professional training, as recently called for by the Surgeon General, and incentives for individuals with pertinent expertise to work in settings with young children are essential first steps toward more effective screening, early detection, treatment, and ultimate prevention of serious childhood mental health problems.

Early Environments Matter and Nurturing Relationships Are Essential

The scientific evidence on the significant developmental impacts of early experiences, caregiving relationships, and environmental threats is incontrovertible. Virtually every aspect of early human development, from the brain's evolving circuitry to the child's capacity for empathy, is affected by the environments and experiences that are encountered in a cumulative fashion, beginning early in the prenatal period and extending throughout the early childhood years. The science of early development is also clear about the specific importance of parenting and of regular caregiving relationships more generally. The question today is not whether early experience matters, but rather how early experiences shape individual development and contribute to children's continued movement along positive pathways.

Conclusions

• The long-standing debate about the importance of nature *versus* nurture, considered as independent influences, is overly simplistic and scientifically obsolete. Scientists have shifted their focus to take account of the fact that genetic and environmental influences work together in dynamic ways over the course of development. At any time, both are sources of human potential and growth as well as risk and dysfunction. Both genetically determined characteristics and those that are highly affected by experience are open to intervention. The most important questions now concern how environments influence the expression of genes and how genetic makeup, combined with children's previous experiences, affects their ongoing interactions with their environments during the early years and beyond.

• Parents and other regular caregivers in children's lives are "active ingredients" of environmental influence during the early childhood period. Children grow and thrive in the context of close and dependable relationships that provide love and nurturance, security, responsive interaction, and encouragement for exploration. Without at least one such relationship, development is disrupted and the consequences can be severe and long-lasting. If provided or restored, however, a sensitive caregiving relationship can foster remarkable recovery.

• Children's early development depends on the health and well-being of their parents. Yet the daily experiences of a significant number of young children are burdened by untreated mental health problems in their families, recurrent exposure to family violence, and the psychological fallout from living in a demoralized and violent neighborhood. Circumstances characterized by multiple, interrelated, and cumulative risk factors impose particularly heavy developmental burdens during early childhood and are the most likely to incur substantial costs to both the individual and society in the future.

• The time is long overdue for society to recognize the significance of out-of-home relationships for young children, to esteem those who care for them when their parents are not available, and to compensate them adequately as a means of supporting stability and quality in these relationships for all children, regardless of their family's income and irrespective of their developmental needs.

• Early experiences clearly affect the development of the brain. Yet the recent focus on "zero to three" as a critical or particularly sensitive period is highly problematic, not because this isn't an important period for the developing brain, but simply because the disproportionate attention to the period from birth to 3 years begins too late and ends too soon.

• Abundant evidence from the behavioral and the neurobiological sciences has documented a wide range of environmental threats to the developing central nervous system. These include poor nutrition, specific infections, environmental toxins, and drug exposures, beginning early in the prenatal period, as well as chronic stress stemming from abuse or neglect throughout the early childhood years and beyond.

Recommendations

• **Recommendation 4** — Decision makers at all levels of government, as well as leaders from the business community, should ensure that better public and private policies provide parents with viable choices about how to allocate responsibility for child care during the early years of their children's lives. During infancy, there is a pressing need to strike a better balance between options that support parents to care for their infants at home and those that provide affordable, quality child care that enables them to work or go to school. This calls for expanding coverage of the Family and Medical Leave Act to all working parents, pursuing the complex issue of income protection, lengthening the exemption period before states require parents of infants to work as part of welfare reform, and enhancing parents' opportunities to choose from among a range of child care settings that offer the stable, sensitive, and linguistically rich caregiving that fosters positive early childhood development.

• **Recommendation 5** — Environmental protection, reproductive health services, and early intervention efforts should be substantially expanded to reduce documented risks that arise from harmful prenatal and early postnatal neurotoxic exposures, as well as from seriously disrupted early relationships due to chronic mental health problems, substance abuse, and violence in families. The magnitude of these initiatives should be comparable to the attention and resources that have been dedicated to crime prevention, smoking cessation, and the reduction of teen pregnancy. They will require the participation of multiple societal sectors (e.g., private, public, and philanthropic) and the development of multiple strategies.

• **Recommendation 6** — The major funding sources for child care and early childhood education should set aside a dedicated portion of funds to support initiatives that jointly improve the qualifications and increase the compensation and benefits routinely provided to children's nonparental caregivers. These initiatives can be built on the successful experience of the U.S. Department of Defense.

Society Is Changing and the Needs of Young Children Are Not Being Addressed

Profound social and economic transformations are posing serious challenges to the efforts of parents and others to strike a healthy balance between spending time with their children, securing their economic needs, and protecting them from the many risks beyond the home that may have an adverse impact on their health and development.

Conclusions

• Changing parental work patterns are transforming family life. Growing numbers of young children are being raised by working parents whose earnings are inadequate to lift their families out of poverty, whose work entails long and nonstandard hours, and whose economic needs require an early return to work after the birth of a baby. The consequences of the changing context of parental employment for young children are likely to hinge on how it affects the parenting they receive and the quality of the caregiving they experience when they are not with their parents.

• The developmental effects of child care depend on its safety, the opportunities it provides for nurturing and stable relationships, and its provision of linguistically and cognitively rich environments. Yet the child care that is available in the United States today is highly fragmented and characterized by marked variation in quality, ranging from rich, growth-promoting experiences to unstimulating, highly unstable, and sometimes dangerous settings. The burden of poor quality and limited choice rests most heavily on low-income, working families whose financial resources are too high to qualify for subsidies yet too low to afford quality care.

• Young children are the poorest members of society and are more likely to be poor today than they were 25 years ago. Growing up in poverty greatly increases the probability that a child will be exposed to environments and experiences that impose significant burdens on his or her well-being, thereby shifting the odds toward more adverse developmental outcomes. Poverty during the early childhood period may be more damaging than poverty experienced at later ages, particularly with respect to eventual academic attainment. The dual risk of poverty experienced simultaneously in the family and in the surrounding neighborhood, which affects minority children to a much greater extent than other children, increases young children's vulnerability to adverse consequences.

Recommendations

The challenges that arise at the juxtaposition of work, income, and the care of children reflect some of the most complex problems of contemporary society. Rather than offer recommendations for specific actions, many of which have been made before and gone unheeded, the committee wishes to underscore the compelling need for a focused, integrative, and comprehensive reassessment of our nation's child care and income support policies.

• **Recommendation 7** — The President should establish a joint federal-state-local task force charged with reviewing the entire portfolio of public investments in child care and early education. Its goal should be to develop a blueprint for locally responsive systems of early care and education for the coming decade that will ensure the following priorities: (1) that young children's needs are met through sustained relationships with qualified caregivers, (2) that the special needs of children with developmental disabilities or chronic health conditions are addressed, and (3) that the settings in which children spend their time are safe, stimulating, and compatible with the values and priorities of their families.

• **Recommendation 8** — The President's Council of Economic Advisers and the Congress should assess the nation's tax, wage, and income support policies with regard to their adequacy in ensuring that no child who is supported by the equivalent of a full-time working adult lives in poverty and that no family suffers from deep and persistent poverty, regardless of employment status. The product of this effort should be a set of policy alternatives that would move the nation toward achieving these fundamental goals.

Interactions Among Early Childhood Science, Policy, and Practice Are Problematic and Demand Dramatic Rethinking

Policies and programs aimed at improving the life chances of young children come in many varieties. Some are home based and others are delivered in centers. Some focus on children alone or in groups, and others work primarily with parents. A variety of services have been designed to address the needs of young children whose future prospects are threatened by socioeconomic disadvantages, family disruptions, and diagnosed disabilities. They all share a belief that early childhood development is susceptible to environmental influences and that wise public investments in young children can increase the odds of favorable developmental outcomes. The scientific evidence resoundingly supports these premises.

Conclusions

• The overarching question of whether we can intervene successfully in young children's lives has been answered in the affirmative and should be put to rest. However, interventions that work are rarely simple, inexpensive, or easy to implement. The critical agenda for early childhood intervention is to advance understanding of what it takes to improve the odds of positive outcomes for the nation's most vulnerable young children and to determine the most cost-effective strategies for achieving well-defined goals.

• The scientific knowledge base guiding early childhood policies and programs is seriously constrained by the relatively limited availability of systematic and rigorous evaluations of program implementation; gaps in the documentation of causal relations between specific interventions and specific outcomes and of the underlying mechanisms of change; and infrequent assessments of program costs and benefits.

• Model early childhood programs that deliver carefully designed interventions with well-defined objectives and that include well-designed evaluations have been shown to influence the developmental trajectories of children whose life course is threatened by socioeconomic disadvantage, family disruption, and diagnosed disabilities. Programs that combine child-focused educational activities with explicit attention to parent-child interaction patterns and relationship building appear to have the greatest impacts. In contrast, services that are based on generic family support, often without a clear delineation of intervention strategies matched directly to measurable objectives, and that are funded by more modest budgets, appear to be less effective.

• The elements of early intervention programs that enhance social and emotional development are just as important as the components that enhance linguistic and cognitive competence. Some of the strongest long-term impacts of successful interventions have been documented in the domains of social adjustment, such as reductions in criminal behavior.

• The reconciliation of traditional program formats and strategies—many of which emphasize the importance of active parent involvement and the delivery of services in the home setting—with the economic and social realities of contemporary family life is a pressing concern. Particularly urgent is the need to ensure access to these intervention programs for parents who are employed full-time, those who work nonstandard hours, and those who are making the transition from public assistance to work.

• Early childhood policies and practices are highly fragmented, with complex and confusing points of entry that are particularly problematic for underserved segments of the population and those with special needs. This lack of an integrative early childhood infrastructure makes it difficult to advance prevention-oriented initiatives for all children and to coordinate services for those with complex problems.

• The growing racial, ethnic, linguistic, and cultural diversity of the early childhood population requires that all early childhood programs and medical services periodically reassess their appropriateness and effectiveness for the wide variety of families they are mandated to serve. Poor "take-up" and high rates of program attrition that are common to many early intervention programs, while not at all restricted to specific racial, ethnic, or linguistic groups, nonetheless raise serious questions about whether those who design, implement, and staff early childhood programs fully understand the meaning of "cultural competence" in the delivery of health and human services.

• The general political environment in which research questions are formulated and investigations are conducted has resulted in a highly problematic context for early childhood policy and practice. In many circumstances, the evaluation of intervention impacts is largely a high-stakes activity to determine whether policies and programs should receive continued funding, rather than a more constructive process of continuous knowledge generation and quality improvement.

• As the rapidly evolving science of early child development continues to grow, its complexity will increase and the distance between the working knowledge of service providers and the cutting edge of the science will be staggering. The professional challenges that this raises for the early childhood field are formidable.

Recommendations

• **Recommendation 9** — Agencies and foundations that support evaluation research in early childhood should follow the example set by the nation's successful approach to clinical investigation in the biomedical sciences. In this spirit, the goals of program-based research and the evaluation of services should be to document and ensure full implementation of effective interventions, and to use evidence of ineffectiveness to stimulate further experimentation and study.

• **Recommendation 10** — The time is long overdue for state and local decision makers to take bold actions to design and implement coordinated, functionally effective infrastructures to reduce the long-standing fragmentation of early childhood policies and programs. To this end, the committee urges two compelling first steps. First, require that all children who are referred to a protective services agency for evaluation of suspected abuse or neglect be automatically referred for a developmental-behavioral screening under Part C of the Individuals With Disabilities Education Act. Second, establish explicit and effective linkages among agencies that currently are charged with implementing the work requirements of welfare reform and those that oversee the provision of both early intervention programs and child and adult mental health services.

• **Recommendation 11** — A comprehensive analysis of the professional development challenges facing the early childhood field should be conducted as a collaborative effort involving professional organizations and representatives from the wide array of training institutions that prepare people to work with young children and their families. The responsibility for convening such a broad-based working group or commission should be shared among the fields of education, health, and human services.

RESEARCH AND EVALUATION

Research has historically played a significant role in enhancing human development and preventing, ameliorating, and treating a range of conditions that can begin prenatally, at birth, or during the early years of life. To identify priorities among the many possible recommendations that could be made for promising further research, the committee was guided by three goals.

First, it is clear that the capacity to increase the odds of favorable birth outcomes and positive adaptation in the early childhood years would be strengthened considerably by supporting creative collaborations among child development researchers, neuroscientists, and molecular geneticists. Second, there is a pressing need to integrate basic research aimed at understanding developmental processes with intervention research that assesses efforts to influence developmental outcomes. Such collaborative initiatives hold the promise of advancing both understanding of environmental effects on development and improving the effectiveness of the nation's early intervention strategies. Third, the entire early childhood evaluation enterprise warrants a thorough reassessment in order to maximize opportunities for valid causal inference and generalization, to assess what has been learned cumulatively across the full array of evaluation studies, and to establish a constructive environment for discussion of ongoing research and its application to policy. The themes and issues presented below are elaborated in the committee's full complement of research priorities in the final report.

Integrating Child Development Research, Neuroscience, and Molecular Genetics

Enormous potential exists at the intersection of child development research, neuroscience, and molecular and behavioral genetics to unlock some of the enduring mysteries about how biogenetic and environmental factors interact to influence developmental pathways. These include: (a) understanding how experience is incorporated into the developing nervous system and how the boundaries are determined that differentiate deprivation from sufficiency and sufficiency from enrichment; (b) understanding how biological processes, including neurochemical and neuroendocrine factors, interact with environmental influences to affect the development of complex behaviors, including self-regulatory capacities, prosocial or antisocial tendencies, planning and sustained attention, and adaptive responses to stress; (c) describing the dynamics of gene-environment interactions that underlie the development of behavior and contribute to differential susceptibility to risk and capacity for resilience; and (d) elucidating the mechanisms that underlie nonoptimal birth outcomes and developmental disabilities.

Integrating the Basic Science of Human Development and the Applied Science of Early Childhood Intervention

There are currently few avenues for integrating knowledge gained from basic developmental science and from evaluations of early interventions. Yet both enterprises ultimately seek to improve children's early outcomes and life opportunities. A great deal stands to be gained from deliberate efforts to forge ongoing interactions among scientists engaged in these complementary yet largely disconnected research traditions. Among the important objectives to be addressed are: (a) enhanced understanding, detection, and treatment of early precursors of psychopathology; (b) improved preventive and ameliorative interventions for women and children who are exposed to biological insults and adverse environmental conditions, as well as for children with identified disabilities; (c) the identification of modifiable mechanisms that link impoverished family resources to both adverse outcomes for individual children and persistent disparities across groups of children in learning skills and other developmental capacities; and (d) refined understanding of how interventions and the staff that implement them can work effectively with families that differ along dimensions defined by race and ethnicity, immigration status, religion, or other cultural characteristics. The capacity of research to address these objectives will hinge in part on investments in improving the available tools for measuring important, but generally neglected early developmental outcomes, such as the multiple components of self-regulatory and executive capacities, and the ability to make friends and engage with others as a contributing member of a group, as well as on increased efforts to evaluate the biological systems that are affected by early interventions.

Improving Evaluations of Early Childhood Interventions

To improve the nation's capacity to learn from evaluations of early childhood interventions, the committee recommends substantially increased attention to program implementation as an integral component of all early childhood evaluation research, the adoption of higher standards for the use of rigorous and appropriate evaluation study designs, the inclusion of early childhood outcomes in evaluations of broad-based community and economic interventions, and the convening of regular forums at the National Institutes of Health to synthesize evaluation research evidence across programs and strategies that share similar developmental aims.

CONCLUDING THOUGHTS

As this report moved to completion, it became increasingly clear to the members of the committee that the science of early childhood development has often been viewed through highly personalized and sharply politicized lenses. In many respects, this is an area in which personal experience allows everyone to claim some level of expertise. Moreover, as a public issue, questions about the care and protection of children confront many of the basic values that have defined our country from its founding—personal responsibility, individual self-reliance, and restrained government involvement in people's lives. In a highly pluralistic society that is experiencing dramatic economic and social change, however, the development of children must be viewed as a matter of intense concern for both their parents and for the nation as a whole.

In this context, and based on the evidence gleaned from a rich and rapidly growing knowledge base, we feel an urgent need to call for a new national dialogue focused on rethinking the meaning of both shared responsibility for children and strategic investment in their future. The time has come to stop blaming parents, communities, business, and government, and to shape a shared agenda to ensure both a rewarding childhood and a promising future for all children.

The charge to this committee was to blend the knowledge and insights of a broad range of disciplines to generate an integrated science of early childhood development. The charge to society is to blend the skepticism of a scientist, the passion of an advocate, the pragmatism of a policy maker, the creativity of a practitioner, and the devotion of a parent—and to use existing knowledge to ensure both a decent quality of life for all of our children and a productive future for the nation.

I Setting the Stage

1 Introduction

Parents have always been captivated by the rapid growth and development that characterize the earliest years of their children's lives. The first responsive smile, the first wobbly step, the first recognizable word—each is a significant personal achievement and an occasion for family celebration. As the months turn to years, unsteady toddling across the living room turns into powerful sprinting across the soccer field, spontaneous smiles evolve into rich friendships, and single words become the building blocks of simple storytelling and, eventually, complex conversations. As the infant becomes a toddler and then a preschooler and finally arrives at his or her first day in kindergarten, parents exclaim, "I can't believe how quickly my baby has grown up!"—and they frequently wonder about whether they have done a good enough job.

Scientists also have had a long-standing fascination with the process of early childhood development. The systematic study of infant behavior can be traced back to the early to mid-19th century, when researchers in both embryology and evolution raised fundamental questions about the origins and course of human development across the life span (Cairns, 1998; Kessen, 1965; Maccoby, 1980). By the 1920s, practice-based investigators in the professions of pediatrics, education, and social work were increasing their interaction with psychologists in the world of child study, which led to the establishment of a vibrant, multidisciplinary, scientific discipline that has continued to grow as a blend of theory, empirical investigation, and insights derived from professional experience (Richmond, 1967).

One of the most abiding issues explored by developmental scientists, and the subject of this report, concerns how biological endowment and early experience combine to affect later developmental outcomes. Are the seeds of extraordinary talent present at birth, or are they planted in early childhood? When do early delays in development signal serious problems later in life? Does early intelligence predict lifelong achievement? Do childhood bullies turn into adult criminals? Do early advantages, such as a sunny disposition and skilled parents, inoculate a child from subsequent adversity? Do early harms, such as repeated exposure to family violence, impose irrevocable constraints on subsequent outcomes?

Interest in these questions is not new, but there have been significant advances in the understanding of the kinds of changes that occur, and the way those changes are grounded in both "nature" and "nurture." Over the past three decades, the rate of generation of new knowledge about early childhood development has been staggering. It has led to a number of advances in both concepts and methods—and it promises to increase even further in the near future. This scientific explosion has been fueled by multiple contributions, ranging from theoretical and conceptual advances to dramatic leaps in both the measurement technology and the computer-based analytic capacity available to the behavioral and biological sciences. We are, for example, on the threshold of a revolution in molecular biology grounded in the decoding of the human genome. The prospect of increasing collaboration among neurobiologists, geneticists, and social scientists offers the exciting promise of still greater breakthroughs in understanding the complex interplay between nature and nurture as they jointly influence the process of human development during early childhood.

Most recently, increasing interest in the developmental significance of early life experiences has been fueled by extensive media coverage of research on the developing brain. From governors and state legislators to business leaders and entertainers, virtually everyone is talking about the importance of the early childhood period, particularly the first three years of life. This growing excitement has fueled a proliferation of media campaigns and policy activities focused on infants and toddlers, as well as a host of entrepreneurial efforts to capitalize on the demand for materials and experiences to enhance early competence. At the same time, skeptics have stepped forward to question this intense interest in very young children, to point out the limits of contemporary neuroscience, and to underscore the evidence of continuing brain development far beyond the infant-toddler period (Bruer, 1999; Kagan, 1998a).

To update what science now tells us about these important issues, the Board on Children, Youth, and Families of the National Research Council and the Institute of Medicine established the Committee on Integrating the Science of Early Childhood Development. The charge to the committee was to review what is now known about the nature of early development and the role of early experiences, to disentangle established knowledge from erroneous popular beliefs or misunderstandings, and to discuss the implications of this knowledge base for early childhood policy, practice, professional development, and research. The goal, then, is not purely one of summarizing what's new or what's fascinating, but rather one of connecting developmental science to its implications for action and continued inquiry.

This is a familiar task for developmental scientists, albeit one that is fraught with difficulties (National Research Council, 1978, 1982; Shonkoff, 2000). Indeed, one of the most distinctive features of the science of early childhood development is the extent to which it evolves under the anxious and eager eyes of millions of parents, policy makers, and professional service providers who seek authoritative guidance as they address the challenges of promoting the health and well-being of young children.

Within the framework of its charge, the committee confronted the following kinds of questions. What are the most important developmental achievements that occur from the prenatal period up to school entry? Are there truly "windows of opportunity" in the early years when critical experiences are required for healthy development? When does early adversity seem to have lasting effects? Which aspects of development are relatively robust, and which are more sensitive to differences in the environments in which young children grow up? What aspects of these environments have the most significant influence on early development? What does it take to alter the course of development for the better, and what can we realistically expect from such efforts? How do the answers to these questions vary for children with different strengths and weaknesses, and who are growing up in different circumstances? The answers to these questions define the nature of early development and the responsibilities of adults. Although the committee was most familiar with, and thus most sensitive to, the context in the United States that is now shaping discussion of these issues, it is our firm hope that this review of the scientific evidence will be seen as pertinent to children around the world.

The body of research that addresses these questions is extensive, multidisciplinary, and more complex than current discourse would lead one to believe. It covers the period from before birth until the first day of kindergarten. It includes efforts to understand how early experience affects all aspects of development—from the neural circuitry of the maturing brain, to the expanding network of a child's social relationships, and to the cultural values of the society in which parents raise children. It includes efforts to understand the typical trajectories of early childhood, as well as the atypical developmental pathways that characterize the adaptations of children with disabilities. As the knowledge generated by these multiple perspectives has evolved, a number of core concepts have come to frame our understanding of the nature of early human development. They are summarized here and reemerge repeatedly throughout the report.

CORE CONCEPTS

Defining the boundaries of science in early childhood development is not an easy task. However, this task can be facilitated for policy makers, practitioners, and parents by differentiating among established knowledge, reasonable hypotheses, and unwarranted assertions (Shonkoff, 2000). Established knowledge is determined by strict rules of evidence and rigorous peer review. It evolves continually over time. Reasonable hypotheses are educated guesses that are derived from, but extend beyond the boundaries of, established knowledge. Although they may be confirmed or disproved by subsequent investigation, they make up a large proportion of the knowledge base that guides responsible policy, service delivery, and parenting practices at any given point in time. Unwarranted assertions distort or misrepresent current knowledge, undermine its credibility, and have the greatest potential to be harmful when they are advanced by those who are viewed as reputable scientists. They are often made to advance commercial goals or an ideological agenda. Ultimately, informed early childhood policy making, effective service delivery, and successful parenting are all dependent on mastery of the existing knowledge base, sound judgment based on reasonable hypotheses, the avoidance of irresponsible practices, and continuous reassessment over time.

Understanding of child development is based on multiple sources of knowledge that include theoretical models, empirical research, program evaluation, and professional experience. The role of theory is to provide a framework for organizing what is known and for guiding further investigation. The role of empirical research and program evaluation is to ask important questions (e.g., How do children learn number concepts?) and to test specific hypotheses (e.g., High-quality child care results in language gains for toddlers from high-risk homes), using a variety of quantitative and qualitative methods. The role of professional experience is to tap the wisdom and judgment of people who work with children in a variety of service settings. Taken together, these diverse sources of knowledge advance understanding of the process of child development and enhance the capacity to promote competence, prevent disorders, and correct maladaptive patterns.

A set of core concepts frames our understanding of the nature of human development during the earliest years of life and lays a foundation for addressing the following questions:

• Is early development highly programmed, so that certain events must

happen at predetermined times, or is it more loosely open to environmental influences and primed to seize those that matter most
whenever they occur?

- Do infants follow a smooth and predictable path toward the preschool years (and beyond) or is early growth and development characterized by bumps, detours, and unanticipated turns?
- Are infants initially incompetent, passive creatures or individuals
  who are born with an active capability to learn from the surrounding world?
- Are young children highly vulnerable, highly resilient, or both?

The discussion provided in this section reflects the prevailing views of
researchers, theorists, and clinicians who study young children. This multidimensional knowledge base has grown exponentially over the past 25
years, fueled by an explosion of scholarly work across a wide variety of
disciplines. Its richness lies in the extent to which diverse perspectives have
converged on a set of core concepts. Its limitations rest on the extent to
which the science is based largely on studies of typical development in
white, middle-class samples and developmental vulnerability in samples
that do not disentangle race, ethnicity, or socioeconomic status.

Focusing on the underlying principles that guide the developmental
process, this report highlights ten guiding principles or core concepts.

**1. Human development is shaped by a dynamic and continuous inter-
action between biology and experience.** Early pioneers in the field of child
study approached the complexity of human development by devising simple
models and testing them. Some, such as Arnold Gesell (1925, 1929), believed that the emergence of skills is driven primarily by genes. Others, such
as John B. Watson (1928), believed that all behaviors are determined by the
environment. These early models reflected a mechanistic conceptualization
of development that was derived from the physical sciences. Over time, it
became increasingly clear that humans do not behave like machines (neither
the prewired nor the programmable type), and children began to be viewed
through the lens of modern biology, rather than that of classical physics or
chemistry. Consequently, human development is now described in interactive terms (i.e., "dynamic"), reflecting the essential characteristic of a living
organism.

Virtually all contemporary researchers agree that the development of
children is a highly complex process that is influenced by the interplay of
nature and nurture. The influence of nurture consists of the multiple nested
contexts in which children are reared, which include their home, extended
family, child care settings, community, and society, each of which is embedded in the values, beliefs, and practices of a given culture. The influence of

nature is deeply affected by these environments and, in turn, shapes how children respond to their experiences.

In simple terms, children affect their environments at the same time that their environments are affecting them. Moreover, no two children share the same environment, and no environment is experienced in exactly the same way by two different children. Two youngsters living in the same home influence each other and are affected by the other members of the family in unique ways. If one child is active and aggressive and the other is passive and subdued, each will elicit different responses from the parents— and each will be influenced differently by the behavior of the other.

These concepts reflect what Sameroff and Chandler (1975) characterized as the transactional nature of the developmental process and what Bronfenbrenner (1979) described as the ecology of human development (also see Horowitz, 1999). This transactional-ecological model of development provides a useful framework that moves far beyond the misleading and tired old nature-nurture debate. It helps people think in more sophisticated ways about the complex determinants of successful adaptation and health as well as those of maladaptation and disorder. It offers insights into how the same behavioral disposition may be adaptive in one context and not in another. It also fits well with what scientists are learning about the dynamic nature of the development of the brain.

Children vary in their behavioral style. Some are high-strung and some are laid-back; some are agile and some are clumsy. Children are raised in a wide variety of social circumstances and cultural contexts. Some conditions are secure and others are unstable; some encourage competition and others promote cooperation. Behaviors that are highly adaptive in one society (e.g., competitiveness among preschoolers in the United States) may not be so in another (e.g., individual assertiveness among preschoolers in Japan). Different childrearing environments promote distinctive patterns of skill development in some children and not in others (e.g., some may reinforce active, physical performance while others encourage quiet, artistic expression).

At every level of analysis, from neurons to neighborhoods, genetic and environmental effects operate in both directions (Gottlieb, 1992). On one hand, the gene-environment interactions of the earliest years set an important initial course for all of the adaptive variations that follow. On the other hand, this early trajectory is by no means chiseled in stone. The considerable degree of developmental plasticity that characterizes an immature organism is embodied in the capacity of its cells to adapt in very specific ways, in both the short and the long run, to changing demands. Neurons grow new axons, sprout new dendrites, form new synapses, and modify the strength of some established connections while eliminating others selectively over time. The impacts of varied experiences are also reflected in observed differences in the brain's blood supply, its cellular (glial) support systems, its intercellular insulation (myelin), the neurochemicals that it produces, and the specific receptors that recognize each individual substance. These concepts are taken up in more detail in Chapters 2 and 8.

2. **Culture influences every aspect of human development and is reflected in childrearing beliefs and practices designed to promote healthy adaptation.** The influence of culture on the rearing of children is fundamental and encompasses values, aspirations, expectations, and practices. Understanding this realm of influence is central to efforts to understand the nature of early experience, what shapes it, and how young children and the culture they share jointly influence each other over the course of development. The effects of culture on child development are pervasive. It prescribes how and when babies are fed, as well as where and with whom they sleep. It affects the customary response to an infant's crying and a toddler's temper tantrums. It sets the rules for discipline and expectations for developmental attainments. It affects what parents worry about and when they begin to become concerned. It influences how illness is treated and disability is perceived. It approves certain arrangements for child care and disapproves others. In short, culture provides a virtual how-to manual for rearing children and establishes role expectations for mothers, fathers, grandparents, older siblings, extended family members, and friends.

Given the magnitude of its influence on the daily experiences of children, the relative disregard for cultural influences in traditional child development research is striking. The literature on typical development is based overwhelmingly on studies of middle-class children of European-American ancestry, often involving samples drawn from university communities. In contrast, much of the research on children of color has focused on the impacts of poverty, drawing its samples from homogeneous communities in high-risk urban environments. Moreover, relatively little is known about the impacts of racism and other forms of systematic discrimination on early childhood development, independent of the adverse effects of low maternal education and socioeconomic status. Consequently, knowledge of the full range of environmental influences on young children and their relation to typical variations during early childhood is highly skewed and incomplete. Similarly, the ability to disentangle the confounding impacts of economic hardship and minority group status is severely compromised (García Coll and Magnuson, 2000).

The influence of cultural context on early childhood development is widely acknowledged. The empirical literature in this area, however, is underdeveloped. This weakness in the knowledge base is particularly problematic in view of the increasing racial and ethnic diversity of the population of the United States. In short, the basic concept is compelling, the database is thin, and the imperative for extensive research is clear. These issues are taken up in more detail in Chapter 3.

3. The growth of self-regulation is a cornerstone of early childhood development that cuts across all domains of behavior. Regulation is a fundamental property of all living organisms. It includes physiological and behavioral regulations that sustain life (e.g., maintenance of body temperature and conversion of food into energy), as well as those that influence complex behaviors (e.g., the capacity to pay attention, express feelings, and control impulses). Regulatory processes modulate a wide variety of functions to keep them within adaptive ranges. The simultaneous operation of these multiple systems at different levels of organization is an essential feature of human development, as we discuss at length in Chapter 5.

A broad range of everyday experiences in early childhood are subject to regulation. In addition, for some children, atypical stresses can overwhelm their baseline regulatory capacities. Experience with manageable challenges (e.g., briefly having to wait to be fed or soothed) promotes healthy regulatory abilities. Repeated exposure to stresses that are overwhelming (e.g., severe malnutrition, chronic abuse) may result in significant maladaptation or disorder. Individual differences in regulatory capacities are rooted in both biological endowment and life experience. For example, the underlying neurobiology of irritability and poor attention may be affected by neurotransmitters in the central nervous system that are determined by either genetics or a chaotic environment. More commonly, regulatory dispositions involve the interplay between both endowment and experience.

As children mature, their capacity to exert their own autonomous control over key regulatory functions is essential. Advances in motor skills make it possible for preschoolers to feed themselves when they are hungry and put on a sweater when they are cold. Cognitive and emotional maturation signals a greater ability to delay gratification, to sit still to read a book, and to cope with the stresses of separation or loss. Thus, development may be viewed as an increasing capacity for self-regulation, not so much in the specifics of individual behaviors but in the child's ability to function more independently in personal and social contexts (Bronson, 2000; Kopp, 2000; Sameroff, 1989; Sroufe and Waters, 1977).

The behaviors children use to regulate themselves and their environments change in meaning as they get older. What is considered typical and adaptive at one age may not necessarily be viewed in a comparable fashion at another age. Crying, for example, is an early regulatory behavior that in infancy sends important signals to caregivers, yet it may become a sign of social immaturity if it is used repeatedly to express frustration in middle childhood. Adaptive behaviors also can have costs, such as the hypervigilance needed to survive in a physically dangerous environment. Finally, the socialization process and meaning of some regulatory behaviors, such as physical aggression and delayed gratification, differ across cultures. Consequently, adaptations essential to survival in one context may be maladaptive in another.

4. Children are active participants in their own development, reflecting the intrinsic human drive to explore and master one's environment. The inborn drive to master the environment is a basic feature of human development throughout the life cycle (White, 1959), as we illustrate throughout Part II of this volume. Shortly after birth, children begin to learn about the world through their remarkable capacities to create their own knowledge from early experience. This inborn thrust is facilitated by the extent to which their environments provide opportunities and supports for growth. Parents and the general public wonder about which experiences are necessary for healthy development to unfold. Must these experiences be costly? Do they require expensive educational toys and early access to computers? The simple answer to such questions is generally "no." Given the drive of young children to master their world, most developmentalists agree that the full range of early childhood competencies can be achieved in typical, everyday environments. A cabinet with pots and pans, for example, seems to serve the same purpose as a fancy, "made for baby" musical instrument.

An extensive body of multidisciplinary research supports the notion of powerful inborn tendencies toward mastery that are apparent in earliest infancy. Piaget (1952) labeled this characteristic *cognitive assimilation* and considered it to be a basic fact of life. Others have called it *mastery motivation* (e.g., MacTurk and Morgan, 1995), emphasizing the experience of pleasure in performing newly acquired behaviors and skills. Fraiberg pointed out that this developmental thrust enhances efforts to direct development along positive pathways, commenting, "it's a little bit like having God on your side" (Fraiberg et al., 1980, p. 53). Reviewing previous research on early development, Emde (1990) specified aspects of this developmental thrust and proposed that they act as key ingredients for behavioral interventions throughout the life span. In this regard, all forms of early childhood intervention are most effective when they counteract obstacles to growth and promote the expression of a child's natural drive toward mastery.

5. Human relationships, and the effects of relationships on relationships, are the building blocks of healthy development. From the moment of conception to the finality of death, intimate and caring relationships are the fundamental mediators of successful human adaptation. Those that are created in the earliest years are believed to differ from later relationships in that they are formative and constitute a basic structure within which all meaningful development unfolds. Because many of the regulatory systems that are essential for infant survival and emotional organization require consistent caregiving attention, it has been said (perhaps too dramatically) that without the caregiver-infant relationship, there would be no infant (Winnicott, 1965).

The essential features of healthy, growth-promoting relationships in early childhood are best embodied in the concepts of contingency and reciprocity. That is to say, when young children and their caregivers are tuned in to each other, and when caregivers can read the child's emotional cues and respond appropriately to his or her needs in a timely fashion, their interactions tend to be successful and the relationship is likely to support healthy development in multiple domains, including communication, cognition, social-emotional competence, and moral understanding (Brazelton et al., 1974; Emde, 1980; Stern, 1977).

Developmental or behavioral disturbances in infants and toddlers are embedded in disturbances of the caregiver-infant relationship (Ainsworth, 1973; Bowlby, 1973; Sameroff and Emde, 1989). Because babies depend for their survival on the care of adults, it is difficult, if not impossible, to consider their problems independent from their relationships with their primary caregivers. For example, a young child may be difficult to soothe, but whether this characteristic expresses itself as a disorder that requires therapeutic attention will depend on the way it affects and is handled by the child's primary caregivers. Some adults may view such behavior as overwhelmingly negative ("he is spoiled, selfish, and unreasonable"), whereas others may see it as a positive trait ("she knows her own mind and won't settle for less than what she wants"). Most successful interventions, whether they are primarily preventive or therapeutic, are based on facilitating that relationship and helping both the child and the caregiver learn to adapt successfully to each other's individuality. These issues are taken up in more detail in Chapters 9, 11, and 13.

6. The broad range of individual differences among young children often makes it difficult to distinguish normal variations and maturational delays from transient disorders and persistent impairments. Developmental competencies vary significantly across a wide range of individual differences, and the rank ordering of children according to their abilities changes over time. Within this broad continuum, it often can be difficult to make clear distinctions among individual differences within a normative or typical range (e.g., variations in communication skills), transient delays related to maturational lags (e.g., speech articulation errors), and diagnosed developmental disabilities (e.g., true disorders of language or cognition), especially in the early childhood years. A related issue is the fact that so many defining symptoms for disorders are also nonspecific indications that something is not quite right. This applies to depression, inattention, overactivity, and anxiety—all of which can be displayed by a child who has a fever or is overly tired, as well as by a child with a specific disorder. In part, these difficulties are related to the limitations of existing developmental measures. To a large extent, however, diagnostic dilemmas are inherent in the complex and unpredictable nature of early childhood development (Boyce, 1996).

All children have built-in capacities to attain developmental goals in multiple ways and under varying conditions. This is illustrated in the phenomenon of alternative developmental pathways, which provides a useful model for understanding the distinctive competencies that children develop in diverse cultural contexts, as well as the different family patterns of interaction that promote their unfolding (Erikson, 1950; Pumariega and Cross, 1997).

The concept of alternative developmental pathways offers a framework for viewing individual differences, maturational delays, and actual disabilities as part of a unified continuum that applies to the development of all children. The early child-caregiver relationship, for example, can be stressed by either biological or environmental threats, yet the processes governing the relationship are organized in a comparable manner, even for children with significant impairments or for those whose development is at very high risk (Cicchetti and Beeghly, 1990; Sameroff and Emde, 1989). Similarly, all developmental transitions are susceptible to the adverse impacts of a wide range of risk factors that can produce a sense of elevated uncertainty, regardless of the nature of the child or the caregiving context (Wishart, 1993). Ultimately, such patterns are understood best when they are viewed as variations within a common developmental framework.

Children born with significant biological impairments (e.g., blindness, deafness, severe motor deficits) also attain a range of basic abilities, such as representational thinking and language competence, in ways different from those experienced by children without such limitations. Greater understanding of these alternative pathways can provide guidance for interventionists in their attempts to facilitate the adaptive development of young children with a wide variety of special needs, as well as in their efforts to extend constructive support to their parents (Decarie, 1969; Fraiberg, 1977; Gleitman, 1986). These issues are further discussed in the context of the specific developmental tasks described in Part II.

7. **The development of children unfolds along individual pathways whose trajectories are characterized by continuities and discontinuities, as well as by a series of significant transitions.** The process of development is essentially a process of change. In some cases (e.g., increasing memory functions), that change appears to be gradual, cumulative, and continuous.

In other cases (e.g., the beginning of expressive language and self-awareness in the second year), the gains are so far-reaching that they represent a qualitative discontinuity from what has come before (Brim and Kagan, 1980; Rutter and Rutter, 1993). Such transformations are often referred to as developmental transitions. These transitional phases, which may be either smooth or characterized by stress and turmoil, have been viewed as important periods of psychological reorganization that provide useful opportunities for intervention (Brazelton, 1992). Developmental transitions occur throughout the life span, but in the early childhood years they are more frequent and involve profound psychobiological changes.

A developmental transition can be thought of as a time when change is pervasive and enduring, and when it involves a major reorientation in how a child relates to the environment. It is a time when the emotional communication between children and caregivers is particularly significant (Emde, 1998). Developmental transitions are periods of psychological disequilibrium that reflect elements of both the stage that is being completed and the stage that is about to begin. The intense negativism of toddlers, who are attempting to reconcile strong feelings of attachment to their parents and a powerful drive for personal autonomy, is a familiar example of this complex phenomenon. These issues are taken up in more detail in Part II.

8. Human development is shaped by the ongoing interplay among sources of vulnerability and sources of resilience. Individual developmental pathways throughout the life cycle are influenced by interactions among risk factors that increase the probability of a poor outcome and protective factors that increase the probability of a positive outcome (Garmezy et al., 1984; Rutter, 2000; Werner, 2000). Risk factors may be found within the individual (e.g., a temperamental difficulty, a chromosomal abnormality) or the environment (e.g., poverty, family violence). Protective factors also may be constitutional (e.g., good health, physical attractiveness) or environmental (e.g., loving parents, a strong social network). The cumulative burden of multiple risk factors is associated with greater developmental vulnerability; the cumulative buffer of multiple protective factors is associated with greater developmental resilience. Sameroff, Seifer, Barocas, Zax, and Greenspan (1987) have demonstrated that the total number of risk factors in a child's life is a better predictor of IQ scores than the specific nature of those factors. The double burden of both biological and environmental risk produces an unusually high level of vulnerability (Escalona, 1982; Parker et al., 1988; Shonkoff, 1982).

Some developmental pathways follow trajectories or patterns that are deeply ingrained and thus less amenable to influences that may deflect them in a positive or negative direction. Others are highly susceptible to such risks and protective influences. Waddington (1966) compared these pathways to the valleys and ridges that are formed by a ball rolling downhill. The further the ball rolls along a given path, the deeper are the valleys and the steeper are the ridges. Developmental characteristics that are embedded in deeply chiseled trajectories (e.g., basic motor capacities, such as crawling and walking) are less amenable to environmental modification and are described as canalized. Other trajectories have valleys that are more shallow or ridges that are less steep, which leave them more susceptible to change (e.g., basic self-care skills, early literacy). Ultimately, the extent to which any existing pathway can be modified or redirected is determined by both biological and environmental influences. The child's own expectations, and those of the significant people in his or her life, often play an important role in maintaining or changing direction. These concepts are especially pertinent to the literature reviewed in Part III regarding the contexts for early development.

9. **The timing of early experiences can matter, but, more often than not, the developing child remains vulnerable to risks and open to protective influences throughout the early years of life and into adulthood.** Human adaptation derives from both the rapid consolidation of essential capacities and lifelong flexibility to adjust to changing circumstances (see Chapter 8). Efforts to understand which aspects of development become set early on and which remain open to change have been shaped by notions of critical and sensitive periods, as well as by a growing research literature on the malleability or plasticity of the human organism.

The concepts of both critical and sensitive periods refer to unique episodes in development when specific structures or functions become especially susceptible to the influence of particular experiences (Bornstein, 1989; Thompson, in press(a)). Although critical periods have been well described for several behaviors in a variety of animal species (e.g., imprinting in newborn geese), the term "sensitive period" is preferred when studying humans because it implies less rigidity in the nature and timing of the required experiences, as well as less inevitability in its developmental outcome (Immelmann and Suomi, 1982). Current knowledge suggests that, although developmental progress in some domains may be relatively more amenable to facilitation or vulnerable to harm during certain periods in comparison to others (see, for example, the discussion of institutionalization in Chapter 9 and of family income in Chapter 10), advances can occur at virtually any age.

The concept of developmental plasticity refers to the capacity of the brain to reorganize its structure or function, generally in response to a specific event or perturbation. Although it is determined fundamentally by genetic modification, plasticity often comes about as a result of a change in the environment (see Chapters 2 and 8). Times of developmental transition, which are often characterized by major alterations in person-environment relationships, provide important opportunities for understanding this critical adaptive phenomenon. Neurodevelopmental plasticity varies inversely with maturation. That is to say, there is more multipotentiality (i.e., greater capacity for alternative developmental adaptations) in the early childhood period than in the later years.

10. The course of development can be altered in early childhood by effective interventions that change the balance between risk and protection, thereby shifting the odds in favor of more adaptive outcomes. Although the desire to learn, grow, and "become" is inherent in the biology of early childhood, it is also a characteristic that is open to modification based on individual experience. When the environment supports a child's emerging sense of agency (i.e., the feeling of being able to influence events and thus having an impact on one's own life), his or her motivation to act on the world flourishes. When experience fails to support (or punishes) such action, a child's motivation diminishes, shifts, or finds problematic outlets. Early environments that facilitate competence and a sense of personal efficacy are more likely to foster children who do well. When opportunities for agency are limited, psychological growth is more likely to be compromised.

A wide variety of early intervention policies and programs have been designed to create growth-promoting environments for young children whose development is threatened by biological vulnerability or adverse life circumstances (see Chapter 13). Different models employ varying combinations of strategies focused on providing direct experiences for the child, influencing the behaviors of the child's primary caregivers and/or working directly on the child-caregiver relationship. The basic objective underlying all interventions in the early childhood years is to increase the probability of a more favorable developmental trajectory for each child. This is accomplished by attempting to identify and mitigate the influence of existing risk factors, as well as to identify and enhance the buffering capacity of available protective factors. This often occurs in the context of specific therapeutic or educational services. Individual goals are determined in terms of each child's and family's baseline status in conjunction with an assessment of the extent to which relevant risk and protective factors are susceptible to change. In the final analysis, early childhood intervention is viewed most appropriately as an individualized strategy designed to increase the probability of a desired outcome, and not as a developmental panacea for all children under all circumstances. It is the art of the possible, based on the science of early childhood development.

SCOPE OF THE STUDY

The committee's charge to identify the implications of its scientific review was directed at three interrelated goals: (1) to inform the design and implementation of policies, services, and professional training to support the health and development of young children and their families; (2) to stimulate the formulation of an integrated research agenda to advance both the basic science of early childhood development and the applied science of early childhood intervention, extending from the prenatal period through the preschool years; and (3) to educate the public about state-of-the-art knowledge regarding human development during early childhood.

The committee did not set out to produce a comprehensive handbook on early childhood development, nor did we seek to provide explicit parenting advice. We selected topics that are especially pertinent to current debates about the early childhood years and sought to help readers understand young children rather than to offer directive statements about how to raise them. Indeed, with such understanding comes humility about the complexity of the task undertaken by anyone who brings up a child, and an appreciation for the value of a firm grounding in "what develops?" and "how?" as a departure point for highly personal decisions involved in day-to-day childrearing.

To select the issues on which it would focus, the committee conducted a series of interviews with practitioners and policy makers to assess their views of the most pressing issues facing contemporary early childhood practice and policy, as well as with scientific colleagues in fields ranging from basic neuroscience to anthropology and sociology. The committee also reviewed a broad range of previous reports produced by the National Research Council and the Institute of Medicine and, with few exceptions (e.g., child care, prenatal alcohol exposure), did not conduct new reviews of areas addressed previously (see Appendix A for a listing of pertinent reports). Appendix A includes a number of reports that address issues of physical health and nutrition that, while not explicitly addressed in this report, are a vitally important foundation for every aspect of development we discuss. The science summarized in this report reflects the expertise and judgment of the members of the committee, who were themselves selected for their breadth of knowledge and interdisciplinary scope.

The analyses that contributed to this report draw on a variety of sources. The committee reviewed a wide body of research through targeted literature searches and direct correspondence with investigators known for their work on specific topics. Between October 1998 and February 2000, the committee met six times to identify critical issues, analyze available data, discuss research findings, seek additional information on specific areas of concern, formulate conclusions and recommendations, and prepare this report. Three additional subcommittee meetings were convened to discuss pertinent literatures on neuroscience, culture and early human development, and methodological issues. Three workshops—on home visiting interventions, precursors of antisocial behavior, and the science of early childhood intervention (National Research Council and Institute of Medicine, 2000)—and five commissioned papers[1] also contributed valuable scientific input to the committee's work.

PLACING THE STUDY IN CONTEXT

One hundred years ago, the transition from the 19th to the 20th century marked a time of significant energy, creativity, and attention to the health and well-being of the nation's children. The overlapping emergence of child development as a focus within the field of psychology, pediatrics as a specialization within the practice of medicine, and child welfare as a defined domain within the purview of both the judicial system and the world of social work provides just a few examples of the extent to which the distinctive needs of children began to appear more clearly on the social and political agenda (National Research Council, 1981, 1982). In 1912, Congress established the Children's Bureau in the Department of Labor, which proceeded to conduct studies in such diverse areas as infant mortality, day care, institutional care, and mental retardation (Lesser, 1985). Ten years later, as a growing database documented the strong association between socioeconomic factors and infant and maternal deaths, public health nursing services and state child hygiene divisions were expanded under the provisions of the Sheppard-Towner Act of 1921 (Steiner, 1976).

As the crown jewel of the New Deal, the passage of the Social Security Act of 1935 formalized an expanded federal responsibility for the health and well-being of children and their mothers. Title V of the act authorized financial assistance to the states to support: (1) a broad array of maternal and child health services, including prenatal care, well-baby clinics, immunization programs, and nutrition services, with a special emphasis on underserved rural and low-income populations; (2) comprehensive services for "crippled children"; and (3) a range of child welfare services for the care and protection of homeless, dependent, and neglected youngsters (Magee

---

[1]Topics were: the demographics of the birth to five age group, atypical language development, the developmental consequences of community violence, regulation of attention and executive function in young children, and the effects of prematurity on early brain development. In addition, over two dozen experts in the area of culture and early development were invited to respond to a brief questionnaire about key topics developed by the committee.

and Pratt, 1985). Another provision of the act, Aid to Dependent Children (later renamed Aid to Families with Dependent Children) ensured a federal entitlement to a guaranteed baseline of economic security for vulnerable children and their mothers.

Three decades after the onset of the New Deal, under the broad umbrella of the Great Society and the War on Poverty, the modern era of early childhood intervention was launched with the creation of Head Start and the initiation of the Handicapped Children's Early Education Program (Smith and McKenna, 1994; Zigler and Valentine, 1979). Whereas Title V of the Social Security Act had strengthened the nation's medical focus on the consequences of low income and childhood disability, the policies of the 1960s spearheaded an education strategy. Fifteen years later, during a period of significant reduction in federal social programs and devolution of authority to the states, Head Start continued to be funded as a part of the government's "safety net," and a new federal entitlement to early intervention services for infants and toddlers with disabilities was enacted under Part H of the Education for All Handicapped Children Act Amendments of 1986 (Public Law 99-457), and reauthorized in 1997 as Part C of the Individuals with Disabilities Education Act (Public Law 105-107) (Meisels and Shonkoff, 2000).

The current social, economic, and political contexts within the United States in which this report will be read and interpreted have once again changed. In recent years, federal legislation has been enacted to expand the financing of child health care through the State Children's Health Insurance Program under Title XXI of the Social Security Act (Public Law 105-33), yet the 60-year entitlement to welfare support for families with young children has been terminated by the Personal Responsibility and Work Opportunity Reconciliation Act of 1996. Greater investment in education reform garners strong public support, universal school readiness is ranked first among the nation's education goals, and the demand for higher standards and stricter accountability in the public schools is widely endorsed. And yet, despite two high-profile White House conferences on child care and early childhood development and significant increases in public funding for early child care and education at both the federal and state levels, there is still widespread and well-entrenched resistance to the formulation and enforcement of more rigorous standards for child care providers and the settings in which they work. And despite the creation and expansion of Early Head Start for infants and toddlers, services for 3- and 4-year-olds are still available to less than half of the eligible children in the United States, more than 30 years after the opening of the first Head Start center in 1965 (Meisels and Shonkoff, 2000).

Beyond specific government policies and programs, the context of this report is reflected in a set of highly interrelated social, economic, and

political challenges presently facing children, their parents and other caregivers, and U.S. society in general. These include: (1) dramatic changes in
the nature of work, an increasingly strong link between education and
employability, and greater difficulty for families at all income levels in
balancing workplace and family responsibilities; (2) ongoing increases in
the racial and ethnic diversity of the U.S. population and the persistence of
significant racial and ethnic disparities in health and developmental outcomes; (3) the persistent poverty of young children and a growing gap
between the wealthy and the poor; (4) continued high rates of community
and family violence, as well as serious mental health problems that impose
significant burdens on family functioning; (5) an increased reliance on market solutions to address complex social problems; (6) the devolution of
some important responsibilities for the implementation of child and family
policy to the state and local levels; and (7) conflicting views about the role
of government and the balance between public and personal responsibility
for the health and well-being of children.

The release of this report also comes at a somewhat sensitive time in the
politics of early childhood intervention in the United States. Evaluations of
a wide range of model programs and community-based replications have
produced results both encouraging and disappointing, posing a critical challenge to those who are seeking to understand the conditions under which
success is more likely than failure. This is also a time of significant expansion in state and local initiatives designed to improve the life chances of
very young children. Fueled by headlines about the importance of the early
years, as well as by increased national interest in school readiness, education reform, and the early roots of antisocial behavior and violent crime,
this heightened public concern raises critical questions about which investments are most likely to make a significant difference for the most vulnerable young children. In this context, the most important task facing the
committee is not to differentiate specific intervention programs that "work"
from those that do not. Rather, it is to provide a scientifically grounded
portrait of the most important achievements of early childhood and the
environmental conditions that either promote or impede their accomplishment, and to point to directions for both action and further research toward those ends.

This report addresses two complementary agendas. The first is focused
on the future and asks: How can society use knowledge about early childhood development to maximize the development of the nation's human
capital and ensure the ongoing vitality of its democratic institutions? The
second is focused on the present and asks: How can the nation use knowledge to nurture, protect, and ensure the health and well-being of all young
children as an important objective in its own right, regardless of whether
measurable returns can be documented in the future? The first agenda

speaks to society's economic, political, and social interests. The second speaks to its ethical and moral values. The committee is clear in our responsibility to speak to both.

ORGANIZATION OF THE REPORT

The organization of this report reflects its charge. Part I sets the stage for understanding the material that follows. This introduction has presented an overview of the core concepts that guided the committee's inquiry. Chapter 2 takes up a reconceptualization of the long-standing debate about the interaction between nature and nurture. Chapter 3 summarizes current thinking about the multifaceted concept of culture and its role in early human development, and Chapter 4 raises important methodological issues regarding efforts to explore questions about causality in early development and early intervention.

Part II addresses the central question of the nature of early development. What develops during the earliest months and years of life? What are the major behavioral and developmental tasks of the early childhood period? When should we worry? This part of the report starts with the child's emerging capacity for self-regulation, reflecting a shift in what developmentalists now believe to be a hallmark of early development (Chapter 5). Next, we turn to the remarkable accomplishments in language and learning that characterize this age period (Chapter 6) and the critical challenges associated with getting along with other children (Chapter 7), both of which represent areas of heightened interest on the part of parents, practitioners, and policy makers alike. Chapter 8 provides an updated review of research on early brain development. It comes last, reflecting the fact that developmental neuroscience is a recent addition to the study of the child. Furthermore, processes of brain development are better understood when considered in relation to the significant and concurrent emotional, mental, and social advances of early childhood.

Part III turns to the role of early environments as they shape early development. The chapters review research on the multiple, overlapping contexts in which development unfolds, beginning with the most active ingredient of early environmental influences, namely the parent-child relationship (Chapter 9). We then discuss the contribution of the economic niche occupied by the family (Chapter 10), the influence of child care (Chapter 11), and the role of the community in which the child lives (Chapter 12). Together, these chapters paint a vivid picture of the environments and experiences that foster or impede adaptation and well-being. Chapter 13 is a critical overview of the scientific foundations of early childhood intervention, thereby complementing what is known about early development as it unfolds naturally over time with a view based on efforts to alter its course.

The committee's charge to draw out the implications of its research review is addressed in the final chapter (Chapter 14), which provides conclusions and makes recommendations for policy, practice, and professional development, as well as for research.

2 Rethinking Nature and Nurture

s developmental psychologists stand at the threshold of a new era in understanding the biological bases for human growth and continue to address fundamental questions about parenting influences, it is time for a new appreciation of the coactivity of nature and nurture in development. Beginning at the moment of conception, hereditary potential unfolds in concert with the environment. The dynamic interplay between gene action and environmental processes continues throughout life. Although their influences are so often distinguished in ancient philosophy and modern science, the inseparability of nature and nurture has profound implications for how we study and understand human development.[1] In this chapter, we trace these implications drawing first on the literature on developmental behavioral genetics, then undertaking a discussion of molecular genetics. We close with a brief discussion of brain development, foreshadowing the focused attention that is given to this topic in Chapter 8.

Nature and nurture are partners in how developing people interact with the surrounding environment. Nature and nurture are partners also in

---

[1]Although this chapter focuses primarily on genetic influences that contribute to individual differences among children, it is essential to remember that genetic influences also account for the characteristics that humans share as a species, such as upright walking and language. Indeed, the inseparability of nature and nurture is also reflected in the fact that both nature and nurture are required for children to acquire these and other attributes that all humans share.

the transactions between the gene[2] and the variety of internal environments that surround it within the body (Greenough, 1991; Greenough and Black, 1992). The environment of the cell influences which of the tens of thousands of genes are expressed to affect cell characteristics. Hormones and growth factors in the cell can turn some genes on and turn others off. These substances can arise from the nucleus of the cell, its cytoplasm, or the surrounding cells or organs. The substances that influence gene expression arise also from the functioning of other genes within the cell (so-called regulator genes) and the products of earlier protein synthesis.

It is impossible to think of gene expression apart from the multiple environments in which it occurs. It is impossible to think of the manifestation of hereditary potential independently of the hierarchy of environments that shape its appearance. It is impossible to think of an organism that interacts with the environment without considering the genotypical uniqueness of that individual. It is impossible, in short, to consider nature apart from nurture.

Why, then, are these two forces of human development so persistently differentiated in efforts to understand human development? From ancient Platonic and Confucian philosophy to the present, the dichotomy between inherited capabilities and environmental incentives and pressures has guided human self-understanding in Western and Eastern thought. All contemporary scientists acknowledge the interaction of heredity and environment (see Elman et al., 1996, for a recent and sophisticated version of the interactionist view). Yet an emphasis on whether hereditary constraints or environmental incentives are the preeminent influence in human development can still be observed not only in scholarship in psychology but also, more significantly, in public discourse concerning the importance of parenting and early education, and in policy debates about early intervention programs, family support, delinquency and criminality, and other issues of child and family policy.

---

[2]Within the nucleus of every cell are chromosomes containing genes, which are segments of DNA. Genes direct the synthesis of proteins that are incorporated into the structure of the cell, regulate its biochemistry, and guide other genetic activity. Genes ultimately affect physical and behavioral characteristics through these influences on the cells within every living being. Although each cell contains genes that are identical to the genes of every other cell, not all genes function in the same way, and this accounts for why cells function differently from one another. Some genes act continuously, for example, while other genes in the same cells turn on temporarily, and others are never expressed. As one colorful description notes, if each gene is represented as a light bulb that is either activated or not, we would see a distinct twinkling of lights within each cell during its normal functioning (Leger, 1992). This is why organisms can have trillions of cells, all of which have the same DNA but many different forms and functions.

It is time to reconceptualize nature and nurture in a way that emphasizes their inseparability and complementarity, not their distinctiveness: it is not nature *versus* nurture, it is rather nature *through* nurture. If gene expression is inconceivable apart from the environment, then it is useless and potentially misleading to try to finely distinguish the relative importance of nature and nurture in the course of human development. Nature is inseparable from nurture, and the two should be understood in tandem. Moreover, by contrast with a traditional view that heredity imposes limitations and environments induce change in developmental pathways, research in developmental psychobiology shows that the coactivity of nature and nurture accounts for both stability and malleability in growth. This view is, indeed, one important way of integrating the science of early childhood development, and it is also reflected in recent scientific advances in some of the research fields that are currently generating greatest interest among developmental scientists: developmental behavioral genetics, molecular genetics, and brain development.

DEVELOPMENTAL BEHAVIORAL GENETICS

In animal species, the importance of genetic influences on behavior can often be studied directly through selective breeding research. In humans, less intrusive procedures are necessary, and for the past several decades developmental behavioral genetics has provided a powerful means of understanding the strength of heritable influences on individual differences in human development, and the environmental contexts in which they are expressed (see Lemery and Goldsmith, 1999; Plomin et al., 1997a; and Rutter et al., 1999a, for overviews of this field). By taking advantage of naturally occurring variation in genotypes and environments, behavioral geneticists seek to partition behavioral variability into its genetic and environmental components and describe their interaction.

They have two primary research strategies for doing so. In adoption research, genetic contributions are estimated by comparing the characteristics of an adoptive child with those of the birth mother (to whom the child is genetically related, but they do not share an environment) and the adoptive mother (who shares the child's environment, but not genes). Sometimes biologically related and unrelated siblings are also studied. The second approach is twin research. Because identical (monozygotic) twins are genetically identical, comparing the similarity of their characteristics with those of fraternal (dyzygotic) twins, who on average share half their genes, is another way of estimating genetic contributions.

Twin and adoption research designs each have assumptions or limitations that can make the interpretation of findings difficult and sometimes controversial. In adoption research, for example, prenatal influences (e.g., teratogenic exposure) can also account for the resemblance of biological mothers to their offspring, and this can inflate estimates of genetic contributions. In addition, adoption designs assume that the selective placement by adoption agencies of children into the homes of parents who are like them (or their biological parents) does not occur. It is possible to estimate the potential biases introduced by selective placement or prenatal influences, but this is very difficult in most research designs. Twin studies also have certain assumptions: that identical twins do not share a more similar environment than do fraternal twins, and that the development of twin pairs is fairly representative of the growth of children in general. These assumptions, too, have been tested, with some researchers concluding that these assumptions are valid and others disagreeing.

Adoption and twin studies each provide means of estimating quantitatively the proportion of variance in human characteristics that is attributable to heredity and to the environment, and of examining how these influences interact in development. During the past decade, developmental behavioral genetics research has expanded considerably in sophistication and analytic methods, using variations on the basic adoption and twin research designs (sometimes combining these methods) and employing structural equations modeling and other quantitative model-fitting methods for estimating genetic and environmental contributions to behavioral variability. These efforts have yielded important new insights into the heritability of individual differences in cognitive abilities, extraversion, emotionality, self-control, and other characteristics and have shown how inherited propensities to childhood disorders like autism, schizophrenia, attention deficit hyperactivity disorder, and antisocial behavior need to be considered by practitioners (see reviews by Plomin et al., 1997b and Rutter et al., 1999b).

Even more important is how this research contributes to an appreciation of how nature and nurture influence development in concert. A recent study of the development of antisocial behavior in children by Ge, Conger, Cadoret, Neiderhiser, Yates, Troughton, and Stewart (1996) is exemplary. Using an adoption design, these researchers found that when biological parents had substance abuse problems or antisocial personality disorder, their adopted children were much more likely to be hostile and antisocial than were adoptees from untroubled biological parents. Children's inherited antisocial tendency may have been manifested as difficult temperaments, problems with emotional self-control, impulsivity, or other difficulties. It was not surprising, therefore, that children's antisocial tendency was also associated with greater harshness and less nurturance and involvement by their adoptive mothers and fathers. This illustrates how children's inherited characteristics can evoke complementary responses from their parents (called "gene-environment correlation").

Parents and children in these adoptive families influenced each other.

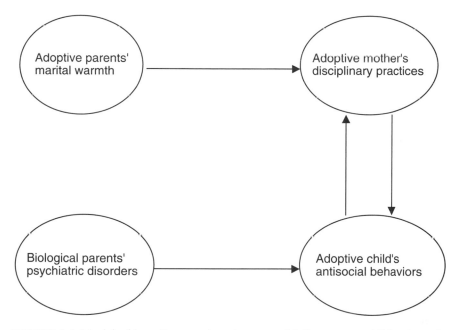

FIGURE 2-1 Model of hereditary and environmental influences on children's anti-social behaviors. SOURCE: Adapted from Ge et al. (1996).

Children with greater hostility tended to evoke more severe disciplinary responses, but harsh discipline also tended to exacerbate children's antiso-cial behavior. Parents' treatment of their adoptive offspring was influenced not only by the child's demandingness, but also by influences that were found to be independent of the child's inherited characteristics, such as the quality of the parents' marital relationship (see Figure 2-1). Thus the devel-opment of antisocial behavior in children was influenced by heritable char-acteristics—which altered the childrearing climate of the home—and by family influences that arose independently of the child. Other studies offer a similar portrayal of the coactivity of nature and nurture in human devel-opment (see Cadoret et al., 1996; O'Connor et al., 1998; Pike et al., 1996; and Reiss, 1997).

These studies have important practical implications. Since parenting and other environmental influences can moderate the development of in-herited tendencies in children, efforts to assist parents and other caregivers to sensitively read a child's behavioral tendencies and to create a supportive context for the child are worthwhile. A good fit between environmental conditions and the child's characteristics is reflected, for example, in family routines that provide many opportunities for rambunctious play for highly active children, or in child care settings with quiet niches for shy children to take a break from intensive peer activity. Thoughtfully designed caregiving routines can incorporate helpful buffers against the development of behavior problems among children with inherited vulnerabilities by providing opportunities for choice, relational warmth, structured routine, and other assists. Interventions to assist children at risk for other psychological disorders must also be individualized and emphasize the creation of a good fit between inherited vulnerabilities and behavioral demands, especially for children at greater heritable risk for problems like antisocial behavior, depression, and attention deficit hyperactivity disorder.

Heritability

Twin and adoption research designs each permit behavioral geneticists to calculate a heritability statistic (h^2), which is an estimate of the proportion of variability in individual characteristics that is due to genetic differences. A heritability of .45, for example, indicates that 45 percent of the measured variability in a particular characteristic is due to genetic differences in the sample. There are comparable statistics that estimate environmental contributions to individual characteristics. Unfortunately, the distillation of many complex findings in behavioral genetics research to a single heritability figure has led to considerable misunderstanding of its meaning, especially when heritability estimates in the range of 30 to 70 percent are derived from studies of the genetic contributions to individual differences in intelligence, personality, and psychopathology. This misunderstanding derives, in part, from the traditional tendency to seek to distinguish the effects of nature and nurture in development. Thus it is important to appreciate several principles:

• *Heritability estimates are proportions based on environmental as well as genetic diversity.* As a proportion, heritability reflects the extent of environmental influences as well as genetic influences. On one hand, if the environment could be made the same for everyone, heritability would inevitably be large because individual differences would then be due entirely to genetic factors (Lemery and Goldsmith, 1999; Plomin et al., 1997b). On the other hand, if people are studied in environments with diverse influences on them (varying significantly in socioeconomic status, ethnicity, or culture, for example), environmental contributions are magnified and heritability is lower. In short, a heritability estimate is uninterpretable without an appreciation of the extent of the environmental variability that also influences behavior in a particular sample.

• *Heritability estimates are sample- and context-specific.* Heritability estimates reflect the environmental diversity of the sample under study, as well as their genetic diversity. Heritability estimates tend to be higher in samples with greater variability in relevant genetic influences and, conversely, lower in samples that are genetically homogeneous. Because research samples can vary in both their environmental and genetic diversity, a heritability estimate must always be understood as pertaining to observed differences between individuals in a particular sample at a particular time in a specific environment.

   • *Heritability estimates change with development.* A characteristic that is highly heritable at one age may not be particularly heritable at another (Lemery and Goldsmith, 1999). There are many reasons for this, including the changes that occur in gene activation with human growth, changes in environmental influences with increasing age, and changes in the nature of a person's engagement with the environment over time. The heritability of variations in general cognitive ability tends to increase with age, for example, as does the heritability of certain behavioral difficulties, such as those associated with antisocial behavior (Goldsmith and Gottesman, 1996; Plomin et al., 1997b). Heritability estimates are thus not consistent over the course of development.

   • Perhaps most important, *heritability estimates describe what is in a particular population at a particular time, rather than what could be* (Plomin et al., 1997b). Changes in either genetic influences or environmental influences are likely to alter the relative impact of heredity and environment on individual characteristics. Phenylketonuria is a highly heritable genetic disorder that leads to mental retardation. But with a combination of early detection and environmental interventions, retardation can be completely prevented (Birch et al., 1992). Thus contrary to the common belief that highly heritable characteristics are impervious to environmental modification, interventions that alter the relevant environment—such as educational opportunities, therapeutic support, improved nutrition—can significantly alter the development of that characteristic.

   Moreover, it is important to remember that a heritability estimate describes influences on individual differences in a characteristic. Environmental influences can have a profound effect on that characteristic, however, even when heritability is high. During the past century, for example, there have been significant increases in *average* height owing to improved nutrition and medical care, even though *individual differences* in height are strongly influenced by heredity. This is because environmental changes (such as improved diet and medical care) have markedly increased average height from one generation to the next, while individual differences in height have remained highly heritable (i.e., smaller parents still have smaller children; see Figure 2-2). In a similar manner, other research (see Chapter 10) indicates that the socioeconomic status of adoptive homes has a powerful effect in elevating the IQ scores of adopted children, even though the

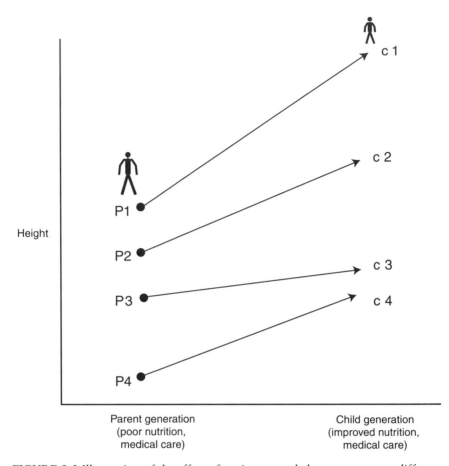

FIGURE 2-2 Illustration of the effect of environmental changes on group differences and genetic influence on individual differences over time. NOTE: Each line represents a family lineage, with P representing parents, and c representing offspring.

heritability of individual differences in IQ remain high (see Maccoby, 1999; Schiff et al., 1982).

High heritability therefore does not mean low malleability. Environmental interventions—which can include improved education, health care, nutrition, and caregiving—can significantly improve developmental outcomes for children, even though individual differences in those outcomes may be strongly influenced by genetic processes. Heritability does not imply constraints on change. It is instead more relevant to appreciating *how* developmental outcomes can be changed. In particular, heritability may be relevant to considering the kinds of interventions that might be most effective in relation to the genetically based characteristics of children.

Some developmental behavioral genetics researchers are dissatisfied, however, with the heritability estimate because it provides a quantitative but frequently misunderstood index of genetic influence that distracts attention from the ways that behavioral genetics research can contribute to a better understanding of risk and protective factors in development (e.g., Rutter, 1997; Rutter et al., 1999a; Wahlsten, 1990; Wahlsten and Gottlieb, 1997). An authoritative review of this field noted (Rutter, 1997:391):

> It has gradually come to be accepted that the precise quantification of heritability has little value because it provides no unambiguous implications for theory, policy, or practice. . . . There is little to be gained by merely quantifying the relative importance of the contributions of genetic and environmental influences because any estimates will be specific to the population studied and will be subject to change if environmental circumstances alter.

Shared and Nonshared Environmental Effects

Research in developmental behavioral genetics has also elucidated features of environmental influence on individual differences. In particular, researchers have helpfully distinguished between shared and nonshared environmental influences. Shared environmental influences are those that make individuals similar in their common environment. Nonshared environmental influences are those that distinguish among individuals within the same environment. Within a family, for example, shared environmental influences make siblings alike independent of their genetic similarity, while nonshared environmental influences make siblings different independent of genetic factors. For instance, parental divorce is a source of shared environmental influence if siblings within the family are affected similarly by this event (e.g., because of moving to a new neighborhood, loss of contact with one parent). Parental divorce can also be a source of nonshared environmental influence if siblings are affected differently by the same event (e.g., older and younger children may interpret their parents' divorce differently). This example illustrates how the terms "shared" and "nonshared" refer not to events or people, but to the *effects* they have on different children within the family.

Both shared and nonshared environmental influences can be estimated from adoption and twin research designs, although in different ways and with different assumptions. Within each design, however, shared and nonshared environmental effects are inferred from the resemblances among genetically related family members and are rarely observed directly or experimentally manipulated. This has caused some scholars to criticize how shared and nonshared environmental influences are estimated (see, e.g., Baumrind, 1993; Rutter et al., 1999a) and to caution that direct measurement is necessary before firm conclusions can be drawn about shared and nonshared influences (e.g., Plomin et al., 1997b).

Like heritability estimates, the difference between shared and nonshared environmental influences is often misunderstood. Some studies have shown, for example, that within families the most important environmental influences are nonshared, making siblings different from each other (Plomin and Daniels, 1987; Rowe, 1994). Some commentators have interpreted this to mean that conventional portrayals of parenting influences (such as the view that parents who use reasoning and gentle sanctions raise responsible children, or that parents who read frequently inspire their offspring to do so) are no longer valid because the important parental influences are those that make siblings *different* rather than alike in their characteristics (e.g., Rowe, 1994; Scarr, 1992; see also Harris, 1995, 1998). But parenting influences have long been understood by developmental scientists as sources of differences between siblings for many reasons (Collins et al., 2000; Maccoby, 1999). Parents develop unique and special relationships with each of their offspring, their childrearing efforts are experienced differently by siblings because of each child's distinctive characteristics (e.g., temperament, personality, gender, age), and good parents take these characteristics into account in adapting their general childrearing practices to their specific encounters with each child (Grusec and Goodnow, 1994). Indeed, even when parents use the *same* child-rearing practices with different children, they evoke *different* reactions because of each child's temperament, age, and other characteristics. These influences contribute to why, as every parent knows, siblings develop unique and distinctive characteristics, and parental practices help to account for these differences.

The distinction between shared and nonshared family influences is important to refining an understanding of how family processes affect children. Most importantly, it emphasizes that parental practices and family events are unlikely to have uniform effects on offspring because of how children experience, understand, and respond in individualized ways. But the distinction between shared and nonshared influences does not radically change current views of the importance of parental influences in the context of genetic individuality (see Box 2-1). Moreover, until findings about the nature of shared and nonshared family influences are based on observational and experimental studies, strong conclusions from developmental behavioral genetics research about how parents influence their children in shared or nonshared ways must remain tentative. Furthermore, current research indicates that it is extremely difficult to identify objective features of the environment that are "shared" or "nonshared" between siblings, and that shared and nonshared effects may depend, in part, on the hereditary

BOX 2-1
Understanding—and Misunderstanding—Parenting Influences

Most parents are concerned about doing the right things for their children. In recent years, however, they have had reason to question whether what they do really matters. In public (Harris, 1998) and scholarly forums (Rowe, 1994; Scarr, 1992), some developmental scientists have called into question whether parenting influences are as significant in the lives of children as commonly believed.

Most of the reason for questioning the impact of parenting comes from developmental behavioral genetics research. Studies emphasizing the importance of nonshared family influences suggest that it is not how parents treat offspring *similarly* that matters (such as their childrearing style, parental income or education, or socioeconomic status); it is their *differential* treatment of siblings that is developmentally influential. This is contrary to how most parents understand their influence on offspring. Moreover, behavioral genetics researchers observe that traditional studies of parenting confound the influence of heredity with the influence of childrearing practices. Children become interested in reading, for example, not only because of a home environment in which parents model reading, but also because of shared genes related to intelligence, activity level, and other characteristics that underlie reading interest and ability. From this view, therefore, parents' most significant contributions to the development of children are the genes they contribute, not the home environment they create.

Clearly, parents respond to the genetically driven characteristics of their offspring (a phenomenon called a "gene-environment correlation"). Indeed, doing so is a characteristic of good parenting. Adults *should* treat their offspring differently because of their unique personalities, age, sex, and other characteristics. But gene-environment correlation typically accounts for only a small part of the variability in children's characteristics, and parental behavior remains a large independent influence on offspring (Plomin et al., 1997b; Rutter et al., 1999a; see, e.g., Ge et al., 1996). The importance of parenting is further underscored by experimental studies that directly modify parental practices to create changes in the behavior of children that cannot be explained by the hereditary characteristics of offspring (Baumrind, 1993; see, e.g., van den Boom, 1994). This means that when parenting changes significantly (independently of gene-environment correlation), the behavior of children adjusts accordingly.

In the end, research shows that parenting *does* matter to children's development (Collins et al., 2000; Maccoby, 1999). At the same time, developmental scientists are increasingly recognizing the need to consider the influence of a child's heredity characteristics as moderators of parental influence, and to incorporate into their research designs attention to hereditary influences. As a result, a new generation of parenting research is emerging that more thoughtfully illustrates the developmental integration of nature and nurture in the family environment.

characteristics of the child (Rutter, in press; Rutter et al., in press; Turkheimer and Waldron, 2000). This form of gene-environment interaction is discussed in the next section.

Like the focus on the heritability estimate, a strong emphasis on the relative influence of shared and nonshared family influences risks missing the important conclusion of developmental behavioral genetics research: specifically, that the action is in the *interaction* between heredity and environment. The manner in which the family environment accommodates to and modifies a child's heritable characteristics shapes the development of those characteristics in a family environment that is also evolving over time.

MOLECULAR GENETICS

Developmental behavioral genetics examines nature and nurture indirectly through the behavioral characteristics of genetically related and unrelated individuals. But it would be far more informative if researchers could identify specific, individual genes associated with distinctive human characteristics, examining their behavioral consequences in concert with particular environmental influences. That goal is slowly being realized because of advances in molecular genetics, a relatively new science that is based on significant technological advances in mapping the human genome and conceptual advances in studying the connections between genes and behavior.

Molecular genetics begins with the scientifically complex task of identifying DNA markers for specific genes and connecting genes and behavior through relative linkage studies and association strategies (for overviews of these procedures, consult Plomin et al., 1997a; Plomin and Rutter, 1998; Rutter et al., 1999a). There have been significant advances in molecular genetics during the past decade owing to advances in mapping the human genome and the development of less intrusive and expensive technologies for extracting and genotyping DNA from human biological samples. There is every reason for confidence that further advances in genetic mapping and in linkage and association studies will soon provide a strong foundation for the integration of molecular genetics into the behavioral research of psychologists.

For developmental psychologists of the future, therefore, molecular genetics offers the remarkable possibility of identifying the genetic markers associated with specific behavioral propensities in children and examining the manifestations of these propensities in relation to environmental factors, developmental changes, and the influence of other genes. Molecular genetics will also enable researchers to develop more powerful analytic methods and theoretical models for understanding the influence of heredity on behavioral development. Perhaps most important, molecular genetics will help developmental psychopathologists understand the genetic bases for childhood disorders, which will include a better appreciation of the continuities between typical variability in personality functioning and atypical deviation, improved detection of continuities in psychopathological risk across developmental transitions, and the potential of reconceptualizing clinical syndromes according to their genetic bases (Plomin and Rutter, 1998). There have already been promising discoveries, such as advances toward the identification of a susceptibility gene for autism and autistic-like characteristics, and research findings suggesting inherited propensities to attention deficit hyperactivity disorder through genes regulating neurotransmitter receptors (Rutter et al., 1999b). Furthermore, impending discoveries from molecular genetics studies will provide added evidence that: (a) hereditary influences are polygenic and multifactorial, involving the impact of multiple genes coacting with environmental influences to increase the likelihood of certain behavioral propensities; (b) genetic bases for developmental disorders reflect, in most cases, extreme variations on a continuum that includes normal variants of the same characteristics; and (c) genetic effects on behavior are *probabilistic* (rather than predetermined) because they increase the likelihood that certain characteristics will occur, but do not directly cause them (Plomin and Rutter, 1998).

Consistent with the more complex portrayal of nature and nurture emerging from molecular genetics is a new appreciation of the importance of gene-environment interaction. Gene-environment interaction indicates that genetic susceptibility may increase an individual's sensitivity to specific environmental influences. Such an interaction is especially important in understanding hereditary vulnerability to environmental stresses that might lead to psychopathology. Gene-environment interaction is demonstrated when researchers find, for example, that there is small to moderate risk for antisocial behavior in individuals who have *either* a genetic susceptibility for this disorder *or* grow up in a stressful environment, but for individuals with *both* genetic and environmental risk for antisocial behavior, the probability of pathology is sharply higher (Cadoret et al., 1995a, 1995b, 1996; Rutter et al., 1999b).

Comparative studies with animals can specify these gene-environment interactions more precisely. In one investigation, for example, rhesus monkeys with a specific genetic vulnerability affecting neuroendocrine functioning who grew up under adverse (peer-rearing) conditions consumed more alcohol in experimental conditions (Campbell et al., 1986a) than did monkeys without this vulnerability. However, monkeys raised under advantageous (mother-reared) conditions with the same genetic vulnerability consumed *less* alcohol than those without it, suggesting that a genetic risk factor under adversity was a protective factor in advantaged conditions. Other forms of gene-environment interaction were apparent with respect to dominance-related assertive behavior in this sample, showing that positive early rearing significantly buffered the detrimental social impact of specific genetic vulnerability in young rhesus monkeys (Bennett et al., 1998; Suomi, 2000). These studies underscore how significantly developmental outcomes depend on the interaction of heredity and environment, rather than the direct effects of either. They also indicate how the behavioral effects of genetic vulnerability can be altered in the context of positive or negative early rearing.

As this research shows, the identification of gene-environment interaction is important not only to understanding developmental psychopathology but also to its prevention, since it indicates how individuals with a genetic propensity to the development of a disorder may be buffered from its emergence if their environments are made more protective. A child with an inherited vulnerability to antisocial personality is much less likely to develop this disorder in supportive, nonstressful family, school, and community environments.

Typical research designs in developmental behavioral genetics lack power to detect these interactions and, in fact, they are often not measured at all (Lemery and Goldsmith, 1999), but molecular genetics research has the potential for identifying gene-environment interactions, as the susceptibility genes to personality characteristics become identified. Behavioral studies suggest the existence of many such gene-environment interactions, such as the heightened responsiveness of temperamentally fearful, inhibited young children to maternal discipline efforts (Kochanska, 1993, 1995, 1997), the stronger impact of mother-infant synchrony on the growth of self-control of temperamentally difficult children (Feldman et al., 1999), and other illustrations of what Belsky (1997) describes as children's differential susceptibility to rearing influences. As the field of molecular genetics matures, in other words, it will become possible to understand how the hereditary characteristics of children influence their responsiveness to parental incentives, their susceptibility to environmental stresses and demands, and their vulnerability (in concert with environmental risk) to psychopathology.

Psychology is thus at the dawn of a new era. Not only will molecular genetics enable scientists in the near future to better understand how the interaction of multiple genes influences behavioral characteristics, but it will also illuminate how gene action can augment vulnerability or resistance to environmental demands. This view of the multifactorial origins of behavior, reflected especially in gene-environment interaction, is another reflection of the essential integration of nature and nurture in behavioral development.

BRAIN DEVELOPMENT

Brain development also reflects the coaction of nature and nurture. The traditional view of early brain development describes a process under tight genetic control, and to a great extent this portrayal is true. Important regulatory genes, such as the "homeobox" genes discovered in the fruit fly, control the timing of the expression of other genes and can direct the development of an entire segment of the insect's anatomy, such as an eye or a limb. Comparable genes have been shown to exist in mammals, including humans, which play similarly significant developmental roles. There is no question that there are genetically driven developmental processes that guide the basic organization of the body and the brain, and these processes influence the growth of single cells and entire systems.

But as the opening paragraphs of this chapter illustrate, gene expression always occurs within the context of the intracellular and extracellular environments within the body, and in the context of experience in the outside environment. These multilevel environmental influences are necessary to coordinate the complex behavioral and developmental processes that are influenced by heredity, as well as to provide catalysts to gene expression that enable behavior to become fine-tuned to the external settings in which the organism lives. When songbirds first hear their species' song, or when patterned light first hits the retina of the human eye, these experiences provoke a cascade of gene expression that commits neural development to certain growth patterns rather than others. This is because the genetically guided processes of neural development are designed to capture experience and to incorporate the effects of experience into the developing architecture of the nervous system. This is especially true of human brain development.

The purpose of a brain is to store, use, and create information. The amount, complexity, and contingency of the information required for humans is far greater than that of the fruit fly, and this is one reason why the strong regulatory influence of homeobox genes in the fruit fly provides a poor model for human brain development. A limited amount of information is required to enable a fruit fly to function successfully for a short life span, and much of the necessary information can be encoded genetically. By contrast, humans acquire information primarily from experience, including their systems for thinking, feeling, and communicating. Most of human knowledge cannot be anticipated in a species-typical genome (e.g., variations in culture, language, and technology), and thus brain development depends on genetically based avenues for incorporating experience into the developing brain. This developmental integration of nature and nurture enables humans to grow and adapt as a species in a manner unequalled by any other (fruit flies don't have books, movies, radio, or television from which to learn, and the only webs available to them are danger-ous ones), permitting unparalleled flexibility in behavior and development. The incorporation of experience into the genetically driven plan for human brain development helps to account for many of the unique qualities of the species.

Developmental neurobiologists have begun to understand how experi-ence becomes integrated into the developing architecture of the human brain (see Chapter 8 for further details). First, developmental processes of brain growth are based on the expectation that certain experiences will occur that will organize and structure essential behavioral systems. These developmental processes have been called "experience-expectant" because normal brain growth expects and relies on these forms of environmental exposure (Greenough and Black, 1992). Not surprisingly, the experiences that are incorporated into normative brain development are ubiquitous in early life: exposure to patterned light and auditory stimulation are two of the best studied, and there are likely to be others (such as acquiring physical coordination in gravity). Deprivation of these essential forms of environ-mental exposure can cause life-long detriments in behavioral functioning.

Second, throughout life, new experiences also help to trigger new brain growth and refine existing brain structures. This is, in fact, how learning, memories, and knowledge are acquired and retained throughout the life course. These developmental processes are called "experience-dependent" because they rely not on species-typical environmental exposures but in-stead on the idiosyncratic and sometimes unique life experiences that con-tribute to individual differences in brain growth (Greenough and Black, 1992). For example, there is evidence that brain functioning is changed in subtle ways if a person is a stringed instrument musician, which can alter neural areas governing the finger movements of each hand (Elbert et al., 1995). Experience-dependent brain development is thus a source of the human brain's special adaptability and lifelong plasticity (Nelson, 1999). Each person has a unique history of experience-dependent influences on brain growth.

Brain development therefore depends on an intimate integration of nature and nurture throughout the life course. Indeed, processes of brain development that were traditionally regarded as genetically hard-wired (such as visual capability) have now been discovered to depend on an exquisitely coordinated dance between experiential catalysts and the he-reditary design for brain growth. Both nature and nurture are essential to the development of a brain of uniquely human capacities and potential. These developmental processes are discussed in further detail in Chapter 8.

CONCLUSION

The integration of nature and nurture, revealed in the findings of behavioral genetics, molecular genetics, and brain development research, should significantly influence how human development is understood. Contrary to the traditional view that heredity imposes constraints and environments induce change in developmental pathways, research in developmental psychobiology shows that nature and nurture are each sources of stability and malleability in human growth. More importantly, their coaction provides the impetus for development, whether it is viewed from the perspective of "experience-expectant" brain growth or the interplay between of genes and environments. The developmental action is in the interaction of nature and nurture.

Although work in developmental psychobiology has contributed most significantly to a revised view of hereditary influences, it also causes us to regard the environment in a different way. Most importantly, we now appreciate that how children respond to environmental incentives is based, in part, on hereditary predispositions (gene-environment interaction), that the social environment adapts itself to a child's inherited characteristics (O'Connor et al., 1998), and that one of the most important ways of understanding environmental influences is how children are individually affected (the nonshared environment). Environmental influences are not just externally "out there": a child's responses to the family, the neighborhood, and the culture hinge significantly on genetically based ways of feeling, interpreting, and responding to environmental events. For parents and practitioners, this underscores the importance of taking into account each child's individuality to create conditions of care that accord with the child's inherited attributes and which, for some children, provide buffers to modify the expression of heritable vulnerabilities. Indeed, the importance of the goodness of fit between the environment and heritable characteristics also shows why human relationships are so profoundly important in early development, since human partners who know a child well are the environmental influences that can most easily accommodate helpfully to a child's individuality.

The inextricable transaction between biology and experience also contributes to a better understanding of developmental disorders and the effects of early intervention. Hereditary vulnerabilities establish probabilistic, not deterministic, developmental pathways that evolve in concert with the experiential stressors, or buffers, in the family, the neighborhood, and the school. That is why early experiences of abuse, neglect, poverty, and family violence are of such concern. They are likely to enlist the genetic vulnerabilities of some children into a downward spiral of progressive dysfunction. By contrast, when children grow up in more supportive contexts, the hereditary vulnerabilities that some children experience may never be manifested in problematic behavior. Understanding the coaction of nature and nurture thus contributes to early prevention.

Early intervention, especially when it is well tailored to a child's individual characteristics, can be helpful in shifting the odds toward more optimal pathways of later growth, but because the nature-nurture interaction is dynamic over time, there are no guarantees. Each new developmental stage provokes new forms of gene-environment transactions that may alter, or maintain, previous pathways. This means that giving young children a good early start increases but does not guarantee later success, and that children who begin life at a disadvantage are not doomed to enduring difficulty. The interaction of nature and nurture underscores the importance of creating current conditions of care that respect inherited characteristics, recognizing that nature-nurture is a source of continuing potential change across the life course.

Finally, research in developmental psychobiology emphasizes the continuity that exists between typical and atypical variability in human characteristics. One of the important emerging insights of molecular genetics is that many psychological difficulties arise not from single-gene mutations, but instead from extreme variations on a biological continuum that includes normal variants of the same characteristics. There is, in other words, a very broad range of individual differences in which the boundaries between the normative and the atypical are matters of degree rather than quality. This means that, in studying the growth of typical children, researchers gain insight into the developmental dynamics of atypicality and that, conversely, efforts to understand the challenges of children with developmental disorders yield insights into normative growth.

These conclusions are consistent with the broader themes of this report and of the findings of research on early childhood development. Taken together, they indicate that despite a long historical tradition of dissociating the effects of nature and nurture on human character and development, their influences are, in the end, indissociable.

3

The Challenge of Studying Culture

evolutionary advances in communications technology and increasing globalization have resulted in unprecedented access to the richness of human variation. In this context, as understanding of the dynamic interaction between nature and nurture continues to grow, the concept of culture offers a promising framework for thinking about the full meaning of nurture in the process of human development.

Interest in the influence of culture on child development, particularly as it is mediated through early childrearing practices, extends across a range of scholarly disciplines, including anthropology, sociology, philosophy, and psychology. Building on the seminal contributions of Margaret Mead, to Murchison's *Handbook of Child Psychology* (Murchison, 1931), and Carmichael's *Manual of Child Psychology* (Carmichael, 1946), all of the leading authoritative volumes on child development research had incorporated a cross-cultural perspective by the middle of the 20th century (e.g., Greenfield and Suzuki in Damon et al., 1998; Whiting in Lindzey, 1954; Whiting and Whiting in Mussen, 1960), and specialized volumes on infancy began to appear (e.g., Mead and Macgregor, 1951; Whiting and Child, 1953).

Notwithstanding this early establishment of a firm cross-cultural foundation for the science of early childhood development, the explosion of cognitive psychology in the 1960s paid relatively little attention to the effects of environmental influences on the emerging competencies of young children. Dominated by the revolutionary thinking of Jean Piaget (1952) and Noam Chomsky (1965), this new generation of psychologists celebrated the role of young children as active agents in their own development and attributed early skill acquisition to the universal emergence of innate cognitive and linguistic structures that required relatively modest environmental guidance.

In the early 1980s, following the publication of *Mind in Society* (Vygotsky, 1978) and *The Ecology of Human Development* (Bronfenbrenner, 1979), the pendulum swung back toward a greater appreciation of the extent to which all human development unfolds within a wide variety of cultural contexts. In his analysis of the child development research literature based largely on the findings of highly controlled laboratory experiments, Bronfenbrenner (1979:19) underscored the limitations of most empirically based developmental psychology, characterizing it as "the science of the strange behavior of children in strange situations with strange adults for the briefest possible periods of time." Subsequently, in contrast to Piaget's image of the young child as a solitary scientist, a growing subgroup of child development researchers returned to the concept of human development as a socially embedded phenomenon, thereby emphasizing the importance of culture (e.g., Rogoff and Chavajay, 1995).

Building on this evolving framework, the committee began its work with a strong conviction about the importance of culture as a highly salient influence on early childhood development. As our examination of the knowledge base progressed, we became increasingly appreciative of its complexity. In part, this complexity is related to the multidisciplinary nature of the field and its reliance on a wide array of qualitative and quantitative methods. Beyond methodological diversity, however, the committee was struck by the extent to which much of the research on the role of culture in child development is tied to values and personal beliefs.

Thus, the task of assessing the science of culture was exceedingly more complicated than assessing the neurobiology of brain development. This complexity was particularly apparent when the committee attempted to define and disentangle the concepts of culture, ethnicity, and race, and to seek greater understanding of the effects of racism, discrimination, and minority status on the development of young children. Consequently, this report presents a more bounded analysis of culture than it does of neuroscience. It is important that this discrepancy not be interpreted as an indication of the relative importance of these two domains of study. Quite the contrary, it should be viewed as a strong message both about the significant challenges that face those who investigate the role of culture in early childhood development and the critical need for ongoing methodologically rigorous research in this area.

THE SPECIAL CONTEXT OF THE
EARLY CHILDHOOD PERIOD

Most definitions of culture have focused on the intergenerational transmission of various combinations of symbolic (e.g., ideas, beliefs, and values) and behavioral (e.g., rituals and practices) inheritances (Shweder et al., 1998). In the realm of early childhood development, symbolic inheritances include (but are not limited to) parents' expectations, goals, and aspirations for their children; the values that govern differential approaches to discipline; gender roles; religious or spiritual values; and ideas and beliefs about health, illness, and disability. Behavioral inheritances, in turn, are embodied in the "scripts" that characterize everyday routines for such common activities as sleeping, feeding, and playing, among others, and the distinctive contexts that shape cognitive, linguistic, and social-emotional development and thereby influence the acquisition of specific skills or behaviors. Some observers have directed their attention preferentially to values and beliefs. Others have focused primarily on behaviors and practices. Shweder et al. (1998) emphasize the importance of integrating both—"the beliefs and doctrines that make it possible for a people to rationalize and make sense of the life they lead" and "patterns of behavior that are learned and passed on from generation to generation" (p. 867).

One of the most extensively studied examples of contrasting developmental values is the difference between cultures that promote individualism (found predominantly in European and European-American societies) and those that favor interdependence (reflected most prominently in Asian, African, and Latin American societies) (Greenfield, 1994; Greenfield and Suzuki, 1998; Markus and Kitayama, 1991; Triandis, 1988). Although all cultures must find a balance between individual autonomy and shared interests, there is considerable variation in each society's location along the continuum. Those that place greater emphasis on the former socialize their children in a way that promotes a greater sense of independence and a strong orientation toward individual achievement and self-fulfillment. Those that favor the latter socialize their children to focus on the importance of their responsibilities to others and the value of viewing personal achievements in terms of their contribution to collective goals. Neither orientation is intrinsically more adaptive or more "normal" than the other. Each reflects the desire for a certain kind of society, with both benefits and costs. When greater emphasis is placed on interdependence, there is a stronger sense of connectedness, sharing, and solidarity, but there may be a real cost in the form of suppression of individual development. When greater autonomy and self-reliance are promoted, there is often a considerable level of material productivity and individual liberty, but there may be a serious cost in the form of strained relationships and social alienation (Kim, 1987).

Central to the process of intergenerational culture transmission during the early childhood years is the translation of cultural belief systems ("parental ethnotheories") into parenting practices (Goodnow and Collins, 1990; Harkness and Super, 1992; Sigel et al., 1992). Whiting and Child (1953) noted both similarities and differences in approaches to childrearing in different cultures, and identified distinctive parenting practices as important reasons for the variations in child outcomes found across diverse populations. LeVine (1977:20) proposed a hierarchy of three universal goals that all parents have for their children: (1) physical survival and health, (2) development of the capacity for economic self-maintenance, and (3) development of the "behavioral capacities for maximizing other cultural values—e.g., morality, prestige, wealth, religious piety, intellectual achievement, personal satisfaction, self-realization—as formulated and symbolically elaborated in culturally distinctive beliefs, norms, and ideologies." In a society in which threats to physical survival are significant, caregiving is focused primarily on protection. When survival is assumed, childrearing practices reveal a process of socialization that reflects the values of the culture and the aspirations of parents for their children.

Miller and Goodnow (1995) defined cultural practices as "actions that are repeated, shared with others in a social group, and invested with normative expectations and with meanings or significances that go beyond the immediate goals of the action" (p. 7). They further noted their appeal as "a construct that will both contextualize development and provide a way of bringing together what are often described under the separate labels of thinking, doing, feeling, and becoming" (p. 7). Thus, according to Miller and Goodnow, their value for child development researchers is reflected in the way cultural practices: (1) provide a vehicle for studying development-in-context, without separating child and context and without separating development into a variety of separate domains; (2) reflect a particular social and moral order; (3) serve as a route by which children come to participate in a culture, allowing the culture to be reproduced or transformed within each child; (4) have a history and a relation to both supporting and competing practices; and (5) have consequences based on the nature of participation in a given practice.

One of the most extensively studied cultural practices in early childhood is the routine sleeping arrangements that are made for babies and young children (see Chapter 5). In the United States, where autonomy and independence are highly valued traits, most children sleep alone in a separate room away from their parents (Abbott, 1992; Lozoff et al., 1984; Morelli et al., 1992). In most of Asia, Africa, and Latin America, where interdependence and solidarity are preferred, children routinely sleep with one or more of their parents or siblings, even when separate rooms are available (Caudill and Plath, 1966; Konner and Worthman, 1980; Shweder et al., 1995). In two-thirds of the cultures surveyed in one international study, mothers routinely slept in the same bed with their infants, and the percentage was even higher when sleeping in the same room was included (Barry and Paxon, 1971; Burton and Whiting, 1961). This pattern was found not only in developing nations, but also in highly industrialized societies such as Japan, where children typically sleep with their parents until age 5 or 6 years (Caudill and Plath, 1966).

Despite the relatively unusual nature of typical U.S. sleeping practices compared with the rest of the world, there is also considerable subgroup variability within the country. In a Cleveland, Ohio, study, only 3 percent of babies in white, urban, middle-class, two-parent families slept in their parents' bedroom under one year of age, and only 1 percent did so in the second year. In contrast, parent-child cosleeping was reported for black children in the same urban area at a rate of 55 percent for children in the first year and 25 percent between 1 and 5 years of age (Litt, 1981). A subsequent study in a predominantly white, blue-collar community in Appalachian Kentucky found cosleeping among 71 percent of children between 2 months and 2 years of age, and 47 percent between 2 and 4 years (Abbott, 1992). Lozoff et al. (1984) found that babies in white, middle-class families are more likely to sleep with their parents when they are ill, when the family moves, or when there is marital conflict.

Both cosleeping with a parent or sleeping alone appear to be adaptive in a variety of cultural contexts. For example, !Kung children have been observed to be more independent than their counterparts in the United States, notwithstanding their early cosleeping experiences (Klein, 1995; Konner, 1982). It is of interest to note, however, that parental concerns about sleep problems in young children are common in the United States, less frequent in Japan (Nugent, 1994), and nonexistent in Kenya (Super and Harkness, 1982). It is not clear whether these differences reflect parent perceptions or actual sleep disturbances. Moreover, although the Japanese mother-child relationship remains relatively strong into adulthood, the husband-wife bond is typically less close than in the United States (Lebra, 1994). In short, cultural differences in early childhood sleeping arrangements are neither better nor worse; they simply reflect contrasting preferences and differential trade-offs.

Differences in early caregiver-child interaction patterns and communication styles further illustrate alternative childrearing strategies, as well as the futility of searching for universally normative or optimal practices. Mothers of Gusii toddlers in Africa and Zinacantecan toddlers in Central America, who use a great deal of imperatives when they speak *to* their offspring, generally have children who grow up to be relatively obedient and nonquestioning (Greenfield et al., 1989; LeVine et al., 1994). Toddlers in the United States, whose mothers typically speak *with* them using interrogatives, often grow up to be more questioning and self-assertive (LeVine et al., 1994). Americans would judge Gusii parents as excessively authoritarian and punitive, and their toddlers as passive. The Gusii would view American parents as overindulgent, and their toddlers as undisciplined (LeVine et al., 1994). In a study of mother-infant dyads playing with toys, Fernald and Morikawa (1993) observed that American mothers tended to name the objects, in contrast to Japanese mothers, who produced soft, easily imitated sounds and encouraged positive feeling toward the toys. Greenfield and Suzuki (1998) characterized these differences as a behavioral manifestation of the American value preference for cognitive stimulation (i.e., "technological intelligence") versus the greater Japanese interest in interpersonal relationships (i.e., "social intelligence").

The take-home message from this evolving literature is clear. Cultural practices related to early childrearing are highly variable and lead to different developmental outcomes. Many of those who embrace a particular practice typically do so because they believe in its relative superiority, although there is generally scant evidence to support the conclusion that one practice is inherently better than others. Yet this message does not mean that any and all beliefs and practices are equivalent in the extent to which they promote the health and development of young children. Some differences are trivial, some are matters of preference or style, and some have important consequences that may be particularly helpful or destructive to individuals or to society. Indeed, some practices can pose significant threats to children's physical or emotional well-being (e.g., binding the feet of young girls, using severe physical punishment to enforce obedience to authority, or imposing highly restricted diets that result in malnutrition). Ethnocentric arrogance leads to the firm belief that one's way is "the only right way." Sound scientific thinking asks how and why cultural practices differ and assesses their differential developmental consequences, in both the short and long term. It is therefore essential that the full range of possible effects of contrasting childrearing practices be evaluated objectively.

CULTURAL DIVERSITY IN THE UNITED STATES

Although much can be (and has been) learned about the relation between culture and child development from cross-national studies, there is also much to be learned from the rich diversity of childrearing beliefs and practices exhibited by families in the United States. A great deal of that variability can be found in that part of the population whose ancestors emigrated from Europe. Significantly more resides among those whose ancestral origins can be traced to various countries in Africa, Latin America, and Asia and who continue to be self-identified or socially identified with those origins. In fact, except for the contributions of the Native American population, most aspects of mainstream culture in the United States have been transported from another society. As such, American culture is modified and reshaped by each newly arrived group, as well as by each successive generation. In this respect, like most open societies in the world today, the United States is a nation whose culture remains a continuous work in progress.

The complex amalgam of cultures that encompass the contemporary U.S. population includes the contributions of a variety of groups whose initial arrival reflected a mixture of circumstances, including voluntary immigrants, involuntary slaves, grateful refugees, and conquered indigenous peoples. Some communities reflect more than two centuries of acculturation since the original departure from their homeland; others can measure their date of arrival in months. Some experience a sense of genuine welcome; others bear the burdens of hostility and overt discrimination. Some blend more easily into the mainstream; others feel more isolated at its fringes. Within this multilayered context, research on the role of culture in the development of young children in the United States is exceedingly complex and challenging.

Central to greater understanding is the need to identify the diverse and frequently overlapping elements of ethnicity, which include national origin, race, minority status, language, and religion. Ethnicity can be an amalgam of any or all of these, and the task of defining it is not an easy one. Helms (1990:293) defined ethnicity as "a social identity based on the culture of one's ancestors' national or tribal groups and modified by the demands of the larger culture or society in which one currently resides." Entwisle and Astone (1994) proposed ethnic categories for research purposes based on race and place of origin. García Coll and Magnuson (2000) described ethnicity as a group status defined by a common nationality, culture, or language. Phinney (1996) noted that the boundaries of ethnicity are blurred and flexible, and that its implications vary widely across individuals. Consequently, she suggested that it be treated not as a categorical variable but as a dynamic aspect of human experience (Goodchilds, 1991). Three dimensions of difference that vary within and across groups, as well as within individuals over time, are suggested for examination—ethnicity as culture, ethnicity as identity, and ethnicity as minority status (Phinney, 1996).

Equating ethnic status with distinctive cultural characteristics is highly problematic. Central to the problem is the common finding of significant variation within ethnic groups in values, beliefs, and practices—variations that can often exceed the magnitude of differences between groups. Most attempts to describe the culture of different ethnic groups in the United

States typically begin with the general characteristics of their native region (e.g., Asia, Africa, Europe, Latin America). This is usually followed by the identification of distinguishing features related to their specific country of origin, the generation and timing of immigration, the region of settlement in the United States, religious affiliation and practice, current community structure, and current socioeconomic status. Different members of a given ethnic group generally demonstrate varying degrees of adherence to its identifiable values, beliefs, and practices, thereby making it virtually impossible to characterize "the culture" of the group.

Individuals can claim ethnicity as an identity, independent of the extent of one's adherence to its cultural values and practices, which has been characterized as "symbolic ethnicity" or "ethnic loyalty" (Keefe, 1992; Keefe and Padilla, 1987). Embedded in this construct is a sense of membership in an ethnic group and a positive feeling about the affiliation (Bernal and Knight, 1993; Phinney, 1990, 1996). Like culture, ethnic identity is a complex phenomenon that varies among the members of a group, as well as in individuals over time. Its psychological correlates also vary, depending on the quality of the identity (Phinney, 1996) and whether it is the result of self-labeling or labeling by others.

Some ethnic groups are characterized as minority groups. This characterization implies a position of relative disadvantage with respect to power and status, often accompanied by previous or ongoing experience with racism or other forms of prejudice and discrimination (Phinney, 1996). It too varies among individuals and over time. In selected cases, it may be correlated with any of a variety of historical experiences that differentiate specific groups, such as slavery, internment, relocation, and refugee or immigrant status.

The concept of race can be especially difficult to define. García Coll and Magnuson (2000) defined race as a term used in the United States to describe a group of people who are defined mainly by physical characteristics, such as skin color, hair type, and other features. In reality, a significant proportion of the U.S. population is of mixed racial descent, and many individuals only marginally resemble the physical prototype of a distinctive race.

Although preschool children do not have well-formulated ideas about race, it is among their earliest emerging social categories. By the time they are 4 years old, children appear to realize that race is an enduring feature that is inherited from parents and established at birth. They also seem to be aware that race is a dimension along which humans are arranged hierarchically, but they do not have a very clear idea about who belongs to which category. Unlike gender, race is not a particularly salient or important dimension by which preschoolers spontaneously categorize people, especially when it comes to choosing playmates. The translation of racial categories into racially based behavior appears to occur after the preschool years (Hirschfeld, 1994). The early development of perceptions and attitudes about race (both one's own and that of others) is a highly sensitive concern in a pluralistic society. This critical issue, which was not addressed by the committee, demands extensive, multidisciplinary investigation.

DEMOGRAPHIC CHALLENGES AND OPPORTUNITIES

Notwithstanding the absence of clear definitions of race and ethnicity, they persist as prominent demographic markers for categorizing children and families, even as the blending of cultures increases and the racial and ethnic diversity of the U.S. population grows. Over the past two decades, the proportions of Asian and Hispanic children in the United States have increased while the young black population has remained stable and the percentage of whites has declined. Much of this growing diversity of young children is the result of increased immigration and higher birth rates among immigrants and their descendants, who represent more than 100 different ethnic and linguistic groups (National Research Council and Institute of Medicine, 1998a). These trends are projected to continue, if not accelerate, through the early decades of the 21st century, such that current notions of majority and minority groups will become less meaningful for children and, as they age, for adults as well.

By the year 2030, children in families of European origin will make up less than 50 percent of the population under age 5 (National Research Council and Institute of Medicine, 1998a). These demographic realities suggest both promising opportunities and potentially sobering challenges. The opportunities offered by a multicultural society that is cohesive and inclusive are virtually limitless—including the richness that comes from a broad diversity of skills and talents, and the vitality that is fueled by a range of interests and perspectives. The challenges posed by a multicultural society that is fragmented and exclusive are daunting—including the wasted human capital that is undermined by prejudice and discrimination, and the threat of civil disorder precipitated by bigotry and hatred.

The changing demographics of the early childhood population in the United States present both the opportunity and the challenge of a great social experiment. The outcome of this experiment will be influenced to a large extent by how human diversity is addressed in the rearing of children. The foundations of relationships and the fundamentals of socialization are culturally embedded and established during the early childhood years (see Chapter 9). Consequently, further research on how young children learn about and develop attitudes toward human differences will help to elucidate both the roots of categorical discrimination and the origins of social inclusion.

CULTURALLY COMPETENT POLICIES
AND SERVICE DELIVERY

As the population of young children in the United States becomes increasingly diverse, policy makers and service providers face the complex task of tailoring their efforts to build on the strengths and address the needs of a wide variety of constituencies. Central to this challenge is a recognition that significant cultural distance between providers and recipients of health and human services can make it difficult to build and sustain the kinds of relationships that often determine the short-term acceptability and ultimate success of an early childhood intervention or family support program. In an effort to respond to these new and growing challenges, the concept of "cultural competence" has been formulated to guide and evaluate professional performance in a broad range of service settings. Despite its intuitive appeal and theoretical validity, however, this concept has not been investigated empirically.

Multiple terms have been used to address the need for responsiveness to diversity, including "cultural sensitivity," "cultural relevance," and "cultural awareness," among others. Unlike these alternatives, cultural competence has been popularized as a knowledge base and set of skills that go beyond the realm of simple respect and sensitivity. A culturally competent professional is defined as one who is able to facilitate mutually rewarding interactions and meaningful relationships in the delivery of effective services for children and families whose cultural heritage differs from his or her own (American Medical Association, 1994; Roberts, 1989). Notwithstanding its current salience in the domains of policy and practice, however, there is little scientific evidence to support this definition.

Beyond the level of individual practice, notions of cultural competence have also been applied to systems and programs that deliver responsive and accessible services to culturally diverse populations. Once again, although the following characteristics have not been evaluated systematically, a culturally competent service system: (1) monitors assessment procedures and evaluation instruments to assure their appropriateness and validity for the children and families who will be assessed; (2) identifies groups that are underserved and eliminates cultural barriers that interfere with service provision; (3) facilitates policy planning, staff training, and community participation in order to ensure the development, delivery, and maintenance of culturally competent services; (4) defines the location, size, characteristics, resources, needs, and ethnography of culturally diverse populations within its service area; (5) builds cross-cultural communication skills; and (6) helps a broad diversity of communities organize themselves to enhance the availability and utilization of needed services. In a culturally competent system of care, the family, as defined by the cultural perspective of the target population(s), becomes the principal vehicle for support and the preferred agent of intervention (Coates and Vietze, 1996). In a health care setting, cultural competence is demonstrated further by the inclusion of cultural considerations in history taking and the formulation of differential diagnoses, and by adapting communication patterns in response to different cultural beliefs, practices, or traditional roles (Oosterwal, 1994). This framework can be used successfully for bicultural as well as multicultural families.

Isaacs and Benjamin (1991) suggested five additional traits that mark a culturally competent service system or institution: (1) the ability to express an appreciation for diversity; (2) the capacity for cultural self-assessment; (3) awareness of the dynamics that occur when cultures interact; (4) the availability of institutionalized cultural knowledge; and (5) availability of adaptive practices, such as the appropriate use of interpreters and sensitivity to cultural celebrations. Proposed guidelines for implementing such practices are available from a variety of sources (Bernard, 1991; Cross et al., 1989; Isaacs, 1986; Isaacs and Benjamin, 1991; Mason, 1989; Orlandi, 1992; Rider and Mason, 1990; Roberts, 1989).

The true sign of a culturally competent system of service delivery is its capacity to recognize the fine line between sensitivity to group differences and the danger of stereotypic or paternalistic approaches in the service of greater individualization. To this end, the ultimate goal should not be a society that develops different policies for different ethnic or racial groups, but a society that takes a families' cultural values and practices into account when it acts on their behalf. At the present time, this perspective is shaped by values and personal beliefs. The underlying science remains to be developed.

EVOLVING PERSPECTIVES ON THE STUDY OF CULTURE AND DEVELOPMENT

One of the fundamental choices facing those who study the complex relation between culture and child development is the need to find an appropriate balance between the identification of universals and the task of cataloging its variations (Cocking, 1994). As noted by Kessen (1991), "No psychologist can ignore the eternal tension between the Search for Uniform Being, on one hand, and the Celebration of Diversity, on the other" (p. 188). Early pioneers in *cross-cultural psychology* identified and described differences among societies. Investigators at the cutting edge of contemporary *cultural psychology* recognize that culture can be studied within a single group, and seek greater understanding of the dynamic interaction between individuals and their contexts in a diverse array of settings

(Greenfield, 1997; Jahoda and Krewer, 1997; Miller, 1997; Poortinga, 1997).

Among the most important tensions that arise in the study of cultural diversity is the struggle between those who view differences as advantages or deficits versus those who adopt a more "situated" and less ethnocentric perspective on human variability (Cole and Bruner, 1971; Ogbu, 1994). Central to the latter approach is a recognition that development is largely adaptive in nature and therefore must be viewed within the context in which it takes place and within which it evolves over time. That is to say, "2-year-old skills" and "3-year-old behaviors" are best understood by taking into account the learning opportunities and expectations that are embedded in the important social interactions in the child's typical environment. Thus, the development of cognitive-linguistic abilities and the achievement of emotional well-being are linked to a child's everyday experiences, which are embedded in the cultural practices or "scripts" of his or her family and society.

Closely related to the movement away from a focus on deficits toward an interest in assets is the emergence of a new subfield of cross-cultural research known as "indigenous psychology" (Berry, 1995). The defining feature of this emerging field is the study of specific cultural traditions by investigators whose personal background matches the cultural group that is the subject of study.

CONCLUSIONS

Similar to the evolving understanding of the reciprocal interaction between nature and nurture, researchers who study human development and culture are developing a greater appreciation for their interdependence as well. That is to say, as children grow up, they are not simply passive products of the culture in which they are reared. Quite the contrary, they are active agents who pick and choose selectively from among the influences to which they are exposed, thereby shaping their own distinctive cultural context over time (Miller and Goodnow, 1995). Fundamental to this concept is the increasing recognition that cultures themselves are also dynamic and continually modified by the people who experience them.

This phenomenon is most obvious in the acculturation of immigrant children, as they navigate the borders between their native and adopted cultures. It is also highly visible in any society during times of social change, as individuals adjust their practices and scripts to the pressures of newly prescribed values and behaviors. The significant social and economic transformations that have affected U.S. society over the past few decades (see Chapter 1) provide vivid examples of such powerful influences on the lives of children and families. Increases in maternal employment and greater utilization of nonparental child care, for example, have dramatically altered the daily life experiences of infants and toddlers by introducing a greater variety of adult relationships and earlier exposure to organized peer group activities, particularly with same-age playmates. The proliferation of early childhood enrichment activities and intense competition for admission to prestigious preschool programs for children from affluent families have increased performance demands within a relatively narrow range of competencies at increasingly younger ages; and the considerable amount of time that toddlers and preschoolers spend watching television and playing with video games have transformed the nature of imagination and play during the preschool years.

The lessons from these examples are clear. Culture is not a static phenomenon. It is sustained, challenged, or modified over time. Culture is also not a neutral construct. It draws much of its influence from the conviction that its values and practices are inherently right and preferable to those of others. In a pluralistic and rapidly changing society like the United States, culture is a highly charged and constantly moving target that is difficult to investigate in an objective manner. Numerous examples of its influence on early childhood development are included throughout this report, but much further work remains to be done. However, unlike research in the neurobiology of early childhood development, studies of the relation between competence and culture are heavily infused with values and personal beliefs. The extent to which both the capacity and the resolve to learn more about this critical relation are strengthened will determine the ability to understand the rich diversity of human cognitive, social, emotional, and moral development, beginning in the earliest years of life.

4 | Making Causal Connections

tudies of child development encompass an enormously varied universe of research strategies drawn from disciplines as diverse as economics and anthropology. These strategies include moment-by-moment ratings of interactions between adults and children and among peers, administration of psychological tests and questionnaires, ethnographic field work, laboratory research using standardized protocols, and clinical observations. Researchers select these strategies to address different goals. They may be most interested in elucidating associations among different facets of development, identifying emerging capacities of children as they develop, or describing the contexts in which children grow up, to name several objectives that studies are designed to address. In this chapter, we focus on studies that seek to identify causal connections between a specific influence (e.g., mothers' talk to children, an intervention program) and child development (e.g., the child's vocabulary, scores on a test of school readiness).

The subset of studies that attempt to establish causal connections are often critical in testing theories about the role of early experience in child development, and they absorb much of the interest of policy makers and practitioners. They can, however, be exceedingly difficult to implement in practice and sometimes involve ethical problems. Currently, a great deal of controversy surrounds the role of experimental studies in understanding the effects of early interventions, in part as a result of the high-stakes policy decisions regarding program funding that are often involved. In this context, our discussion aims to clarify the logic and contributions of studies of causality to the understanding of developmental processes and to interventions aimed at affecting these processes. Something close to a consensus has emerged within statistical science on the logic of causal inference: its definition, the conditions required for valid causal inference, and generalization of causal inferences. Appendix B discusses the statistical issues involved in defining and estimating causal effects. In the committee's view, this consensus has implications for all studies making causal comparisons, basic and applied, experimental and nonexperimental. Here we sketch the essential ideas in this emerging consensus and consider how these ideas can be applied to improving early childhood research. This focus is not intended to minimize the importance of other research strategies and goals. Research is most appropriately viewed as a sequential process, properly starting with exploratory observation, moving through correlational work aimed at tracing associations among variables of interest, to more rigorous designs permitting causal inference. Indeed, the richness of developmental science derives from the field's reliance on multiple methods of inquiry, and its greatest insights often emerge at the convergence of diverse strands of evidence.

We begin by considering causal inference in basic and applied developmental research. Basic research attempts to uncover fundamental processes of development and change, while applied research aims to help policy makers and practitioners evaluate practical efforts to improve children's experiences and outcomes. We emphasize the importance of integrating basic and applied research in building a strong science of early childhood development. Insights from basic science are crucial in the design of practical programs, while the evaluation of programs can provide new evidence essential to basic science about casual connections. We then discuss the problem of generalizing from intervention studies to the populations of children, to the settings and personnel, and to the historical times and social contexts that might ultimately characterize a new program if its adoption became more widespread. Well-designed studies can answer important questions about the generalizability of a study result. Nevertheless, because strong generalizations typically can emerge only from a stream of related studies, we also discuss the importance of synthesizing evidence across multiple studies. Finally, we consider the particularly thorny issue of causal inference as it applies to growing children.

CAUSAL INFERENCE IN BASIC RESEARCH

The theory and evidence contained in this report are connected by chains of causal reasoning. We consider how prenatal and neonatal environments affect early brain development and behavior and how these early effects, together with the child's early relationships, affect self-regulation, social competence, language development, and reasoning. The consequences of early experiences for later behavioral functioning, including the ability to initiate and sustain relationships and to succeed in school and at the workplace, are of central interest to theory and policy. This report and developmental science more generally integrate empirical findings regarding such causal propositions and evaluate alternative theoretical explanations that tie these propositions together.

Despite their importance, however, causal connections are difficult to nail down. Suppose, for example, that we are interested in how high-quality relations between caregivers and infants affect later cognitive or social functioning. For simplicity, we refer to the quality of such relations as "quality of care." Let us assume that we have taken great pains to define and validly measure quality of care as well as the outcome of interest: a specific aspect of cognitive or social functioning. When quality of care is found to be associated with an enhanced outcome, we may be inclined to think that the quality of care is the *cause* of this outcome. But children who enjoy high-quality care are likely to have other advantages that may also shape such outcomes. For example, they may benefit from favorable genetic endowment, highly involved parents, or ample family incomes, all of which may contribute to the cognitive and social outcomes of interest. These other causal factors are called "confounding variables" or "confounders" for short. A confounding variable in the context of this example is a child characteristic or feature of the child's environment that (a) predicts who will receive high-quality care and (b) also predicts the outcome of interest. The failure to control for confounders leads to an error called "selection bias."

Scientists try hard to devise research strategies that reduce or eliminate selection bias. That is, they try to separate the effects of the main variable of interest—in this case, quality of care—from effects of confounders. The surest way to eliminate selection bias is to conduct an experiment. In it, one would randomly assign children to either high-quality or low-quality care, carefully provide the kind of care assigned, and then, at some later point, assess the outcome of interest. Random assignment would eliminate all confounding variables. To be quite specific, random assignment would ensure that the probability of assignment to high-quality or low-quality care is utterly unaffected by any preexisting characteristic of the child.[1]

---

[1]Some have argued that random assignment eliminates selection bias only in large samples, but this is not true. By ensuring that previous variables are unrelated to the probability of assignment to each treatment condition, random assignment ensures that tests of statistical significance accurately quantify the uncertainty about the causal question. Thus, when treatment groups are compared on the outcome of interest, significance tests yield p-values that

It is, of course, unethical to assign children to receive low-quality care. Thus, many of the causal factors that are most important to theory are not amenable to experimentation for ethical reasons. Prenatal substance use, poor nutrition, and lack of early affection are three such examples of potentially important causal factors whose effects on humans cannot be assessed experimentally. Moreover, even when it might be ethically defensible to experiment, it may be practically impossible. For example, a controversial hypothesis is that keeping a 3-year-old at home with his or her mother is better for the child than sending him or her to child care (even if the quality of care is good). Since it is not known which kind of experience is superior, one might ethically conduct an experiment. Yet it is usually impossible to assign children at random to stay at home or attend child care; parents will not allow it.

When experiments on humans are impossible for ethical or logistical reasons, scientists use a variety of alternative strategies to eliminate selection bias. One is to create special circumstances in which human experimentation becomes both ethical and feasible, for example, by using wait-list controls.[2] Another possibility is to conduct experiments on animals. A great deal has been learned, for example, about the effects of highly stressful rearing circumstances on infant development using randomized experiments on monkeys (see Chapter 5). The key problem, of course, is that findings from such experiments may not generalize to human populations.

In another example, pregnant women who smoke could be randomly assigned to a smoking-cessation program to evaluate the effects of prenatal smoking on child outcomes. Again, however, generalization may be tenuous, as the special circumstances may not represent the contexts of greatest interest scientifically. Those who volunteer to participate in the evaluation and are assigned to either the experimental or control group may be different from other mothers who smoke but do not volunteer to participate. The results of the experiment may not generalize to those other mothers. Moreover, not all participants will "comply": some assigned to quit smoking will smoke anyway, and some not assigned to the program will quit, leading to a biased estimate of the effect of smoking.

---

convey the probability of obtaining a sample result of the type actually obtained if there were no causal effect. In small samples, these p-values will, appropriately, tend to be larger than in large samples, but in either case, the p-value and related confidence intervals are fair indicators of uncertainty about the causal effect of interest.

[2]A possible scenario for experimentation arises when a large number of parents seek child care and only a small number of places in child care centers are available. Then children can be randomly assigned to receive child care or to be placed on a waiting list. Constructing a wait-list control in this way can be a very effective research strategy, but any conclusions must be restricted to the set of parents who are actively seeking care. Such parents may provide a different kind of home care than would parents who are not interested in child care.

The strategy that is perhaps most common for coping with selection bias, however, abandons experimentation entirely. Now the goal is to identify and control for the most plausible confounding variables, preferably by design or, alternatively, by clever statistical analysis, such as propensity score analysis or reliance on other statistical techniques that adjust estimates of treatment impact for other influences related to the outcome. To return to the quality of care example, researchers would ideally take great care to obtain information on many aspects of a child's experience, including the prenatal behavior of the mother, the child's birthweight, early nutrition, the parents' cognitive skill, parenting behavior, education, occupation, and income level. They would also assess the child's previous status on the outcome variables of interest at least once (see discussion of time-series designs below). They would then make a concerted effort to construct comparison groups of treatment and control children or families that are as similar as possible on these pretreatment variables. In addition, they may attempt to adjust for such confounding variables ex posteriori, using statistical adjustments when assessing the effects of quality of care.

Studies using these nonexperimental designs and analytic strategies are extremely numerous and have yielded a wealth of evidence about the predictors of key childhood outcomes. In these nonexperimental approaches, statistical adjustments after the fact can seldom make up for failures to design as strong a quasi-experiment as possible, particularly if the groups being compared are highly disparate prior to program participation. As others have noted, "no matter how precise your measurement or how sophisticated your analyses, you risk failure if your research is not well planned. You can't fix by analysis what you have bungled by design" (Light et al., 1990). Unfortunately, even with a strong quasi-experimental design, one can never be sure whether key confounders have been overlooked or whether the method of adjustment has effectively removed potential selection biases.

Selection bias is not the only threat to valid causal inference. Another is called "simultaneity bias." Consider a study in which the quality of a child's relationships with his or her parents as well as the child's behavior are repeatedly assessed. Suppose one finds that changes in the quality of parenting predict changes in the child's behavior. Selection bias is not an issue because comparisons are made within the same children. That is, the child's behavior when parents are providing the best care is compared with the same child's behavior when the parents are not doing such a good job. The problem, however, is that the causal variable—parental care—will to some extent be caused by previous child behavior (see Bell, 1968; Bell and Chapman, 1986; Lytton, 1990; Rutter et al., 1997). Thus, parents will have learned to tailor their care to the past behavior of their child. It then becomes very difficult to ascertain the extent to which parental care is truly a cause of future child behavior, rather than a result of past child behavior. This is often called the problem of simultaneous causation, and ignoring it can lead to simultaneity bias. As a result, researchers have come to appreciate the crucial importance of testing for the direction of causal influence. Simultaneity bias can lead to absurd findings. For example, one might infer that talking baby talk to a 3-year-old slows down expressive vocabulary when, in fact, a child's failure to speak has driven a parent to use baby talk in a frantic attempt to elicit speech.

As in the case of selection bias, researchers have devised a variety of clever strategies for controlling simultaneity bias (Duncan et al., 2000). The most satisfactory is the randomized experiment, but again, such experiments on humans may be impossible for ethical or practical reasons. Careful, repeated assessments of both the causal factor and the outcome, combined with sophisticated statistical analyses, can be very helpful, although, once again, undetected sources of simultaneity may always exist (Robins and Greenland, 1992).

In sum, detecting causal connections is basic to developmental science, yet threats to valid causal inference, including selection bias and simultaneity bias, are often substantial. A variety of strategies can cope with these biases, including experimentation on animals, experimentation on humans under special circumstances, and nonexperimental studies that are designed to address threats to causal inference and may also rely on statistical adjustments. Studies using these strategies have different strengths and weaknesses. For this reason, strong causal inferences are rarely justified by a single study. Rather, evidence in favor of a causal connection becomes convincing when the findings from a variety of studies having varied strengths and weaknesses converge, especially when the evidence is consistent with the best available theory. The connection between prenatal substance use and infant outcomes is a good example: although experimentation on humans is difficult, convergent evidence from a variety of animal and human studies supports quite strong conclusions about effects.

CAUSAL INFERENCE IN APPLIED RESEARCH

The evaluation of interventions designed to improve children's early experiences and outcomes is an important component of early childhood research. Intervention studies can provide an especially strong means for testing theories about the developmental significance of early experiences. Government-subsidized early childhood intervention programs, nutritional supplements, home visitation programs, and parent training programs are but a few examples. Program evaluations enable policy makers to assess how program funds are being spent, whether and to what extent programs are being implemented as planned, and, ultimately, whether program participation is having positive effects on those served and, if so, why. Knowing that an intervention met its goals is a step in the right direction, but the real need is to move from this general conclusion to specific conclusions about which aspects of the intervention have which effects, to what degree, and under which circumstances (Rutter et al., in press). Assessing program impact on those served is once again a causal question. As in more basic research, threats to valid causal inference arise. Selection bias occurs when characteristics that predict program participation are also associated with outcomes. Simultaneity bias can also occur, especially when program activities and outcomes are studied over time.

There is, however, an important distinction between the kinds of causal questions that arise in basic research and those that arise in program evaluations. Basic developmental science typically assesses causal connections between events that unfold naturally over time. Opportunities for experimentation are limited. In contrast, program evaluations assess the effects of deliberately planned interventions—activities that would not occur in the absence of a new policy. For this reason, it is often more plausible, both ethically and logistically, to conduct experiments in program evaluation than in basic developmental science.

Such experimentation not only provides strong causal inferences about the impact of the program, but it can also provide new insights of great relevance to basic research. Experiments such as the Infant Health and Development Program (Gross et al., 1997), the High/Scope Project (Schweinhart et al., 1993; see Chapter 13) study of the long-term effects of high-quality child care, the Abecedarian Program (Campbell and Raney, 1994, 1995), and the Nurse Home Visitation Program (Olds et al., 1986, 1999) provide a wealth of knowledge about how early environmental enrichment affects short- and long-term cognitive and social development, knowledge that would otherwise be unavailable. Experimental evaluations have also shown that some promising ideas do not appear to translate into better childhood outcomes, a result that requires a deeper reflection on the validity of the theory behind the program, as well as on program implementation. This interplay between basic and applied research is essential to the vitality of the field.

This discussion may seem to imply that all program evaluations should be randomized experiments. Although we strongly suspect that randomized experiments are underutilized in program evaluation research, they are not the right tool for addressing all questions about interventions and special conditions must hold before a randomized experiment is feasible or desirable. Moreover, well-planned experiments can unravel.

Randomized experiments are of use when a clearly stated causal question is on the table. Many program evaluations are designed to answer other kinds of questions. Early in the life of a new program, the key question may be whether the program can be implemented as planned, whether the participants for whom the program is designed actually participate, and how much the program costs. A test of the impact of the program generally makes sense only when the program is based on sound theory regarding modifiable mechanisms that are associated with the outcomes of interest (e.g., reducing maternal smoking will enhance newborn outcomes), when one is confident that the program can be faithfully implemented, and when there is reasonable assurance that the children and families of interest will participate as planned. A premature and expensive test of impact can be a waste of money and can demoralize those who are trying to invent promising new programs. The results from such an evaluation are difficult to interpret, creating confusion rather than clarification about policy and theory. Indeed, premature causal evaluation can undermine potentially promising programs.

Logistical and political considerations are also extremely important. Suppose that a new program is ready for a test of its impact. A randomized experiment often becomes an attractive option, yet the decision about how to design a causal-comparative study must be made on a case-by-case basis. Randomized experiments are often feasible and ethically defensible. For example, when funds become available for a promising new intervention, there will often be considerable interest among parents in participating but insufficient resources to accommodate all interested families. In this setting, a lottery can be used to select who will participate—in effect, a randomized selection. If the results of the randomized experiment are promising, resources may then become available to accommodate more families. However, in other cases, randomized experiments may not be feasible or desirable for logistical or political reasons. In still other cases, it may already be known from previous experimentation that a program works under the special conditions of the experiment. The question then may be whether the program produces significant effects in a routine (nonexperimental) setting. Nonexperimental methods are then required to cope with selection and simultaneity biases.

It is also important to recognize that an initially randomized experiment can deteriorate under the impact of noncompliance, becoming a nonrandomized experiment, also called a "quasi-experiment." An intervention often calls for a degree of investment on the part of participants that some, or many, find difficult to manage; they may drop out quickly, or attend training meetings sporadically, or "forget" to be at home when the home visitor is scheduled to arrive. The same processes are not at work with the comparable set of control families not receiving the program. Thus, in longitudinal evaluations, "differential attrition" arises and selection bias remains a problem despite efforts to conduct a randomized experiment. Even in these cases, however, it is important to keep in mind that the resulting quasi-experiment is likely to be much less biased than if no random assignment is attempted and parents are free to enroll children in the program or not. Moreover, few experimental evaluations are now implemented without ongoing monitoring of attrition and other forms of treatment attenuation. This means that attrition can be detected early, efforts can be undertaken to reduce it, and these efforts can be used to improve the quality of subsequent implementation (see Shadish et al., in preparation). Finally, statistical techniques are now available for obtaining relatively unbiased estimates of program effects despite noncompliance (see Little and Yau, 1998). In brief, they involve assessing effects of "the intent to treat" and examining the effects of the program on participants who received different "dosages" or amounts of the program. These advances have gone a long way toward addressing some of the problems to which randomized experiments can succumb.

Even when a randomized experiment is impossible or unadvisable, however, "experimental thinking" is central to success of causal or comparative studies. Nonexperimental evaluations of program impacts can be viewed as more or less accurate approximations of "the experiment we wish we could conduct but cannot." The more accurate the approximation, the stronger the confidence that the evaluation has produced a valid causal inference. To understand why this is so requires an understanding of current thinking in statistical science about the nature of causation and the logic conditions for valid causal inference (see Appendix B).

In short, this involves thinking hard about the randomized study one would conduct if it were feasible and ethical. First, we must be able to imagine an experiment in which each participant is randomly assigned to the treatment groups. In studying the effects of divorce on children, for example, we cannot randomly assign parents to obtain or not obtain a divorce. But we can imagine such an experiment and thus conceive of a child's potential outcome under both conditions (the child's outcome if the parents were or were not divorced). In a randomized experiment, the propensity for one's parents to divorce would be independent of the potential outcomes—the outcomes that would be observed if divorce did or did not occur. Although such an experiment is impossible, it can be approximated by studying the propensity of couples to get divorced. For example, it might be possible to find, for each child of a divorced family, a child in a nondivorced family whose parents had the same predicted propensity to be divorced. These matched pairs might then be compared on outcomes.

In imagining this study of divorce, it becomes clear that there will be many children of nondivorced parents with very low propensities to be divorced. In an analysis using propensity-score matching, such cases are likely to be discarded, because there may be no good match—no child whose parents were divorced but who had a low propensity to be divorced.

One might ask whether discarding those cases with low risk of divorce is sensible. Although statisticians generally dislike throwing away data, the argument here is that discarding those cases is indeed sensible. The causal question really has meaning only for those families for which divorce is a plausible course of action. It makes little sense to compare children of parents with strong marriages to children of parents who divorce as a strategy for understanding the effects of divorce. A vivid demonstration of this point is available in Cherlin et al. (1991).

This last paragraph raises a crucial point about causal inference. There are often causal questions that are of interest only for a subset of the population. Whether to have heart bypass surgery is not a relevant question for persons with good cardiovascular health. And no one would conduct a randomized experiment in which persons with such good health, along with others, were randomly assigned to heart bypass surgery. This is not only an ethical concern. The impact of heart bypass surgery on persons with good cardiovascular health is not an interesting question for policy. Yet it is quite common to find researchers using survey data, for example, to examine "the effects of divorce" or the effect of low birthweight or the effects of infant care in an analysis using all participants. Such an analysis would use statistical procedures to control for extraneous variables. Yet participants with no chance or a very small chance of experiencing divorced parents or low birthweight or infant child care really contribute little or no useful information about the causal question of interest. Thus, the inclusion of such cases may distort findings. Thinking about the populations for whom the "treatment" is relevant is intimately connected to the problem of generalizing from an experimental study to a different population, with a different variant of the intervention or treatment, with a different kind of outcome measure, in a new setting, and sometime in the future. We now turn to these issues of causal generalization.

CAUSAL GENERALIZATION

Studies of causal connections in early childhood research involve explicit generalizations from the sampled domains of people, settings, times and contexts, causes, and effects to other situations in which the results might be applied (see Cook, 1990, 1993). Generalizability involves the inference that a research result arising in a given setting at a given time for a given set of participants, under a specific version of a treatment and for specific outcomes is likely to hold in some other setting at a later time with some other participants, under somewhat different versions of the treatment, and for somewhat different ways of assessing the outcomes. When applying research results from an intervention study to a natural setting, one is assuming that: (a) the "treatment" would be implemented in the natural setting similarly, but not necessarily identically, to how it was implemented in the study, (b) the participants in the natural setting would respond similarly to how the participants in the study responded, (c) the effects of the treatment would be assessed similarly, and (d) events have not transpired over time to change the broader context in which the treatment is being implemented and assessed. In research on early childhood interventions, the effectiveness of the intervention often depends on the knowledge and skill of the practitioners—those who provide home visits, child care, or parental counseling—and on other services available in the community (see Olds et al., 1998). It is essential that researchers vividly describe the characteristics of those implementing the treatments; the training, skill, and supervision required to implement them effectively; and the resources available within the community where the program is being replicated. Such descriptions will help determine whether the conditions that may facilitate the success of the program are present in the natural setting.

Defining the target population—that is, the families and children intended to benefit from a program (or assumed to be affected by the risk factor of interest)—is also essential, and a well-crafted statistical analysis can provide useful information on how children of varying backgrounds respond to a causal variable. Ideally, study participants would be a probability sample randomly selected from a well-defined target population—that is, the universe of families and children for whom the causal question is relevant. A probability sample is obtained when every element (e.g., family or child) in the target population has a known, nonzero probability of being included in the study. Such a sample makes it possible to compute estimates of effects that are unbiased for the target population.

Randomized experiments, however, rarely involve probability samples from well-defined populations. Some effort is generally required to convince child care providers or pediatricians or parents or children to participate in a randomized experiment, generally making random selection from a population impossible. And cost concerns and logistics generally require that randomized experiments be carried out in local settings. A nationally or regionally representative sample is generally far too dispersed to be used in an experiment.

The trade-off between causal credibility and representativeness is known in the methodological literature as the trade-off between internal and external validity (Cook, 1993; Cook and Campbell, 1979). "Internal validity" is the validity of a causal inference, the kind of credibility obtained from a well-run randomized experiment. "External validity" is the validity of generalizations made from the study to the practical setting in which a new treatment or program might be implemented, the kind of credibility that might come from a survey based on a probability sample. The trade-off arises in part because it is usually impossible to conduct experiments on participants who have been sampled with known probability from the population of interest. It also arises because the special circumstances required to construct a randomized experiment often create a research scenario (settings, implementers, and participants) that is quite different from the settings of practical interest. Yet even having a probability sample of settings, implementers, and participants from the population of interest would not, in itself, guarantee a high level of external validity—what is called "generalizability."

To illustrate this point, suppose that a home visitation program works very well for families of type A but very badly for all other families (families of type B). Also suppose that the researcher is unaware of this fact and has the luxury of conducting a true experiment on a random sample of families. The researcher might then report that "the average treatment effect is near zero." While such a statement may be true, it would disguise the reality that the treatment had a very good or a very bad effect, depending on the type of family. Thus, the conclusion, even though based on a seemingly perfect design, would be misleading. The generalization would apply to no one, neither to families of type A nor of type B.

In this situation, it is essential to consider the concept of a "moderator," a preexisting characteristic of families or children on which the impact of the treatment and magnitude of the treatment effect depend. It is possible, for example, that seriously depressed women are less responsive to home visiting interventions. In this case, maternal depression moderates the treatment effect and it would be advisable to assess effects separately for depressed and nondepressed mothers. Using the concept of a moderator, one can assess the generalizability of a treatment effect in some detail within a single-site study, across sites of a multisite study, and across studies in a research synthesis. This kind of investigation is far more manageable when randomization is feasible and ethical in each study, because nonrandomized studies involve confounders as well as moderators. Moderators can, however, be overused. It is critical to choose a priori moderators suggested by previous research that are most plausible theoretically for subsequent exploration in order to avoid random hunts for moderating influences in the absence of evidence of program effectiveness.

One of the most common procedures for studying the generalizability of findings from multiple studies is "meta-analysis" (see the comprehensive review of Cooper and Hedges, 1994). A meta-analysis can be thought of as an unplanned multisite study. If it had been jointly planned by all of the investigators, care would have been taken to ensure that similar outcome variables were used in every study; that treatment conditions were standardized; and that key dimensions of site-level variation were incorporated into the design. As a retrospective form of inquiry, meta-analyses do not have the luxury of capitalizing on such planning. Nevertheless, a stream of inquiry on a common set of hypotheses in developmental research usually includes interesting variation in participants, implementers, sites, and treatment conceptions, as well as interesting variation in methodological approaches. Using meta-analysis, it is possible to exploit this variation to study intensively the degree of generalizability of a treatment effect and the specific sources of variation in the treatment effect.

CAUSAL INFERENCE AND GROWING CHILDREN

Growth and change are pervasive and typically rapid during early childhood. For this reason, studies using repeated measures on each outcome are common. There are good reasons to do longitudinal studies: cross-sectional differences in height, weight, vocabulary, quantitative reasoning, and motor control may be of little interest compared with understanding children's growth trajectories on each of these outcomes. An intervention to enhance growth in any of these areas can affect cross-sectional status only by deflecting the growth trajectory. Over time, a shifted trajectory—what we refer to throughout this report as shifting the odds—will produce substantial shift in expected status, but the shift in *growth rate* is the leading indicator. Studies of causal effects on growth may be significantly more powerful than studies of status, particularly when the number of participants is strongly constrained by cost or logistical issues.

In principle, all of the ideas we have discussed apply to studies of growth as well as developmental status, if we simply reconceive the outcome as some interesting aspect of growth, such as an average rate of change or an acceleration rate rather than a cross-sectional outcome. However, assessing growth poses special problems of measurement, design, and analysis. Measuring growth is challenging for such psychological outcomes as vocabulary or quantitative reasoning, less so for physical characteristics such as height and weight. New design challenges arise in experimental studies because repeated measurements pose a risk of attrition, and because subtle forms of confounding can arise that are not present in cross-sectional research. Methods of analysis are typically more challenging as well.

Growth curve analysis has a long history in biology and medicine. Models for growth in stature during childhood, for example, have been developed and refined over many years. In measuring human height (or weight or lung capacity, for example), there is little disagreement about the meaning of the construct being measured or about the units of measurement (e.g., centimeters, grams, cubic centimeters). Unreliability of measurement is not a large problem.

Measuring growth in psychological domains (e.g., vocabulary, quantitative reasoning, verbal memory, hand-eye coordination, self-regulation) is more problematic. Disagreement is more likely to arise about the definition of the construct to be assessed. This occurs, in part, because there are often no natural units of measurement (i.e., nothing comparable to the use of inches when measuring height). As a result, units of measurement must be created and defended, and errors of measurement are likely to be quite large. This becomes especially problematic when the outcome of interest changes as children mature—as is the case with achievement outcomes—or when transitions are involved, as with the development of literacy. For example, once a child acquires visual recognition memory (between 3 and 9 months), it becomes more appropriate to assess the number of words the child knows and, later, to assess prereading skills. To compound this problem, it can be hard to reach agreement about the appropriate age range for which a particular psychological construct is relevant. Nevertheless, growth in these psychological domains is of great interest. Many important interventions are designed to enhance psychological growth, and theories of development depend on hypothesized causal chains that explain human variation in the rates of such growth.

Another obstacle to studies of change is the cross-sectional orientation of psychometrics. When social scientists speak of reliability of measurement, they are almost invariably describing cross-sectional reliability: that is, the reliability with which one can distinguish among individuals at any given time. The study of cross-sectional individual differences, especially differences in cognitive functioning, has had a powerful and enduring influence on the theory and practice of measurement in psychology. Only recently have researchers begun to take seriously the reliability with which one can distinguish among individuals in rates of change, acceleration, or other aspects of developmental trajectories (see Willett, 1988, for a review).

An example may prove instructive. Consider Figure 4-1, which displays expressive vocabulary as a function of age for three children, based on the work of Huttenlocher et al. (1991). The researchers took pains to estimate the total number of words in a child's expressive vocabulary on each of multiple occasions during the second year of life, a period during which vocabulary rapidly grows from a starting point near zero at age 12 months. Note that a curved line with positive acceleration neatly fits the repeated measures for each child. What is distinctive about each child's growth record is not the starting point (vocabulary is near zero at age 12 months for all three children) nor the standing of the child at any time point, but rather the rate of acceleration for each child. This rate of acceleration is increasingly well measured as time points are added. Subsequent analyses found a strong relationship between maternal speech and vocabulary acceleration. The statistical power of such analyses was strengthened by the fact that it effectively incorporated all the data in a single analysis. That is, every occasion of measurement contributed to understanding a single crucial aspect of growth (acceleration), enabling the researchers to discover relations that had proved elusive in studies of change in relative status.

The following appear to be the key ingredients in studies of quantitative growth:

- A clear definition of the outcome variable or construct on which children are believed to be growing.
- A measurement unit or scale that has constant meaning over the age range of interest (e.g., height in inches or the number of words in a child's expressive vocabulary).
- An outcome that can be measured on a common scale across ages, such that the alternative, age-appropriate forms of the assessment can be equated, that is, put onto the same meaningful scale.[3]
- A statistical model for individual change over time. During the second year of life, for example, the appropriate model for vocabulary is a positively accelerating curve, as depicted in Figure 4-1.
- A longitudinal study that is optimally designed to ensure a given level of statistical precision for the question at hand. Trade-offs among the length of the study, the frequency of observation, and the sample size are invariably involved.

These design choices strongly affect the reliability and validity of individual measures of change.

These choices can also affect the internal validity of quasi-experimental studies. Experts on developmental change have emphasized the value of interrupted time-series designs when children are growing, especially when randomized experiments are not feasible (Bryk and Weisberg, 1977; Campbell and Erlebacher, 1970; Glass et al., 1972; Porter, 1967; see also Blumberg and Porter, 1983). In these designs, multiple pretreatment observations are taken in order to establish a pretreatment trajectory for the children. Figure 4-2 illustrates the value of this approach. Designs that include only one pretest before a treatment or intervention, followed by a posttest after the treatment (see shaded portion), cannot distinguish whether the apparent gains made by the participants (thick line) compared with the

---

[3]Standardization within age, as is common in IQ tests, eliminates the possibility of a meaningful scale with respect to the construct of interest (e.g., cognitive ability) and therefore distorts the study of growth on that construct. Such standardized scales can exhibit shifts in the relative standing of persons, but they cannot reveal rates of growth with respect to the behavioral domain. One typical result is that individual differences in estimates of change become substantially less reliable after standardization, undermining the capacity of intervention studies to discover effects.

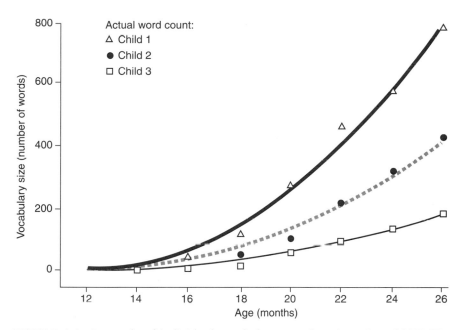

FIGURE 4-1 A sample of individual vocabulary growth trajectories. SOURCE: Huttenlocher et al., 1991. NOTE: •, Δ, and □ represent actual word counts for three individual children.

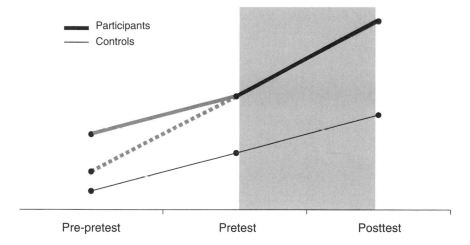

FIGURE 4-2 Distinguishing treatment effects from growth in time-series designs.

controls (thin line) are attributable to the intervention. If an additional pretest had been given, however, it would be possible to tell if the treatment actually accelerated the growth of the treated children relative to the controls (see thick line from the pre-pretest to the pretest for the participants) or if the children were already showing different rates of growth prior to the treatment (see dashed line). In this later case, the treatment actually had no effect; these patterns of growth would have been predicted without the intervention.

In sum, it is often essential in studies of early childhood development to recognize that children are rapidly growing. Causal inference on aspects of child growth poses important issues that extend beyond efforts to make causal connections between an intervention and a set of child outcomes at a given age. When the growth of interest is psychological, it is challenging to define clearly the dimensions on which children are growing, to devise assessments that are sensitive to growth, and to evaluate the capacity of alternative designs to reliably gauge individual differences in growth. Formulating and criticizing statistical models is essential to defining causal effects and considering threats to valid inference. Explicit models are especially important in cases in which participants are rapidly growing, because the meaning of growth and of causal effects on growth must be made explicit if progress is to be made in assessing the quality of the assessments or the utility of alternative designs for capturing these causal effects.

CONCLUSIONS

At the beginning of this chapter, we emphasized the importance of combining insights from basic and applied research to gain a fuller understanding of early development and the influences that guide and affect it. Basic research is designed to provide detailed observations of development and to test theories about causal mechanisms. It is often difficult, however, to meet the conditions that lead to strong causal inferences. In contrast, applied research avails itself of interventions and natural experiments that can often provide better evidence of causation and, when studies are designed appropriately, can help to specify the mechanisms involved. The challenge to researchers is twofold. The first involves designing studies and evaluations that successfully capture causal information. The second is to integrate the evidence from basic and applied research to evaluate alternative explanations for development and discern their implications for policies aimed at improving children's life chances.

In the final analysis, knowledge is advanced not through a single, decisive study, but by integrating evidence generated by different strategies, with different strengths and weaknesses. The research that generates this knowledge is, under the best of circumstances, a cumulative process that starts with rich descriptive data about the phenomena of interest, moves to understanding connections between outcomes and important influences on them, and finally seeks to identify causal relations and mechanisms. This chapter has focused on the final stage of this sequence, given its importance to both theoretical and political debates about the role of early experience in child development. Its purpose has not been to assert the superiority of causal studies, but rather, *when* causal questions are being addressed by research, to illustrate the key issues that arise and the critical importance of being tough-minded about ensuring that the conditions for making valid causal inferences are met. Only when the limits of current knowledge and the best thinking about improved designs are clear can we plan research that will contribute significantly to knowledge in the future.

II The Nature and Tasks of Early Development

etween the first day of life and the first day of kindergarten, development proceeds at a lightning pace like no other. Consider just a few of the transformations that occur during this 5-year period:

- The newborn's avid interest in staring at other babies turns into the capacity for cooperation, empathy, and friendship.
- The 1-year-old's tentative first steps become the four-year-old's pirouettes and slam dunks.
- The completely unself-conscious baby becomes a preschooler who not only can describe herself in great detail but also whose behavior is partially motivated by how she wants others to view and judge her.
- The first adamant "no!" turns into the capacity for elaborate arguments about why the parent is wrong and the preschooler is right.
- The infant, who has no conception that his blanket came off because he kicked his feet becomes the 4-year-old who can explain the elaborate (if messy) causal sequence by which he can turn flour, water, salt, and food coloring into play dough.

It is no surprise that the early childhood years are portrayed as formative. The supporting structures of virtually every system of the human organism, from the tiniest cell to the capacity for intimate relationships, are constructed during this age period. The fundamental capabilities that enable human beings to explore and learn about the world around us emerge and become remarkably sophisticated. The child becomes a social being with an array of deeply important relationships. Language is acquired and powerful communicative capacities develop. And, the child's emotional repertoire and awareness grow to encompass both tremendous joy and deep sadness. The tasks to be accomplished range from developing day-night rhythms to acquiring a rudimentary moral code to learning how to negotiate and sustain friendships.

At the same time, virtually no one argues that a given child's life course is set by the time of school entry. People are not like rockets whose trajectory is established at the moment they are launched. Indeed, it is the lifelong capacity for change and reorganization that renders human beings capable of dramatic recovery from early harm and incapable of being in-oculated against later adversity. This lifelong plasticity renders us both adaptive and vulnerable.

Development depends on both stability and flexibility—it is not a zero-sum game that sets the importance of the early years against the value of the later years. The real question is not which matters more—early or later experience—but how is later experience influenced by early experience? This directs attention to the early childhood years not because they provide an unalterable blueprint for adult well-being, but because what is learned at the beginning of life establishes a set of capabilities, orientations to the world, and expectations about how things and people will behave that affect how new experiences are selected and processed. The infant who has learned that he can engage his parent in play and make objects do what he wants them to do acquires a fundamental belief in his ability to affect the world around him. The toddler who has learned that the people she de-pends on for comfort will help her when she is distressed is more likely to approach others with empathy and trust than the toddler whose worries and fears have been dismissed or belittled. The preschooler who has rou-tinely cuddled into an adult's lap and read books before going to bed is more likely to enter kindergarten with a keen interest in reading. The child who has missed these experiences may have a hard time recapturing them later in life. In short, getting off to a good start in life is a strategy for increasing the odds of greater adult competence.

What do we know about how many young children are getting off to a good start? It would seem logical in a report of this nature to include information about trends in the well-being of young children. In fact, as a nation, we have surprisingly little information of this nature. We know far more about trends in the conditions, such as poverty and use of child care (see Part III), that affect young children than we do about the children themselves.

The data that are available present a very mixed picture (for an excellent overview, see U.S. Department of Health and Human Services, 1999a). While the nation has made impressive inroads in reducing infant mortality, rates of premature births and low-birthweight babies are increasing (see Chapter 8). Among other health indicators (not covered in this report), immunization rates have increased and lead exposure and unintentional injuries have declined substantially, but the percentage of young children living in poverty with activity limitations has risen and the incidence of asthma and chronic sinusitis has increased substantially for all children. The incidence of overweight school-age children is increasing, but data are not available on children under age 6. While there are a few signs that young children's early literacy is improving, the positive trends appear only for children who are not growing up in poverty and whose parents speak English as their native language (see Chapter 6). Rates of child abuse and neglect have remained constant for children under age 6 over the past decade (see Chapter 9). We know virtually nothing about trends in the incidence of mental health or behavioral problems affecting young children. Many groups before us have highlighted the tremendous need for better early childhood indicators in this country (see Hauser et al., 1997; National Research Council and Institute of Medicine, 1995a), for two recent reports on this issue); and we enthusiastically concur.

Developmental science does, however, allow us to address the question of what getting off to a good start means, and it can guide efforts to improve the nation's data on young children. These are the issues that we address in this part of the report. What are the most significant developmental changes that occur during these early years and that, if absent or seriously delayed, are cause for concern? What early experiences foster these developments, which undermine them, and how might this differ for different children?

There are libraries full of books on child development. Our intent was not to produce a comprehensive handbook that describes every facet of early development or a guide for parenting that addresses every milestone. Our review was more circumscribed. We sought to identify and discuss early developmental tasks that, if mastered, appear to get children started along adaptive pathways and, if seriously delayed or problematic, can lead a child to falter. We drew heavily on the legacy of research that has followed children over time, starting in infancy and preschool, to discern early precursors of later (and even lifelong) resilience and sustained competence (see Anthony and Cohler, 1987; Egeland et al., 1993; Garmezy and Rutter, 1983; Masten, 1994; Rutter, 1994; Werner, 1995, 2000). The internal resources and capabilities and external supports that characterize children who develop well despite adversity struck us as a fitting departure point for the exploration of the significant accomplishments of the early childhood years. Others have conducted similar reviews in recent years (see Carnegie

Task Force on Meeting the Needs of Young Children, 1994; Damon, 1998; Ramey and Ramey, 1999), and we benefited tremendously from their work as well. This led us to emphasize three domains among the many accomplishments that characterize the years from birth to age 5:

• Negotiating the transition from external to self-regulation, including learning to regulate one's emotions, behaviors, and attention. This captures the emergence of self-control and independence and can provide an analogy for the movement toward competent functioning that characterizes development as a whole (Chapter 5).
• Acquiring the capabilities that undergird communication and learning. This includes the early development of language, reasoning, and problem solving (Chapter 6).
• Learning to relate well to other children and forming friendships. This highlights the emerging capacity to trust, to love and nurture, and to resolve conflict constructively (Chapter 7).

The behavioral evidence on these topics provides a rich portrait of how early development unfolds in interaction with people, things, places, and events; the conditions under which it appears to get off track; and the factors that seem to make a difference in whether the child is equipped to learn, make friends, and enjoy life as a 5-year-old. We close this part by looking inward at the developing brain (Chapter 8). Not only has the research on early brain development generated tremendous public excitement, but it also complements what we have learned from behavioral research and points to some areas of special concern. Considered together, these two streams of behavioral and neuroscience research offer a fuller portrait of early childhood than does either one considered alone.

5   Acquiring Self-Regulation

uman infants start life as remarkably helpless individuals who elicit powerful protective responses from their caregivers. On their own, they would die. In relationships with protective, nurturing adults, they thrive. Supporting their development, however, requires sustained patience and adaptation as infants move gradually and unevenly from needing help in order to do anything, to doing—and even insisting on doing—many things for themselves. Scientists have found it useful to capture this transition from helplessness to competence in terms of the child's growing regulatory capacity. What does this mean? Initially, it refers to the mastery of tasks that were accomplished by the mother's body or in concert with the mother's body when the child was in the womb, but now must be accomplished by the child's body and through signaling needs to responsive adults. These tasks include everything from maintaining a normal body temperature to orchestrating physiology and behavior to conform to the day-night rhythm of human existence, to learning to soothe and settle once basic needs are met. Later, it means developing the capacity to manage powerful emotions constructively and keep one's attention focused. This chapter addresses these regulatory tasks.

Regulation cuts across all aspects of human adapatation. Living and learning require people to react to changing events and then to regulate their reaction. The capacity to react and the toll that reaction takes depend on the capacity to recover from the reactions. For example, getting upset by things that are upsetting can be very useful. It motivates people to act to make life better. But staying upset, ruminating, or carrying negative emotions around like a talisman can be very destructive to oneself and others. Mobilizing efforts to explore a new problem or situation is very important and useful; staying mobilized while working on a problem to the point of exhaustion and collapse is unhealthy. Adequate adaptation and development require reaction and regulation. Infants and young children are often good at the reaction part, but need help with regulation. Children increasingly develop the ability to regulate their reactions, particularly in supportive environments. To reiterate one of our core concepts, development may be viewed as an increasing capacity for self-regulation, seen particularly in the child's ability to function more independently in a personal and social context.

Reaction and regulation can be seen in all aspects of life, from the capacity to work harder when one is rested better to the capacity to fight diseases better when one is able to both turn on and turn off the immune system more efficiently. Regulation in early development is deeply embedded in the child's relations with others. In caring for infants, parents are acting as extensions of their internal regulatory systems. Establishing the connection between parent and child can be seen as the basic task of the early months of life. Making that connection is not always easy, however. It requires the ability to read and understand the baby's needs and the knowledge, energy, and resources to respond in ways that are helpful. Providing the experiences that allow children to take over and self-regulate in one aspect of their lives after another is a very general description of the job of parents, teachers, and protectors of children that extends throughout early childhood and into the adolescent years. The first step in the earliest days of children's lives is to establish regulatory connections with them and then gradually shift the responsibility of regulation over to them in the day-to-day domains of sleeping, waking, and soothing.

In this chapter, the development of self-regulation is profiled with respect to managing physiological arousal, emotions, and attention. These are fundamental tasks for the early years, but they entail very different influences and developmental processes. The reason for considering each a component of developing self-regulation is that these are the earliest ways that infants and toddlers learn to manage themselves and begin to acquire the behavioral, emotional, and cognitive self-control that is essential to competent functioning throughout life (Bronson, 2000; Kopp, 2000). Each is important also because it reflects the growing maturity and integration of several brain areas (particularly in the frontal regions) that enable increased self-monitoring and deliberate inhibition of undesired behavior (Diamond, 1996; Diamond and Taylor, 1996; Diamond et al., 1994).

These neurobiological changes are consistent with the common observation that, between birth and age 6, children become increasingly proficient at exercising self-control and applying rules consistently to their own behavior, whether this is manifested in their success at "Simon Says," their ability to wait for a cookie, their capacity to remain quiet and still during religious services, or their capacity to ignore distractions while concentrating on a task. Further advances in the same brain regions are thought to be related, at older ages, to the growth of higher-level reasoning, problem solving (Case, 1992), and planning and executing complex actions, sometimes called "executive control" (Stuss, 1992), which we profile in the final section of this chapter.

EARLY REGULATORY TASKS

Some cultures celebrate a child's first birthday at about 3 months after birth. This recognizes the fact that the child's life history began at conception. But interestingly, it also corresponds to what has been called the first biobehavioral shift in development (Emde et al., 1976). Between 3 and 4 months after birth, there are marked changes in almost every aspect of infant functioning, from the electrical patterns of brain activity (EEG) (Emde et al., 1976) to the regulation of visual attention (Rothbart et al., 1994a). Sharper focus on the first 3 months of life suggests that the entire period is one of transition, as the baby's behavior and physiology shift from intrauterine to extrauterine regulation (Mirmiran and Lunshof, 1996). The full-term newborn of normal weight comes into the world well-prepared to negotiate this transition.

As with all developmental tasks, however, cultural variations in caregiving practices and individual family differences within cultures affect how this early transition is worked through. The full range of childrearing practices around the world appears to confront newborns with markedly different contexts in which to manage the transition from intra- to extrauterine regulation (Barr et al., 1987). Nevertheless, babies adapt, and indeed thrive, in a wide variety of culturally normative caregiving niches. This theme of developmental adaptation within cultural variation applies to virtually all developmental tasks for which we have pertinent data.

Take the !Kung San—a hunter-gatherer culture from the Kalahari Desert—as an example. The young infant is in constant skin-to-skin contact with her mother, sleeping with her at night and being carried continually during the day. She is fed breast milk in small amounts approximately every 15 minutes. Fusses are responded to immediately before they build to cries. Little or no emphasis is placed on getting the baby to sleep through the night. At arguably the other extreme, in North America and Europe, early care typically separates the baby from the caregiver for varying periods of the day and night. Feedings are larger but more widely spaced. Not all cries, and certainly not all fusses, are responded to immediately. And there is a strong emphasis on encouraging day-night behavioral organization and sleeping through the night.

Although intriguing, there are few data on whether or how these different practices influence children's development in the long term. In the short term, it seems likely that both cultural and individual differences in caregiving influence what caregivers view as regulatory problems in this early period. Unfortunately, most of what is known about this has been based on studies in North America and Europe, where two regulatory concerns permeate the pediatric and child development literature: (1) concerns about establishing day-night rhythms, typically labeled "sleep problems" (Anders, 1979) and (2) concerns about excessive crying (Barr, 1993; Keefe, 1988; St. James-Roberts and Halil, 1991). These concerns, however, take different forms even within European-American cultures, as illustrated by comparisons between Dutch and U.S. (white) mothers (Super et al., 1996). While concerns about their child's sleep patterns were much more evident among the Dutch mothers, who focused on their own role in imposing regularity on sleep times, the U.S. mothers were much more likely to use the terminology of "problems" when discussing their child's sleep and to ascribe the problems to innate tendencies of the child rather than to their own parenting practices.

While parents raise issues about sleep and crying throughout infancy, they are particularly evident during this early birth-to-3-month transition period. Much of the research on these concerns has focused on identifying the underlying pathology in the child (Lehtonen et al., in press), yet there is very little evidence that early sleep and crying problems strongly predict later physiological or behavioral problems for otherwise healthy, full-term babies (Elliot et al., 1997; Rautava et al., 1995; Stifter and Braungart, 1992).

This has led to a more recent, albeit still controversial, approach that views these problems not as expressions of infant pathology, but as reflections of how normal individual differences are expressed when infants attempt to accomplish early regulatory tasks in the context of the dominant North American/European style of caregiving (Barr, 1990). This perspective shifts the unit of interest from the baby to the family, and from the behavior (i.e., crying per se) to what the behavior sets in motion within the family (Papoušek and von Hofacker, 1998; St. James-Roberts et al., 1995a; Stifter and Bono, 1998). There is, in fact, some evidence in support of this more dynamic perspective. These early sleep and crying problems can pose serious challenges to parents, which create tension among family members, fuel negative perceptions of the infant, and undermine the parents' confidence in their caregiving abilities. These detrimental repercussions remain measurable, at least in some families, later in infancy after the precipitating behavior has largely passed (Papoušek and von Hofacker, 1998; Raiha et al., 1995; Rautava et al., 1995).

The regulatory challenges of this period are heightened for premature or medically fragile infants (see Chapter 8 for a fuller discussion). There is a general consensus that the lower the birthweight, the more difficult the adjustment to extrauterine life, especially for the babies who are small for their gestational age and for those born to mothers with low educational attainment (Georgieff et al., 1989; Ment, 2000; Saigal et al., 1991). Among very-low-birthweight infants, there are the added risks of serious medical conditions and long stays in neonatal intensive care nurseries. Thus, each partner contributes vulnerabilities to the establishment of the mother-infant dyadic relationship. It is easy to understand that the mother would be stressed and anxious. The infant, in addition, tends to be much less adept than the normal newborn in organizing and stabilizing biological rhythms of sleep, waking, and feeding. He is likely to be more unpredictable, to be fussier during social interactions, to make less eye contact, to smile less, to vocalize less, and to show less positive affect—in other words, to be more difficult and harder for the parent to read (Beckwith and Rodning, 1992; Barnard and Kelly, 1990). Under these circumstances, the caregiver's ability to respond sensitively and to cooperate with the infant's ongoing behavior can be seriously compromised. But even here, a shift in emphasis from focusing on what is wrong with the baby to identifying caregiving strategies that provide support for the child's emerging regulatory competencies can be most helpful.

Because early intervention efforts, such as home visiting, often begin during this period, accurate information about early regulatory challenges may help service providers short-circuit potential corollary problems. Looking in more depth at what is now known about day-night rhythms and crying can expand the focus from the problem of getting the infant to sleep or stopping the infant from crying, to a better appreciation of the magnitude of the task that the infant is attempting to accomplish, individual differences in how infants respond during this time of transition, and the contribution of caregivers' responses to the success with which these transitions will be made. Accomplishing early regulation is an example of how the outcomes of developmental processes depend on the relationship between children and their caregivers.

Acquiring Day-Night Wake-Sleep Rhythms

Humans are diurnal beings who are typically active during the day and quiet at night. Through eons of evolution, human physiology has come to reflect this day-night rhythm (Moore-Ede, 1986). Day-night rhythms are due to both endogenous factors (clocks inside the body) and exogenous influences (the day-night rhythms in the physical and social world) (Ikonomov et al., 1998). The internal clock lies deep in the brain in a part of the hypothalamus called the suprachiasmatic nucleus (Dickstein et al., 1998a). It receives information about what time it is outside the body, generates signals that set the timers or pacemakers of different systems, and coordinates or synchronizes those various systems.

Newborns don't seem to know day from night (Anders, 1975). Is this because their internal clocks aren't fully mature? Is it because these clocks, although fully mature, still need to be set to the light-dark, activity-rest periods of family life? Does the fact that the newborn's energy needs require her to eat in the middle of the night keep her clocks from generating robust day-night rhythms (Wright et al., 1983)? Is she working on pulling together and orchestrating the rhythms of multiple systems—temperature, blood pressure, hormone, kidney, liver—that are themselves still maturing (Price et al., 1983)? We do not know the full answers to any of these questions yet. However, this list, which could be much longer, gives some of the flavor of the complexity of the task that faces both the newborn and the family in sorting out how to differentiate day from night.

Something is known about the facet that affects parents the most: infant sleep-wakefulness (Coons and Guilleminault, 1982; Elligson and Peters, 1980; Schectman et al., 1994). Both the structure and temporal organization of sleep evolves rapidly in the first 3 to 4 months after birth (Anders, 1975; Elligson and Peters, 1980; Gehart and Maccoby, 1980). Newborns sleep a lot, typically 16-17 hours per day (Coons and Guilleminault, 1982; Hoppenbrouwers et al., 1982), and the structure of sleep-wakefulness more strongly reflects a basic 90-minute rest-activity cycle than it does a day-night rhythm (Anders, 1982; Coons and Guilleminault, 1982). Total sleep time decreases to about 14-15 hours by 3 months, and sleeping and waking bouts begin to lengthen and consolidate (Anders et al., 1992; Bernal, 1973; Coons and Guilleminault, 1982). At birth, the longest sleeps last about 4 hours, while by 3 months they can be as long as 8 to 10 hours and, for most babies, they occur during the night (Anders et al., 1992; Bernal, 1973).

Like adults, during long periods of sleep, babies drift up to brief periods of waking or near waking. Videotaped studies of infant sleep suggest that one big difference between babies who sleep through the night and those who don't is what happens during these brief waking periods (Anders et al., 1992). Babies who sleep through rouse briefly and then settle themselves back into sleep, while those who don't then cry out and waken their parents. There is some evidence that babies who fall asleep in their cribs establish patterns of self-settling, while those who fall asleep in contact with a parent signal when they wake to circumstances that are different from those when they fell asleep. Patterns of feeding also influence nighttime signaling (and thus parental sleeping through the night) (Wright et al.,

1983). Bottle-fed babies lengthen the duration of their longest bout of sleep a bit faster than do breast-fed babies. While this can sound attractive to the sleep-disrupted parent, bottle-fed babies also get sick more than do breast-fed babies (Beaudry et al., 1995). Because the rhythms of other systems, like growth hormone, cortisol, body temperature, and so on, are orchestrated in relation to sleep, many suspect that the development and organization of sleep helps orchestrate the day-night rhythms in these other systems (Finkelstein, 1971; Koob, 1992; Weitzman et al., 1979).

Poets and philosophers have long been intrigued by the similarities between sleep and death. Parents find these similarities more terrifying than intriguing. Many a parent has probably poked or nudged his or her soundly sleeping infant to bring about reassuring signs of life. Although controversial, some suspect that the shorter bouts of sleep characteristic of early infancy may be protective for babies whose neural systems regulating breathing, swallowing, and airway clearing are still maturing (McKenna, 1990; Trevathan and McKenna, 1994).

Concerns that very young babies will sleep so deeply that they will fail to react when air is blocked and oxygen levels get too low have led to the recent pediatric advice to avoid placing babies on their stomachs during sleep (American Academy of Pediatrics Task Force on Infant Positioning and SIDS, 1992). Similar concerns have led researchers to reexamine what happens when babies sleep alone and when they sleep with others (i.e., cosleeping) (McKenna et al., 1993, 1994). Mothers and their 3-month or older infants have been brought into sleep laboratories, where brain waves, heart rate, and respiration for both mother and infant can be monitored throughout the night. Perhaps not surprisingly, mothers and babies don't sleep as soundly when they sleep together.

Because both breast-feeding and cosleeping induce shorter bouts and less sound nighttime sleep, several researchers have speculated that they protect the very young baby from such things as sudden infant death syndrome (SIDS) (McKenna, 1990; McKenna and Mosko, 1990). This is virtually impossible to prove. Nevertheless, differences in cultural practices surrounding cosleeping and breast-feeding abound. In this context, it may be useful to think broadly about how culturally normative variations mesh with the infant's developing capacities. On one hand, it is instructive to recognize that human infants have remarkable capacities to adapt to a wide range of caregiving practices. On the other hand, understanding practices that have evolved and been sustained around the world, but are less common in the United States, can be extremely valuable. Cultural differences are not arbitrary, nor do they reflect any simple translation from beliefs into practices; rather they reflect different trade-offs among several goals that can, in turn, have differing consequences for the infant.

Learning to Regulate Crying

Crying serves to signal caregivers. Infants of many species produce calls that serve similar functions. However, only humans cry for no reason at all (paroxysmal crying) and keep crying after being picked up, fed, and otherwise apparently made comfortable (Barr, 1990). Folk wisdom says that there are hunger cries, pain cries, irritable cries, and so on. In fact, when one hears cries out of context, the likelihood of identifying the cause of the cry is very poor (Green et al., 1995). Beyond what is causing crying, caregivers usually want to know how to stop the cries and soothe the infant.

Although there are marked cultural variations in beliefs about responding to all fusses and cries, once people do respond, they follow remarkably similar soothing patterns (Barr, 1990). They say something, touch, pick up, search for sources of discomfort, and then feed. Parents run through this repertoire so often in those early weeks and months of a baby's life that they could do it in their sleep—and often do, or so it seems. Infants cry in all of the cultures that have been studied, and interestingly, crying follows a similar developmental course (Barr, 1990; Barr et al., 1987, 1996). In caregiving settings as different as the !Kung and North America, crying makes up more and more of the baby's (and caregiver's) day until it peaks, often around 6 to 8 weeks, and then begins to decline (with the timing of the peak and decline varying for different babies). But cultural variations in caregiving practices may influence the amount of crying that characterizes infants. Comparing the !Kung and North American and Northern European babies, although crying peaks at about the same time, !Kung babies cry less, even at their peak. Furthermore, it is not that !Kung babies cry less often, rather that they are soothed more quickly.

Researchers in Canada tested whether they could help North American babies settle more readily by providing them with more of a !Kung-like caregiving experience (Hunziker and Barr, 1986). They randomly assigned families to a condition in which caregivers increased by 2 hours how much they carried the baby each day. Compared with babies in the control condition (in which caregivers kept on with their regular practices), babies who were carried around more shifted their crying toward the !Kung level of the curve. They did not cry less often, but began to be soothed more quickly. Unfortunately, the rather dramatic results of this study were not replicated when something similar was tried in England (St. James-Roberts et al., 1995b). The Canadian and English studies weren't identical, and researchers are still puzzling over whether the differences (in baby slings/packs, instructions to families, control group rates of carrying, or something else) might explain the lack of replication. This failure to replicate, however, probably suggests what parents have long suspected—there is no magic bullet, except perhaps time. By 12 to 16 weeks, most babies have settled down, spend less of their days crying, seem easier to read, and much easier to soothe.

There is also some evidence that individual differences in caregiving can affect crying in the earliest months of life. Babies whose caregivers have been responsive to their distress and sensitive in reading the meaning of their somewhat ambiguous cry communications shift more smoothly into patterns of noncrying communication and spend more time in happier, less distressed states as the first year proceeds (Crockenberg, 1981). This may sound like babies have never heard of the laws of learning (i.e., reward the behavior and it should increase). However, babies who are never responded to, such as those who grow up in institutions, often cease crying almost completely by about the time they are 3 months old. Babies evidently do learn to stop crying if it is never "rewarded." The laws of learning actually say that the most powerful way to keep a behavior going is to reward it sometimes and not others, termed "intermittent reinforcement." The laws of learning would argue that less, but intermittently, responsive parenting should create a baby who is more fussy and whiny. This, indeed, appears to be the case. The evidence that responding consistently and readily to the infant's cries reduces crying in the long run is not as strange as it first seems.

Not all crying is the same. Some parents live in dread of having an infant with colic. Colic is a syndrome that has perplexed parents and physicians for ages. It describes a syndrome of excessive, uncontrollable crying that, following the normal crying curve, also peaks around 6 to 8 weeks and resolves between 12 and 16 weeks (with lots of variation among babies in timing and duration) (Barr et al., 1992; Karofsky, 1984; Miller and Barr, 1991). Like other crying, it also clusters in the late afternoon and evening hours. It differs from noncolic crying primarily in being difficult if not impossible to soothe. Somewhat arbitrarily, colic is often defined for research purposes by Wessel's rule of three: fussing or crying for more than 3 hrs/day, for 3 days/week, for 3 weeks (Wessel et al., 1954). How much a baby with colic cries varies from one day to the next, and from one baby to the next. Using diaries kept by parents in which they record each crying bout of 5 minutes duration or more, the crying of infants with colic has been documented to vary from 3 hrs/day to as much as 6 or more hrs/day. This compares to the 1 to 2 hrs/day of crying that parents report for babies without colic. At its worst, a baby with colic may cry most of the time she's awake, and, adding insult to injury, she seems to sleep less than babies without colic (Lehtonen et al., 1994).

The word colic refers to what has seemed to be the obvious source of this crying: something to do with the digestive system. However, despite many attempts to identify what is wrong with the baby (i.e., sensitivity to cow's milk protein, incomplete lactose absorption, gastroesophageal reflux, gastrointestinal immaturity, including allergic reactions) thoughtful reviews of the data suggest that no more than 5 percent of colic can be attributed to identifiable pathologies (Gormally and Barr, 1997). That's not much, especially considering that the rate of colic may be as high as 10 to 20 percent in Western cultures.

Even if convinced that babies with colic are not suffering from a physical disorder, scientists, like the parents, wonder about its implications for who the baby is and who she will become. By definition, infants with colic are difficult. But does this mean that they are biologically or constitutionally predisposed to have difficult, irritable temperaments once the colic has passed? The weight of the evidence suggests that this is not true (Elliot et al., 1997; Rautava et al., 1995; Stifter and Braungart, 1992), but there is still argument over this conclusion primarily because of the difficulty of measuring both crying and temperament.

It must be a relief to parents of babies with colic to find that, by about 3 to 4 months, they have an emotionally quite different baby on their hands. No longer irritable or hard to soothe, the baby's true temperament begins to be more apparent. This is true not only of infants with colic. In general, it is difficult to predict later temperament from behavior in the first 3 to 4 months of life, as infants are going through so many transitions. Stability in infant temperament appears to increase by 4 months of age.

Recently, developmental psychologists have become quite interested in identifying the roots of a temperamental pattern that is known as behavioral inhibition. Inhibited toddlers and preschoolers are very shy in social encounters (Calkins et al., 1996; Rubin et al., 1997), wary of and upset by novel stimuli, and are thought of by parents and peers as anxious and fearful (García Coll et al., 1984). The impetus for this interest is twofold. First, there is growing concern with understanding the developmental pathways that lead to later anxiety and depressive disorders. Second, neuroscience research is revealing the specific neural pathways and neurochemical processes that underlie fear responses. This work is suggesting hypotheses about why some children may be extremely anxious and fearful from an early age.

This has led to several programs of research (see Fox et al., in press; Kagan and Snidman, 1991; Kagan et al., 1998) on young children who display fearful, shy, inhibited temperaments to identify both the antecedents and consequences of these characteristic patterns of responding to people and events. Kagan and his colleagues developed a set of challenges for 4-month-olds that included highly stimulating sounds, sights, and smells that are presented to the baby in a set order. Some babies think these stimuli are great. They smile, coo, and wave their arms around as if to say, "Give me more!" At the other end of the spectrum, some babies find the stimulation to be too much. They fuss, arch their backs, cry, and struggle, as if to say, "Take them away!" When babies are tested at 2 months, how they react to these challenges doesn't predict later temperament. However, by 4 months, reliable differences emerge. Babies who react positively are more likely to become busy, active, boisterous toddlers—some would say a handful, others refer to them as exuberant. In contrast, those who find the stimulation to be too much are more likely to be fearful and shy as toddlers and preschoolers. This evidence suggests that, for some children, negative reactivity to novel stimuli as infants evolves into a shy, inhibited, anxious temperamental pattern by toddlerhood.

This is not a trivial phenomenon. About 20 percent of healthy, European-American samples display negative reactivity to novel stimuli as young infants (Kagan et al., 1998). About one-third of the reactive infants studied by Kagan and his colleagues remained highly fearful of unfamiliar events at 14 and 21 months, and 13 percent of these infants continued to show subdued and shy behavior with unfamiliar adults and peers at 4 $1/_2$ years of age (Kagan et al., 1998). At age 6, the inhibited children continued to be socially wary and reticent during their interactions with peers and an adult experimenter, and they exhibited signs of physiological stress (Kagan et al., 1987). Researchers who have focused on the socially reticent behavior of these children have found contemporaneous associations with maternal reports of both shyness and internalizing behavior problems (Coplan et al., 1994). Recently, inhibited temperamental patterns have been associated with a physiological pattern of resting right frontal EEG activation (Calkins et al., 1996; Fox et al., 1995, 1996; Schmidt and Fox, 1994), which appears to be associated with a tendency to respond to stressful events with negative affect or depressive symptomatology (Davidson, 1992). Fox and his colleagues (in press) have recently linked this physiological pattern at 9 months of age to continuity in behavioral inhibition up to age 4. We refer to the same physiological pattern when we discuss the developmental consequences of maternal depression in Chapter 9.

Once caregivers and babies have ridden the roller-coaster of rapid developmental change through the first 3 months of life and the baby's behavioral style or temperament seems to be easier to discern, the next task is to support the baby's developing abilities to regulate his or her emotions and behavior.

Although learning to sleep through the night might seem far afield from controlling outbursts of emotion, learning to wait before acting, self-monitoring, and acquiring the ability to organize segments of behavior sequentially—all of which are embraced by the term "self-regulation"—they all involve various forms of self-monitoring and response inhibition that, in turn, reflect the growing maturity of the brain, as we discussed at the beginning of this chapter. The infant's emerging ability to replace crying with other forms of communication is just the first step along a developmental progression that recruits the child's increasing competencies into more and more mature self-regulatory functioning.

UNDERSTANDING AND REGULATING EMOTIONS

Emotions color the life experience of young children. They account for the peaks and valleys of daily life as they are manifested in exuberant peals of laughter during play, angry defiance when faced with unfamiliar food, or distress and frustration after a fall. Emotions can contribute to or undermine the growth of new skills and competencies in young children. The interest and pleasure a child brings to mastering new tasks motivates the development of new abilities. Angry conflict with a parent or a peer can be a catalyst for new understandings of others' feelings and motives. On other occasions, however, heightened emotion undermines a young child's capacities to function competently, as any parent witnessing a toddler's tantrum can document. Much of the current interest in early emotional development revolves around the young child's growing ability to regulate and integrate emotions adaptively into the fabric of social interactions. Both parents and the public, for example, are interested in ensuring that young children learn to handle anger and resolve conflicts without resorting to aggression, to "use their words" instead of hurling a block across the room. At the same time, understanding the development of emotion regulation requires a broader understanding of emotional development.

Early emotional development provides the foundation for psychosocial well-being and mental health. Just 20 years ago, the thought that very young children could manifest serious psychological disorders was unimaginable. Today people recognize that toddlers and preschoolers are subject to many of the same kinds of emotion-related disorders that have long been studied in older children, adolescents, and adults. In 1994, a diagnostic classification scheme was developed to assess emotional and developmental problems in the first three years of life (Zero to Three's Diagnostic Classification Task Force, 1994), and scientific inquiry into questions of young children's mental health has increased exponentially in recent years. Young children can experience problems related to sad, depressed affect (Cicchetti and Schneider-Rosen, 1986; Cicchetti and Toth, 1998; Kovacs, 1989), anxious fear (Albano et al., 1996; Thompson, in press(b); Vasey, 1998) and angry behavioral problems (Shaw et al., 1994, 1996; White et al., 1990). This emerging knowledge is bringing issues of early emotional development and regulation to the forefront of discussions about prevention, early detection, and early treatment of disorders in young children.[1] Over recent years,

---

[1]Reports of extensive pharmacotherapy for preschoolers with behavioral disorders have raised critical questions about existing diagnostic and treatment practices for social and emotional problems in young children and related concerns about the general lack of scientific evidence to guide appropriate intervention (see, for example, the recent NIH Consensus Statement on the Diagnosis and Treatment of Attention Deficit Hyperactivity Disorder, 1998).

there has also been a growing appreciation for the fact that children growing up in very different sociocultural contexts develop emotionally in different ways as a result of how emotions are socialized. Children learn to construe their emotional experience in culturally relevant ways (Eisenberg, 1986; Miller, 1994; Miller et al., 1996; Ochs, 1986).

After a brief overview, we describe in more detail what is known about how young children come to understand their own and other's emotions and about the early development of emotion regulation. Throughout, it is clear that just as it is impossible to understand the construction of a 50-story building apart from the scaffolding that supported its emerging structure, it is impossible to understand early emotional development apart from the parent-child or caregiver-child relationship within which this process unfolds. In addition, the task of learning how to manage one's emotions constructively is a different challenge for children with different temperaments, as well as for their parents.

Emotional Development

Compared with efforts to understand how children learn, the study of emotion in young children is relatively new. Researchers are still asking (Mascolo and Griffin, 1998): What is emotional development the development *of*? The answers range from the capacity to identify one's own feelings, to the development of empathy, to the ability to constructively manage strong emotions. All are correct. As more is learned, we are struck by the richness and complexity of young children's emotional lives, as well as by the remarkable accomplishments that they make in this area prior to school entry.

The ways in which researchers learn about emotional development are diverse and, in some cases, ingenious. Some have conducted fine-grained analysis of the facial expressions of young infants in interaction with their mothers; others have observed family interactions during dinnertime or bedtime (to obtain rich profiles of the family emotional climate), or engaged in conversations with young children about their understanding of emotion (often centered around hypothetical stories); still others have interviewed parents or other caregivers about the emotions they commonly observe in the children they care for. Few of these studies have followed

---

The committee did not specifically address these vitally important issues and does not include a discussion of them. This is not to imply, however, that we minimize their significance. To the contrary, these issues constitute an urgent topic for both scientific inquiry and guidelines for practice.

children over more than brief periods of time, however, so knowledge of emotional development is based largely on looking separately at infants, toddlers, and preschoolers and piecing together a picture of development from these cross-sectional data. Moreover, the broad mix of approaches to studying emotional development has not been matched by attention to the variety of contexts in which emotions develop and are socialized. Unfortunately, most of what is known has been based on studies of middle-class white children, despite suggestive evidence that socioeconomic and cultural contexts confer significant variability in how children learn to interpret and express their emotions.

Emotions are biologically basic features of human functioning. They are governed by very early-developing regions of the human nervous system, including structures of the limbic system and the brainstem that have a long evolutionary history. The capacity of a newborn to exhibit distress, fear, and rage reflects the early emergence of these biologically deeply rooted emotional brain systems. Chapter 8 discusses the richly interconnected brain structures and hormonal influences that organize the arousal/activation and regulatory/recovery interplay of emotional reactions (LeDoux, 1996; Panksepp, 1998; Schore, 1994). Throughout early childhood, other brain regions (especially in the frontal neocortex) progressively mature and become interconnected with these early-developing brain regions to contribute to the development of more accurate emotion appraisals, growing capacities for emotion self-regulation, complex emotional blends, and other developing features of mature emotional experience.

Individual differences in emotion, insofar as they derive from differences in temperament, are also biologically rooted. Temperamental qualities, including a child's typical ways of reacting to events, general mood, capacities for self-regulation, and activity level, appear early in infancy and, as mentioned earlier, show signs of stability starting at 4 months. Although the ways that temperament is manifested in behavior change significantly as the child matures—the fearful child practices being brave, the highly active child learns to sit still—these qualities are biologically or constitutionally based. Some of the most distinctive temperamental features that characterize infants at birth are based on emotional response tendencies, whether they concern the baby's dominant mood, adaptability, soothability, sociability, or fearfulness of novelty (Goldsmith and Campos, 1982; Goldsmith et al., 1987). Temperamental individuality is descriptive not just of response tendencies, but also of self-regulation (Rothbart and Bates, 1998). Young children who are reticent or withdrawn in response to new or challenging situations are displaying a temperamental attribute that is both emotional in quality (i.e., fearful) and self-regulatory (i.e., inhibited), with profound implications for their social as well as biological functioning (Kagan, 1998b). Emotions are, in short, one of the most ancient and enduring features of human functioning, and they develop significantly during the first years of life in the context of social interactions and relationships.

Emotional development during the first five years offers a window into the psychological growth of the young child (Denham, 1998; Lieberman, 1993; Saarni et al., 1998; Sroufe, 1996). Newborns' emotional lives center on feeling hungry or sleepy, too cold or too hot, and other manifestations of "state," and their emotional repertoires seem to range narrowly from crying to cooing. In contrast, physical states rarely determine the emotions of preschoolers. Their feelings hinge on how they interpret their experiences, what they think others are doing and thinking, and how others respond to them. In early infancy, emotions can be extreme and are not easily regulated by the child or, for that matter, by the parents. By the end of the preschool years, young children are capable of anticipating, talking about, and using their dawning psychological awareness of their own and others' emotions to better manage everyday emotional experience (Thompson, 1990, 1994). Their emotional repertoires have expanded dramatically and now include such feelings as pride, shame, guilt, and embarrassment that reflect developing self-understanding and social awareness. Preschoolers have also become proficient at anticipating other's emotions, adjusting their behaviors accordingly, and even hiding their emotions from others, all important social skills of which the young infant is incapable.

Emotions are, by their nature, relational (Emde, 1987, 1998). They both emerge from and provide the basis for human attachments, social communication, and prosocial as well as antisocial encounters with adults and children (Emde, 1987, 1998; Izard, 1991). A baby's cries of distress bring his caregivers to his side; his coos and gurgles illicit playful interaction. Even young infants smile in response to a smile and cry in response to a cry (Thompson, 1998a). By the end of the first year, infants are acutely sensitive to the emotional cues of other people, especially in uncertain or potentially threatening circumstances. In a process that researchers call social referencing, infants take their cues from the reassuring or anxious expression of a caregiver, which, in turn, can affect whether they continue to play comfortably or freeze in their tracks (Baldwin and Moses, 1996; Bretherton et al., 1981; Feinman, 1992; Saarni et al., 1998; Sorce and Emde, 1981; Sorce et al., 1985; Tomasello et al., 1993; Trevarthen and Hubley, 1978). By age 2, children begin to show genuine empathy towards others (Thompson, 1998a; Zahn-Waxler and Radke-Yarrow, 1990). They not only read and adjust their own responses to others' emotions; they try to make others, even their dolls and stuffed animals, feel better. In the years that follow, a child's emotional life is shaped by relational influences as diverse as the security of attachment relationships (Cassidy, 1994; Laible and Thompson, 1998), parent-child conversations about emotional events

(Kontos et al., 1994), and parental coaching of appropriate emotional expressions in social situations (Miller and Sperry, 1987). Emotional development is thus a window into how, early in life, developmental change and responsive relationships are entwined.

The cultural meanings expressed in these relationships also profoundly affect how children learn to construe and react to their emotional experiences (Eisenberg, 1986; Miller, 1994; Miller et al., 1996; Ochs, 1986). Cultural values affect how young children learn to interpret and express their experiences of fear, anger, shame, pride, embarrassment, and other emotions. They also guide the construction of new emotions and emotional blends (such as fear-shame, anger-guilt) that color emotional life and reflect these values. The sociocultural context also guides how emotions are socialized so that, for example, in some contexts experiences like teasing can serve constructive purposes and in other contexts they can be debilitating to the socialization of emotion and its expression (Briggs, 1992; Corsaro and Miller, 1992; Eisenberg, 1986; Miller and Sperry, 1987). As we discuss in the context of language development (see Chapter 6), emotions are also socialized in the context of parent-child discourse, as well as in the conversations that young children overhear among the adults around them. Chinese and Chinese-American mothers, for example, are more likely than European-American mothers in the United States to emphasize moralistic themes and the shame inherent in misbehavior when recounting their children's mischievous behavior to other mothers in the child's presence (Miller et al., 1990, 1996). In each case, mothers are interpreting the child's experience consistently with the broader values of their culture.

Because of the diverse and powerful ways that parents socialize emotional development, researchers have devoted considerable attention to the broader emotional climate of the home environment and its impact on young children (e.g., Gottman et al., 1997). In typical circumstances, young children are faced with a variety of emotional demands at home and are assisted in understanding and managing them by the support of their caregivers. When the emotional climate of the home is undermined—such as when parents experience marital dysfunction (Cummings, 1987; Cummings and Davies, 1994a; Davies and Cummings, 1994; Grych and Fincham, 1990; Lieberman and Van Horn, 1998), or parent-child interactions are conflictual, coercive, or abusive (Gaensbauer and Sands, 1979; Patterson et al., 1989, 1992), or the parent suffers from depression or other affective disorders (Dawson et al., 1994; Garber et al., 1991; Zahn-Waxler and Kochanska, 1990; Zahn-Waxler et al., 1991)—young children are confronted with conflicting, confusing, and sometimes overwhelming emotional demands. To make matters worse, they are often deprived of the parent as a resource for managing these powerful emotions (Thompson and Calkins, 1996; Thompson et al., 1995). It is not surprising to find that children from homes with serious marital conflict, or who are raised by a depressed parent, or who are maltreated are more likely than children who are spared these experiences to experience difficulties in emotion regulation and, for a small but significant minority, to develop affective disorders of their own.

What has not been appreciated until recently is that these disorders can be apparent early in life, as emotional experience is becoming organized in infancy and early childhood (Emde et al., 1993). Young children growing up with a parent with an affective disorder are themselves at risk for depression and other affective disturbances, partly as a consequence of the child's overinvolvement with the parent's emotional state and difficulties in managing the emotional demands this presents (Zahn-Waxler and Kochanska, 1990; Zahn-Waxler et al., 1988). Some young children (especially those who are dispositionally fearful or inhibited) are prone to anxiety-related disorders, especially when their temperamental vulnerability is coupled with anxious or hostile attachments to their caregivers (Cassidy, 1995; Thompson, in press(b); Vasey, 1998). Young children who are abused or neglected by their caregivers can experience significant emotional and psychosocial problems, including the display of intense, maladaptive emotions, difficulties in understanding emotion in others, and social incompetence (e.g., Beeghly and Cicchetti, 1994; Cicchetti, 1990; Rogosch et al., 1995; Shields et al., 1994). Seriously problematic parent-child interactions are also one of the cluster of features that distinguish young children who display conduct problems (Shaw et al., 1994, 1996).

These and other illustrations of the development of emotion dysfunction in early childhood suggest that, as a result of their reliance on the emotional support of their caregivers in understanding, experiencing, and managing their own feelings, young children may be particularly vulnerable to emotion-linked disorders when parent-child relationships are insecure, coercive, or otherwise troubled. This is especially so because of limitations in their independent capacities for emotional and behavioral self-regulation (Cole et al., 1994). Not only are these children failing to receive the positive supports they require for healthy emotional development; they are grappling, sometimes on a daily basis, with circumstances that undermine the well-being of many adults.

Learning to Understand Emotions

How do the indiscriminate cries of the infant become the preschoolers' differentiated feelings of anger, shame, embarrassment, and loss? Researchers have made some inroads into understanding how the generalized arousal conditions of early infancy mature into the more refined emotional states apparent in older children and adults. Social experiences are a central part

of the answer (Saarni et al., 1998). In practice, a child's emotional repertoire is socially constructed.

As parents and other caregivers respond to an infant's emotional expressions, manage the child's feelings, and later label and discuss emotional
experience, they help to organize and give meaning to early emotional
experience. For example, parents who discuss emotions more frequently
and elaborate on emotional experiences (e.g., Why do you think Sally is
sad? Do you think she misses her sister? What do you think you could do
to cheer her up?) tend to have children with more accurate and elaborated
understandings of emotion (Brown and Dunn, 1996; Brown et al., 1996;
Denham, 1998; Denham et al., 1994; Dunn, 1994; Dunn et al., 1991;
Nelson, 1993, 1996). Research on children with developmental disabilities
indicates that such conversations are crucially important. However, looking specifically at children with Down syndrome, their mothers are significantly less likely to refer to inner states (feelings and cognitive states) during
everyday conversations compared with mothers of normally developing
children, and the children are significantly less likely to talk spontaneously
about feelings and more likely to have delayed expressive language skills
(Beeghly and Cicchetti, 1997; Tingley et al., 1994). Parents also help their
children understand that "how I feel" is not necessarily the same as "how
you feel" and thus foster a growing awareness of other people as their own
actors—an essential building block of social understanding. Parental behavior can also serve as a catalyst for early empathic responding, especially
when parents fix their children's attention on another's distress and explain
the causes of that person's feelings (Zahn-Waxler et al., 1992).

Emotion understanding grows in concert with the development of other
forms of knowledge and learning in early childhood. Emotions are objects
of children's thinking as well as of their feelings. Take, for example, the
burgeoning research on "theory of mind," which focuses on children's
developing frameworks for inferring what other people (or children) are
thinking, intending, believing, and feeling and then making predictions
about how they will respond (Astington, 1993; Bartsch and Wellman, 1995;
Flavell and Miller, 1998). Young children, it turns out, are remarkably
perceptive. Even 2-year-olds, for example, understand that people have
inner experiences of perceiving, feeling, and desiring and that they will feel
good if they get what they want and feel bad if they don't. Four- to 5-year-
olds appreciate the more complex connections between emotions and an
individual's thoughts, beliefs, and expectations (Bartsch and Wellman,
1995; Flavell and Miller, 1998; Wellman, 1990; Wellman et al., 1995).
They understand, for example, that individual tastes and preferences guide
how people respond emotionally to rock music or a symphony. Their
appreciation of the connection between emotions and expectations appears

also in their delight in fooling others—such as telling a sibling that the thermos contains hot chocolate, when water is really inside.

In the years that follow, children begin to understand the dynamics of emotional experience, including how emotional intensity gradually dissipates over time, how specific emotions are related to certain prior events, and how a person's background, experiences, and personality can yield unique emotional reactions to events (Gnepp and Chilamkurti, 1988; Harris et al., 1985; Thompson, 1989). Eventually children also begin to understand how a person can experience simultaneously multiple or conflicting emotions, but this is a conceptual achievement beyond the grasp of most preschoolers. These are momentous achievements, but the more important point is that children's emotional and cognitive development support each other. Certain emotional understandings and capacities (including regulatory capacities) are simply beyond their reach until they have reached certain levels of cognitive maturity. The combination of emotional difficulties and communication problems (e.g., major speech delays, hearing problems) in young children provides a more troubling example of how different facets of development interact to facilitate or undermine their overall functioning (Prizant et al., 1993).

Understanding emotion is also closely linked to the growth of self-understanding and, with it, the capacity to experience self-conscious emotions such as pride and shame. Late in the second year and during the third year, young children begin to call themselves by name, to use "I" and "mine," and to assert their new feelings of competence and independence by insisting on "doing it myself" (Bates, 1990; Bullock and Lutkenhaus, 1988, 1990; Stipek et al., 1990). Along with this newly emergent self-consciousness, young children begin to exhibit pride, guilt, shame, embarrassment, and other self-referent emotions (Barrett et al., 1993; Lewis, 1993; Tangney and Fischer, 1995). Once they have a self, in other words, young children begin to respond to experiences—good and bad—on behalf of the self. Catching a ball prompts not only glee, but also pride; spilling food in one's lap brings not only discomfort, but also shame and embarrassment. Interestingly, this is also the beginning of self-regulation and self-control (Kopp and Wyer, 1994). These self-conscious emotions are advanced by the young child's capacity to see the self as an object of observation and evaluation by others, to understand behavioral standards, and to apply those standards to an evaluation of their actions (Kochanska and Thompson, 1997; Kochanska et al., 1995). Guilt derives, for example, from the realization of how one's behavior has departed from an accepted standard, while pride arises from awareness of how one's actions have exceeded what might reasonably have been expected. With these transitions in self-awareness, the young child is an emotionally much different person than before. Her emotional life is now colored by the feelings evoked by others' evaluations and by her own self-judgments. Emotional development thus depends on and affects the development of the self.

Learning to Regulate Emotions

As young children acquire a better understanding of emotions, they become more capable of managing their feelings (Fox, 1994; Garber and Dodge, 1991; Kopp, 1989; Thompson, 1990, 1994). Emotion regulation is perhaps the most challenging aspect of emotional development. Regulating feelings depends on putting understandings about emotion to work in real-life contexts that can be extremely frustrating, upsetting, or embarrassing. Even positive emotions require regulation; exuberance is appropriate on the playground but not in a hospital. The task of emotion regulation is not simply a matter of learning to suppress emotions. It is more broadly one of deploying emotions effectively in relationships, while playing and learning, and in a wide range of settings. The fact that cultures and even individual families differ in their standards for the appropriate display and management of emotions makes this task especially challenging for children who cross over from one cultural environment (e.g., their immigrant family) to another (e.g., their preschool, which may or may not reflect their home culture).

Children start life completely incapable of modulating the expression of overwhelming feelings, integrating emotions adaptively into the fabric of social interactions, and deploying emotions in the service of focusing and sustaining attention. From a very early age, however, infants develop rudimentary skills for managing their own emotional experiences, in part by learning to enlist others who can help them. This can be observed initially in the comfort seeking of a distressed infant or toddler (Thompson, 1990). By the middle of the second year, toddlers can already be observed making active efforts to avoid or ignore emotionally arousing situations, engaging in encouraging or reassuring self-talk, changing or substituting goals that have been frustrated, and other quite sophisticated behavior strategies for managing emotions (Braungart and Stifter, 1991; Bretherton et al., 1986; Buss and Goldsmith, 1998; Calkins and Johnson, 1998; Cummings, 1987; Grolnick et al., 1996; Smolek and Weinraub, 1979; Stein and Levine, 1989, 1990). By the time of school entry, children's regulatory repertoires have become increasingly proficient and flexible as they learn, for example, that their interpretations of events can affect how they react and that they can camouflage their emotions if need be (Harris, 1993).

Children who learn to manage their emotions constructively not only have an easier time with the disappointments, frustrations, and hurt feelings that are so prevalent when they are young—and are presumably happier as a result—but they also have an easier time relating to others at home, in child care, and on the playground, as we discuss in more detail in Chapter 7. Indeed, the close correspondence between emotion regulation and relationships with peers has critical implications for efforts to foster positive social interactions and help young children who have problems in this area. Acquiring the capacity to regulate emotions also helps children believe that emotions are manageable, controllable, and can be appropriately mobilized and expressed—in short, that one's feelings need not be overwhelming, undermining, or disorganizing —what Saarni (1990, 1999) calls "emotional self-efficacy." Children who do not feel in control of their emotions are more prone to outbursts, inattention, and rapid retreats from stressful situations, thereby creating a self-fulfilling prophecy (Garber et al., 1991). Finally, the capacity for self-regulation is a prerequisite for the critical task of learning to comply with both external and internalized standards of conduct (Zahn-Waxler and Radke-Yarrow, 1990; Zahn-Waxler et al., 1992). Compliance is dependent on the child's ability to control his reactions, as well as his motivation to do so.

Parents contribute in multiple ways to children's developing capacity for emotion regulation. As with the infant's emerging ability to regulate states like crying, the parents' role in socializing emotion regulation is one of gradually handing over the reins to the child. At first, parents and other caregivers intervene directly to soothe or pacify the infant, organizing the child's experiences around routines that are manageable and predictable. These behaviors lend predictability to the infant's world, reduce the emotional demands of daily experiences, and "scaffold" the infant's own efforts at emotion regulation. Later, parents and others coach children in strategies for mobilizing their emotions to fit the needs of a given situation, whether it involves comforting a hurt friend, learning to take turns, or dealing with the frustration of attempting a task that is just beyond their capabilities (Thompson, 1990). This involves a subtle blend of give-and-take with the child (i.e., you hide and learn that you can handle the anxiety of doing without me momentarily, and then I'll find you and dispel your anxiety), the provision of supportive challenges (i.e., this puzzle may be a little frustrating, but I'll help you do it), and respect for the child's unique ways of dealing with emotions (i.e., I'll let you blow off some steam before I try to calm you down). Equally important, however, are the more subtle ways in which the reassurance that young children derive from their attachments to caregivers constitute an important resource for emotion regulation (Cassidy, 1994, 1995; Cassidy and Berlin, 1994; Nachmias et al., 1996). Emotion regulation is fostered, in other words, not only by the parent's immediate interventions but also by the security and confidence that the relationship with the caregiver inspires in children as they grapple daily with feelings that, initially without even a vocabulary to describe them let alone strategies for managing them, can be confusing and frightening (Case, 1992; Diamond, 1996; Diamond and Taylor, 1996; Diamond et al., 1994; Johnson, M.H., 1998; Rothbart et al., 1990, 1994; Stuss, 1992).

Parents, however, do not operate in a vacuum. Research is revealing the large extent to which the task of learning how to manage one's emotions and integrate them into daily life is a different challenge for children with different temperaments, as well as for their parents. The ability to inhibit a response one is all set to perform, sometimes called effortful control, has been of special interest to researchers who seek to understand how individual differences in children's tendencies to respond to stressful or exciting events affect the growth of emotion regulation. Effortful control is one component of a larger set of inhibitory competencies, termed "executive functions," discussed later in this chapter.

Effortful control is what enables the preschooler to take a response that is "primed" and inhibit it. Examples include acting only when it is appropriate to the rules (such as when the game leader says "Green light!"), constraining negative emotional outbursts, and planning a long-term strategy for a desired reward (such as saving an allowance to buy a Nintendo game). A game like Red Light, Green Light or Simon Says, for example, involves getting one type of behavior going (like walking quickly to the finish line or doing whatever Simon says as fast as you can) and then suddenly inhibiting or stopping those actions. Doing well at these games requires paying sharp attention for a long time, keeping track of the rules of the game, and interrupting actions that you are all set to perform. The more excited children get about playing these games, the harder it is for them to play them well. The faster they get going, the harder it is to stop. In the language used at the beginning of this chapter, the stronger the reaction, the greater the challenge for regulation.

The ability to play these games (and to use these competencies in general) seems to involve the development of structures in the prefrontal areas of the brain (Rothbart et al., 1995). An area of the frontal lobe called the anterior cingulate gyrus becomes very active any time one effortfully attempts to inhibit a thought or action for which one is primed. This area of the brain, like many areas in the frontal lobe, develops slowly over the course of childhood. People get better at performing the cognitive tasks that involve the anterior cingulate as they get older, and they also get better at controlling their emotional expressions as they get older. What researchers are now trying to determine is whether these two phenomena go together. Children of the same age exhibit differences in behaviors that should reflect the development of the frontal lobe. Parents and teachers report that some children are better than others at inhibiting inappropriate behavior, playing games like Red Light, Green Light and so on. So far, for normally developing children, the most evidence that effortful control is involved in emotion regulation comes from studies using parent and teacher questionnaires and observational tasks (i.e., not peeking while an experimenter wraps a present for you) involving behaviors that should reflect these competencies. There is very little evidence as yet that relates data obtained from these methods to activity in the anterior cingulate or other areas in the frontal lobes. Thus, the link to brain development is still only a theoretical one.

Children develop effortful control competencies gradually over the preschool years, and the full expression of these competencies requires development that extends into adolescence. From early in their development, some children seem to be better at effortful control than others, and there appears to be reasonable stability in this aspect of temperament and regulatory capacity (Kochanska et al., 2000). There is also growing evidence that individual differences in these capacities have meaningful implications for several aspects of early development that parents and others who work with young children care a great deal about. For example, young children who are higher on measures of effortful control tend to perform better on measures of early conscience and moral behavior (Kochanska et al., 1996, 1997). Conversely, infants and young children who have difficulties with inhibiting more compelling, negative impulses also tend to elicit aversive responses from others which, in turn, recreate precisely the kinds of experiences that lead to impulsive and negative behaviors (Rothbart and Bates, 1998). Not surprisingly, children who are not good at effortful control have a hard time with peer relations (see Chapter 7). In each of these examples, the response biases that come with a young child's unique temperamental profile provide the intrinsic context within which developing capacities for self-regulation emerge.

In sum, self-regulatory skills have important implications for how well children negotiate many other tasks of early childhood. Identifying and intervening with children who need extra help in developing these competencies may be important. However, determining who really needs help, as opposed to just more time to grow up, may be difficult. Furthermore, it seems possible that children who have more to regulate (i.e., those who are more exuberant and more active, more anxious and inhibited) may appear to be delayed or deficient in self-regulatory abilities, when in fact they are not. They may simply need to reach more mature levels of these abilities to be able to adequately manage who they are.

REGULATION OF ATTENTION AND EXECUTIVE FUNCTION

Just as infants and young children must learn to control their emotions, they must also learn to control behavior and regulate mental processes. The ability to think, retrieve, and remember information, solve problems, and engage in other complex symbolic activities involved in oral language, reading, writing, mathematics, and social behavior is dependent on the development of attention, memory, and executive function (Lyon, 1996). Difficulties with these more cognitive aspects of self-regulation can lead to problems in school, in relationships, and in life.

Self-regulation of attention and cognitive abilities is often described as a form of executive function. Executive function is an umbrella term used to refer to a variety of interdependent skills that are necessary for purposeful, goal-directed activity, such as learning to hold a crayon and scribble on paper, string beads, or hand a cup of juice to a friend without spilling (e.g., Luria, 1966; Shallice, 1982). To engage in these sorts of behaviors, the child must be able to deploy a series of relatively complex skills. They include generating and maintaining an appropriate mental representation that guides goal attainment ("I need to hold up the string and put the end through the hole in the bead"), monitoring the flow of information about one's progress ("I've got one on, now I'll try another"), and modifying and flexibly adapting problem-solving strategies so that behavior is continually directed toward the goal ("Oops, that bead was too hard to string; maybe I need to find a bead with a bigger hole"). These skills are needed whether the task involves correctly sorting colored blocks, gaining entry to a peer group, or successfully riding a tricycle. The construct of executive function is difficult to define, in part, because executive function, attention, and memory are interdependent and have fuzzy boundaries (Lyon, 1996). Despite difficulty in establishing a clear definition, there is growing consensus among researchers as to what executive functions entail: self-regulation, sequencing of behavior, flexibility, response inhibition, planning, and organization of behavior (see Eslinger, 1996). Control and modulation of behavior are fostered by the abilities to initiate, shift, inhibit, sustain, plan, organize, and strategize (Denckla, 1989).

Emerging Capacities for Executive Functioning

Early researchers did not study executive functioning in young children, believing that executive skills were not functional until the brain reached maturity in adolescence (Golden, 1981). It is now generally recognized that early precursors of these skills are present in infancy (Welsh and Pennington, 1988), and there is a growing body of research that demonstrates that performance on executive tasks improves in a stage-like manner that coincides with growth spurts in frontal lobe development during infancy and through the early childhood years (Anderson, 1998; Bell and Fox, 1992, 1994; Levin et al., 1991; Posner et al., 1998; Thatcher, 1991; Welsh and Pennington, 1988). This evidence for the early emergence of executive skills is further supported by findings from the neuropsychological literature that link deficits in executive function to early frontal lobe dysfunction (Benton, 1991; Eslinger and Grattan, 1991; Tranel et al., 1994).

What are the first signs of emerging executive skills, and when do they develop? At a very basic level, executive functions cannot emerge before the child is able to orient to relevant and important features in the environment, anticipate events, and represent the world symbolically (Barkley, 1996; Borkowski and Burke, 1996; Denckla, 1996; Pennington et al., 1996). Recent methodological advances have made it possible to study some elements of these abilities in infants. For example, Haith and his colleagues have demonstrated that infants as young as 6 weeks are capable of anticipating a sequence of events (Dougherty and Haith, 1997; Haith and McCarty, 1990; Haith et al., 1988). When they are shown pictures that appear and disappear in predictable locations at predictable times, 6-week-old infants quickly form expectations and demonstrate they can anticipate the location of the next picture by shifting their eyes to the predicted location before the picture appears (Haith et al., 1988). The ability to make anticipatory eye movements using these simple sequences improves with age, becoming consistent by $3 \frac{1}{2}$ to 4 months (Haith et al., 1988; Johnson et al., 1991), but then it reaches a plateau in which there is no improvement between 4 and 10 months (Posner et al., 1997). It is not until age 18 months that infants can anticipate ambiguous, context-dependent sequences (e.g., learning to look at a target that moved from location 1 to location 2 and then back to locatoin 1 before moving to location 3) that would require focused attention in adults (Posner et al., 1997). These emerging abilities to control attention underlie the development of executive functions that entail, for example, planning and executing sequences of behavior.

Means-ends behavior, another precursor to executive functioning, commonly emerges around ages 8 to 12 months, when the infant will, for example, remove an obstacle to retrieve a toy (Piaget, 1952). Research aimed at linking the emergence of goal-directed behavior to early brain development has provided evidence that frontally mediated, goal-directed, planful behavior is present as early as 12 months in infants (Diamond, 1988; Diamond and Goldman-Rakic, 1989; Goldman-Rakic, 1987). At about the same time, children learn to use language and to represent the world through symbols. Symbolic representation and language are the means through which a child can link the present with past knowledge and a future goal (e.g., Baron and Gioia, 1998; Kopp, 1997). They are believed to be the cornerstone for working memory and a necessary component for executive problem solving (Goldman-Rakic, 1987).

A third skill that emerges in infancy and continues to develop through childhood is self-control (Kopp, 1982). Research on self-control examines the child's emerging ability to comply with a request, to inhibit or delay an activity, and to monitor behavior according to the situational demands

(Kopp, 1982). The ability to exercise self-control increases from 18 to 30 months and becomes more stable across time and across situations (Vaughn et al., 1984).

The capacity to use developing executive function to regulate behavior and emotions in the service of social goals and situational demands is sometimes referred to as inhibitory or effortful control, as discussed above. Because many skills, competencies, and experiences affect whether a child can regulate his or her emotions and behavior, researchers have used a wide variety of tasks to assess individual differences in effortful control. These tasks include being able to shift with ease from doing something as "fast as you can" to "as slow as you can" to being able to "not peek" when waiting for a surprise gift, to being able to play games like Simons Says. When individual differences on such tasks are assessed and averaged, they provide one window into why some children comply more readily with adult requests not to touch interesting things even when the parent is not watching and more readily resist the temptation to cheat on games even when they think they will not be caught. Being good at effortful control tasks, including those that more directly assess executive functioning, doesn't mean that a child will behave in compliance with social rules that require self-control, however. Aspects of children's relations with others that motivate them to want to adopt the rules of their group also matter (Kochanska, 1990).

A number of researchers have investigated the developmental trajectories of executive function by presenting children with a battery of tests purported to measure different aspects of this domain of regulatory behavior (e.g., Gnys and Willis, 1991; Levin et al., 1991; Welsh et al., 1991). The focus here is not on precursors of executive function, but on manifestations of behaviors that constitute components of this construct. These studies have demonstrated that the different component skills involved in executive functioning show different developmental trajectories and mature at different rates. In one of the first studies to include preschoolers, children ages 3 to 12 were presented with a series of tasks that involved visual searching, verbal fluency, motor planning, planning sequences, the ability to respond flexibly to changes in the environment, and the capacity to inhibit responses (Welsh et al., 1991). Patterns of performance on these measures indicated that three underlying factors captured children's responses: (1) fluid and speeded response (2) hypothesis testing and impulse control and (3) planning. The investigators interpreted their findings as evidence for stage-like development, with the first stage beginning around age 6, the next stage around age 10, and the final stage during adolescence. Six-year-olds, for example, were able to perform as well as adults on tasks that involved visual searching and planning simple sequences, whereas it was not until adolescence that the ability to plan complex sequences, verbal fluency, and motor planning reached maturity.

In contrast to the research on children's emerging capacities to regulate states and emotions, relatively little is known about how parents, other adults, and features of children's early environments affect the development of attention regulation and emerging executive functions. These influences clearly matter (Carlson et al., 1995), but researchers have yet to identify the mechanisms that account for individual differences among young children. Research on school-age children demonstrating that it is possible to teach attentional skills and executive functions to individuals with developmental disabilities (Borkowski and Burke, 1996; Graham and Harris, 1996) also indicates that they are amenable to environmental influence.

Deficits in Executive Function and Attention

The importance of understanding how children learn to plan and organize new actions, remember past experiences and bring them to bear on new experiences, and maintain attention to tasks is underscored by the consistent relation of deficits in any one of these processes to problems in school (Lyon, 1996). Of great interest to educators and parents alike is growing evidence that deficits in attention regulation and behavioral control are integral to disorders such as attention deficit hyperactivity disorder (ADHD). They also have vast implications for social and emotional behavior given the highly permeable boundaries between cognitive abilities and social competence. For example, forethought and planning are intimately involved in making friends, seeking attention, and solving interpersonal conflicts. Because social interactions involve people and people are often unpredictable and have their own goals that may interfere with one's own, flexibility is essential for achieving social goals (Goodnow, 1987). To be a competent social problem solver, one must be able to detect obstacles that will interfere with social goals, generate and evaluate alternative strategies to overcome or prevent these obstacles, and be able to flexibly adapt behavior to meet the challenges presented by the constantly changing social environment (Rubin and Krasnor, 1986). These are extremely challenging tasks for young children.

Designing appropriate, individualized interventions for young children who are displaying early deficits in organizational, planning, and attention-related capacities depends on understanding the processes that underlie their development and manifestation. Taking ADHD as an example, this is generally considered to be a relatively common disorder, with prevalence estimates ranging from 0 to 16.7 percent with a median of 2 percent for school-age children (Lahey et al., 1999). Yet the true prevalence and the cause of ADHD remain unknown (Zametkin and Ernst, 1999). According to the *Diagnostic and Statistical Manual of Mental Disorders* (DSM-IV; American Psychiatric Association, 1994), the diagnosis of ADHD requires evidence of either inattention or hyperactivity and impulsivity. There are three subtypes of ADHD, the predominantly hyperactive-impulsive type, the predominantly inattentive type, and the combined type. Most of the research to date is on the hyperactive-impulsive and combined types. Focus on the inattentive subtype is an emerging research topic.

Tests of the validity of the three DSM-IV subtests of AHDH for preschoolers have been conducted with children 4 to 6 years of age. The findings show that the subtests are valid for children of these ages (Lahey et al., 1998). Yet diagnosis is complicated by the fact that many of the behaviors associated with ADHD are normal for preschoolers who often have difficulty paying attention and are impulsive and fidgety by nature. And there is no information about the validity of ADHD diagnosis below age 4. The absence of a nationally representative epidemiological study of mental health problems in the childhood population leaves us in the dark with regard to efforts to distinguish children who are at the ends of a typical spectrum from those who are manifesting serious delays. A related critical issue in both research and practice concerns how to differentiate ADHD from other frequently coexisting conditions, such as learning disabilities, oppositional-defiant disorder, conduct disorders, and anxiety disorders and also how to individualize treatment when ADHD occurs in conjunction with these and other disorders. A recent study of 7- to 9-year-old children shows that different types of treatments for ADHD benefit individuals with different combinations of problems (MTA Cooperative Group, 1999). Finally, recalling the core concepts in Chapter 1, it is critically important to note that many of the symptoms of ADHD are also nonspecific indicators that something is not quite right. Heightened activity can also occur, for example, when a child is overly tired or upset. This can make the clinician's task of sorting out true disorder from other problems exceedingly difficult, perhaps especially with a diffusely defined disorder such as ADHD (Rutter and Sroufe, in press).

In sum, understanding the constructs of attention, memory, and executive function is critical for understanding how children think, learn, and develop. Because these constructs are hard to define and have overlapping boundaries, there is a pressing need to develop more refined definitions of executive function and its component skills, and for valid measures of early manifestations of pertinent behaviors and abilities (Weinberg et al., 1996). The capacity to map specific executive functions onto specific areas of the brain and to distinguish normal development from emerging disorders is dependent on such efforts to lend greater precision to the analysis of task demands and individual children's responses. For these important capacities, there is much to learn about the emergence, integration, and consolidation of the skills that serve as building blocks for adaptive behavior and provide a yardstick against which to evaluate what is abnormal neurological or cognitive development.

It is clear at this point that the various components of active, internally guided regulation of attention, behavior, and emotion emerge in intricately interrelated ways at the end of the first year of life and then develop more rapidly during the toddler and preschool years (Kopp, 1982; Rothbart and Bates, 1998). They emerge in the context of caregiving relationships that explicitly guide the child from her dependence on adults to regulate virtually every aspect of functioning to gradually taking over and self-regulating her own behaviors and feelings in one aspect of her life after another. Parents don't tell their 3-year-olds to clean up their rooms and then leave them to their own devices. They help by suggesting that they start with the clothes and throw them in the hamper and then put away their blocks on the shelf. They praise them at each step along the way and then move on to pulling the covers up on the bed. They repeat these patterns over and over, day after day, and then begin to pull back the scaffolding as the child begins to do it himself. Some children need more scaffolding than others and for longer times. Some children have serious disorders, such as mental retardation, that interfere with their ability to benefit from parents' and others' efforts to help them practice and then extend their emerging competencies. Sorting out children who don't have sufficient help from those with serious disorders is extremely challenging. In attempting to distinguish normal development from emerging disorders in these regulatory domains, it is crucially important to consider the contexts within which children's executive functioning and self-regulatory behaviors have been struggling to develop.

SUMMARY AND CONCLUSIONS

The capacity for self-regulation, ranging from sleeping and settling in the earliest weeks of life to the preschooler's emerging capacity to manage emotions, inhibit behavior, and focus attention on important tasks, reflects young children's transition from helplessness to competence. Stated simply, early development entails the gradual transition from extreme dependence on others to manage the world for us to acquiring the competencies needed to manage the world for oneself. Research on this transition has focused on the triad of regulatory tasks captured by emotion regulation, behavior regulation, and attention regulation. In reality, however, these dimensions of self-regulation are highly interrelated. Success in one area can fuel success in another; problems in one area can undermine development in another. There is much to learn about normative patterns of regulatory development, as well as the adjustments made by young children with a range of developmental disabilities, and the mechanisms that under-lie the successful navigation of the many challenges encountered en route to well-regulated behavior.

Regulation in early development is deeply embedded in the child's relations with others. Providing the experiences, supports, and encourage-ment that enable children to take over and self-regulate in one area of functioning after another is one of the most critical elements of good caregiving. Indeed, the locus of regulatory problems during the early months of life is increasingly seen as residing not in the infant's behavior (e.g., excessive crying, irregular sleeping) but in the transactions that tran-spire between infants and their caregivers and the more enduring percep-tions and patterns of interaction that are subsequently set in motion in the family. These transactions, in turn, provide a promising entry point for early interventions aimed at getting new parents and their infants off to a good start.

There is also growing appreciation of the fact that learning to regulate one's emotions, behaviors, and task-oriented capacities is a different chal-lenge for children with different temperaments, for children with a variety of diagnosed disabilities, and for their caregivers. While overly active and disinhibited children often come to the attention of adults, those who fall at the other end of the spectrum all too often are overlooked.

Recent attention to problematic regulatory behavior has, in fact, been prompted by growing concern about early precursors of conduct problems, attention deficits, depressive and anxiety disorders, and other psychological problems of childhood. While emerging evidence suggests that regulatory problems can offer early warning signs, there are many pitfalls on the road to early diagnosis. Virtually all young children display "poorly regulated" behavior simply as part of being a little kid. Children with temperaments that give them more to regulate can appear to be deficient in self-regulatory abilities when, in fact, they are not. In this context, identifying and inter-vening with children who need extra help is fraught with ambiguity and runs the risk of overdiagnosis and unnecessary treatment.

Nevertheless, some young children are struggling with serious mental health problems and need help urgently. These issues were highlighted recently by the Surgeon General's report on mental health (U.S. Depart-ment of Health and Human Services, 1999b), which includes an extensive discussion of children's vulnerability to mental health problems, the impor-tance of understanding these problems in the context of children's social environments, and the nation's serious personnel shortages that constrain the capacity to address them. Recent reports of extensive use of pharmaco-logical treatments for preschoolers with behavioral disorders (Zito et al., 2000) have raised urgent questions about how best to address social and emotional problems in young children and further highlight how poorly equipped the nation is to respond to these issues. For children whose problems do not fall within the clinical range, early interventions to address regulatory behavior focused on "fixing" the environment to reduce demands on the child warrant serious attention to balance the current focus on "fixing" the child. It is also clear that focusing on young children's relationships with adults and peers is a promising and complementary, yet poorly exploited, approach.

Finally, cultural dimensions of regulatory development have been neglected by most scientists and practitioners alike. Nevertheless, cultural values have a profound impact on how young children learn to interpret and express their emotions, and on the behaviors that are seen as appropriate in different circumstances. Cultural expectations about self-regulatory behavior can even affect the boundaries of what is considered "childhood." The Yoruba, for example, define childhood in terms of self-reliance and no longer refer to children who can talk, walk, dress themselves, and do certain other things around the house as children (Zeitlin, 1996). These cultural dimensions have important yet unexplored implications for children whose home culture is not the same as the dominant culture in other settings they inhabit (e.g., child care, homes of friends, intervention programs) and for adults who work with diverse groups of young children and whose responses to their behaviors are highly contingent on their own cultural expectations.

6 Communicating and Learning

hrough the early childhood years, emerging communication skills and capacities for learning support other critical developments. The infant who learns more readily to replace crying with rudimentary attempts at other forms of communication (e.g., pointing and directing her gaze) spends more time in happier states and is an easier baby for parents to manage during the early months of life (Crockenberg, 1981). Preschoolers who speak clearly and communicate their ideas more effectively are better able to sustain bouts of play with other children (Guralnick et al., 1996). Even before children enter school, weak academic skills are associated with, and over time appear to exacerbate, behavioral and attention problems (Arnold, 1997; Hinshaw, 1992; Morrison et al., 1989). This is not to say that efforts to support language and cognitive development or to remediate delays in speech, hearing, and learning, will fix all other early developmental problems. Rather, without attention to problems in these domains of development, important and sometimes powerfully influential avenues to addressing emotional and behavioral problems may be neglected. Scientists are, however, only beginning to understand how these intersecting strands of development operate to either foster or undermine development as a whole during the early years of life.

The young child's growing skills in communication, language, and learning are also vitally important in their own right. No one disputes that success and persistence in school are major contributors to constructive life pathways (Stipek, in press). Children who do not complete high school, for example, are significantly more likely as adults to display a host of behaviors that are destructive to themselves and others, including substance abuse, unemployment, low income, welfare dependency, delinquency, and crime (Haveman and Wolfe, 1984; Hawkins and Lishner, 1987; Hinshaw, 1992; Loeber and Stouthamer-Loeber, 1987; Rutter et al., 1998; Steinberg et al., 1984).

One of the most significant insights about educational attainment in recent years is that educational outcomes in adolescence and even beyond can be traced back to academic skills at school entry (Chen et al., 1996; Cunningham and Stanovich, 1997; Luster and McAdoo, 1996; Weller et al., 1992). Academic skills at school entry can, in turn, be traced to capabilities seen during the preschool years and the experiences in and out of the home that foster their development. Children's cognitive skills before they enter kindergarten show strong associations with achievement in elementary and high school (Hess and Hahn, 1974; Stevenson and Newman, 1986) and during early adulthood (Baydar et al., 1993). Preschool general cognitive ability has also been shown to predict high school completion (Brooks-Gunn et al., 1993). This evidence underpins the national commitment to school readiness and has fueled the proliferation of public prekindergarten programs (Schulman et al., 1999).

It is important to note that children who start school lagging behind their peers in language and cognitive abilities are not doomed to be school failures and dropouts. To the contrary, early interventions can make substantial contributions to the academic skills of young children (see Chapter 13). Moreover, the associations found between early and later achievement leave substantial unexplained variance. This means that there is plenty of room for children to defy the odds, and many do.

Both language development and the emergence of early learning capabilities appear to be relatively resilient processes. This means that they are relatively protected from adverse circumstances, that it may take more to undermine these processes than is the case for other aspects of development, and that they can show surprising recovery if children exhibiting delays are placed in more advantageous environments. Nevertheless, some aspects of language and cognition appear to be less resilient and more open to environmental influence than others, including vocabulary and attentional capacities. These aspects are particularly important to school success, in part because of what they can set in motion once a child enters formal schooling. They are also characterized by striking socioeconomic differences and therefore contribute to inequities in children's life chances. Moreover, the prospects for children with serious delays in language and cognition resulting from developmental disabilities and specific disorders can be seriously constrained and are heavily dependent on early detection and intervention. This chapter illustrates these points first with a discussion of what is now known about the development of communication and language, and then with a discussion of how children learn about the world and come to view themselves as competent individuals.

LANGUAGE ACQUISITION AND COMMUNICATION

Starting from the first day of life, the development of communication skills, language, and literacy are significant accomplishments. The child's first word is a cause for celebration. Parents watch in amazement as these words multiply exponentially, turn into phrases and then sentences, and ultimately allow them to have almost adult like conversations with their preschoolers. The transition from a newborn who can barely keep his eyes focused on a book to a preschooler who laughs and cries when his parent reads or tells a story, moves his fingers along a page and pretends to read, and, in some cases, can read himself is equally impressive. Almost all children learn to talk without explicit instruction, suggesting that language acquisition is a relatively resilient process, although they do not all learn to talk well, suggesting that language acquisition includes some more fragile elements. In contrast, reading as a component of literacy is a much more fragile process. Not everyone achieves fluent reading, and instruction seems to be essential. Indeed, some cultures don't even have a written system. The development of reading is addressed in a pair of recent reports from the National Research Council: *Preventing Reading Difficulties in Young Children* (National Research Council, 1998a) is written primarily for a research audience, and *Starting Out Right* (National Research Council, 1998b) is geared to parents and practitioners.

Only recently has information about trends in young children's literacy development become available, and the data span only 6 years (Nord et al., 1999). Unfortunately, the information comes exclusively from parent reports, which can contain biases, but the sample is nationally representative. They tell us that 3- to 5-year-olds in 1999 have somewhat better knowledge of the alphabet and are able to count a bit higher (i.e., 57 versus 52 percent in 1993 can count to 20 or higher) than their counterparts in 1993, but they are no more likely to be able to write their own names or to read or pretend to read. Moreover, the majority of the statistically significant changes are for children who are less at risk of school failure, namely, those who are not poor and whose mothers speak English. The somewhat good overall news must thus be tempered by the fact that the children for whom we most want to see progress are still being left behind. In this discussion, we do not attempt to recount all of the accomplishments of young children in the realm of literacy; rather, we focus on the ways in which (and for whom) language development is and is not resilient, the role of the environment—particularly that provided by the parent—and implications for intervention.

To study the process of language learning, the most common technique is to do nothing more than observe children as they talk. Early studies consisted of diaries that researcher parents made of their own child's first utterances. The goal was to write down all of the new utterances that the child produced. Diary studies were later replaced by audio and video samples of talk from a number of children, usually over a period of years. The most famous of these studies is Roger Brown's longitudinal observations of Adam, Eve, and Sarah (Brown, 1973). Because transcribing and analyzing child talk is so labor-intensive, language acquisition studies typically focus on a small number of children, often interacting with their primary caregiver at home. Naturalistic observations of children's talk can be supplemented with experimental probes that are used with larger numbers of children. For example, Berko (1958) gave children nonsense words and asked them to generate novel forms in different contexts (e.g., "This is a wug. Now there are two of them. There are two ____?" The child who understands English plurals should supply the word "wugs"). Unlike many areas of developmental research, language acquisition studies have been conducted across the globe, although typically the studies focus on a small number of children in each culture (see Slobin, 1985).

Language Learning is a Resilient Process

Language learning turns out to be remarkably similar across cultures. Children exposed to markedly different languages follow similar developmental trajectories as they learn their native language. Six-month-old infants can distinguish the full range of sounds used in the world's languages, but by age 1 they have lost many of these distinctions as they focus in on their own culture's language. Children the world over produce their first words between 10 and 15 months ("mine," "shoe"); they then learn that the word can be composed of smaller, meaningful parts (morphology, e.g., "shoe" + "s") and that the word is a building block for larger, meaningful phrases and sentences (syntax, e.g., "my shoe"). Most 18-month-olds have begun a word-learning explosion, acquiring (on average) 9 new words a day, every day, throughout the preschool years (Carey, 1978). They also begin to produce two-word strings that are highly similar across languages in two respects. First, the content is the same. Children note the appearance and disappearance of objects, their properties, locations, and owners and comment on the actions done to and by objects and people. Second, the words in these short sentences are consistently ordered in ways that mirror adult word orders (e.g., "drink juice," "Mommy give").

By the time children are 3 years old, full sentences are the norm ("I wish I could sit on a horse and ride him to every house in the world"; Hoff-Ginsberg, 1997). These sentences often involve elaborating one element of a single proposition ("baby drinking big bottle") or combining two propositions with a conjunction ("maybe you can carry that and I can carry this"). Three-year-olds can also show some remarkably subtle capabilities for language comprehension. For example, consider a child who is told that a little girl fell and ripped her dress in the afternoon and reported the event to her mother later that night. When 3-year-olds are asked, "When did the girl say she ripped her dress?" they will provide one of two possible answers (in the afternoon, or at night), but when asked "When did the girl say how she ripped her dress?" they will provide only one (at night). By age 4 or 5, children all over the world have mastered the fundamental (and many of the fine points) of the grammatical system of their native language, including verb declensions, gender agreement, embedded clauses, and the like (Brown, 1973; Slobin, 1985).

This common trajectory of language acquisition is particularly striking given the variability in input that children receive across cultures. In all cultures, language is one of the most powerful symbolic systems through which children learn to understand and interpret human behavior (Harwood et al., 1995). How language is used in the context of social interaction is just as important as what is said. For example, in some cultures, children are commonly spoken to directly as participants in conversation; in other cultures, children primarily overhear talk that is directed toward others. Despite large differences of this sort, children proceed quite uniformly with the task of language learning (Ochs and Schieffelin, 1984). Another example is cross-cultural research on narrative constructions, which reveals both considerable overlap across cultures in the narratives that caregivers use with their children and also striking differences that have an impact on the child. For example, Taiwanese mothers tend to tell narratives that make explicit reference to moral rules and point out the child's wrongdoing. European-American mothers, by contrast, emphasize the entertainment function over the didactic function and go to great lengths to portray the child in a positive light (Miller et al., 1996). Children who hear stories of this sort not only learn how to build their own culturally appropriate narratives, but they also learn the social value of their behaviors, as noted in Chapter 7.

Language learning proceeds apace even when the child is faced with learning two languages simultaneously (de Houwer, 1995; Hakuta, 1986; National Research Council and Institute of Medicine, 1997). Children becoming bilingual from birth are not dramatically slowed in their development and appear to develop each language as they would had it been their only tongue. The problematic issue in the case of bi- or multilingualism is less one of language acquisition than of language retention, which can be made difficult when one language is not used or valued by nonfamily adults or institutions, such as the schools, peer groups, and the broader society

(National Research Council and Institute of Medicine, 1997, 1998b). For example, language loss (of Spanish) among Mexican-American children increases rapidly across first-, second-, and third-generation children (Hakuta and D'Andrea, 1992). Finally, although language development is markedly delayed among children raised in low-stimulating orphanages (Rutter, 1981a), once placed in supportive families, children develop language even with the added challenge, in most of the cases that have been studied, of learning a new language.

Thus, language learning is apparently a very robust process. Where does this robustness come from? One way to address this question is to systematically vary either the learner or the learning environment, observing the effects of these variations on subsequent language development. As an example from another species, Marler raised two closely related but genetically distinct varieties of sparrows from the egg in identical environments, exposing them to a common collection of songs typical for both (Marler, 1990). He found that the two varieties learned different songs out of the same collection, each variety apparently zeroing in on different aspects of the input. The range of possible outcomes in the learning process, for this species and for this skill, appears to have been narrowed by the organism itself.

For obvious ethical reasons, researchers cannot deliberately manipulate the conditions under which human language is learned. One can, however, take advantage of variations that occur naturally in language-learning conditions in order to explore the boundary conditions under which language learning is possible. And many studies have done just that, each exploring a particular deviation from typical language-learning circumstances and its effect on the development of language (Gleitman and Newport, 1995).

Three types of deviations from the norm might be expected to have effects on the language-learning process: (1) deviations in the environment that affect the quantity or quality of the linguistic input children receive (e.g., children raised under conditions of relative deprivation of access to linguistic input), (2) deviations in the organism that affect the way children process their linguistic input (e.g., intermittent conductive hearing loss, which affects the way the child processes speech), and (3) deviations in the organism that affect the general endowment of the learner (e.g., children with Down syndrome, autism). Interestingly, in many cases, the cause of the deviation does not appear to be what is important—just its effect. Thus, deviations in the language-learning environment often lead to the same effects—or noneffects—on children's language as deviations in the organism.

In general, language learning is remarkably resilient even under extremely altered learning circumstances. However, there are some conditions that are not compatible with the development of language independent of the learner, and some learners who are not capable of language acquisition independent of their environment. As one example, children raised under conditions of extreme social and linguistic deprivation do not develop language during their periods of deprivation (Brown, 1958; Skuse, 1988); many of them, however, do achieve some linguistic proficiency after recovery and rehabilitation, findings that bear on the issue of a critical period for language learning, discussed below. As another example, some children with severe autism are deviant in every aspect of speech, language, and communication despite apparently normal language input (Fay, 1988). Thus, there appear to be both environmental and organic limits on language learning in children.

Perhaps the clearest example of the resilience of language comes from the fact that it is not tied exclusively to spoken language (Klima and Bellugi, 1979). Children who are exposed to a conventional sign language such as American Sign Language from birth acquire that language as effortlessly, and along the same developmental course, as children acquiring a spoken language (Newport and Meier, 1985). This fact is notable, as it suggests that children are completely "equipotential across modality" with respect to language learning. In other words, if language is offered via hand and eye, it is learned and processed as easily as if it is presented via mouth and ear. Thus, in an appropriate environment, deaf children are not at all handicapped with respect to language learning, and the capacity for language learning appears to be modality independent.

However, most deaf children are not born into an environment in which signing is the language of communication. About 90 percent of deaf children are born to hearing parents and thus are not immediately exposed to a sign language. If exposed only to input from a spoken language, profoundly deaf children (even if given intensive training) are not likely to acquire that spoken language (Mayberry, 1992), suggesting that the visual channel cannot compensate for a lack of auditory input in the acquisition of spoken language.

It is important to point out, however, that deaf children who cannot learn spoken language do indeed communicate—even if their hearing parents do not expose them to conventional sign language until later in life. Such children have no usable linguistic input, although in other respects their home environments are quite typical. Despite these children's lack of a language model, they learn to use their hands to communicate—they gesture, as do all humans when they communicate. However, the deaf children's gestures are structured very differently from the gestures that speakers typically produce to supplement their talk (Goldin-Meadow et al., 1996) (see Box 6-1). The deaf children's gestures resemble the early communication systems of children learning conventional languages, signed or spoken (Goldin-Meadow, 1997). For example, the children's gestures are

BOX 6-1
The Resilience of Language

What happens if a child has hearing losses so severe that he or she cannot learn the surrounding spoken language, and does not have access to sign language? Such a child might not be able to communicate at all. It turns out, however, that the need to communicate is so strong that such children invent gesture systems to get their ideas and desires across. Deaf children who have not seen sign language and cannot learn speech have been studied in both Taiwan and the United States (Goldin-Meadow and Mylander, 1998). Both Chinese and American children produce gestures to communicate with the hearing individuals in their worlds, and do so to fulfill many of the functions typically assumed by language—to make requests, comments, and queries, and even to describe events in the past and future. Moreover, children in both cultures often convey their messages via strings of gestures, akin to sentences, rather than single gestures—and those "sentences" do not follow either English or Mandarin work order. For example, the child pictured below first gestures the action, "eat" and then the actor, "you" and then "you" again for emphasis. A typical pattern for English or Mandarin would be "you eat" rather than "eat you."

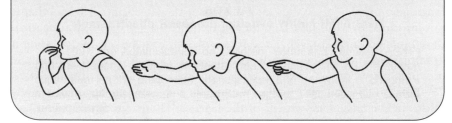

used to request and to make comments about the present and the nonpresent and even to "talk" about their own gestures. The gestures display sentence-level structure (following order and deletion regularities, and with structures for both simple and complex gesture sentences), word-level structure (hand shape and motion morphemes), and grammatical categories (distinctions among nouns, verbs, and adjectives). These characteristics are not found in the spontaneous gestures their hearing parents use when communicating with them, and thus may be the default system that children themselves bring to the language-learning situation. The fact that children will produce a communication system with structural properties, even without guidance from a conventional language model, suggests that these properties are not maintained in human language merely by being transmitted from one generation to the next. Rather, these particular linguistic properties can be introduced de novo by a child attempting to communicate with other people.

Language learning also proceeds in the face of variation in the amount and consistency of linguistic input that children receive, and in the communicative situation in which language is learned, whether that variation is caused by environmental or organic factors. For example, hearing children of deaf parents, who themselves are not fluent speakers, can acquire spoken language normally if they receive as little as 5 to 10 hours per week of exposure to hearing speakers (Schiff-Myers, 1988). Moreover, hearing children do not reproduce the idiosyncrasies of their deaf parents' speech, but rather regularize their language toward the norms of the spoken language they are learning. Twins most often share their language-learning situation with one another, making the typical twin situation triadic (e.g., a parent and two children) rather than dyadic. Nevertheless, normal language development is observed in most twin pairs, although mild delays are common (Mogford, 1988). As an example of variation in input created by internal or organic factors, children who have intermittent conductive hearing losses that cause their intake of linguistic input to vary in amount and pattern, for the most part, acquire language normally (Klein and Rapin, 1988). Children who are blind from birth might be expected to have difficulty learning language simply because they map the words they hear onto a world that is not informed by vision. In fact, they have little difficulty with grammatical development, suggesting that the formal learning involved in acquiring a grammatical system does not depend in any crucial respect on the precise mapping between that system and the world (Landau and Gleitman, 1985).

Finally, language learning can even survive some rather major alterations in the basic endowment of the learner. Language development can proceed normally after focal brain damage even if the left cerebral cortex is removed, provided the brain damage necessitating this operation is sustained very early in life (Feldman, 1994). It appears that speech and language are affected by brain injury only when the damage occurs bilaterally (i.e., to both hemispheres). In the face of unilateral damage prior to age 5 or 6, aphasic symptoms may result initially, but are not permanent. In fact, extensive left-hemisphere damage sustained prenatally or in the immediate postnatal period, i.e., before the onset of speech, has not been reported to result in any lasting language deficits despite some delays in the development of speech (Gadian et al., 1999; Rasmussen and Milner, 1977; Taylor, 1991; Vargha-Khadem and Mishkin, 1997; Vargha-Khadem and Polkey, 1991). Indeed, Bates and colleagues have reported that even significant focal brain injuries that occur perinatally to the left hemisphere appear to spare most language functions (see, e.g., Bates and Roe, in press). Moreover, language development does not proceed in lockstep with the development of other mental abilities. For example, children with Down syndrome are delayed in language learning relative to mental age (Fowler et al., 1994). Yet children with Williams syndrome (a rare metabolic disorder), who are as mentally retarded in terms of IQ as children with Down syndrome, display considerably better grammatical skills (Bellugi et al., 1988). Thus, low intelligence does not, in all cases, preclude grammatical development.

The inverse is true, as well: language difficulties do not inevitably imply cognitive difficulties. For example, children with specific language impairment, by definition, have no cognitive disabilities but do have difficulty learning language. As a final piece of evidence, adults, who are cognitively mature, typically have difficulty learning a second language (Johnson and Newport, 1989), suggesting that cognitive maturity is not sufficient to guarantee grammatical development (and after some sensitive period may even become an impediment, as discussed below). In general, in fact, the growth of cognitive, language, and literacy skills is much more domain-specific, constrained, and modular than previously thought (Christian et al., in press). A similarly complex pattern holds for social skills. For example, children with Down syndrome are relatively adept socially (in comparison to children with autism) yet have difficulty learning grammar (Fowler et al., 1994). In contrast, autistic children's social interactions are atypical, yet when they are able to learn language, their grammatical skills are intact (Tager-Flusberg, 1994).

Language learning is robust in the same way that developing an attachment to a caregiver is robust. Only in aberrant conditions of care, such as extreme neglect or institutional deprivation, do children fail to form attachments to anyone (see Chapter 9). However, not all infants develop *secure* attachments—secure attachments are formed in a more restricted set of circumstances. Similarly, children acquire language with very little environmental support (deaf children inventing their own gesture systems are a good example). However, the specific language that they learn and certain qualities of their language depend on specific features of the environment in which they learn language. And these aspects of language are often instrumental to subsequent cognitive and social growth. Children can be at risk in society, not because they do not have mastery of a language, but because they do not have complete mastery of the dominant language of their society, particularly at the time of formal school entry.

Not All Language Learning Is Resilient

It is important to recognize that language is not a unitary phenomenon. Certain aspects of language may turn out to be more susceptible to variations in learning conditions (both internal and external) than others. If, across a variety of exceptional circumstances, the same components of language tend to be delayed while others remain intact, one might begin to argue that certain components of language are resilient in the face of either environmental or organic deviations from the typical language-learning circumstances, while other components of language are relatively fragile (Goldin-Meadow, 1982). For example, clinical notes on language development in children who have been adopted from institutions suggest that despite becoming proficient in the language of their new homes, these children may not use language as readily for expressing emotion, requesting aid from adults, or expressing ideas and fantasy (Provence and Lipton, 1962). It is not known if they are as likely as other children to use language to guide problem solving, although this might be one reason for their poorer executive functioning (Gunnar, in press).

Perhaps the most dramatic example of how language is vulnerable to environmental influences concerns the role of the timing of language inputs in language proficiency. This literature is highly relevant to current debates about critical or sensitive periods in development. There is, in fact, a considerable amount of evidence suggesting that early exposure to a language results in greater proficiency in that language than late exposure. For example, deaf children of hearing parents, as mentioned earlier, are typically not exposed to a conventional sign language at birth and may not receive their first exposure to such a system until adolescence or later. These individuals thus provide an excellent "experiment of nature" to test the effects of learning a first language at varying times in the life course. Findings from these studies suggest that certain aspects of language—morphological properties, for example, which involve how smaller parts of words make up bigger words and affect word meaning (e.g., "eat" + "ing" = "eating")—are affected by the age at which the learner is first exposed to sign language. An example of a morphological property in sign is movement added to a sign such as "eat" to create the meaning "eat continuously over time." Late learners, although perfectly capable of conversing in sign, do not have complete productive control over many of the complex morphological properties of the language (Newport, 1991). Interestingly, however, certain properties of language—such as the order of signs in a sentence—appear to be completely unaffected by the age at which the learner is first exposed to the language. In other words, native-like competence is possible for sign order whether or not the learner is exposed to sign early in life—but is far less likely for morphological properties.

Similar patterns arise in second-language learning (Newport, 1991). Learners who are first exposed to their second language after puberty find that certain aspects of that language (often morphological aspects) are difficult, if not impossible, to master even after decades of use, while others (like word order) are relatively easy to control. For example, learning to systematically produce endings such as "-ed" in "walked," which adds the past meaning, or "s" in "shoes," which adds the plural meaning, is far more difficult for late learners than learning that "cats chase mice" has a different meaning from "mice chase cats." We see the same trend when we look at Genie, a child who experienced extreme deprivation for the first 13 years of her life. During this deprivation, Genie made essentially no progress in developing a communication system (she had, after all, no one to talk to). After discovery and rehabilitation, Genie was found to make progress in acquiring certain components of language (word order among them), but little progress in acquiring other components of language, including morphology (Curtiss, 1977; Goldin-Meadow, 1978).

This developmental pattern again suggests that certain components of language may be resilient—here in the face of variations in the timing of acquisition—while other components may be relatively fragile. The ability to learn the fragile components of language does not drop off precipitously. Rather, there appears to be a decline after age 6 or 7—a decline that begins to plateau and become less steep in late adolescence. Importantly, unlike early learners who tend to follow the same developmental trajectory (that is, there is strikingly little variability across them), late learners vary quite a bit. Some achieve native-like competence even on the fragile properties of language, while others do not. This research is providing a much more refined understanding of the ways in which early language experience provides a foundation for later language facility.

Studies of brain activity patterns (using event-related brain potentials, called ERPs, which measure electrical activity recorded at the scalp) provide further evidence that language is not a single entity and that developmental mechanisms may differ for different properties of language (see Neville and Mills, 1997). For example, Neville and her colleagues have found, in normal, right-handed, monolingual adults, that nouns and verbs (words that provide semantic information—that is, about meaning) elicit a markedly different pattern of brain activity than do prepositions and conjunctions (functional words that provide grammatical information). These findings suggest that different neural systems mediate the processing of semantic and grammatical information in adults (in particular, a greater role for more posterior temporal-parietal systems in semantic processing and for anterior temporal systems within the left hemisphere in grammatical processing). Impressively, these findings are robust across languages, including sign languages (although there appears to be more right-hemisphere involvement in processing a sign language like American Sign Language than in processing a spoken language like English).

The work of Neville and her colleagues also bears on issues of the timing of environmental inputs. In studies of cerebral organization in individuals who learned English at different times in the life span, Neville and colleagues have found that aspects of semantic and grammatical processing differ markedly in the degree to which they depend on the timing of language input (Neville and Mills, 1997). In particular, in a group of Chinese-English bilinguals, delays as long as 16 years in exposure to English had very little effect on the organization of the brain systems important in lexical semantics. That is, the brain system underlying the organization of nouns and verbs was disrupted very little. However, delays of only 4 years had significant effects on aspects of brain organization linked to grammatical processing. Brain organization underlying function words, such as prepositions and conjunctions, was severely disrupted. Similar patterns have been found in studies of congenitally deaf individuals who learned English late and as a second language (American Sign Language was their first language). Deaf individuals displayed ERP responses to nouns and to semantically anomalous sentences that were indistinguishable from those of normally hearing individuals. However, the same deaf individuals displayed aberrant ERP responses to grammatical information. These findings suggest that the systems that mediate the processing of at least some types of grammatical information are much more modifiable by—and therefore vulnerable to—variations in language experience. This is demonstrated again below, in the discussion of interventions with children with specific language disorder.

In general, it seems important that practitioners consider the data generated from studies of the effects—and noneffects—of exceptional circumstances on language learning, for they provide important information on the boundary conditions of language learning. Moreover, these phenomena are the anchor points for theories of language development that take into account the resilience of language learning within more normal ranges of both environmental and organic variation.

The Impact of Linguistic Input on Language Learning and Language Production

As noted earlier, conventional language input is not essential for a young child to develop a language-like system and use it to communicate with others. However, a language model may play a central role in determining how often and when those linguistic properties are used. We noted above, for example, the infrequent use of language to express emotions among children who had been institutionalized. Another example concerns the ability to communicate about objects and events in other than the here and now. Deaf children who are not exposed to usable linguistic input (because their parents do not know American Sign Language, for example) not only use gesture to convey information about the here and now, but they also use it to converse about past, future, and hypothetical events (Morford and Goldin-Meadow, 1997). Linguistic input is thus not essential for a child to communicate about the nonpresent. However, the amount and nature of the linguistic input a child receives has large effects on how *often* the child actually uses talk about the nonpresent, particularly the past. And the amount and type of talk children hear, in turn, can influence how well they remember events in the past (Reese et al., 1993).

A great deal of attention is now being paid to research indicating that the amount of talk mothers direct to their children is strongly associated with the children's vocabulary growth (Hart and Risley, 1995; Huttenlocher et al., 1991), as well as with the children's performance on measures of emergent literacy and print-related skills (De Temple and Snow, 1992). For example, during the period from 11 to 18 months, children in one study heard, on average, 325 utterances addressed to them per hour (Hart and Risley, 1995). But the range was enormous—one child heard as many as 793 utterances per hours, another as few as 56. And these differences tend to be stable over time. The amount of speech children heard from their parents at 18 months was strongly correlated with the amount of speech they heard at age 3. Moreover, these differences tended to be associated with socioeconomic status, although it is important to recognize that the sample of 42 participating families was small and not representative and so cannot provide firm evidence regarding social class differences.

Often researchers videotape mothers and their young children to explore parental verbal input and child output. One study (Hoff-Ginsberg, 1991), for example, videotaped mothers while they dressed, fed, and played with their 18- to 29-month-old children. They all talked when they played with their children, but there were big differences in how much they talked and whether they used a rich vocabulary and asked questions during dressing and feeding. The children whose mothers talked more during the mundane activities had larger vocabularies, indicating the importance of integrating conversations throughout the day.

Although differences in mother's talk are associated with their social class, it is critical to recognize that other characteristics that can be more easily targeted by early interventions are as strongly related to children's accomplishments as the advantages conferred by socioeconomic status. A composite of parental behaviors that included "just talking," "trying to be nice," "telling children about things," "giving children choices," and "listening" accounted for over 60 percent of the variance in the rate of children's vocabulary growth and vocabulary use and almost 60 percent of the variance in their IQ scores at age 3 (Hart and Risley, 1995). Moreover, it is important to recognize that even the large differences in mother talk and child vocabulary that characterized the children in this study had more specific than pervasive effects on the children's school-related outcomes. For example, while the children's vocabulary use at age 3 was strongly associated with their vocabulary test and reading comprehension scores in third grade, the rate of vocabulary growth was not associated with children's third grade scores in the academic skill areas of reading, writing, spelling, or arithmetic.

It is important to recognize that this research on language input focuses largely on white, middle class children in the United States and on mothers' speech directed to their children. It does not explore the role that talk around and about the child might play in language acquisition. This may be particularly important in other cultures, in which children are more likely to be involved in relationships in which skilled conversation takes place around them, but is not directed at them (Rogoff et al., 1993). For example, in a Mayan Indian community studied by Rogoff and her colleagues, adults communicated to their children primarily through shared activity and group conversations, rather than in the context of one-on-one lessons or explanations directed to the child. Although, as we noted earlier, virtually all children learn language, the issue is whether there are qualitative differences across individuals that are correlated with differing types of input.

It is also important to note that this area of research is open to the criticism that it has not considered the sizeable role that genetic influences undoubtedly play in the development of verbal abilities. Mothers who talk more to their children may also share genetic endowments that facilitate language learning. One study, which took advantage of the fact that twins tend to lag behind singletons in language development, ruled out a variety of competing hypotheses to conclude that the quality and complexity of mother-child communicative interaction was responsible for the twin-singleton differences in language development (Rutter et al., 2000). Measures of mother-child verbal interaction at 20 months predicted language level at 36 months in both twins and singletons, and they accounted for the twin-singleton differences in language level. Nevertheless, the relative inattention to genetic factors in this area of research is a shortcoming that needs to be addressed.

Evidence of the importance of verbal input during the years when verbal development is proceeding rapidly has also emerged from research on child care. Children whose teachers talk with them a lot (and many don't!) have higher scores on tests of both verbal and general ability. This is especially the case when the talking consists of the teacher encouraging, questioning, and guiding the children's exploration and learning. Positive inputs are positive inputs, whether they happen at home or in child care. Vocabulary size, in turn, is highly correlated with IQ. Thus, environmental input can play a large role in determining the rate at which children acquire and use a particular aspect of language, and rate of acquisition and use may be an important factor in cognitive growth and cognitive functioning.

Furthermore, taking vocabulary as an example, the individual differences that characterize children at school entry are enormous. In one large, longitudinal study, children tested at kindergarten when they were 5 years old displayed receptive vocabularies (i.e., word comprehension, as distinct from the ability to produce words) that ranged from the level of a typical 1 year, 9-month-old to the level of a 10 year, 8-month-old (Morrison et al., 1997, 1998). These individual differences not only emerge early, but they also appear to be stable over time. It is hard to imagine that such striking differences would not affect how children fare and are treated during their early years of school, in ways that perpetuate the initial differences. In fact, children's scores on early literacy tasks at kindergarten entry consistently predict academic performance throughout the first three years of formal schooling and beyond (Morrison et al., 1995; Stevenson et al., 1976). Similar patterns have also been reported for early mathematical abilities (National Research Council, 2000).

That these early emerging and quite stable individual differences in language skill are consistently linked to the social class of children's families lends them even greater importance in a society that established its educational system in part to promote equity of opportunity. There is some evidence to suggest that socioeconomic factors exert their most powerful effects on children's achievement during early childhood and that these early influences contribute to sustaining socioeconomic effects on achievement throughout the school years and beyond.

It is also important to note that these aspects of early language development (e.g., vocabulary, semantics), unlike morphology, grammar, and phonology, do not show critical or sensitive periods. In these domains, children can, in principle, catch up given appropriate and sufficient exposure. As Hart and Risley point out, however, the amount of additional exposure a child needs to catch up increases over time. With each passing year, the gap widens and, at some point, may become insurmountable for all practical purposes.

The studies just described explore the effects of linguistic input on child output by examining the natural range of variation found in mother talk to children. But what would happen if one were to augment the amount of input children typically receive? As an example, Nelson (1977) enriched the input children received in forming questions and found that this enriched experience selectively increased the children's production of this type of construction. However, it is not clear from such studies whether the enriched input is actually teaching children a new construction or merely teaching them to produce an already known construction in a particular context. Thus enriched input may be important, not to establish a particular construction in a child's linguistic repertoire, but to influence the production of that construction in a given context. Given that production of language is what teachers hear and base their judgments of competence on, strategies that improve production warrant substantial attention in early invention programs.

In another example of an enrichment study, Goodwyn and Acredolo (1998) attempted to accelerate young children's production and comprehension of spoken words by teaching them symbols in another modality—gestures. The findings suggest that gesture training does indeed accelerate word use and word understanding at the beginning stages of language learning, although the gains appear to be short-lived. The important finding, however, is that gesture training does absolutely no harm to word learning and, in fact, has the potential to enrich parent-child early communications. Many parents in the gesture-training condition reported that the gestures improved communication with their children and made them feel more involved in their children's lives. Enriched input may be important, again, not for direct benefits to language learning, but, in this instance, for the indirect effects it has on parent-child interaction.

It is clear that, under typical circumstances, parents do not need to arrange linguistic inputs according to a particular plan in order for language learning to proceed on course. They do not need to think about when to introduce particular syntactic constructions (e.g., questions, imperatives, passives) into the talk they use with their children. Parents across the globe seem intuitively to provide children with input that is adequate for them to learn how to talk. To the extent that problems arise, it is generally not because parents are doing the wrong things, but because they are not doing enough of the right things. The more children are talked to, the more they themselves talk and the more elaborate that talk becomes (Hart and Risley, 1995). But what happens when language learning goes awry? How can one tell, and what does one do? How, as we noted in the core concepts outlined in Chapter 1, can we distinguish persistent impairments from typical variations and maturational or otherwise transient delays?

Language Impairment

A language impairment during childhood is usually defined as a significant limitation in language ability as indicated by poor performance on language tests (the psychometric criterion) and concern about the child's language skills on the part of family members and educators. Both criteria are used in considering whether a child is language impaired. The language tests used for this purpose are typically comprehensive batteries that include semantic (e.g., vocabulary) abilities and grammatical abilities, as measured in both comprehension and production. Some comprehensive tests at the preschool-age level assess phonological abilities (i.e., speech pronunciation and clarity) as well. As children reach school age, narrative abilities are sometimes included in tests. Although pragmatic abilities—the social uses of language—are important, these abilities have not yet been incorporated into tests of language ability.

How frequent is language disability? In the most extensive epidemiological study conducted to date, the prevalence of specific language impairment—children with language problems but no other documented developmental problems—at age 5 was determined to be 7.4 percent (Tomblin et al., 1997). This figure is somewhat higher than previous estimates, in part because earlier studies have relied on clinically referred children. Studies relying principally on clinically referred children also report a lower percentage of girls with specific language impairment than was reported in the epidemiological study. Boys with a language disorder may be more likely to be referred than girls simply because of the kinds of behaviors that they exhibit in response to their communication difficulties. Boys frequently react with more exuberance and activity to being misunderstood than do girls.

By the late preschool years, it is not always easy to distinguish children whose language problems constitute a true disorder and may persist from children whose abilities fall on the extreme low end of a normal distribution and who may catch-up to their expected levels of language development over time. Children with persistent language impairments are at risk for social and academic problems, making the task of distinguishing them from those with more transient delays extremely important. Recent research has uncovered at least two measures that might serve as clinical markers of a true impairment. One measures the use of finite verb morphology—forms such as the present third person singular verb inflection "-s" ("he walks"), the past inflection "-ed" ("he walked"), and the copula and auxiliary forms such as "is," "are," and "am." These forms are extraordinarily weak in many English-speaking children with specific language impairment (e.g., Leonard et al., 1997; Oetting and Horohov, 1997; Rice and Wexler, 1996). Even by school age, they are not used with consistency by many of these children (e.g., Marchman et al., 1999).

The second measure is a task in which the child is asked to repeat multisyllabic nonsense words (e.g., Gathercole and Baddeley, 1990; Kamhi et al., 1988; Montgomery, 1995). Both of these measures show excellent sensitivity and specificity in distinguishing children with specific language impairment from their normally developing peers (for finite verb morphology, see Bedore and Leonard, 1998; Rice, 1998; for nonsense word repetition, see Bishop et al., 1996; Dollaghan and Campbell, 1998). It is interesting that verb morphology, a property of language that is vulnerable to variations in learning conditions, as discussed above, is also implicated in specific language impairment.

Thus, children with clinically significant language difficulties are not just less good language-learners than children who are developing on course; they appear to have particular deficits that lead to their language difficulties. There is, moreover, some evidence that the combination of genetic and environmental factors at the extreme of language delay is different from those operating in the normal range. In a large twin study, Dale and colleagues (1998) found that language delay at age 2 is highly heritable and that language delay is much more heritable than individual differences within the normal range of language ability. These findings suggest that extreme language delay is qualitatively different from typical language learning, and that it reflects a strong genetic contribution. However, two caveats are important with regard to this study. First, age 2 is much too early to determine whether the language deficit will or will not persist and, in many cases, it probably will not. Second, there was severe attrition from the sample of young mothers and of mothers who were socially disadvantaged or less well educated than average. As a result, the results, interesting and potentially important though they are, were based on a sample that was not representative of environmental risk. Moreover, it is essential to stress the point, made in the broader discussion of genetic influences in Chapter 2, that genetic causes do not imply that language delay is inevitable or unchangeable. Interventions can be implemented that affect the course of language delay.

What Can be Done?

Most of the therapy procedures designed for children with specific language impairment focus directly on language itself. Approaches to language difficulties range from structured, drill-like techniques to what may appear to be relatively unstructured play. For example, in imitation-based approaches, the clinician produces the exact sentence or phrase required of the child, and the child is asked to repeat it. In conversational recasting, the clinician and child participate in play activities. The clinician responds to utterances produced by the child in a manner that serves as a relevant conversational turn and contains some linguistic form serving as the focus of therapy. Focused approaches of this sort are adopted when there are specific therapy goals, such as assisting the child in the production of particular semantic or grammatical forms. However, more intensive programs that children attend for several mornings per week, 3 hours per morning, are also available. In these programs, specific approaches may take up a portion of the child's day, but much of the time is spent in group activities that have both education/enrichment and general language stimulation as goals.

How effective are these therapies? The controls used to evaluate programs vary from study to study. The gains of children who receive treatment are compared with gains made by similar children in no-treatment control groups or by children receiving therapy unrelated to the linguistic forms of interest. In other cases, a multiple-baseline design has been used in which the child's progress is assessed on forms that have been explicitly taught, as well as forms that were not part of the instruction. Still other studies have made use of statistical estimation as a means of determining the amount of gain that could be expected by maturation alone, so that added gains attributed to therapy can be deciphered. Each of the therapy approaches described above has been shown to be effective (Farran, 2000; Leonard, 1998; McLean and Cripe, 1997). The gains with these approaches are greater than can be expected through maturation without therapy. In addition, each approach leads to the children's use of target forms in sentences that were not explicitly taught, and in speaking contexts that differ from those used during therapy.

In spite of this generally positive picture, two important qualifications must be made. First, the more specific the focus of therapy, the narrower the scope of the rules or patterns that are learned. For example, therapy that concentrates on helping the child use "wh-" questions, such as "Where is the girl taking the dog?" and "Why is the man crying?" will result in the child's use of similar untaught questions, but gains may not be seen in other details of the child's grammar (e.g., Wilcox and Leonard, 1978). More intensive programs tend to avoid this problem but, of course, intensive programs are just that—programs that not only occupy a good portion of the child's week, but can also extend for as long as 2 years.

The second qualification is that, whereas most children in therapy begin to progress at an accelerated rate, the gains are often not enough to bring them to age-appropriate ability levels. It is not unusual for children to remain a full standard deviation behind their peers (Rice and Hadley, 1995). Indeed, there appears to be great stability in language impairments over time. For example, in a 14-year follow up study, Johnson and colleagues (1999) found that 73 percent of the children who were language impaired at age 5 continued to perform in this range at age 19. Long-term outcomes were better for those with initial speech impairments than for those with language impairments—that is, for those whose impairments involved problems with speech sounds rather than problems with the structural aspects of language. In addition, interventions that are successful in facilitating grammatical expression in preschoolers with language impairments do not always minimize the risk that these children have in their social adjustment and academic achievement upon entering school (Fey et al., 1995).

One last intervention must be mentioned. In recent years, an approach developed by Tallal, Merzenich, and their colleagues has attracted considerable attention (Merzenich et al., 1996; Tallal et al., 1996). This treatment approach is based on earlier findings that children with specific language impairment have significant difficulty on tasks requiring them to process auditory information that is presented rapidly, and auditory information in which contrastive stimuli differ only in acoustic details that are brief in duration. The approach takes the form of computer games in which the children must first make discriminations based on stimuli of greater duration and intensity. As the children progress through the program, the stimuli begin to approximate their typical duration and intensity values. Impressive gains on standardized tests of language have been reported for children who participated in this program. Because measures of language in natural settings, such as spontaneous speech samples, have not yet been part of the testing protocol with this approach, it is difficult to determine if the test gains made by children with this approach are gains in language ability or gains in attention skills.

Is early intervention better than later intervention? The working assumption is yes, but it has been difficult to test empirically. Some portion of the children diagnosed with specific language impairment at young ages will, in fact, grow out of it—these are the late talkers who will catch up to peers even without intervention. It is always difficult to know whether intervention was effective, or whether the child just grew out of his or her problems. For example, following a period of intervention, 28-month-olds with expressive language limitations were found to make larger gains in expressive language ability than a comparable group of children not receiving intervention; by 34 months, these children approximated age-level expectations. However, 10 months later, the control children, too, caught up to age level (Whitehurst et al., 1992). Unfortunately, therapy effectiveness as a function of age has not been investigated systematically, in large part because of the problems inherent in diagnosing children with specific language impairment at an early age.

When should parents take language and speech delays seriously? Children are often regarded as being late talkers if at 24 months they use fewer than 50 words and produce no word combinations (Paul, 1991; Rescorla, 1989; Thal and Bates, 1988). However, many of these late talkers will be normal language users in 1 to 3 years. For example, 50 percent of late talkers are likely to exhibit typical language use by age 3, and another 25 percent will be functioning normally when they enter school (Rescorla and Schwartz, 1990; Thal and Tobias, 1992). Thus, a good proportion of children who have language difficulties at a young age will grow out of those problems even without intervention. Early language delay is not sufficient for a child to have severe language problems later in development. However, early language delay does appear to be a necessary condition for later language problems. Most, if not all, children with specific language impairment have a history of slow, protracted language development (Trauner et al., 1995). Virtually all such children come from the ranks of the late-talking.

Considerable research has been aimed at discovering the factors that distinguish late talkers who will and will not outgrow their language limitations. No factor has proven foolproof. However, several factors are associated with better as opposed to poorer outcomes. Children with age-appropriate language comprehension who use recognitory gestures (e.g., pretending to drink from an empty cup) are more likely to outgrow their language difficulties (Thal and Bates, 1988; Thal et al., 1991). In contrast, children with family members who have a language-related problem or a history of such a problem are less likely to outgrow their language difficulties and more likely to be diagnosed as having a specific language impairment (Tallal et al., 1989; Tomblin, 1989; van der Lely and Stollwerck, 1996; Weismer et al., 1994).

Given the difficulty in discriminating children who will grow out of language difficulties from those who will not, the most prudent (although perhaps not the most cost-efficient) strategy may be to intervene whenever a child shows early language impairment. There is, of course, always the possibility that labeling children as "language delayed" may affect how others view them and may, in the end, have adverse effects on them. Very little is known about this potential problem. However, it is known that intervention can do considerable good. It may be important to foster these benefits as early as possible, before the gap in language development widens.

Of particular significance is evidence showing that wide individual differences at school entry in vocabulary and other early literacy skills are seldom reduced as children move through school, and they can be exacerbated. This is true for children within the normal variation of language ability as well as for those with specific language delays. Evidence discussed below with respect to early learning that these initial differences set in motion very negative chains of events reveals the critical importance of language interventions that start prior to school entry. Moreover, early intervention that moves children toward normal linguistic functioning as quickly as possible may be able to forestall some of the problems with social skills that are demonstrated by children who are slow to develop language. Indeed, early intervention can have benefits, not only in vocabulary and multiword combinations, but also in areas not specifically targeted for intervention, such as social skills, speech intelligibility, and parental stress (Robertson and Weismer, 2000). Early intervention may be important, not because doors remain permanently closed without it, but because with it, doors swing open that might otherwise have been inaccessible at that moment in the child's development.

THINKING AND LEARNING DURING EARLY CHILDHOOD

As with language learning, children's early capacities to make sense of the world around them and learn from their experiences appear to be relatively robust features of early development. Studies that examine cultural variation often find similar developmental progressions across cultures in cognitive development, although this is not uniformly true (Avis and Harris, 1991; Diamond, 1991; Fernald et al., 1989; Flavell et al., 1983; Gelman, 1998; Slobin, 1997). This may be due to certain fundamental commonalities in cultures across the world, such as opportunities to interact with other people, to observe physical events, to observe countable numbers of things, and to hear language. Moreover, despite dramatically delayed cognitive development among children reared in highly depriving institutions, their recovery upon adoption into stable and loving families is equally dramatic (see Chapter 9). At the same time, however, some aspects of early learning are more susceptible to variations in children's environments, as well as to early insults arising from exposures to prenatal toxins and other damaging influences (see Chapter 8). Finally, early interventions can have significant effects on what children know and can do at school entry and, perhaps as a result, sometimes have lasting influences on their school trajectories.

We first portray aspects of early cognitive development and learning that proceed apace for almost all children who grow up in supportive early environments. We then describe aspects of early learning that are characterized by individual differences and discuss the debate about early learning and sensitive periods. Next, following a brief discussion of early achievement motivation, we review what is known about features of environments that foster or undermine early learning, including the influence of socioeconomic status. We close with a discussion of measuring early cognitive development. A companion report from the National Research Council titled *Eager to Learn: Educating Our Preschoolers* (National Research Council, 2000) discusses what science now tells us about instruction and teaching during the early years.

Early Intellectual Competence

Infancy, toddlerhood, and the preschool years are times of intense intellectual engagement. Even 30 years ago, it would have seemed absurd to suggest that infants have memories, that they explore cause-and-effect sequences, or that they can engage in numerical reasoning. Today, thanks to the efforts of scientists who have developed new techniques for studying cognitive development, we know that they have these and many other amazing mental capacities.

Children from birth to age 5 engage in making sense of the world on many levels: language, human interactions, counting and quantification, spatial reasoning, physical causality, problem solving, categorization. Indeed, even preverbal infants show surprisingly sophisticated understandings in each of these areas. Complex human reasoning is thus rooted in early childhood. For example, infants less than a month of age can imitate others' gestures that are no longer in view, such as sticking out their tongues or opening their mouths (Meltzoff and Moore, 1989). By 9-12 months of age, infants can learn new behaviors simply by watching others, such as remembering how to unlock a container up to 24 hours after observing a peer do it (Bauer and Wewerka, 1995; Mandler and McDonough, 1995; Meltzoff, 1988). Six- to eight-month-olds can represent numbers: they match the number of objects visually depicted on a display with the number of drumbeats emanating from a loudspeaker (Starkey et al., 1983), and, when shown first one toy and then another hidden behind a screen, 5-month-olds expect to see two toys when the screen is lifted (Wynn, 1992). By the second half of the first year of life, infants have already learned about the properties of physical objects (Baillargeon et al., 1995). They know, for example, that objects cannot pass through one another and that objects fall when they are not supported.

Within the first year of life, infants become highly attuned to causal relations between objects. They distinguish events involving a causal sequence from other, noncausal events. For example, babies are more surprised when a video of one object colliding into another is run backward than when an object changing color is run backward (Leslie and Keeble, 1987). Furthermore, babies are aware of the effects of their own behaviors, in that they prefer consequences that they control directly over those that are uncontrollable (e.g., Parritz et al., 1992). For example, a child interacting with a noisy mechanical monkey perceives it as mildly threatening when it moves unpredictably, but enjoys it when he himself controls the toy's movements (Gunnar-vonGnechten, 1978). Similarly, infants 12 and 18 months old respond more positively to strangers who act in predictable ways that allow them more control than to strangers who are less predictable (Mangelsdorf, 1992).

In addition to distinguishing cause from effect, infants can distinguish accidental from intentional actions (Leslie and Keeble, 1987; Oakes and Cohen, 1990; Tomasello et al., 1996). In one study, 18-month-old children viewed an adult attempting to perform a series of target actions (e.g., pulling the ends off a tube) (Meltzoff, 1995). The adult was shown trying, but failing, to perform the target acts. When children imitated the event, they imitated the intended action—*not* the observed behavior. In a control experiment, children viewed a machine performing the same failed target acts. In this case, children did not attempt to perform the target acts at all.

These results suggest that 18-month-olds situate people, but not machines, within a psychological framework that differentiates between the surface behavior of people and a deeper level involving goals and intentions. This feature of imitative learning, which appears to be unique to human beings (see Tomasello, 1996), has been highlighted as crucial to the acquisition of cultural knowledge. As Tomasello notes (2000:37): "Children grow into cognitively competent adults in the context of a structured social world full of material and symbolic artifacts . . . structured social interactions . . . and cultural institutions such as families and religions" (see also Rogoff and Chavajay, 1995). The capacity to learn from others, by perceiving their goals and attempting to reproduce their strategies to achieve the same goals, initiates for the 1-year-old the process of being socialized as a member of a particular cultural group that reflects the accumulated wisdom of its ancestors.

Surprisingly, given the usual image of toddlers as egocentric, this mentalistic framework also allows even 2 1/2-year-olds to take on the perspective of another person, for example, recognizing that someone may have different tastes or preferences from their own (Flavell et al., 1990; Repacholi and Gopnik, 1997). By age 5, this has developed into a full-blown theory of mind, in which children can predict others' intentions, deceive others successfully, and recognize that beliefs don't always correspond to reality. The appearance-reality distinction is understood quite broadly by age 4 or 5, extending to children's way of reasoning about categories of objects and animals in the real world. Thus, 4-year-olds recognize that everyday categories (such as dinosaurs or living things) are not just perceptually based. They can readily learn that a pterodactyl is a dinosaur, not a bird, and infer from this information that it behaves like other dinosaurs (Gelman and Markman, 1986).

Given the wealth of abilities present even in infancy, it is not surprising that researchers now describe babies as "wired to learn," "computers made of neurons," and as "having inborn motivation to develop competencies." The policy issue is therefore not one of getting children ready to learn, but rather one of appreciating that they are born to learn and crafting policies and programs that actively build on their considerable capabilities (see National Research Council, 2000). Children's intrinsic drive to master the environment is probably no more evident than in relation to their efforts to understand and control the world around them. Indeed, infants' need to be active agents in their own learning becomes abundantly evident when you take away their control over stimulation. By a year of age, give a baby a metal spoon and a bunch of pots to bang on and she will happily make a considerable din. Let her hit a panel to turn on a toy monkey that claps cymbals loudly and she will do so with much glee. Record when she hits the panel, though, and use her record of *hits* to turn the toy (unpredictably) on for another child and, instead of smiles and laughter, that child will likely cry and attempt to escape to the safety of her parent's lap. Provide a *beep* before the toy comes on each time (to add predictability), and although the child lacks control, she will be less likely to cry and try to escape, but she still won't be likely to smile and reach for the toy. This clever research suggests that early learning environments should be set up to provide ample opportunities for young children to be active agents in their own learning and to receive predictable responses from their surroundings.

But not all aspects of cognitive development emerge with such predictability. As with language development, cognitive development consists of numerous components, some of which appear to be more affected by varying early environments than others. Unfortunately, the majority of research on cognitive development, particularly during the earliest years of life, has focused on the identification of universal patterns. By the time children are on the verge of school entry, however, research exploring individual differences becomes more prominent.

Virtually all children develop the capacity to understand causality, adopt the perspective of another person, and sort objects by categories. But just as children arrive at school with widely varying vocabularies, they also arrive at school with vast individual differences in their understanding of number concepts, familiarity with the alphabet and its relationship to sounds and printed words, capacity to reason through problems, knowledge of different notational forms (i.e., print, 3-D models, maps), and even familiarity with question-answer formats (National Research Council, 1998a, 2000). Another example of individual differences is provided by research on early conceptual development. While all preschoolers, for example, can categorize objects, only children who have been exposed to substantial knowledge about dinosaurs can sort them according to whether they are meat-eaters or not, land-dwellers or not, and so on (Gobbo and Chi, 1986).

One of the more striking differences among children starting kindergarten is in the area of executive functioning, discussed in the previous chapter. Some children are far more capable than others of the self-regulatory, sequencing, planning, and organizational skills that the research refers to as executive functioning. Deficits in any of these processes typically result in problems in school (Lyon, 1996), and they can create a snowball effect, with problems growing greater over time and extending to other areas of cognitive, academic, social, and emotional development. Year after year of failing to "stop, look, listen—and think" (Douglas, 1980:71) will inevitably diminish the richness of children's intellectual growth and experience and will interfere with their ability and motivation to be effective problem solvers.

Are There Sensitive Periods in Cognitive Development?

Perhaps a surprising point to many interested in early cognition is that there is no evidence for critical or sensitive periods in any aspect of cognitive development, in contrast to recent discoveries regarding processes in perception and language that are linked to the timing of inputs. This is not to say that sensitive periods in cognition do not exist; rather, scientific tools have not yet identified them if they do exist. Indeed, scientists have generally not even studied sensitive periods in cognitive development. Thus, there is an absence of relevant studies, rather than an absence of positive evidence. This gap reflects the difficulty of manipulating, in any precise way, the timing of input deemed relevant to cognitive development.

Consider, as a contrasting example, studies of sensitive periods in language acquisition. The most successful of these studies exploit certain experiments of nature, in which children are effectively *barred* from linguistic input (for example, due to deafness in a nonsigning environment). The problems inherent in studying comparable cases in cognition are multiple. First, everyday interactions and observations are rich with evidence that children exploit to further their cognitive growth (e.g., other faces or voices to imitate; sights and sounds to remember; problems to solve, including even those so mundane as an infant attempting to find her fingers to suck; similarities and differences to note and classify). Thus, it is difficult to imagine a context in which a child could be deprived utterly of cognitive input. Second, those cases in which cognitive deprivation of some sort does occur tend to be confounded with social, emotional, and language deprivation (for example, children who suffer extreme isolation). One implication of this gap is that strong claims regarding inherently irreversible effects of early experience on later cognition in humans, no matter how appealing, are not scientifically well founded.

In addition to the lack of evidence regarding sensitive periods for cognition, it is clear that important intellectual developments take place throughout childhood and even adulthood. To give just one striking example: researchers studying memory capacity have been able to train ordinary adults to achieve prodigious memory feats. In one well-documented case study (Kliegl et al., 1987), two young adults were trained, over a period of many months, to extend their digit span (that is, the number of single-digit numbers they could recall without error, after hearing them spoken aloud only once, without any opportunities to study, practice, or rehear the list). They started with a digit span of typical length (about 7, the length of a telephone number) and by hours of practice extended it over tenfold. In other words, by the end of training they could hear any *new* list of 80 single-digit numbers, one time only, and repeat the entire list, flawlessly, in order.

More usual (yet still remarkable) examples concern the striking growth of scientific knowledge and reasoning, mathematical understanding, and reading and writing skills of children past age 5, typically in school contexts. Likewise, although children from birth to age 3 engage in complex reasoning, it is well documented that major developments continue into early school age and well beyond. For example, there is a major shift between the ages of 3 and 7 in children's understanding of social relationships, in their understanding of biological principles (Carey, 1985), in their capacity to be self-reflective, and in their capacity to self-regulate. Learning is characterized by remarkable plasticity over the life span; learning during the earliest years is not unique.

This picture is complicated, however, by the recognition that early developmental sequences may provide important foundations for later development. Consider, for example, the case of early motor development. Researchers Joseph Campos and his colleagues have discovered that infants' experience with crawling appears to affect their fear of heights. In particular, crawling experience predicts wariness of heights, controlling for age; experience moving about in a walker leads to wariness of heights; lack of locomotor experience (due to physical disability) yields lack of wariness of heights; and regardless of the age when infants began to crawl, it is the duration of locomotor experience and not age that predicts avoidance of heights (Campos et al., 1992a).

Another quite different example of the importance of early sequences concerns the implications of impoverished verbal communication for development of reasoning about others' mental states. In one study (Peterson and Siegal, 1999), normal 4-year-olds were compared with a sample of deaf children averaging 9 years of age and to a sample of autistic (hearing) children averaging 9 years of age. The deaf children included a group of deaf signers from hearing families, none of whom had experienced daily conversational access to fluent signers, as well as children with access to more enriched conversations (either in homes with at least one native deaf signer or as oral deaf children with a moderate to severe hearing loss and the assistance of amplifying hearing aids). All children participated in a series of experimental tasks designed to tap their understanding of others' mental states. For example, in one task, children discovered that a candy box actually (and unexpectedly) contained pencils inside. They were then asked to predict what a naive observer would think was inside the closed box. A correct understanding of mental states would lead a child to answer "candy"; an incomplete understanding would lead a child to answer "pencils" (i.e., the child would attribute his or her own belief state to that of the naive observer).

Results indicated that native deaf signers performed as well as the hearing children. Oral deaf children also performed well. In contrast, the signing children from hearing homes, all of whom had limited access to enriched conversations, and the autistic children performed much more poorly, at about half the level of the other two groups. These results suggest that the availability of discourse about invisible mental states contributes to children's capacity to make sophisticated inferences about these constructs. The authors also suggest the possibility of a neurobiological basis for these group differences in performance, as deaf children who have been restricted in early conversational exposure differ in their patterns of language-related brain activity from both hearing adults and deaf native signers (Marschark, 1993; Neville et al., 1997). Findings such as these certainly do not argue for a sensitive period of development. Nonetheless, they emphasize the importance of early screening of sensory, perceptual, and motor abilities. These seemingly mundane skills are the foundation for later learning and problem solving and, if not addressed early, can constrain or alter consequent aspects of learning.

Motivational Dimensions of Early Learning

The vast majority of young children think they are just wonderful, capable of doing almost anything, and headed for success (Harter and Pike, 1984; Stipek, 1992). Most kindergarten children, for example, will tell you that they are the smartest child in their class (Stipek, 1993). Even when they approach tasks on which they have previously failed, young children usually predict that they will succeed (Stipek and Hoffman, 1980; Stipek et al., 1984). Why is this so? Ironically, the self-confidence of most preschoolers derives, in part, from their limited capabilities to distinguish among their strengths and weaknesses, to recognize that ability is not infinitely malleable (i.e., they confuse effort and ability), and to use social comparisons to make realistic judgments of their skills and competencies. Indeed, one reason why young children are so buoyantly optimistic about themselves is that when they compare what they can do with what they were able to do when they were younger, they can easily see how much more competent they are now (Frey and Ruble, 1990). In effect, they conclude that "every day, in every way, I am getting better and better!"

Young children thus appear to be disposed toward positive motivation-related cognitions. This applies across the board to children from families with both high and low socioeconomic status (Stipek and Ryan, 1997). But not all young children display this positive bias, and not all aspects of achievement motivation in the early years are so robust. Achievement motivation encompasses a set of constructs, including: (1) mastery motivation, or the child's propensity to explore, manipulate, persist, and derive pleasure in mastery-related behaviors and achievement (White, 1959); (2) intrinsic motivation, or the child's engagement in an activity without pressure or rewards for doing so (Deci and Ryan, 1985; Lepper, 1981); and (3) cognitive aspects of motivation, including expectations for success, challenge seeking, and self-perceptions of competence (Atkinson, 1964).

Despite the optimistic and positive picture of young children's motivation, their positive beliefs decline precipitously upon school entry (Stipek and Hoffman, 1980; Stipek and Tannatt, 1984; Wigfield et al., 1997). While some studies find that girls are more likely than boys to succumb to declining self-perceptions of their abilities (Entwisle and Baker, 1983; Ladd and Price, 1986), this is not always the case (Phillips, 1984), at least during the elementary years. A blend of developmental and contextual factors seems to be involved, including children's developing ability to make social comparisons, exposure in school to explicit and comparative standards for performance, and individual differences in the tendency to ascribe failure to one's ability or to more transient (i.e., effort) or external (i.e., the test was unfair) factors. Researchers have, however, continued to search for early indicators of motivational problems.

Individual differences in facets of behavior that are closely aligned with motivational tendencies can be detected as early as 6 months of age (see MacTurk and Morgan, 1995 and Morgan and Harmon, 1984 for reviews). Some infants, for example, persist in goal-directed behavior and seem to derive more pleasure from attaining goals (e.g., slipping a ball into a hole) than do other infants. These early differences, moreover, are closely tied to constructs assessed in the literature on temperament, such as inhibition around novel stimuli, persistence, and sustained attention (Fox et al., in press; Kagan et al., 1987). It is possible that individual differences seen in infants' mastery-related behaviors reflect differences in temperament. Whether these differences set in motion interactions that, over time, lead to motivational differences in the preschool and elementary years remains to be seen. Longitudinal studies of motivation that follow children from infancy into school are, surprisingly, missing in the developmental literature, despite recognition of the critical role played by motivational tendencies in children's achievement (see Stipek and Greene, in press).

The one chink in the armor of motivational resilience that has been detected in children as young as age 4 concerns their reactions to failure. Carol Dweck and her colleagues have examined a broad set of negative cognitions, behaviors, and emotional variables that they refer to as learned helplessness (Cain and Dweck, 1995; Diener and Dweck, 1978, 1980; Dweck, 1991; Smiley and Dweck, 1994). Children who display learned helplessness are highly impaired by failure experiences, showing displays of negative affect, challenge avoidance, and low expectancies for future success. Some preschoolers exhibit learned helplessness in achievement-related contexts. In one of the studies that first demonstrated this, children first completed a series of puzzles in which three unsolvable puzzles were followed by a fourth solvable puzzle, which all children were given sufficient time to complete. They were then again presented with all four puzzles and asked to choose a puzzle to work on. About one-third to one-half of the children not only chose the puzzle that they had previously completed (thus avoiding the puzzles on which they failed), but also expressed a coherent set of negative attitudes about their ability and future achievement. For example, they indicated that they would not be able to complete puzzles in the future even if given more time, were likely to describe themselves as "not so good" at puzzles even when they had said they were "good" at puzzles prior to failure, and to express "very sad" feelings about their performance. These individual differences among preschoolers emerged despite the fact that there were no prior differences among the children in puzzle-solving ability, in the number of pieces they fit into unsolvable puzzles, or in post-failure puzzle-solving ability. Moreover, the children who were negatively affected by failure generalized their diminished self-confidence to tasks that were unrelated to puzzles.

Unlike older children, however, preschoolers who display learned help-lessness do not show performance decrements following failure; in fact, their use of effective problem-solving strategies seems to bounce back once presented with a solvable task. Still, their negative self-appraisals may have implications for their orientations to learning as elementary students. In one study (Smiley and Dweck, 1994), children who responded negatively to failure as 4-year-olds were found to have significantly lower expectations for success and poorer appraisals of their abilities as third and fourth graders than did the children whose motivation was not impaired as preschoolers.

In sum, many aspects of achievement motivation fail to show individual differences prior to school entry, suggesting that young children either lack the cognitive abilities or experiences that can lead some to give up easily, anticipate poor performance, and disparage their abilities. Yet there is some evidence that children as young as age 4 are sensitive to failure experiences and, although subsequent performance does not appear to be affected, their internalized views of themselves as effective students do appear to remain vulnerable over time.

Early Learning Environments

The exciting discoveries that have characterized research on cognitive development have led some to argue that young minds—so active and capable—require special, heightened cognitive stimulation. Certainly, as more is learned about the remarkable capabilities of young children and their eagerness to learn, one naturally wants to provide them with environments that will support them in their task of becoming the most competent children, and ultimately adults, that they can be. As mentioned earlier, this does not imply that specific inputs are required at specific times during early development. But what is known about how best to ensure that children's early learning is on track? And to what extent do efforts to accelerate learning have lasting effects?

Early Learning and Early Environments

There is no question that enriched inputs can lead to enhanced learning, at least on a short-term basis. To give a trivial example, a 4-year-old child who is coached on the names of different species of birds can develop a more extensive vocabulary of bird names than a child who does not receive such input. However, it is not clear what the longer-term implications of such inputs are, nor which skills are being transmitted. It is also not clear that early learning is any more efficient, enduring, or effective than later learning. For example, there is to date no scientific evidence that teaching children to count at age 2 versus age 4 has any implications for their mathematical understanding or later mathematical achievement. Moreover, as discussed below, some activities embarked on in the name of enrichment may actually have some unintended detrimental effects.

As much as parents and other caregivers may wish for a toy or a tape or a lesson that would accelerate cognitive development, there isn't one yet. In fact, there is no magic bullet for brain stimulation and early learning. For example, there is no credible scientific foundation to the popular belief that listening to classical music will raise a child's IQ (see Box 6-2). Rather, it appears that, just as the vast majority of children all around the world grow up in homes and communities that provide them with the inputs they need to develop language, most grow up in environments that support their natural inclinations and abilities to learn. Indeed, children's curiosity about how the world works and their basic understandings in these domains routinely emerge without special prompting or instruction. Children, for example, spontaneously begin organizing objects into categories before 2 years of age, neatly sorting a pile of toys into cars and marbles and blocks (Sugarman, 1981; Waxman, 1999). Likewise, 2-year-olds spontaneously count arrays of objects, both in the service of solving problems (i.e., has someone taken one of my marbles?) and because it is fun for its own sake (Gelman and Gallistel, 1978). All they need are the small objects to manipulate and the opportunity to play with them.

Accordingly, the literature on early learning environments is not about accelerating learning with expensive toys and explicit early instruction. Instead, it focuses on how adults interact with young children and set up relatively ordinary environments to support and foster early learning. While this sounds like a subtle distinction, it captures the difference between a

BOX 6-2
The Mozart Effect

Does listening to classical music improve a young child's cognitive performance? Belief in the so-called Mozart effect has already had far-reaching consequences for public policy, not to mention the musical choices of first-time parents. In Georgia and Tennessee, for example, a classical music CD is given to every new mother, and in Florida, a new law requires that children in state-run child care facilities listen to classical music daily. Many parents are now wondering whether they should be playing classical music to their infants and toddlers—or whether their failure to do so earlier has blunted untapped intellectual potential in their offspring.

The possible effects of classical music on cognitive performance were first suggested by a study of college students showing that adults who listened to a Mozart sonata performed slightly—though significantly—better on a brief spatial reasoning task than did students listening to a relaxation tape or sitting in silence (Rauscher et al., 1993). The effect on performance was measured immediately after exposure to the music; longer-term effects were not studied. Many studies have attempted to replicate and extend these findings, but there has been no research with infants or toddlers, none involving assessments of brain functioning, and few examining effects of more than a day's duration. Even research with adults that has used the same particular Mozart sonata as the original study (Sonata for Two Pianos in D Major, K 448) has yielded inconsistent findings, with some researchers replicating the effect for performance on a brief spatial-temporal reasoning task but most failing to do so, and others finding that the effect can be induced by other pleasant events, such as listening to a story (Chabris, 1999). There have been no studies with infants or young children showing long-term cognitive gains attributable to early exposure to classical music.

In the end, although listening to music and learning to play a musical instrument may have important benefits for children, it is important to realize that there is no shortcut on the path toward developing early intellectual skills.

child who is taught to recite the alphabet and a child who is read to every night and becomes interested in letters and words because they are associated with the joy of being in her father's lap, seeing beautiful pictures, and hearing a wonderful story.

As with every other task of early development that we have discussed, the elements that support early learning revolve around relationships and the resources they provide for children. This literature emphasizes parents' interactions with their young children, their beliefs about learning and their children's capabilities, the home learning environment, and family organization. We discuss these aspects of the child's environment in more depth in Part III. Here, it is important to note that these features of families account for sizeable differences in the learning opportunities that children are exposed to prior to school entry and, in turn, for the wide disparities in knowledge and abilities that characterize kindergarteners (Duncan et al., 1994).

Child care and preschool experiences also matter, as do children's peer groups and the degree to which their communities support and provide opportunities for learning. Cognitive outcomes have, in fact, been a central focus of research on the effects of child care and more comprehensive early interventions. There is ample documentation in this literature of early environmental influences on concurrent cognitive development and, in some cases, on later learning and such important outcomes as special education placement and staying at grade level in school (see Chapters 11 and 13). But even for children who spend hours every day in child care or preschool, the home environment accounts for the lion's share of the variation in what young children know and are ready to learn when they start kindergarten (NICHD Early Child Care Research Network, 2000).

Motivation and Early Environments

There is also evidence regarding the effects of early learning environments on motivational aspects of early development (see Phillips and Stipek, 1993; Stipek and Greene, in press). Studies have found systematic effects of both the home environment and the instructional and social climate of early childhood education programs on a variety of motivation-related outcomes. For example, infants' mastery motivation has been associated with the number of toys in the home that are responsive to infants' manipulations and with maternal physical and auditory stimulation (Busch-Rossnagel et al., 1995; Yarrow et al., 1982), as well as to parental support of autonomy in task situations (e.g., nonintrusive assistance and encouragement) (Frodi et al., 1985; Grolnick et al., 1984). For toddlers and preschoolers, intrusive behavior on behalf of parents and teachers discourages mastery behavior, as does criticism and directive comments instead of using praise, giving suggestions and information, and demonstrating effective strategies (Fagot, 1973; Farnham-Diggory and Ramsey, 1971; Hamilton and Gordon, 1978; Henderson, 1984). These same relations appear to hold for young children with disabilities (Hauser-Cram, 1996).

With regard to classroom settings, although there is minimal variation in achievement motivation among preschool-age children, the variation that exists is significantly associated with classroom context. Specifically, highly didactic, performance-oriented early childhood classrooms have been found to depress young children's motivation. Children in these classrooms characterized by strong teacher control over activities, discouragement of collaborative work, a strong emphasis on getting correct answers, and relatively low levels of teacher warmth have been found to rate their abilities lower, to avoid challenging tasks, to expect poorer performance from themselves, and to show less enjoyment while working on achievement tasks compared with children in classrooms characterized by minimal pressure to perform, ample child choice in activities, encouragement of collaboration, and more nurturant teacher-child interactions (Stipek et al., 1995, 1998). They also showed more evidence of stress (e.g., nail biting, frowning, turning away from a task) and were less compliant in the classroom. It remains to be seen if highly didactic instruction in preschool has enduring effects on motivation or achievement. This research also fails to untangle the influence of didactic instruction and low levels of nurturance, because they were highly associated. Perhaps didactic instruction in the context of more nurturant teacher-child interactions would not be harmful to motivation.

In light of the very early age at which children in the United States are first exposed to a school-like setting (see Chapter 11), there has been a growing appreciation of the importance of studying children whose home language or culture differs substantially from the norm in early childhood classrooms. How do these differences manifest themselves in children's classroom behavior, motivation to learn, and achievement? A child who has been taught that it is disrespectful to ask questions of adults or who is unaccustomed to playing in mixed-sex peer groups is likely to feel some initial discomfort and confusion in classrooms that embody different rules and norms for behavior. Japanese students, for example, are more reluctant than their counterparts in the United States to ask questions because this suggests that they did not work hard enough to understand the material or that they are implicitly criticizing the teachers' ability to communicate information (see Greenfield and Cocking, 1994). Parents' beliefs about when and how children learn school-related skills and the social rules that guide learning interactions—termed "funds of knowledge"—are also based in culture (Moll et al., 1992), and they affect how much parents emphasize explicit early learning opportunities that map onto what kindergarten teachers in the United States expect children to know and be able to do (Goldenberg et al., 1992; Heath, 1983; Laosa, 1980; Shanahan and Rodriguez-Brown, 1993). Classroom adaptations that are designed to accommodate young children's differing approaches to learning have been found to reduce disruptive and inattentive behaviors (Au and Mason, 1981; Gallimore et al., 1974; Vogt et al., 1987; Weisner et al., 1989), but effects on achievement remain to be demonstrated.

In sum, despite the generally positive motivational orientations of young children, both home and classroom environments, as well as the lack of "fit" between them, have the capacity to undermine their natural optimism and enjoyment of learning. Motivation suffers when parental behavior is intrusive, highly directive, and critical, and when teachers stress individual performance and deemphasize interpersonal warmth.

The Contribution of Family Socioeconomic Status

Of all aspects of children's early environments, the family's socioeconomic status (SES) is most powerfully associated with children's cognitive skills when they enter school. We consider this literature separately and return to these issues in Chapter 10. Because lifelong educational attainments can be traced back to academic skills at school entry, these class-related differences at the beginning of school are cause for serious concern (Stevenson and Newman, 1986; Stipek, in press). Thus, even though there is no evidence that early cognitive attainments are characterized by sensitive periods that are inherent to development, school entry can be viewed as an important social transition when SES-linked individual differences can become solidified and amplified or initial gaps can be narrowed. In this sense, what children know and can do at school entry matter, not because development becomes less amenable to environmental influence once the preschool years have passed, but because there is, in effect, a manufactured critical transition at which point individual differences begin to predict longer-term patterns of learning and achievement.

Indeed, there is good evidence to suggest that the long-term prediction of academic achievement, school dropout, and even adult literacy from the socioeconomic status of one's family during the early childhood years is attributable to the effects of social class on early school achievement (Stipek, in press). For example, when researchers explore causal sequences in their data (e.g., does A explain C, or does A explain B, which then explains C?) they find, for example, that the significant effect of income on early adult literacy is mediated or influenced by the effects of income on early childhood cognitive level, which in turn predicts adult literacy (Baydar et al., 1993). Similarly, while mothers' SES-linked interactions with these young children predict the children's achievement in sixth grade, an even stronger relationship is found between children's preschool academic skills and their sixth grade achievement (Hess et al., 1984). As we discuss in Chapter 10, SES during the early childhood years appears to be more predictive of educational attainments than SES during other periods of childhood.

Several mechanisms have been proposed to explain the long-term predictive power of a child's academic skills at school entry and, in particular, the extent to which class-linked differences at school entry are perpetuated—even exacerbated—as children move through school. These include effects of children's initial performance on teachers' expectations for their subsequent learning, teacher behaviors and decisions that derive from these expectations, associations between low academic skills and conduct problems that further impede learning, and self-defeating perceptions and expectations that children hold for themselves that undermine effort, persistence, and therefore learning (Stipek, in press). These processes are not the focus of this report. They do, however, further illustrate the importance of narrowing the gap prior to school entry between children whose families occupy different economic niches in society.

Measurement Issues

The learning capacities of young children, discovered by researchers over the past 30 years, complicate efforts to measure early intellectual and cognitive development. Yet the measurement of early learning and cognition, primarily with global measures of developmental status or IQ, has been a staple of efforts to evaluate the effects of early interventions. This final discussion raises concerns about traditional approaches to assessing the effectiveness of early interventions and identifies alternative constructs that would provide firmer evidence of effective programs. We return to these questions when we discuss the early intervention literature in Chapter 13.

IQ tests are not, in fact, well suited for studying development. They are not designed, for example, to capture the enormous cognitive growth that is taking place during the early years in such areas as increased knowledge, memory, speed of processing, and sequencing and planning abilities. Rather than assessing individual growth over time, or growth in response to an intervention, the IQ is designed to be stable over time and to assess the relative standing of an individual with respect to others of the same age. Indeed, because the IQ is hard to push around, an intervention that finds reliable improvements in IQ has accomplished something noteworthy, particularly if these improvements endure over time (which they seldom do).

Standard IQ tests are also not designed to assess intelligence in infancy, and scores within the normal range on standard measures of infants' developmental status (such as the Bayley Scales of Infant Development) have poor predictive value for later functioning. Indeed, later IQ cannot be reliably predicted by early measures of ability until the child is about 4 years of age. In contrast, the speed with which infants habituate to stimuli and their preference for novelty are predictive of later childhood IQs (Bornstein, 1989; Fagan, 1984; McCall and Carriger, 1993; Rose et al., 1992; Thompson et al., 1991).

Finally, many of the early intellectual abilities that have been the focus of research on cognitive development over the past 30 years are not evaluated directly by standard IQ tests. These include children's regulatory and attentional capacities, certain aspects of memory, and abilities that relate to theory of mind. Moreover, as researchers have learned more about what can go wrong with cognitive development, it becomes imperative to assess the specific dimensions of early cognitive functioning that can reveal serious problems and register the effects of efforts to intervene. For example, understanding of others' intentions and mental states seems to be a quite separate intellectual domain, which is impaired in autism but spared in Down syndrome. Children with autism also display failures to engage in protodeclarative pointing, low rates of direct eye contact with others, low levels of pretend play, language delays, and deficits in reasoning about others' mental states (Baron-Cohen, 1995; Tager-Flusberg, 1989). The research on early biological insults, reviewed in Chapter 8, further calls attention to the importance of assessing the attention, memory, and abstract thinking abilities that appear to be affected by a number of these insults, as well as by prolonged exposure to stress. These are not the outcomes that are typically measured in research on early intervention, despite their relevance to the populations that are typically targeted by these initiatives.

SUMMARY AND CONCLUSIONS

The years from birth to school entry mark a period of remarkable linguistic and intellectual growth. Children make the transition from having no language at all to understanding and expressing the subtleties of intentionality, cause and effect, and emotional states. The motivation and capacity of the newborn to act on and learn about the surrounding world and the people in it flourish during the early childhood years and ultimately transform the newborn into a 5-year-old who is usually well prepared to embark on the formal school curriculum. At the same time, there is no evidence to confirm or disconfirm that the age of 3 or 5 marks the end of a sensitive period in human cognition and, with respect to language development, evidence for sensitive periods is largely restricted to pronunciation and the complex morphological properties of language. In fact, both language development and early learning appear to be relatively resilient processes, largely protected from adverse circumstances and quick to recover when these circumstances are removed, and to be characterized by lifelong capacities for growth and learning.

Nevertheless, some critical aspects of language and learning remain vulnerable to environmental variation even within the normal range that encompasses families at different socioeconomic levels in society. Indeed, evidence reviewed in Part III, suggests that young children's academic attainments may be even more susceptible to the negative influence of poverty than is the case for older children (at least up to adolescence). These less resilient aspects include the extent of the child's vocabulary, language proficiency (i.e., uses of language), understanding of number concepts, familiarity with letter-sound associations, and executive functioning. Importantly, these are precisely the aspects of early communication and learning that distinguish children at school entry and are thus strong candidates for the aspects of early school performance that become consolidated over time, accounting for linkages between preschool capabilities and educational outcomes in adolescence and beyond. Early interventions can attenuate these individual differences at school entry, although the subsequent school environment plays a crucial role in either sustaining or undermining early gains. Children with specific disabilities (as contrasted with transitory developmental delays) can also benefit to varying degrees from specially designed interventions, although the early initiation of these efforts may be especially important (as has been demonstrated by research on deaf children) and the extent to which normal functioning can be approached remains unclear (as illustrated by children with specific language impairments).

Despite the substantial interest that research on the developing brain has stimulated in finding materials that can accelerate early talking and learning, there is no evidence that any specialized kind of short-term input improves intelligence or learning in an appreciable way. Put in crude terms, there is no magic bullet to boost intelligence. Likewise, there is no scientific evidence that any sort of mobile, toy, computer program, or baby class has a long-term impact on reasoning, intelligence, or learning. Rather, under typical circumstances, parents around the globe seem intuitively to talk to children in ways that work quite well in fostering language development and to provide children with the interactions and materials that promote early learning. To the extent that problems arise, it is usually not that parents are doing terribly wrong things, but that they are not doing quite the right things or enough of them. This includes talking to children more and using more elaborate talk, taking advantage of everyday interactions to introduce number concepts, and not only spending more time reading but also exploring the words and pictures in the book.

7 | Making Friends and Getting Along with Peers

Establishing relationships with other children is one of the major developmental tasks of early childhood (see Rubin et al., 1998, for an excellent review). How well children fare at this task appears to matter. It matters to the children themselves, creating a context in which they evaluate their self-worth, competence, and view of the world as pleasant or hostile (Harter, 1982; Ladd and Price, 1986). It matters to their future, as the patterns of peer interaction in early childhood increasingly predict whether children will walk pathways to competence or deviance in the tasks of middle childhood and adolescence (Barclay, 1966; Kupersmidt and Coie, 1990; Ollendick et al., 1992). And it matters to the other children a child comes into contact with, as the experience of children in peer groups depends in good measure on the nature of the other children with whom they interact (Wright et al., 1986). Yet playing nicely, making friends, and being a good friend are not all that easy for young children. These tasks confront them with increasing demands on their developing cognitive and emotional capacities (Howes and Matheson, 1992).

Developmental psychologists use a variety of techniques to understand the landscape of early peer relations. Teachers and parents have often been used as informants. However, their ratings correlate only modestly (Achenbach et al., 1987). Teacher and parent ratings reflect how adults, not children, think about what it means to be competent, nice, or fun to play with (Rubin et al., 1998). Direct observation helps get beyond problems of adult interpretation, and it has been a staple of research on early peer relations. Several observational instruments have been used fairly widely, and these include measures of the type (e.g., solitary, parallel, coordinated) and complexity (e.g., exploring things, constructing things, pretending things) of play (see Ladd and Price, 1993, for a review), as well as assessments of how well children appear to be getting along (e.g., prosocial exchanges, aggressive exchanges, withdrawn behavior) and the emotions they are expressing (e.g., positive, angry, sad). Observational measures are not appropriate, however, for the study of enduring relationships since they capture only brief episodes of interaction. Researchers have also asked groups of children whom they like and dislike, which can be done effectively with children as young as age 3 (Coie and Dodge, 1983; Newcomb and Bukowski, 1983). Children are classified as popular (many "like" and few "dislike" nominations from their peers), rejected (many dislike and few like nominations), neglected (few of either kind of nominations), controversial (many of both kinds of nominations), or average. These classifications and the continuous measurement of liking and disliking can be used to explore the emotional, behavioral, and cognitive competencies that influence peer acceptance. These ratings may not generalize, however, beyond the group tested. For example, a child who isn't popular at preschool may be popular in her neighborhood. Unfortunately, we know little about how variation in acceptance across different peer groups affects children.

Peer status is not written in stone, even when assessments are focused on a child's standing in the same group over time. Among preschool children, the number of liking and disliking nominations a child receives at one time accounts for only about 25 percent of the variation in the number of nominations she receives even a short time (3 weeks) later (Olson and Lifren, 1988). Classifications based on such measures are also only modestly stable, with popular, rejected, and average classifications typically being more stable than controversial and neglected classifications (Newcomb and Bukowski, 1984). These methods are also probably culturally bound. Making decisions about who you like and don't like may make sense to children in cultures in which common topics are deciding who does and doesn't get to come to one's birthday party, who does and doesn't get invited over to play, and who can and cannot be "my friend today." For children from cultures that encourage them to like all the children in a group, however, asking such questions may make little sense.

Despite these limitations, these so-called sociometric measures have yielded important findings. This is especially true with regard to children who end up in the rejected classification. Most of the work on peer rejection comes from studies of school-age children, so extrapolation from these studies must be done with caution when considering younger children. By the early school years, peer rejection is clearly a risk factor. Rejected children are overrepresented among adults with psychiatric problems (Cowen et al., 1973), among children who do poorly at school (Coie et al.,

1992; Ollendick et al., 1992; Wentzel and Asher, 1995), and among those who come into contact with the law (Kupersmidt and Coie, 1990). Whether it is the rejection that causes the later problems or the behaviors that get the child rejected that cause these problems is difficult to disentangle. Both are likely to be true. Importantly, however, not all, nor even most, children who are rejected by other children at some time in their childhood have difficulties of this sort (Parker et al., 1995). In addition, rejected children are not all cut from the same cloth. At least two bases for rejection appear to be important by middle childhood (Cillessen et al., 1992; French, 1988). Some children are rejected because they are mean and aggressive, others because they are shy and withdrawn. The trajectories for these two kinds of rejected children differ. The most is known about rejected aggressive children, who appear to be at risk for all types of externalizing behavioral and emotional problems. Less is known about rejected withdrawn children, although they may be at greater risk for psychiatric problems of the internalizing type (i.e., anxiety, depression) (Hymel et al., 1990; Rubin and Mills, 1988).

Efforts to improve the quality of peer relations have focused largely on school-age children, with few exceptions (Webster-Stratton, 1990). Yet problematic patterns of social interaction can be discerned well before school entry. To facilitate efforts to design appropriate interventions for young children, it is important to understand how their interactions and play with one another change over the early years of life, and why some children negotiate this changing landscape more easily than others.

PLAY AND THE DEVELOPMENT OF PEER RELATIONS

Views about the development of peer relations have changed over the past half-century or so (Rubin et al., 1998). A report based on what was known in the 1950s would begin by stating that babies really aren't interested in one another, and when they do interact, they treat each other more like objects than like people. It would state that from 24 months onward, while children could have playmates, the development of friendships is beyond their capabilities.

Thousands of hours of observation have modified these views, leading to a much richer appreciation of the interest, capacity, and skills young children bring to their relations with other children, including their friends. Observations have also led to a richer appreciation of the challenges that face children when they try to join into and sustain play with other children of similar age. This increased awareness of the landscape of early peer relations has developed over a period in U.S. society when the amount of time children spend with other unrelated children has increased significantly. For example, as recently as the 1980s, researchers estimated that only 10 percent of a 2-year-old's interactions involved peers. Today, given that approximately 40 percent of children under age 3 are in part- or full-time child care with other children, this is probably an underestimate (Capizzano et al., 2000; U.S. Bureau of the Census, 1996).

The increasing salience of the peer group must also be placed in the context of the large decrease in family size that has characterized recent decades. In 1965, the average family in the United States had 2.44 children under 18. By 1998, the average family had 1.85 children—a 25 percent decline (U.S. Bureau of the Census, 1998). Young children today are thus more likely to grow up as "onlies" or with only one sibling. Siblings provide daily opportunities for children to practice social interaction (although not necessarily positive interaction—see Buhrmester, 1992; Dunn and Kendrick, 1982), can play a protective role for each other under highly stressful circumstances (Anderson et al., 1999), can be an important source of child care (see Chapter 11), and, in general, are an important influence on children's emotional, cognitive, and behavioral development (Dunn, J., 1993; Dunn and Kendrick, 1982). We don't really know whether and to what extent unrelated peers fulfill some of these functions for young children with few or no siblings.

Babies are interested in one another from at least as early as 2 months of age. Young infants get excited by the sight of other infants and, when given the opportunity, they will stare avidly at one another (Eckerman, 1979). By 6 to 9 months, babies seem to try to get the attention of other babies. By this age, they will smile and babble at other babies, sometimes initiating and sometimes returning social bids (Hay et al., 1982; Vandell et al., 1980). By 9 to 12 months, babies begin to imitate each other, and this imitation seems to serve as the coin of the infant realm of play ("see, I know what you are doing, let's do it together") (Mueller and Silverman, 1989).

From ages 1 to 2 years, there are tremendous strides in what children can do with one another. Bouts of interaction get longer and more complex ("see, I know you are doing what I am doing, so I'll do it again—now you do it."). Bouts of reciprocal imitation indicate that toddlers are aware, at least on some level, of the intent of others consistent with their emerging theory of mind (DiLalla and Watson, 1988). Reciprocity ("you do it, I do it, you do it") reveals their developing turn-taking abilities. These very simple abilities to share meaning, be aware of another's intent, and take on reciprocal roles probably lay the groundwork for coordinated play (Howes, 1992). In establishing these early play routines, language certainly helps. Indeed, throughout the preschool years, children who speak more clearly and communicate their ideas better have an easier time getting and keeping play going (Mueller, 1972).

For toddlers, social play is hard, and play bouts are fragile experiences.

A brief distraction, someone bumbling into your play area, a few miscues, and the pattern is broken. For these reasons and others, how well adults structure play environments for toddlers makes a difference in how much and how well they can play together (Howes and Unger, 1989). Cognitive development also facilitates the growth of early peer skills. Interactional skill depends, for example, on the child's capacity to distinguish her actions from events and actions in the world and to plan and execute sequences of behavior, both of which develop rapidly during the second and third years of life as major strides are made in peer relations (Brownell, 1988; Brownell and Carriger, 1990). Importantly, toddlers seem to find it easier to play with the children they play with often (Howes, 1996). Experience playing together seems to expand what two toddlers can do together, perhaps explaining why they show their most mature play when playing with someone they know well.

Just putting two toddlers together on a regular basis does not ensure that play will happen. They find it easier to play with others who are emotionally and cognitively compatible and who share their play preferences (Rubin et al., 1994). The importance of familiarity and compatibility to toddler play suggests that some form of at least rudimentary friendship may be as critical to toddlers as it is to older children. Toddlers are readily capable of establishing relationships (not just encounters) with age mates (Rubin et al., 1998). They are more likely to initiate play, direct positive affect to, and engage in complex interactions with familiar than with unfamiliar playmates (Howes, 1988a). Beyond mere familiarity, they develop reciprocal relationships in which positive interactions beget other positive interactions in a manner that distinguishes specific pairs of children and not others (Ross et al., 1992). Toddler friendships are not ephemeral. When asked, many parents of 4-year-olds say that their child is currently friends with children he met as a toddler. Although these early friendships are unlikely to carry the same emotional significance as do later friendships, they provide children with their earliest lessons about how to establish and maintain relationships.

Toddler play and friendships, of course, are not all sunshine and light. Conflict happens. Indeed, conflict and aggression initially increase as children try to play together, peaking between years 2 and 3 before they decline (Brown and Brownell, 1990; Hay and Ross, 1982). It may come as some relief to parents that in the toddler and early preschool period, moderately aggressive children are often the most socially outgoing; they are the children who try more to play with other children (Brown and Brownell, 1990). Furthermore, while aggression seems to be a correlate of peer rejection beginning as early as it has been studied, this does not mean that children who are completely nonaggressive are well liked. In fact, observations of withdrawn, submissive children show that peers rebuff them more than they do socially outgoing children (Rubin, 1985).

Both cognitive and social theories of peer relations argue that conflict (at least a certain amount of it) is often benign and may play a positive role in children's development (Azmitia, 1988; Hartup, 1996; Piaget, 1932; Roy and Howe, 1990; Vygotsky, 1978). Conflict, arguments, and outright physical aggression disrupt the flow of play, indicate that something is wrong, and challenge children to figure out what needs to happen to get play back on track. When conflict happens, younger children, like older children and adults, can walk away, slug it out, give in, argue and negotiate, or appeal to higher powers. Researchers who have observed what toddlers and preschool children actually do during conflicts find that most often play dissolves, either because the children stop trying to be together or an adult intervenes (Hartup et al., 1988). However, when conflict happens among friends, the rules seem to change. Friends are more likely to try to stick it out, negotiate, compromise, and continue to play (Hartup and Laursen, 1993). Friendship, as distinct from familiarity, is again seen to support competent social behavior. However, conflict of the "beat 'em up, drag 'em down" variety is not good for anyone involved, and a young child who engages frequently in highly aggressive peer interactions warrants concern.

As children move into the preschool years, their social skills expand dramatically. Play among preschoolers increasingly involves pretense, and pretense increasingly includes playing with things that don't depend on the props available (Howes, 1992). By age 5, most children can quickly set up elaborate pretend play, making almost anything stand for almost anything else (Göncü, 1993). The number of children who can be included in play at one time also expands. At age 2 and 3, working out play themes with just one other child is challenging. Indeed, as noted by one savvy 3-year-old, "Hunter, me, Juliet (pointing to each). That's three. I can't do three." By age 5, children can often do three and more at a time, keeping track of what roles all are playing, how their roles fit the overall theme, and negotiating conflicts to decide together what is and isn't supposed to happen next (Garvey, 1990).

Certainly children's developing cognitive and language abilities play a role in the increasing complexity of play, as does their developing ability to regulate their emotions. However, experience with peers may also be important. It seems unlikely that a 5-year-old who has not spent time with age mates would fare well, at least initially, if suddenly dropped into a room full of other 5-year-olds. In line with this reasoning, greater experience in adult-supervised play groups is associated with more frequent and more complex peer interactions among toddlers (Holmberg, 1980; Howes, 1988a; Mueller and Brenner, 1977).

As distinct from play groups, however, efforts to examine the role of early child care experience in young children's social competence has produced contradictory findings (see Chapter 11 for a fuller discussion). On one hand, preschool children with prior experience with peers in child care have been found to be more involved, positive, and cooperative with peers than preschoolers without such experience (Harper and Huie, 1985; Lamb et al., 1988; Volling and Feagans, 1995) and to engage in more complex forms of play (Rubenstein and Howes, 1983). This is especially the case when children remain with the same group of peers over time (Galluzzo et al., 1990). Indeed, toddlers who establish friendships in child care tend to remain friends right up to school entry, even when the two youngsters are of the opposite sex (Howes, 1983, 1988a; Howes and Phillipsen, 1992).

On the other hand, extensive child care in the first two years of life has been associated with lower social competence and heightened aggression in preschool and beyond (Bates et al., 1994; Haskins, 1985; Schwartz et al., 1974; Vandell and Corasaniti, 1990). The clue to these contradictory findings seems to lie in the quality of care that is provided and, in particular, in the sensitivity of the relationships that caregivers establish with their young charges. Higher-quality child care is generally related to more competent peer relationships during early childhood and into the school years (Holloway and Reichart-Erickson, 1989; Howes, 1990; NICHD Early Child Care Research Network, submitted; Phillips et al., 1987a). This is consistent with evidence that infants' attachments to their caregivers are important correlates of emerging peer relations (Goossens and van IJzendoorn, 1990; Oppenheim et al., 1988).

HOW DO ADULTS HELP?

Arguably, the more that is learned about the complexity of the peer landscape in early childhood, the less surprising it is that some children have problems with it, and the more amazing it is that so many children do so well. What helps them? Researchers have paid the most attention to what parents, especially mothers, do to help their children negotiate the early peer environment and to how the child's own personality or temperament helps or hinders them. Secure attachment relationships with parents (see Chapter 9) certainly seem to help. Secure attachment in infancy is associated with social competence for toddlers (Pastor, 1981) and preschoolers (Booth et al., 1991; Erickson et al., 1985). Secure attachment relationships in infancy also predict greater popularity with peers during the preschool years (LaFreniere and Sroufe, 1985) and more harmonious, supportive friendships with other preschool children (Park and Waters, 1989). Insecure attachment, in contrast, seems to limit children's social competence, yet the problems of insecurely attached children are not all alike.   Infants who avoid contact with their parents in the moderately stressful circumstances in which attachment is assessed later tend to be more hostile, angry, and aggressive with other children in preschool settings that do their secure counterparts (LaFreniere and Sroufe, 1985; Troy and Sroufe, 1987). Infants who display more ambivalent attachments, appearing to be both preoccupied and angry with their mother, tend to develop into whiny, easily frustrated, and easily rebuffed toddlers and preschoolers (Erickson et al., 1985; Fox and Calkins, 1993).

Presumably, these associations between the security of attachment and behaviors with peers reflect the ways that young children's experiences in their primary attachment relationships affect the ideas they develop about themselves and others (i.e., so-called inner working models of relationships), the skills they bring with them to the peer group, and their emotional state. Angry children who feel unloved and unlovable, not surprisingly, make poor playmates, as do whiny, easily frustrated children. Unfortunately, although a number of interventions have been designed to improve the mother-infant attachment relationship in high-risk samples, few studies have examined effects on children's peer relationships (see Stams et al., in press, for an exception in which an isolated effect was found for 7-year-old girls' peer competence). Thus, while these correlations abound and they are consistent with theories about the ways that parent-infant attachment should affect how children get along with other children, it cannot yet be proved that they are causal.

Beyond attachment security, parents do many other things that support or impede their children's relations with other children. Parents of socially competent toddlers and preschoolers believe that helping their children learn to play well is part of their role as parents (Goodnow et al., 1985). In the context of the United States, this translates into arranging chances for their children to play with others and socializing their children in competent play behavior (Rubin et al., 1989). In other parts of the world, this translates into honing the child's observational skills (Briggs, 1991; Ellis and Gauvain, 1992; Ochs, 1988). Interestingly, parents of socially adroit children attribute their children's social gaffes to transitory, fixable factors (e.g., she's tired, we let them play too long, the group is too large) (Goodnow et al., 1985). In contrast, parents of socially maladroit children see social competence or its lack as more inherent (i.e., aggressive children are born that way), devalue the importance of social skills, and argue that teaching social skills is the job of the schools or others with formal training in teaching such skills (Rubin et al., 1989).

Of course, parents of socially incompetent children may form beliefs in response to their history with that child, their failures in previous attempts to improve the child's social behavior, and their feelings of embarrassment (Bugenthal, 1992). This, in turn, may lead parents to respond punitively, setting up circular patterns of hostility that can feed children's aggressive and angry behavior (Hart et al., 1992; Rubin and Mills, 1990). Indeed, highly aggressive, poorly regulated behavior with peers has repeatedly been found to correlate with parental rejection, the use of power-assertive and inconsistent discipline, permissiveness, indulgence, and a lack of supervision, at least in the Westernized cultures that have been studied (see Rubin et al., 1995a for a review). Parents of popular children, in contrast, are more feelings-oriented, warmer, and more likely to use reasoning and explanations to encourage compliance (Hart et al., 1990; MacDonald and Parke, 1984; Putallaz, 1987). Less well understood are parental reactions to shyness and social wariness, although, among preschoolers, there is interest in parents who are both overcontrolling and overprotective (East, 1991; Hart et al., 1992; LaFreniere and Dumas, 1992).

Parents also influence the development of their children's social behavior through direct interventions in their lives. They provide opportunities for peer interactions, monitor their children's encounters with peers, coach their children to deal competently with peers, and sanction unacceptable peer-related behaviors (see Bhavnagri and Parke, 1991; Ladd et al., 1992; Pettit and Mize, 1993). In one study, for example, mothers who were moderately involved in arranging and monitoring the peer contacts of their preschool sons fostered their son's growing popularity with peers over time, in contrast to mothers who were either over- or underinvolved (Ladd and Hart, 1992). The intriguing possibility that training parents in these peer monitoring and coaching skills could be an effective intervention for young children who appear to be getting off to a poor start in peer relations is suggested by Webster-Stratton's work. In a small-scale intervention that was subjected to a randomized trial, she effectively trained parents of preschoolers who were displaying serious conduct problems to modify their children's behavior (Webster-Stratton, 1990; Webster-Stratton et al., 1989). Persistent effects on the children's social behavior were found at a one-year follow-up assessment and, three years after the intervention, parents who participated in the intervention continued to report more favorable perceptions of their children's behavior, particularly if they were in a variation of the intervention that was staffed by a professionally trained therapist.

THE CONTRIBUTION OF TEMPERAMENT

So fixing the parent will fix the child? Perhaps. But that ignores the possibility that some parents and some children face greater challenges in getting to the point at which the child can easily get along with other children. Only recently have researchers begun to examine how a child's temperament influences peer relations and friendships. Most of the attention has been paid to the small group of extremely anxious, inhibited children—discussed earlier in relation to regulatory capacities—who do find it a real struggle to feel comfortable with other children (Fox et al., in press; Kagan et al., 1987). When children characterized by this temperamental pattern are followed into the preschool and early elementary years, a sizable share remain cautious and vigilant during interactions with peers, which appears to be part of an overall tendency to display wariness and fear when presented with unpredictable and unfamiliar situations (Kagan et al., 1987). Because these children's inhibition tends to be elicited more by social encounters than by novel and unfamiliar objects as they get older, the term "social reticence" has been coined to describe their behavior (Fox et al., 1996; Rubin et al., 1995b). Their reticence tends to be accompanied by signs of anxiety and, as we described with regard to regulatory capacities, by patterns of brain activity that suggest a tendency to react to mild stress with negative affect, such as sadness and anger.

Many initially inhibited children, however, do not remain so (Fox et al., in press). Specifically, about one in four infants who display highly negative responses to novel stimuli early in the first year continue to show highly inhibited behavior as preschoolers. This raises the question of what accounts for the divergent pathways of children who display consistent versus declining inhibition as they move through the preschool years. As toddlers, before their social behavior diverged, the continuously inhibited children were more likely to display the unique pattern of brain activity described above and to be described as socially fearful by their mothers compared with the children who went on to become less shy and more sociable. It is not known if the differing maternal perceptions of the children reflected earlier changes in behavior seen at home and on the playground (but not in the research laboratory), or if they contributed in some way to the direction of change in the children's behavior over time. There is some evidence that when parents overprotect these children, they seem to learn to lean on adults in ways that can sustain their inhibited behavior and interfere with their acceptance by other children (Arcus et al., 1992; Park et al., 1997). However, many shy children do quite well when they have plenty of time to develop relationships (Asendorpf, 1989). They may not be social butterflies, but they can develop close, often supportive relationships with other children.

Recently, rambunctious and highly active children who relish new and slightly scary things have received attention from researchers (Rubin et al., 1995b). These children have characteristics that are valued in the majority culture, especially among boys. Such children can be identified as early as 4 months of age by their happy, exuberant reactions to novel stimulation. Perhaps because this behavior is valued, about half of them tend to remain exuberant throughout infancy and the preschool years (Fox et al., in press).

Although exuberant, these children are not hard to manage, nor are they rated as having behavior problems of either the internalizing or externalizing variety.

Children on the far extremes of this temperament dimension, however, face additional challenges in getting along with other children. Their exuberance, while sometimes attractive to other children, can also be overwhelming. Not surprisingly, teachers sometimes note that these children are slightly more aggressive than other children in the early preschool years, perhaps because they are usually smack in the middle of whatever is going on socially (Gunnar et al., 1997). Children who approach other children readily and seem to have little anxiety about new or novel experiences are more likely to score higher on externalizing or "acting out" kinds of behavior problems, but only if they also have trouble with self-control (Rubin et al., 1995b). Thus, although exuberance is sometimes valuable in children, highly exuberant children may create challenges for themselves and for others.

The real issue may not be whether children are shy and anxious or overwhelmingly outgoing, but how they learn to regulate how they express who they are. Temperament may play a role here as well. It has proven useful in research to distinguish among three dimensions of temperament during the preschool years (Rothbart and Bates, 1998). One is the dimension of shy to extroverted, just discussed. Another includes how readily children show negative emotions (e.g., fearful, anxious, sad). The third, which becomes increasingly obvious from about 18 months onward, is how well the child can sustain focused attention and inhibit certain actions. We discussed this dimension of self-regulation, which is often called "inhibitory" or "effortful control," earlier in the context of how temperament affects the young child's emerging capacity for emotion regulation (see Chapter 5).

At least within the range that is typically seen among children, this dimension of temperament supports children in their attempts to play nicely and make friends (Fabes et al., 1999). Furthermore, this dimension seems to temper and even reverse the influence of other aspects of the child's temperament. Exuberant children who can control and modulate expression of their exuberance seem to be valued as playmates; indeed, they can be a lot of fun (Rubin et al., 1995b). Those who cannot receive mixed reviews from playmates. Children who tend to feel things more intensely than others, especially angry, sad, or fearful emotions, but who can control them don't have many problems with other children, while those who cannot control those emotions end up doing things that get them disliked and rejected (Fabes et al., 1999).

IMPACT OF DISABILITY ON PEER INTERACTIONS

Children with developmental disabilities are often the least preferred play partners of typically developing children. This is reflected both on sociometric measures and in direct observations of children's interaction patterns. Although outright rejection of children with disabilities is uncommon, a pattern of exclusion is most evident (Guralnick, 1999). While they may not be so disliked that they fall into the rejected category, they do consistently score as less preferred (fewer "liked" and more "disliked" nominations) on sociometric measures. Even children with only mild delays tend to participate less in sustained play in preschool classes, spend more time alone or off to the side when other children are playing, express more sadness and negativity when playing (or not being allowed to play) with other children, get angry more, and use less effective strategies when conflicts arise. Children with language delays have more trouble communicating with other children, and this impedes their ability to participate in the flow of activities with other children in preschool classrooms (Craig and Washington, 1993; Gertner et al., 1994; Guralnick et al., 1996; Hadley and Schuele, 1998). Children born with very low birthweight also have difficulties with social skills and are disproportionately rated as exhibiting both internalizing (depressive-anxious) and externalizing (hyperactive-aggressive) behaviors independent of IQ and social class (Breslau et al., 1988).

For children with obvious disabilities, such as those with sensory or physical impairments, exclusion may be partly a consequence of negative attitudes toward people with disabilities and the absence of a framework for interpreting developmental differences (Stoneman, 1993). For the most part, however, even for the large group of young children with mild developmental delays, it appears that the pattern of exclusion relates to their unusual difficulties related to peer-related social competence—problems that go beyond those expected based on their developmental levels. In particular, children with disabilities have special difficulty mastering the social tasks of gaining entry into peer groups, maintaining play, and resolving conflicts. Friendship formation is similarly affected and the overall pattern of social interaction with peers is highly fragile. As a consequence, social isolation and negativity follow.

Given what is now understood about how complex and challenging social exchanges can be for any young child, the fact that children with disabilities get off track is hardly surprising. What is surprising, however, is the unusual nature of these problems and their magnitude. An array of social-cognitive and emotional regulation processes are implicated in these children's diminished ability to support the generation of appropriate and effective social strategies. Concerns about these processes can be partly traced to intrinsic child characteristics such as those related to attention, working memory, and temperament. External factors also contribute to peer competence problems among children with disabilities and include more limited peer social networks and parent-child interactions stressed by a variety of factors (Guralnick and Neville, 1997).

Knowing what to do to support these children's social skills is highly challenging and undoubtedly requires knowing more about where and how children with different types of developmental challenges need help. For typically developing children who appear to need more help, targeted interventions focused on training social-cognitive skills have had some modest success (Mize and Ladd, 1990). Likewise, with typically developing children, efforts to improve peer social competence by making changes in parent-child interactions have also shown some success (LaFreniere and Capuano, 1997). For young children with disabilities, however, programs to improve social skills, while showing some promise, often fail to produce substantive or sustained gains or improvements that generalize beyond the therapeutic setting.

Changes in the ecology of early childhood programs to remove physical or structural barriers to social interaction, to select toys and materials that encourage social exchanges, and to design activities that enhance the social focus of a program have been valuable for children with disabilities, as have structured programs directed by teachers, even those enlisting the assistance of more socially skillful peers (Chandler et al., 1992; Grubbs and Niemeyer, 1999). But as noted, despite the many creative approaches, the absence of sustained and generalizable effects remains a significant issue. More comprehensive, developmentally oriented, and intensive approaches, involving both a family and community intervention component in conjunction with more child-focused interventions, may be needed.

As we acknowledged with respect to young children who display problems with self-regulation, children who may look like they are headed for long-term problems often are not. This should make us cautious about rushing in to fix children who may not be broken. We do not know if this is as true for children who are developmentally delayed or have other disabilities as it is for their typically developing peers. Finding settings in which children play competently with others, monitoring play to avert disasters, coaching children in what works, attributing their failures to situations and not to flaws in the children themselves, and searching for creative solutions that build on what they can do well seem to build social competence for most children. Good child care and preschool programs do these things, effectively providing universal interventions for all children who attend them. Some children, however, may need more.

EARLY CONDUCT PROBLEMS

Interest in understanding and addressing serious behavior problems in young children has increased substantially in light of growing evidence that recidivist offending in adolescence and adulthood, as well as persistent patterns of aggression and peer rejection during the early and middle school years, have their roots in disruptive behavior that can be detected as early as age 3 (Campbell et al., 1986a; Olson and Hoza, 1993; Rutter et al., 1998). Some scientists who study this issue point to evidence that antisocial behavior with a very early age of onset, compared with antisocial behavior that arises in the adolescent years, is more likely to persist into adolescence and adulthood (Caspi and Moffitt, 1995; Maughan and Rutter, 1998; Moffitt, 1997). For boys, early-onset conduct problems are moderately predictive of such adolescent outcomes as drug abuse, depression, juvenile delinquency, and school dropout (Campbell, 1991; Campbell et al., 1986b; Egeland et al., 1990; Rose et al., 1989; Wadsworth, 1976; White et al., 1990). The evidence on early-onset delinquency is, however, a matter of active debate within the field (see Loeber and Hay, 1997).

Deciding when to worry and who to worry about is not a simple matter. It is much easier to look back and say "he was always getting in trouble" or "he's always been a loner" than to predict the future trajectories of children who always seem to be getting in trouble. It is uncertain whether serious and enduring conduct problems can be predicted during the preschool years, and with what reliability. As soon as children begin to interact with one another, they begin to dislike children who hurt them. But we don't know whether or when the factors that get very young children in trouble with their peers begin to constrain the pathways they walk on the way to adulthood. What is fairly clear is that beginning in the preschool years, the social reasoning of rejected children, the skill or lack of it they display in social interaction, their ability to control their behaviors and emotional outbursts, and the nature of their interactions and relationships with adults (in particular parents) do differ from their peers in ways that are similar to differences noted for older children (Rubin et al., 1998). Thus, even if prediction from the preschool years may be tenuous, rejected-aggressive children seem to have a toehold on the pathway to later problems.

Furthermore, although rejected-aggressive children are just as likely as popular children to tell researchers that they are competent, they view others as mean, unkind, and hostile (Crick and Dodge, 1994; Dodge and Frame, 1982). This may explain why, in a recent study (Megan Gunnar, University of Minnesota, unpublished data), all of the rejected-aggressive 3- to 5-year-olds who were examined had stress hormone levels in the top third of those shown by children in the classroom. On many days the hormone levels of these children spiked to a stress range. Thus, even if one can't predict that they will go on to experience problems later, rejected children appear to be struggling in the here-and-now.

Thus, a focus on serious conduct and interpersonal problems in the years prior to school entry is warranted for reasons of understanding developmental pathways but, more importantly, for the prevention opportunities that it may identify. Nevertheless, because most young children who display serious behavior problems do not turn into deviant school children or adult criminals, concerns about overlabeling young children and perhaps creating self-fulfilling prophecies are also well warranted. Indeed, one of the major challenges facing those who study these issues is to distinguish the conditions that contribute to the emergence of early conduct problems from the conditions under which they persist.

The numbers of young children involved are far from trivial. Various studies have reported rates of serious conduct problems ranging from 5 to 10 percent of school-age children (Kaiser and Hester, 1997), with perhaps even higher rates among preschool children (Offord et al., 1986, 1987). These difficulties are strongly associated with early academic competencies (Arnold, 1997; Hinshaw, 1992; Morrison et al., 1989). Children with conduct problems and problems with hyperactivity do poorly in school, and poor academic performance, in turn, appears to exacerbate these problems. These reciprocal relationships can be seen in children as young as 3 and 4 years of age (Arnold, 1997). Children who display disruptive behavior in preschool have been found to pay less attention to academic tasks, which, in turn, undermines learning. Sometimes teachers contribute to the problem by calling on children with conduct problems less often, asking fewer questions of them, providing less information to them, and thus providing them with fewer learning opportunities.

More is known at this point about the factors that are associated with the early emergence of these problems than about the factors that promote or prevent their persistence, although the peer group seems to play an important role in older children (Rowe et al., 1994; Rutter et al., in press; Thornberry and Krohn, 1997). This is a complex story that illustrates the extent to which individual differences among children interact with their early environments in and out of the home to produce adaptive or maladaptive behavior patterns. It is quite clear that young children who have failed to master the early regulatory tasks of learning to manage interpersonal conflict and modulate aggressive and disruptive impulses are more likely than their self-regulated peers to display early conduct problems. Rejection by peers is likely to be both a cause and an effect of conduct problems. Children with serious behavior problems have a higher probability than other children of coming from families in which there is a family history of psychiatric illness, such as depression and bipolar disorders, adult criminality, and substance abuse, suggesting a genetic component (Rutter et al., in press; Webster-Stratton, 1990). These children also appear to process information from social encounters in ways that are less common among children without behavior problems. Specifically, when they are presented with possible scenarios in the form of hypothetical stories followed by a series of questions, children with conduct problems tend to overattribute hostile intent to other children, more readily provide aggressive rather than socially competent responses to "What would you do?" queries, and place a high value on gaining dominance over peers as a desirable outcome (Dodge et al., 1986, 1990; Sancilio et al., 1989; Slaby and Guerra, 1988). Finally, early-onset conduct disorders combined with early signs of hyperactivity may be especially problematic (Hinshaw and Anderson, 1996; Hinshaw et al., 1993).

The settings and social interactions of children with serious behavior problems, which they undoubtedly contribute to eliciting, appear to play an instrumental role in turning their difficult and disruptive behavior into more serious problems. In other words, characteristics that make a child susceptible to conduct disorders become highly problematic in interactions with adults and peers that amplify these characteristics and, in turn, are exacerbated by the negative exchanges that ensue. Family factors matter as well: exposure to physical abuse is a strong predictor of early behavior problems (Dodge et al., 1990), as are other forms of family conflict and coercion seen under conditions of marital discord, spousal violence, and extremely hostile and inconsistent parenting (Campbell and Ewing, 1990; Campbell et al., 1986a; Cummings and Davies, 1994a; Egeland et al., 1990; Richman et al., 1982; Shaw et al., 1996). Extreme forms of disengagement and very lax monitoring also predict conduct problems (Coie et al., 1992, 1995; Hawkins et al., 1992; Dishion and McMahon, 1998). If, in addition to these other factors, a child is growing up in poverty (Sameroff et al., 1987) or in a crime-ridden neighborhood (Rutter, 1981a), the likelihood that he will engage in highly aggressive and disruptive behavior as a preschooler is amplified.

Any of these factors in isolation from the others is unlikely to contribute to either the initial appearance or the persistence of these behaviors. Rather, it is the number of so-called risk factors operating in concert with each other that produces behavior problems and probably plays a critical role in their stability. The question, then, is not which of the individual and genetic variables (family, peer, and community factors) are the most important influences, but rather how these factors interact and either amplify or dampen each other. As stated by Rutter, "How is the child who is born with a tendency to be rather overactive, oppositional, and impulsive subsequently trained by the world to behave well or, alternatively, coerced into behaving badly?" (Rutter et al., 1998, pg. 379).

What can be done? Fortunately, some promising inroads have been made toward helping these children. Interventions with children in the early elementary grades have been very effective in reducing children's negative social attributions and aggressive interactions with peers (see Asher, 1985; Asher et al., 1996; Bond and Compas, 1989; Eisenstadt et al., 1993; Forehand et al., 1982; Kazdin, 1993; Olweus, 1991, 1993). Work with preschoolers, such as that of Webster-Stratton and others (Kaiser and Hester, 1997; Odom et al., 1994), which is generally focused on parenting but is increasingly moving into child care environments, is also emerging (see Box 7-1) and should be a high priority for future intervention research. Interventions that focus on multiple early environments and multiple peer groups may be more promising than those that are directed at only one setting. Moreover, different manifestations of antisocial behavior in the early years (e.g., isolated conduct disorder, conduct disorder accompanied by hyperactivity) may require different approaches. Growing recognition that young children can engage in relatively sophisticated thinking about

---

BOX 7-1
Mental Health Research Initiative Within Head Start

In 1997, the Administration on Children, Youth and Families (ACYF) and the National Institute of Mental Health (NIMH) created a research consortium on the prevention, identification, and treatment of children's mental health disorders in a Head Start context. The initial five studies are exploring:

- The validity of an early screening project for a diverse group of families, including African-American, European-, Hispanic-, and Native Americans.
- The efficacy and the effectiveness of an intervention designed to both prevent and address severe behavior problems in preschool children.
- The effectiveness of an early detection and prevention intervention designed to improve the mental health of Head Start children and their families.
- The frequency, in Head Start 3-year-olds, of behavioral and communication problems that place these children at risk of developing conduct disorders, and the effectiveness of an intervention designed to improve children's social and communication skills.
- How external influences, such as type of neighborhood, exposure to violence, and child care and family characteristics, affect the emotional health of children.

SOURCE: ACYF/NIMH Collaborative Mental Health Research Initiative (2000).

others' emotional states and intentions (see the discussion of theory of mind in the previous chapter) suggests that interventions that help children make constructive attributions about others' behavior may also be beneficial in the early years. In addition to efforts focused on the reduction of conduct disorders, parallel efforts are needed to create early childhood environments that foster caring, emotionally responsive interactions among all children (see Asher et al., 2000).

SUMMARY AND CONCLUSIONS

Establishing relationships with other children is a central task of the early childhood years. The success with which young children accomplish this objective can affect whether they will walk pathways to competence or deviance as they move into the middle childhood and adolescent years. Learning to play nicely, make friends, and sustain friendships are not easy tasks, and children who do them well tend to have well-structured experiences with peer interactions starting in toddlerhood and preschool, and, in particular, opportunities to play with familiar and compatible peers. They are also more likely to have secure relationships with their parents who, in turn, believe they have an instrumental role to play in fostering their children's social relationships, deliberately creating opportunities for peer interactions, encouraging keen observational skills, and coaching their young children in constructive attitudes and skills. Temperament also plays a role. For example, shy children, compared with those who are rambunctious and highly active, tend to have different patterns of relationships with other children.

As American culture becomes ever more diverse, a higher priority needs to be granted to research on cultural issues in peer acceptance, rejection, and friendship and their effects on the social development of young children who are increasingly experiencing culturally diverse groups of peers in their child care and early education settings. Finally, it is vitally important to recognize that children with developmental disabilities face major hurdles with peer relations. They tend to be excluded from peer activities by typically developing children and to lack friends. Moreover, their more limited peer networks and often stressed parents can contribute unwittingly to their poor peer relations. These children warrant much greater attention in both research and intervention in the area of peer relationships.

Peer rejection is a risk factor for an array of subsequent problems ranging from conduct disorders to depression. Beginning in the preschool years, the social reasoning of rejected children, their lack of skill in social interactions, and their difficulty with controlling emotional outbursts set them apart from other children. Yet there is a serious dilemma. On one hand, the fact that early signs of serious adolescent and adult behavioral problems and criminality can be traced back to the preschool years provides a tantalizing opportunity for preventive interventions. On the other hand, many children who display early warning signs of high levels of peer aggression and hostility, persistent noncompliance, and callousness to other's distress, for example, become perfectly normal school-age children who go on to productive adult lives. Shifting from group-level associations to individual prediction, in other words, is a very risky business.

It is a difficult task to understand what mix of conditions contributes to stabilizing early conduct disorders for which children. Judging from what is known about other problematic conditions early in life, the answer is likely to involve the juxtaposition of the child's inherited predispositions, early peer encounters, performance in school, family environment and parental monitoring, neighborhood environment, and association with productive or deviant peer groups over time. Without good prediction, the appropriate perspective to adopt for early intervention may be one of fostering prosocial behavior for all children rather than trying to prevent delinquency for a few. Along these lines, approaches that involve all children in a setting, work simultaneously on eliminating disruptive child behaviors and developing prosocial behaviors, and give serious attention to creating early environments that reduce barriers to positive peer interactions will avoid stigmatizing some children, ignoring others who might also be in trouble, and have reasonably good odds of success.

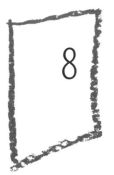

8 The Developing Brain

The brain is the ultimate organ of adaptation. It takes in information and orchestrates complex behavioral repertoires that allow human beings to act in sometimes marvelous, sometimes terrible ways. Most of what people think of as the "self"—what we think, what we remember, what we can do, how we feel—is acquired by the brain from the experiences that occur after birth. Some of this information is acquired during critical or sensitive periods of development, when the brain appears uniquely ready to take in certain kinds of information, while other information can be acquired across broad swaths of development that can extend into adulthood. This spectrum of possibilities is well captured by coinciding evidence of both the remarkably rapid brain development that characterizes the early childhood period and the brain's lifelong capacity for growth and change. The balance between the enduring significance of early brain development and its impressive continuing plasticity lies at the heart of the current controversy about the effects on the brain of early experience.

The past 20 years have seen unprecedented progress in understanding how the brain develops and, in particular, the phenomenal changes in both its circuitry and neurochemistry that occur during prenatal and early postnatal development. As discussed in Chapter 2, knowledge of the ways in which genes and the environment interact to affect the maturation of the brain has expanded by leaps and bounds. The years ahead will bring even more breathtaking progress as, for example, knowledge of the human genome is increasingly transformed into knowledge about how genes are expressed in the brain. This promises a dramatic expansion in the ability to understand the interweaving of genetic and environmental influences as they affect both brain and behavioral development (see Nelson and Bloom, 1997).

Growth in brain knowledge naturally leads to questions about what it means for raising children and, specifically, for improving their development. Accordingly, efforts to translate this emerging knowledge for public consumption have proliferated in recent years. Some of this information has been portrayed well and accurately, but some has not. The challenge of deciphering what this information means for what parents, guardians, and teachers of young children should do is enormous. There are actually few neuroscience studies of very young children, and those that exist have not usually focused on the brain regions that affect cognition, emotions, and other complex developmental tasks.

Much of the fundamental knowledge about brain development is based on experimental studies of animals. The translation of this information from basic neuroscience into rules for application to humans can be quite straightforward when the mechanisms involved are very similar in humans and animals, as is the case with the developing visual system. But the interpretation of other data from animals, or even some data from humans (such as estimates of the density of synapses in various brain regions at various ages), can be extraordinarily complex or inappropriate when the brain mechanisms of cognition, language, and social-emotional development are addressed. In this context, it is essential to balance excitement about all the new learning with caution about the limits of what is understood today.

This chapter about the developing brain focuses on the role of experience in early brain development. Following a brief discussion of how to study the developing brain is an overview of early brain development from conception through the early childhood years. We then turn to a discussion of how early experiences contribute to brain development. Four themes run throughout this section:

1. Developmental neuroscience research says a great deal about the conditions that pose dangers to the developing brain and from which young children need to be protected. It says virtually nothing about what to do to create enhanced or accelerated brain development.

2. The developing brain is open to influential experiences across broad periods of development. This openness to experience is part of what accounts for the remarkable adaptability of the developing mind. Although there are a few aspects of brain growth that require particular kinds of experience at particular times, as far as we know at present, this is more the exception than the norm for human brain growth.

3. The kinds of early experiences on which healthy brain development depends are ubiquitous in typical early human experience—just as nature intended. This means, however, that concern should be devoted to children who, for reasons of visual impairment, auditory processing problems, major perceptual-motor delays, and other basic deficits cannot obtain these experiences on which the developing nervous system depends.

4. Abusive or neglectful care, growing up in a dangerous or toxic environment, and related conditions are manifest risks for healthy brain development. Beyond these extremes, the nature and boundaries of the environmental conditions necessary for healthy brain growth are less well known, partly owing to the complexity and the cumulative achievements of cognitive, language, and socioemotional growth. Exploration in this area is cutting-edge research.

STUDYING THE DEVELOPING BRAIN

Neuroscience techniques have advanced significantly, rendering studies of young children's brains more feasible and informative than in the recent past. These techniques have enabled scientists to learn more about how babies' brains change with development and how vulnerable or resilient they are to environmental harm. However, the repertoire of techniques that can be used with preschool-age and even younger children is still limited. Some of the more direct methods (i.e., looking into the brain) are either invasive (e.g., positron emission tomography requires the injection of a radioactive substance) or require long periods of remaining still (e.g., functional magnetic resonance imaging). Nevertheless, by tracking the brain's activity from the outside with the electroencephalogram, event-related potentials, and magnetic encephalography, researchers can learn about brain functioning in very young children. For instance, scientists can record the electrical or magnetic activity of the brain while the child is presented with different stimuli (e.g., speech sounds) and identify which parts of the brain are active and how active they are when children are doing different things. This approach has been used to reveal that the neural substrate for recognizing faces and facial expressions is remarkably similar in infants and adults (de Haan and Nelson, 1997, 1999), and that babies' brains change as they learn their native language (Neville et al., 1998).

In addition, children with localized brain damage can be studied using neuropsychological tools. These entail giving young children behavioral tasks that have been shown to involve specific brain functions (e.g., working memory, spatial planning) and observing how performance varies with the particular part of the brain that is damaged (Luciana and Nelson, 1998). This approach, used in a longitudinal study of language development in children who suffered focal brain damage in the first months of life, revealed the extensive capacity for recovery of language functioning in these children (Bates and Roe, in press). Finally, among children whose medical conditions have required that their brains be studied, positron emission tomography has revealed metabolic patterns consonant with synaptic growth and pruning occurring in early development (Chugani and Phelps, 1986). (See Appendix B, as well as Nelson and Bloom, 1997, for a fuller discussion of technologies for studying the developing human brain.)

WHAT DEVELOPS IN EARLY BRAIN DEVELOPMENT?

The development of the brain has a long trajectory, beginning within a few days after conception and continuing through adolescence and beyond. The nervous system undergoes its most dramatic development during the first few years of life. Yet the processes that establish the structure and functioning of the brain, made possible by the developing networks of synapses that interconnect nerve cells and by the progressive fine-tuning of the neurons for the roles they will play within their synaptic networks, continue well into adolescence. The milestones of brain development from the prenatal period until school entry involve the development and migration of brain cells to where they belong in the brain, embellishments of nerve cells through the sprouting of new axons or by expanding the dendritic surface; the formation of connections, or synapses, between nerve cells; and the postnatal addition of other types of cells, notably glia. Fascination with the earliest stages of brain development is understandable. During this period, the spinal cord is formed, nearly all of the billions of neurons of the mature brain are produced, the dual processes of neural differentiation and cell migration establish the neuron's functional roles, and synaptogenesis proceeds apace. These processes represent an elaborate interplay between gene activity and the surrounding environments both inside and outside the child.

There have been significant changes over time in the aspects of brain development that have captured public attention. Twenty years ago, people were fascinated by the ability to measure developmental changes in the degree to which neurons in different areas of the brain become wrapped in the white, fatty matter—myelin—that insulates nerve cells and affects the speed with which nerve impulses are transmitted from one cell to another. Myclination is, in fact, affected by the young child's behavioral experiences and nutrition, as discussed below. Today, the public is more focused on information, not all of it new, about the rate of synapse development, particularly on studies showing that there is a tremendous burst of synapse formation early in life, followed by a decline in synapse number, apparently extending into adolescence in some areas of the brain. Combined with evidence that synapses that are used are retained and those not used are eliminated, there has been a frenzy of concern expressed as "use it or lose it" in the first years of life. It turns out, however, that synapse elimination is a normal part of development. In comparison to the brain's wiring, far less attention has been paid to the neurochemistry of early brain development, which is essential to the brain's capacity to learn from experience and is likely to play an important role in the regulation of behavior.

Development of the Brain's Wiring Diagram

Brain development proceeds in overlapping phases: making the brain cells (neurulation and neurogenesis), getting the cells to where they need to be (migration), growing axons and dendrites, which are structures needed to link with other nerve cells (neuronal differentiation and pathfinding), developing synapses or points of communication with other cells (synaptogenesis), refining those synapses (maturation and pruning), and, finally, forming the supportive tissue that surrounds the nerve cells and makes for efficient communication among them (gliagenesis or myelination).

The brain and spinal cord arise from a set of cells on the back (dorsal part) of the developing embryo called the neural plate. Two rows of rapidly dividing cells arise from the plate on each side along its length and fold over centrally into the neural tube. The anterior or head end of the neural tube forms a set of swollen enlargements that give rise to the various parts of the brain—the forebrain containing the cerebral hemispheres, the midbrain containing important pathways to and from the forebrain, and the hindbrain containing the brainstem and cerebellum. The remainder of the neural tube becomes the spinal cord, peripheral nerves, and certain endocrine, or hormone, glands in the body. Under the control of regulatory genes, the brain cells migrate to where they belong in accord with the functions they will ultimately serve. These genes provide developmental directions to particular groups of cells, which tell them what to do and where to go in the embryonic brain.

Within the neural tube, the innermost cells divide repeatedly, giving rise first to the cells that primarily become nerve cells, or neurons, and later giving rise to both neurons and the supportive tissue components called glia. Once the nerve cells are formed and finish migrating, they rapidly extend axons and dendrites and begin to form connections with each other, called synapses, often over relatively long distances. These connections allow nerve cells to communicate with each other. This process starts prenatally and continues well into the childhood years. There is evidence in many parts of the nervous system that the stability and strength of these synapses are largely determined by the activity, that is, the firing, of these connections. The speed with which neurons conduct nerve impulses is determined by the development of myelin, a substance that wraps itself around nerve axons. By insulating the nerve cell axon, myelin increases conduction velocity. The development of myelin is a protracted process extending well into the postnatal period. The rate and extent of myelination is also affected by experience. Most myelinated pathways are laid down in the early years, but for some, as in the frontal cortex, myelination continues into the third decade of life. The unique wiring diagram that brain development produces in each individual brain guides thoughts, memories, feelings, and behaviors.

Synaptic Overproduction and Loss

Beginning 20 years ago, Huttenlocher (e.g., Huttenlocher, 1979; Huttenlocher and Dabholkar, 1997) first showed that there is a pattern to synaptogenesis in the human cerebral cortex characterized by the rapid proliferation and overproduction of synapses, followed by a phase of synapse elimination or pruning that eventually brings the overall number of synapses down to their adult levels. This process is most exuberant during the first few years of life, although it can extend well into adolescence. Within this developmental span, however, different brain regions with different functions appear to develop on different time courses (see Figure 8-1). Huttenlocher estimated that the peak of synaptic overproduction in the visual cortex occurs about midway through the first year of life, followed by a gradual retraction until the middle to the end of the preschool period, by which time the number of synapses has reached adult levels. In areas of the brain that subserve audition and language, a similar although somewhat later time course was observed. However, in the prefrontal cortex (the area of the brain where higher-level cognition takes place), a very different picture emerges. Here the peak of overproduction occurs at around one year of age, and it is not until middle to late adolescence that adult numbers of synapses are obtained.[1]

Scientists have pondered the purpose of synaptic overproduction and loss for a very long time. One of the earliest observations was made by

---

[1]Many of the human findings regarding synaptic overproduction and loss were based on measurements of the density of synapses, rather than on measurements of the actual number of synapses. Density measures reflect both how many synapses are present and how many other things (e.g., nerve cell bodies, dendrites and axons, glial cells, and blood vessels) are present in addition to synapses. The human brain adds lots of cells to the cerebral cortex postnatally (almost two-thirds of the mass of the cerebral cortex is added after birth), and this makes density estimates very difficult to interpret. Thus, evidence available to date does not enable determination of how ubiquitous synapse overproduction and loss are in brain development generally or in humans specifically.

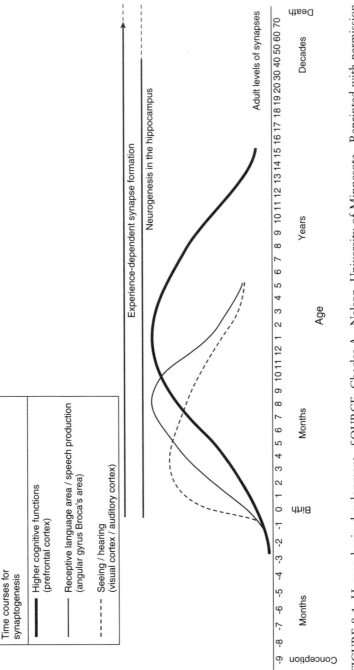

FIGURE 8-1 Human brain development. SOURCE: Charles A. Nelson, University of Minnesota. Reprinted with permission.

Spanish neuroanatomist and Nobel laureate Santiago Ramon y Cajal (Ramon y Cajal, 1989[1917]):

> I noticed that every ramification, dendritic or axonic, in the course of formation, passes through a chaotic period, so to speak, a period of trials, during which there are sent out at random experimental conductors most of which are destined to disappear. . . . What mysterious forces precede the appearance of the processes, promote their growth and ramification . . . and finally establish those protoplasmic kisses, the intercellular articulations, which seem to constitute the final ecstasy of an epic love story?

A more modern formulation of the love story began with the Cragg (1975) report that the cat visual cortex produced a greater number of synapses during development than it actually retained into adulthood. Subsequent work in monkeys and cats by Hubel and Wiesel and their collaborators (e.g., LeVay et al., 1980) demonstrated that as the physiological functioning of the visual cortex became more refined and precise, the anatomical synaptic connections were also refined. Those that fit the intended pattern were retained, and those that did not were eliminated.

Scientists also showed that visual experience played a necessary role in this process. If experience was distorted, so that one eye got much more stimulation than the other, for example, its connections were pared back less drastically than usual, and the connections with the inexperienced eye were pruned more than usual. In short, the development of patterned organization in the visual cortex was dependent on visual experience and involved the selective loss of connections that were not appropriate to the pattern. Synapses appear to be programmed to be eliminated if they are not functionally confirmed, based on some not fully known aspects of their activity history. In general, frequently active connections, like those of the more experienced eye, are more likely to survive.

While the data are not as complete for other senses, it is reasonably clear that building the organized neural systems that guide sensory and motor development involves the production of excess connections followed by some sort of pruning that leaves the system in a more precisely organized pattern. Moreover, in both humans and animals, the effects of experience on these systems—normal or abnormal—become increasingly irreversible over time. In kittens, irreversible deficits in vision will result with deprivation lasting for only 2-3 months after birth. In humans, irreversible deficits in vision are present when corrections for such optical conditions as strabismus (in which, due to muscular weakness, one eye deviates from and cannot be brought into alignment with the other normally functioning eye) are not made by the time the child reaches elementary school. Deficits become more pronounced with more prolonged visual deprivation. Thus, a sensitive period exists for vision, but rather than being sharply demarcated, it gradually tapers off.

A useful way to consider how experience becomes incorporated into the developing synaptic connections of the human brain, discussed briefly in Chapter 2, has been offered by Greenough and Black (Black and Greenough, 1986; Greenough and Black, 1992). They distinguish between experience-expectant and experience-dependent mechanisms guiding brain development. Experience-expectant synaptogenesis refers to situations in which a species-typical experience (that is, something that all members of a species experience, barring highly aberrant conditions) plays a necessary role in the developmental organization of the nervous system. Normal brain growth relies on these forms of environmental exposure. For example, the visual cortex "expects" exposure to light and patterned visual information and is genetically programmed to utilize these inputs for normal development. Deprivation of these ubiquitous and essential forms of environmental input can permanently compromise behavioral functioning, which is why it is essential to detect and treat early sensory deficits (e.g., cataracts, strabismus, auditory deficits) that interfere with the detection and registering of expected experiences.

Experience-dependent synaptogenesis, in contrast, refers to encoding new experiences that occur throughout life, foster new brain growth and the refinement of existing brain structures, and vary for every individual. This process optimizes the individual's adaptation to specific and possibly unique features of the environment. Whereas in experience-expectant development, all brains depend on the same basic experiences to develop normally, in experience-dependent development, individual differences in brain development depend on the idiosyncratic experiences that are encountered across the life span. Experience-dependent development is also linked to synaptogenesis, but in this case all we know is that experience triggers more plentiful connections among neurons. We do not know if this occurs through a process of overproduction and pruning, or if a more continuous pattern of growth is involved. Whatever the specific mechanism, experience-dependent brain development is a source of enduring plasticity and of adaptability to the demands of everyday life. And it is important to note that there appears to be no abrupt transition from utilization of experience-expectant processes to utilization of experience-dependent processes of brain development. In fact, it seems likely that the greater potential for recovery from deprivation or damage that characterizes young animals probably reflects the availability of both mechanisms.

Postnatal Neurogenesis

We now need to add the possibility of postnatal neurogenesis—the postnatal production of new nerve cells—to the repertoire of mechanisms by which the human brain continues to develop after the early childhood years. Prevailing knowledge about brain development, notably that the adult human brain does not produce new neurons, has recently been challenged by new insights into adult brain development. Specifically, important forebrain regions, such as the hippocampal dentate gyrus (which is involved in establishing memory for facts and relationships among events and places in one's experience), continue to receive new nerve cells into adulthood in humans (e.g., Eriksson et al., 1998). Recent findings in monkeys indicate that new neurons are also being formed each day and migrating to areas that include the prefrontal cortex, the seat of planning and decision making (Gould et al., 1999). Although it remains to be determined how significant neuronal additions in adulthood are to the functioning of the brain, it certainly lends further support to the argument that the brain continuously remodels itself.

Neurochemistry of Early Brain Development

The sending and receiving of messages in the nervous system depends on chemical messengers. A number of these chemical messengers affect gene expression in nerve cells in ways that have long-lasting effects on how nerves grow, respond to stimulation, and function. They are thus intimately involved in the growth and development of the nervous system and in neural plasticity. The past two decades have seen an explosion of information about these chemical messengers. In addition to the classic neurotransmitters, over 60 other peptide and steroid molecules have been identified that have direct effects on the brain. Currently, what can be confidently applied from this field directly to human development is limited. However, the study of neurochemistry is already revolutionizing the way people think about the nervous system, and a brief overview of some basic ideas from this work is warranted.

Chemical messengers that affect the brain operate through receptors, most of which are located in the dendrites and synapses of nerve cells. Like locks and keys, the physical structure of the messenger (the key) has to fit the physical structure of the receptor (the lock) for the chemical messenger to have any effect on the nerve cell. Receptors are specific. They typically recognize or bind with only one natural molecule. For many years, this type of specificity gave rise to the hope that science would be able to link specific neurochemicals to specific behaviors, allowing highly focused manipulations of behavior through drug therapy. However, despite what filters its way into the popular press (e.g., low serotonin levels cause aggression), the way the biochemistry of the brain operates is vastly more complex than a match of one chemical with one behavior. For example, it now appears that many of the chemicals that affect brain function are able to unlock several different receptors. This allows the same (or quite similar) chemical to have different functions and to play a role in multiple (often related) behavioral systems.

The brain is also able to alter its sensitivity to a chemical messenger by changing the presence, conformation (structure), and availability of the chemical's receptors. Receptor changes often reflect the history of the nerve cell's experience with its neurochemical. High levels of the chemical operating on the receptor frequently result in a decrease in the nerve's receptors for that chemical (a process called down-regulation); sometimes a dearth of a chemical important in a nerve's functioning results in an increase in receptor number (i.e., up-regulation). Up- and down-regulation takes place over hours and days, partially explaining why some psychoactive drugs take time before they begin to influence behavior and why some drugs, with time, need to be taken in higher and higher dosages to have the same effects. Some of these shifts in chemical messenger-receptor systems appear to be relatively permanent, perhaps especially those that occur during periods of rapid development; others are more transient, reflecting the normal turnover (production, decline, replacement) of receptors. This complexity may complicate things for those who are trying to decipher the mysteries of the brain, but it does allow the brain to be highly plastic, toning its functioning in highly nuanced ways, often quite rapidly.

Neurochemical-receptor systems also lie at the heart of how the brain alters its physical structure. A variety of different nerve growth factors (i.e., chemicals that play a role in the growth of dendrites and synapses) have been identified. These growth factors are present in different quantities and locations at different points in development of the brain, regulated by genes involved in normal brain development. They also change in their concentration in response to nerve damage, playing a role in the brain's attempts to adapt to and restore functioning following trauma. Receptor systems play critical roles in both experience-dependent and experience-expectant neural plasticity. The NMDA (N-methyl-D-aspartate) receptor is one receptor, but not the only one, that plays a role in neural plasticity. It appears to support learning by helping to foster what is termed "long-term potentiation." Long-term potentiation, a memory "model" involving increased synaptic strength, is brought about by sustained, rapid activity in the neural circuits involved in newly acquired information, analogous to repeating a new phone number in order to memorize it. It also appears that at critical points in the development of neural systems, there is sometimes an increase in NMDA receptors. This increase seems to open the window for the development of that neural system, allowing stimulation to have large effects, with the window closing when the number of NMDA receptors decreases.

Changes in chemical messenger systems and their receptors tend to tone the nervous system, altering sensitivity to stimuli and probabilities of responses, rather than necessarily causing particular behaviors. The following thought experiment provides a good example. You have been on a low-calorie diet (and have stuck to it) for several weeks. Numerous neurochemical changes in your brain have been set into motion by this semi-starvation. All of these changes do not mean that you will eat that luscious steak the waiter just set in front of you (the fact that you are dieting, are a vegetarian, and did not order the steak will hopefully rule the day). But the myriad of neurochemical changes in your brain set into motion by semi-starvation will probably make you more sensitive to how good the steak smells, make you salivate more, make you remember that steak for a long time, and so on; all changes orchestrated to help increase the probability that you will break down and eat the steak that your body might, in fact, "need." As this thought experiment indicates, the behavioral impact of changes in neurochemistry are dependent on the context and the individual's history. Like one's temperament, the changes tend to orchestrate a bias or propensity to respond in particular ways rather than rigidly determine that a behavior will always be expressed. A number of researchers believe that in order to understand the neural bases of temperament and emotions, they will need to understand the genetic and experiential processes that regulate these complex neurochemical systems of the brain throughout development.

Characteristically, the neurochemical systems of the brain are open both to input from the environment and to events occurring in the body other than the brain. There is increasing animal evidence that the environment plays a role in regulating aspects of brain neurochemistry. For example, the licking and grooming that the mother rat does of her pups (infant rats) appear to enhance the production of serotonin and thyroid hormone, both important in the neurochemistry of brain development. There is also increasing evidence that elements of early caregiving may help modulate the neurochemicals involved in pain and distress. Thus, the fats and sugars in breast milk appear to stimulate taste receptors linked to central opioid (natural painkiller) pathways, stimulating mild analgesia. Similarly, tactile stimulation of the mouth appears to operate through neurochemical mechanisms, not involving opioids, that affect brain pathways controlling distress. Some of these effects have been demonstrated in human infants. The evidence that the regulation of neuroactive chemical systems extends into basic caregiving activities is exciting, even though much of it still has been demonstrated only in animals. This evidence promises to help explain how alterations in the environment early in life may have wide-ranging effects on brain development and may alter patterns of behavioral responding for children with different rearing histories.

HOW THE BRAIN IS AFFECTED BY EARLY EXPERIENCE

This account of early brain development emphasizes the ways in which the nervous system is designed to recruit and incorporate experience into its developing architecture and neurochemistry. Normal experience (e.g., good nutrition, patterned visual information) supports normal brain development, and abnormal experience (e.g., prenatal alcohol exposure, occluded vision) can cause abnormal neural and behavioral development (Black et al., 1998). Plasticity is a double-edged sword that leads to both adaptation and vulnerability. The process of synaptic overproduction and loss is dependent on environmental information, although the evidence is largely restricted to sensory systems. Similarly, the brain's neurochemistry is exquisitely sensitive to behavioral and environmental stimuli. Scientists are far, however, from linking specific types or amounts of experience to the developing structure or neurochemistry of the immature human brain, and, conversely, from understanding how early brain development affects the ways in which young children process the abundance of information and experiences that their environments present to them. Answers to questions about when during development particular experiences must occur and when, in fact, timing is important and when it is not also lie, to a large extent, beyond the boundaries of current knowledge. Research on the developing brain can nevertheless provide a framework for considering the effects of early experience on development more generally. The questions that have been asked by neuroscientists have their parallels in research on behavioral development.

Two issues have played pivotal roles in guiding scientific inquiry about early experience and the brain. The first concerns the nature of early experiences. Those who raise and work with young children are deeply concerned about whether they are providing them with the right experiences and protecting them from harmful ones. What harm is done by exposure to inappropriate experiences, and how reversible are the effects? What degree of enhancement can be achieved by exposure to enriched experiences, and how long do beneficial effects last? Much more is known about the negative consequences for brain development of harmful environments than about the benefits of advantageous environments. And relatively more is known about the effects of pre- and perinatal environments on the developing nervous system than about environmental influences after the first few months of life.

The second issue concerns the timing of experience and is often expressed in terms of critical or sensitive periods. Much of the contemporary discussion of the importance of the first three years of life is framed in the terminology of sensitive periods. But does it really matter when the child is exposed to particular experiences? Do specific experiences need to occur during specific windows of time in order for the brain to develop normally? Can the brain recover or compensate when critical experiences are missed? In addition to the examples regarding the visual system described above, there are some very dramatic instances of timing effects, again primarily in other species. For example, an injury to the rat's cortex on the first day after birth causes more ultimate damage to brain tissue and greater loss of normal behavioral functioning than a similar injury on day 5 (Kolb and Whishaw, 1998). The presence of testosterone in the third trimester of human fetal development organizes the physiological characteristics of brain regions such as the hypothalamus in the male direction, so that release of hormones that govern sexual and reproductive functions follows the noncyclic pattern seen in the post-adolescent male (Cooke et al., 1998). Although estrogen and testosterone can affect neural structures after this time, nothing can duplicate or reverse the effects of this in utero hormone exposure. Normal development of the zebra finch's song (reviewed in Clayton, in press) requires exposure of the young male to an adult tutor during a sensitive period in juvenile life (Immelmann, 1969). The shortest period demonstrated to be sufficient for development of a relatively normal song extends from approximately day 20 to day 35 (Böhner, 1990). Zebra finches continue to be sensitive to the effects of further tutoring up to the age of about 65 days (Jones et al., 1996).

In developmental science, the term "sensitive period" is generally preferred to "critical period" because it implies less rigidity in the nature and timing of formative early experiences (Immelmann and Suomi, 1982). Sensitive periods can be defined as unique episodes in development when specific structures or functions become especially susceptible to particular experiences in ways that alter their future structure or function (Bornstein, 1989; Thompson, in press(a)). This susceptibility can operate in two ways: first, certain early experiences uniquely prepare the young children for the future by establishing certain capabilities at a time when development is most plastic and responsive to stimulation. Second, the young child is highly vulnerable to the absence of these essential experiences, and the result may be permanent risk of dysfunction.

In fact, it is extraordinarily difficult to study issues of timing in human development given that it is profoundly unethical to deprive children of needed experiences in order to introduce them at different developmental stages. We are thus dependent on animal studies, which are generating fascinating evidence of timing effects (see, for example, Bornstein, 1989; Knudsen, 1999) but have limited translations to humans, and on so-called experiments of nature, such as prenatal exposures that occur at different points in fetal development (discussed below) and research on children with sensory deficits, such as the case of deaf children who do not experience normal spoken language inputs, and children who have sustained brain injuries. In the latter case, as we saw in Chapter 6, unilateral brain lesions incurred prior to age 5 or 6 appear to have few lasting effects on language development, whereas when damage occurs after this age language development is often compromised. However, there can be significant deficits in certain aspects of memory and verbal functioning when these lesions are accompanied by seizure disorders and these deficits do not appear to be sensitive to the age at which the seizures occur (Vargha-Khadem et al., 1997, 1992). This exemplifies the complexity of what is presently known about sensitive periods in childhood.

Within these limitations, it is well known that a variety of environmental factors play a significant role in modulating early brain development. Some of the greatest insights have come from research on the detrimental consequences of early biological insults, deprivations, and stress. We have also learned a great deal from research on the neurobiological consequences of prematurity. We turn to this research following a brief overview of the studies that generated excitement about the brain's receptivity to environmental influence.

The Contribution of Environmental Variation

Documented differences in the brains and behaviors of animals that have experienced markedly discrepant early environments have emerged from the laboratory of Greenough and his colleagues (Black and Greenough, 1998; Black et al., 1998; Greenough and Black, 1992). Rats, not babies, were the subjects of study. They were either housed from the time of weaning or placed as adults in cages that varied in the degree of stimulation offered. The "complex" cages contained play objects and other animals. Animals reared since weaning or placed in these cages as adults outperformed rats raised alone or placed in typically barren laboratory cages on a variety of learning and problem-solving tasks. The brains of the rats reared in the complex environments also showed more mature synaptic structure, more dendritic spines, larger neuronal dendritic fields, more synapses per neuron, more supportive glial tissue, and increased capillary branching that increases blood volume and oxygen supply to the brain (see Box 8-1).

It is important to note that these effects did not appear to be characterized by a critical period. The indicators of both superior performance and more developed brains characterized the rats exposed to the complex environments as adults, as well as those housed in these environments since weaning. Both early and later exposure to greater environmental stimulation had beneficial consequences, although the effects occurred more rapidly and to a greater degree in the younger animals. Moreover, while long-term neuron and synapse studies have not been conducted, the effects of exposure to a complex environment on learning ability diminished over

---

BOX 8-1
Experience, Learning, "Exercise," and the Brain

Some neuroscientists are trying to understand learning at the level of the nerve cells and the synaptic connections through which they communicate. As noted in the text, early work found that rats reared in a complex environment exhibited substantial increases in the numbers of synapses in various parts of the brain. These studies have shown, however, that formation of new synapses is probably one of the mechanisms underlying memory. Follow-up studies examining motor skill learning in adult rats found that animals that performed a lot of effortful exercise without significant learning formed new blood vessels in their brains but no new synapses. If they learned motor skills, with minimal exercise, they formed synapses but not new blood vessels (Black et al., 1990). This shows both that (1) there are components to the brain's adaptation to the environment beyond neurons and synapses and that (2) making new synapses is associated with learning. In addition, this research has shown that the ability to add synapses in response to housing in a complex environment or learning something new is a lifelong property of the brain—not something lost at an early age—which is precisely what we would expect for memory.

---

time if the rats were removed from the environment. The intervention provided by the complex cages thus functioned more like the tetanus vaccine, which requires regular boosters, than the smallpox vaccine, which inoculates against disease with a single injection. As this book shows, most early interventions for humans act more like the tetanus than the smallpox vaccine.

Studies of complex environments in rats have also revealed the role that such environments can play in processes of recovery. For example, the detrimental behavioral effects of prenatal exposure to low to moderate levels of alcohol in rats (e.g., motor dysfunction and impairments in learning spatial tasks) can be greatly attenuated by raising the animals in a complex environment (Hannigan et al., 1993). A program of forced motor skill training in alcohol-exposed rats nearly eliminated motor dysfunction, and it also increased synapse number in their cerebellar cortex (Klintsova et al., 1997, 1998). Finally, increasing the complexity of the environment before or after brain damage in developing and adult rats enhanced recovery from the impairments produced by damage to various brain areas, probably through mechanisms that involve the development of alternative strategies rather than the direct recovery of lost functions (see Kolb and Whishaw, 1998).

This research on complex environments certainly suggests that better environments with greater diversity can have beneficial effects. However, it would be misleading to locate the complexity of the animal environments near the enriched part of the continuum from deprivation to enrichment. In fact, the environments in these experiments were probably less complex than the rats' natural wild habitats. Nevertheless, these studies do point to the existence of a multidimensional continuum of environments and indicate that development (and recovery) is improved as one moves toward the anchor point of enrichment. Moving from these animal studies to research on the neurological aspects of human cognitive, linguistic, and social-emotional development is a big leap, but one that warrants a major investment of time and resources. The need for research that can illuminate how environments that exceed some minimal threshold of adequacy affect human brain development is especially needed, in light of the fact that most of the research on how experience affects the developing brain explores the detrimental consequences of harmful experiences.

Early Biological Insults and the Developing Brain

Research on early biological insults provides fundamental insights into the vulnerability and resilience of the developing central nervous system. This area of research also offers a compelling illustration that plasticity cuts both ways, leaving the developing fetus and young child simultaneously vulnerable to harm and receptive to positive influences. It also suggests that the current emphasis on the years from birth to age 3 may have unwittingly bypassed an important stage of development: the prenatal period is when damaging environmental conditions may have some of the most devastating effects on development and, consequently, is when preventive efforts may have the greatest benefits.

Environmental factors that play a significant role in modulating prenatal and early postnatal brain development include substances and circumstances that are necessary for normal brain development, as well as exposures to chemicals, diseases, and stressors that are toxic or disruptive. As with psychosocial risks, such as poverty and family violence, their effects on development are probabilistic; they increase, but do not seal, the odds of impaired development. Table 8-1 lists some of the environmental factors that are beneficial and some that are detrimental. The factors listed, by no means exhaustive, are examples selected on the basis of clinical importance, availability of basic research on brain effects, and existence of relevant clinical studies of human infants. We consider below a few of these detrimental conditions and substances in more detail: an infectious disease (rubella); a developmental neurotoxin (alcohol), and a nutrient deficiency (lack of iron).

TABLE 8-1   Conditions and Substances that Affect the Developing Brain

Needed for Normal Brain Development	Detrimental or Toxic
Oxygen	Alcohol
Adequate protein and energy	Lead
Micronutrients, such as iron and zinc	Tobacco
Adequate gestation	Prenatal infections
Iodine	Polychlorinated biphenyls (PCBs)
Thyroid hormone	Ionizing radiation
Folic acid	Cocaine
Essential fatty acids	Metabolic abnormalities (excess phenylalanine, ammonia)
Sensory stimulation	Aluminum
Activity	Methylmercury
Social interaction	Chronic stress

Note: The listed factors are not intended to be exhaustive.

Infectious Disease

Rubella (German measles) is a classic example of an infectious disease that causes harm in utero. Exposure to rubella early in prenatal development affects the organs (e.g., eyes, ears) that are developing at the time that the virus crosses the placental barrier. Because the development of most organs is largely complete by the end of the first trimester, fetal development during the second and third trimesters of pregnancy is relatively more protected from the negative effects of the rubella virus.

The rubella story demonstrates how long it has often taken to recognize that a particular condition or exposure can put the fetus or child at risk. It was widely believed that few diseases were as benign as rubella until 1942, when the first report of the devastating effects of maternal infection during pregnancy was published (Gregg, 1942). One of the puzzles is why the medical community did not figure out the link between maternal rubella and congenital malformations earlier. Some qualities of rubella, which exist in other conditions as well, made it difficult to make the connection (Beswick et al., 1949). For example, it is not always clear that a fetus has been exposed to a particular infectious illness or toxic agent during pregnancy. In the case of rubella, there are many causes of fever, rash, and other symptoms that are seen. To complicate matters further, effects on the developing fetus or child may also be quite variable. For instance, rubella may affect the fetus's eyes, ears, brain, or heart, among other organs. Furthermore, the very idea that the fetus could be vulnerable to harm was novel before the rubella syndrome was accepted. This is now known to be true for many conditions, such as some of those in Table 8-1.

The rubella story also illustrates a triumph in prevention. As better methods of diagnosing rubella became available in the 1960s (Forbes, 1969), there was more certainty about which rashes and nonspecific symptoms in early pregnancy were due to rubella and which were not. Today, public health policy requiring universal immunization against rubella has virtually eliminated the problem of the congenital rubella syndrome in the United States.

Developmental Neurotoxins

Substances such as drugs and chemicals that are damaging to the developing nervous system are known as developmental neurotoxins. Table 8-1 indicates a number of these agents. Their effects on brain and behavior have been summarized in several comprehensive volumes (Kimmel et al., 1990; Slikker and Chang, 1998), as well as in thousands of original research reports. We use prenatal alcohol exposure as an example of this class of early biological insult. The effects of prenatal alcohol have been studied extensively, and the current state of knowledge was recently considered in depth in an Institute of Medicine report (Institute of Medicine, 1996). Major points related to questions of early brain and behavior development are highlighted here.

The adverse effects of prenatal alcohol exposure are now so widely known and accepted that it is hard to believe that the first report was issued only 30 years ago. Fetal alcohol syndrome was first described in the English-language medical literature in 1973 (Jones and Smith, 1973). Maternal alcohol consumption during pregnancy can lead to facial deformities, loss of neurons, severe neurobehavioral impairment, and impaired cognitive functioning, among other problems. Its consequences appear to persist throughout life (Connor and Streissguth, 1996; Institute of Medicine, 1996; Jacobson et al., 1993; Sampson et al., 1994; Streissguth et al., 1996a). They are not, however, inevitable. One of the perplexing aspects of fetal alcohol exposure is that, even with high doses of alcohol, not all fetuses develop symptoms of fetal alcohol syndrome or alcohol-related neurodevelopmental disorder (see below). Its importance lies in its prevalence and preventability, not its inevitability. Nonetheless, this is a very common cause of harm to the fetus that can be prevented.

Survey data collected by the Centers for Disease Control and Prevention show that the incidence of drinking at levels sufficient to put the fetus at risk for neurobehavioral impairment was 3.5 percent in 1995 (the most recent year for which data are available), with binge drinking the predominant pattern (87 percent of the cases) (Ebrahim et al., 1998). The proportion of women who consume alcohol during pregnancy has decreased since the mid-1980s (Serdula et al., 1991), although much of the decline is due to the changed habits of light drinkers. Women who drink heavily, who pose the greatest risk to their fetus, appear to be more resistant to prevention efforts. Heavy drinking and the consequent incidence of fetal alcohol syndrome are much higher among black Americans than among white Americans (Abel, 1995; Faden et al., 1997) and are also high among American Indians (Duimstra et al., 1993).

Fetal alcohol syndrome is the most severe form of prenatal alcohol effects. Defined by a specific pattern of facial and other physical deformities accompanied by growth retardation, fetal alcohol syndrome identifies a relatively small proportion of children prenatally affected by alcohol. The Institute of Medicine (1996) recently suggested that the term "alcohol-related neurodevelopmental disorder" be used to focus specifically on brain dysfunctions in the presence of significant prenatal alcohol exposure but without physical deformities. Fetal alcohol syndrome is estimated to occur at a rate of 1-3 per 1,000 live births; alcohol-related neurodevelopmental disorder is estimated to be at least 10 times more prevalent. Brain dysfunctions in alcohol-exposed children without fetal alcohol syndrome are often as severe as those in children with the full impairment.

A variety of neurobehavioral changes have been observed in children exposed to alcohol prenatally. These effects range from problems with attention and memory to poor motor coordination to difficulty with problem solving and abstract thinking. Infants and toddlers may be delayed in reaching important milestones, may have difficulty tuning out excess sensory stimuli, and often are hyperactive. About half of all individuals with fetal alcohol syndrome are mentally retarded (IQ < 70). Both severely and more mildly affected children demonstrate slower information processing and longer reaction times and appear to have specific problems with arithmetic (Jacobson et al., 1994). These effects have been documented through the early adolescent years and into adulthood. Such results demonstrate the importance of assessing functions other than IQ. In fact, these measures often detect effects of early biological insults in the absence of IQ differences, and behavioral disturbances may create more functional impairment than a lower IQ. In addition, more specific and sensitive measures may indicate differing effects of various developmental neurotoxins (Jacobson, 1998).

The importance of considering timing (when a condition occurs during development), severity (degree or dose), and chronicity (how long it lasts) in attempting to understand the effects of early biological insults is well illustrated by prenatal alcohol exposure. In general, the prenatal period appears to be distinguished by its sensitivity to a large array of harmful conditions. But even within the prenatal period, timing matters. For instance, alcohol exposure early in gestation has different effects on the developing brain from similar exposure later on. Case reports from autopsies and, more recently, neuroimaging studies (Riley et al., 1995; Sowell et al., 1996; Swayze et al., 1997) give an indication of central nervous system effects in humans. However, animal models—with experimental manipulation of alcohol exposure and direct examination of brain tissue—continue to provide crucial information. In the mouse, for example, exposure to alcohol on days 7 and 8 of gestation results in not only the typical facial deformities of fetal alcohol syndrome but also brain anomalies, such as small overall size and deficiencies in cerebral hemispheres, striatum, olfactory bulbs, limbic structures, the corpus callosum, and lateral ventricles. Exposure later in gestation generally does not produce such gross structural malformations but nonetheless kills nerve cells and interferes with synaptogenesis, formation of myelin, and other biochemical processes, including reduction of NMDA receptor binding in the hippocampus.

Research with humans also shows that the timing of prenatal alcohol exposure has differential effects (Connor and Streissguth, 1996; Institute of Medicine, 1996; Jacobson et al., 1993, 1998; Sampson et al., 1994; Streissguth et al., 1996a, 1996b). The unusual facial features of fetal alcohol syndrome in the human infant (e.g., low-set ears, short philtrum, cleft palate, cleft lip) appear to be due to heavy exposure early on, in the first trimester, when the structures that come together to form the face are developing. Fetal exposure to alcohol during the second and especially the third trimester of pregnancy appears to be a time of particular vulnerability for the impaired neurobehavioral development, although some data suggest that these effects extend throughout pregnancy. Dividing cells appear to be particularly sensitive to the toxic effects of alcohol, and hence a period during which extensive neurogenesis occurs would be a time of acute sensitivity to the effects of alcohol. The cognitive effects associated with exposure to alcohol later in pregnancy, for example, may be associated with the high level of neuronal cell division in pertinent parts of the brain that occurs during the third trimester.

The severity of exposure is another important factor in understanding ill effects, perhaps as important as the timing. For prenatal alcohol use, greater exposures are associated with worse effects. In addition, episodic binge drinking appears to be more harmful to the developing brain than equivalent levels of alcohol consumed steadily. Experimental animal studies indicate that ingestion of a given dose of alcohol over a short period of time generates a greater peak blood alcohol concentration than the same dose ingested over several days (Bonthius and West, 1990). Thus, the developing fetus is actually exposed to a higher level of alcohol in binge drinking and has been found in animal research to experience greater neuronal (Bonthius and West, 1990) and behavioral (Goodlett et al., 1987) impairment. In humans, binge drinking is more of a problem than is usually recognized, because moderate drinkers, who consume 1-2 drinks per day on average, in fact, tend to concentrate their drinking on 1-2 days per week, thus drinking 4 or more drinks per occasion (Jacobson and Jacobson, 1999). When juxtaposed with evidence on the timing of alcohol exposure, the detrimental effects of binge drinking suggest that any bouts of drinking during pregnancy run the risk of damaging some aspect of the developing brain.

Chronicity is another important factor in understanding the effects of early biological insults. In the case of prenatal alcohol exposure, it appears that the effects on the fetus worsen with successive pregnancies. Specifically, older mothers who are moderate-to-heavy drinkers are at higher risk for having an affected offspring (Institute of Medicine, 1996). This may be due to reduced ability to metabolize alcohol by women who have been drinking heavily for several years (Jacobson et al., 1993, 1994). In the case of alcohol exposure, chronicity should thus be thought of as a dimension of risk both within and between pregnancies.

Research on early biological insults has also yielded information on modifiability or brain plasticity. Environmental interventions to reduce the effects of alcohol exposure (other than specific treatment of a toxin or deficiency) have been studied for only a few conditions. Prenatal alcohol exposure is perhaps the best researched in recent years. In animal models, a variety of interventions has been shown to ameliorate some of the central nervous system effects of alcohol (Greenough and Black, 1992; Hannigan et al., 1993; Klintsova et al., 1997; Weinberg et al., 1995). Effective interventions include motor training, procedures that enhance maternal caregiving behaviors, and a postweaning environment that is physically and socially stimulating. However, one should not conclude that the process is trivial. For instance, getting a rat to do motor training may require quite heroic efforts on the part of the investigator, and interventions typically do not bring the brain and behavior of exposed animals fully back to the levels of animals who never experienced the biological insult. As common sense would suggest, protecting the developing brain from early biological insults is a more desirable and effective strategy than trying to correct the deficits once they have occurred. Fetal alcohol research provides a particularly compelling case for preventive interventions, as well as for early detection and treatment of associated difficulties.

Nutrient Deficiency

Both before and after birth, nutritional adequacy is important for optimal brain development and function (see Georgieff and Rao, 1999, and Morgan and Gibson, 1991, for recent reviews). The effects of generalized undernutrition (lack of sufficient protein, energy, and other nutrients) on the developing brain have been studied extensively over several decades

(Dobbing and Smart, 1974; Morgane et al., 1993; Strupp and Levitsky, 1995; Winick and Rosso, 1969). This research has demonstrated that the timing of nutrient supplementation or deficiency is important. For example, nutritional deprivation in the second trimester of pregnancy has been shown to result in deficient numbers of neurons, whereas deprivation in the third trimester affects numbers of glial cells and the maturation of neurons (e.g., Dickerson, 1981). Postnatal nutrition also appears to show timing effects, with the first 2 to 3 years of life being an especially vulnerable time for effects on brain growth. The earlier the malnutrition occurs, the greater the reduction in brain size, and the longer the malnutrition continues, the greater the effect on the brain (Morgan and Winick, 1985; Winick, 1976). Nevertheless, as the literature on orphanage-reared infants illustrates (reviewed in the next chapter), young children can show remarkable recovery in growth and behavior even after gross early (postnatal) generalized malnutrition when they are fed adequately.

Although sufficient nutrient intake is important throughout life, certain nutrients have a more profound effect on the developing brain than others. The following discussion summarizes research on iron deficiency, an area in which there has been a recent burst of relevant research. Iron deficiency is probably the world's most common single nutrient disorder. Approximately 20 to 25 percent of babies worldwide have iron-deficiency anemia, and a much higher proportion have iron deficiency without anemia (deMaeyer and Adiels-Tegman, 1985; Joint Committee on Health Policy of the World Health Organization and UNICEF, 1994). The latter is common even in countries where public health interventions have reduced anemia. In the United States, for instance, the prevalence of iron-deficiency anemia has decreased dramatically (Looker et al., 1997), due to fortification of infant formula and cereal and increased breast-feeding, among other factors. However, poor and minority children are still at considerable risk for iron deficiency with or without anemia (Ogden, 1998). In a recent U.S. national survey, nonpoor white toddlers had the lowest prevalence of iron deficiency (about 3 percent), while Mexican-American toddlers were at highest risk regardless of economic status, affecting approximately 18 percent of poor and 12 percent of nonpoor Mexican-American children (Ogden, 1998).

Altered behavior and development are among the most worrisome concerns about iron deficiency in infancy. Iron-deficient anemic infants generally test lower in mental and motor development (see review by Nokes et al., 1998). Other behavioral differences, such as increased fearfulness, fatigue, and wariness, have also been noted (Honig and Oski, 1984; Lozoff et al., 1985, 1986, 1996, 1998; Walter et al., 1983, 1989). Although one study reported that test scores improved with a full course of iron treatment (Idjradinata and Pollitt, 1993), the other available studies found that a majority of infants with iron-deficiency anemia continued to have lower developmental test scores (Aukett et al., 1986; Lozoff et al., 1987, 1996; Walter et al., 1989), despite iron therapy for 2-6 months and correction of anemia; other behavioral differences were also still observed (Lozoff et al., 1998). Differences thus appear to persist.

Follow-up studies have sought to determine if differences persist beyond infancy. Several studies have shown that, at early school age, children who were anemic as infants continue to have lower test scores than their peers who did not experience anemia (Dommergues et al., 1989; Lozoff et al., 1991; Palti et al., 1983, 1985; Walter et al., 1990). A comprehensive follow-up at the transition to adolescence (Lozoff et al., 2000) found that children who had been treated for severe, chronic iron deficiency in infancy still scored lower on measures of mental and motor functioning, specifically in arithmetic achievement and written expression, motor functioning, and some specific cognitive processes such as spatial memory and selective recall. They were also more likely to have repeated a grade. Parents and teachers rated the formerly iron-deficient children as showing more anxiety or depression, social problems, and attention problems. In a different, population-based study (Hurtado et al., 1999), children who were anemic in infancy (presumably due to iron deficiency) were at increased risk for mild to moderate mental retardation at age 10. Thus, severe, chronic iron deficiency in infancy identifies children who continue to be at developmental and behavioral risk more than 10 years later.

Basic research and animal studies indicate some possible mechanisms for such behavioral and developmental differences. Iron is required for many processes, including neurotransmitter synthesis (dopamine being the most studied), myelination, and oxidative metabolism (reviewed in Georgieff and Rao, 1999). Maximal transport of iron into the brain corresponds with the brain growth spurt, and iron deficiency during this period results in a deficit of brain iron in animal models. These observations suggest that the developing brain may be particularly vulnerable to the effects of this nutrient deficiency. Conversely, free or excess iron is toxic to cell membranes and may contribute to neuronal damage following a brain injury.

New studies that utilize neurophysiological and electrophysiological methods are now providing data on iron-deficient human infants and demonstrating close links to results in animal models. In one such study (Roncagliolo et al., 1998), 6-month-old infants with iron-deficiency anemia had slower nerve conduction in the auditory pathway. Differences in nerve conduction velocity between anemic and nonanemic infants increased over the following year despite iron therapy. A disruption or defect in myelination was considered to be a promising explanation, given that brain iron is required for myelination, young iron-deficient animals have been noted to be hypomyelinated, and the auditory system is rapidly myelinating in the first two years after birth in the human infant (reviewed in Roncagliolo et al., 1998).

The hippocampus, which is a key structure in the circuit that subserves recognition memory, also appears to be vulnerable to early iron deficiency (de Ungria et al., 2000; Erikson et al., 1997). In animal models, iron deficiency results in markedly reduced neuronal metabolism (as indicated by cytochrome coxidase activity) in all subareas of the hippocampus and other regions involved in higher cognitive functions (de Ungria et al., 2000). Preliminary evidence from a study of infants of diabetic mothers (who are at risk for lower levels of iron in the liver, heart, and brain in addition to hyper- and hypoglycemia and hypoxia), using electrophysiological techniques, has revealed impaired recognition memory despite normal iron status at 6 to 8 months of age (de Regnier et al., in press). These findings are consistent with a hippocampally based memory deficit, and iron deficiency may be a contributing factor. Disruptions in recognition memory, in turn, may be a subtle early effect that could contribute to learning disabilities later on.

It is important to emphasize that early biological risks and insults, such as iron deficiency, often do not occur in isolation (see Figure 8-2). In fact, they typically are increased among infants who also grow up in disadvantaged environments. Iron deficiency, for example, is more prevalent among poor infants in the United States (McLoyd and Lozoff, 2000). Thus, in human studies, it can be exceedingly difficult to disentangle poor development and behavioral outcomes that are due to the biological exposure, from those due to the problematic environment.

Prematurity and Early Brain Development

One of the true marvels of human brain development is that an infant can be born prematurely in the early part of the third trimester and not only survive, but also achieve something resembling his or her potential in mental and motor behavior. Highly sophisticated intensive care techniques have improved survival rates of premature infants. The KidsCount data of the Annie E. Casey Foundation shows that the percentage of low-birthweight babies increased in each of the 50 states between 1990 and 1997 (Annie E. Casey Foundation, 2000). Low-birthweight babies were 7.5 percent of all births in 1997, compared to 7.0 percent in 1990. This represents a 7 percent increase over just this 7-year period (National Center for Health Statistics of the Centers for Disease Control, 1993, 1999).

The borders of viability (approximately 24 weeks of gestation), however, have not changed since 1980 (Richardson et al., 1998). Greater than 95 percent of infants born after 28 weeks of gestation and greater than 50

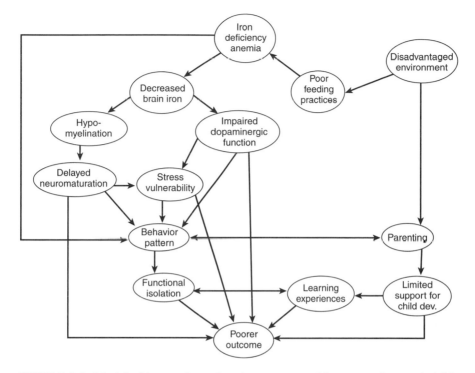

FIGURE 8-2 Model of interaction of environment, nutrition, parenting, and child characteristics on outcomes. SOURCE: Lozoff et al., 1998. Reprinted with permission.

percent of infants born at 24-28 weeks survive (Hack et al., 1991). At the very borders of viability (22-24 weeks of gestation), mortality remains high. Of the infants who survive, a high percentage have sustained damage to developing neurological structures and have significant neurological morbidity (Allen et al., 1993). Moreover, recent research with toddlers suggests that even low-risk preterm infants (those born between 27 and 34 weeks gestational age) cannot be assumed to have caught up with their full-term counterparts in all aspects of cognitive development (de Haan et al., 2000). Nevertheless, it is safe to say that, over the past decade, neonatology has begun to concern itself less with survival (mortality) and more with outcome (morbidity) (Richardson et al., 1998). The corresponding challenges that these infants at the border of viability present to society are only beginning to be addressed.

It is useful to consider preterm infants as fetuses who develop in extrauterine settings at the time when their brains are growing more rapidly than at any other time in their life (Als, 1997; McClellan, 1972). Prematurity has two main negative effects on brain development. First, premature birth predisposes the infant to pathological events that directly injure the brain. These events can be thought of as damage committed by factors that the human at this gestational age would not normally encounter. These can be as seemingly benign as the wrong mixture of nutrients to more obvious neuropathologies such as intracranial hemorrhage. Second, premature birth interrupts the normal process of intrauterine brain development by denying it expected intrauterine stimuli and factors important for growth (e.g., nutrients such as docosohexaenoic acid). One can consider this to be disruption due to omission of factors that are critical for normal development. Ultimately, the morbidity seen at any gestational age is the result of the combination of the number and severity of exposure to both types of influence.

The first principle of assessing the effect of prematurity on neurological outcome is to note that the child's general developmental status and intelligence scores decrease with reductions in gestational age (Saigal et al., 1991). Thus, an infant born at 24 weeks is at greater risk than an infant born at 26 weeks, who in turn is at higher risk than an infant born at 28 weeks. Infants born at 24 weeks not only have a less complete brain than those born at 26 weeks, but they also are far more prone to intracranial hemorrhage, hypoglycemia, and postnatal malnutrition, all of which adversely affect the more primitive parts of the brain. Once one moves out of the high-risk groups, however, outcomes become highly variable.

Insults Due to Prematurity

The literature on neonatal outcomes is replete with studies assessing the effects of intracranial hemorrhage (Papile et al., 1983), periventricular leucomalacia (Feldman et al., 1990; Lowe and Papile, 1990), hypoglyecmia (Duvanel et al., 1999), and malnutrition (Georgieff et al., 1985, 1989; Hack and Breslau, 1986) on head growth and developmental outcome. Besides gestational age and socioeconomic status, the next most important factor in assessing risk of adverse neurological outcomes is the degree of illness of the infant during the newborn period. Infants whose overall physiology is more compromised are more developmentally delayed at 2 years and appear to be at greater risk of prefrontal deficits at age 8 (Brazy et al., 1991; Luciana et al., 1999).

Intracranial hemorrhage (also known as intraventricular hemorrhage) is the most extensively studied noxious event that affects the premature infant's brain. This is probably due to the fact that it is easily visualized by cranial ultrasonography and quantifiable into Grades I (least severe) to IV (most severe). Approximately 20 percent of infants between 28 and 34 weeks gestation have intraventricular hemorrhage, with the vast majority

(> 60 percent) rated as Grade I or II. In contrast, 60 percent of infants born between 24 to 28 weeks have intraventricular hemorrhage, and their hemorrhages tend to be the more severe Grade III and IV varieties. Accordingly, the risk of major handicaps, both motor and cognitive, is increased. Infants with lower-grade hemorrhages do not appear to be at any greater risk of major handicap (cerebral palsy, mental retardation) than infants who did not bleed (Papile et al., 1983), although they are at higher risk of minor handicaps (e.g., behavior problems, attention problems, memory deficits) (Lowe and Papile, 1990; Ross et al., 1996).

Omission of Factors Important for Normal Brain Development

A premature infant with a benign neonatal course nevertheless remains at increased risk of neurological morbidity. Although one can never be assured that all noxious events (both prenatal and postnatal) have been accounted for in any given study, there is mounting evidence that transferring brain growth and development from an intrauterine to an extrauterine environment prematurely is less than optimal even in the absence of other definable neurological risk factors (Chapieski and Evankovich, 1997; Cherkes-Julkowski, 1998; Huppi et al., 1996). Recent research, for example, has demonstrated poorer performance on elicited imitation tasks (a medial temporal lobe function) at age 18 months in 27- to 34-week gestational age preterm infants with completely benign neonatal courses compared with term infants tested at the same post-conceptional age (de Haan et al., 2000). These emerging data strongly suggest that the human brain continues to develop in a unique way in utero until the end of gestation and that early termination of pregnancy disrupts that development with subsequent behavioral consequences.

A more pernicious effect of extrauterine life on brain development in small preterm infants is the general problem of malnutrition. Neonatal illness not only predisposes preterm infants to definable adverse events (e.g., intraventricular hemorrhage, hypoxia) but also blocks provision of adequate nutritional substrates to promote normal brain growth and development. Studies have estimated that greater than 50 percent of very low-birthweight infants fall below the 5th percentile for head growth sometime during their hospitalization (rendering them, by definition, microcephalic) (Georgieff et al., 1985). Fortunately, one of the most amazing aspects of early human life is the ability of the head (and brain) to demonstrate catch-up growth. After a period of no growth, the head exhibits a remarkable increase in growth velocity to double or triple normal rates, given adequate protein-energy intakes (Georgieff et al., 1985; Sher and Brown, 1975). There is, however, a point of diminishing return. If the infant has had no growth for more than a month, the subsequent catch-up rate is markedly reduced, almost as if the potential for catch-up has been lost (Georgieff et al., 1985; Hack and Breslau, 1986; Sher and Brown, 1975). Premature infants with more striking postnatally acquired microcephaly due to malnutrition indeed have smaller head circumferences and poorer scores on the Bayley Scales of Infant Development at age 12 months (Georgieff et al., 1985). Reduced head circumference at 8 months postnatally bodes poorly for developmental outcomes measured at age 3 and 8 years (Hack and Breslau, 1986). These studies suggest that although catch-up head growth is a marvelous compensatory response, it is better to have never experienced the growth deficit in the first place. Extrapolating further, it argues for important windows of opportunity for brain growth late in the third trimester that, if interrupted by premature birth and lack of head growth, may result in the brain being "constructed" in an alternative manner (de Haan et al., 2000).

In sum, prematurity confers a significant risk to the developing brain. The risk emanates from both insults that arise during the course of illness in the premature infant and from interruptions of the provision of the expected substrates and environment apparently necessary for normal brain development. We have used examples for which there is a substantial literature (e.g., intraventricular hemorrhage), but hasten to add that other potentially neuropathological factors that are more difficult to isolate and quantify (e.g., hypoxia-ischemia, hypoglycemia, neurotoxic medications such as steroids) are likely to play important roles as well. The ultimate risk to any single premature infant is likely to be a composite of all the known and unknown risk and protective factors that characterize that infant, and on the infant's general extent of biological and environmental vulnerability. Thus the premature infant born to a lower-income mother with few resources who received poor prenatal care is likely to have a much more difficult neonatal course, and therefore be at higher neurodevelop-mental risk, than an infant of the same gestational age born to a mother who received better prenatal care and has more resources. Perhaps this helps explain the overall down-shifting of developmental scores in premature infants from families of lower socioeconomic status (Saigal et al., 1991).

Growing awareness of environmentally based differences in the outcomes of premature infants has fueled multiple intervention efforts ranging from dramatic changes in the care these infants receive in neonatal intensive care units (see reviews by Als, 1997; Hernandez-Reif and Field, 2000) to comprehensive initiatives that provide a range of services to the infants and their families from the time they leave the hospital to several months or years after discharge. The best known of the comprehensive approaches is the Infant Health and Development Program (see Box 8-2) (Gross et al., 1997), which included a randomized trial and extensive follow-ups of the participating families.

BOX 8-2
Infant Health and Development Program

Premature babies with low birthweight are more likely than babies with normal birthweight to have a range of health and developmental problems, including lower IQ, cerebral palsy, less emotional maturity, less social competence, and attentional difficulties. Many low-birthweight, premature infants are also considered doubly vulnerable because they are also more likely to experience environmental risks such as living in poverty, having a single parent, or being the child of a teenage mother.

The Infant Health and Development Program was a large, randomized clinical trial to determine the efficacy of an intervention designed to promote the physical health, and cognitive and socioemotional development of low-birthweight, premature children. The program provided services for 985 children from birth through age 3 at 8 different sites throughout the United States. All of the children received pediatric surveillance and community referral services. The families of one-third of the children also received family support through home visits throughout the program. Beginning at age 1, the children from these families participated in full-day educational child care in eight child development centers, and their parents participated in regular group meetings. Data on the health, behavior, and cognitive development of all of the children were collected during the 3 years of the program, as well as at ages 5 and 8.

Infants participating in the intervention demonstrated improved behavioral functioning (e.g., higher IQ scores, vocabulary gains, and fewer behavioral problems) at the conclusion of the intervention, when they were 3 years old (Infant Health and Development Program, 1990). At age 5, only the heavier low-birthweight infants (i.e., 2,000-2,500 grams) continued to show gains that distinguished them from the children that did not receive the intervention (Brooks-Gunn et al., 1994). By age 8, even the gains of the heavier infants had been substantially diminished (McCarton et al., 1997). The authors have speculated about the outcomes that might have emerged if they had continued the program up to school entry.

SOURCES: Brooks-Gunn et al. (1994); Gross et al.(1997); McCarton et al. (1997).

The evaluation literature on these interventions offers good news about the capacity of early childhood programs, which emphasize individualized developmental care, as well as initiatives focused on parental coping and training in optimal parenting skills, to improve health outcomes and decrease developmental delays in premature infants. It thus appears that the developmental problems associated with prematurity and low birthweight can be mitigated by intervention. However, this is such a complex biological phenomenon that relatively nonspecific interventions may not be the most productive approach. Moreover, virtually all experts in this area agree that efforts focused on preventing low birthweight need to be the top priority.

Stress and the Developing Brain

Research on premature infants has provided substantial evidence of the importance of the caregiving environment for the baby's later progress. This theme emerges, as well, from research on animals regarding how stress affects the developing brain. This research provides preliminary insights into how alterations of the early caregiving environment affect neurochemical aspects of early brain development. Extending this evidence to the human species is not yet warranted, however. There is, for example, only one scientifically reviewed study that has imaged the brains of maltreated children (De Bellis et al., 1999a) (discussed in Chapter 9). The animal evidence, however, is suggestive of the physiological processes that may underlie associations found between highly dysfunctional caregiving and problematic child outcomes, particularly those that lie in the realm of self-regulatory behaviors. This, in turn, points to promising directions for future collaborative research among behavioral and brain scientists.

The term "stress" is used by psychologists, physiologists, and the lay public and means different things to each (Engle, 1985). In this report, stress refers to the set of changes in the body and the brain that are set into motion when there are overwhelming threats to physical or psychological well-being (Selye, 1973, 1975). Stress can have dramatic effects on health and development (Johnson et al., 1992). This happens because the physiology of stress produces a shift in the body's priorities. When threats begin to overwhelm one's immediate resources to manage them, a cascade of neurochemical changes that begin in the brain temporarily puts on hold the processes in the body that can be thought of as future-oriented: finding, digesting, and storing food; fighting off colds and viruses; learning things that don't matter right now but may be important sometime in the future; reproducing and rearing offspring. Many of these neurochemical changes take place in the very same brain structures (e.g., hypothalamus and brainstem) that function to regulate heart rate, respiration, food intake and digestion, reproduction, growth, and the building up versus breaking down of energy stores (Stratakis and Chrousos, 1995).

These brain regions also play a role in regulating the production of stress responses in the rest of the body. Specifically, the adrenal glands, located on the top of the kidneys, produce adrenaline and cortisol (Axelrod and Reisine, 1984). Adrenaline is part of the sympathetic nervous system. Increases in sympathetic nervous system activity support vigilance, focus attention, increase heart rate, shunt blood to muscles and away from the digestive system, break down fat stores making energy available to cells, and dampen activity of the immune system. Cortisol is a steroid hormone that plays a myriad of roles in stress physiology. It helps to break down protein stores, liberating energy for use by the body. It suppresses the immune system, suppresses physical growth, inhibits reproductive hormones, and affects many aspects of brain functioning, including emotions and memory.

Current understanding of how psychological stimuli, such as experiences of fear and anxiety, set in motion stress physiology is centered on an area of the brain called the amygdala (Miller and Davis, 1997; Rolls, 1992; Schulkin et al., 1994), which has close back-and-forth communication with areas of the brain involved in attention, memory, planning, and behavior control. In animals, experimentally causing a hyperstimulation of the amygdala (a process termed "kindling") seems to create a hypersensitization of the fear-stress circuits of the brain and changes in behavior that look like an animal version of posttraumatic stress disorder (Rosen et al., 1996). It is as if the fear circuits get locked in the "on" mode and have trouble shutting off. These circuits course through the amygdala and an area called the bed nucleus of the stria terminalis. They appear to be pathways through which circumstances outside the body set in motion the cascade of events inside the body and the brain that undergird fear-stress responses. These events involve the elevation of cortisol and stimulation of the sympathetic arm of the stress response. In animals, flooding the brain with cortisol for prolonged periods of time produces changes in this process that may lower the threshold for activating the fear-stress system (Makino et al., 1994). The result is an animal that more readily experiences fear, anxiety, and stress and may have a harder time dampening or regulating these responses.

The amygdala is a fairly mature brain area at birth in humans and seems to be fully mature at least as early as a child's first birthday. All anatomical evidence suggests that by the end of the first year, young children should be capable of experiencing psychologically driven fear, anxiety, and stress. Indeed, fear reactions to strangers (Bronson, 1971; Schaffer, 1966; Waters et al., 1975) and anxiety reactions to separation from familiar caregivers (Ainsworth and Bell, 1970; Bowlby, 1973; Sroufe, 1979) are hallmarks of emotional development in late infancy. Brief periods of stress are not expected to be problematic. Indeed, survival requires the capacity to mount a stress response. However, because the stress system functions to put growth-oriented processes on hold, frequent or prolonged periods of stress may negatively affect development.

Evidence from research on rodents and primates suggests that experiences of neglect early in life constitute the kinds of stressful experiences to which young offspring are especially sensitive and may result in a more reactive stress system. In studies of rats, for example, when experimenters do things to the nest that affect maternal behavior (such as handle the pups), they can affect the development of the rat's stress system (Denenberg, 1999; Levine and Thoman, 1970). Doing things to the nest that result in better organized maternal behavior results in infant rats that develop into less fearful, less stress-reactive adults, whereas doing things that disrupt maternal behavior results in more fearful and stress-reactive adult rats. Researchers have also shown that strains of rodents that are known to be more stress-reactive are characterized by maternal care that involves less licking and grooming (Liu et al., 1997; Meaney et al., 1996; Plotsky and Meaney, 1993). Cross-fostering genetically high stress-reactive infants to mothers from low stress-reactive strains results in the development of a more stress-resilient animal. These effects of early experience in the rat appear to operate through the development of the receptor system in the brain that influences the reactivity of the fear-anxiety circuits. Plenty of input early in life that keeps the stress system dampened down results in the development of a stress-modulating receptor system that can quickly turn off stress reactions. Without this input, the fear-stress system appears to get "shaped" so that the rat pup becomes a more highly reactive adult who has difficulty modulating these responses. In short, the development of a less stress-reactive rat seems to revolve around enhancing and supporting qualities of the caregiving environment.

There are monkey analogues of these rat studies, although details of the biobehavioral mechanisms have not been worked out as thoroughly. Infant monkeys deprived of normal social stimulation grow into socially incompetent, fearful adults (Harlow et al., 1971; Young et al., 1973). More recent studies have documented that monkeys reared on cloth surrogates, but exposed every day to several hours of play with other infant monkeys, are not as socially incompetent as monkeys raised in isolation, but they show numerous physiological signs of being very anxious and fearful (Suomi, 1991). They produce higher levels of stress hormones when threatened and they have high levels of anxiety-related brain neurochemicals in the cerebrospinal fluid, which bathes and nourishes the brain and spinal cord. Monkeys reared only with other infant monkeys (i.e., no cloth surrogates to call their own), show similar patterns of high reactivity to stress (Champoux et al., 1989, 1992).

A high stress-reactive adult monkey can also be produced by procedures that cause stress to its mother (Coplan et al., 1995, 1996; Rosenblum and Andrews, 1994; Rosenblum et al., 1994; Schneider, 1992a, 1992b; Schneider et al., 1992, 1998). One technique for stressing the mother is to make her food resources unpredictable. This has the effect of deeply disturbing the mother's social relationships with other adult monkeys in her group. The infant monkeys in these unpredictable food studies (who are roughly equivalent in developmental age to 1- to 2-year-old human children) experience high levels of stress hormones (like their mothers) and grow up into highly fearful, socially less competent adult animals (Rosenblum and Andrews, 1994; Rosenblum et al., 1994). These effects were obtained even though food was never uncertain for the young monkeys themselves, and thus seem to be influenced by what this uncertainty and disturbance in the social environment does to their mothers.

There is a great deal to learn about how the social environment connects with the biology of growth and the regulation of stress physiology in human infants and children. Intriguing research is emerging, however, to suggest that the development of stress regulation in young children may be a very promising place to look for brain-experience dynamics. For example, both failure to thrive and psychosocial dwarfism (Gohlke et al., 1998; Skuse, 1985), in which children's pituitary glands fail to secrete sufficient growth hormone (Skuse et al., 1996), are associated with failures in the social environment (Alanese et al., 1994). Removing the child from the problematic social system reverses the disorder and growth increases rapidly. This research, as well as that on orphanage-reared infants discussed in Chapter 9, raises extremely important questions about the plasticity and self-righting tendencies inherent in the human (as well as the animal) brain. In general, there is much to learn about the extent to which the neurological pathways between caregiving environments and dysfunctional behavior that are emerging in the animal literature apply to human offspring and about the effects of remedial experiences that attempt to enhance the development of children from early abusive and neglectful environments.

In sum, neuroscience evidence from animal research is increasingly pointing to experiences of neglect, stress, and trauma within the caregiving environment as a source of compromised brain development. Research on rodents and primates indicates that the ways in which the brain learns to respond to stressful and fear-inducing circumstances are profoundly affected by the capacity of the infant's caregivers to regulate the developing stress system. Disruptions to the caregiving environment that produce stress in the mother appear to alter the offspring's developing reactivity to stress, as seen behaviorally in high levels of fearfulness and neurologically in how the brain releases and modulates stress hormones. Alternatively, supportive and nurturant caregiving can protect offspring from these consequences. Although this evidence is compelling with regard to the significance of early rearing environments as they affect the developing brain, we are barely at the beginning of exploring these issues in human babies (Kimmel et al., 1990; McLoyd and Lozoff, 2000; Morgane et al., 1993).

SUMMARY AND CONCLUSIONS

Basic research on the development of the brain is a rapidly moving frontier. Abundant evidence indicates that brain development begins well before birth, extends into the adult years, and is specifically designed to recruit and incorporate experience into its emerging architecture and functioning. For some systems, environmental inputs need to occur prenatally or relatively early in life, after which time the brain becomes decreasingly capable of developing normally. But available evidence indicates that such critical periods are more exceptional than typical in human development. For the vast majority of brain development, including areas of the brain involved in cognitive, emotional, and social development, either questions regarding critical or sensitive periods have not been explored or it appears that the brain remains open to experiences across broad swaths of development. This makes sense. Adaptation depends on the rapid consolidation of capabilities essential to survival and the life-long flexibility to adjust to changing circumstances and learn new skills. As a result, assertions that the die has been cast by the time the child enters school are not supported by neuroscience evidence and can create unwarranted pessimism about the potential efficacy of interventions that are initiated after the preschool years.

Nevertheless, what happens early matters. Concerns about protecting the developing brain need to begin well before birth. During the prenatal months, the developing brain is highly vulnerable to intrinsic hazards (such as errors of neural migration) and external insults resulting from drug or alcohol exposure, viral infection, malnutrition, and other environmental harms. This directs attention to efforts to protect brain development during pregnancy and the earliest months of life, including the importance of prenatal and postnatal medical care, as well as expanded public health efforts to improve nutritional quality and reduce drug and viral exposure. It also argues for continued efforts to reduce the incidence of premature births and to ameliorate the adverse consequences of prematurity. Neuroscience evidence also directs attention to the early detection, identification, and treatment of problems such as visual impairments, auditory deficits, and major perceptual-motor delays that have profound effects on children's capacity to access and incorporate the stimulation needed to organize the developing nervous system. For these aspects of development, there is solid evidence that the timing of corrective efforts matters a great deal.

Beyond this evidence regarding detrimental influences on brain development, neuroscience offers few insights into how early environments can function to enhance development beyond what might otherwise be expected. The experiments with complex environments conducted on rats reveal the benefits of more enriched environments, indicate that younger brains react more rapidly and to a greater degree to environmental variation, and suggest that removal from complex environments results in decreasing benefits over time. Nevertheless, we do not yet have the evidence on infant brains to translate these findings from animal research into tangible recommendations for early interventions aimed at children's cognitive or social-emotional development. For these insights, additional behavioral evidence from human development is needed.

A final implication of research on early brain development concerns the detrimental effects of early and sustained stressful experiences, particularly those that derive from aberrant or disrupted caregiving environments. Evidence from research on animals suggests that such experiences overactivate neural pathways that regulate fear-stress responses in the immature brain, perhaps placing them on a "high alert" setting that may alter patterns of behavioral responding in adult animals with different rearing histories. Translations of these findings to human development are largely speculative. However, emerging evidence regarding the physiology of children subjected to serious deprivation and trauma early in life are consistent with the animal studies, as is the richer body of behavioral data on young children exposed to such early adverse experiences. This is an especially promising area for research that integrates animal and human studies, using both neuroscience and behavioral approaches, and explores not only the negative consequences of early stress and trauma but also the capacity of the brain to reorganize itself following highly depriving circumstances early in life.

In sum, the neuroscientific research on early brain development says that the young children warranting the greatest concern are those growing up in environments, starting before birth, that fail to provide them with adequate nutrition and other growth-fostering inputs, expose them to biological insults, and subject them to abusive and neglectful care. Children with undetected sensorimotor difficulties (whose developing brains may not receive the stimulation they need) also warrant concern. The brain research also reassures that brain development is probably on course for the vast majority of young children who are protected from these conditions and, in many instances, can be affected positively by timely corrective interventions focused on early insults and deficits.

III

The Context for Early Development

Early interventions are premised on a belief in the power of environmental influences on early development. Our review of the research on early development in areas as disparate as behavior genetics, neurobiology, and social and cognitive development has supported this belief. Genetic susceptibilities are activated and displayed in the context of environmental influences. Brain development is exquisitely attuned to environmental inputs that, in turn, shape its emerging architecture. The environment provided by the child's first caregivers has profound effects on virtually every facet of early development, ranging from the health and integrity of the baby at birth to the child's readiness to start school at age 5. Documenting and understanding environmental influences, however, are not the same tasks as changing environments. Indeed, as we discuss in this report, it is decidedly not a simple task to shift the developmental pathways of young children through interventions that affect their environments, particularly when the interventions are modest in scope, poorly implemented, and inadequately staffed—which is all too often the case.

In Part III we expand our lens on young children to encompass the contexts that influence early development. We start with the nurturing relationships that are forged between the growing child and his or her caregivers at home. Early development is inextricably tied to this most proximal, interpersonal context. In fact, active debates now characterize discussions of the extent to which parenting and the family environment affect child development (Harris, 1995, 1998; Rowe, 1994). Our reading of the literature, as discussed in the next chapter, calls attention to the myriad ways in which children's relationships with their parents (or those who otherwise serve as the child's primary caregivers), the parents' behavior toward their children, and the home environment in which children grow up profoundly affect what children learn and can do, what they expect and believe, and how they approach others during the early years and start them off along differing pathways as they move into the school-age years.

Arguably, young children now growing up in the United States are exposed to an unprecedented number and variety of out-of-home environments. School entry used to mark a major transition when the balance of a child's time spent at home and with parents was profoundly altered. Today this happens for the majority of children before the end of their first year, given trends in parental employment and early reliance on child care. It is certainly plausible that, as a result, adults other than parents, care settings other than the child's home, and peers and neighborhood settings are becoming increasingly influential sources of early developmental variation. We do not yet, however, have any evidence bearing on this speculation. In fact, studies of both child care settings and neighborhoods have reaffirmed the powerful influence of the family and studies of socioeconomic influences have emphasized the large extent to which they affect young children through effects on their caregivers.

While there has been a long-standing agreement among those who study children that development cannot be understood out of context—the so-called ecology of human development (Bronfenbrenner, 1979, 1986)—concerted efforts to understand influences that derive from contexts other than the immediate family are relatively new. These efforts include studies of children as they grow up in families that occupy different socioeconomic niches, experience nonparental child care, and reside in communities and neighborhoods with widely differing characteristics and resources. Research that tracks the natural trajectories of young children, particularly longitudinal studies that follow the same children over time, tell us about how these environments affect the natural unfolding of development. Do these beyond-the-family contexts matter, and if so, how much do they matter in shaping the early direction of children's lives? We also learn about contextual influences from studies of efforts to change these environments, ranging from providing infants and toddlers with enriched child care to moving families out of dangerous neighborhoods. This research tells us about the malleability of early development. Can we change development by changing its contexts, and what does it take? We discuss both of these streams of research and argue for their integration.

Research on the context for early development that is provided by parents and other primary caregivers in the home (Chapter 9) provides the point of departure. We then summarize the research on socioeconomic influences on early development (Chapter 10), including the influence of income and poverty, parental schooling and employment, and family structure. Next, we consider the influence of child care (Chapter 11). Although we introduce the literature on child care in Chapter 9, particularly as it bears on young children's attachments to important caregivers, we dedicate a separate chapter to examining child care as an important setting that supplements the care children receive from their parents. Nevertheless, as we illustrate, families blend and switch among various forms of exclusive parental care and care that is shared with others, making distinctions between these two contexts fuzzy at best. We close Part III with a discussion of neighborhood influences on development (Chapter 12).

There is one very important context for early development that is not addressed in this report, namely the media. Today's children spend more time with more media (e.g., television, VCRs, CD players, game systems, computers, among others) than any generation before them, and there is every reason to believe that their media use and exposure will continue to increase (Roberts et al., 1999). Children ages 2 to 4 spend well over 4 hours every day, on average, exposed to the media (primarily television) and over a quarter have televisions in their bedrooms. In many instances, these are noninteractive experiences. For example , almost 15 percent of 2- to 7-year-olds watch television mainly alone (Roberts et al., 1999). We are only beginning to understand the repercussions of these trends for family life and child well-being. Our neglect of this topic is not a signal of any lack of concern; this is clearly an issue that warrants substantial attention.[1]

The science reviewed in this part of the report is more interdisciplinary than that reviewed in Part II, particularly as it moves beyond parents and the home environment. Efforts to understand the effects on development of economic influences, and notably of poverty, have brought together the full spectrum of social and behavioral scientists. Child care has been studied primarily by developmental psychologists, but also by sociologists and economists. As a result, the science base undergirding the understanding of contextual influences has benefited from different methodologies, theoretical perspectives, and standards of evidence, making it both rich and full of controversy.

This literature is not without its shortcomings, however. The major challenge facing those who seek to understand how beyond-the-family contexts affect early development is that parents select these environments. They decide where to live, where and how much to work, whether and

---

[1]A few recent references for interested readers include: Anderson et al. (2000, forthcoming); Calvert (1999); Huston and Wright (1998); Huston et al. (in press); Roberts et al. (1999); Schmitt et al. (1999).

when to place their babies in child care and which child care settings to use, and how to invest their resources. Thus, effects on children that are ascribed to such factors as child care and neighborhoods may, in fact, really be effects of parent selection.

This distinction is extremely important for policy purposes. If, for example, quality child care is associated with children's development because parents who also provide more for their children at home place their children in higher-quality programs, then efforts to improve quality will produce smaller improvements in child well-being than anticipated. If this were true, a more effective strategy would be to provide family-based benefits to more children. Researchers deal with this problem in two ways. First, they measure the family environment and control for it statistically when examining the effects of nonfamily environments, effectively measuring the effects of child care, for example, net of at least some of the effects of the family and home environment. These controls, however, can never capture all of the family environment. Second, they also conduct experiments in which children are more or less randomly assigned to different child care programs (as is the case with early intervention studies) or to different neighborhoods. Of course, children cannot be assigned to different social classes, but one can measure the effects of changes in socioeconomic status (SES) and the effects of SES on siblings who experienced different socioeconomic contexts during the early years of life.

The second challenge concerns genetic influences. Behavior geneticists, in particular, have argued that parents exert their influence on children primarily through their genetic contributions (Rowe, 1994), yet it is increasingly clear that the expression of heritable traits depends substantially on experience, including how parents behave and what they provide for their children (Collins et al., 2000). Behavioral geneticists also argue that socioeconomic status and the benefits it confers on children (including the neighborhoods they live in) largely reflect parents' genetic endowments. As such, efforts to relate children's family SES to their achievement, for example, that do not somehow adjust for parent and child genetic endowments risk overattributing to SES causation what ought to be attributed to genetic influences. Although this argument has merit, we discuss research that places genetic factors in the context of substantially larger SES-based environmental influences on children's development.

With these challenges in mind, our synthesis of research on family-based caregiving influences, socioeconomic influences, child care, and neighborhood influences on early development focuses on the role of experience in early development. The themes that emerge reflect several presented in previous chapters:

- There is a firmer understanding of what constitutes "deprivation," in contrast to "enrichment," during the early years. At the most general level, it is clusters of influences that undermine development rather than isolated or temporary exposures to harm. Far less is known about how bad or enduring these influences need to be in order for change to be done, about factors that enable some children exposed to extremely detrimental circumstances to avoid harmful consequences while others succumb to serious problems, and about capacities and opportunities for recovery.

- At the other end of the spectrum, beyond numerous associations between better environments and better development, little is known about what constitutes "good enough" environments and how the answer to this question varies for different children and families. Similarly, enrichment remains an elusive construct, particularly insofar as it is conceptually linked to contemporary interest in accelerating or improving the development of children who are relatively risk free and on track.

- While there is no evidence that critical or sensitive periods characterize parenting, socioeconomic, child care, or neighborhood influences, there is suggestive evidence that young children compared with older children may be particularly vulnerable to very detrimental experiences that derive from aberrant caregiving and serious economic hardship.

- Children's early pathways can be shifted by efforts to change the contexts of their lives. Less is known, however, about what it really takes to shift the odds, and very little is known about the factors that keep children moving along adaptive pathways once they leave the early childhood years behind.

9 Nurturing Relationships

In this report, we have emphasized the remarkable achievements of young children and the strong developmental thrust that characterizes these accomplishments. Each achievement—language and learning, social development, the emergence of self-regulation—occurs in the context of close relationships with others. These close relationships are typically with parents or those who serve the parenting role in the child's life. We turn our attention to these relationships in this chapter and explore their influence on early development. Although we address young children's relationships with their child care providers given their pervasive and significant role in the earliest years of life, we reserve the fuller discussion of child care for Chapter 11. We start the discussion of parenting with a focused synthesis of the extensive literature on parent-infant attachment, followed by a discussion of other aspects of parenting that extend beyond the provision of emotional security. Next, we examine disruptions in parenting. We include an examination of the orphanage-to-adoption research as a demonstration of the extent to which young children can recover from early adverse experiences when the contexts of their lives change dramatically. We use this as a backdrop for an initial discussion of parenting interventions, which is placed in a broader context in Chapter 13.

INTRODUCTION

Starting with the mother's reproductive health and behavior, the child's primary caregivers—be they parents or grandparents or foster parents—structure the experiences and shape the environments within which early development unfolds. A vast store of research, summarized in this chapter, has confirmed that what young children learn, how they react to the events and people around them, and what they expect from themselves and others are deeply affected by their relationships with parents, the behavior of parents, and the environment of the homes in which they live (Bradley et al., 1988; Collins and Laursen, 1999; Dunn, J., 1993; Hartup and Rubin, 1986; Maccoby and Martin, 1983). Even when young children spend most of their waking hours in child care, parents remain the most influential adults in their lives. We shall also see, however, that efforts to change the course of development by strengthening parenting have met with mixed success. Shifting parental behavior in ways that shift the odds of favorable outcomes for children is often remarkably difficult. This perplexing mismatch between the power of parenting and the difficulty of altering it in ways that are sufficient to affect development is one of the major dilemmas confronting developmental scientists and interventionists alike.

It is important to clarify that we use the term "parenting" to capture the focused and differentiated relationship that the young child has with the adult (or adults) who is (are) most emotionally invested in and consistently available to him or her. Usually this is a birth or adoptive parent (thus the use of the term "parenting"), but sometimes it is a grandparent, a foster parent, or another primary caregiver. *Who* fills this role is far less important than the quality of the relationship she or he establishes with the child. The hallmark of this important relationship is the readily observable fact that this special adult is not interchangeable with others. A child may not care who cuts his hair or takes his money at the toy store, but he cares a great deal about who is holding her when she is unsure, comforts her when she is hurt, and shares special moments in her life.

Understanding Parenting

Parenting has been a centerpiece of developmental inquiry from the beginning of the field, reflecting the firm belief that childrearing makes the child. Only in the 1990s has this belief come under intense scrutiny, in debates over the influence of parenting relative to that of genetics and peers (Borkowski et al., in press; Harris, 1995, 1998; Rowe, 1994). While these debates have focused on children of school age and older (few dispute the significant role of parents during the earliest years of life), they have implications for the understanding of the more enduring influences of parenting in adolescence and adulthood. The controversy, moreover, highlights important shifts in studying and understanding the role of parents in early development.

The classic, early studies of childrearing sought to identify styles of parenting that promoted competent behavior in preschoolers (i.e., a child who is happy, self-reliant, self-controlled, friendly, and cooperative as distinct from withdrawn or immature) (see Baldwin et al., 1945; Baumrind, 1967, 1971, 1973; Emmerich, 1977). The answers yielded by this research highlighted the combined influence of clear standards of conduct, firm control, and ample warmth. The heritage of this research is an abiding interest in both the management or control function and the emotional quality of parent-child relationships. In the ensuing 25 years, however, static characteristics of parents as restrictive or warm have been challenged by substantial evidence that parenting changes over time, varies from one child to another, and is not just received, but is also shaped, by the child's own behavior (Grusec and Goodnow, 1994; Holden and Miller, 1999).

The result is a concept of parenting and parental influence that is more complex and conditional than that which emerged from prior eras of research (Collins et al., 2000; Maccoby, 2000). Succinct formulas for good parenting have been replaced by an appreciation for the many ways in which parents adjust what they do in response to the needs and characteristics of their children, the conditions in which they live, and the circumstances of their own lives (Cowan and Cowan, 1992; Elder, 1991; Holden and O'Dell, 1995). Whereas scientists used to study parenting in isolation, contemporary researchers take into account the network of contexts in which parenting is embedded. These contexts include the child care programs that children attend, the peers they associate with, the stability and socioeconomic strata of their families, their parents' marital relationship, the neighborhoods they live in, and the times they live in.

Challenges to the notion that children are relatively passive players in the socialization process (Bell, 1968; Bell and Chapman, 1986; Engfer et al., 1994) have led to a substantial body of evidence showing the many ways in children contribute to their rearing environments, including influences on the parenting they receive. Researchers now realize that they need to consider the ways in which parents affect children and children affect parents. The growing reliance on research designs that address the interplay of genetics and socialization has both confirmed the substantial influence of parenting on child development and increased awareness of the complex ways in which parenting intersects with the child's inherited strengths and vulnerabilities to affect the pathways that are followed en route to adulthood (see Collins et al., 2000; Rutter et al., in press). The methodological challenges involved are considerable, as discussed in more detail in connection with the effects of impaired parenting. Accordingly, research on parenting has become a very complex endeavor.

Bringing Fathers into the Picture

The research discussed in this chapter on the multifaceted dimensions of parenting is primarily focused on mothering. Fathering, in contrast, has received less attention, and this literature has tended to focus on men's economic contributions to their families, the developmental consequences of father absence, and distinctions between the roles of fathers and mothers (Lamb, 1999; Parke, 1996; Pleck and Pleck, 1997). This began to change in the 1970s with a growing emphasis on family dynamics, including the marital relationship, as they affect child development (see Belsky, 1984; Cummings and O'Reilly, 1997; Dunst, 1985) and is continuing to change as an increasingly interdisciplinary group of scholars is exploring how fathers affect developmental trajectories (see Cabrera et al., 2000).

Contemporary research on fatherhood has highlighted several themes. First, fathers seem to be both more and less involved in their children's lives today than was true even a decade ago, revealing a growing dichotomy in children's experiences of fathering. On one hand, there is evidence that paternal involvement has increased over the past three decades, as seen in higher rates of single fathers raising children, greater involvement of fathers in child care while their wives are in the labor force, and more self-reported time spent by fathers with their children (Pleck, 1997; Yeung et al., 1998). At the same time, unprecedented numbers of children are now spending part or all of their childhoods in families headed by single mothers (see Chapter 10). While there is a growing appreciation of the extensive father involvement that can characterize children in single-mother families and extensive policy interest in the issues involved, scientists are only beginning to explore the factors that predict this involvement (Coley and Chase-Lansdale, 1999; W. Johnson, 1998) and its effects on children (see Garfinkel et al., 1994). It certainly appears to be the case that fathers' economic situation is closely involved. The consequences of these markedly different experiences of fathering for children's development, for their conceptions of parenting, and for their assumption of parenting roles remain largely unexamined.

Second, fathering is increasingly viewed as involving multiple functions that go well beyond the role of breadwinner (Amato and Rivera, 1999; Lamb et al., 1985a; Parke, 1996; Parke and Buriel, 1998). Indeed, there is growing acceptance that father involvement per se is not necessarily linked to positive outcomes for children (see, for example, Hoffman et al., 1999). Rather, it is the variety of ways in which fathers take responsibility for their children that many now believe to be the most important component of fathering (Lamb, in press). This entails not only financial responsibility, but also functions that have typically been thought of as the purview of mothers—tasks such as taking children to the doctor or to lessons, arranging for and transporting the child to and from child care, monitoring the child's safety and whereabouts, and scheduling play dates. As with mothers, the emotional quality of the father-child relationship also appears to be extremely important to children's adjustment and well-being and may, in fact, influence the benefits of increased involvement and responsibility.

Finally, despite the rapid changes affecting the ethnic and racial composition of the nation's families, there is almost no research on how the roles of fathers and other men in young children's lives are evolving in the context of diverse values and family structures (Cabrera et al., 2000). Both theoretical models and empirical work need to incorporate culturally diverse conceptions of fatherhood related to race and ethnicity, as well as other dimensions of culture such as immigrant status and religion.

In the following discussion of parenting, we note the research that specifically addresses fathers. The examples are far from plentiful, but we are hopeful that the renewed attention to fathering that is now characterizing developmental science will foster expanded efforts to study parenting in all of its varieties and certainly as it involves both mothers and fathers.

ATTACHMENT RELATIONSHIPS

What gives the parent a special place in the young child's life? What does the close emotional relationship with the parent provide that other adults cannot replicate? To answer such questions, researchers have focused on the development of security, confidence, and trust between infants and toddlers and their parents. This central feature of early relationships is captured by the concept of "attachment security." In the rare situations in which infants do not have the opportunity to form an attachment with even one trusted adult, their development can deteriorate rapidly and dramatically. The remarkable recovery that these infants display once they receive stable care and loving attention further reveals the importance of the child's earliest intimate relationships. Indeed, long ago the field was riveted by evidence that toddlers who were languishing in institutional settings could be made to thrive cognitively, emotionally, and physically simply by providing them with loving care—even if this meant that they were moved onto wards for young women with mental retardation who held them, played with them, hugged them, and lavished attention on them. As dramatic, the remarkable recovery observed today in children adopted from orphanages in Romania and other areas of the world speaks to the power of consistent care, attention, and affection in the lives of young children.

Virtually all infants develop close emotional bonds, or attachments, to those who regularly care for them in the early years of life. These early attachments constitute a deeply rooted motivational system that ensures close contact between babies and adult caregivers who can protect, nurture, and guide their development. Indeed, the infant appears to be so strongly motivated and prepared to develop attachments to one or more caregivers that, given the opportunity to interact regularly with even a modestly responsive caregiver, he or she will develop an emotional tie to that person.

Those who study attachment believe that children's first relationships, especially with their parents or other primary caregivers, address two fundamental needs (Ainsworth, 1973; Ainsworth et al., 1978; Belsky and Cassidy, 1994; Bowlby, 1969; Cassidy, 1999; Sroufe, 1996). First, the caregiver's company reduces a young child's fear in novel or challenging situations and enables the child to explore with confidence (so-called secure base behavior) and to manage stress (Ainsworth, 1967; Emde, 1980; Emde and Easterbrooks, 1985; Gunnar, in press; Gunnar et al., 1996). "Stay here so I can do it myself!" captures this emotional regulation function of early attachments in the words of a toddler. Second, attachment relationships strengthen a young child's sense of competence and efficacy. The adult's contingent responding strengthens a young child's awareness of being able to influence others and affect the world (Carson and Parke, 1996; Cassidy et al., 1992; Denham et al., 1997; Hooven et al., 1994). This might be called, therefore, the self-efficacy function of early attachment relationships.

Well before the first birthday, infants clearly exhibit preferences for and special responsiveness to certain adults. About the time children become more mobile (i.e., 6-12 months), they organize their behavior to maintain proximity to one or a few people. They advance into the world to explore, but return periodically to touch base with these people. If frightened, they seek proximity and physical contact, and when forced to be separated from them, they often protest, sometimes frantically. In short, they appear to use these people as secure bases. Secure base behavior describes the presence of an attachment bond, and toddlers show in these behaviors that they are gradually acquiring an awareness of the psychological qualities of other people (Stern, 1985; Tomasello et al., 1993) and constructing expectations for their behavior (Gekoski et al., 1983; Lamb and Malkin, 1986).

Security of Attachment

Although virtually all infants become attached to their caregivers, attachment relationships differ in how much security they provide. Assessments of attachment security, whether conducted in a laboratory or at home, focus on the child's exploratory behavior in the presence of the caregiver, responses to separation, and reactions upon reunion. A secure attachment is assumed to exist when the infant or toddler explores comfortably in the presence of his or her caregiver, keeps track of and seeks proximity with the caregiver, happily and eagerly seeks contact after having been separated, and, in general, shows signs of trust and delight in the caregiver's presence. In contrast, children whose exploratory play is disrupted because they are preoccupied with the caregiver, who avoid or resist contact after separation, display distress and anger upon reunion, and are not easily comforted are considered insecurely attached. An insecure attachment is not, however, equivalent to no attachment at all. Even a young child who is insecure about the caregiver's nurturance derives important emotional support from her presence that is not derived from the company of someone to whom the child has no attachment at all. After all, even a resistant infant turns to the caregiver for help.

Recent research on children who have experienced highly disruptive, sometimes abusive care has led to important refinements in views of insecure attachment. Studies of physically abused infants and toddlers have noted significantly elevated proportions of insecure attachments (Crittenden, 1988; Lyons-Ruth et al., 1987), as have studies of children of clinically depressed mothers (DeMulder and Radke-Yarrow, 1991; Lyons-Ruth et al., 1990, 1991). Studies of neglected children, such as those reared in orphanages or removed from their homes because of severe neglect, have shown that some, but certainly not all, of these children do not seem to organize their behavior in meaningful ways around one or a few adults. They do not fit typical patterns of insecurity, but rather display inconsistent and disorganized responses to their caregivers. The field is just beginning to document these unusual patterns of attachment behavior and to explore their clinical roots and implications for children's development. We are far from being able to say anything definitive about these disordered patterns of attachment behavior, but they form one of the cores of the nascent field of infant mental health (Osofsky and Fitzgerald, 2000; Zeanah, 2000). This field of clinical research, albeit new, highlights what has become increasingly evident: infants and young children have rich emotional/psychological lives and can suffer in ways that heretofore had never been realized.

The interest in documenting unusual patterns of attachment behavior in search of a better understanding of infant mental health and disorder increases the need to broaden cultural understanding of attachment and the assessment of its security. It is important to realize that the laboratory assessments that have formed the basis for much of the research on attachment security have been designed to produce only mild challenges for the infant. The meaning of the laboratory assessment depends on whether the challenges are both mild and meaningful within the child's culture and life history.

For example, the standard laboratory assessment (termed the "strange situation") relies on brief (e.g., 3 minute) separations from the parent. In cultures in which infants are frequently separated from parents for brief periods, the child's reactions are presumably influenced by expectations, based on previous history, that the parent will return and be helpful. In cultures in which separations rarely occur, it is presumed that these experimentally imposed separations may take on a very different meaning for the infant. Indeed, research on Japanese infants who are rarely separated from parents during their first year initially demonstrated high rates of presumably insecure attachment (Takahashi, 1986, 1990). Later reinterpretations of the results, however, emphasized the vast difference in the strange situation between the Japanese and European-American cultures (van IJzendoorn and Sagi, 1999).

A study of desirable and undesirable attachment behavior among white and Hispanic (Puerto Rican) mothers provides a compelling illustration of these differences (Harwood et al., 1995). The white mothers preferred that toddlers balance autonomy and relatedness (playing at a distance and involving the mother prior to separation and greeting the mother happily during the reunion), and they disliked clinginess (clinging to the mother prior to separation, crying continuously during separation, and being unhappy during the reunion). In contrast, Puerto Rican mothers preferred that toddlers display respectfulness (sitting near the mother and waiting for a signal before playing with the toys prior to separation, waiting quietly for the mother to return during separation), and they disliked highly active or avoidant (ignoring the mother before, during, and after separation) behavior.

This and other cross-cultural evidence on attachment raises significant issues regarding the ways in which parents and young children form expectations about each other and, in turn, behave and react in each other's presence (and in the strange situation). We strongly suspect that, across all cultures, children form attachments and use parents as sources of security and comfort. Even when the relationship is somewhat insecure, children seek comfort and maintain proximity to parents, deriving important emotional support from the caregiver's presence that other adults cannot provide; however, they do not derive the same developmental benefits that accrue from a secure attachment.

Specific attachment patterns result from an intricate interplay among characteristics of the child, the capacities of the parent, and the broader context of their relationship (see Isabella, 1995; Lamb et al., 1985b; Thompson, 1999a, for reviews). Secure attachments are seen more often in the context of parenting that is dependable and sensitive to the child's intentions and needs, enabling the child to count on the caregiver's future availability and assistance (Ainsworth et al., 1978; Belsky, 1999; De Wolff and van IJzendoorn, 1997; Isabella, 1995; Thompson, 1997, 1998a). Infants and toddlers are less likely to establish secure attachments with caregivers who are generally detached, intrusive, erratic, or rejecting. The important role of sensitive caregiving in the establishment of secure attachments is compellingly illustrated by a recent intervention that randomly assigned low-income mothers of infants who were observed in the first two weeks of life to be irritable to a program designed to enhance maternal sensitivity and responsiveness or to a control group. After 9 months, the mothers who had received the programs were significantly more responsive and stimulating than the control group mothers and their infants engaged in more sophisticated exploratory behavior and were significantly more likely to be securely attached (van den Boom, 1994, 1995). A follow-up when the children were $3^1/_2$ years old documented sustained effects in maternal sensitivity, attachment security, and the children's observed cooperation with the mother. Interestingly, the husbands of mothers who participated in the intervention were also more responsive to their preschoolers. Adoption studies add to the evidence regarding the importance of sensitive, responsive care. Toddlers fostered or adopted from conditions of extreme neglect have been found to reorganize their attachment behavior over time, exhibiting behavior reflective of secure expectations of support and comfort as they adapt to foster or adoptive parents who provide sensitive, responsive, and consistent care (Chisholm, 1998; Dozier, in press a, in press b; O'Connor et al., 1999).

Providing sensitive, responsive, and consistent parenting of infants and toddlers is challenging work. Both characteristics of the child and of the parent can make this type of parenting difficult to achieve. For example, newborns who continue to react to repeated stimuli after other newborns have tuned out or habituated to the repeated stimulation are somewhat more likely to form insecure attachment relationships to caregivers (Warren et al., 1997). Babies who become disorganized when stressed and those who get very upset when limits are placed on their actions are also somewhat more likely to develop insecure attachments (Fox, 1985; Gunnar et al., 1996; Izard et al., 1991). These infant characteristics don't predestine children to insecure attachment; rather they shift the odds. This may be because it is harder for people to provide the sensitive parenting such children need. It may be because it is not clear what the baby needs or because the needs of such infants exceed the time, attention, and sensitivity that the parents can provide given all of the demands on them. Indeed, when parents can manage to maintain high degrees of sensitivity and responsiveness, even temperamentally difficult infants develop secure and trusting relationships (Goldberg, 1990; Mangelsdorf et al., 1990; van IJzendoorn et al., 1995). Challenging parental life circumstances can also result in an imbalance between the infant's needs and what the parent can provide. Emotional problems such as depression, economic stress, and marital conflict can interfere with sensitive and responsive parenting, be disruptive of secure attachments (see Belsky and Isabella, 1988; Thompson, 1999b; Waters, 1978), and constitute a significant source of instability over time in attachment security.

It also appears to be the case that atypical attachments are more common among atypical samples, including premature infants, children with Down syndrome, and children with autism (Atkinson et al., 1999; Capps et al., 1994). In particular, a significantly larger share of children at the extremes of reproductive risk or who have an identifiable developmental disability display disorganized or unclassifiable patterns of attachment to their mothers. Much remains to be understood about the meaning and consequences of atypical attachments. They may arise from problems parents experience in being sensitive to their child (i.e., difficulty of reading the infant's cues), from these children's cognitive limitations, from the added stress that can accompany raising a child with special needs, or from limitations of the typical model for studying attachment when applied to these special populations. There is a tremendous need for research in this area, given its role in elucidating child factors and surrounding conditions that impinge on early attachments, as well as the developmental significance of behavioral differences in patterns of relating to important others among both atypically and typically developing children (see Vondra and Barnett, 1999).

Mothers and Others

The large majority of research on early attachments has focused on the parent-child relationship and, specifically, on the mother-infant relationship, despite the fact that young children establish close relationships with a surprising variety of people, including relatives, child care providers, and friends. Children certainly develop secure attachments to their fathers that do not depend on the security they derive from their attachments to mothers (Thompson et al., 1985). Grandmothers are also important attachment figures, and their support of the mother can facilitate secure attachment in infants (Crockenberg, 1987; Myers et al., 1987). Grandmothers are an especially important source of child care during the earliest months and years of life, as we discuss in Chapter 11.

Howes (1999) proposed the following three criteria for identification of attachment figures other than the mother: provision of physical and emotional care, continuity or consistency in the child's life, and emotional investment in the child. We do not know whether there is a specific limit to the number of people with whom very close emotional connections can be established at different ages. Regardless of their number and variety, from the child's perspective, close personal relationships are not interchangeable. The child may turn to a substitute attachment figure or even a relatively unfamiliar but friendly person when the preferred one is not available, but the distress about the loss of one beloved person is not easily alleviated by the ongoing availability of the others, as many parents faced with their children's reactions when a beloved babysitter or child care teacher goes out of their lives can attest.

Young children clearly benefit from opportunities to develop close relationships with different caregivers. As with the mother, the security of these relationships is based primarily on the trust and confidence that each adult has inspired in the child. It is also clear that the child's primary caregiver (usually the mother) remains central in this constellation of attachment relationships (Berlin and Cassidy, 1999; Howes, 1999; NICHD Early Child Care Research Network, 1997a). The security of attachment between a mother and her child is more influential on early psychosocial growth than are the relationships a child has with other caregivers at home or outside the home, and even children in extensive child care continue to show an overwhelming preference for their mothers (Easterbrooks and Goldberg, 1990; NICHD Early Child Care Research Network, 1997a, 1998a, 1998b, 1999a, in press(a)). Although there once was concern that spending many hours in nonparental care might undermine the child's primary relationships, recent studies now reassure parents that this is not the case (Berlin and Cassidy, 1999; Easterbrooks and Goldberg, 1990; Howes, 1999; NICHD Early Child Care Research Network, 1997a).

Moreover, attachment relationships are specific to each adult, so that an insecure attachment to one caregiver may develop at the same time that a secure relationship grows with another (Howes et al., 1988; Suess et al., 1992). For example, children often exhibit secure attachment behavior with one parent but not the other (Belsky et al., 1996a). Infants and toddlers who develop secure attachments either to their mothers *or* their child care providers are observed to be more mature and positive in their interactions with adults and peers than are children who lack a secure attachment. However, the most socially skilled children are those who have established secure attachments with both their mothers and care providers (Howes et al., 1995a). In this context, it is important to recognize that child care can be used effectively to provide respite for highly stressed parents who may be prone to child abuse or at risk of having their children placed in foster care (Crittenden, 1983; Kempe, 1987; Roditti, 1995; Subramanian, 1985). Unfortunately, as a result of pervasively high turnover in child care providers and frequent changes in arrangements, children are more often insecurely than securely attached to their child care providers (Galinsky et al., 1994; Howes, 1999; Seltenheim et al., 1997; Whitebook et al., 1990).

At a minimum, this knowledge indicates that the significance of a young child's attachments to caregivers other than their mothers and fathers merit respect and consideration. It also raises very significant issues for intervention efforts focused exclusively on parent-child relationships and suggests the value of extending these efforts to embrace other significant adults in the young child's life.

Links to Development

Early attachments are important not only as an indicator of the parent-child relationship, but also for their significant effects on other aspects of the child's functioning. They appear to have their most consistent and enduring influence on young children's social and emotional development, although they also foster the exploratory behavior that is so vital to early learning and seem to bolster parents' efforts to support learning (Matas et al., 1978; also, see Thompson, 1998b and 1999a, for reviews). We are, however, only beginning to understand the mechanisms that underlie these connections between parent-child attachment and developmental outcomes.

Longitudinal studies suggest that early attachments set the stage for other relationships, as children move into the broader world beyond the immediate family (Bretherton and Munholland, 1999; Sroufe and Fleeson, 1986, 1988; Thompson, 1998a). This occurs as young children acquire the ability to encode their early attachment relationships at the level of mental representations, which, in turn, guide their expectations about the availability and responsiveness of other partners. In this sense, research on internal representations of relationships converges with cognitive research on the child's unfolding theory of mind, as reviewed in Chapter 6. Securely attached young children compared with their insecurely attached peers have an easier time developing positive, supportive relationships with teachers, friends, and others whom they encounter as they grow up (Sroufe and Egeland, 1991; Sroufe et al., 1993; Thompson, 1998a, 1999a). Securely attached children may respond more positively to unfamiliar people (such as new classmates, a family acquaintance, or a substitute teacher) as well. It appears, however, that the positive expectations for close relationships that are inspired by a secure parent-child relationship—or, in the case of insecurely attached children, their distrust or ambivalence—are most apparent in their encounters with familiar partners.

There is also emerging evidence that securely attached young children are found, for example, to have a more balanced self-concept (Cassidy, 1988; Verschueren et al., 1996), more advanced memory processes (Belsky et al., 1996b; Kirsh and Cassidy, 1997), a more sophisticated grasp of emotion (Laible and Thompson, 1998), a more positive understanding of friendship (Cassidy et al., 1996; Kerns, 1996; Park and Waters, 1989) and they show greater conscience development (Kochanska, 1995, 1997; Laible and Thompson, in press) than insecurely attached children. These associations are especially evident when attachment security and other behaviors are measured at the same point in time, thus displaying a dense web of associated outcomes.

Beyond these specific developmental outcomes, secure attachments seem to play a very important role in shaping the systems that underlie children's reactivity to stressful situations. As discussed in Chapter 8, experiments with animals have yielded similar findings (Suomi, 1997) and further suggest that early mothering can affect the neural circuitry that governs behavioral stress responses in the offspring (Caldji et al., 1998; Liu et al., 1997). The development of noninvasive means of studying the activation of the stress-hormone system that produces cortisol has allowed the study of stress physiology in the everyday lives of infants and young children. The results of these studies indicate that, as in the work on nonhuman primates (Gunnar et al., 1981; Levine and Wiener, 1988) and human adults (Cohen and Wills, 1985), stress in young children is intimately linked with social experiences. About the time that infants begin to form specific attachments to adults, the presence of caregivers who are warm and responsive begins to buffer or prevent elevations in stress hormones, even in situations that elicit behavioral indicators of distress in the infant (Gunnar et al., 1996; Nachmias et al., 1996; Spangler and Schieche, 1994). In contrast, insecure attachment relationships are associated with higher cortisol levels in potentially threatening situations (Gunnar et al., 1992; Hertsgaard et al., 1995; Nachmias et al., 1996; Tout et al., 1998).

For example, in one study, toddlers were exposed to a live clown who entered the room and invited them to "come over and play." Toddlers who were securely attached to the parent who accompanied them showed no rise in stress hormones to this strange event, even if they were frightened and wary of the clown and were generally described by the parent as more temperamentally fearful and anxious. In contrast, toddlers who showed the same behavioral signs of fear and wariness and were described as having a similarly fearful and anxious temperament, but who had an insecure attachment to the parent who was with them, showed significant elevations in this stress hormone. This was true despite the fact that the security of the attachment relationship was assessed separately, on a different day, and in a different context (i.e., the strange situation; Nachmias et al., 1996). These studies with infants and young children seem to be saying that secure emotional relationships with adults appear to be at least as critical as individual differences in temperament in determining stress system reactivity and regulation.

Beyond this emerging evidence regarding physiological reactions to stress, there is much to learn about how secure attachments function to promote and protect early development. Some have proposed that secure attachments enhance the child's receptivity to other facets of parents' socialization efforts. From this standpoint, a secure attachment inducts the child into what has been characterized as a "mutual orientation of positive reciprocity" between parent and child (Kochanska, 1997; Maccoby, 1983, 1992; Maccoby and Martin, 1983). This mutuality, in turn, heightens the child's receptivity to the many ways in which parents socialize their children to get along with others, deal effectively with conflict, and become motivated early learners (Kochanska, 1997; Kochanska and Thompson, 1997; Waters et al., 1991). The children, in effect, are more receptive to the parent's instruction, guidance, and teaching, which then reinforces the parent's sensitive parenting and, in all likelihood, further binds their secure attachment.

This evidence of the developmental significance of secure attachments supports the focus on relationship building in early intervention studies with high-risk populations of children. It is also important to recognize, however, that the effects of early attachment relationships are provisional and contingent on many other influences on psychosocial growth, as well as on continuity or change in the parent-child relationship itself (Sroufe et al., 1990, 1999). The security or insecurity of attachment relationships can change in the early years of life. A child who begins with an insecure relationship may, for example, later have opportunities to develop a sense of secure confidence in the same caregiver. Changes in attachment may arise from changing family circumstances, such as the birth of a sibling or periods of family stress (Cummings and Davies, 1994a; Teti et al., 1996a; Vaughn et al., 1979). There is therefore no guarantee that the influence of early attachment security will endure, unless that security is maintained for the child in the years that follow. The instability of early attachments renders efforts to trace long-term consequences very difficult. At best, we can conclude that the effects of early secure attachments are conditional. They shift the odds toward more adaptive development, but subsequent experiences and relationships can modify their longer-term impacts, sometimes substantially.

BEYOND ATTACHMENT SECURITY

Although the attachment relationship may bolster the parent's attempts to produce desired behavior in the child, fostering a secure attachment relationship is far from all that parents do in the early years of the child's life to promote healthy development. In essence, parents must have the personal skills to interact constructively with their children, the organizational skills to manage their lives inside and outside the home, and the problem-solving skills to address the many challenges that children invariably present. Doing this well requires sensitivity to the child and an ability to read, interpret, and anticipate what the child needs and how the child is responding to the world. It also requires supports, like child care and social networks, and resources that come with economic security.

Capturing the almost infinite variety of ways in which parents carry out their childrearing responsibilities is, of course, an impossible task. Some variations are related to the cultural context in which the family lives. Others are related to the economic resources that are available to them. Still others are forged in response to the characteristics and needs of individual children, or represent the best efforts of parents who are struggling with problems of their own. Even within relatively homogenous groups, parents deploy their childrearing responsibilities in widely differing ways. Confronted with this task, researchers have continued to pursue the dimensions of control and warmth, but they have also extended their reach to capture the ways in which parents support learning and make investments and choices that affect the well-being and future prospects of their children. There is also a growing interest in the ways in which parents convey cultural values and traditions to their children and adjust what they do in light of the attributes they want their children to have. We have organized our discussion of these issues by addressing parents' role in fostering cooperation and the development of a conscience, encouraging exploration and learning, and raising their children to live adaptively in differing cultural contexts.

Fostering Cooperation and the Development of a Conscience

The growth of cooperation in the context of close relationships has been studied much less intensively in young children than has the growth of love in the context of attachment. Yet at the same time that attachment security is taking shape late in the first year through the sensitivity and warmth of the caregiver, another dimension of the relationship is being forged by the negotiation of conflict between parent and child. Developmental scientists are showing renewed attention to this aspect of the parent-child relationship because of its relevance to the early origins of psychosocial problems in young children, including defiance, withdrawal, and conduct problems (Caspi et al., 1995; Moffitt, 1990; White et al., 1990), as well as its contribution to the emergence of conscience, moral values, and consideration for others (Kochanska and Thompson, 1997).

Young children can experience conflict with virtually every family member, as well as with the peers with whom they play. As noted earlier, for example, getting along with peers is one of the central developmental tasks of early childhood. Sibling relationships are also a potent arena for conflict between young children, as well as for empathy, cooperation, and social comparison (Dunn, 1993; Dunn and Kendrick, 1982). How parents manage these episodes of conflict can be significant for how young children learn about the feelings of others, the skills of competent sociability, and how to negotiate and cooperate. Even more important, however, is conflict between a young child and a parent because of the significance of their attachment relationship and the adult's capacity to guide the child in learning how to manage disagreement and defiance.

Young children's conflicts with caregivers who are skilled at helping them learn to manage experiences of disagreement and defiance early in life can provide a foundation for the growth of empathy and prosocial motivation, as well as the development of skills for negotiating and successfully resolving conflicts with others (Eisenberg and Murphy, 1995; Goodnow, 1996, 1997). These conflicts do not need to be momentous; in fact, they often arise in the context of everyday exchanges in which, for example, parents say "no" to a child's request (e.g., for a snack, for a particular dress) or attempt to gain the child's cooperation (e.g., picking up toys or taking a bath). In this light, how young children experience conflict with their caregivers provides a forum for learning how to address conflict in their encounters with others throughout life. Conflicts and the negotiations they entail also provide essential practice as children learn acceptable ways to elicit help and to be assertive about their own needs and interests. They also provide opportunities for parents to learn how best to issue directives and make requests of their child. Little is currently known with assurance about how these experiences become catalysts for the growth of prosocial behavior and the rudiments of conscience, or the development of dysfunctional social behavior. It is clear, however, that nothing focuses a young child's attention on what others are thinking, feeling, and expecting better than the realization that conflict with that person must be resolved.

Research in this area has moved away from static characterizations of parenting style (e.g., authoritarian, permissive) toward a more dynamic understanding of what parents are doing when they set limits, create incentives, and administer punishments. As a result, researchers are now trying to understand how parents and others work with young children to foster capacities for safe, socially acceptable, self-regulated behavior in the context of conflict. This, in turn, shifts attention from whether parents are doing the right things or the wrong things to limit unacceptable behaviors, to how they encourage the joint resolution of conflict and the social understanding and skills that come with it. The focus of inquiry is thus less on the moment of conflict, anger, or frustration and more on what happens next.

This perspective also focuses attention on moments of "negotiable disagreement" (Goodnow, 1996), in which children try out a variety of strategies and in which parents—North American parents at least—teach children about the more or less acceptable ways to phrase a dissent or to negotiate a compromise (Kuczynski, 1993; Kuczynski and Kochanska, 1990). Among the strategies that children learn are deferral ("later, ok?"), offering a compromise, offering a reason for not complying, and acting as if no directive or request had been made (Kuczynski and Kochanska, 1990; Leonard, 1993). The phenomenon of interest then becomes the particular areas on which negotiation or divergence in values are more or less acceptable, and the particular ways in which differences are accepted, negotiated, or encouraged (Goodnow, 1997). The second and third years of life appear to be pivotal for the child's emerging capacities and inclination to be cooperative and considerate toward others. Toddlers are developing the cognitive skills to understand parental standards and apply them to their own behavior and achieving capacities for self-regulation that enable them increasingly to comply with internalized standards of conduct (Kopp, 1982, 1987; Kopp and Wyer, 1994). They are also becoming increasingly aware of the feelings and perspectives of others, which provides a resource for empathic responding to another in distress (Zahn-Waxler and Radke-Yarrow, 1990; Zahn-Waxler et al., 1992).

At the same time, the parent-child relationship is changing, as the child's growing assertiveness and the parents' growing use of prohibitions and sanctions lead to what can sometimes seem like endless conflicts of will (Biringen et al., 1995; Campos et al., 1992b). Parents now use emotional signals to convey approval or disapproval, sometimes before the obviously contemplated act of misbehavior even occurs (Emde and Buchsbaum, 1990; Emde et al., 1987). All young children internalize messages from these interactions; what is of interest is what they internalize.

These experiences during the toddler years provide the first opportunities for the child to answer the question, "What must I do to maintain good relations with others?" In the years that follow, the child's understanding of how to manage conflict becomes elaborated as the behavioral expectations of parents expand to incorporate consideration for others, basic skills at self-care, safety concerns, and compliance with family routines and manners (Gralinski and Kopp, 1993). The strategies used by parents to elicit cooperation also change to build on the child's maturing capacities for self-regulation. Specifically, they begin to rely more on explanations, bargaining, indirect guidance, and other nonassertive strategies (Belsky et al., 1996c; Crockenberg and Litman, 1990; Kuczynski et al., 1987). At the same time, however, children are also asserting their own independent judgment, making the preschool years ones of greater cooperation and greater conflict between parents and their offspring (Kuczynski and Kochanska, 1990; Kuczynski et al., 1987). Young children tend to comply more with behavioral standards as they reach the preschool years, but they also show a greater tendency to refuse before they comply and to negotiate, compromise, and display other indicators of self-assertion (Gralinski and Kopp, 1993; Vaughn et al., 1984).

Complicating this process is the fact that young children want to feel that they are in control of their lives. Long before babies understand that *they* are the ones making things happen, the controllability and predictability of stimulation affects their attention, emotions, and behavioral reactions (Sullivan et al., 1991). In studying face-to-face interactions between young infants and their caregivers, for example, researchers have noted that after a period of back and forth smiles and vocalization that often build in intensity, babies will look away. Skilled caregivers react by remaining quiet for a moment. The baby then looks back and the two begin to interact again. Unskilled caregivers or ones who are depressed sometimes ignore the cue or try even harder to get the baby's attention when he looks away. This often makes the baby fussy and irritable and increases the time he looks away. Overall, in pairs in which the baby controls the action (by looking toward and away), the caregiver keeps the infant's attention longer and elicits more smiles, coos, and active infant participation. Social interaction with a baby, however, is somewhat of a one-way street. Let the adult be the one to turn away and ignore the baby (e.g., to answer the phone), and the baby often doesn't wait patiently for the adult to look back; he gets more demanding.

By 1 year of age, being able to control the action can actually alleviate fearful responses to potentially frightening events. In one study discussed earlier (Gunnar, 1980), 12-month-olds were presented with a toy monkey that clangs symbols and flashes its eyes and can be quite frightening to children this young. The infants who were able to turn the toy on for a few seconds at a time did so repeatedly and often smiled and laughed. They liked it. In contrast, the children who could not control its actions were often upset, cried, and tried to get away from it. For older children, issues of control have been studied in the context of more subtle situations in which, for example, adults offer rewards if children engage in certain activities or are highly directive and intrusive while children are at work on a task (Fagot, 1973; Hamilton and Gordon, 1978; Lepper et al., 1973). These circumstances presumably undermine children's sense of autonomy and feelings that they are engaged in an activity because they want to do it. In fact, following these manipulations, children's levels of interest and persistence decline significantly. These situations are not unlike those in which a parent insists that a child clean up his room before he can play outside or finish her dinner before she can have dessert. The challenge for parents is one of encouraging cooperation while also fostering feelings of control and self-determination that lead the child to cooperate because he or she wants to. This also entails learning when to push for cooperation and when not to; when to go along with the child's requests and when to say "no." As we saw earlier (Parpal and Maccoby, 1985), children are more likely to cooperate with parents who have on a previous occasion shown that they are willing to follow a child's interests.

Beginning in early childhood, as these examples illustrate, cooperation is not primarily a matter of whether parents consistently and firmly enforce their intentions on offspring, but is rather an interactional process in which a child's capacities to understand, agree with, and be motivated to comply by a positive parent-child relationship are also important (Grusec and Goodnow, 1994; Kuczynski et al., 1997). Interactions that, at one extreme, become highly coercive and engage parents and children in escalating battles of will can contribute to the mix of factors that place children on a path toward dysfunctional social behavior (Dodge, 1990; Patterson et al., 1992). Alternatively, when these interactions are characterized by clear and consistently enforced limits, low levels of emotional arousal, ample affection, and a deemphasis on the use of power, threats, and criticism (Campbell, 1997; Herrera and Dunn, 1997; Lepper, 1981; Maccoby, 1992; Zahn-Waxler et al., 1979), children learn to observe and ultimately internalize their parents' standards of conduct.

Caregivers who are warm and provide clear expectations for child behavior that are consistently enforced also encourage early conscience development (Eisenberg and Murphy, 1995; Kochanska, 1991, 1993, 1995). At times, this can involve directly focusing the child's attention on the consequences of misbehavior (especially when those consequences involve harm to others) or their responsibility for harm, explaining why certain actions are inappropriate or harmful, or drawing attention to the needs of another person whom the child can assist (Hoffman, 1983, 1988; Zahn-Waxler and Kochanska, 1990; Zahn-Waxler et al., 1979). The benefits of these activities for the child are enhanced when parents themselves model morally responsible behavior and respond prosocially to others. In short, when parents are clear about their expectations (e.g., "you need to put your action figures back in the box before we eat lunch") and direct but noncoercive in enforcing them (e.g., "we'll eat lunch as soon as you are done"), rather than threatening (e.g., "if you don't hurry up, you won't see those action figures for a week") in the context of a warm relationship with the child, early moral understanding is most likely to thrive (Eisenberg and Murphy, 1995).

Early conscience also grows significantly in contexts other than direct conflict over misbehavior. When parents and offspring converse about the day's events, for example, moral lessons are often implicit in what the adult conveys and what the child learns from their conversation (Dunn, 1987, 1988; Dunn et al., 1995). In these situations, moreover, children can reflect on what they hear—whether the conversation concerns the reasons for a sibling's outburst, the parent's response to being wronged, or a recounting of the child's own previous misbehavior—without the heightened emotion that may make it difficult for a young child to learn the same lessons in the context of a discipline encounter. Moreover, everyday family life is characterized by routines that enlist the young child's cooperation in rituals like bedtime, storyreading, waking, mealtimes, bathing, and other recurrent, predictable events (Fiese et al., 1999; Miller and Goodnow, 1995). The presence of these routines is one way of making expectations known and of avoiding constant confrontations. Children thus learn cooperation not only in the context of conflictual encounters and occasions for mutual give and take, but also in the predictable flow of daily life.

Interactions with siblings as well as parents are also important catalysts to early moral understanding, especially in relation to disputes over rights, possessions, and territory (Dunn and Munn, 1987; Slomkowski and Dunn, 1992; Tesla and Dunn, 1992). And at times, parents foster early conscience development when they devise alternative control strategies, such as avoiding a discipline encounter by proactively structuring circumstances or providing anticipatory guidance, each of which succeed in enlisting the child's cooperation in a nonconfrontational manner (Belsky et al., 1996c; Holden, 1983). Although these influences have been studied almost exclusively in the context of parent-child relationships (especially mother-child interactions), there is reason to believe that they are also important in the child's relationships with other caregivers, including fathers, grandparents, child care providers, and teachers.

The ways that caregivers can best support early conscience development also depend on the young child's temperamental characteristics (Kochanska, 1991, 1993, 1995). Depending on the extent to which a child is dispositionally more inhibited and fearful, for example, the parent's disciplinary efforts may either provoke cooperation or distressed withdrawal. Relatively gentle discipline characterized by suggestions and reasoning appears to be especially important for these children, for whom power assertive techniques are neither necessary nor effective. It is important for caregivers to calibrate their response to misbehavior according to the child's personality attributes, as well as the child's tolerance for stress and capacities for understanding. Regardless of temperament, however, developmental researchers have found that a secure, positive relationship with the parent is the best predictor of early moral growth. In a sense, a relationship of warmth and mutual responsiveness provides a context in which the parent's values and standards are most likely to be believed, accepted, and adopted by the young child (Kochanska, 1991, 1993, 1995).

Encouraging Exploration and Learning

Our prior discussion of children's emerging capacities for communication and learning (Chapter 6) documented the many ways in which parents support young children's linguistic and cognitive development. Much of early learning, in short, requires environmental supports, and children are dependent on their parents for providing them.

Starting in infancy, researchers have sought to identify the facets of parenting that are associated with higher scores on various tests of developmental status and cognitive abilities. The contingency and sensitivity with which parents respond to their baby's cues emerge consistently as important correlates of early cognitive outcomes (Beckwith and Cohen, 1989; Beckwith and Parmelee, 1986; Donovan and Leavitt, 1978; Landry et al., 1997; Vietze and Anderson, 1980). Infants whose parents can interpret, adjust their own behavior, and respond appropriately to their bids for attention, moods and states, expressions of interest, and efforts to communicate their needs are more advanced on virtually all assessments of developmental and cognitive status. Sensitive give and take between parent and infant appears to get children off to a good start on early markers of cognitive growth, just as it facilitates secure attachments. Other aspects of parenting that have shown positive associations with these outcomes include encouragement of exploration (in contrast to highly restrictive parenting), provision of a rich verbal environment, and ample amounts of nurturance and warmth (Clarke-Stewart et al., 1979; Cowan et al., 1991; Olson et al., 1986; Pettit et al., 1997). These features point to parents' role in creating an environment that is playful and nurturing, is rich in conversation, strikes a balance between safety and freedom to explore, and, in general, builds a belief in the child that the world is a receptive and responsive place.

A related literature has focused more directly on the interplay between the child's emerging capacities and the parents' ability to structure learning opportunities to both bolster and challenge these capacities. Originally proposed by the Russian psychologist Vygotsky (e.g., Vygotsky, 1978), children's learning is assumed to proceed optimally when parents (and teachers) present material in the child's "zone of proximal development." This zone is defined in terms of tasks that are difficult for the child to perform independently but have components that can be accomplished with assistance. These kinds of processes, which have been portrayed as scaffolding (Wood, 1986; Wood et al., 1976), emphasize the ways in which parents orchestrate children's experiences to provide them with the most effective levels of support. Although most of the studies in this area have been concerned with cognitive development, parents have been observed to engage in the same kinds of supportive activities as they facilitate their children's entry into peer groups, with demonstrated benefits for the child's later social skills (Finnie and Russell, 1988). They undoubtedly apply, as well, to other situations in which parents attempt to manage or shape children's experiences—from making play dates to arranging child care—so that they remain within the child's tolerances for stimulation and challenge, while also fostering new capabilities (see, for example, Parke and Buriel, 1998).

These processes have also been examined in the cross-cultural literature on the teaching and learning roles of children and parents. This research has directed attention to the culturally organized ways in which adults involve children in routine activities and interactions, supportively structure their activities, and gradually transfer responsibility for specific tasks as the children acquire understanding and expertise (Goodnow, 1996; Ochs, 1992; Rogoff, 1990). In this sense, early learning is portrayed as a form of apprenticeship that is enacted in different ways in different cultures (Rogoff et al., 1991). For example, in some cultural communities, parents directly instruct children, play with them, and engage in conversations with them that are structured around materials and activities geared to the children's interests and abilities. In other communities, children are expected to learn through observation and participation in adult activities and through play with siblings and peers.

The cross-cultural literature has also called attention to the role that parents' expectations about the importance of various forms of achievement play in children's early learning—their familiarity with particular task strategies, their investments of effort in some tasks and not others, and their readiness to interpret various instructional or learning situations in particular ways (Goodnow, 1998). There are, for example, differences across cultures (e.g., China, Japan, and the United States) in the importance placed on reading compared with mathematics, and in the importance placed on being a well-rounded and happy child compared with being a good student (Stevenson and Lee, 1990). Subgroups within cultures—boys and girls, for example—also encounter different expectations, and children's own assessments of importance can influence what parents and others in their community view as important, as any nonsports-minded parent with a child who excels at baseball can attest.

As children reach the preschool years, researchers have turned their attention to the ways in which parents foster skills and abilities that are considered basic elements of school readiness, namely, literacy and number skills. For example, as mentioned earlier, maternal speech patterns predict vocabulary growth during the first three years of life (Hart and Risley, 1995; Huttenlocher et al., 1991), as well as prekindergarten measures of emergent literacy and print-related skills (De Temple and Snow, 1992). Parents encourage learning very explicitly through frequent visits to the library, routines that include regular reading to the child, and involvement in activities that allow children to play with notions of quantity. These behaviors show strong associations with early literacy and numeracy skills and later academic achievement (Ginsberg et al., 1998; Griffin and Morrison, 1997). Children generally benefit from parenting practices that expose them to high amounts of rich discourse and lots of print-related experiences (Beals et al., 1994; Gallimore and Goldenberg, 1993), as well as opportunities to experiment with numerical concepts (Saxe et al., 1987; Starkey and Klein, 1992). Of particular importance for the early acquisition of literacy and numeracy skills are the language and social interactions that surround such activities as storybook reading and board games that involve number concepts (Case and Griffin, 1990; Snow, 1993).

This work on parent-child interactions per se has been extended to encompass the next broader level of influence, namely the quality and quantity of stimulation and support that the overall home environment provides to a child. The home environment is most commonly assessed with the Home Observation for Measurement of the Environment (HOME) Inventory (Caldwell and Bradley, 1984), which assesses the materials, activities, and transactions that occur within the family setting and are supportive of early learning, defined largely in terms of IQ and traditional academic skills. Literally hundreds of studies have reported significant associations between HOME scores and children's IQ, cognitive and language development, and school performance (Bradley, 1985; Bradley et al., 1989; Clarke-Stewart, 1979; Gottfried, 1984; Linver et al., 1999; Smith et al., 1997; Wachs and Gruen, 1982). These relations hold for white, black, and Hispanic children from low and middle socioeconomic groups, although the patterns of relations may vary somewhat across ethnic groups (Bradley et al., 1989). Virtually every item on the HOME inventory distinguishes poor from nonpoor families both within and across white, black, and Hispanic families.

Efforts to assess the home learning environment raise the question of resources more broadly. Parents play an instrumental role in providing both social (i.e., opportunities for peer interactions, access to other supportive adults) and material (i.e., food, books, vacations, lessons) resources for their children. Economists and sociologists, in particular, have been interested in how the resources that families provide for their children influence their life trajectories (Becker and Tomes, 1986; Haveman and Wolfe, 1994). These family decisions are, of course, constrained by the decisions of government policy makers and employers, much more for some families than for others. Unfortunately, with the major exceptions of research on child care and family income (reviewed in the next two chapters), the influence on *early* development of the investments that parents make remains unexamined.

Parenting Practices and the Transmission of Cultural Values

Efforts to understand the importance of cultural practices in the rearing of young children, as described in Chapter 3, emphasize the extent to which culture is both reproduced and transformed within each child (Miller and Goodnow, 1995). That is to say, the socialization process that is embedded in the development of early relationships is influenced by the transmission of values and behaviors from one generation to the next, the "transformation" of those values and behaviors by the contemporary social context, and individual differences among caregivers (García Coll and Magnuson, 2000; Harkness and Super, 1992, 1996; Miller and Goodnow, 1995; Super and Harkness, 1997). These processes are of particular importance with respect to immigrant families (Portes, 1996; Rumbaut, 1994; Waters, 1997; Zhou and Bankston III, 1998). There is also a growing appreciation for the ways in which children themselves are not simply passive recipients of cultural influences, but rather active agents who bring both the ability and the willingness to accept, modify, or resist those influences.

Current research on differences in childrearing beliefs and practices is directing increased attention toward the scripts that characterize the daily routines of children and their primary caregivers (Farver, 1993; Farver and Wimbarti, 1995; Farver et al., 1995; Greenfield and Suzuki, 1998; Weisner, 1999). These routines are imbued with expectations that are designed to establish a moral order within which the child is expected to adapt (Schieffelin and Ochs, 1986; Shweder et al., 1995). They also create learning environments that vary dramatically across different cultural settings and groups (Rogoff, 1990). In this context, parents and other important caregivers introduce children to both informal routines and formal institutions that reinforce their cultural values and goals. When confronted by outside influences that they perceive to be undermining these efforts, caregivers can become highly threatened.

Parent belief systems and modes of parent-child interaction provide some of the most important ways in which culture is embedded in the process of child rearing during the early years of life (Levine, 1989; Super and Harkness, 1986). A wide range of cultural practices are salient in this regard, ranging from those related to sleeping, crying, and breast-feeding to those that affect the way parents talk with their children, the way emotion is acknowledged and expressed, and the way a child is expected to respond to praise for an individual achievement (see Chapters 3, 5, 6, and 7 for more detailed discussion). Inuit children are led, through adults' repeated teasing, to learn not to display anger (Briggs, 1992). Gusii mothers seldom gaze into the eyes of their infants, and their children are discouraged from looking adults in the eye (which is seen as an act of disrespect), yet they readily establish secure attachments (Levine, 1990). The widely varying views about sleep arrangements are discussed in Chapter 5.

The ways in which parents talk with children have been portrayed as one of culture's most powerful symbol systems (Harwood et al., 1995; Schieffelin and Ochs, 1986). As we discussed in Chapters 5 and 6, ways of storytelling have emerged as a prime site for exploring the socialization of values (Goodnow, 1997). Parents encourage some forms of storytelling and not others, sometimes to the point of labeling as "lies" stories that teachers portray as "imaginative" (Heath, 1983). In one study of black families, parents often recounted their everyday experiences in ways that presented themselves in a feisty light—a style that was repeated by their children in their own stories (Miller and Sperry, 1988). The impact, it is argued, extends beyond the kinds of stories that are transmitted from adult to child, to the child's emerging views of the self (e.g., If I'm feisty, that's good; if I'm reticent, that's bad), built up by way of the everyday events that are recounted and endorsed among family members (Miller et al., 1990). One very interesting issue that this raises is how children react when they are confronted with differing or even competing messages between parents or among the various important adults in their lives (Goodnow, 1997).

Individual differences in parents' previous and current interactions with the larger sociocultural context also affect how they raise their children (Parke and Buriel, 1998). The socialization of ethnic minority children, for example, has been conceptualized as a highly complex process that is influenced by the socioeconomic resources (i.e., housing, employment, health care, education, jobs) available to the family and the childrearing goals and adaptive strategies that the parents adopt in this context, among other factors (Harrison et al., 1984, 1990; Hughes and Chen, 1997, 1999). Extended family members, notably grandmothers, play a particularly important role in these processes, contributing, for example, material support, income, child care, and social regulation (Wilson, 1986, 1989).

This model highlights the need for greater attention to the efforts that parents make to help their children meet the challenges they will face as members of a minority group in a race-conscious society. In some cases, this leads parents to encourage their children to adapt to two cultural contexts—that of the child's primary ethnic group and that of the larger "mainstream" society (Boykin and Toms, 1985). This strategy is observed commonly in the lives of many ethnic minority groups in the United States (see, for example, LaFromboise et al., 1993).

Most empirical data on biculturalism and on the use of alternative strategies by ethnic minority parents to facilitate their children's adaptation have been collected from adult and adolescent samples (Parke and Buriel, 1998). It is therefore essential that this kind of research be conducted with samples of younger children, be extended to encompass nonminority parents, and be used to investigate distinctive strategies that are used by specific groups for raising children in an increasingly multicultural society.

An appreciation of the broad range of circumstances in which parents rear young children brings with it tremendous admiration for those who do it well. Conversely, conditions that pose significant challenges to the efforts of parents to get their children off to a good start in life warrant serious concern. We next turn to examine circumstances that seriously threaten and often undermine the parenting process.

DISRUPTIONS IN PARENTING

The challenges associated with parenting become abundantly evident when we take a look at parents who are struggling. There is an extensive literature on the effects of maternal depression, a relatively common, but potentially very serious, problem for parent-child interactions and child development. Child abuse and neglect represent a more unusual and far more extreme disruption in parenting. The long-standing literature on orphanage-reared children can inform questions about situations that undermine the basic and powerful tendency of infants to form relationships and the young child's capacity to recover from the effects of extremely aberrant care. These examples illustrate circumstances that place young children at risk of highly compromised development. In addition, the behaviors that are seen in young children exposed to these circumstances may be usefully considered as "canaries in the mineshaft"—that is, as early warning signs of serious problems in children who experience less extreme, but nonetheless harmful, early rearing experiences.

Research on the developmental consequences of disrupted parenting is part of a broader literature on environmental influences leading to psychopathology (see Rutter, in press; Rutter et al., in press). This is an exceedingly complex literature that is fraught with challenges regarding, for example, the need to elucidate how genetic factors interact with environmental factors to affect susceptibility to risk and the need to consider how children themselves contribute to parental behavior, including behavior that poses risks to their development. A good example of this latter point is provided by the discussion of the work by Ge and colleagues (1996) in Chapter 2, which links children's inherited antisocial tendencies to more harsh parenting by their adoptive mothers and fathers. Another example of how genetic and environmental influences interact is provided by a study of Scandinavian adoptees (Bohman, 1996). The children who were characterized by neither genetic (indexed by criminality or alcoholism in one or both biological parents) nor environmental risk (indexed by the same in adoptive parents, together with serious adversities in rearing) had a 3 percent rate of adult criminality, the children characterized by only one source of risk had rates of 6-12 percent, and those characterized by both genetic and environmental risk had a 40 percent rate of adult criminality. Environmental risk, in other words, led to negative outcomes primarily in the presence of genetic risk.

Sorting out genetic contributions and the direction of effects in research on parent-child relationships is a daunting task. Longitudinal designs, studies of adoption, and intervention studies are among the approaches that can be enormously useful; we rely on these when we can in this discussion of disruptions in parenting and in the following section on efforts to improve parenting, but they are seldom a panacea. Finally, this discussion focuses on the role of environmental influences deriving from parenting on individual differences among children. Equally important questions about why overall rates of particular childhood behaviors may be rising or falling (e.g., Is the increase in childhood poverty associated with increasing rates of maternal depression and, if so, is increased depression leading to higher rates of childhood disorders?) are not addressed, in large measure because there are virtually no data on secular trends in the relevant young child outcomes.

Early Development and Maternal Depression

A variety of methods have been used to assess maternal depression, ranging from self-reports to clinical diagnoses. They typically gather information about the mother's mood as well as other symptoms of depression, such as sleep disturbances, difficulties with concentration, loss of motivation, and appetite changes (Campbell et al., 1995). Approximately 1 in 10 women with young children experience depression (Dickstein et al., 1998b; Gelfand et al., 1996), with prevalence rates often reaching two times these levels among mothers living in poverty.[1] Descriptive data from several recent studies of welfare samples have identified rates of moderate to severe depression in the 13 to 28 percent range (Danziger et al., in press; Lennon et al., 1998; Moore et al., 1995; Olson and Pavetti, 1996). These high prevalence rates are cause for concern about the effects of maternal depression on young children. This focus for this discussion, however, is not meant to minimize the need for societal attention to other forms of mental illness that can disrupt parenting (e.g., anxiety disorders, bipolar disorders, alcoholism).

Compared with children of nondepressed mothers, those with depressed mothers show greater risk of developing socioemo-tional and behavior problems, which translate into difficulties in school, poor peer relationships, reduced ability for self-control, and aggression (Campbell et al., 1995, Cummings and Davies, 1994b, Dawson and Ashman, in press; Zeanah et al., 1997). Children of depressed parents are also at heightened risk of serious psychopathology (Cummings and Davies, 1994b; Downey

---

[1]Prevalence rates vary widely from one study to the next, depending on the measure of depression used and the population being studied, with some as low as 12 percent and others as high as 55 percent (Lennon et al., 1998; Wolf et al., submitted).

and Coyne, 1990; Zeanah et al., 1997). For example, children of clinically depressed parents are several times more likely to develop major depression then children of parents without such symptoms (Downey and Coyne, 1990).

Depression is not a static state. Mothers with major depressive disorders have periods when their symptoms abate, along with periods of greater suffering. Examining changes in child functioning in conjunction with changes in maternal functioning can help to disentangle genetic and experiential contributions to child outcomes. Work of this sort is being conducted in some cases using physiological measures.

In adults, depression is associated with changes in neural activity measured over the frontal areas of the brain that control emotion regulation (Davidson, 1994), as well as with altered day-night patterns that are evident in disordered sleeping, eating, and cortisol production. When EEG measures are taken, nondepressed adults typically show evidence of greater activity over the left compared with the right frontal region. But negative emotions evoked using movie clips produce a shift in this asymmetry, resulting in greater right than left frontal activity (Davidson et al., 1990). Depressed adults, in contrast, routinely exhibit greater right than left frontal activity, thus resembling the pattern evoked by negative emotionality in healthy adults.

Frontal asymmetry has been studied in infants and toddlers as well as adults (Dawson et al., 1992). Young children, like adults, show increased activity in the right frontal region relative to the left frontal region when negative emotions are evoked (Fox and Davidson, 1987). However, children of depressed mothers have been observed to display this asymmetry even when they are at rest or engaged in an activity with someone other than their mother (Dawson et al., 1992). Furthermore, the magnitude of this asymmetry was related to the timing of the mother's depression. Frontal EEG asymmetry in 3-year-olds was more highly related to maternal depression in the child's second and third years of life than to maternal depression in the child's first year of life. Interestingly, among three-year-olds, cortisol levels in the children were more highly related to maternal depression in the children's first year than to maternal depression in the year prior to testing. Thus, the neurobiology and neuroendocrinology associated with adult depression is observed in young children of depressed mothers in ways that may be somewhat specific to when, during the young child's life, the mother (and presumably the child) suffered most severely from the mother's depressive disorder (Dawson and Ashman, in press; Dawson et al., 1994; Zeanah et al., 1997).

This evidence has led some to suggest that infants and toddlers who are acutely dependent on their mothers, whose frontal lobes are experiencing rapid growth, and whose attachment, social-emotional, and regulatory capacities are developing, are particularly vulnerable to the negative effects of maternal depression (Dawson and Ashman, in press; Dawson et al., 1994; Goodman and Gotlib, 1999; Murray and Cooper, 1997; NICHD Early Child Care Research Network, 1998a; Weinberg and Tronick, 1998; Zeanah et al., 1997). While the severity and chronicity of maternal depression are clearly predictive of disturbances in child development (Campbell et al., 1995; Cummings and Davies, 1999; Frankel and Harmon, 1996; NICHD Early Child Care Research Network, 1998a), there is no definitive evidence regarding how the timing of maternal depression in the course of a child's life affects the child (Cummings and Davies, 1994b; Gelfand and Teti, 1990; Seifer et al., 1996). The neurobiological data suggest, however, that this is an area in which careful study of the timing question is warranted.

Efforts to understand the processes that underlie the developmental consequences of maternal depression have, not surprisingly, focused on mother-child interactions. Many depressed mothers show disrupted patterns of interaction with their infants. They also express self-doubts about their ability to parent well and are more likely than nondepressed mothers to perceive their children as being difficult (Teti et al., 1996b). Maternal depression affects both the emotional availability of the mother and the emotional tenor of her interactions with her child. Specifically, depressed mothers are more likely either to withdraw from their children and respond with little emotion or energy, or to become intrusive and hostile toward them (Frankel and Harmon, 1996; Tronick and Weinberg, 1997; Zeanah et al., 1997). These behaviors undoubtedly contribute to the higher rates of insecure attachment, as well as the withdrawal, reduced activity, and dysphoria that are observed in infants of depressed mothers (Cummings and Davies, 1994b, 1999; Dawson et al., 1992; Frankel and Harmon, 1996; Murray and Cooper, 1997; Seifer et al., 1996; van IJzendoorn et al., 1992).

These disrupted interactions and, more generally, the adverse effects of maternal depression are not seen uniformly. Many depressed women are very good mothers who raise children who are securely attached, do well in school, and do not misbehave (Cummings and Davies, 1994b, 1999; Frankel and Harmon, 1996). This raises important questions about the conditions that either prevent the damaging processes from occurring or protect children from their effects. Parenting by depressed mothers tends to be disrupted primarily when it occurs in conjunction with other sources of stress or adversity. Accordingly, a child of a depressed mother who also experiences poverty, marital discord, or maltreatment, or whose mother is also abusing substances or is an adolescent, is much more likely to exhibit some form of compromised development than is the child of a mother whose depression occurs in the context of an otherwise supportive environment (Cummings and Davies, 1994b; Seifer et al., 1996; Zeanah et al., 1997).

Unfortunately, depression often goes hand in hand with poverty, substance abuse, and other factors that place early development at risk (Campbell et al., 1995; Seifer, 1995; Zeanah et al., 1997).

The role of marital discord and of fathers is especially noteworthy in this regard. When maternal depression occurs in a family experiencing marital harmony, mothers are better able to sustain healthy interactions with their children and the children are less likely to display adverse consequences (Cummings and Davies, 1999; Teti, 1999; Teti et al., 1996b). In fact, the occurrence of marital discord in a child's family may predict certain developmental problems more accurately than maternal depression. Relatedly, involved, psychologically healthy, and supportive fathers can buffer children from the detrimental effects of maternal depression, whereas absent or psychologically unhealthy fathers can amplify the effects (Goodman and Gotlib, 1999).

Beyond its direct effects on children, maternal depression can be a major barrier to the effectiveness of early interventions. The high rates of depression among low-income mothers combined with emerging evidence that depression can be a major deterrent to enrollment and full participation in intervention programs, such as home visiting, highlights the critical importance of this relatively hidden issue for those who design, implement, and evaluate early childhood programs (Teti, 1999). Maternal depression can also undermine the intended benefits of early intervention, as illustrated by the New Chance Demonstration. Mothers who participated in this comprehensive program for poorly educated teenage mothers on welfare not only felt more stressed than mothers who did not participate in the program, but the program actually had negative effects on the children of the depressed participants (Quint et al., 1997). It appears that New Chance overwhelmed the capacity of depressed mothers to cope with their situations, with detrimental consequences for their children (Lennon et al., 1998). Early intervention is clearly a complex undertaking for depressed mothers who are also experiencing other sources of stress and for whom mental health services may be a more appropriate first step (see Teti, 1999).

Children Exposed to Abuse and Neglect

Child abuse and neglect can be devastating for children's development (Cicchetti and Carlson, 1989; Cicchetti and Toth, 2000; Goodman et al., 1998; Kolko, 1996; National Research Council, 1993). In 1996, nearly 1 million children were involved in substantiated reports to child protective services agencies (National Center on Child Abuse and Neglect, 1997), and, based on reports from just 21 states (National Committee to Prevent Child Abuse, 1997), over 64,000 children were removed from their homes and placed in alternate care. Extrapolating from data from 40 states that provided figures by age of the child, over one-third of these victims were 5 years old or younger and, of the child victims killed in 1995, 77 percent were under age 3 (National Center on Child Abuse and Neglect, 1997). These official figures do not include community violence or the incidence of children who witness domestic violence, which also have pervasive detrimental impacts on young children (Osofsky, 1999). Moreover, many children are assumed to suffer multiple forms of maltreatment (Thompson and Wyatt, 1999).

Child maltreatment is associated with both short- and long-term adverse consequences for children (see reviews by Kolko, 1996; Malinosky-Rummell and Hansen, 1993; Pianta et al., 1989; Thompson and Wyatt, 1999). Physical abuse extracts a substantial toll on young children's social adjustment, as seen in elevated rates of aggression that are apparent even in toddlers (George and Main, 1979) and appear to derive, in part, from biases in social information processing that lead victims of physical harm to overattribute hostile intent to others (Dodge et al., 1990). On average, children who have experienced physical abuse also have lower social competence, show less empathy for others, have difficulty recognizing others' emotions, and are more likely to be insecurely attached to their parents. Deficits have also been noted in IQ scores, language ability, and school performance, even when the effects of social class are controlled.

These adverse effects are not short-lived. Although the vast majority of abused children do not become abusive adults, abused children are overrepresented among adults involved in both nonfamilial and familial violence (Malinosky-Rummell and Hansen, 1993). Among females, long-term effects manifest themselves as depression, anxiety disorders, and suicidal and self-injurious behaviors. Both men and women who were maltreated as children are at heightened risk for multiple forms of psychopathology (Cicchetti and Lynch, 1995; Kaufman, 1996; National Research Council, 1993). There is less research on physical or emotional neglect, although similar patterns across the same spectrum of outcomes have been reported (see Erickson and Egeland, 1996; Gaudin, 1993; Hoffman-Plotkin and Twentyman, 1984; Maxfield and Widom, 1996, for reviews).

As with maternal depression, abuse that occurs in the context of other adverse circumstances, such as multiple out-of-home placements, additional life stressors, and parental depression, reaps worse consequences. Coping and adaptation in the face of abuse are more likely when abuse is relatively isolated from other sources of adversity and, in particular, when the child receives emotional support from another important adult in his or her life (Garmezy, 1983; Rutter, 2000; Werner, 2000). As we discuss in the section below on institutionalization, the presence of a consistently available and emotionally invested adult appears to have a remarkably restorative influence on children who might otherwise be expected to succumb to the deleterious circumstances of their early lives.

Recent work has explored the presence of posttraumatic stress symptoms in maltreated children, with a special concern for potential alterations in fear-stress physiology that have been found to accompany reactions to trauma among adults and older children. Work is currently ongoing with children 3 years and under to discover how trauma manifests itself in preverbal children (Scheeringa and Zeanah, 1995). By 4 and 5 years of age, however, trauma symptoms typically assessed in older children and adults can be observed (Pynoos and Eth, 1985; Scheeringa et al., 1995). Many children who show these symptoms following traumatic experiences appear to recover when their circumstances improve. In others, however, there is evidence of fairly long-term alterations in the physiology of the fear-stress system, seen in higher levels and atypical daily patterns of cortisol and adrenaline production, that correspond to the duration of maltreatment (De Bellis et al., 1999b; Hart et al., 1996; Kaufman, 1996; Kaufman and Charney, 1999; Pynoos et al., 1996a, 1996b). More severe physiological changes are noted when children suffered for longer periods before rescue (De Bellis and Putnam, 1994; De Bellis et al., 1999b).

Do these changes in the physiology of fear-stress in children have developmental consequences? Certainly chronic abuse in childhood is associated with problems in emotion and behavioral regulation (Pynoos et al., 1995). In addition, maltreatment in childhood is a risk factor for multiple forms of psychopathology that are often seen to co-occur with post trauma symptoms (Cicchetti and Lynch, 1995; Kaufman, 1996; National Research Council, 1993). Many suspect that chronic activation of the physiology of stress during periods of rapid brain development may be producing pathology because of the effects of stress physiology on brain development (e.g., Cicchetti, 1994). However, there has been only one peer-reviewed scientific study that imaged the brains of maltreated children.

The 44 children in this study had all been sexually abused, typically beginning between ages 2 and 6, and most had also been physically abused beginning between ages 1 and 3 and had witnessed violence in the home. The duration of abuse varied but averaged around 3 or more years. These children, who were all of school age at the time of testing and had been living in stable, presumably nonabusive circumstances for several years, were all selected to meet clinical criteria for posttraumatic stress disorder, and many also met criteria for depression and other clinical syndromes (De Bellis et al., 1999a). The imaging data showed that, compared with physically and mentally healthy children matched for age and sex, these children had smaller brain volumes, larger lateral ventricles (i.e., the fluid-filled cavities of the brain), and smaller areas of connection (i.e., the corpus callosum) between the left and right sides of the brain. Most importantly, these findings were correlated with the duration of trauma (although not with age of onset), with children who had been abused longer showing greater differences from their matched controls than children who were rescued after shorter periods of abuse.

These results are preliminary and require replication, but they suggest that a history of chronic and severe trauma in early childhood can be associated with alterations in fear-stress physiology and in brain development. At the same time, there is no reason to interpret these results as indicating permanent impairment. Indeed, there is no evidence on whether or how therapeutic interventions may affect the fear-stress system or the neurological development of children who suffer maltreatment early in life. There is, however, compelling evidence from research on children reared in orphanages and then later adopted into loving families of the remarkable capacity of the young child to recover from aberrant early care.

Orphanage Rearing and Later Adoption

Children growing up in institutions have been the focus of a long-standing literature on early privation (Rutter, 1981a; Skeels, 1966). Studies of orphanage-reared children are now focusing on the wave of Romanian children adopted into families during the early 1990s (Benoit et al., 1996; Groze and Ileana, 1996; Morison et al., 1995; Rutter and the English and Romanian Adoptees [ERA] Study Team, 1998). This literature tells a compelling story about the severe developmental consequences of institutional care that affords neither stimulation nor consistent relationships with caregivers, which often confronts children with other physical adversities, including malnutrition, exposure to pathogens, and untreated chronic illness. It also reveals the remarkable recovery that characterizes many children exposed to these environments once they are adopted into loving homes, as well as the long-term impairments that continue to plague some of them many years after their life circumstances have improved. On both accounts, the fundamental message concerns the vital importance of consistent and committed adults in young children's lives.

Orphanage-reared infants and toddlers who have received adequate medical care and nutrition, but virtually no social or cognitive stimulation and few opportunities to establish a relationship with a consistent caregiver, show striking delays in motor and cognitive growth over the period of institutionalization (Provence and Lipton, 1962). They become extremely unresponsive, showing minimal crying, cooing, babbling, or motor activity. When tested in the orphanage, the deficits increase over time (Ames, 1997; Dennis, 1973; Provence and Lipton, 1962; Rutter and the English and Romanian Adoptees [ERA] Study Team, 1998).

When adequate physical care and developmentally appropriate stimulation are provided and only the availability of *stable* caregivers is lacking, development is substantially less delayed (Hodges and Tizard, 1989a, 1989b; Tizard and Hodges, 1978; Tizard and Joseph, 1970; Tizard and Rees, 1974). This suggests that stable relationships, as distinct from social-cognitive stimulation, are *not* required to ensure adequate physical, sensorimotor, cognitive, and language development. Children who have lacked stable and consistent caregiving, however, are not free of problems. Using parent and teacher reports, these children have been found in several studies to show impairments in regulatory aspects of thinking that involve concentration, attention regulation, and inhibitory control, generalizing problem solutions, and excessive concreteness of thought (Hodges and Tizard, 1989b; Tizard and Hodges, 1978, as reviewed in Gunnar, in press).

Importantly, removing children from institutions and placing them in stable families with adequate resources can produce remarkable catch-up growth on developmental milestones and in general cognitive (i.e., measures of IQ) and language development (Ames, 1997; Rutter, 1972, 1981b; Rutter and the English and Romanian Adoptees [ERA] Study Team, 1998). Even children delayed a year or more in behavioral and physical development can achieve normal levels of functioning once they are given the opportunity to live with a loving family.

Nonetheless, a persistent minority of institutionalized children across all studies and samples fails to show this dramatic recovery. They continue to exhibit multiple, debilitating problems in cognition and behavior years after entering their new families. Multiple, often unknown factors are likely to constrain developmental outcomes for this persistent minority. Case by case, these factors may include varying mixtures of genetic, prenatal, and postnatal conditions. If institutional rearing is involved, the continuing deficits found in some children should show a consistent dose-response relationship with the duration of privation experienced. Duration of orphanage exposure is highly confounded with illness, maltreatment, repeated changes in caregiving, and so on, making it exceedingly difficult to isolate duration as the causal factor. However, recent findings based on the Romanian children offer a reasonable test of this hypothesis (O'Connor et al., 2000; Rutter and the English and Romanian Adoptees [ERA] Study Team, 1998). In fact, a strong dose-response relationship was found (with a 24-point IQ difference between the extremes), in which children who spent more time in the institutions showed more persistently poor outcomes. The study controlled for a series of alternative explanations, including the possibilities that later-adopted children might have had greater impairments at birth and that the differing outcomes may have been due to the children's degree of malnutrition, which adds to the credibility of the conclusion.

The outcomes of institutionalized children may also be constrained by the capacity of the adoptive family to provide for the special needs of the child and the availability of appropriate remedial treatment. Surprisingly little is known about post-adoption effects on the recovery of children from such neglectful early environments. As with any family of a child with special needs, however, the challenge for such families may tax their emotional and financial resources. This may be one reason why the recent work on Romanian adoptees has shown that persistent problems were more common for children when two or more were adopted simultaneously from the orphanage by the same family (Ames, 1997).

In contrast to the rapid recovery from gross cognitive and language deficits that is often seen in formerly institutionalized children, social and emotional development appears to be more compromised or more susceptible to long-term impacts (Ames, 1997; Hoksbergen, 1981; Rutter and the English and Romanian Adoptees [ERA] Study Team, 1998; Tizard and Rees, 1974; Verhulst et al., 1990, 1992). Specifically, children from the most depriving conditions, which often included illness, malnutrition, frequent relocations, and thus disruptions in care, appear to be at increased risk for enduring behavioral problems and difficulties in peer relationships that have been seen well into adolescence (Ames, 1997; Fisher et al., 1997; Hodges and Tizard, 1989b; Tizard and Hodges, 1978; Verhulst et al., 1992). Once again, however, many of the children, including some with the most depriving and adverse early backgrounds, do remarkably well when taken out of those circumstances and given the opportunity to develop in stable, loving, and economically resourceful families.

The natural experiment provided by orphanage-reared children also affords the opportunity to ask if children deprived of stable, consistent attachment relationships early in life remain capable of forming such relationships when opportunities arise later in childhood (see Thompson, in press(a)). In contrast to expectations from early attachment theory, the window for forming attachments appears to remain open for a rather long period, at least through the early childhood years, and possibly later. Children seem to be capable of forming their first attachments to parents even when adopted or fostered later in development, although it is unknown how long this adaptive capability endures. Nevertheless, the quality of these children's attachment relationships varies considerably. A substantial minority have difficulties establishing secure attachments with adoptive or foster parents (Chisholm, 1998; Hodges and Tizard, 1989b; O'Connor et al., 1999). Some also display quite shallow relations with others and reduced likelihood of forming intimate relationships with peers later in development (Hodges and Tizard, 1989b). This implicates the importance of stable relationships during infancy for organizing competencies that support the development of attachments that entail strong emotional commitments to specific partners (Gunnar, in press).

A final look at whether the problems seen in institutionalized children derive from their institutionalized rearing or from other factors is provided by another study of Romanian children (Roy et al., 2000). These investigators compared children reared from infancy in residential group homes and those brought up in individual foster homes. Almost all of the children had biological parents with overt psychopathology. The rearing provided by the foster parents differed significantly and in positive ways from the rearing received by the institutionalized children. The findings showed that the institutional children had a much higher level of overactivity and inattention than the foster family children, suggesting that the institutional rearing was the more probable culprit. It is important to note that this finding applies to the children who were studied, namely, those who also came from very high-risk backgrounds.

In sum, the literature on orphanage rearing and later adoption illustrates the dual nature of early experiences. On one hand, highly disrupted or aberrant experiences of early care can have devastating effects on development. On the other hand, the impacts of even these extreme environments are modified by subsequent experiences. Indeed, the rebound shown by orphanage-reared children when they are adopted into loving homes highlights the vital role that caregiving in all of its facets plays in the lives of young children. The literature attests that early deprivation does not doom children to lives of compromised development. It also reveals, however, that not all children escape unharmed. Some children institutionalized as infants continue to show lingering, persistent, and even severe problems, and a substantial minority show traces of their conditions of early care in what appear to be problems in their capacity or willingness to form intimate, secure, and deep relationships with others. Improving care can certainly improve child outcomes, but given the massiveness of the change entailed in adoption (most families involved in international adoptions are middle to upper income, given the expense involved) and the lingering problems of some children, questions are raised about what can realistically be expected from far more modest attempts to alter the consequences for children of adverse early life experiences.

EFFORTS TO IMPROVE PARENTING

Some of the strongest evidence available on the efficacy of parenting behavior in fostering positive developmental outcomes comes from evaluations of interventions focused on parenting. For example, a long-standing parent management training program focused on elementary-age and older children has been instrumental in demonstrating that coercive parenting plays a role in the causal mechanisms leading to antisocial behavior (Dishion et al., 1992; Forgatch, 1991; Forgatch and DeGarmo, 1999; Patterson and

Forgatch, 1995). There have been a number of recent reviews of the literature on parenting interventions (Barnard, 1997; Barnes et al., 1995; Benasich et al., 1992; Brooks-Gunn et al., 2000; Cowan et al., 1998; Farran, 2000; Gomby et al., 1999; Heinicke, 1993; McCollum and Hemmeter, 1997; Olds and Kitzman, 1993). They converge on two fundamental conclusions. First, parenting is open to change. A number of carefully evaluated interventions have successfully improved various dimensions of parenting and, for some, have linked these changes to improved child outcomes. Second, it is not easy to change parenting. There are at least as many failures as there are success stories. Learning from the unsuccessful efforts is vitally important to the intervention enterprise, as well as to understanding the many influences that impinge on parenting. This brief discussion emphasizes the implications of this literature for understanding parenting generally. Chapter 13 discusses this literature in the broader context of interventions aimed at improving young children's well-being and life chances.

Parenting interventions do not constitute a coherent field or delimited set of strategies. They range from relatively brief (several months), intensive interventions focused on highly specific objectives to multiyear initiatives that provide a range of services to families aimed at the broad goal of supporting family functioning. The focal points of intervention range from parent literacy to the sensitivity of parent-child interactions to maternal health behaviors. The interventions often, but not always, take place in the home; they rely on a multiplicity of service providers ranging from nurses and highly trained parent educators to paraprofessionals recruited from the same neighborhoods as the clients, who are sometimes (but not always) given substantial training. Increasingly, intervention approaches that were developed on largely middle-class white populations are being extended to families from different ethnic and culturally defined groups and to families at many levels of risk (Cowan et al., 1998).

There are surprisingly few studies of efforts to improve parenting that have simultaneously examined the causal influence of changes in parental behavior on child outcomes. The exceptions have, however, provided compelling evidence that successfully applying what is known about beneficial parenting to intervention efforts can improve outcomes for children. Carefully designed intervention programs have proven successful in improving the sensitivity and reciprocity of care that parents give their infants and toddlers, with some programs also succeeding in strengthening the security of attachment in young children as a consequence (van IJzendoorn et al., 1995). The most effective of such interventions (e.g., Heinicke et al., 1998, 1999; Lieberman et al., 1991; Quint and Egeland, 1995; van den Boom, 1994, 1995) strive to improve a caregiver's sensitivity through sustained, individualized sessions that take into account the mother's broader life circumstances and needs. The Family Development Service Program in Los Angeles, for example, places a strong emphasis on helping mothers work with the child's father and with institutions outside the nuclear family (Heinicke and Ponce, 1999) and has documented that a relationship-based intervention can have a significant impact on parent-child interaction and on the infant's security of attachment. The Infant-Parent Psychotherapy Program in San Francisco emphasizes intergenerational patterns of attachment and devotes substantial resources to helping mothers cope with life issues in the world outside the family (Lieberman et al., 1991). It remains difficult, however, to delineate the key mediators involved in the positive findings that these studies are producing.

These successful approaches confirm correlational evidence of the extent to which parenting sensitivity is tied to the extent of marital support, socioeconomic stress, demands in the neighborhood, and other life circumstances that can compete for the adult's energy and attention to a young child's needs (Belsky, 1984, 1999). It is therefore not surprising that such intensive strategies also improve child functioning indirectly by improving the sensitivity of the care they receive. It is also important to note that these interventions typically rely on professional staff who are clinically trained to deal with parent-child issues and place a strong emphasis on staff continuity as essential to the central task of supporting relationships.

Other similarly intensive, localized programs have been successful in teaching low-income parents to facilitate their young children's early literacy skills (Whitehurst et al., 1994) and improve parents' behavior management strategies (Webster-Stratton, 1992), with significant program effects on young children's reading and vocabulary and reduced aggressive and oppositional behavior, respectively. Cowan and Cowan (2000), in a randomized design, showed that largely middle-class parents' participation in 16-week therapist-led discussion groups on effective parenting just prior to their children's entry into kindergarten resulted in better school adjustment and higher academic achievement for kindergartners and first graders, compared with children whose parents attended discussion groups without an emphasis on effective parenting.

While these model programs with explicitly defined goals and painstaking attention to implementation and service quality can be effective in changing parenting practices and affecting targeted child outcomes, the literature on larger-scale parenting interventions is substantially less consistent. This is not to say that promising results are never found; rather, they are more sporadic and of smaller magnitude. Nevertheless, there are important exceptions among the larger-scale efforts. Randomized trials of the Nurse Home Visitation Program (Olds et al., 1999), for example, have reported reduced maternal smoking, positive changes in maternal attitudes and behaviors related to abuse and neglect, and improved safety of home environments, as well as fewer reported cases of child abuse and neglect and reduced hospital visits due to injuries and ingestions in the first four years of life. One evaluation of the national Even Start Family Literacy Program that randomized treatment at five sites found positive program effects on school readiness and language scores for 3- and 4-year-olds (St. Pierre et al., 1995a), despite weak effects on the aspects of parenting that were measured.

There is, however, little empirical documentation that nonspecific, general family support interventions for high-risk families are able to produce significant or enduring changes in parenting behavior. For example, a review of 15 randomized trials of home visiting programs aimed at promoting the cognitive and linguistic development of young children in low-income families found that only 6 produced significant benefits for children and 5 of the 6 programs employed professional staff (Olds and Kitzman, 1993). A more recent review of six high-quality evaluations (i.e., primarily randomized experiments) of home visitation programs that are being, or have been, implemented nationally called for "a dedicated effort, led by the field, to improve the quality and implementation of existing home visiting services, and a more modest view of the potential of the broad array of home visiting programs" (Gomby et al., 1999:24). Widely implemented programs that have extended their services beyond home visiting to provide a mix of adult education, job training, parenting education, and child care have also yielded, at best, modest results (Berrey and Lennon, 1998; St. Pierre and Layzer, 1998; St. Pierre et al., 1995a), particularly when they do little to address the multiple risk factors that often characterize the families they are trying to reach and do not focus extensive resources on addressing the parent-child relationship (Cowan et al., 1998).

In sum, the question today is not whether interventions focused on parents can be effective, but rather what does it take to change parenting behavior in ways that will be sufficient to produce improved child outcomes (and for whom is this unlikely to be the right approach). The complex evidence on parenting interventions suggests that this is not an easy task for which success can be readily assumed. The challenges become even more daunting in light of the multiple problems that face many at-risk families today. The committee agrees with others (see Cowan et al., 1998; Teti, 1999) who have suggested that these families are likely to require more intensive services than the typical parenting intervention program provides, interventions that go beyond the enhancement of parenting skills to address the serious life issues (e.g., poverty, hopelessness and depression, substance abuse, troubled relationships) they face and involve adults other than just the mother and utilize program staff who are specifically qualified to work with multiproblem families. The growing diversity of families with young children also raises profoundly important questions about how best to match programs to the needs, values, and goals of various ethnic and cultural groups. A final challenge to parenting interventions is posed by the demographics and circumstances of working parents, for whom finding the time to participate in these programs is exceedingly difficult.

Evaluations of the next generation of parenting interventions also face a new set of challenges: (1) the importance of subjecting to direct assessment the underlying assumption that improving parenting will produce meaningful changes in children's functioning, (2) the need to thoroughly document program implementation and, in particular, to study the interactions that transpire between program staff and participating families, and (3) the need to distinguish children and families for whom parenting interventions are effective from those for whom an alternative intervention strategy holds more promise. Figuring out the conditions and mechanisms that underlie successful efforts to change parenting will contribute not only to more successful interventions but also to efforts to understand parenting more generally.

SUMMARY AND CONCLUSIONS

Relationships are among the most significant influences on healthy growth and psychological well-being. The mother-child relationship is the primary one for most children, but relationships with others inside and outside the home have become increasingly important as young children receive care from many different individuals. These are not new conclusions, but research during the past quarter-century has highlighted how early relationships are influential, how diverse are their consequences, and how significant are the harms resulting from relational abuse or neglect on young children.

Early in life, a young child enjoys relationships that are unique to different partners. Relationships with mothers are different from relationships with fathers, grandparents, and a caregiver in child care, but each relationship can be supportive and secure in its own way. Moreover, relationships are established and sustained in a cultural context in which how children and adults regard each other is influenced by the beliefs, values, and expectations of the wider social community. Indeed, a central function of early caregiving relationships addresses the child's socialization into a specific cultural niche within society. In these ways, early relationships are diverse and multifaceted and have different effects on young children.

Despite their diversity, however, all young children seem to require certain things from early abiding relationships. These include: (a) reliable support that establishes confident security in the adult, (b) responsiveness that strengthens a young child's sense of agency and self-efficacy, (c) protection from the harms that children fear and the threats of which they may be unaware, (d) affection by which young children develop self-esteem, (e) opportunities to experience and resolve human conflict cooperatively, (f) support for the growth of new skills and capabilities that are within the child's reach, (g) reciprocal interaction by which children learn the mutual give-and-take of positive sociability, and (h) the experience of being respected by others and respecting them as human beings. In these ways, relationships shape the development of self-awareness, social competence, conscience, emotional growth and emotion regulation, learning and cognitive growth, and a variety of other foundational developmental accomplishments.

Relationships are also important because these attachments buffer young children against the development of serious behavior problems, in part by strengthening the human connections and providing the structure and monitoring that curb violent or aggressive tendencies. But strong, supportive early attachments do not inoculate young children against later difficulty. Relationships may begin well but decline over time, and many other influences affect early psychosocial growth.

Stability and consistency in these relationships is important, as are the adult's sensitivity, love, availability, and unflagging commitment to the child's well-being. Fulfilling these responsibilities does not always come naturally, nor is it easy. The circumstances that surround parents and other caregivers, as well as their own mental health, exert a powerful influence on their capacity to fulfill the responsibilities that are entailed in raising children. Characteristics of the child can also make good parenting difficult to achieve. It should come as no surprise that early child-caregiver relationships can go awry in many ways. When they do, children suffer and the harms they experience can be life-threatening. Short of this, they include alterations in fear-stress physiology, blunted capabilities for emotion and attention regulation, delays in cognition and learning, and social dysfunction. Remarkably, when young children are removed from these deleterious conditions, many recover amazingly well. The capacity to rebound in supportive relationships speaks to the growth-fostering importance of close relationships for young children. Nonetheless, not all children who experience harmful care early in life rebound so well. Why one child recovers while another struggles is difficult to know without being privy to all the harmful influences the child experienced prior to being rescued. But there is evidence that the longer children remain in care that is threatening or fails to meet their basic needs, the greater the challenge in getting them on a healthy trajectory.

Early relationships can improve if they begin badly. It is thus vitally important for society to do everything possible to enable parents to establish good relationships with their children from the beginning and, when this fails, to help parents become better caregivers. The quality of an adult's caregiving can be strengthened, but it is not easy to do. Because the quality of caregiving has diverse roots in the family ecology, marital relationship, and the adult's individual past, improving the quality of care requires carefully designed interventions that take these contextual features of families into consideration. It also involves reducing the stresses that impinge on parents from circumstances beyond the family unit, ranging from work-related pressures to community violence. The central and irreplaceable nature of young children's close relationships also point to the importance of evaluating the impact of programs affecting families (such as welfare reform, child care policies, and economic/child support policies) through the prism of young children's relational needs.

10   Family Resources

The previous chapter illustrated the many ways in which young children's relationships with their caregivers at home influence the course of their development. A central message was that parenting and its consequences always occur in a context larger than the family unit. In this chapter and the next two, we examine these contexts, looking first at the socioeconomic resources available in children's families and then at the child care and community settings in which children grow up. Questions about the developmental consequences of parental education, family income, parental work and occupational status, and family structure—the indicators of family socioeconomic resources—have long occupied the attention of scientists. They have also been an enduring focal point of policy making on behalf of children and families, starting with the War on Poverty in the 1960s and leading up to present-day welfare reforms.

Today, this work is undergoing a transition from asking *whether* family resources affect child development to asking *why* research shows so consistently that they do. This shift in emphasis is described in this chapter, starting with the evidence linking family resources to developmental outcomes and then summarizing what has been learned about the mechanisms that account for the links. New in this research is an emphasis on the dynamic nature of resources—including changes in family income and employment and movements in and out of poverty—as well as the differential impact of poverty depending on the child's age. Questions are now being asked, as well, about how much improvement in income or parental education is needed in order to produce measurable improvements in children's developmental outcomes.

Finally, with welfare reform has come a growing interest in the families of the working poor. This vast natural experiment has also created new opportunities to learn about how various approaches to increasing work and income among families living in poverty affect both child and adult outcomes of paramount interest to the nation. Increasingly, research addressing questions about how resources change over time and their impact on children's development is relying on longitudinal data and experimental designs.

DO RESOURCES MATTER FOR CHILDREN'S DEVELOPMENT?

Understanding how different family resources affect young children's lives necessitates distinguishing among them; connecting them to such resources as money, time, and access to the learning opportunities that they represent; and identifying the different pathways through which these resources might influence young children's development. Taking poverty as an example, it is important to know how it manifests itself in young children's lives, how it affects the extent to which their basic needs are met, and through what processes it promotes or undermines their capacity to accomplish the basic developmental tasks outlined in the previous chapters of this report.

It would be surprising if the odds of healthy, adaptive development did not differ for children growing up in families with ample, compared with impoverished, resources. Families who occupy different socioeconomic niches because of parental education, income, and occupation have strikingly different capacities to purchase safe housing, nutritious meals, high-quality child care, and other opportunities that can foster health, learning, and adaptation (Becker, 1981; Brooks-Gunn et al., 1995). A two-parent family with one highly paid wage earner who makes it possible for the other parent to stay at home with the children is in an entirely different situation from a single parent with a poverty-level wage, for example (Becker and Lewis, 1973; Mason and Kuhlthau, 1992; Timmer et al., 1985). How the trade-offs that families make among employment, cash income, and child care time affect young children is a controversial and poorly understood question.

The psychological well-being of mothers and associated patterns of parenting are also much more likely to suffer in families with limited resources (Brooks-Gunn and Duncan, 1997). Research has focused increasingly on connections among family resources, psychological aspects of family functioning, and child well-being (McLoyd, 1998). Finally, there is growing interest in how families' access to different social resources, such as relatives, supportive friends and neighbors, and community organizations (churches, family resource centers, safe recreational settings), affects parenting and child development (Coleman, 1985; Edin and Lein, 1997; Jarrett and Burton, 1999; Jencks and Mayer, 1990; Sampson, 1992; Yoshikawa, 1999). We reserve discussion of resources outside the family for Chapter 12.

In this section, we describe what is known about the extent to which parental employment, income and poverty, parental schooling, and family structure affect the developing child. We couch the discussion in the context of trends that have altered, in many instances dramatically, the socioeconomic landscape of young children in the United States. We close our discussion of connections between socioeconomic resources and child development by addressing the challenges raised by behavioral geneticists (e.g., Rowe and Rodgers, 1997), who argue that genetic factors are at the heart of associations between family resources and child outcomes. In the final section, we review evidence on the various ways in which socioeconomic resources affect young children's development.

Work and Children's Development

Maternal and paternal employment play a powerful role in determining the time and money that families devote to their children. Long-standing concerns about the developmental impacts of fathers' unemployment and mothers' employment have now been supplemented by research focusing on the developmental consequences of how parents configure their work, the circumstances of parental work, and the increasing decoupling of work and economic security, illustrated by the growth in working-poor families.

Increases in paid maternal employment over the past quarter-century are one of the most dramatic—and best-known—social trends. Between 1975 and 1999, the proportion of children under 6 years of age with mothers in the labor force increased from 38.8 percent to 61.1 percent—a 36 percent increase (Figure 10-1).[1] The proportion of young children with mothers working full-time and year-round nearly tripled, from 11 to 30 percent. The increase in maternal employment (including both full- and part-time workers) over this 24 year period was most rapid for infants, rising from 24 to 54 percent, compared with older children. The proportion of young children with a mother working part time changed relatively little (ranging between 36 and 40 percent) over that period. A much larger share of young Hispanic (48 percent) than white (29 percent) or black (26 percent) children lived with mothers who did not work for pay in 1997.

---

[1]These data are based on all young children who are living with their mothers.

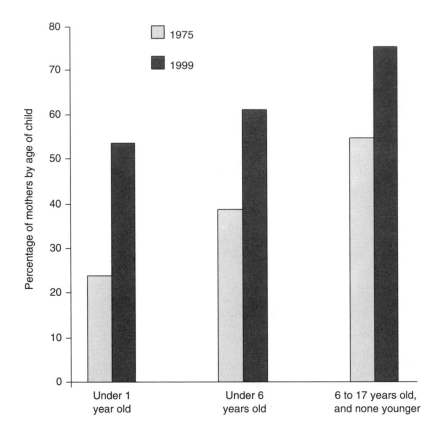

FIGURE 10-1 Trends in the proportion of mothers in the labor force, by age of child, 1975-1999. NOTES: Since 1975 data for mothers with children under 1 year of age are not available, the data for this column are from the June 1977 Current Population Survey. CPS was redesigned in 1994, so data in this table for 1999 are not strictly comparable with the data shown for 1975 and 1977. SOURCES: Data from 1999 Current Population Survey (annual averages), available online at www.bls.gov/news.release/famee.t05.htm and www.bls.gov/news. release/famee.t06.htm; Hayghe (1997); U.S. Bureau of the Census (1982).

Parental employment often, but not always, entails supplementing parental care with substantial amounts of care by others, and herein lies many of today's concerns about its effects on very young children, as we discuss in Chapter 11. While employment may increase the cash income of families, work-related expenses may increase as well, leaving them with a differing composition of time and money, but not necessarily greater resources overall.

Employment, of course, can take many different forms. Some parents work full-time, full-year in low-wage jobs that fail to lift their families out of poverty. In other cases, work is intermittent, or multiple low-wage jobs are held by multiple family members, including older children, who all contribute to family income. As we discuss in the chapter on child care, it is not unusual for parents to organize their work hours so that they can keep child care within the family, particularly during infancy. Even among mothers who have received public assistance, a recent analysis found that over a 24-month period, 43 percent either combined work and welfare receipt or cycled between the two, and another 23 percent were not employed but spent substantial time looking for work (Spalter-Roth et al., 1995).

What do employment trends mean for young children? Research on maternal employment has been based primarily on middle-income families (Gottfried and Gottfried, 1988; Hoffman, 1989) and has been inconclusive. Most of the evidence indicates that children are either positively affected or unaffected by growing up in a family with an employed mother. Evidence is accumulating,[2] however, that suggests that maternal employment in the child's first year, especially if mothers work long hours, can indeed be a negative factor for infant development (Baydar and Brooks-Gunn, 1991; Belsky and Eggebeen, 1991; Ruhm, 2000; Desai et al., 1989; Vandell and Corasaniti, 1988; Han et al., 2000; Waldfogel et al., 2000). Efforts to determine which infants are most affected have been inconclusive, but the negative findings emerge more often for those in two-parent and middle-income families than for those with fewer family resources. Interestingly, one report (Ruhm, 2000) hinted at similar effects of paternal and maternal employment, suggesting the importance of time investments by fathers as well as by mothers. How strong these negative effects are can, of course, be affected by the quality of the alternative care that the child experiences in the mother's absence (see next chapter)

Research on the children of working-poor parents is just beginning to emerge, despite the fact that this is one of the fastest growing groups of children in the United States. In 1996, about 5 million children lived in a working-poor family, defined as a family with an income below the poverty line and two parents who work the equivalent of a full-time job or a single

---

[2]Much of the evidence is based on analyses of the National Longitudinal Survey of Youth (NLSY) The NLSY is a national sample of 12,686 youth who were 14 to 22 years of age when first interviewed in 1979. Beginning in 1986 and every 2 years since, developmental measures were administered to children of civilian mothers in the NLSY (4,971 children of 2,922 mothers in 1986). See Chase-Lansdale et al. (1991) for a fuller description. The survey does not include measures of child care quality.

parent who works at least 20 hours per week (Wertheimer, 1999). Over half of children in poor, married-couple families and 30 percent of poor children in single-mother families have parents who work these substantial hours. Both Hispanic and black families are more likely than white families to be poor, despite the presence of working adults.

The few studies that have focused on maternal employment among low-income children suggest that they are not hurt by and may benefit from maternal employment, particularly with regard to cognitive outcomes (Alessandri, 1992; Hoffman et al., 1999; Moore and Driscoll, 1997; Vandell and Ramanan, 1992). In fact, there appears to be a more consistent advantage of maternal employment for children in working class than in middle class families (Desai et al., 1989; Gold and Andres, 1978; Hoffman, 1979; Zaslow, 1987), perhaps as a result of its positive effects on the mother's sense of well-being, the father's involvement in child-care activities, and the quality of parenting (Hoffman et al., 1999). The limited evidence that is available suggests that infants and toddlers fare better in working-poor families than in poor families in which the parents do not work or work minimally (NICHD Early Child Care Research Network, 1999b). Yet those in working families that are not living in poverty do substantially better than either group of children living in poverty. The children's better adjustment is seen on measures of cognitive, language, and social development. This pattern of child outcomes is, however, largely attributable to differences across these three groups of families in demographic characteristics (e.g., mothers' education, family size), mothers' depression and social support, and parenting quality and attitudes. New evidence from experimental studies of welfare reform (discussed below) are beginning to expand understanding of how parents' transition to work—often substantial hours of work—affects young children living in poverty.

The corresponding literature on how fathers' loss of work and unemployment affect children has emphasized the influence of these circumstances on harmful family dynamics. Unemployment increases financial strain, which in turn may compromise parent-child relationships by creating tension and hostility as well as reducing warmth and supportiveness in the home. These adverse home environments have been found to have negative consequences for children's development in the short and long term (Conger and Elder Jr., 1994; McLoyd, 1989; Tomblin et al., 1997).

Investigators have also explored to what extent the circumstances and features of work, such as the flexibility of one's work hours, the extent of control over the day-to-day nature of work and the absence of repetitious and boring tasks or the presence of challenging tasks, account for the effects of maternal employment on children (Alessandri, 1992; Greenberger and O'Neil, 1991; Howes et al., 1995a; Jencks et al., 1988; Menaghan and

Parcel, 1995; Parcel and Menaghan, 1994; Parke and Buriel, 1998). Research has linked these features of work to parental cognitive skills, such as intellectual flexibility, and other personal characteristics, such as self-direction (Kohn and Schooler, 1973), and more recently to children's cognitive achievement and social behavior (Parcel and Menaghan, 1994). In one longitudinal analysis, for example, single mothers' entry into low-complexity, low-wage jobs was associated with declines in the quality of the home environment (Menaghan and Parcel, 1995). This evidence is cause for concern when juxtaposed with projections that the second highest rate of job growth over the next decade will occur in the service economy. These jobs often entail very low wages, few benefits, little autonomy, and nonstandard hours (e.g., shift work). They are also disproportionately filled by less-well-educated women who now constitute a sizeable group of mothers who are entering the labor force as a result of welfare reform.

In 1994, close to half (41 percent) of children under age 5 whose mothers were employed had mothers whose principal job involved a "nonday" work shift (defined as the majority of work hours being outside the 8 a.m. to 4 p.m. time period). Young children living in poverty are much more likely to have a mother who works a nonday shift (59 percent of children) compared with young children living above the poverty line (39 percent of children) (Presser and Cox, 1997). We know very little about the developmental implications of shift work. One recent study has reported an association between shift work and marital instability, with the odds of separation or divorce three to six times higher among mothers and fathers who are engaged in shift work, compared with otherwise similar parents not engaged in shift work (Presser, 2000). These findings did not appear to be attributable to spouses in more troubled marriages electing to move into shift work. This is, however, an isolated study that needs to be replicated, particularly in light of the fact that many parents are motivated to engage in shift work as a way of keeping child care within the family.

In sum, the familiar trends in parental employment can bode well or ill for young children depending on features of the work, the income it generates, the nature and structure of the job, its timing and total hours—and, as we see in Chapter 11, on the environments and relationships that children experience when they are not in the care of their parents. Of concern is the fact that the growth in parental employment appears to be in precisely those circumstances that have been found to pose risks to early development. It is thus critically important to recognize that the characteristics and experiences of working families have changed substantially over the past 25 years. It is especially troubling that young children whose parents are making considerable work efforts are more likely today than in the recent past to be living in poverty.

TABLE 10-1 Risk of Adverse Child Outcomes and Environmental
Conditions Associated with Poverty Status

Child Outcomes	Risk for Poor Relative to Nonpoor Children
Lead poisoning	3.5[a]
Birth to unmarried teenager	3.1[b]
Short-stay hospital episode	2.0[c]
Grade repetition and high school dropout	2.0[c]
Low birthweight	1.7[d]
Mortality	1.7[d]
Learning disability	1.4[c]
Parent report of emotional or behavior problem that lasted 3 months or more	1.3[e]
SES Mediators	
Child abuse and neglect	6.8[f]
Depression	2.3[g]
Experiencing violent crimes	2.2[h]
Substance abuse	1.9[i]

[a]Data from NHANES III, 1988-1991 (Brody et al., 1994). Poor children living in families with incomes less than 130 percent of the poverty threshold are classified as poor. All other children are classified as nonpoor.

[b]Data from the Panel Study of Income Dynamics (PSID) Based on 1,705 children ages 0-6 in 1968; outcomes measured at ages 21 to 27 (Haveman and Wolfe, 1994, p. 108, Table 4.10c).

[c]Data from the 1988 National Health Interview Survey Child Health Supplement (NHIS-CHS), a nationwide household survey. The household member who knew the most about the sample child's health, usually the child's mother, reported children's health status. Figures calculated from Coiro et al. (1994) and Dawson (1991).

[d]Data from the National Maternal and Infant Health survey collected in 1989 and 1990, with 1988 as the reference period. Percentages were calculated from the number of deaths and number of low-birthweight births per 1,000 live births as reported in Federman et al. (1996, p. 10).

[e]Data from the National Health Interview Survey Child Health Supplement (NHIS-CHS). The question was meant to identify children with common psychological disorders, such as attention deficit disorder or depression, as well as severe problems, such as autism.

[f]Data from Children's Defense Fund (1994, p. 87, Tables 5-6). Poor families are those with annual incomes below $15,000.

[g]Data from a New Haven Epidemiological Catchment Area in 1980 (Bruce et al., 1991). Poverty status was determined by comparing respondent's 1980 income to the 1980 poverty threshold. Odds ratio of having depressive episode in six months after first interview. Depressive episode was diagnosed by the DIS. The odds ratio was corrected for age, sex, race, and previous history of depression.

TABLE 10-1 Continued

*b*Data from the National Crime Victimization Interview Survey. Results are for house-holds or persons living in households. Data were collected between January 1992 and June 1993 with 1992 as the reference period. Percentages are calculated from the crimes per 1,000 people per year. Reported in Federman et al. (1996, p. 9).
*i*Data from the National Comorbidity Survey 1990-1992 (Kessler et al., 1994). Parental sample was restricted to respondents between age 15 and 54. Substance abuse included both alcohol and drug abuse or dependence in the past 12 months, as diagnosed by the Composite International Diagnostic Interview. Poor respondents were those with incomes of less than $20,000 compared with those with $70,000 or more.

Poverty and Children's Development

One of the most consistent associations in developmental science is between economic hardship and compromised child development. The influence of family income, and specifically of poverty, has been of special interest in light of the numerous policies that address poverty in the United States and the intractability of—indeed, the increase in—the child poverty rate.[3] In 1997, some 5.2 million young children (22 percent of all young children) in the United States were poor, and 42 percent lived at or below 185 percent of the poverty line.[4] The strength and consistency of associations between poverty and critical aspects of child development are striking (Brooks-Gunn and Duncan, 1997) (Table 10-1).

Developmental research on children in poverty has grown exponentially in recent years (see Brooks-Gunn and Duncan, 1997; Chase-Lansdale and Brooks-Gunn, 1995; Huston, 1991; Huston et al., 1994; McLoyd, 1998). This research has yielded suggestive evidence that increasing the incomes of low-income parents with young children will improve the odds of successful early development. What remains to be understood is the nature of the impact and optimal strategies for increasing the incomes of poor parents that best promote their children's development. Even though most children living in poverty grow up to be productive adults, some do not and, without intervention, individual differences among children at school entry that are linked to poverty often persist over time (Stipek, in press). When this evidence is combined with the basic facts about early

---

[3]This "official" poverty count is based on a Census Bureau comparison of total family income with a poverty threshold that varies by family size. Expressed in 1997 dollars, the respective poverty thresholds for families with three and four persons were roughly $13,000 and $16,500. Young children living in families with total cash incomes below these thresholds were counted as poor.

[4]Children in families with incomes between 100 and 185 percent of the federal poverty line are designated near poor because they are served by a number of government assistance programs that use 185 percent of the poverty line as the upper limit to determine eligibility.

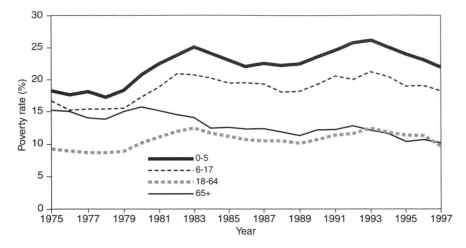

FIGURE 10-2 Poverty rates by age, 1975-1997. SOURCE: Bennett et al. (1999).
Reprinted with permission.

childhood poverty, there is considerable cause for concern: (1) young children are now the poorest age group in U.S. society (see Figure 10-2); (2) poverty is considerably more prevalent among children now than 25 years ago,[5] despite an unprecedented period of macroeconomic prosperity and substantially higher rates of parental employment; (3) poverty has increased much more for minority than nonminority children; and (4) children living in poverty are falling farther behind their more affluent peers. The United States now has both more poor *and* more affluent children than it did 25 years ago, creating a widening disparity between the haves and have nots among young children. Our country also has more poor and more affluent children than most other Western countries (Table 10-2).

Assessing the developmental consequences of poverty and of differing family incomes more generally is not as straightforward as one might think. Contrary to popular belief, and in contrast to most other measures of socioeconomic status, family income is often quite volatile across a family's life cycle and, in particular, a child's childhood (Duncan et al., 1998a). For example, only half of children and families who are poor in a given year are

---

[5]As discouraging as these poverty figures are, they would have been worse had it not been for certain changes in government taxes and transfer programs. In 1997, taking into account the effects of all taxes, tax credits (including the earned income tax credit), means-tested income transfers, and non-means-tested income transfers reduces the poverty rate for families with young children by about 9 percentage points, to leave 14 percent living in poverty.

TABLE 10-2 Poverty and Affluence Among Young (Under 6 Years of Age) Children in 16 Countries

Nation	Percent Poor	Percent Affluent	Year
United States	26.0	6.0	1997
United Kingdom	24.2	6.6	1995
Italy	19.2	4.6	1995
Canada	17.4	2.8	1994
Germany	12.4	2.8	1994
Israel	11.7	6.2	1992
Spain	11.6	8.3	1990
Netherlands	8.6	1.3	1994
France	8.0	4.7	1994
Finland	7.7	1.7	1995
Belgium	6.4	1.7	1992
Austria	5.9	0.7	1987
Denmark	5.6	1.3	1992
Norway	5.3	1.3	1995
Sweden	3.7	1.0	1995
Luxembourg	3.0	3.6	1994

NOTE: "Poor" is defined as family-size-adjusted income less than 50 percent of country median income. "Affluent" is defined as family-size-adjusted income greater than 200 percent of country median income. Equivalence scale is the square root of family size.

SOURCE: Calculations by Lee Rainwater based on data from the Luxembourg Income Study.

persistently poor (Duncan et al., 1994). On average, family incomes increase as children age, but average patterns conceal a great deal of year-to-year volatility, making it important to consider how economic resources at different points during the childhood years affect development. The malleability of young children's development and the overwhelming importance of the family (rather than school or peer) context suggest that economic conditions in early childhood may be far more important for shaping children's ability, behavior, and achievement than conditions later in childhood.

Efforts to understand the developmental effects of poverty have relied on both experimental and nonexperimental studies. Experimental designs involving manipulation of family incomes are extremely rare. In four income maintenance experiments in the 1960s and 1970s, experimental treatment families received a guaranteed minimum income. Impacts on preschool children, however, were not assessed. School performance and attendance were affected positively in some sites for school-age children, but not for high school adolescents. In two sites reporting high school completion and advanced education, these were higher for the experimental group (Institute for Research on Poverty, 1976; Kershaw and Fair, 1976; Salkind and Haskins, 1982; U.S. Department of Health and Human Services, 1983).

Experimental Studies

A new generation of experimental welfare reform programs have undergone recent evaluations. Three incorporate designs that include income-based incentives to work, such as wage supplements and income disregards. Milwaukee's New Hope Program involved experimentation with a package of work supports that included wage supplements, child care subsidies, health insurance, and supportive case workers (Bos et al., 1999) for families living in two poor inner-city neighborhoods. Large positive impacts (.25 to .50 standard deviation) were found on teacher-reported behavior and achievement of school-age boys but not girls. Changes outside the family, such as expanded use of after-school and community youth programs, rather than changes inside the family, such as parenting quality, maternal mental health, and family routines (which were unaffected), appeared responsible for the child impacts. Given the multifaceted nature of the New Hope treatment, it was impossible to determine how much of these impacts were caused by the increased family incomes, other components of the intervention, or New Hope's particular bundling of these resource components. Unfortunately, preschool outcomes were not assessed.

The Minnesota Family Independence Program (Gennetian and Miller, 2000; Miller et al., 1997) and the Canadian Self-Sufficiency Program (Lin et al., 1998; Morris and Michalopoulos, 2000) are among those that are assessing impacts on young children's well-being. In the Minnesota program, children were ages 2 to 9 when their families were enrolled, with two-thirds age 6 and younger. The Canadian study involved a broader age range, including a group of children who were less than 3 years old when their parents were enrolled. They were assessed when they were 3 to 5 years of age. Like New Hope, both programs adopted a welfare reform strategy that emphasized rapid entry into work combined with provisions to ensure that family income improved as well.[6] Preliminary findings from the two studies are remarkably similar. The youngest children were largely unaffected by their mothers' participation in the program. This was true of cognitive outcomes, social behavior, emotional well-being, and child health. While both programs increased the time young children spent in child care

---

[6]The Minnesota program enabled families to keep both their wages and a generous amount of their former welfare benefits through an income disregard mechanism. The Canadian program supplemented earnings.

and, in particular, time in center-based arrangements, they had no effect on parenting behavior, the high rates of depressive symptoms that characterized the mothers in both programs, or the home environment (as measured by the HOME scale). To the extent that positive child outcomes emerge from these experiments, they are restricted largely to school-age children.

A fourth set of studies were based on work and education strategies that did not include economic incentives, such as those included in the three experimental programs described above (Hamilton, 2000; McGroder et al., 2000). These were conducted in 11 sites of the National Evaluation of Welfare-to-Work Strategies (NEWWS). There were no consistent impacts on young children's development.

Nonexperimental Studies

Nonexperimental research using longitudinal data has shifted from studying poverty as an unchanging status (poor versus not poor) to understanding how particular characteristics of poverty affect development for different age groups. This has focused attention on the depth, duration, and timing of poverty in childhood (Brooks-Gunn and Duncan, 1997; McLeod and Shanahan, 1993). What have we learned? Of particular importance is emerging evidence suggesting that family income may exert its most powerful influence on children during the earliest years of life (Duncan et al., 1998b). Using data from a nationally representative sample of children and families, Duncan and his colleagues related children's completed schooling to family income averaged over three age spans: 0-5, 6-10, and 11-15 years. Family income during children's preschool years, which are most distant from their decisions about leaving school, appeared far more important than income during middle childhood. Income during adolescence mattered, but primarily for entry into college. Moreover, early childhood income effects were particularly strong in the lower income ranges. Controlling for income later in childhood as well as for demographic characteristics of households, a $10,000 increment to income averaged over the first five years of life for children in low-income families was associated with a 2.8-fold increase in the odds of finishing high school. This analysis suggests that for children in families experiencing economic hardship, income in the preschool years matters more for children's education attainment than does income later in childhood.

We have also learned that a household's long-term economic status has a much greater association with achievement and behavior problems than do single-year income measures (Blau, 1999). There appear to be larger impacts of income increments on low-income than higher-income families (Duncan et al., 1998b; Mayer, 1997; Smith et al., 1997), although this is not found consistently (Blau, 1999). Finally, although we've seen that poverty combined with parental work appears to be more beneficial for children than nonworking poverty, correlational evidence suggests that young children's outcomes may be affected positively by a transition from welfare to work only if that transition lifts the family's income above the poverty line (Moore and Driscoll, 1997; NICHD Early Child Care Research Network, 1999b). What we don't yet know, but hope to untangle with forthcoming evidence from welfare experiments that include child assessments, is whether these work- and poverty-related developmental patterns are due to work or income per se. They may instead be due to preexisting differences among parents who fail in their efforts to secure employment, work in low-wage jobs, or secure higher-wage jobs that are also, not inconsequentially, more likely to provide health insurance, family leave, and other benefits.

In sum, young children are more likely than any other age group in this society to live in poverty, and poverty during the early years is more powerfully predictive of later achievement than is poverty at any subsequent stage of development. Children living in poverty are more likely today than in the recent past to have working parents, many of whom work consistently and for substantial hours. While the weight of the evidence indicates that parental work is usually a neutral or positive influence in the lives of young children, particularly for those living in poverty, its benefits appear to be attenuated or lost in the presence of low wages that sustain rather than ameliorate poverty, low job complexity, and perhaps employment that occurs during a child's first year of life.

The new generation of welfare reform studies provides some of the only experimental evidence available about the effects of providing increased income to working-poor families with young children, particularly those who previously had a history of reliance on public assistance. They suggest that, in the absence of positive effects on young children's home environments, parental mental health, and parenting, increases in family income and reductions in poverty are not in and of themselves sufficient to benefit young children. Yet there is no evidence that the children are harmed, and the evidence of positive outcomes for school-age children raises hopes for improved outcomes for the young children as they reach school age. At the same time, this evidence raises the question of "what would it take?" to improve the well-being of younger children in the context of efforts to improve the work effort and earnings of their mothers. The research on parents' mental health reviewed in Chapter 9 and the early intervention literature reviewed in Chapter 13 suggests that a promising answer would involve making the most of the opportunity that welfare reform presents to link families to both mental health and early intervention services.

Parental Schooling

Large, positive associations between parental schooling levels and children's achievement and behavior are among the most substantial and replicated results from developmental studies. It would thus be reasonable to expect that the recent increases in the educational attainment of parents of young children would bode well for them. Between 1974 and 1997, the proportion of children whose mothers had not graduated from high school dropped nearly in half, from 30 to 17 percent, while the proportion whose mothers had graduated from college nearly doubled, from 13 to 24 percent (Figure 10-3). Trends in fathers' schooling were similar, although not quite as dramatic. Changes in parental schooling levels among young black children were even more favorable than among white children, although in 1998 it was still the case that much larger fractions of black (21 percent) than white (8 percent) children had mothers who had not completed high school. In stark contrast, however, the low schooling levels of Hispanic

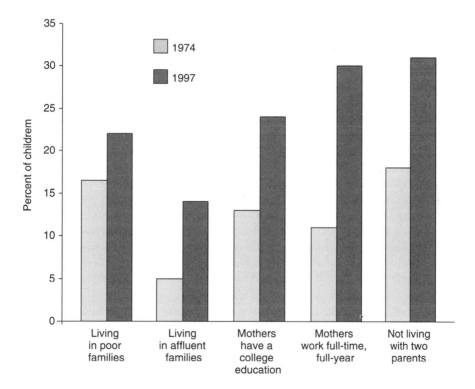

FIGURE 10-3 Trends in the socioeconomic resources of young children, 1974-1997. SOURCE: Untabulated data from the Current Population Survey.

immigrant parents led to distressingly low maternal schooling levels for Hispanic children as a whole; in 1998 nearly half (45 percent) of young Hispanic children had mothers who lacked a high school diploma.

Parental education levels are strongly associated with the home literacy environment, parental teaching styles, and investments in a variety of resources that promote learning (e.g., high-quality child care, educational materials, visits to libraries and museums) (Bradley et al., 1989; Laosa, 1983; Michael, 1972). These dimensions of what economists refer to as human capital are indisputably linked to early learning and educational attainment once children begin formal schooling.

Nevertheless, surprisingly little is known about the developmental implications of these trends. In policy terms, if a program could somehow increase the number of young mothers completing high school, how many spillover benefits would be expected in their children's development? Evidence from developing countries indicates that educating mothers through at least the primary grades benefits public health, reduces fertility, and improves their children's literacy and verbal skills (Dexter et al., 1998; Hobcraft et al., 1984; Richman et al., 1992). For the purposes of this U.S.-based review, the issues are more subtle, with policy changes typically involving the mother's completion of a general education development (high school equivalency) certificate, a final year or two of formal high school, or a year or two of junior college. What evidence is there that these kinds of changes benefit children?

Two studies have taken advantage of the fact that young mothers may acquire more formal schooling between the births of first and subsequent children to estimate whether achievement and behavioral differences between earlier- and later-born siblings are related to increases in mother's formal schooling. The results are mixed, however, with one study (Kaestner and Corman, 1995) reporting no effect of increased maternal education on young children's achievement scores, and the other (Rosenzweig and Wolpin, 1994) reporting that an additional year of maternal schooling had a modestly positive effect, and more specifically that a mothers' enrollment in school during a child's first three years had a significant and large positive effect on children's receptive vocabulary.

Thus, the jury is still out regarding the role of increased parental education in promoting the well-being of children. From a policy point of view, it may well be that the increments in skills associated with the completion of high school or an associate degree are too small to make much of a difference for children. This does not, however, answer the question of whether larger changes in parental education or changes that involve acquiring basic literacy would benefit young children.

Family Structure

Family structure is often included among the dimensions that scientists study when trying to understand how the availability or lack of resources in families affects child development. Not surprisingly, the configuration of resources in single-parent families is often quite different from that in two-parent families (McLanahan and Sandefur, 1994). Single parents are most often mothers, and single-mother families face much higher rates of poverty than two-parent families. Among working adults, unmarried women maintaining families have the highest risk of living in poverty (Klein and Rones, 1989; Thompson and McDowell, 1994). Many children in single-parent households have fewer relationships with male role models or nonmaternal adults that might be important for their social development (Levine-Coley, 1998). Time constraints faced by single parents may affect their ability to supervise their children and participate in their activities (Amato, 1993; Levine-Coley, 1998). These factors may, in turn, be associated with diminished emotional supports and lower levels of cognitive stimulation in the home environment (Amato, 1993; Levine-Coley, 1998; Miller and Davis, 1997).

The circumstances and adaptations of parents vary greatly among single-parent families, as do the amount and types of resources they make available to their children. Accordingly, there is growing interest in how single parenting comes about and what alternative forms of support exist. On average, children raised by single parents have lower levels of social and academic well-being than do children from intact marriages (Cherlin, 1999; McLanahan and Sandefur, 1994)—a finding that has fueled widespread concern about the large and persistent decline in the proportion of young children living with two parents. Between 1974 and 1997, the proportion not living with two parents rose from 18 to 31 percent (Figure 10-3). Two-parent family structures have declined much more rapidly among black (a 16 percentage point decline) and Hispanic (18 percentage points) than white (10 percentage points) families. As of 1998, only 35 percent of young black children lived with two parents, compared with 63 percent of young Hispanic and 79 percent of young white children. Most of this decline can be accounted for by the increase in the proportion of young children living with never-married mothers rather than divorced or separated mothers. Indeed, in 1998, more than three-quarters of young children living in mother-only families had mothers who had never been married.

What do we know about how these trends may be affecting the development of young children? Studies focused on divorce find that most children have a difficult time during and shortly after the divorce process (Hetherington and Stanley-Hagan, 1999), and that the problems are larger for their behavior than for school achievement (McLanahan, 1997). Nevertheless, although difficulties may reemerge later in life, recent reviews suggest that the vast majority of children from divorced families do not exhibit severe or enduring problem behaviors (Amato and Keith, 1991). The very few studies that have investigated the effects of divorce on preschool children have found that divorce typically has small negative effects on preschoolers' social adjustment, but no effects in other domains. The largest effects of divorce on children are found among children in primary school (Amato and Keith, 1991). It is also of interest that studies using better designs (e.g., better controls for differences between divorcing and stable couples, more representative samples) tend to find smaller effects (Amato and Keith, 1991).

Divorce is but one of several routes into single parenthood, and it is important to distinguish it from other routes, particularly childbearing by unmarried women. Unfortunately, most research has focused only on the effects of divorce on children or has pooled together all single-parent families (McLanahan, 1997). The few studies that have addressed this question have found few differences between children of divorced and never-married parents; both groups are at risk for poorer achievement and behavior compared with children from intact families (Cooksey, 1997; McLanahan, 1997). As already noted, this risk is largely accounted for by differences in the socioeconomic resources available to single parent families. A forthcoming study on "fragile" families will focus directly on children born to never-married parents (see Box 10-1).

But many questions remain unanswered. Are these differences caused by the family structure, or do they reflect preexisting differences between children in intact and single-parent families? Does the effect of single-parent family structure depend on the age of the child? Unfortunately, research to date has not supplied clear answers to these questions.

In sum, the central challenge facing those who study children of single parents is one of disentangling the effects of family structure from the effects of the diminished resources that typically characterize single-parent families. Those who have tackled this challenge largely agree that, while growing up in a single-parent family increases the odds that children will do less well in school and exhibit behavior problems, these outcomes derive largely from the socioeconomic realities of single parenthood (e.g., lower income, less parental time from both mothers and fathers), rather than from any direct effects of living only with one parent. Nevertheless, this topic remains an area of active controversy among scientists and politicians alike.

Role of Genetic Factors

As a part of a review of evidence linking differences in family resources to differences in child outcomes, it is critical to address the challenges to this literature that have been raised recently by behavioral geneticists. If

BOX 10-1
The Fragile Families and Child Well-Being Study

The Fragile Families and Child Well-Being Study is designed to study unmarried parents—their relationship and their resources—to learn more about them generally and to determine how outside factors and public policies affect them and the health and well-being of their children. Researchers are particularly interested in examining how Temporary Assistance to Needy Families (TANF) work requirements and time limits, as well as stricter paternity establishment and child support enforcement (as set down in the Personal Responsibility and Work Opportunity Reconciliation Act) will affect unmarried parents and their children.

Specifically, the Fragile Families and Child Well-Being Study will be examining four major issues:

1. The circumstances and resources of new, unmarried parents, especially fathers (i.e., How many parents have steady jobs? How many fathers want to be involved in raising their children?)

2. The nature of the relationship between unmarried parents. (i.e., How many of these couples are involved in stable relationships? Do they expect to marry? Are they experiencing high levels of conflict or domestic violence?)

3. Factors that affect new, unmarried parents' relationship (i.e., What pushes new unmarried parents together or pulls them apart? How are their living arrangements and parents' behavior affected by public policies?).

4. The long-term consequences for parents, children, and society of new welfare regulations, especially the implementation of stronger paternity establishment rules, stricter enforcement of child support payment requirements, and changes in the delivery and financing of health care and child care.

The study began in 1997, and data will continue to be collected through 2004. More than 3,600 unmarried couples are participating in the study, which is being conducted in 21 cities across the United States. In addition, information is also being collected from more than 1,100 married couples to be used as a comparison group. Researchers sought out participants in the hospital and interviewed the mother within 24 hours of her child's birth. The fathers were then interviewed as soon as possible after that. Follow-up interviews will be conducted with both the mother and the father when their child is 12, 30, and 48 months old. In addition, the children's health and development will be assessed at home when they are 48 months old.

Funding for the study is provided by the National Institute of Child Health and Human Development and a consortium of national and local foundations. Principal investigators are Sara McLanahan and Irving Garfinkel (see McLanahan and Garfinkel, 2000).

family resource differences derive primarily from parents' genetic endowments (e.g., cognitive, mental health) as behavioral geneticists argue (see, for example, Rowe, 1994), then any putative effects of resources on children's development could in fact derive from genetic endowments rather than from any of the features of families that we have just discussed. This in turn would render policy efforts aimed at these features either moot or exceedingly difficult.

There is little doubt that genetic influences need to be added to the long list of potentially important factors that deserve attention in studies that assess the effects of family resources on children's development. The issue is how to ask the pertinent questions and how to explore them in research. Two kinds of evidence suggest that, even net of genetic endowments, family resources have important impacts on child development. These studies have used measures of family socioeconomic status (SES) (i.e., parental education and occupational status, income, family structure, and other measures of the family environment) to capture family resources.

The first study compares the importance of socioeconomic factors on children's achievement before and after statistical adjustments for parental genetic endowments. Phillips et al. (1998) used data from a nationally representative sample of mothers (the National Longitudinal Survey of Youth) to do exactly this. Specifically, they adjusted for what they called the "mother's cognitive genotype index" using her score on the battery of Armed Forces Qualifying Tests (numerical operations, arithmetic and math knowledge, paragraph comprehension), her class rank in high school, and the interviewer's assessment of the mother's understanding of the interview when assessing the association between socioeconomic status and children's achievement. They found that genetic factors accounted for only about one-quarter of the SES-achievement association. Although far from trivial, this finding suggests that maternal cognitive endowments do not account for most of the socioeconomic contributions to children's achievement.

The second approach compares the association of socioeconomic status to child outcomes between children raised by biological and adoptive parents. If this association is due primarily to genetic factors, then the correlation between child outcomes and the SES of adopted (and thus genetically unrelated) parents should be much lower than the correlation between child outcomes and the SES of their biological parents. Loehlin, Horn, and Willerman (1989) found that the correlation between SES and child IQ for their sample of adopted children was only 18 percent less than the correlation for biological children. Scarr and Weinberg (1976) found similar patterns in their sample of black adopted and biological children. The magnitude of these reductions are in line with those found in the direct approach of Phillips et al. (1998), and also suggests that SES impacts on childhood IQ cannot be attributed primarily to genetic factors.

An even more dramatic illustration of the role of parent SES is provided by a recent study of children adopted between 4 and 6 years of age into families that varied widely in socioeconomic status (Duyme et al., 1999). This study directly addresses the question of the extent to which the environment, defined by the SES (father's occupation) of adoptive families, can alter the cognitive development of children who tested in the very low range (IQs between 60 and 86) prior to adoption. The results are compelling. All children, whether adopted by low-, middle-, or high-SES families, had higher IQs after adoption. But more to the point, the children adopted by higher-SES families had significantly larger gains in IQ than did children adopted into lower-SES families (see Figure 10-4). Because the children and their adoptive parents are genetically unrelated, these SES effects carry no genetic influence.

A very different line of reasoning leads many behavioral geneticists to doubt that family socioeconomic status matters for children's development. Key here are the striking similarities in the abilities and personalities of twins and other siblings reared apart from one another. Indeed, these similarities are almost as large as those found for siblings who grow up together and, in the language of the behavioral geneticists, share the same environment (see Chapter 2). By behavioral geneticists' accounting, children's "shared environments" account for very little (almost always less than 10 percent, usually less than 5 percent) of the variability of ability and personality found in the population (Bouchard et al., 1990). Some have concluded from this evidence that the developmental consequences of per-

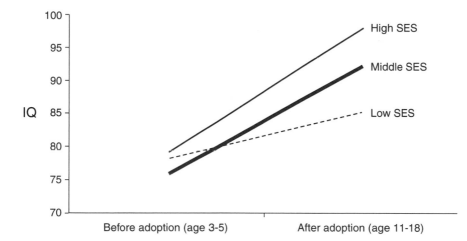

FIGURE 10-4 Mean differences in IQ by SES of adoptive family. SOURCE: Duyme et al. (1999).

sistent family environmental influences, such as socioeconomic status and parenting, are remarkably small. Scarr (1992), for example, argues that family environments in the "normal developmental range" have little or no effect on children's development. Harris (1995, 1998) relies, in part, on this evidence to argue that "parents don't matter."

Problematic in this reasoning is that socioeconomic status is not a permanent family characteristic shared by siblings. There is abundant evidence that the nature and effects of family socioeconomic influences vary sufficiently across time and among children to suggest that they are more properly conceived as belonging to the "nonshared" than the "shared" environmental category. Specifically, longitudinal studies based on nationally representative data have shown that family income is quite volatile (Duncan, 1988) and that siblings several years apart in age often experience quite different childhood incomes (Duncan and Raudenbush, 1999). Few children who live in single-parent families do so for their entire childhood (Duncan and Rodgers, 1998). This leads to the possibility that the effects on child development of economic conditions and single-parent family structure, for example, may depend on the stage of childhood in which they are experienced. In fact, a study of the completed schooling of siblings in a national sample found that differences in family income specific to stages of childhood accounted for approximately 17 percent of the variation in differences in completed schooling (Teachman et al., under review). Thus, socioeconomic status contributes importantly to both the shared and nonshared environments of children, and one cannot use evidence on the unimportance of siblings' shared environments to argue that socioeconomic status does not matter for children's development.

In sum, the review of current thinking about genetic influences presented in Chapter 2 reminds us of the importance of understanding the interplay between genetic and environmental influences over the course of development. This discussion of genetics and family resources counters more extreme portrayals of socioeconomic status as primarily reflecting genetic influences on development. At the same time, by revealing that environmental influences tell only part of the SES story, the evidence also reminds us that genetic influences warrant greater attention in studies that assess the effects of both shared and nonshared family resources on child development.

INFLUENCES ON YOUNG CHILDREN'S DEVELOPMENT

The processes by which family resources matter for children's well-being have been difficult to elucidate (Belsky et al., 1986; Brooks-Gunn and Duncan, 1997). In this section, we summarize evidence on three pathways by which they may affect children's development. The first focuses on the parent's own mental health. The second involves parental beliefs about childrearing. The third focuses not on parents directly, but rather on the home environments they create for their children. Although we discuss these pathways separately, it is likely that they interact and accumulate within families in disparate ways. Moreover, the processes we describe presume that parents and parental environments affect children, but not vice versa. However, as we have discussed throughout this report, children actively shape both their personal relationships and their environments more broadly (Bell, 1968, 1974; Sameroff and Fiese, 1990). Thus, some of the apparent associations between parental factors and children's development undoubtedly reflect the pervasive and reciprocal ways in which children and parents affect each other.

Parent Psychological Distress

One way in which families' economic resources may shape children's lives is through their impact on parents' mental health. Low-income parents are at greater risk for depression and other forms of psychological distress, such as low self-worth and negative beliefs about control (see bottom panel of Table 10-1; Gazmararian et al., 1995; Pearlin and Schooler, 1978; Rosenberg and Pearlin, 1978). Over 40 percent of the poor women in two large samples participating in work and training programs, for example, scored at or above the cutoff for clinically significant depressive symptoms (Quint et al., 1997; U.S. Department of Health and Human Services, 1995). Nationally representative estimates of mental health problems indicate that approximately 10 percent of poor and less-educated people in the United States have current major depressive episodes—twice the rate of others who are more advantaged (Blazer et al., 1994).

The psychological cost of economic hardship is compellingly portrayed by ethnographic work with poor families. Based on hundreds of interviews with low-income welfare recipients and working single mothers living in three cities, Edin and Lein (1997) describe their constant struggles to provide food, housing, and other necessities, as well as to keep their children out of danger. Despite ongoing hardship, most of the mothers in the study adapted to their situations. They budgeted carefully and spent considerable time and energy making money in alternative ways. Despite their efforts, however, arrangements for child care, housing, and medical care were often precarious. Any one of a number of events, such as a family or extended-family illness, could cause major disruptions to their employment and family lives. The chronic and pervasive stress that Edin and Lein document suggests important potential links among economic hardship, mental health, and parenting.

Psychological distress is more prevalent among low-income populations because they experience more negative life events and have fewer resources with which to cope with adverse life experiences (Kessler and Cleary, 1980; McLeod and Kessler, 1990). In addition, Kessler (1982) demonstrated that low levels of education, income, and occupational status each make independent contributions to the variation seen in maternal psychological distress. While all socioeconomic dimensions may play a role, most developmental research has emphasized the effects of economic hardship on parents' mental health (McLoyd, 1997).

The connection between economic hardship and mental health is important because, as discussed in Chapter 9, poor mental health is related to harsh, inconsistent, and detached parenting. Research in this field has emphasized the associations among economic decline, economic strain, parental psychological well-being, and children's outcomes (e.g., McLoyd, 1997). For example, in the case of depression, mothers' responses to the needs of their children tend to be less consistent and positive. Consequently, research on low-income families has explored whether depressive parenting patterns, or elements of these patterns, account for the relationship between economic hardship and children's maladjustment. These associations are often dependent on the age and gender of the children and, as with each aspect of socioeconomic status, they account for only part of the association between poverty and child well-being (McLeod and Shanahan, 1993; Watson et al., 1996).

The work of Elder and colleagues (Elder, 1979; Elder et al., 1984, 1985) on children of the Great Depression found strong associations among economic hardship, parental psychological well-being, and children's well-being in intact families. Fathers who experienced job loss and economic deprivation were more distressed psychologically and prone to explosive, rejecting, and punitive parenting. Preschool-age children in these families, especially boys, were more likely to exhibit problem behaviors, while adolescent girls were more likely to have lower feelings of self-adequacy and to be less goal-oriented. Adolescent boys fared better than either adolescent girls or younger children. Elder and colleagues (1985) speculated that the gender and age differences reflected different experiences in families during the deprived times. During this time of economic hardship, adolescent boys sought economic opportunities outside the home, which reduced the time they spent with their families, gave them a useful role to play, and may have reduced the amount of negative family interactions they experienced. Younger children and adolescent girls did not have the same access to buffers provided by extrafamilial activities.

In more recent applications of Elder's framework, similar processes have been found to operate in Midwestern farm families experiencing economic decline (Conger et al., 1992, 1994) and single-parent black families that experience chronic economic strain (McLoyd et al., 1994). These studies confirmed the cluster of economic insecurity and decline, poor parental mental health, punitive and less involved parenting, and poor adolescent outcomes. But there are important exceptions. Among the farm families and children, some became more involved in social institutions, such as schools and churches, and the adolescents' resilience had much to do with their connections to these social influences (Elder Jr. and Conger, 2000).

Two studies have focused on young children. In one, reduced financial resources among black, rural, single-parent families were associated with lower maternal self-esteem, and lower self-esteem was associated with deterioration in family routines and the quality of mother-child interactions (Brody and Flor, 1997). These family processes were related to 6- to 9-year-olds' self-regulation, which in turn was associated with both academic and behavioral problems. A second study (Harnish et al., 1995) of ethnically diverse low-income children entering first grade found that the quality of mother-child interaction partially accounted for the effects of socioeconomic status and maternal depressive symptomatology on children's externalizing behavior.

Substance abuse constitutes another risk factor associated with decreased mental health and economic hardship among parents (Table 10-1). Research on children of substance-abusing parents has focused largely on drug exposure during pregnancy and children's subsequent developmental outcomes (Harden, 1998; Mayes, 1995; U.S. Department of Health and Human Services, 1999c). Since the effects of drugs vary dramatically by drug type, substance-abusing parents may display a variety of patterns of impaired parenting. For example, drugs such as alcohol or marijuana may depress parents' moods, possibly resulting in withdrawn behavior, whereas cocaine may increase activity and elevate moods, possibly resulting in unpredictable or impulsive behavior.

Few empirical studies have evaluated parenting among substance-abusing parents. Most of the evidence comes from studies that have documented high occurrences of abuse and neglect among these parents; more harsh, negative, angry, threatening, and punitive interactions; and less responsiveness to their children (Bauman and Dougherty, 1983; Bernstein et al., 1986; Colten, 1980; Leif, 1985). However, because drug abuse often co-occurs with other psychiatric problems and disadvantaged circumstances, it is hard to know whether the parenting practices of substance-abusing parents are uniquely impaired by their drug habits (Mayes, 1995).

Finally, both the reporting and incidence of child maltreatment are higher among low-income than high-income families (Table 10-1; Trickett et al., 1991; Waldfogel, 1998). Studies of the etiology of child maltreatment suggest that while child abuse and neglect capture different behaviors, children who are abused are also often neglected, and differences in co-occurrence patterns may have both different causes and different effects (Aber, 1994; National Research Council, 1993). Some have speculated, for example, that persistent poverty is more closely related to neglect, while abuse is precipitated by sudden economic loss (Aber, 1994). Research suggests that economic hardship is only one of several risk factors that may contribute to child abuse and neglect. Others include parental beliefs about childrearing and unrealistic expectations of children's capabilities, social isolation, and psychopathology (Aber, 1994). Nevertheless, the contribution of economic hardship to child maltreatment suggests that some of the negative effects of poverty on children may result from higher rates of abuse and neglect (McLoyd, 1997).

In sum, the toll that low socioeconomic status takes on parents' mental health appears to have important effects on child well-being. This implies a pressing need to integrate economic and mental health policy at numerous levels, ranging from federal decision making to the implementation and evaluation of both economic interventions, such as welfare reform, and early interventions for children and families in local communities. We also have much more to learn about connections among low socioeconomic status, parental mental health, parenting behaviors, and child well-being. Important questions concern the differential effects of economic hardship on parents of infants, toddlers, older children, and adolescents; the progression of effects on parents and children over time; and identification of factors that assist or undermine coping. In light of the more serious problems that are associated with cumulative risk (Sameroff et al., 1987; Seifer, 1995), we also need to understand how different types and manifestations of psychological distress—which often occur together and in conjunction with protective factors—combine to affect child development.

Parental Beliefs

Only modest differences have been found in the typical parenting practices and parent-child interactions of low-income and higher-income parents (Miller and Davis, 1997; Radziszewka et al., 1996). Higher-SES parents have been found to rely more than lower-SES parents on shame, guilt, and reasoning as disciplinary strategies and less on commands and imperatives (Kohn, 1969). These modest differences have been ascribed to parents' values or beliefs (Hoff-Ginsberg and Tardif, 1995; Kohn, 1959, 1963, 1969, 1976; Kohn and Schooler, 1973). One of the most often cited differences thought to affect parenting practices and childrearing is that lower-class parents value conformity, whereas higher social-class parents value self-direction (Gecas, 1979). In fact, mothers who value conformity have been found to voice more concern that being too responsive to a child's crying and fussing will spoil the child (Luster et al., 1989). These mothers were also less likely to emphasize the importance of reading and more likely to endorse controlling their child's activities, with discipline if necessary. Mothers who valued self-direction, in contrast, were more likely to emphasize reading and exploration and were less concerned about disciplining children or spoiling them by responding to their crying.

Unfortunately, much of this work has stopped short of relating parenting values to children's developmental outcomes (e.g., Harwood, 1992; Holden, 1995; Sigel et al., 1992). Consequently, it is unclear how much social class differences in values, beliefs, and parenting practices account for the differential development of children. Further complicating this research are the facts that important parental values (e.g., about academic achievement) do not differ by social class (Warren et al., 1993) and that social class is only one of many potential influences on parent's belief systems (Sigel et al., 1992). Finally, class differences in values have declined over time, suggesting that values may be a less important source of differences in parenting practices than they once were (e.g., Alwin, 1984; Hoff-Ginsberg and Tardif, 1995; Wright and Wright, 1976).

In sum, although researchers have consistently found a modest relationship between socioeconomic status and some parental beliefs, research has failed to establish that these differences in values explain differences in parenting, or are consequential for young children. All told, class-related differences in parental values are unlikely to explain more than a small portion of variation in the development of children.

The Home Learning Environment

Family socioeconomic resources are closely associated with the home learning environments of poor children. Seminal work by Bradley and Caldwell (1980) identified important aspects of the home environment that are related to children's well-being (see Chapter 9). Their widely used HOME (Home Observation for Measurement of the Environment; Bradley and Caldwell, 1984) scale assesses the type and frequency of interactions and learning experiences parents provide for their children, both inside and outside the home. Stimulation, emotional support, structure, and safety are associated with the well-being of both low-income and high-income children (Bradley et al., 1994). Although there is considerable overlap between the HOME scores of high- and low-income families, on average, high-income families received higher scores. This may be due in part to the fact that several of the HOME items depend on having more income (e.g., books in the home; Bradley et al., 1994). Poverty and persistent poverty are strongly associated with less optimal home environments (Garrett et al., 1994).

Recent work has suggested that the home learning environment (as distinct from other aspects of the home environment, such as warmth and safety) might be particularly important for understanding children's cognitive development. Several studies have found that the more positive home learning environments of high-income versus low-income children account for as much as half of the gap in test scores of preschool children, and as much as one-third of the gap in the achievement scores of school-age children (Smith et al., 1997). Miller and Davis (1997) found stronger associations between a child's poverty history and the quality of the home learning environment than between poverty and parent-child interactions.

While income is a strong correlate of the home learning environment, so too are education and occupation. Miller and Davis also found that, after controlling for history of poverty, maternal educational attainment was still significantly and positively associated with the cognitive stimulation provided to the child at home. For example, mothers' provision of verbal stimulation differs by education and occupation. As we discussed in more detail in Chapter 6, higher-SES mothers, compared with lower-SES mothers, "talk more, provide more object labels, sustain conversational topics longer, respond more contingently to their children's speech and elicit more talk from their children" (Hoff-Ginsberg and Tardif, 1995:177; see also Hart and Risley, 1995; Hoff-Ginsberg, 1991).

Efforts to understand why maternal education might be a particularly important aspect of socioeconomic status in determining mothers' verbal interactions with their children have pointed to the fact that a mother's educational attainment, but not her occupational status, correlates with her teaching style (Laosa, 1983). Specifically, mothers with higher levels of education use more verbal reinforcement, inquiry, modeling strategies, and reading with their preschool children. What remains to be understood is whether these findings are attributable to mothers' relative schooling per se, or to genetic differences or other characteristics that distinguish mothers who acquire different levels of schooling and might affect such relevant aspects of parenting as the use of complex verbal strategies with their children (see Borduin and Henggeler, 1981).

As described earlier, Parcel and Menaghan (1994) argue that jobs that are routinized, have low autonomy, and provide little opportunity for substantively complex work erode parents' cognitive skills and, in turn, decrease the likelihood that they will provide a cognitively stimulating environment for their children. In a longitudinal study, Parcel and Menaghan (1994) show that the complexity of mothers' and fathers' occupations has a positive association with the home learning environment that is independent of parental education, wage rate, and hours of work. However, they also found that the positive effects of job complexity on the home environment depend on family and work demands and stresses, such as the birth of an additional child and the spouse's work conditions.

In sum, the support for learning that characterizes young children's home environments is strongly associated with both their cognitive development and their family's socioeconomic niche. As with maternal mental health, therefore, improving the literacy and learning environment of the home offers a potentially promising focus for efforts to promote early learning in poor families. The challenge, as illustrated by our review of parenting interventions (see Chapters 9 and 13), is finding effective approaches to accomplishing this goal.

SUMMARY AND CONCLUSIONS

The past quarter-century has produced many changes—some favorable, many not—in families' time, money, education, and other socioeconomic resources. Income inequality has increased, producing both more poverty and more affluence among families with young children. The average parental schooling level has increased. More young children are growing up in single-parent homes, and many more mothers with young children now hold full-time jobs than before. Finally, more children are growing up in poverty today than was the case 25 years ago.

These trends hold both the promise of improved child well-being and the risk of increased problems. Their effect on an individual child will depend on the mix of positive and negative influences affecting his or her own family. Their effect on this generation of young children will depend on the broader landscape of how many children are affected by which influences, and what steps society takes in response to them. On balance, however, the evidence suggests that while improved maternal education may have modestly positive effects on early development, the effects of shifting family structures and, to an even greater extent, of maternal employment will depend on a number of accompanying conditions. However, the persistent economic hardship that affects so many children is likely to be highly detrimental, especially during the earliest years of life.

If confirmed in future research, this evidence that poverty during the early childhood years is especially harmful suggests that tax and transfer policies affecting family economic status should pay much more attention to improving families' incomes while children are young. The emerging evidence from welfare reform experiments suggests, however, that the success of such efforts (when the criteria for success emphasize the well-being of young children) may hinge on simultaneously linking families and children to early intervention and mental health services. Nevertheless, because many children growing up in poverty become productive adults, it is most accurate to portray low socioeconomic status as reducing the chances of success rather than leading inevitably to diminished attainments.

We found suggestive associations, but little strong evidence, that an intervention aimed at generating modest increases in parental education would produce measurable benefits for children's development. Associations found between parental occupation and children's development suggest that characteristics of employment may have a modest impact on children's development The literature on single-parent family structure shows that children living in single-parent families are at greater risk for poor developmental outcomes compared with children reared in two-parent families, although we have a limited understanding of the processes involved.

The research on maternal employment and children's development is generally reassuring to working parents. Nevertheless, we have learned that maternal employment is too complex a phenomenon for simple comparisons between young children with and without working mothers to reveal consistent differences. Rather, it is the circumstances of work, such as the income it generates, the proportion of the day the infant is spending in the presence of a security-giving, trusted caregiver, and related effects on family functioning that lie at the heart of how maternal employment affects young children. In particular, there is now evidence that nonstandard working hours—which now make up a major share of jobs for poor working women—pose risks for children; and that going to work for long hours during the child's first year poses a risk to child development perhaps especially when trade-offs are involved from time in sensitive and stable parental care at home to time in poorer quality alternative care, as they often are.

Some of the most promising efforts to understand how a family's resources affect young children have focused on the mental health of parents, associated effects on their parenting, and the quality of the home environment, notably the support it provides for learning. Punitive parenting, reduced monitoring, parental psychological distress, and substance abuse, as well as less parental support for children's early learning, are all more prevalent in low-income families. While these factors have often been studied in isolation, they are likely to occur in clusters which, in turn, place children at higher risk of poor outcomes.

Growing Up in Child Care

11

econd only to the immediate family, child care is the context in which early development unfolds, starting in infancy and continuing through school entry for the vast majority of young children in the United States. It is the setting in which most children first learn to interact with other children on a regular basis, establish bonds with adults other than their parents, receive or fail to receive important inputs for early learning and language development, and experience their initial encounter with a school-like environment. Early and extensive enrollment in child care has become the norm in U.S. society. Indeed, if children were only sporadically or briefly exposed to child care, it would not be the visible policy issue that it is today.

In 1994, 10.3 million children under the age of 5 were in child care while their mothers worked, including 1.7 million infants under 1 year of age (U.S. Bureau of the Census, 1997). The vast majority of 5-year-olds are in kindergarten (88.5 percent in 1995) (Hofferth et al., 1998). Younger children have also been enrolling in center-based child care, preschool, and pre-kindergarten programs at increasing rates so that, by 1997, 45 percent of 3- and 4-year-olds and 22 percent of children younger than 3 were in these types of programs (Capizzano et al., 2000; Ehrle et al., 2000). But enrollment in child care begins long before this. In 1999, the National Household Education Survey, which asks all families about nonparental child care arrangements regardless of the employment status of the mother, reported that 61 percent of children under age 4 were in regularly scheduled

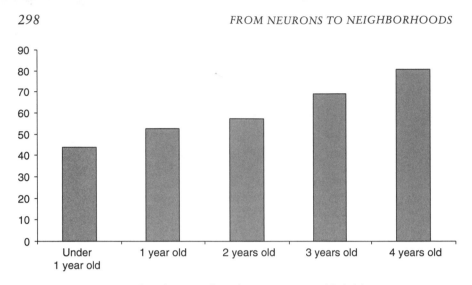

FIGURE 11-1 Percent distribution of newborn to 4-year-old children in nonparental care on a regular basis, by age, 1999. SOURCE: Unpublished tabulations from the 1999 National Household Education Survey; generated for the committee by DeeAnn Brimhall, National Center for Education Statistics, U.S. Department of Education.

child care, including 44 percent of infants under 1 year, 53 percent of 1-year-olds, and 57 percent of 2-year-olds (see Figure 11-1).

This is a dramatic change from the recent past. With it have come both growing acceptance of child care as supplementing rather than competing with parental care and persistent worries about the effects of child care on children's development. The dilemmas that today's parents are facing are not new, however. Decisions about the care and supervision of young children are among the oldest problems faced by human society (Lamb, 1999; Rossi, 1977). Over the history of family life and across cultures, mothers have had multiple duties that have necessitated sharing the hands-on care of their infants and toddlers with others, primarily other women relatives and older children (Lancaster and Lancaster, 1987; LeVine et al., 1994; Weisner and Gallimore, 1977).

What is new is the rapid growth in reliance on paid care by nonrelatives in center-based settings and the expansion in public subsidies for child care. While parents and relatives continue to provide vast amounts of early child care, rapid growth in reliance on center-based arrangements as the primary source of child care has occurred for children of all ages, accompanied by a decline in the use of home-based care by nonrelatives. The ramifications of welfare reform—the Personal Responsibility and Work Opportunity Reconciliation Act (PRWORA) of 1996—for child care are also changing the landscape in unprecedented ways. Prior to the 1996 legislation, states were prohibited from requiring recipients who were single parents caring for infants to participate in work-related activities. As of June 2000, 14 states have used the new flexibility granted by the legislation not to exempt automatically from work requirements parents whose youngest child is less than 1 year old (and most of them require work when the infant reaches 3 months of age). An additional 23 states require mothers receiving benefits to work when their children reach age 1 (State Policy Documentation Project, 2000). Moreover, for single mothers, over half of the states require 30 or more hours of work per week. As a result, the population of children in child care is likely to include more very low-income infants than has ever before been the case.

WHAT IS CHILD CARE?

What do we mean by child care? It is not just *day care*, given the growing numbers of children who require supervision while their parents work nontraditional and shifting hours. It is also not just *care*. Beneficial outcomes for children in child care are associated with settings that provide both nurturance and support for early learning and language development. Accordingly, previous distinctions between "early education" or "pre-school" and "day care" have unraveled. In fact, child care may be seen as providing a number of services, including the provision of nurturance and learning opportunities for children, preparation for school, support for working parents and reduction of poverty, respite care in child welfare cases, and access to supplemental services such as vision and hearing screening, developmental testing, feeding programs, and even parent support and literacy programs (Fein and Clarke-Stewart, 1973; Lamb, 1998; Scarr and Eisenberg, 1993).

While many of these purposes are complementary, the distinction between child care as a developmental program for children and child care as a support service for working parents continues to guide different emphases in policy debates (Blau, 2000). This is most apparent with respect to the differing attention given to issues of the quality of care supported by different policies. For example, 25 percent of all new funds for Head Start, which emphasizes developmental goals, is set aside for quality improvement initiatives. In contrast, only 4 percent of the funds for the Child Care and Development Fund (CCDF)—the major source of child care support tied to welfare reform—is dedicated to quality improvements. There are indications, however, that the political divide between these two tiers of child care policy making is becoming less distinct, as funding streams for state prekindergarten, Head Start, and CCDF-funded child care programs are increasingly being merged at the federal, state, and program levels (Kagan and Cohen, 1996; Raden, 1999; Schulman et al., 1999).

The research reviewed in this section covers the broad array of programs and services that provide for the care and early development of young children while their parents work or, for other reasons, rely on others to provide care for their children on a regular basis. Recognizing that substantial controversy surrounds nomenclature in this area of research, practice, and policy, we use the term "child care" throughout this report to encompass the blend of care, nurturance, and early education that the best child care provides. We focus on naturalistic studies of community-based child care settings—ranging from grandparent care to preschool programs—given that these, in all of their diversity, constitute most of the child care for children in the United States. They also are the focus of concern regarding the developmental effects of child care. Within this literature, we emphasize studies that have examined the effects of child care net of family influences on development. We also include evidence from planned interventions, discussed more extensively in Chapter 13, when they supplement and sharpen knowledge about child care. Research on school-age child care is not included in this synthesis, given the focus of this report on children prior to school entry (for excellent recent reviews on school-age child care, see Vandell and Posner, 1999; Vandell and Shumow, 1999). Following a brief discussion about the timing of entry into child care and factors that impinge on this decision, we synthesize the literature on the effects of child care on both the mother-child relationship and child development. We then discuss research on the ingredients of quality care that promote beneficial development, the availability and distribution of higher-quality arrangements, and child care for children with disabilities.

ENTRY INTO CHILD CARE

Parental decisions about child care are an important component of parental influence in the early childhood years. The first decisions about child care that face new parents are whether and when to place their child in nonparental child care and what specific arrangement to select. Corresponding to the rapid growth in labor force participation of mothers with children age 1 and younger (see Chapter 10), the majority of parents now enroll their children in child care during the first year of life. National survey data reveal that, as of the mid-1990s, approximately 1.7 million infants under 1 year of age were in child care while their mothers worked (Hofferth et al., 1998; U.S. Bureau of the Census, 1997). Data from the NICHD Study of Early Child Care (see Box 11-1 for a description of the study), which is the only prospective study of parents' child care decisions, further reveal that enrollment in child care occurs very early in the first

---

BOX 11-1
The NICHD Study of Early Child Care and Youth Development

Aware of the growing use of child care and the increasing public and policy concern about this issue, the National Institute of Child Health and Human Development (NICHD) of the U.S. Department of Health and Human Services set out to develop a comprehensive, longitudinal study about the relationships between the children's experiences in child care and their development over time. The NICHD Study of Early Child Care is the most comprehensive child care study conducted to date in the United States. A total of 1,364 children and their families from diverse economic and ethnic backgrounds, living in 10 locations around the country, were enrolled in the study beginning in 1991, at the time of the children's birth. The children are now entering the third grade, with 1,100 families still participating.

In the study, parents—not the researchers—selected the type and timing of child care that their children received. They were placed in a wide variety of child care settings: care by fathers, other relatives, in-home caregivers, child care home providers, and center-based care. The research team observed these settings at regular intervals (6, 15, 24, 36, and 54 months) to assess quality of care, which was found to be highly variable. Family characteristics were also regularly assessed, including the family's economic situation, family structure, the mother's psychological adjustment and childrearing attitudes, the quality of mother-child interactions, and the extent to which the home environment contributed to the optimal development of children. Various aspects of individual children, such as their gender and temperament, were also considered.

The children's developmental outcomes were assessed using multiple methods (trained observers, interviews, questionnaires, and testing) that provided measures of many facets of their development (growth and health, cognitive and language development, school readiness and achievement, relationship with their mothers, self-control and compliance, problem behaviors, and peer relations).

The findings are reported on a regular basis at scientific meetings and in scientific journals and books (see, for example, NICHD Early Child Care Research Network, in press[c]). To obtain further information contact: Sarah L. Friedman, Ph.D., Project Scientist/Scientific Coordinator at FriedmaS@exchange.nih.gov or (301) 435-6946. Ongoing updates about the study are available at http://public.rti.org/secc.

---

year. In this study, 72 percent of the infants experienced some nonparental child care in the first year of life, with an average age at entry of 3.31 months (NICHD Early Child Care Research Network, 1997b). About three-quarters of those who entered care during the first year of life entered prior to age 4 months and they were in care for an average 28 hours per week. The picture these data provide is thus one of very early entry into extensive child care.

The extent to which the high use of child care at early ages reflects parents' desire to return to work quickly or financial constraints on their ability to remain at home with their infants remains an open question. Pertinent information is available, however, regarding access to and use of family leave benefits, as well as about families who adjust their work schedules to curtail their reliance on nonparental child care for their babies.

The Role of Parental Leave

It is well documented that use of infant care is substantially lower in countries that have generous parental leave policies (Kamerman and Kahn, 1995). Prior to passage of the Family and Medical Leave Act (FMLA) in 1993, the United States was the only industrialized country without a federal law guaranteeing a job-protected maternity leave. In the absence of federal legislation, 23 states had passed leave laws that cover both private- and public-sector workers, but with varying provisions (Commission on Family and Medical Leave, 1996). The federal law requires employers with 50 or more workers to offer a job-protected family or medical leave of up to 12 weeks to qualifying employees (those who have worked at least 1,250 hours in the previous year) who need to be absent from work for reasons that meet the terms of the law, including the need to care for a newborn or a newly adopted or new foster child.

It is estimated that these provisions of the FMLA leave 89 percent of all private-sector work sites and 53.5 percent of the nation's private-sector employees uncovered (Commission on Family and Medical Leave, 1996). Nevertheless, the law appears to have had a major impact on the number of companies who are now offering job-protected leaves for maternity and other family and medical reasons, as well as on increased use of leave by employees (Waldfogel, 1999a, 1999b). Much of this increased use has been among men who appear to be using the leave for "other" family and medical reasons (i.e., for reasons of their own health or to care for an ill family member). There is also evidence that more leave is being used by women with infants as a result of the FMLA, although this appears to be due not so much to more women taking infant care leave as to women taking more leave (Klerman and Leibowitz, 1998; Rossi, 1998).

The law does not require the leave to be paid, but it does require that employers who provide health insurance coverage to continue to do so during the leave period. This raises questions about who avails themselves of leave and who does not. National survey data collected by the U.S. Department of Labor following implementation of the FMLA (see Cantor et al., 1995) reveals that only 17 percent of covered employees took leave during 1994-1995 and an additional 3.4 percent indicated that they needed but did not take leave. Two-thirds of workers who needed but did not take a leave indicated that they could not afford the associated loss of wages. Parents who have access to parental leave benefits and can afford to make use of them do so, suggesting that the enrollment of very young infants in child care is not entirely voluntary. Results from the NICHD Study of Early Child Care mentioned earlier indicating that the families who placed their infants in child care at the youngest ages (before 3 months) were heavily or entirely dependent on the mother's wages to escape poverty, and that many had previously been poor or dependent on public assistance, lend support to this possibility (NICHD Early Child Care Research Network, 1997c).

Parents' Arrangements for Child Care

The arrangements that parents make for the care of their children span every conceivable combination of care by mothers, fathers, and others, the complexity of which tends to get lost in efforts to categorize and portray them. In some countries, the predominant form of child care is sibling care (Harkness and Super, 1992; Nsamenang, 1992; Zeitlin, 1996). In Cameroon, for example, infants and toddlers are usually cared for by preadolescent girls, often older siblings or relatives, as part of the girls' preparation for their adult roles. After weaning, the peer group becomes the ubiquitous socializer and caretaker of children. While sibling care is much less common in the United States, it does occur.

Most young children in the United States are, however, with adults. Figure 11-2 provides information on the care arrangements used by families where the primary caretaker of the child was employed in 1997 (Capizzano et al., 2000; Ehrle et al., 2000). There are two very different ways of looking at these data. One view focuses on the large extent to which infant and toddler care, and to a lesser extent preschool care, remains within the family, shared equally by parents and other relatives. The other view focuses on the extent to which parents rely on nonfamilial care and move their children rapidly into formal group care arrangements.

As has historically been the case, a surprisingly large number of employed parents with young children do not rely on others for child care at all. In 1997, for example, a little over one-quarter of families with at least one employed parent and an infant or toddler under age 3 relied primarily on parental child care while the primary caretaker was working. Hispanic families are somewhat more likely than others to rely on parents for infant and toddler care (32 percent did so in 1997; Ehrle et al., 2000), but it is also very common among white (27 percent) and black families (22 percent).

Child care provided by fathers (while mothers work), for example, has

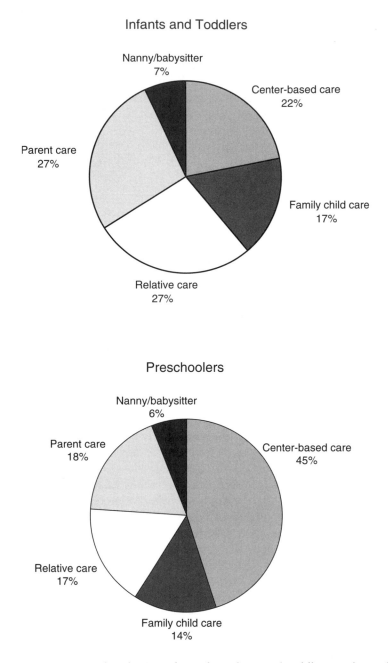

FIGURE 11-2 Current distribution of care for infants and toddlers, and preschoolers with employed mothers, 1997. SOURCE: Capizzano et al. (2000).

crept upward from 15 to 21 percent of all infant and toddler care arrangements between 1977 and 1994 (U.S. Bureau of the Census, 1997). Fathers provided one in four of the first child care arrangements made for the infants in the NICHD Study of Early Child Care (NICHD Early Child Care Research Network, 1997b). While reliance on parent care is much more common among two-parent families in which only one parent works or both parents work part-time (44 percent of families with children under 3 and 30 percent of families with children ages 3 to 4), it is also surprisingly common among two-parent families in which both parents work full-time (16 percent of families with children under 3 and 12 percent of families with children ages 3 to 4) and in one-parent families that get by with part-time employment (26 percent of families with children under 3 and 7 percent of families with children ages 3 to 4) (see Figure 11-3). Clearly, a considerable number of parents are making the effort to care for their own children, usually at home, perhaps at considerable cost to their family incomes.

Once parents turn to others for assistance with child care, grandparents and other relatives are the caregivers for many families, including 27 percent of children under age 3 and 17 percent of 3- and 4-year-olds. Hispanic

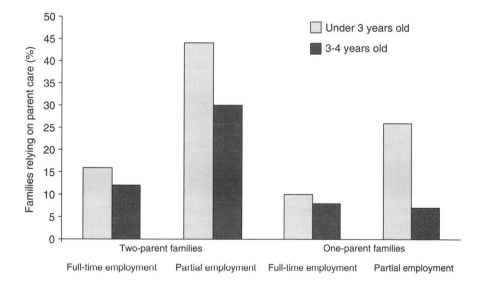

FIGURE 11-3 Reliance on parent care by family structure and extent of employment, 1997. SOURCE: Unpublished tabulations from the 1997 National Survey of America's Families; generated for the committee by Gina Adams and Jennifer Ehrle, The Urban Institute.

families are particularly likely to rely on relatives for infant and toddler care (39 percent of Hispanic families do so; Capizzano et al., 2000; Ehrle et al., 2000), compared with black (27 percent) and white families (25 percent).

At the same time, as noted above, there has been extremely rapid growth in reliance on center-based care not only for preschoolers, but also for infants and toddlers (see Figure 11-4). The share of children under age 3 in child care centers, preschools, Head Start programs, and other early childhood education programs tripled between 1977 and 1994, from 8 percent to 24 percent of children with employed mothers (U.S. Bureau of the Census, 1982, 1997). In contrast to patterns of family-based care, center-based care is used much more by black and white families than by Hispanic families, with the largest discrepancies appearing for infant and toddler arrangements (rates of use are 30, 24, and 10 percent, respectively; Capizzano et al., 2000; Ehrle et al., 2000). The increased use of center care has been accompanied by declining use of family child care providers. Nevertheless, as of 1997, 39 percent of infants and toddlers and 59 percent of preschoolers were in center-based or family child care arrangements with nonrelatives (see Figure 11-2), revealing the rapid movement of children into formal care settings and peer groupings during the earliest years of life.

In sum, vast numbers of infants spend substantial portions of their time in child care, often starting within a few months after birth. While much of this very early care remains within the family—with parents who are juggling their work schedules and with relatives—young children move rapidly into nonrelative care as they enter the toddler and preschool years. Al-

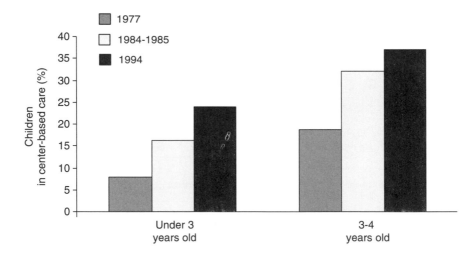

FIGURE 11-4 Growth in use of center-based care, 1977-1994. SOURCE: U.S. Bureau of the Census (1982, 1987, 1997).

though we know virtually nothing about the factors that impinge on parents' decisions about when to first rely on child care, it appears that these decisions are affected by a complex mix of factors including access to parental leave, the capacity to forgo wages for a period of time, new policies requiring work from mothers formerly dependent on public assistance, and the availability of child care arrangements (including sharing care between two parents) with which the parents are comfortable. The emerging evidence on these issues belies the hesitancy and ambivalence that accompanies new parent's decisions about infant child care and renders questions about the consequences of child care for young children especially compelling. In this context, issues concerning equity of access to family leave benefits become important, as do questions about the extent to which families in differing circumstances (e.g., those without a partner available to share child care responsibilities) feel that they are able to exert their preferences regarding when and how they arrange for the care of their infants.

THE EFFECTS OF CHILD CARE

Two concerns have guided research on the developmental effects of child care. The first focuses on the mother-infant relationship and asks, "Will this relationship be harmed or diminished in significance as a result of the daily separations that are entailed when a baby is placed in child care?" This concern is not unfounded. Child care, insofar as it reduces the amount of time available for the mother to learn the baby's signals and rhythms, might also adversely affect her ability to respond sensitively to the baby and establish a secure attachment relationship (see Brazelton, 1986). The other concern focuses directly on the children: "Will the young child's cognitive, language, and social-emotional development be compromised as a result of spending time in child care?" Today, this concern is riveted on infants and toddlers, for whom early and extensive enrollment in nonfamilial child care is a relatively recent phenomenon. The National Research Council summarized the evidence on these issues a decade ago (National Research Council, 1990). The intervening decade of research has both confirmed and expanded on the earlier panel's conclusion that the effects of child care derive not from its use or nonuse but from the quality of the experiences it provides to young children. (For additional, recent reviews of research on child care see Lamb, 1998; Love et al., 1996; Scarr and Eisenberg, 1993, and Smith, 1998.)

Child Care and the Mother-Infant Relationship

Evidence from child care research of the 1990s is reassuring to those who have been concerned that child care might disrupt the mother-infant relationship. Not only does the mother remain the primary object of attachment for infants in child care (Ainslie and Anderson, 1984; Farran and Ramey, 1977; Howes and Hamilton, 1992; Kagan et al., 1978), but also the attachment relationship appears to be largely protected from possible negative effects emanating from early entry into and extensive hours of care, as well as poor-quality care (NICHD Early Child Care Research Network, 1997a; Roggman et al., 1994; Symons, 1998). The primary influence on the attachment relationship derives not from child care but from the sensitivity of the care that is provided by the mother (namely, her supportive presence, positive regard, and lack of intrusiveness and hostility). This is equally true for children experiencing very little child care and children experiencing a lot of child care (NICHD Early Child Care Research Network, 1998b).

But the mother-child relationship is not necessarily unaffected by child care. In addition to studying the attachment between mother and infant, researchers have made direct observations of mother-infant interaction. Although many studies find no effects of child care on mother-infant interaction, some report positive effects and still others report that child care appears to create or compound problems that are seen in these interactions. Looking again at the NICHD study, infants and toddlers in more hours of child care, regardless of its quality, experienced somewhat less sensitive mothering and were less positively engaged with their mothers than other children who were not enrolled in child care (NICHD Early Child Care Research Network, 1999a). Among infants and toddlers enrolled in child care, however, those in higher-quality arrangements (regardless of hours in care) experienced greater maternal sensitivity. Moreover, the negative relation between the amount of child care and maternal sensitivity and child engagement with mother was not of sufficient magnitude to disrupt the formation of a secure infant attachment. When considered in conjunction with the data presented in the previous chapter, suggesting detrimental effects of maternal employment in the first year of life, there would seem to be cause for concern about early infant care, particularly in light of its highly variable quality in the United States (discussed below).

A number of other studies have found that when very young children (i.e., infants and toddlers under 2 years of age) are exposed to risk factors at home and to extensive or poor-quality early child care, their odds of experiencing insensitive mothering increase (Belsky et al., 1996c; Clark et al., 1997; Tresch Owen and Cox, 1988). The direction of effects underlying these findings is not yet clear: that is, there have been some suggestions that early reliance on child care undermines the mother's ability to respond sensitively to her child and, as a result, diminishes the child's involvement with her mother (see Clark et al., 1997; NICHD Early Child Care Research Network, 1999a; Stifter et al., 1993; Tresch Owen and Cox, 1988), but other studies fail to find these associations between early child care and maternal sensitivity (Burchinal et al., 1992; Egeland and Hiester, 1995; Goldberg and Easterbrooks, 1988; Gottfried et al., 1988; Rabinovich et al., 1986; Stith and Davis, 1984; Zaslow et al., 1985). It may also be the case that less sensitive mothers are more likely to enroll their infants in child care at a very early age, although this hypothesis has not been tested.

Child care can also protect children from family-based risk. This has been a primary rationale for early intervention programs that provide high-quality center-based child care for children living in poverty and for children in the child welfare system. Naturalistic studies of typical child care have also demonstrated protective influences. For example, mothers participating in the NICHD study who were living in or near poverty and whose infants were in full-time, high-quality child care were observed to show more positive involvement with their 6-month-olds (i.e., spontaneously vocalizing, responding verbally to the child, voicing positive feelings, hugging, kissing, praising) compared with similarly poor mothers who were rearing their babies at home or were using full-time, lower-quality infant care (NICHD Early Child Care Research Network, 1997d). Others have found that child care can protect infants and older children from the detrimental effects of both poverty (Caughy et al., 1994) and maternal depression (Cohn et al., 1986, 1991).

In sum, despite persistent concern about the effects of child care on the mother-infant relationship, the weight of the evidence is reassuring, with the possible exception of emerging findings regarding very early, extensive exposure to care of dubious quality. Mothers themselves play the lead role in determining the quality of their relationship with their infants, toddlers, and preschoolers. If anything, the child care research of the past decade has enhanced appreciation of the potent influence of parents on early development. When child care effects are examined net of parental effects on child outcomes, parent's behaviors and beliefs show substantially larger associations with their children's development than do any features of the child care arrangement. These efforts to control for family influences when examining how child care affects child development might appear to be an obvious and straightforward approach. Nevertheless, it has only become common in the past decade. In fact, even with extensive controls for family influences on development, it is impossible to be assured that we are capturing the effects of child care untainted by influences that result from the fact that families with different features (e.g., higher incomes) are able to place their children in child care with different features (e.g., higher-quality care).[1]

---

[1]These selection biases, which arise from the fact that parents select their children's child care environments and do not do so randomly, can contribute to both over- and underestimates of associations between child care and child development (see Chapter 4, as well as Blau, 1999, and Duncan et al., 2000).

When child care is found to be associated with the mother-child relationship, the link is as likely to be positive as it is to be negative. The
challenge now facing those who study child care is to clarify when child
care protects children from family-based risk (such as poverty, maternal
depression, high levels of conflict), when it compounds risk, and when it
poses risks to children who otherwise are growing up in supportive home
environments. In other words, we need to ask more complicated questions
regarding how child care intersects with what transpires at home (Hoffman,
1989; Zaslow et al., 1985).

Effects of Child Care on Children's Development

Ultimately, questions about child care turn on its consequences for
child development. Under what conditions does child care contribute to or
undermine children's social skills, emotional well-being, and readiness for
school? The answer is "it depends," but a great deal more is known about
what it depends on than was known a decade ago.

One of the most consistent and ubiquitous findings in this literature
links the quality of child care that children receive to virtually every measure of development that has been examined. While hours of care, stability
of care, and type of care are sometimes associated with developmental
outcomes, it is the quality of care and, in particular, the quality of the daily
transactions between child care providers and the children for whom they
are responsible, that carry the weight of the influence of child care on
children's development. This conclusion, based largely on correlational
studies of typical child care, is confirmed by experimental evidence linking
enrollment in very high-quality early intervention programs to both short-
and longer-term outcomes in both academic attainment and prevention of
delinquency for high-risk children (see Barnett, 1995; Currie, 2000;
Shonkoff and Meisels, 2000; Yoshikawa, 1994, 1995; as well as the discussion in Chapter 13). What remains to be understood is whether investments in quality that fall substantially short of the levels entailed in the
intervention programs can produce meaningful benefits not just for high-
risk children, but for all children. Let's look at the evidence.

Effects on Cognition and Language

As a result of concerns about school readiness (or, in the case of early
intervention programs, hopes for promoting readiness), emerging competencies in cognitive and language domains have been a long-standing focus
of study in child care research. Outcomes that have been assessed range
from IQ and general developmental levels to specific learning and communication skills.

The strongest and most compelling evidence regarding the developmental effects of high-quality child care on early cognition and language has come from experimental studies of planned early interventions for economically disadvantaged children or for those at risk of developmental problems. The findings from this literature are consistent. Intensive, high-quality, center-based interventions that provide learning experiences directly to the young child have a positive effect on early learning, cognitive and language development, and school achievement (Barnett, 1995; Brooks-Gunn et al., 1994; Burchinal et al., 1997; Feagans et al., 1995; Lamb, 1998; Ramey and Ramey, 1998; Roberts et al., 1989). Sometimes these effects dissipate during the early school years, but the impacts of some programs have been found to continue well into the school years and even into adulthood (Campbell and Ramey, 1994; Currie and Thomas, 1995; Lazar and Darlington, 1982; Luster and McAdoo, 1996; McLoyd, 1997; Yoshikawa, 1994, 1995). Effect sizes in this literature range up to 1.0 standard deviation for outcomes for preschoolers.[2] The early intervention literature further indicates that the strongest effects of high-quality care are found for children from families with the fewest resources and under the greatest stress.

High-quality care in the infant and toddler years is also associated with children's cognitive and linguistic development in the correlational research on typical child care settings (Burchinal et al., 1996; Galinsky et al., 1994; Howes and Rubenstein, 1985; McCartney, 1984; Peisner-Feinberg and Burchinal, 1997; Peisner-Feinberg et al., 2000). One of the few studies that provided effect sizes reported that they ranged from .09 to .14 for associations between child care quality and cognitive and language outcomes for 3-year-olds (NICHD Early Child Care Research Network, 1999c). The evidence associating quality of care and early cognitive and language outcomes is striking in its consistency. The results are often but not always stronger for children from lower-income families and those whose mothers have relatively low levels of education (Peisner-Feinberg and Burchinal, 1997). Sometimes improved language and learning outcomes are short-lived (Chin-Quee and Scarr, 1994; Deater-Deckard et al., 1996) and sometimes they endure into the school years (Andersson, 1989; Broberg et al., 1997; Burchinal et al., 1995; Field, 1991; Larsen and Robinson, 1989; NICHD Early Child Care Research Network, 2000; Peisner-Feinberg et al.,

---

[2]Effect sizes provide an estimate of the fraction of a standard deviation in the child outcome associated with a change in the given quality measure. Effects less than .3 are considered small, .3 to .5 as moderate, and above .5 as large (Cohen, 1988). There is, however, an emerging debate about how best to portray the magnitude of effects in this literature, with several experts now suggesting that effect sizes be interpreted not in absolute terms but in relation to other pertinent effects (McCartney and Rosenthal, 2000).

2000; Rosenthal, 1994; Vandell and Ramanan, 1992). Of central importance to cognitive and language outcomes is the verbal environment of the child care setting (McCartney, 1984; NICHD Early Child Care Research Network, 2000). As with mother care, child care providers who are both supportive and provide more verbal stimulation have children in their care who show advanced cognitive and language development.

In light of the experimental evidence on center-based early intervention programs, it is interesting that evidence is emerging from nonexperimental studies of more typical child care suggesting that cumulative experience in high-quality, center-based care starting in the second year of life may be particularly beneficial for cognitive development (Broberg et al., 1997; Hartmann, 1995; NICHD Early Child Care Research Network, 2000). Some studies find that center-based care is especially beneficial for children from low-income families (Caughy et al., 1994), but others find that all children benefit regardless of their family background (NICHD Early Child Care Research Network, 2000). What might children be getting in child care centers that they are not getting in other settings? One of the features that distinguishes higher-quality from lower-quality care with regard to early cognition and language is the amount of language stimulation that child care teachers provide (McCartney, 1984; Melhuish et al., 1992; NICHD Early Child Care Research Network, 2000). Center-based teachers, who are more likely to have received specialized training in early development and more education generally than providers in other child care settings (NICHD Early Child Care Research Network, 1996, in press b). As a result, they may talk more with children and respond to their efforts to communicate in precisely the ways that foster early language and cognitive skills, but this speculation requires empirical study.

Effects on Social and Emotional Development

Efforts to understand how child care affects children's social-emotional development have assessed a vast array of outcomes that tap children's self-regulatory behavior, their cooperation with and attachments to adults, their social skill (or lack of it) with other children, and the developmental level of their social interactions. For virtually every outcome that has been assessed, quality of care shows positive associations with early social and emotional development (see NICHD Early Child Care Research Network, 1998c and reviews by Lamb, 1998; National Research Council, 1990; Scarr and Eisenberg, 1993) after family influences on development are controlled, albeit to varying degrees. The experimental literature on early intervention also has demonstrated significant effects on young children's social skills and, in particular, on reduced conduct problems (Yoshikawa, 1994, 1995). Indeed, it is in the realm of preventing delinquency in adolescence and early adulthood that the strongest economic effects of early intervention appear to be focused (see Chapter 13). When children enter high-quality child care earlier and spend more time in these arrangements, positive effects on social competence can continue on into the elementary years (Peisner-Feinberg et al., 2000) and even preadolescence (Andersson, 1989; Field, 1991), although this is not consistently the case.

The child's relationship with his or her child care provider seems to play an especially important role with regard to social-emotional development. Children form secure attachments to their child care providers when they are stable and these attachments, in turn, are associated with adaptive social development, just as they are for children and parents (Howes et al., 1992; Oppenheim et al., 1988; Peisner-Feinberg et al., 2000; Pianta and Nimetz, 1991; Sroufe et al., 1983). Howes and her colleagues have found, for example, that children who are securely attached to their providers show more competent interactions with adults and more advanced peer play (Howes and Hamilton, 1993; Howes et al., 1988, 1994), both during the child care years and on into second grade (Howes, 2000).

Others have found associations between the stability of child care providers in center-based programs and the quality of children's interactions with their providers (Barnas and Cummings, 1994), as well as their social competence with peers, active engagement with materials in the classroom, and vocabulary levels (Howes et al., 1992). As reviewed in Chapter 7, the stability of the peer group may matter as well. Children who remain longer with the same group of children are more peer-oriented and less solitary over time than those whose peer groups have changed frequently (Galluzzo et al., 1990; Harper and Huie, 1985; Holmberg, 1980; Howes, 1988a, 1988b) and they are friendlier toward peers in distress (Farver and Branstetter, 1994).

In sum, the positive relation between child care quality and virtually every facet of children's development that has been studied is one of the most consistent findings in developmental science. While child care of poor quality is associated with poorer developmental outcomes, high-quality care is associated with outcomes that all parents want to see in their children, ranging from cooperation with adults to the ability to initiate and sustain positive exchanges with peers, to early competence in math and reading. This conclusion derives from experimental research on high-quality interventions for children at risk, as well as from the weaker correlational designs that assess a broader range of quality and a broader distribution of children. The stability of child care providers appears to be particularly important for young children's social development, an association that is attributable to the attachments that are established between young children and more stable providers. For cognitive and language outcomes, the verbal environment that child care providers create appears to be a very important feature of care.

The influence of child care is not as large as the influence of the family environment, but it emerges repeatedly in study after study, using different measures, and for children of different ages and living in different circumstances. Most studies of typical child care have not, however, followed children on into elementary school, let alone into adolescence. This is an important missing piece in the child care literature that is needed to understand the conditions in schools, families, peer groups, and communities that sustain positive, early child care effects. The studies of typical child care also remain open to criticism, discussed earlier, based on the difficulties associated with the fact that parents select their children's child care settings. To address this criticism, research on typical child care settings using experimental and other stronger designs is needed. In particular, a firmer understanding is needed of the causal impacts of differing amounts and types of investment in child care quality that, for reasons of political feasibility, fall short of providing high-quality interventions for all children.

WHAT IS QUALITY CHILD CARE?

Volumes of both scholarly and popular material have been written about the ingredients of high-quality child care (Lamb, 1998; Love et al., 1996; Phillips and Howes, 1987). Although some have argued that the factors that parents care about differ from the features of child care that researchers tend to study, in fact, the differences appear to be more a matter of terminology than of substance (Hofferth et al., 1998). For example, parents want their children to receive lots of individual attention and to be exposed to materials and interactions that will prepare them for school. Researchers in search of the central features of quality care have identified the relationship between the child and the care provider and the amount of cognitive and language stimulation provided over the course of the day as especially critical. In general, three tiers of variables have been examined in studies of child care quality: the child-provider relationship, the structural features of care, and the surrounding community and policy context. They can be viewed as nested levels in which the quality of child-caregiver interaction is affected by the quality that characterizes the structural features and community context of care.

The Child and the Caregiver

Quality of care ultimately boils down to the quality of the relationship between the child care provider or teacher and the child. A beautiful space and an elaborate curriculum—like a beautiful home—can be impressive, but without skilled and stable child care providers, they will not promote positive development.

Young children whose caregivers provide ample verbal and cognitive stimulation, who are sensitive and responsive, and who give them generous amounts of attention and support are more advanced in all realms of development compared with children who fail to receive these important inputs (see Lamb, 1998; Smith, 1998). This conclusion applies to infants, toddlers, and preschoolers and also applies to all forms of child care, ranging from relatives to center-based programs (NICHD Early Child Care Research Network, 1998c, 2000). Stability and skill appear to go together. More stable providers have been found to engage in more appropriate, attentive, and engaged interactions with the children in their care (Raikes, 1993; Rubenstein et al., 1977; Whitebook et al., 1990). It is not a coincidence that the high-quality intervention programs that have generated strong experimental evidence of positive developmental effects have employed highly qualified staff and experienced virtually no teacher turnover (National Research Council and Institute of Medicine, 2000).

Stable child care providers are rare, however. Turnover rates among them (including those who change settings as well as those who leave the field) are among the highest of any profession that is tracked by the U.S. Department of Labor (U.S. Bureau of Labor Statistics, 1998), hovering at 30 percent per year. By comparison, 6.6 percent of public school teachers and 21 percent of home health aides leave their jobs each year. Multisite, observational studies of child care centers have reported turnover rates in the 1990s ranging from over 40 percent (Whitebook et al., 1990, 1997) to 25 percent (Phillips et al., 1994). In 1977, the annual turnover rate among center-based providers in these same sites was 15 percent (Coelen et al., 1979). The authors of a multisite study of home-based providers (Kontos et al., 1995) reported that 30 percent of care arrangements provided by relatives were no longer available after a year, 25 percent of unregulated family day care providers had gone out of business, and 8 percent of regulated family day care providers were no longer operating.

Structural Features of Care

The next tier of quality consists of features that are associated with warm, sensitive, and stimulating interactions on the part of child care providers and teachers. Solid evidence has documented associations among the provider's behavior, her self-reported training and education, and the immediate context in which she works, including ratios, group size, and the adult work environment (Lamb, 1998; Love et al., 1996; Smith, 1998). Some intriguing recent evidence suggests that the staff-child ratio may be relatively more important for infants and toddlers and that the educational level of the provider may become more important as children move beyond the infant years into toddlerhood and beyond (NICHD Early Child Care Research Network, 1996, in press b).

Both formal education levels and recent, specialized training in child development have been found quite consistently to be associated with high-quality interactions and children's development in center-based, family day care and even in in-home sitter arrangements (Dunn, L., 1993; Fischer and Eheart, 1991; Kontos et al., 1994, 1995; Lamb, 1998; NICHD Early Child Care Research Network, 1996, in press b; Smith, 1998; Whitebook et al., 1990). Caregivers with more child-centered and less authoritarian beliefs about childrearing have also been found to provide warmer and more sensitive care (NICHD Early Child Care Research Network, 1996, in press b; Phillips et al., 1987a). Among home-based providers, the choice of child care as a career (sometimes called "intentionality") has been associated with higher-quality care (Kontos et al., 1995). Experience as a child care provider, in contrast, shows a much less consistent relationship to quality care (Dunn, L., 1993; Galinsky et al., 1994; Kagan and Newton, 1989; Kontos, 1994; Kontos and Fiene, 1987; Ruopp et al., 1979; Whitebook et al., 1990).

The context within which caregivers work has been examined most often using measures of ratio and group size that capture the demands on an individual child care provider's time and capacity to provide sensitive care to her young charges. The ratio of children to caregiver has held up over time as one of the most sensitive indicators of quality care in all settings as, to a somewhat lesser extent, has group size (Burchinal et al., 1996; Galinsky et al., 1994; Lamb, 1998; NICHD Early Child Care Research Network, 1996, in press b; Phillipsen et al., 1997; Ruopp et al., 1979; Smith, 1998; Whitebook et al., 1990). Importantly, it appears that fairly minor changes in ratios and group sizes can affect the quality of care that young children receive. For example, 6-month-olds who are the only child in care have been found to receive significantly more positive caregiving than infants in settings in which one additional child is present, even when the additional child is the caregiver's own (NICHD Early Child Care Research Network, 1996). Infants in centers with ratios of three or fewer children per caregiver have been found to receive significantly more sensitive and appropriate caregiving (Howes et al., 1992), and to score one standard deviation above those in centers with larger ratios on a measure of communication skills, even after adjusting for family factors that affect development (Burchinal et al., 1996). The addition of two school-age children to family day care homes caring for infants, toddlers, and pre-schoolers was observed to result in less sensitive caregiving (Howes and Norris, 1997).

More recently, aspects of the adult work environment of child care, including provider wages and benefits, have been included in studies of child care quality. This research has revealed strong relationships, comparable to those found for training and ratios, between staff wages and child care quality in both center-based and family day care arrangements (Cost Quality and Outcomes Study Team, 1995; Helburn, 1995; Kontos et al., 1995; Phillips et al., 1991, in press; Scarr et al., 1994; Whitebook et al., 1997). Wages are also the primary, although not the only, determinant of staff turnover; when wages are increased, turnover declines (Whitebook and Bellm, 1999; Whitebook et al., 1997).

In light of this evidence, it is of concern that the average hourly wage of child care workers is $6.12 and that of family child care providers is $3.37 (U.S. Bureau of Labor Statistics, 1996). This is less than the hourly wage of parking lot attendants ($6.38) and bus drivers ($11.56), and substantially below the wages of kindergarten teachers ($19.16). Wages are not only low, but they have also not kept pace with inflation, and they often do not reflect the educational levels of child care providers. For example, in 1988, child care teachers in the National Child Care Staffing Study with some college education earned an average of $9,293 per year compared with the average wage of $19,369 for women with some college education in the civilian labor force (Whitebook et al., 1990).

The Community and Policy Environment

The final tier of quality consists of the broader community and policy environment in which child care operates. Important elements of this environment include the financing and regulatory structures that bear on the child care market, community-based planning systems, consumer education and involvement, systems for staff development and leadership training, and interconnections among providers working in different sectors of the market (Gormley et al., 1995; Kagan, 1993; Phillips, 1996). Child care regulations, which have been the focus of study in efforts to understand how the surrounding context of child care affects quality of care, appear to establish a floor of quality for regulated dimensions of care (i.e., ratios, group size), which, in turn, is associated with differing distributions of quality in states with more or less stringent regulatory provisions (Cost Quality and Outcomes Study Team, 1995a; Helburn, 1995; Howes et al., 1995b; Phillips et al., 1992). However, more stringent regulations may have the unintended effect of reducing the supply of regulated programs (Hofferth and Chaplin, 1998).

Voluntary systems may also be effective. Child care centers that voluntarily meet widely accepted guidelines for quality, such as those recommended by the American Public Health Association and the American Academy of Pediatrics (1992) provide better care, and the children in these programs show better outcomes than their peers in programs that do not meet these guidelines. For example, the mean school readiness scores for children in classrooms meeting none of the APHA/AAP standards was about 14 percentage points below the population norm; the scores for children in classrooms meeting all of the standards was just above the population average (NICHD Early Child Care Research Network, 1998c). Children in centers that met more of the standards had higher scores than did children in centers meeting fewer of the standards. In other words, there were no clear thresholds above which outcomes were markedly improved—more was better. Of course, we cannot ascribe the better outcomes directly to the standards. Centers meeting more standards may also be doing other things that foster development, and parent-driven selection bias may also be operating such that children who would do well in any case are more likely to be placed in high-quality settings. It is notable, however, that state child care standards fall far short of the APHA/AAP standards and vary enormously, from mandated ratios for infants ranging from 3 to 1 to 12 to 1 and for 3-year-olds ranging from 7 to 1 to 17 to 1 (for example Azure, 1996). Most states permit infants and toddlers to be cared for by staff who, on average, have not completed high school, have only had some general training in child development, and receive fewer than 5 hours of in-service training annually (Young et al., 1997).

In sum, quality is inherent in the child care provider, whether it is the grandmother, an unrelated sitter, or a center-based teacher. Critical to sustaining high-quality child care for young children are the providers' characteristics, notably their education, specialized training, and attitudes about their work and the children in their care, and the features of child care that enable them to excel in their work and remain in their jobs, notably small ratios, small groups, and adequate compensation. Regulatory and voluntary systems that support higher levels of quality on these dimensions are associated with variation in the quality of care that is found in given states, communities, and programs. Even small improvements in ratios and education are reflected in more sensitive, appropriate, and warm caregiving, suggesting useful targets for investments in quality. The success story provided by the U.S. Department of Defense's efforts to improve its child care programs attests to the feasibility of upgrading the quality of child care in the United States (see Box 11-2). It is important to recognize, however, that other dimensions of quality that are rarely measured (i.e., the leadership skill of the center director, the mental health and motivation of the caregiver, the stability of funding, characteristics of the families served) are, in all likelihood, important ingredients along with the structural dimensions of care that dominate the research literature (Blau, 1997, 2000). Without attention to some of these subtle, but potentially powerful, influences on quality, it is difficult to predict how much can ultimately be

BOX 11-2
Child Care for U.S. Military Families

The U.S. armed services oversee a child care system that serves more than 200,000 children every day at over 300 worldwide locations and includes families from all four branches of the military. The military child care system includes child development centers, family care, and before- and after-school programs.

In 1989, the Military Child Care Act (MCCA) was enacted by Congress in response to General Accounting Office reports and congressional hearings that detailed the extremely poor condition of the child care available to military families. The goal of the act was improve the quality, availability, and affordability of military child care. It addressed the creation of new child care staff positions, staff training and compensation, inspections, parent fees based on family income, and other issues. After just 10 years, the military child care system is now considered a model for the nation.

Because of its link to low-quality care, staff turnover was one of the issues that the MCCA required the armed services to address. In 1989, the average annual turnover rate at military child care centers was 48 percent. By 1993, the turnover rate was reduced to less than 24 percent (Zellman and Johansen, 1998). This remarkable reduction in turnover is attributed primarily to the improvements that were made in child care workers' compensation and training. First, the rate of pay for child care workers was standardized and made comparable to other jobs on base that required similar levels of training, education, and responsibility. Second, advancement and salary increases were made contingent upon completing specific training programs. Third, at least one training and curriculum specialist was added to the staff of every child development center. The training and curriculum specialists are responsible for focusing on child development issues, as opposed to administrative issues. The costs of these quality improvements were not shifted to parents. In fact, because the U.S. military subsidizes the cost of its child care, military families actually pay on average 25 percent less for child care than do nonmilitary families. And 95 percent of all military child care centers (compared with 8 percent of civilian child care centers) meet the accreditation standards developed by the National Association for the Education of Young Children (NAEYC).

SOURCE: Campbell et al. (2000); see also Zellman and Johansen (1998).

accomplished by policy actions that focus on only one or two structural dimensions of care.

THE DISTRIBUTION AND COST OF QUALITY CARE

Some child care settings offer children what they need to feel secure and loved, to learn, and to build social skills and friendships. Many do not. Virtually every systematic effort to characterize the quality of child care in the United States has found that about 10 to 20 percent of arrangements fall below thresholds of even adequate care (Cost Quality and Outcomes Study Team, 1995; Galinsky et al., 1994; Helburn, 1995; Whitebook et al., 1990). This is the case regardless of the type of care being examined. What do researchers see when they go into these settings? They see caregivers who more often ignore than respond to young children's bids for attention and affection, a dearth of age-appropriate or educational toys, and children who spend much of their time wandering aimlessly around, unengaged with adults, other children, or materials. Given the likely possibility that providers who offer extremely poor-quality care do not participate in research, these figures may actually be underestimates of the amount of poor-quality care that exists in this country.

In some cases, infants appear to get the poorest-quality care, but in other cases they have been found to get better care than older children, particularly when they are in a one-to-one arrangement with a competent caregiver. Even the NICHD Study of Early Child Care, which provides a more favorable portrait of child care quality than do other studies, reported that one in four infant caregivers were moderately insensitive, only 26 percent were moderately or highly stimulating of cognitive development, and 19 percent were moderately or highly detached (NICHD Early Child Care Research Network, 1996). Fewer than 20 percent of toddlers and preschoolers were in settings in which caregivers offered care that was "highly characteristic" of positive caregiving.

It is not unusual for basic safety to be compromised in the nation's child care settings, as illustrated by a 1998 Consumer Product Safety Commission (CPSC) study of 220 licensed child care settings. The study reported pervasive health and safety violations: two-thirds of the settings they visited had at least one safety hazard, including cribs with soft bedding, no safety gates on stairs, unsafe (or no) playground surfacing, and use of recalled products (Consumer Product Safety Commission, 1999). An earlier investigation conducted by the Office of the Inspector General (1994) found more than 1,000 violations in 169 child care facilities in five states. Among the hazards were fire code violations, toxic chemicals, playground hazards, and unsanitary conditions.

This range of quality becomes particularly worrisome when juxtaposed with evidence about who experiences better and worse child care in the United States. Children from poorer and more stressed homes receive lower-quality child care than other children (Howes and Olenick, 1986; NICHD Early Child Care Research Network, 1997c; Phillips et al., 1994). There is, however, one exception to this pattern. Among families using child care centers, the working poor and those whose incomes hover just above the poverty line receive poorer-quality care than either families living in poverty or families with solidly middle and upper incomes (NICHD Early Child Care Research Network, 1997c; Phillips et al., 1994). This counterintuitive finding appears to be attributable to differential access to child care subsidies and programs such as Head Start and other publicly subsidized arrangements that are available to the very poor, but not to families with somewhat higher incomes. Quality of care in these programs is significantly higher than in other community-based child care centers (Layzer et al., 1993; Phillips et al., 1994; Whitebook et al., 1990).

The link between subsidized care and quality care is not surprising in light of estimates of what it costs to provide high-quality child care. The cost of providing accredited[3] center-based child care was estimated at $4,797 per child per year in 1988 ($6,764 in 1998 dollars) (U.S. General Accounting Office, 1990). A more recent analysis of the cost of care in Air Force child care centers, about 90 percent of which are accredited, estimated the per hour cost at $3.86 per child in 1997, which would amount to over $7,000 per year for 50 weeks of full time care (U.S. General Accounting Office, 1999). The average cost per child of Head Start was $5,021 in 1998—a largely part-day program serving 3- to 5-year-olds for 34 weeks a year.

Setting aside quality, the average cost (to families) of child care was $60.17 per week for children under age 5 and $66.39 per week for infants under 1 year in 1993. This amounts to costs of $3,609 for preschoolers and $3, 982 for infants for full-year care in 1998 dollars (U.S. Bureau of the Census, 1995). The most thorough analysis of who pays the costs of providing center-based care (similar analyses are not available for other forms of care) found that parent fees cover less than half the full cost of care (Helburn, 1995). A sizable contribution toward the cost of child care (estimated at 20 percent of costs) consists of forgone earnings by child care providers who would receive substantially higher wages in other sectors of

---

[3]The National Association for the Education of Young Children administers an accreditation program for child care centers with well-specified criteria for "developmentally appropriate" care ranging from the structural features discussed above to required elements of teacher-child interaction to dimensions of the curriculum. Centers volunteer to participate, engage in an extensive self-study period, and are then visited by trained experts who assess the center's compliance with the accreditation criteria.

the labor market. A third of the costs (in 1993-1994) were paid by federal and state governments and other subsidies and contributions.

Even though many parents do not pay for child care, it represents a substantial financial burden to those who do pay[4] and, in particular, to those who have meager incomes and lack subsidized care. This is not a small group. The vast majority of children with working mothers and family incomes below 200 percent of the poverty line receive no or almost no federal subsidies for their child care (U.S. Council of Economic Advisers, 1997). In 1998, only 15 percent of the children eligible for the Child Care and Development Fund—the major source of federal child care assistance for low-income families—actually received help through the program (U.S. Department of Health and Human Services, 1999d). Subsidies that lower the price of child care induce low-income mothers to work (Blau and Hagy, 1998; U.S. General Accounting Office, 1995) and lead to increased reliance on paid care rather than unpaid care, although not necessarily higher-quality care (Blau and Hagy, 1998; Hotz and Kilburn, 1992; Ribar, 1995).

Child care expenses are often the second or third largest item in a low-income working family's household budget. In 1993, for example, child care expenses averaged 18 percent of family income, or $215 per month, for poor families paying for care for a preschool-age child (U.S. Bureau of the Census, 1995). Average monthly costs for nonpoor families were higher in absolute terms—$329 per month—but lower as a percentage of the household budget—only 7 percent. The average share of income devoted to child care was even higher—at 25 percent—for families with incomes of less than $14,400. Thus, families with meager incomes not only spend substantially more of their income on child care, but also are priced out of higher-cost forms of care, namely centers and many licensed family day care homes, in many areas of the country (U.S. Department of Health and Human Services, 1999d). This is compounded for families with infants, for whom the cost of care is significantly higher (see above) compared with older children (U.S. Bureau of the Census, 1995).

While the type of care selected by a family is often a matter of personal choice, there is growing evidence that, without access to subsidies, low-income parents are often precluded from enrolling their children in more expensive center-based and other arrangements. Other factors come into play as well, including the high proportion of low-income mothers (41 percent; U.S. Bureau of the Census, 1997) who work nonday shifts and are largely precluded from using centers and regulated family day care homes

---

[4]In 1999, 70.6 percent of parents paid for child care for their children age 4 years or younger. (These data are based on unpublished tabulations from the 1999 National Household Education Survey, which were generated for the committee by DeeAnn Brimhall, National Center for Education Statistics, U.S. Department of Education.)

(Hofferth, 1995; National Research Council and Institute of Medicine, 1995b; Siegel and Loman, 1991) and the low supply of center-based and other arrangements in low-income neighborhoods (Queralt and Witte, 1998). These constraints may be reflected in the results of a nationally representative survey of families using child care (Brayfield et al., 1995), in which 27 percent of parents with children under age 5 and incomes less than $15,000 expressed a desire to change their child care arrangements. Two-thirds reported a preference for care in centers, and 70 percent cited quality as the principal reason for wanting to switch.

In sum, the child care that is available to parents with young children in the United States is highly variable in quality, unlikely to offer stability, and supported primarily by parent fees. Several comprehensive studies have now reported that a sizable minority of children receive substandard care, and two federal investigations have found rampant safety and health violations in regulated programs. Indeed, the most characteristic feature of child care in the United States may not be what many have described as its typically mediocre quality, but rather the immense range in quality that is tolerated. The higher-quality programs are inequitably distributed and often beyond the reach of families with meager incomes, unless they are poor enough to receive heavily subsidized care and can adjust their work schedules to accommodate these arrangements. Finally, it is critical to recognize that prevailing fees for child care depend heavily on child care providers' low wages which often fail to reflect their educational attainments—a situation that fuels extremely high rates of turnover and instability for children and their parents.

CHILDREN WITH DISABILITIES AND CHILD CARE

Only a few decades ago, most children with disabilities were raised in foster or group homes or in specialized institutions. Today, nearly all children with disabilities are raised at home by their parents. As of 1996, a national health survey of households (1996 NHIS) found that 2.5 percent of children under 5 years of age, or 513,000 children, were limited in their activities and living at home. Half of these children experienced major limitations, such as mental retardation and cerebral palsy.[5] Data from the U.S. Bureau of the Census reported by Brandon (submitted) indicate that nearly 4 percent of households included a preschooler with a disability.

This has turned attention toward the needs of working families with

---

[5]The activity limitation data are based on unpublished tabulations from the 1996 National Health Interview Survey, which were generated for the committee by Paul Newacheck, University of California at San Francisco.

young children who have disabilities. As the 1996 welfare reform law affects a growing share of families in poverty, it is likely that even more mothers of young children with disabilities will be returning to work. It is well documented that children with a variety of special needs are overrepresented in poverty samples (Meyers et al., 2000). Consequently, the availability and quality of child care for children with disabilities is likely to become a more significant issue than is the case today. Unfortunately, there is very limited information about the child care arrangements for these children.

Like all families with young children, those whose children have a disability or special health care need are faced with the challenges of finding good-quality, affordable child care. But the inability or unwillingness of many child-care providers to accept children with disabilities (Berk and Berk, 1982; Chang and Teramoto, 1987), transportation and other logistical problems, difficulties with coordinating early intervention and child care services, and the scarcity of appropriately trained caregivers (Kelly and Booth, 1999; Klein and Sheehan, 1987) make the effort to find any child care a tremendous challenge for these families. One multisite study reported that 45 percent of mothers of an infant with a disability reported that they were not planning to work because they could not find child care, and 31 percent indicated that they could not find affordable child care (Booth and Kelly, 1998, 1999). The severity of the child's disability or illness greatly compounds these problems (Breslau et al., 1982; Warfield and Hauser-Cram, 1996).

Not surprisingly, the added caregiving demands of having a child with a disability lead to lower rates and fewer hours of employment among parents (overwhelmingly mothers) of these children compared with other parents (Brandon, submitted; Breslau et al., 1982; Jacobs and McDermott, 1989; Leonard et al., 1992; Wolfe and Hill, 1995). This is particularly true of families who have a severely disabled child or more than one child with a disability (Meyers et al., 2000), yet a large share of mothers of a moderately disabled child also report barriers to work. These relations hold even when other individual and structural factors that predict employment are taken into account. It also appears that mothers of children with disabilities are less likely to have reentered the labor force by the child's first birthday and are employed for fewer hours than mothers of typically developing children (Booth and Kelly, 1999).

When children with disabilities require child care, the expense to the family can be considerable. Recent survey and administrative data from California (Meyers et al., 2000) reveal that child care is the most common form of out-of-pocket expense for families with disabled children from birth to age 5 (with 25 percent of all families paying for child care), even more common than medical expenses. Child care is also the most expensive single category of expense, including medical expenses, for these families, with an average monthly cost of $141.87.

Surprisingly little is known about patterns of child care usage or the quality of care received by children with disabilities. Available evidence suggests that children with disabilities begin child care at older ages, are enrolled for fewer hours, are more likely to be cared for by relatives, including fathers, and less likely to be in child care centers than other children (Booth and Kelly, 1998; Brandon, submitted; Landis, 1992; Warfield and Hauser-Cram, 1996). One study reported that infants with disabilities received significantly poorer-quality care in child care centers than in child care homes or relative care, regardless of whether the centers provided early intervention services. Overall, however, approximately 60 percent of the infants were receiving relatively high-quality care. Moreover, the children in higher-quality care had more advanced motor development and higher adaptive behavior scores than children staying at home with their mothers at 30 months of age (Booth and Kelly, 1998, 1999; Kelly and Booth, 1999). Other studies have also reported benefits to children with disabilities that accrue from child care, as well as benefits to their families (Guralnick, 1976; Ispa, 1981).

In sum, despite the increasing influx of children with disabilities into child care, little is known about the conditions that support or hinder their access to care, their experiences in care, or how factors such as the type or severity of the child's disability or the child's family circumstances affect these issues. Even less is known about these issues from the perspective of child care providers, for whom anecdotal reports are beginning to reveal serious concerns with respect to the administration of medical procedures, inadequate training, and even explicit fears about children with disabilities. Much more research is needed on these concerns to inform parents, policy makers, and the wide range of practitioners who work with children with disabilities and their families.

SUMMARY AND CONCLUSIONS

The topic of care for young children cuts to the heart of conceptions of parental roles and responsibilities. Parents seeking a balance between providing economic resources for their families and providing care and nurturance for their children face competing pressures. Should they forgo income so a parent can remain home full-time with a young child? Should they arrange their jobs so they can combine work and child care without relying on others? Should they combine employment with nonparental child care? For some parents, these options represent real choices, but for others work is less a choice than an economic necessity, and for still others, work is now required. Nevertheless, a sizable minority of parents manage to care for their children during the earliest months and years of life without relying on others, despite the lost income that this may involve.

For the many parents who do arrange for nonparental child care, it is reassuring that child care is not the inevitable risk factor that some have portrayed it to be, nor does it replace parents as the major influence on early development. At its best, child care can be a significant source of nurturance, friendships, and early learning for the fortunate children in high-quality, stable arrangements. At its worst, however, child care can expose children to safety hazards, extremely unstimulating environments, and unresponsive supervision. Not surprisingly, the basic elements of high-quality care closely resemble the qualities of good parenting. Children's basic needs for consistent, sensitive, and stimulating care transcend the difference between home and child care. Moreover, when children's home environments fail to offer them this care, child care environments that do provide it can protect and promote their early development. By the same token, poor-quality child care can compound the consequences of problematic parenting. What remain to be specified for policy purposes are the dollar amounts and types of investments in quality improvements that are sufficient to produce meaningful improvements in developmental outcomes both for children living in high-risk situations and for children who are largely protected from these circumstances. This should be a high priority for future research on child care.

Safety hazards and settings that basically warehouse young children are inherently intolerable. But, even setting aside these programs, most of which refuse to participate in child care research, the wide range of care that is captured in research is associated with varying developmental outcomes. While the associations are seldom large, they are consistent and statistically significant, starting in infancy and continuing through the preschool years, and, in some cases, on into the early elementary grades. When child care is of very high quality, as is the case for model early intervention programs, the positive effects can endure into the early adult years, particularly for children from the poorest home environments. However, the fortunate low-income children who have access to these programs are outnumbered by thousands of others who, for financial as well as other reasons, receive some of the poorest-quality care that exists in communities across the United States. Thus, many children who can benefit greatly from high-quality child care are unlikely to get it.

If young children were only sporadically or briefly exposed to child care, we might not need to be concerned about the portrait of child care quality and its associations with developmental outcomes that emerges from this review of research. But child care is an enduring fixture on the early childhood landscape, starting within the first few months of life, for substantial hours each day, and continuing up to school entry and beyond.

Apart from the evidence that children's developmental trajectories are influenced by the child care they experience, the day-to-day quality of young children's lives is profoundly affected by the quality and continuity of their experiences in child care. It appears that even small improvements in ratios and training, and relatively modest compensation initiatives, can produce tangible improvements in the observed quality of care. But the larger need is for communities to create more viable systems of child care that do not tolerate unsafe and unstimulating settings, actively promote and reward high-quality care, stem the tide of staff turnover, and enable parents at all income levels to avail themselves of quality care for their children (Kagan and Cohen, 1996; National Association of State Boards of Education, 1991; National Research Council, 1990).

12 Neighborhood and Community

An African proverb, popularized by Hillary Rodham Clinton (1996), asserts that it takes an entire village to raise a child. Scientists have had a difficult time documenting "village-level" effects on children's development, yet parents who have the resources to select the neighborhoods in which they raise their families often spend substantial time and energy checking out schools, housing options, parks, children's programs, and other elements of communities that they believe will affect their children's safety, achievement, and friendships. This reflects a belief that community and neighborhood conditions are important determinants of children's experiences and opportunities, and hence, life chances.

Most research on neighborhood effects has focused on adolescents, whose time away from their homes may make them more susceptible than young children to neighborhood influences. Young children's interactions with people and institutions outside their immediate families have been relatively limited in scope and usually controlled closely by parents. This scenario is changing rapidly, however, as very young children are spending increasing amounts of time in settings other than their homes and with adults other than their parents. Moreover, there is substantially less attention paid to rural communities than to urban communities in this area of research and intervention. This chapter focuses on why and to what extent neighborhood contexts influence young children's development and the efficacy of intervention programs directed at them.

WHY NEIGHBORHOOD AND COMMUNITY CONDITIONS MAY MATTER FOR YOUNG CHILDREN

Much of the recent work on neighborhood and community influences has focused on high-poverty urban settings, which have grown substantially in size in recent years. The fraction of poor urban families living in high-poverty neighborhoods (i.e., with 40 percent or more of residents in households with incomes below the poverty line) nearly doubled, from 17 percent in 1970 to 28 percent in 1990 (Kasarda, 1993). During this period, urban poverty has been especially concentrated in the Midwest, in such cities as Chicago, Detroit, Cleveland, and Milwaukee, as well as in New York. This profile of cities may change with the findings from the 2000 census, since concentrated urban poverty is a slowly moving target. Residence in high-poverty urban neighborhoods is much more likely for black and Hispanic than white children (Kasarda, 1993).

Perhaps surprisingly, most poor children do not live in high-poverty urban neighborhoods. The most recent data, from the 1990 census, show that only 15 percent of all poor children live in high-poverty urban neighborhoods (Jargowky, 1997, Table 3.7). More than one-quarter of all poor children lived outside metropolitan areas altogether, while one-third lived in urban neighborhoods with poverty rates below 20 percent. These fractions differed little between young and older children.

The combination of family and neighborhood poverty, however, is much more prevalent among black than either Hispanic or white children. Some 27 percent of poor black children lived in high-poverty urban neighborhoods, compared with 20 percent of Hispanic and only 3 percent of white children. These children thus experience the double risk of family and neighborhood poverty.

William Julius Wilson (1987) galvanized empirical research on community and neighborhood effects with his description and analysis of conditions in high-poverty, inner-city Chicago neighborhoods. He documented the poor employment prospects, poor marriage pool, violence, and high mobility that were endemic to these neighborhoods. He also provided explanations of structural changes that produced these conditions as well as of how life in high-poverty urban neighborhoods affects the families and children living in them. Wilson hypothesized that massive changes in the economic structure of inner cities, when combined with residential mobility among more advantaged blacks, have resulted in homogeneously impoverished neighborhoods that provide neither resources nor positive role models for the children and adolescents who reside in them. Bronfenbrenner's (1979) ecological model of child development portrays nested layers of influence on children emanating from the family out to the more amorphous realms of neighborhoods, policies, and social values. More recently, theories have been proposed to capture the ways in which neighborhood and community processes may affect children's development (Coulton, 1996; Earls and Buka, 2000; Haveman and Wolfe, 1994; Jencks and Mayer, 1990), including:

- stress theory, which emphasizes the importance of exposure to such physical toxins as lead in soil and paint, as well as such social and psychological conditions as community violence;
- social organization theory, based on the importance of role models and value consensus in the neighborhood, which in turn limits and controls problem behavior among young people;
- institutional explanations, in which the neighborhood's institutions (e.g., schools, police protection) rather than neighbors per se make the difference; and
- epidemic theories, based primarily on the power of peer influences to spread problem behavior.

Proponents of stress theory, such as Earls and Buka (2000), emphasize the damaging developmental consequences of exposure to violence and to physiological hazards, such as ambient lead and asthma-inducing air pollutants. For other theorists, the extent of social organization in a neighborhood may well matter for families with young children. Neighborhoods in which parents frequently come into contact with one another and share values are more likely to monitor the behavior of and potential dangers to children (Sampson, 1992; Sampson and Groves, 1989). Contact among parents may lead them to share ways of dealing with the problem behavior of their children, encouraging their talents, connecting to community health and other resources, and organizing neighborhood activities (Klebanov et al., 1997). Others argue further that practices of family management are key to understanding how neighborhood and community conditions may affect children's development (Furstenberg et al., 1998). They point out that families formulate different strategies for raising children in high-risk neighborhoods, ranging from extreme protection and insulation to assuming an active role in developing community-based networks of "social capital" that can help children at key points in their academic or labor market careers.

Institutional models stress the importance for children of neighborhood resources—parks, libraries, children's programs—which provide more enriching opportunities in relatively affluent neighborhoods than are usually available in resource-poor neighborhoods. Here again, the perceived level of neighborhood safety matters, since parents' willingness to take advantage of existing neighborhood resources may depend on their perceptions of the safety and consequences of doing so.

Since adolescents typically spend a good deal of time away from their homes, explanations of neighborhood influences involving peer-based "epidemics," role models, schools, and other neighborhood-based resources would appear to be more relevant for them than for younger children. However, interactions between preschool children and their kin, neighbors, religious communities, child care, and health systems suggest that neighborhood influences may begin long before adolescence (Klebanov et al., 1997).

Despite ample theoretical reasons to suspect that neighborhood conditions influence development and behavior, the task of securing precise, robust, and unbiased estimates of neighborhood effects has proved remarkably difficult (Duncan and Raudenbush, 1999; Manski, 1993). One important difficulty is measuring a neighborhood's social organization, institutions, and levels of violence. A subtler problem arises from the fact that families are not randomly allocated to their residential neighborhoods, which may lead researchers to mistakenly attribute effects to neighborhood factors that are really caused by unmeasured differences in the children's parents. The major challenge facing those who seek to understand how family contexts affect early development is that parents usually select these environments. They decide where to live, where and how much to work, and whether and when to place their babies in child care and which child care settings to use. Thus, effects on children that are ascribed to such factors as neighborhoods may, in fact, really be effects of parent selection. Compounding this problem is the high mobility that characterizes families with young children. Nearly one-fourth of young children ages 1 to 5 move to a new home during the course of a year, with moves only slightly more common among black and Hispanic than among white young children.

A final problem is that of isolating the effects of conditions in the worst urban neighborhoods from effects caused by the more general range of neighborhood conditions. Representative population surveys typically draw relatively few families from high-poverty urban neighborhoods. Analysts using these surveys base estimates of neighborhood effects on relative differences among more advantaged, mostly white families and children. If neighborhood conditions matter more for disadvantaged than advantaged children, as some have found (Cook et al., 1998), then studies of neighborhood effects based on broad population samples may miss an important part of the story.

ASSOCIATIONS BETWEEN NEIGHBORHOOD CONDITIONS AND CHILD DEVELOPMENT

Most broad-based neighborhood studies rely on data gathered in the decennial census. Every 10 years, the Census Bureau provides information that can be used to construct neighborhood-based measures, such as the fraction of individuals who are poor, the fraction of adults with a college degree, and the fraction of adult men without jobs. Such data are available for census tracts (geographic areas encompassing 4,000 to 6,000 individuals, with boundaries drawn to approximate neighborhood areas) as well as larger geographically defined areas.

One striking result in broad-based studies of neighborhood effects on young children is that there are many more differences in families and children *within* neighborhoods than *between* them. As a result, in one study, neighborhood factors such as poverty, male joblessness, and ethnic diversity were found to account for only a small share of the differences across 5- to 6-year-old children in problem behaviors and academic achievement (Klebanov et al., 1997, Table 4.10). The presence or absence of affluent, high-income neighbors, rather than of poor neighbors, related more strongly to child and adolescent outcomes. This may not be a direct effect of income per se; it may derive from the differing social and interpersonal resources that are available in higher-income neighborhoods, as emphasized in social organization theories of neighborhood influence, as well as their greater support for sustaining academic achievement and other positive efforts (Darling and Steinberg, 1993). Yet neighborhood conditions added at most 2 percent to the explained variation in young children's outcomes over and above family conditions.

Neighborhood factors also do not account for much of the variation in parental mental health and family management practices. Using data from the Infant Health and Development Program, Klebanov et al. (1994) found that at most 4 percent of the variation in the depression, social support, and behavioral coping of mothers of preschoolers could be accounted for by neighborhood conditions. With data from a diverse set of Philadelphia neighborhoods, Furstenberg et al. (1999: Table 7.1) found similar results for their measures of the psychological resources of adolescents' care-givers—fully 90 percent of the variance in family management practices was found within rather than between neighborhoods.

These results indicate that even if we could somehow equalize neighborhood conditions, it would have little impact on the dispersion of family mental health and management practices or on individual differences in children's behavior problems and achievement. However, we caution against drawing more practical policy conclusions from these patterns of explained variance (Cain and Watts, 1972; Duncan and Raudenbush, in press; Rosenthal and Rubin, 1982). The cost-effectiveness of a neighborhood intervention depends on effect sizes relative to cost, and socially profitable intervention policies are quite possible in the context of a small amount of explained variation.

The neighborhood study of Sampson, Raudenbush, and Earls (1997) is noteworthy for its focus on the "collective efficacy" of neighborhoods. This potentially important component of a neighborhood's social organization was measured by conducting a survey of adult residents in sampled neighborhoods rather than relying exclusively on demographic census-based measures. Collective efficacy combines social cohesion (the extent to which neighbors trust each other and share common values) with informal social control (the extent to which neighbors can count on each other to monitor and supervise youth and protect public order). It is thus a capacity for collective action shared by neighbors. They find that collective efficacy so defined relates strongly to neighborhood levels of violence, personal victimization, and homicide in Chicago, after controlling for social composition and previous crime. One could imagine that lower levels of neighborhood violence and crime might change parenting practices in ways that benefit young children, although that possibility has not yet been tested with these or other data.

Taken together, this picture of at best modest neighborhood influences based on population samples is at odds with more specialized studies focused on very bad neighborhoods. For example, in a sample of patients in a Boston pediatric clinic, Taylor and colleagues (1992) found that 1 in 10 children witnessed a violent event prior to age 6, while Buka and colleagues (Buka and Birdthistle, 1997; Buka et al., submitted) estimated that about 1 in 4 urban youths reports having seen someone murdered during childhood. There are no corresponding figures for children raised in better neighborhoods. Psychiatric problems ranging from posttraumatic stress and aggression to externalizing behavioral disorders are more common among children and youth who witness violence (Singer et al., 1995). Neighborhood violence may also have indirect effects on development, if mothers in physically dangerous neighborhoods restrict their children's interactions with peers and adults (Lipsey and Wilson, 1993).

Among physiological hazards, lead poisoning continues to pose a threat to the healthy development of children, and disproportionately to low-income children of color living in central cities. As described in Chapter 8, excess lead in blood has been tied to such neurobehavioral problems as attention deficits, and poor children are disproportionately at risk for exposure to lead (Brody et al., 1994). Epidemiologists have linked the elevated levels of lead in poor urban children to old housing stock, which often still contains lead-based paint and other environmental contaminants, such as leaded gasoline. Although discontinued in the 1980s, the legacy of leaded gasoline emissions remains through elevated levels of lead in the soil, especially in central cities that are heavily congested with traffic (Mielke et al., 1997). Combining data from the Massachusetts 1990 statewide screening of children's blood lead levels and the decennial census, Sargent et al. (1995) investigated what characteristics of communities were correlated with heightened risk for lead poisoning. They found that the odds for having elevated levels of lead were nearly 9 times above average in communities in which 20 percent of the children under age 5 were living in poverty, 5.5 times higher if the community was densely populated, and 8 times higher than average if more than 10 percent of the community received public assistance. Similarly, studies in Minnesota (Nordin et al., 1998) and Louisiana (Mielke et al., 1997) have found that poverty, residence in central cities, and old housing stock considerably elevate the risk for high levels of lead in children's blood and pose a threat to their healthy development.

EXPERIMENTAL EVIDENCE ON NEIGHBORHOOD EFFECTS

Three other studies are noteworthy because they evaluate the effectiveness of residential mobility strategies for families living in high-poverty neighborhoods. In contrast to the studies described above, these studies use an experimental or quasi-experimental approach to estimate the influence of neighborhoods on children. Taken together, results from these three studies suggest that neighborhood characteristics may influence children's well-being to a greater extent than nonexperimental studies seem to indicate.

As part of the 1976 Gautreaux court case (Rosenbaum, 1991), nearly 4,000 families living in Chicago's high-rise housing projects volunteered to participate in a subsidized program that arranged for private housing, much of it in predominantly white Chicago suburbs, but some of it in predominantly white sections of the city of Chicago itself. Since participants were assigned to the first available housing and were not allowed to choose between city and suburban locations, their assignment to locations constituted a kind of quasi-experimental manipulation. Rosenbaum (1991) reports an impressive series of positive differences, both in the employment outcomes for adults and in developmental outcomes for their children, for the families assigned to the suburban rather than to the city locations. For example, the high school dropout rate of children moving to suburban locations was one-quarter the size of the dropout rate of children moving to city addresses (20 percent in the city versus less than 5 percent in the suburbs—Kaufman and Rosenbaum, 1992), while the corresponding college enrollment rate was doubled (54 versus 21 percent). These studies did not investigate effects on young children.

With funding for 10 years, the Moving to Opportunity experiment randomly assigned residents of housing projects in five of the nation's largest cities to one of three groups: (1) a group receiving housing subsidies to move into low-poverty neighborhoods, (2) a comparison group receiving a subsidy for moving into higher-rent housing (through the Section 8 program) but not constrained in their locations, and (3) a second comparison group receiving no special assistance. The vast majority of families who volunteered for the program reported that escaping from gangs and drugs was their most important reason for participating in the program. Katz et al. (1999) used the experimental data from the Boston site to evaluate the effects of the program on, among other things, maternal reports of the health and behavior problems of children between ages 6 and 15 and on their own mental health. They found significantly fewer injuries, accidents, and asthma attacks for children in the experimental compared with the control groups. Furthermore, rates of behavior problems among boys in the experimental group were significantly lower than among boys in the control groups. Measures such as "is cruel or mean to others" showed a larger experimental effect than measures such as "is unhappy, sad or depressed." In the case of behavior problems, there were no significant differences in program or control groups for girls. Ludwig et al. (in press) used the experimental data from the Baltimore site to evaluate the effects of the program on the frequency of criminal activity among adolescents, as reflected in the criminal offender records of the Maryland Department of Juvenile Justice. They found a sizable and statistically significant reduction in the proportion of youth who were arrested for violent offenses. However, property crime arrests appeared to be higher for the experimental group, particularly in the first year after the move, perhaps reflecting the greater opportunities for property theft in the new, more affluent locations.

How do we reconcile the large effects found in the Gautreaux and Moving to Opportunity studies with the more modest impacts found in the nonexperimental literature? One possibility is that the effects found in the experimental studies are less biased owing to their experimental designs. Another is that improving neighborhood conditions matters a lot for the development of children in the worst neighborhoods—a finding that could be masked in population-based studies that look at a wide range of neighborhoods. A third possibility is that the nature of the samples for these two interventions—which consisted of voluntary participants who were also, to some extent, screened by those administering the programs—produced larger effects than would be the case for a less selective sample of low-income, inner-city families. Whether beneficial effects extend from school-age to younger children is another critical issue that needs to be addressed in research on neighborhoods.

SUMMARY AND CONCLUSIONS

Although most urban poor families still live outside high-poverty neighborhoods, the past quarter century has produced an alarming growth in the fraction of poor urban families who do live in such neighborhoods. The combination of family poverty and neighborhood poverty poses double risk to a substantial minority of black children and, to a lesser extent, to Hispanic children, who are much more likely than white children to grow up in these circumstances. When juxtaposed with the rapid growth in these populations of children, this becomes a very worrisome finding.

Evidence on the impacts of neighborhood conditions on children's development is complex and continues to raise more questions than answers. For children residing outside the nation's inner cities, neighborhood conditions appear to be far less consequential for children's development than conditions within the family. Population-based studies are consistent in showing much more variation in achievement, behavior, and parenting *within* than *across* neighborhoods. This certainly does not rule out the possibility of cost-effective community-based interventions outside high-poverty urban areas. Nor does it imply that certain children aren't affected in fundamental ways by the events and conditions in their neighborhoods. It may be the case that neighborhoods matter most when other risk factors are present, such as family poverty or mental health problems within families.

Yet for children living in dangerous environments, neighborhood conditions may matter a great deal. Such neighborhood conditions as crime, violence, and environmental health hazards constitute potent risk factors for children. Experimental evidence suggests that moving from high-poverty to low-poverty neighborhoods enhances the physical and psychological health of children and reduces violent crimes committed by adolescents. We do not yet know whether smaller, more easily achieved changes in neighborhood conditions will produce cost-beneficial improvements for young children's development.

13 Promoting Healthy Development Through Intervention

he care and protection of young children are shared responsibilities. At their most intimate level, they require the investment and attention of a limited number of adults. In their broadest context, they depend on an environment that supports the childrearing function of families. In the final analysis, healthy child development is dependent on a combination of individual responsibility, informal social supports, and formalized structures that evolve within a society.

From the time of the nation's founding over 200 years ago, mainstream culture in the United States has viewed the rearing of children largely as a matter of individual self-reliance and family privacy. Consequently, the threshold for government involvement is high and the level of public investment is limited in comparison to that of other industrialized societies. Three prominent examples of this distinctive national characteristic are the absence of universal health care, the relatively limited availability of publicly funded early childhood care and education, and the resistance to paid, job-protected leave for working parents after the birth or adoption of a child (Kamerman, 2000; Kamerman and Kahn, 1995).

Within this social and political context, all families with young children in the United States have needs that extend beyond the boundaries of total self-sufficiency. These range from the universal to the particularistic—from primary health care for all and nonparental child care for a majority, to specialized services for a variety of vulnerable subgroups. Over the past four decades, a wide range of public policies and programs have been designed to address these specialized needs in order to promote healthy development in the preschool years (Shonkoff et al., 2000; Zigler et al., 1996). These highly diverse initiatives have been included under the broad umbrella of what is called "early intervention."

CONCEPTS OF INTERVENTION AND THEORIES OF CHANGE

Disentangling the Concept

Early childhood intervention is more a concept than a specific program (Guralnick, 1998; Shonkoff and Meisels, 2000). Much of its diversity is related to differences in target groups—from the broad-based agendas of health promotion and disease prevention, early child care, and preschool education to the highly specialized challenges presented by developmental disabilities, economic hardship, family violence, and serious mental health problems, including child psychopathology, maternal depression, and parental substance abuse. Within this context, the diversity among and within subgroups is as great as that across the general population.

Generalizations about children with developmental disabilities are particularly problematic. As a distinct population, they represent a markedly heterogeneous group of individuals with a wide variety of impairments that differ in both their defining features and level of severity. These impairments may include various combinations of delayed or atypical skills in cognition, communication, motor performance, emotional reactivity, and social relatedness, among others. Specific disorders range from commonly recognized conditions (e.g., Down syndrome, cerebral palsy, spina bifida, and autism) to relatively rare and less known disorders (e.g., Rett syndrome, trisomy 13, and metachromatic leukodystrophy), with a large proportion of children whose conditions elude both a definitive diagnosis and a known cause (Guralnick, 1997; Shonkoff and Marshall, 2000).

Children with developmental problems that are presumed to be secondary to the influences of an adverse caregiving environment (e.g., poverty, family violence, parental mental illness) comprise a similarly heterogeneous population. In both circumstances (i.e., whether the vulnerability originates primarily in the biology of the child or the stresses in the environment), the cultural values of the family create a distinctive childrearing context that can present yet another set of challenges to the delivery of professional services in a highly pluralistic society (García Coll and Magnuson, 2000; Lewis, 2000). Nevertheless, all children deemed eligible for early intervention programs share a common characteristic—concern about their development or behavior, regardless of the cause, and a belief that formalized services can increase the probability of a more positive outcome.

Another major source of diversity among early childhood interventions is the marked heterogeneity of service formats. These include multiple variations and combinations of center-based and home-based models, guided by different blends of child-focused and family-focused philosophies. Significant differences in staffing configurations contribute additional variability, ranging from the highly professionalized services delivered by educators, developmental therapists, social workers, and nurses with advanced degrees to the highly personalized supports provided by community workers with limited formal education or training. Widely differing views on the definition of "early" provide yet another element of variability, ranging from preschool programs targeting 4-year-olds to prenatal services focused on expectant mothers. The breadth and the depth of these differences illustrate the diversity of the field of early childhood intervention (Guralnick, 1997; Shonkoff and Meisels, 2000; Zeanah, 2000). The extent of this heterogeneity underscores the challenges confronting policy development, service coordination, and evaluation research.

Closely related to the diversity of early childhood programs is the extent to which interventions are defined differently depending on the disciplinary lens through which they are viewed. Early intervention is a collection of service systems whose roots extend deeply into a variety of professional domains, including health, education, and social services (Meisels and Shonkoff, 2000). It is a field whose knowledge base has been shaped by a diversity of theoretical frameworks and scientific traditions, from the instruction-oriented approach of education (Bailey, 1997; Bruder, 1997; Wolery, 2000) to the psychodynamic approach of mental health services (Emde and Robinson, 2000; Greenspan, 1990; Lieberman et al., 2000; Osofsky and Fitzgerald, 2000), and from the conceptual models of developmental therapies (Harris, 1997; McLean and Cripe, 1997; Warren et al., 1993) to the randomized control trials of clinical medicine (Infant Health and Development Program, 1990; Palmer et al., 1988). At its best, early intervention embodies a rich and dynamic example of multidisciplinary collaboration. Less constructively, it can reflect narrow parochial interests that invest more energy in the protection of professional turf than in serving the best interests of children and families.

As its knowledge base has matured, the field of early childhood intervention has evolved from its original focus on children to a growing appreciation of the extent to which family, community, and broader societal factors affect child health and development. A natural outgrowth of this evolution is a recognition that individual programs are always delivered within a multilayered context, and that their effects are always moderated by the influences of more pervasive social, economic, and political forces. Thus, successful policies for children who live in adverse circumstances may have less to do with the impact of specific services and be more a matter of changing the larger environment in which the children are reared. This growing awareness is likely to lead to further expansion of the concept of early childhood intervention to include such wide-ranging policy concerns as housing, employment practices, community policing, and taxation, among many others (Garbarino and Ganzel, 2000; Sameroff and Fiese, 2000).

Theories of Change

All successful interventions are guided by a theoretical model that specifies the relation between their stated goals and the strategies employed to achieve them (Weiss, 1995). Sometimes these frameworks are articulated explicitly; other times, they are implicit but not clearly formulated. After more than a quarter century of remarkable growth and continuing maturation, the basic sciences of child development and neurobiology have converged with the learned experiences of a broad array of intervention policies and programs to generate sufficient knowledge to build an intellectually rigorous, common theory of change for the field.

The essential characteristics of this framework are drawn from the core concepts outlined in Chapter 1 and buttressed by the wealth of information contained in this report. They stand on the shoulders of decades of creative theoretical formulations about the process of human development. Most prominent among these are the transactional model first formulated by Sameroff and Chandler (1975) and later adapted to the challenges of early intervention by Sameroff and Fiese (1990, 2000); the ecological model articulated by Bronfenbrenner (1979) and subsequently expanded to a bio-ecological model by Bronfenbrenner and Ceci (1994); the concepts of vulnerability and resilience applied to a wide variety of biological and environmental conditions by Werner and Smith (1982), Garmezy and Rutter (1983), and Rutter (2000); the process model of parenting developed by Belsky (1984); the social support model for families of children with disabilities popularized by Dunst (1985); the developmental contextual perspective proposed by Lerner (1991); the biosocial model adopted for an intervention targeting low-birthweight, premature infants by Ramey and colleagues (1992); the principles of developmental psychopathology formulated by Cicchetti and Cohen (1995); the social context model constructed by the MacArthur Foundation Research Network on Psychopathology and Development (Boyce et al., 1998); and the developmental framework for early intervention for both biologically and environmentally vulnerable children presented by Guralnick (1998).

Taken together, the substance of these models converges to a remarkable degree and applies equally well across the diverse mixture of policies and programs that characterize early childhood intervention in the United States today. This shared theory of change has several central features:

- All strategies of intervention, regardless of the target group or the desired outcomes, can be derived from normative theories of child development. That is to say, the general principles of development apply to all children, independent of their biological variability or the range of environments in which they live.

- All domains of development unfold under the interactive influences of genetic predisposition and individual experience. The trajectories of experience-expectant skills (e.g., motor development) are relatively less susceptible to intervention effects and those of experience-dependent skills (e.g., literacy) are affected more significantly, but no area of human competence is completely predetermined by intrinsic factors.

- Young children's relationships with their primary caregivers have a major impact on their cognitive, linguistic, emotional, social, and moral development. These relationships are most growth-promoting when they are warm, nurturing, individualized, responsive in a contingent and reciprocal manner, and characterized by a high level of "goodness of fit."

- A young child's environment is both physical and social. Its impact on development is mediated through the nature and quality of the experiences that it offers and the daily transactions that transpire among people inside and outside the home.

- The ability of caregivers to attend to the individualized needs of young children is influenced by both their internal resources (e.g., emotional health, social competence, intelligence, educational attainment, personal family history) and the external circumstances of their lives (e.g., family environment, social networks, employment status, economic security, experience with discrimination). The cumulative burden of multiple risk factors and sources of stress compromises the capacity of a caregiver to promote sound health and development. The buffering function of protective factors and sources of support enhances it.

- Early intervention programs are designed to affect children directly (through the provision of structured experiences) and indirectly (through their impact on the caregiving environment). Child-focused interventions involve developmentally guided educational opportunities or specifically prescribed therapies or both. Caregiver-focused interventions include varying combinations of information, instruction, emotional support, and assistance in securing needed resources and related services.

- The determination of appropriate child and family outcomes, and their assessment, require an appreciation of the importance of individual differences among children, an understanding of the extent to which the caregiving environment is changeable, and a realistic appraisal of the match between the resources of the service program and the goals of the intervention.

• The success of an intervention is determined by the soundness of the strategy, its acceptability to the intended recipients, and the quality of its implementation.

EMPIRICAL FINDINGS, PROFESSIONAL EXPERIENCE, AND CURRENT PRACTICE

A comprehensive review and synthesis of the full corpus of early intervention research was beyond the resource capacity of the committee. The literature analyzed for this report was therefore culled largely from an extensive number of published reviews (Barnett, 1995; Benasich et al., 1992; Berlin et al., 1998; Brooks-Gunn et al., 2000; Casto and Mastropieri, 1986; Currie, 2000; Farran, 1990, 2000; Gomby et al., 1995, 1999; Guralnick, 1997, 1998; Halpern, 2000; Karoly et al., 1998; Lazar et al., 1982; Shonkoff and Hauser-Cram, 1987; St. Pierre et al., 1995b; Yoshikawa, 1995) and supplemented by original publications for a selected number of flagship studies.

In contrast to its rich and widely endorsed conceptual foundation, the empirical knowledge base on the efficacy of early childhood intervention is relatively uneven. The diversity of target populations and service models that have been studied, and the methodological deficiencies of much of the available literature, contribute to this lack of consistency in the existing database. Most important in this regard is the extent to which a large proportion of studies that address questions of causality have suffered from inappropriate research designs, inadequate analytic approaches, or both, as described in Chapter 4. Notwithstanding these limitations, more than three decades of developmental research and program evaluation have generated the following core of replicated findings, whose convergence strengthens their presumed validity:

• In the absence of formal intervention, social class differences in scores on standardized developmental measures that favor children in better educated, higher-income families begin to emerge between 18 and 24 months of age and increase over time (Golden and Birns, 1976; McCall, 1979).

• In the absence of formal intervention, there is a general decline in performance on standardized developmental measures for children with established cognitive disabilities, documented most clearly in toddlers and preschoolers with Down syndrome, across the first five years of life (Guralnick, 1998; Guralnick and Bricker, 1987).

• Well-designed and successfully implemented interventions can enhance the short-term performance of children living in poverty, with reported effect sizes ranging up to 1.0 standard deviation in the preschool years (Farran, 1990, 2000; Guralnick, 1998; Karoly et al., 1998; Ramey and Campbell, 1984; Schweinhart ct al., 1993).

• Well-designed and successfully implemented interventions can promote significant short-term gains on standardized cognitive and social measures for young children with documented developmental delays or disabilities, with reported effect sizes ranging from 0.5 to 0.75 standard deviation (Casto and Mastropieri, 1986; Farran, 1990, 2000; Guralnick, 1998; Shonkoff and Hauser-Cram, 1987).

• Short-term impacts on the cognitive development of young children living in high-risk environments are greater when the intervention is goal-directed and child-focused in comparison to generic family support programs (Farran, 2000; Guralnick, 1998).

• Measured, short-term impacts on the cognitive and social development of young children with developmental disabilities are greater when the intervention is more structured and focused on the child-caregiver relationship, although the effects are highly variable in view of the marked diversity of child impairments and their severity (Farran, 2000; Guralnick, 1988, 1998; Shonkoff and Hauser-Cram, 1987).

• Short-term IQ gains associated with high-quality preschool interventions for children living in poverty typically fade out during middle childhood, after the intervention has been completed; however, long-term benefits in higher academic achievement, lower rates of grade retention, and decreased referral for special education services have been replicated (Barnett, 1995; Karoly et al., 1998; Lazar et al., 1982), with reported long-term effect sizes ranging from 0.1 to 0.4 standard deviation (Ramey and Campbell, 1984; Schweinhart et al., 1993).

• Extended longitudinal investigations into the adolescent and adult years are relatively uncommon but provide documentation of differences between the intervention and control groups for economically disadvantaged children in high school graduation, income, welfare dependence, and criminal behavior (Karoly et al., 1998; Schweinhart et al., 1993; Yoshikawa, 1995).

• Long-term follow-up data on children with disabilities are scarce, although follow-up studies of children with autism demonstrate persistent benefits of intensive preschool interventions that are followed by continuing specialized services during middle childhood (McEachin et al., 1993; Lovaas, 1987).

• Analyses of the economic costs and benefits of early childhood interventions for low-income children have demonstrated medium- and long-term benefits to families as well as savings in public expenditures for special education, welfare assistance, and criminal justice (Barnett, 2000; Barnett and Escobar, 1990; Karoly et al., 1998).

Successful child-focused intervention programs for economically disad-vantaged groups are designed to provide children with cognitively stimulat-ing environments that they are presumed to be less likely to experience at home. Such programs typically offer rich, school-based learning curricula, often in combination with a wide variety of developmentally enhancing activities in a classroom setting. Several recent comprehensive reviews of such interventions have attempted to discern patterns of impact across programs (Bryant and Maxwell, 1997; Farran, 1990, 2000; Yoshikawa, 1994, 1995). Unfortunately, despite a plethora of investigations, most conclude that it is difficult to draw clear conclusions about the effectiveness of any of a variety of specific intervention approaches.

The limitations of this literature are due largely to basic problems in research design (e.g., lack of random assignment, lack of comparable com-parison groups) that make the findings of individual studies less reliable and difficult to compare with each other. A more fundamental barrier to comparisons across studies, however, is the considerable variability among intervention programs on a number of important dimensions, such as the age of the children at time of entry, the characteristics of the target popula-tion, the nature of the program components, the intensity and duration of service delivery, issues regarding comparison or control conditions, and the nature of the staff and their training. Consequently, it is not possible to be certain that differences in outcomes, when they are found, are due to any one (or a combination) of these factors. Generally speaking, programs that have demonstrated the largest and longest-lasting cognitive gains have been administered to children with multiple risks and have offered the most intensive and longest-lasting services. For example, the largest initial IQ gains were documented in the Milwaukee Project, which targeted low-income, black mothers with intellectual limitations and offered full-day infant and preschool child care for the first five years of life, as well as parent education and job training (Garber, 1988). The association between the intensity or duration of service and child outcomes, however, has not been a consistent finding in other studies.

In contrast to the extensive attention paid to cognitive performance, relatively few evaluations of child-focused interventions for low-income children have provided short-term outcome data on social adjustment. Those studies that have reported such information generally have not found much evidence of either reduced problems or increased positive behavior. Nevertheless, some researchers have argued that the subsequent documen-tation of differences in progress through school and into adulthood (as illustrated by differential rates of welfare dependence and criminal behav-ior) reflect a social rather than a cognitive impact (Barnett, 1995; Yoshi-kawa, 1995).

In addition to the broad array of child-focused programs that have undergone extensive evaluation, many interventions for low-income children have focused primarily on parents and parenting, employing various combinations of home visits, group supports, and informational sessions (Brooks-Gunn et al., 2000; Seitz and Provence, 1990). Some of these programs have combined parent-focused components with center-based child care. Despite the considerable diversity of designs, most services are based on the common assumption that parents play a central role in their children's development and that interventions for low-income children are most efficient when they target parents' behavior directly. Such services typically provide some form of social support, both instrumental and emotional, as well as instruction about children's development. The expectation is that reliable support will reduce parental stress and consequently enhance parental mental health and caregiving capacity, whereas instructional materials on children's development will improve parenting behavior by addressing parents' presumed lack of information about what is appropriate and developmentally enhancing for their children (Seitz and Provence, 1990). A recent review by Olds and colleagues (1999) suggests that interventions for socioeconomically disadvantaged families that are largely parent-focused work best when the parents perceive that they or their children need help.

Generally speaking, programs that offer both a parent and a child component appear to be the most successful in promoting long-term developmental gains for children from low-income families. Most of the documented benefits have clustered in the realm of social development, perhaps because of early program impacts on risk factors for antisocial behavior. A review by Yoshikawa (1995) of the effects of early childhood intervention programs found that all four of the programs that showed a long-term impact on chronic delinquency had influenced multiple family risk factors in early childhood, including parent-child interaction. Nevertheless, these findings are suggestive, not conclusive, and comparable information on a broader range of interventions is necessary before meaningful conclusions can be drawn about which program components, and in which combination, are successful in promoting positive long-term social outcomes.

In recent years, a growing number of interventions have focused on family literacy as a key strategy for improving the home learning environment for young children. Some programs (e.g., Even Start) offer intergenerational literacy activities that include child and adult instruction, as well as parenting education (St. Pierre and Swartz, 1995). Others (e.g., the Home Instruction Program for Preschool Youngsters, or HIPPY) emphasize instruction for parents on how to create a stimulating environment for their children, as well as offering model activities and complementary materials such as books (Baker et al., 1999). To date, evaluation results for both types of programs have been modest and inconsistent. In the future, much more rigorous evaluations with randomized assignment will be needed to assess their effectiveness.

In contrast to the marked heterogeneity of program models for children living in socioeconomically disadvantaged circumstances, early intervention services for young children with developmental disabilities operate within a more circumscribed arena, guided by a federal entitlement to services for all children with a diagnosed impairment or a documented developmental delay (with the additional option for states to serve infants at risk for subsequent developmental problems). This entitlement was first established in 1986 under Part H of Public Law 99-457 and reauthorized in 1997 under Part C of the Individuals With Disabilities Education Act (Public Law 105-17). Although the mandate for individualized family service plans provides room for considerable variability, virtually all programs for children with special health or developmental needs employ a family-centered model that combines individual child therapies and educational experiences with an array of parent services, such as support groups, individual counseling, and instrumental assistance in securing materials and related services specific to the child's disability. Finally, unlike interventions for low-income children, programs for children with special needs are required to provide access to a designated array of professional services in natural environments, including those offered by educators, physical and occupational therapists, and speech and language pathologists (Harbin et al., 2000).

Beyond both the prescriptions of the law and the evolving conceptual and empirical foundations of the field, much of the knowledge base that shapes the current practice of early childhood intervention is based on professional experience. Central to this perspective is a firm belief in the benefits of family-centered services, the importance of cultural competence, and the impact of relationships on relationships. In this context, a broad spectrum of policies and programs are implemented by a wide variety of service providers, guided by a clear conviction that the impact of their efforts is determined by the extent to which their relationships with families affect the relationships between parents and their children, which, in turn, have a significant impact on child health and development (Barnard, 1998; Berlin et al., 1998; Gilkerson and Stott, 2000; McDonough, 2000).

ASSESSING DEVELOPMENTAL OUTCOMES AND MEDIATORS

Assessing Child Abilities

The evaluation of development in young children is a complex task. The growing cultural diversity of the early childhood population in the United States intensifies that complexity. Superimposed on this formidable challenge, the high-stakes assessment of competence in children who are adapting to a wide variety of biological vulnerabilities and environmental stressors remains one of the thorniest issues facing the early intervention field. Thus, for more than three decades, researchers and service providers have struggled with both the identification of significant child outcomes and their valid and reliable measurement (Brooks-Gunn and Weinraub, 1983; Cicchetti and Wagner, 1990; Gilliam and Mayes, 2000; Honzik, 1983; Meisels, 1994, 1996; Zigler and Trickett, 1978).

Traditional Emphasis on IQ and Early Skill Acquisition

From its earliest beginnings, the field of early childhood intervention has focused considerable attention on the promotion of intelligence. Although there is still widespread interest in this objective, there is also a great deal of concern about the way in which this elusive construct is conceptualized and measured. Debate on this issue has been lively in both academic and policy circles. It centers on both the general challenges inherent in developmental assessment during the early childhood period and the specific value and limitations of an IQ test as an appropriate measure of program effects (McCall et al., 1972; Meisels and Atkins-Burnett, 2000).

Perhaps the most important limitation of an IQ score in the context of evaluating the performance of children in an early intervention program is the fact that it is standardized for age and therefore is not useful as a measure of *growth* or developmental *change* (see Chapter 4). Nevertheless, its popularity as a measure of intervention impact has been remarkably robust. Moreover, although the evaluation literature is vast and diverse in its focus, highly variable in its methodological rigor, and often inconsistent in its findings, there is a clear pattern regarding short-term impacts on standardized test performance. Specifically, a wide variety of services, both for children living in poverty and for those with biological vulnerabilities, have demonstrated significant gains in IQ during the first five years, followed by a subsequent fade-out of effects during middle childhood (Campbell and Ramey, 1994; Lally et al., 1988; McCarton et al., 1997; Schweinhart et al., 1993; Walker and Johnson, 1988). The magnitude of these initial treatment-control differences has been moderately high, ranging from effect sizes of 0.5 to 0.75 standard deviation (Casto and Mastropieri, 1986; Farran, 1990, 2000; Guralnick, 1998; Shonkoff and Hauser-Cram, 1987).

The most striking exception to the fade-out phenomenon has been demonstrated in an intensive intervention program for children with autism, which produced sustained treatment-control differences in IQ scores well into the middle childhood years, while the children continued to receive special services as needed (McEachin et al., 1993; Lovaas, 1987).

Despite the strength of this study, in the face of significant ethical and practical challenges (Rogers, 1998), legitimate methodological concerns have been raised, including lack of random assignment and questions about the actual intensity and duration of the intervention (Gresham and MacMillan, 1998). A major multisite replication[1] is now in progress and is likely to clarify these and related issues and begin to identify the characteristics of subgroups of children who vary in their response to the program.

Growing Interest in Underlying Functional Capacities

Increasing numbers of early childhood investigators and service providers criticize conventional intelligence testing that relies on the administration of single instruments in standardized settings. Central to this concern is a belief that traditional cognitive measures are unrelated to the everyday context of children's lives, that they impose a linear orientation on a process that is typically characterized by spurts, plateaus, and extensive variability, and that they are particularly inappropriate when used to evaluate the competence of children with disabilities or youngsters who are reared in families that reflect nonmajority cultures (Meisels, 1996).

As an alternative, critics have suggested greater focus on assessing the processes of social and emotional development, as well as the underlying functional capacities that lead to cognitive gains, rather than simply measuring the achievement of concrete milestones (Cicchetti and Wagner, 1990; Hauser-Cram and Shonkoff, 1988, 1995; McCune et al., 1990). Closely linked to this emerging perspective is the call for an approach to evaluation and intervention that is embedded within the child's natural environment and conducted in an ongoing information-gathering manner rather than as a series of disconnected snapshots of competence (Meisels, 1996). This reorientation is particularly important for the evaluation of children with significant motor and sensory impairments, whose progress is often not reflected in standardized test scores (Brooks-Gunn and Lewis, 1983; Shonkoff, 1983).

Although the program evaluation literature in these new domains of interest is extremely limited, the underlying developmental science has grown considerably, as described in Chapters 5 and 6. Among the potential target areas for greater attention in measuring program effects, three are particularly noteworthy: self-regulation, interpersonal skills and relationships, and knowledge acquisition skills and problem-solving abilities.

Self-regulation. As critical early mediators of successful development,

---

[1]Although no data from the multisite replication have been published yet, a description of the project appears in Smith et al. (2000).

self-regulatory behaviors offer an attractive focus for early intervention services (see Chapter 5). Dimensions that appear particularly promising include emotional reactivity, attention and activity level, and other behavioral aspects of school readiness, such as taking turns and following directions. Facilitating the capacity for self-regulation can provide a constructive framework for addressing temperamental differences in all young children, as well as a useful strategy for promoting mastery in those with disabilities (Barton and Robins, 2000). Infants with very low birthweight are particularly vulnerable with respect to regulatory difficulties, most notably in their ability to handle different levels of intensity of interaction (Field, 1979; Goldberg et al., 1980). The hypothesized relation between early disorganization and later attention deficit hyperactivity disorder presents a rich area for investigation as a potential opportunity for preventive intervention in the early childhood years.

Interpersonal skills and relationships. Extensive research has demonstrated that the establishment of stable and secure relationships is a central feature of healthy human development, and therefore a critical goal of developmental promotion and early childhood intervention (see Chapter 6). Beginning with the infant's attachment to his or her primary caregivers and extending to the bonds that young children develop with other adults, siblings, and peers, early relationships are viewed as both the foundation and the scaffold on which cognitive, linguistic, emotional, social, and moral development unfold. Early social interactions serve as an essential vehicle for children to learn about how their actions elicit responses from others, how to explore their environment with confidence, and how to experience and deal with thoughts and feelings. Consequently, increasing numbers of program evaluators are measuring aspects of the parent-child relationship as both mediator and outcome variables (Brooks-Gunn et al., 2000; Kelly and Barnard, 2000; Zeanah et al., 2000).

Knowledge acquisition skills and problem-solving abilities. As an alternative to relying exclusively on standardized cognitive assessments, considerable value lies in an evaluation of the underlying capacities that make it possible for children to learn. Among those that are of greatest potential interest are new methods of measuring mastery motivation, problem-solving strategies, and the ability to generalize learning from one situation to another (see Chapter 5).

Medium-Term Impacts on Subsequent School Achievement

The War on Poverty in the 1960s and the establishment of a federal entitlement to early intervention services for infants and toddlers with developmental disabilities in the 1980s were both motivated by a belief that preschool programs for vulnerable children in the early years could enhance later academic achievement and reduce the subsequent need for special education services. After more than 30 years of empirical study, the research literature on this issue is uneven but promising.

Beginning with the data syntheses of the Consortium for Longitudinal Studies (Lazar et al., 1982), early childhood researchers in growing numbers have looked beyond the disappointing fade-out of early IQ effects after the intervention is completed, focusing increasingly on intervention-control group differences in school performance during middle childhood and adolescence (i.e., differences in later performance between children who received the intervention during the preschool years and those who did not). This approach began with aggregated findings from 11 program evaluations reported by Lazar and his colleagues (1982), which revealed significant impacts of early intervention on both grade retention (i.e., repeating a grade) and the need for special education services, with greater differences found for those studies that had more nearly randomized research designs. More recently, the Abecedarian Project demonstrated a statistically nonsignificant trend toward less grade retention and special education at age 12, which reached significance at age 15 (Campbell and Ramey, 1994, 1995). Notwithstanding their statistical significance, however, the small magnitude of the intervention-control differences in many of these studies have led some critics to question their value (e.g., Locurto, 1991). However, since the one-time costs of repeating a grade are roughly $6,000 per year and the continuing costs of special education are approximately $8,000 per year, relatively small impacts on grade retention and especially the use of special education services can produce substantial financial benefits (Currie, 2000).

The frequently replicated finding of positive impacts of early intervention services on school performance, however, has not been universal. For example, no differences in either special education or grade retention were found in follow-up investigations of the Houston Parent-Child Development Center to age 11 (Johnson and Walker, 1991) or for the Syracuse Family Development Research Program up to age 15 (Lally et al., 1988). Researchers in the Infant Health and Development Program also found no differences in either retention or special education at age 8 (McCarton et al., 1997). However, the sample children were only in first and second grade at the time of the follow-up assessments, and the intervention-control group differences in special education placement for the Perry Preschool sample did not appear until the third grade (Weikart et al., 1978).

The interpretation of these discrepant findings is not entirely clear. Beyond obvious differences in the nature of the preschool intervention and the program participants, it is difficult to determine how much these findings are related to differences in criteria for repeating a grade or for special education assignment among the study sites and across time. Nevertheless, there are sufficient data to conclude that early intervention services for children living in poverty that are provided during the first five years of life can reduce subsequent rates of grade retention and use of special education services in middle childhood. The important research question is to determine why some programs are more successful than others. Comparable longitudinal studies have not been conducted on children with diagnosed developmental disabilities.

Assessments of school achievement provide another set of criteria by which the impact of early intervention services may be measured. Once again, the literature demonstrates positive program effects but the patterns of impact are variable and not detected universally. Graduates of the Abecedarian Project scored significantly higher than controls in reading and knowledge on the Woodcock-Johnson Test of Achievement at age 12 and in mathematics and reading at age 15 (Campbell and Ramey, 1994, 1995). Perry Preschool participants achieved significantly higher scores in reading, arithmetic, and language on the California Achievement Test (Schweinhart et al., 1993). Follow-up studies of children served by Parent-Child Development Centers indicate positive trends in reading, vocabulary, and language on the Iowa Tests of Basic Skills, but the differences did not reach statistical significance (Johnson and Walker, 1991). At age 8, there were no overall differences on the Woodcock-Johnson Test between the intervention and follow-up groups from the Infant Health and Development Program, but the heavier of the low-birthweight intervention group had significantly higher mathematics scores than a matching subset of the control group (McCarton et al., 1997).

Taken together, the follow-up literature provides abundant evidence of intervention-control group differences in academic achievement during middle childhood, but no consistent or distinctive pattern of advantage associated with a particular type of preschool curriculum or program format. Moreover, the nature of the outcomes (i.e., grade retention, special education placements, and academic achievement scores) do not lend themselves to analyses that address questions regarding growth, as described in Chapter 4. Perhaps of greater concern is the possibility that the absence of reproducible patterns of outcomes across studies is a reflection of the extent to which published reports focus primarily on those variables for which statistically significant differences are found, with little attention given to the much larger number of measured outcomes that demonstrate no program-control differences. This criticism was raised by Locurto (1991) in an analysis of data from the Perry Preschool Project and the Milwaukee Project, which noted their mutually inconsistent and counterintuitive findings regarding the relation between IQ scores and academic achievement.

Long-Term Influences on Productive Adult Citizenship

Measuring the relation between participation in a preschool intervention program and long-term outcomes through the adolescent and adult years is a complex and highly speculative venture. On one hand, a hypothesized impact fuels public interest in the potential return on investment in the early childhood period. On the other hand, it raises expectations that may be unrealistically ambitious, tends to downplay the value of the enhanced well-being of children during the intervention itself, and fails to account for the significant impacts of intervening influences on development in middle childhood and early adolescence.

Central to the concept of long-term intervention effects is the notion of shifting developmental momentum prior to school entry in a manner that increases the likelihood that an otherwise vulnerable child will embark on a more positive pathway into middle childhood. Whether this favorable trajectory is sustained into the adolescent and later adult years obviously will depend on subsequent influences at multiple points along the life course. That is to say, significant medium- and long-term benefits of early childhood intervention may be viewed as a continuing developmental pathway that is contingent on a chain of positive effects that increase the probability of remaining on track.

Very few early childhood intervention programs have followed their sample into the adolescent and adult years. The most extensive data have been collected for graduates of the High/Scope Perry Preschool Program, which reveal statistically significant differences at age 27 favoring the intervention group over the controls in income and in rates of high school graduation, criminal arrests, and welfare participation, but no differences in teen pregnancy (Schweinhart et al., 1993). Intervention-control group differences in criminal behavior also were reported for the Syracuse Family Development Research Program (Lally et al., 1988) but were not found in a follow-up of graduates of the Elmira Prenatal/Early Infancy Project (Olds et al., 1997).

ASSESSING FAMILY MEDIATORS OF CHILD WELL-BEING

A variety of family-focused intervention models have been designed to improve the developmental trajectories of children at risk for problems as a result of environmental or biological vulnerability, as well as for those with diagnosed disabilities. The theory of change that guides such programs is grounded in the assumption that strengthened parent-child relationships and enhanced home environments promote positive outcomes for all young children across a broad range of functional domains (Guralnick, 1998; Sameroff and Fiese, 2000). Professional experience indicates that sensitivity to cultural differences is also essential to service effectiveness, although the empirical knowledge base in this area is limited (García Coll and Magnuson, 2000).

Caregiver-Child Relationships and Interactive Behaviors

Extensive research conducted over the past several decades has provided rich documentation of the mutual influences that caregivers and young children have on each other (see Chapter 6). Caregiver characteristics that promote healthy child development include warmth, nurturance, stability, predictability, and contingent responsiveness. Children's characteristics that influence the nature of their interactions with their caregivers include predictability of behavior, social responsiveness, readability of cues, activity level, and mood. Caregiver behavior may be affected adversely by immaturity or inexperience, low educational attainment, or mental health problems (e.g., depression, anxiety) related to family violence, substance abuse, economic stress, or constitutional illness. Child behavior may be affected adversely by prematurity, poor nutrition, illness, disability, or temperamental difficulties. Beyond the significance of any particular attribute (either positive or negative), the quality of the caregiver-child relationship is influenced most often by the goodness of fit between the styles of both contributors. Consequently, helping parents understand their child's unique characteristics and providing guidance on how to build a mutually rewarding relationship that facilitates the child's development and promotes a sense of parental well-being are common goals shared by a wide variety of early childhood programs.

Despite the marked heterogeneity of children, families, and service models that characterize the early childhood field, there is strong consensus on the central importance of child-caregiver relationships. Low income creates a particularly stressful context in which positive interactions with children are threatened, and punitive or otherwise negative relationships may result. The high prevalence of depression, attachment difficulties, and posttraumatic stress among mothers living in poverty serves to undermine their development of empathy, sensitivity, and responsiveness to their children, which can lead to diminished parenting behaviors and thus decreased learning opportunities and poorer developmental outcomes (McLeod and Shanahan, 1993; McLoyd, 1990; Pianta and Egeland, 1990).

Research evidence supporting the potential positive impacts of early childhood programs on parent-child interaction is encouraging. Brooks-Gunn and her colleagues (2000) conducted a recent review of 24 parent-focused programs, 17 of which were home based and 7 of which combined home and center components. Of the 17 home-based programs, 13 assessed parent-child interactions or relationships, and 11 of the 13 documented significant intervention effects. Six of the seven home-center combinations reported similar findings. The majority of the effects reflected increased rates of sensitive parenting behaviors, although these gains were generally not associated with significant differences in child outcomes.

Several investigators have noted the extent to which parents' beliefs influence a wide range of caregiving behaviors, including specific child-rearing practices (e.g., discipline and limit setting), and how cultural differences influence the way in which the home environment is structured to create a variety of learning opportunities (García Coll, 1990; García Coll et al., 1996; Harrison et al., 1990; Thompson et al., 1999).

Home Environment and Family Experiences

The most widely cited and well-documented finding in the early childhood intervention literature is the strong correlation between family socioeconomic status and child health and development (see Chapter 10). Specifically, children in families with lower incomes and lower maternal educational attainment are at greater risk for a variety of poorer outcomes, including school failure, learning disabilities, behavior problems, mental retardation, developmental delay, and health impairments (Aber et al., 1997; Chase-Lansdale and Brooks-Gunn, 1995; Duncan and Brooks-Gunn, 1997; Huston, 1991; McLoyd, 1998). Poor children who are members of racial or ethnic minority groups are particularly vulnerable (McLoyd, 1990; Shonkoff, 1982). Less well appreciated is the disproportionate prevalence of children with biologically based developmental disabilities in low-income and less-educated families. In fact, Bowe (1995) reported that at least one-third of the families of children with a developmental disability are living at or below the poverty line.

Notwithstanding the strong predictive validity of demographic markers, they have relatively limited utility as guides for designing effective interventions because they tell us relatively little about the causal mechanisms that explain their impacts on child development. Thus, researchers and service providers are focusing increasingly on the importance of within-group variability and individual differences among children and families (Berlin et al., 1998; Brooks-Gunn and Duncan, 1997). Closely related to the salience of such variability is the importance of the home environment as a marker of either vulnerability or protection for young children (Bradley, 1995; Bradley et al., 1989).

As a source of risk, the home may reflect an atmosphere of disorganization, neglect, or frank abuse. As a source of resilience and growth promotion, it is characterized by regularized daily routines and both a physical and a psychological milieu that supports healthy child-caregiver interactions and rich opportunities for learning. In a literature review cited earlier

(Brooks-Gunn et al., 2000), 11 of 17 evaluations of parent-focused home-based programs used the HOME inventory (Home Observation for Measurement of the Environment; Caldwell and Bradley, 1984) as a measure of the caregiving milieu, and 8 of the 11 demonstrated at least some positive program influence. In addition, impacts on the quality of the home environment were assessed in four programs that combined home-based and center-based components, two of which (the Infant Health and Development Program and the Houston Parent-Child Development Center) documented modest positive effects (Andrews et al., 1982; Bradley et al., 1989) and two of which (Project CARE and the Teenage Pregnancy Intervention Program) found no intervention-control group differences (Field et al., 1982; Wasik et al., 1990).

The quality of daily family life (e.g., emotional well-being, level of personal control, life satisfaction, and interpersonal relationships) serves as another important protective or risk factor for both child and family outcomes (Crnic et al., 1983; Sameroff et al., 1987). In this context, the protective influences of family cohesion, as well as the adverse impacts of family violence and parental mental illness, are particularly significant. Maternal depression or substance abuse, for example, presents a major threat to child health and development (Bauman and Dougherty, 1983; Downey and Coyne, 1990; Field, 1995; Lester et al., 2000; Mayes, 1995; Seifer and Dickstein, 2000). Similarly, children who witness family violence or who are the victims of physical abuse directly experience significant consequences, such as psychosomatic disorders, anxiety, fears, sleep disruption, excessive crying, and school problems (Cicchetti and Toth, 1995; Osofsky, 1995; Pynoos et al., 1995; Scheeringa et al., 1995).

Few early childhood intervention programs include sufficient professional expertise to treat serious parent or family psychopathology, which can overwhelm the most valiant efforts of a conventional education and support approach. Limited data suggest, however, that attention to such needs may be fruitful. In one example, a home visiting program for socially isolated, pregnant women employed two service models—one focused on providing information and resources and the other on developing a therapeutic relationship between the home visitor and the expectant mother. Follow-up study revealed that women who received the mental health program approach reported fewer depressive symptoms, and the impact was particularly significant for those who experienced multiple risks (Barnard et al., 1988; Booth et al., 1989).

Assessing Community Mediators of Child Well-Being

The concept of community can be defined in multiple ways—as a network of social connections, a target for resource allocation, and simply a physical space. The hypothesized impacts of community factors on child health and development range from the positive effects of an environment rich in social capital and collective efficacy to the adverse influences of one that is burdened by poverty, violence, and other social drains. Although the potential effects of community-level variables on child health and development have been well described, their explicit measurement in early intervention impact studies has been limited, and the extent to which they are amenable to change is unclear (Duncan and Raudenbush, 1999; Earls and Buka, 2000; Manski, 1993). Potential domains of influence include both threats and facilitators and are described in greater detail in Chapter 12. The relative absence of significant attention to community-level interventions, in contrast to the dominant focus on child- and family-oriented strategies, is another indication of the relatively limited scope of early childhood programs in the United States, which are conceptualized within a more individualistic and less interdependent framework (see Chapter 3).

Threats to Physical Health and Safety

Potential threats to the physical health and well-being of young children include poor housing, with its associated risk of increased exposure to infectious diseases and higher incidence of injuries; environmental toxins, such as lead (which can adversely affect brain development); and endemic substance abuse and violence, with their associated risk of child maltreatment (Klerman, 1991; Korenman and Miller, 1997). When safety concerns limit the extent to which children are allowed to play outside their homes, learning opportunities are restricted and development may be compromised. Significant interactions between the adverse physical features of a poor neighborhood and the associated social context of a dangerous environment present a particularly serious threat to children's well-being. Empirical data linked explicitly to early intervention program effects, however, are unavailable.

Threats to Social and Educational Opportunity

Beyond their threats to children's physical health and safety, certain characteristics of communities add further disadvantage by undermining a sense of opportunity or individual possibility, beginning in infancy and extending throughout childhood. Aspects of this burden include the adverse consequences of limited recreational facilities, inadequate child care, and substandard schools. Racism or other forms of discrimination based on ethnic status, social class, or the presence of a developmental disability lead to both overt and subtle messages of social exclusion that can have significant debilitating effects on a young child's emerging sense of self

(García Coll and Magnuson, 2000; Stoneman, in press). Once again, these concepts have been well described, but their empirical documentation has been limited.

Some researchers have hypothesized that the negative impacts of community factors on child well-being may be significant only in the most impoverished environments, and that modest community-level interventions in such circumstances may be of limited benefit (see Chapter 12). Notwithstanding the modest science base in this area, family relocation has been demonstrated to result in positive child outcomes for some children, but results suggest that a large (i.e., 1+ standard deviation) change in neighborhood conditions, as might be reflected in a move from an inner-city housing project to a neighborhood with only half as many poor families, is necessary to produce significant effects (Katz et al., 1999; Ludwig et al., in press).

Severe Deprivation

The concept of environmental deprivation in the early childhood years is complex and highly charged. Several observers have raised concerns about the inappropriate labeling and associated stigmatization of low-income families, many of whom are members of minority groups, who are unfairly and inaccurately categorized as neglectful. This is particularly problematic in circumstances in which children are developing normally in caring and nurturing environments but are not mastering the social behaviors or cognitive skills that are expected by teachers and required by schools (García Coll and Magnuson, 2000).

Nevertheless, some children do indeed grow up in environments that are characterized appropriately as deprived, inadequate, or destructive. Historical examples include institutions for young children with Down syndrome and cerebral palsy; contemporary models are best exemplified by Romanian orphanages and children living in extremely abusive homes dominated by severe mental illness and substance abuse. In both circumstances, research has demonstrated the devastating impacts of early and severe deprivation, as well as the remarkable capacity of children, both with and without biologically based disabilities, to recover from extraordinary developmental assaults if an alternative environment is provided as early as possible (Benoit et al., 1996; Provence and Lipton, 1962; Spitz, 1945) (see Chapter 9).

Facilitators of Growth-Promoting Opportunities

In contrast to strong evidence documenting the adverse impacts of high-risk environments, a number of enhancing community characteristics have been postulated to increase the probability of more positive child outcomes. These include supportive social networks for families, particularly for mothers; inclusive community settings, such as organized programs that offer a welcoming environment for children of diverse backgrounds and make appropriate accommodations for children with special medical or developmental needs; and other manifestations of social capital or collective efficacy that are accessible to children and families (Sampson et al., 1997). These facilitators may be particularly important for victims of systematic discrimination or social isolation. Empirical evidence for such associations, however, has not yet been produced.

The extent to which community resources can promote developmental opportunities for young children is presumed to be determined by both the nature of the offerings and the commitment of the community to ensure their availability. Common examples include accessible and affordable child care and preschool programs of high quality and a diverse selection of recreational activities. As important as the programs themselves are the intangible sense of community and the message of social inclusion, which communicates to all children and families that opportunities are available to them and that expectations for their healthy development and later achievement are high. Such messages are likely to be particularly critical for children with disabilities, children who are poor, and children of racial or ethnic minority status. Promoting such social capital and increasing its accessibility for vulnerable families is an important component of the early childhood intervention agenda. Systematic research in this area has not yet been done.

Social Policies that Affect Families with Young Children

Social policies often have considerable impact on the well-being of young children and their families, directly or indirectly, and by either commission or omission (Shonkoff et al., 2000). Some, such as federally mandated early intervention and special education services under the Individuals with Disabilities Education Act and state-mandated child care regulations, are recognizable components of the early intervention arena. Others, such as the provision of unpaid job leave for parents of newborns under the Family and Medical Leave Act and the time limits and mandated work requirements of Temporary Assistance to Needy Families under the Personal Responsibility and Work Opportunity Reconciliation Act, are not linked directly to the field of early childhood intervention but have a significant impact on its agenda. By the same token, many important social policies do not have their origins in direct government action. Prominent examples include the shift in pediatric health services toward a managed care model and corporate policies and practices that affect working hours, fringe benefits, and other supports for employees with young children.

Some policies (e.g., minimum wage laws, the earned income tax credit) have an impact on child health and development by affecting the availability of material resources and therefore the quality of family life and parents' ability to provide learning experiences for their children. Others (e.g., mandated child safety caps for medicine containers, legal limits on hot water heater temperature settings, the fortification of foods with iron or folic acid) are designed to reduce reliance on individual caregiver behavior by controlling external environmental threats to health and safety. Taken collectively, the range of potential policies that can influence the well-being of young children is considerable. This indicates a need to consider a much broader scope and definition of the concept of early childhood intervention.

LESSONS LEARNED AND FUTURE CHALLENGES

Essential Features of Effective Interventions

Despite the methodological limitations of the existing science base and the marked diversity of disciplinary perspectives and program models that are represented in the research literature, a common set of essential features has emerged across a broad spectrum of early childhood intervention systems. These include a mix of both well-documented empirical findings and state-of-the-art guidelines based on professional consensus.

Before examining the characteristics that are associated with effective interventions, it is necessary to acknowledge the specific problems inherent in the available data. Notwithstanding important exceptions, much of the empirical knowledge base is compromised by incomplete information on sample children and families, inadequate documentation of the services planned or delivered, and substantial methodological limitations in study design and data analysis. These limit their utility for addressing causal questions (see Chapter 4). Moreover, except for selected reports, most intervention studies focus on the quantification of aggregate program effects rather than the more useful analysis of differential program impacts based on complex interactions among child, family, and service variables.

In this context, promising new studies of early childhood intervention are beginning to employ a variety of quantitative and qualitative research methods to address a more focused set of questions. For example, what can be learned about tailoring specific services to children and families in different circumstances and with different needs? How does a policy or program decide when to focus on the child, the family, the community, or other significant influences in the child's life, and in what mix? What can we learn about thresholds of program intensity and levels of parent engagement that are necessary for measurable impact, particularly as they may vary for different populations? What is known about the developmental timing and duration of different interventions? What is required to sustain positive change, both in terms of the processes that must be set in motion and the ongoing services, if any, that must be continued? What are the major barriers and constraints that limit the possibilities for positive change?

Future research will undoubtedly provide answers to these and other compelling questions about the differential impacts of early childhood services. The clear determination of causal connections between specific interventions and specific outcomes, however, will depend on the extent to which investigators adhere to the principles discussed in Chapter 4. Current knowledge points to the need for greater empirical attention to the following essential features of effective interventions: (1) individualization of service delivery; (2) quality of program implementation; (3) timing, intensity, and duration of intervention; (4) provider knowledge, skills, and relationship with the family; and (5) a family-centered, community-based, coordinated orientation.

Individualization of Service Delivery

Extensive research from a variety of service system perspectives converges on the principle that effective intervention demands an individualized approach that matches well-defined goals to the specific needs and resources of the children and families who are served. Thus, there is scant support for a one-size-fits-all model of early childhood intervention. Consequently, there is little justification for an approach to program evaluation that asks generic questions about whether services are effective, in contrast to an assessment strategy that investigates the extent to which specific kinds of interventions have differential impacts on specific kinds of children in specific types of families. Central to this fundamental principle of effective services is the importance of understanding the diverse cultural contexts within which young children grow up, and the need for individualized functional child assessments that measure important capacities that are linked to the intervention in an ongoing, reciprocal fashion.

For young children whose development may be compromised by an impoverished, disorganized, or abusive environment, as well as for those with a documented disability (who themselves represent a remarkably heterogeneous population), interventions that are tailored to specific needs have been shown to be more effective in producing desired child and family outcomes than services that provide generic advice and support (Brooks-Gunn et al., 2000; Farran, 1990, 2000; Guralnick, 1998). Furthermore, programs that directly target the everyday experiences of children appear to be more effective in improving their acquisition of skills than those that seek to promote child development indirectly by enhancing the general quality of the caregiving environment (Farran, 2000). Similarly, services that are focused explicitly on parenting behaviors have greater impact on parent-child interactions than do generic parent education efforts (Brooks-Gunn et al., 2000). These patterns are reflected in the relatively greater child-focused impacts of center-based interventions (Farran, 2000) and greater parent-focused effects of home-based programs (Brooks-Gunn et al., 2000). A confirmatory review of 27 early intervention programs by Benasich and colleagues (1992) found short-term child cognitive benefits in 90 percent of center-based services, in contrast to 64 percent of home-based interventions. One year after program termination, child developmental gains persisted for 67 percent of the center-based programs and 44 percent of the home-based interventions.

Research demonstrating differential effectiveness for specific subgroups of children and families further supports the need for individualization of services to ensure maximum impact. For example, children whose mothers had the lowest IQ gained the most from the Abecedarian Project (Campbell and Ramey, 1994, 1995). Similarly, children whose mothers had less education demonstrated greater benefits from the Infant Health and Development Program, although greater child impacts were also documented for children at lower biological risk as measured by birthweight (Brooks-Gunn et al., 1994; Liaw and Brooks-Gunn, 1993; McCarton et al., 1997). For children with defined disabilities, both the nature of the impairment and its level of severity demand a highly differentiated approach to service planning and delivery. Generally speaking, for both biologically and environmentally vulnerable populations, program impacts are generally greater for more disadvantaged families and for children with less severe disabilities (although the latter may be a function of the developmental measures that are used). More definitive understanding of the causal relations between specific interventions and specific outcomes for specific target populations will require further randomized experimental studies.

Linked to the need for individualized intervention strategies, current practice (and, in fact, federal law for children with disabilities) mandates that service outcomes be tailored to the particular interests of each individual family (Meisels and Shonkoff, 2000). In this context, parents of children with the same developmental disability may have very different goals and aspirations. Similarly, families experiencing comparable levels of economic hardship may have different needs and desires for assistance.

Quality of Program Implementation

The extent to which model demonstration programs are endowed with abundant resources and highly trained staff, evaluated successfully, and subsequently replicated with inadequate budgets and less skilled personnel is a highly problematic burden for the early intervention field. Thus, a second feature of early childhood services that is endorsed widely across all service systems is the fundamental importance of the quality of the intervention that is actually delivered and received by target children and families.

The research literature on child care provides abundant evidence of the positive correlation between quality of care and developmental outcomes for children (see reviews by Lamb, 1998; Love et al., 1996; Scarr and Eisenberg, 1993; and Smith, 1998). Moreover, in the absence of subsidies, children from low-income families who are at greater developmental risk are more likely to receive lower-quality care (NICHD Early Child Care Research Network, 1997c; Phillips et al., 1987b). The impact of quality has been shown to be particularly important for children from families who bear the burden of multiple risk factors, who are also the children with the greatest probability of being enrolled in poor-quality programs (Currie, 2000; Peisner-Feinberg and Burchinal, 1997).

Variations in quality among intervention programs designed to address the problems of economic disadvantage are widespread. One evaluation of a sample of Head Start programs, for example, generated developmentally appropriate ratings for only 3 of the 32 classrooms studied (Bryant et al., 1994). More promising results from the recent FACES data collection reflect greater attention to quality standards in Head Start centers (Administration on Children Youth and Families, 1998, 2000). Generally speaking, concerns about the quality of program implementation have received much less explicit attention in the literature on services for young children with developmental disabilities.

The critical importance of the quality of program implementation is also a key issue with respect to the future of the evaluation enterprise. As noted in Chapter 4, the premature assessment of an intervention impact before one is confident that it can be faithfully implemented is likely to be both a waste of money and a demoralizing influence on those who are trying to develop promising new programs.

Timing, Intensity, and Duration of Intervention

The research literature on service intensity, duration, and age of initiation is perhaps the most complex and inconclusive aspect of the early childhood intervention knowledge base. Many investigators have reported findings that support the value of "earlier" and "more." Others have challenged such conclusions as advocacy-driven research.

The concept of intensity is defined operationally in many ways. Most typically it has been measured by the amount of professional time (e.g., hours per day, days per week, or weeks per year) spent with families or children. Unfortunately, however, relatively few effectiveness studies have collected sufficient data to assess this important variable. One important exception is the Infant Health and Development Program, which has generated a rich database on services received by individual sample members and has documented a positive association between intensity of participation and child cognitive gains (Ramey et al., 1992). The nonrandom nature of the differences in program participation, however, precludes definitive interpretation of intensity effects. In two studies of a home visiting program for poor families with infants in Jamaica, one of which used a random assignment design, weekly visits were associated with higher child developmental test scores than biweekly visits, and children who were visited biweekly scored higher than those who received services at monthly intervals (Powell and Grantham-McGregor, 1989). Intensity effects have also been noted for children with autism, as increased program intensity is associated with more substantial short- and long-term outcomes (McEachin et al., 1993; Lovaas, 1987).

Duration of intervention has also been studied and found to be associated with measurable family impacts. For example, mothers who participated in the Prenatal/Early Infancy Project for 2 years were less likely to maltreat their children than mothers who received 9 months of service. Moreover, a 15-year follow-up revealed an inverse relation between the amount of service received and a number of negative maternal outcomes, including child maltreatment, repeat pregnancy, welfare dependence, substance abuse, and interactions with the criminal justice system (Kitzman et al., 1997; Olds et al., 1997). The Abecedarian intervention plus a follow-up program into the elementary school years was more effective than the preschool intervention alone (Campbell and Ramey, 1994).

For families of young children with developmental disabilities, the variability in service intensity is considerable. Differences in both amount and duration of intervention may be related to the age of referral, the nature and severity of the child's impairment, or the family's resources and needs. In a systematic investigation of services received by families of children with Down syndrome, motor impairment, and developmental delays of uncertain etiology, the Early Intervention Collaborative Study documented an average of 7 hours of service per month over the first 12 months of program participation, with a range from less than 1 hour to over 20 hours monthly (Shonkoff et al., 1992) In this sample of 190 children enrolled in 29 community-based programs, the strongest predictor of service intensity in the first year was the child's score on the Bayley Scales at the time of program entry (i.e., children with more severe impairments received more hours of service).

The measurement of program intensity for children with disabilities also includes parent time spent on developing relationships and acquiring knowledge, as well as the extent to which structured learning opportunities are embedded in typical family routines. Indeed, the ultimate impacts of such programs are presumed to be dependent on the degree to which families are able to incorporate specific intervention techniques into their everyday interactions with their children (Gilkerson and Stott, 2000).

Finally, both empirical data and clinical experience indicate that earlier identification and intervention are more important for some conditions or circumstances than for others. For example, early diagnosis and treatment is clearly effective in reducing the adverse impacts of a hearing loss on functional communication and cognition (Brasel and Quigley, 1977). Similarly, early tactile/kinesthetic stimulation of premature newborns has been associated with greater weight gain, higher survival rates, and higher neurobehavioral scores (Field et al., 1986). Children who are adopted out of institutionalized orphanages before 12 months of age have better developmental outcomes than those who are adopted at an older age (Benoit et al., 1996). The impacts of prenatal home visits have been correlated with enhanced health and safety outcomes and decreased parental interaction difficulties for some groups but have shown minimal effects for others (Olds and Kitzman, 1993). The persistent effects of the Abecedarian Project have been attributed by some investigators to the initiation of the intervention in early infancy and its extension over the first five years of life.

In summary, earlier has been shown to be better (and defined differently) for some conditions than for others. There is no basis, however, for concluding that individualized interventions provided after certain ages can have no positive impacts. Furthermore, notwithstanding the importance of preventing early developmental concerns from becoming more serious problems later, the premature initiation of services may lead in some circumstances to inappropriate labeling or the removal of children from typical experiences, thereby reducing the possibility of self-righting corrections or compensatory growth spurts. Finally, questions about intensity and duration must always be considered in the context of assessing the ratio of costs to benefits. Modest benefits from shorter and less intense services may be small, but their cost is relatively low. In contrast, significantly higher benefits may be derived from longer and more intense services, but the cost of those greater gains may be quite high.

Weighing the difference between costs and benefits in the determination of appropriate program "dosages" is a critical policy challenge. Unfortunately, the data needed to assess this issue are quite limited. Moreover, it is most important to recognize that the only way to provide *definitive* answers to questions about the relative impacts of the timing, intensity, and duration of service delivery is to conduct randomized experimental studies on specific populations.

Provider Knowledge, Skills, and Relationship with the Family

The extent to which service providers have the knowledge and skills necessary to address the needs of their target population is a fundamental challenge facing all human services. This challenge is particularly compelling for early childhood programs, in view of the broad array of conditions and circumstances with which they are confronted. Examples include infants with significant developmental disabilities with or without complex medical concerns, preschoolers with severe behavioral disorders, mothers with clinical depression, and families dealing with the stresses of poverty, marital discord, substance abuse, and recurrent domestic violence. Each of these types of problems typically requires a level of professional expertise that exceeds the generic skills of a child care provider, early childhood educator, child protective services worker, or nonprofessional home visitor.

A substantial body of research in child care settings has clearly linked well-trained, qualified teachers and staff to better child outcomes, particularly for low-income children who are at risk for early developmental problems and later educational underachievement (see Lamb, 1998). However, as greater numbers of children with disabilities are enrolled in programs, child care providers and early childhood educators are increasingly faced with the inadequacy of their professional training and the paucity of expert consultation available to help them address a wide variety of special needs. The massive shortage of mental health professionals to deal with very young children and the uneven level of skills and excessive rate of turnover among child care workers are particularly critical problems in this regard (Knitzer, 2000).

Resource limitations and pressures to "do more with less" present enormous challenges to programs that serve families who are coping with complex developmental and socioeconomic concerns. Marked disparities in the training and skills of home visiting program staff are prominent examples of this phenomenon (Gomby et al., 1999; Olds et al., 1999). In this context, the ultimate impact of any intervention is dependent on both staff expertise and the quality and continuity of the personal relationship established between the service provider and the family that is being served. For example, mothers and children who received high ratings for active engagement in the Infant Health and Development Program were found to have better home environments and higher child IQ scores at 36 months (Liaw et al., 1995), although the direction of effect could not be determined with assurance.

The challenges of establishing relationships with individuals who face varying combinations of child disability and adverse environmental circumstances are substantial. Families of children with special needs seek guidance in understanding how to promote their child's atypical development, and service providers are trained to respect parents' knowledge about their child's unique personal characteristics. Children living in impoverished or disorganized environments are presumed to need compensatory, enriching experiences, and their parents are generally presumed to need help in addressing basic childrearing needs. This tension between intervention models that view parents as the ultimate authority with respect to their children's interests and those that view them as requiring significant assistance demands highly skilled staff and creates a complex challenge for the early childhood field.

Family-Centered, Community-Based, Coordinated Orientation

The concepts of family-centered, community-based, coordinated services are firmly embedded in the professional experience and philosophies that guide all early childhood programs, from the generic child care facility to the most highly specialized intervention for young children with complex developmental disabilities or severely compromised living arrangements. Thus, although the empirical evidence for these concepts is thin, the theoretical and experiential support is strong.

Central to the concept of family-centered care is the notion of empowering parents as the true experts with respect to their own child's and family's needs and the goal of building a strong, mutually respectful, working partnership in which parents and professionals relate comfortably in a collaborative effort to achieve family-driven objectives (Turnbull et al., 2000). The essential characteristics of a community-based model are reflected in the extent to which services are delivered in a nonstigmatizing, normative environment that has both physical and psychological proximity to where young children and their families live. The essence of coordinated services is embedded in the synergistic organization of a variety of programmatic resources in a rational, efficient, and cost-effective manner that minimizes bureaucratic complexity and avoids unnecessary burdens on families.

The essential features of a family-centered approach to early childhood services include: (1) treating families with dignity and respect, particularly with respect to their cultural and socioeconomic characteristics; (2) providing choices that address family priorities and concerns; (3) fully disclosing information so that families can make informed decisions; and (4) providing support in a manner that is empowering and that enhances parental competence. The extent to which a program is viewed as family-centered is generally determined by measures of parent satisfaction, service utilization, and level of participant attrition.

Providing developmental promotion and early intervention services in a community-based context facilitates access and reduces the stigma associated with service provision in a segregated setting. For children with developmental disabilities, the promotion of competence in normative community contexts is particularly important as a vehicle for both acquiring functional skills and gaining social acceptance (Guralnick, in press).

The evolving nature and imprecise measurement of the concepts of "coordinated," "community-based," and "family-centered" underscore the critical need for more descriptive, exploratory investigations in this area, including both qualitative and quantitative research. Indeed, as described in Chapter 4, the level of maturation of the knowledge in this area indicates that experimental, randomized studies would be premature and of less value at the current time.

Opportunities, Constraints, and Challenges

As the concept of early childhood intervention continues to evolve, it faces a multitude of ongoing challenges. Some must await the generation of new knowledge; others will depend on the resolution of old political conflicts. In the final analysis, the future vitality of the field will be served best by a creative blend of critical self-evaluation and openness to fresh thinking. The following seven challenges are particularly important at this point in time: (1) increasing access and participation, (2) ensuring greater quality control, (3) defining and achieving cultural competence, (4) identifying and responding to the special needs of distinctive subgroups, (5) influencing and evaluating the impacts of postintervention environments, (6) strengthening the service infrastructure, and (7) assessing the costs of early childhood investments.

Increasing Access and Participation

Marked inequalities in access to state-of-the-art early childhood services are a serious problem. Diminished accessibility is related to a variety of potential barriers, including cost, language, culture, citizenship status, transportation, eligibility standards, program scheduling, and stigma associated with labeling, among others.

Beyond the failure of existing policies and programs to ensure the identification and enrollment of all children and families who could benefit from available services, many early childhood intervention efforts experience significant participant attrition. For example, in one study of Parent-Child Development Centers, 47 percent of the treatment group dropped out in the first year of the program (Walker et al., 1995). Of the 985 children enrolled in the Infant Health and Development Program, 81 received no services whatsoever (Liaw et al., 1995). Average attendance in the High/Scope Perry Preschool Program was 69 percent in the center-based component (Weikart and Schweinhart, 1992), and only 56 percent of the families enrolled in the Comprehensive Child Development Programs were actively engaged after three years of participation (St. Pierre et al., 1994). A recent review of several model home visiting programs characterized the enrollment, involvement, and retention of families as a common struggle. For example, data from the Hawaii Healthy Start Program and the Nurse Home Visitation Program estimated that 10-25 percent of families who were invited to enroll in these programs chose not to participate. Once the families were enrolled, they received an average of about half of the scheduled visits, regardless of the intended frequency. Between 20 and 67 percent of all the families who enrolled in the home visiting programs reviewed left the program before it was scheduled to end (Gomby et al., 1999).

Significant dropout rates present problems for both service delivery and for the evaluation of intervention impacts. On one hand, less than universal "take-up" is a fact of life and may reflect rational responses by parents who do not perceive the potential benefits of a program to be worth the costs of the time and commitment required of them. In such circumstances, the failure of families to continue to participate in an early childhood program may indicate the need to reevaluate the goals of the intervention, the nature of the services that are provided, and the goodness-of-fit between what the program offers and what the target families perceive as their needs. Thus, assessing the impact of an offer of service could be of great value. On the other hand, an evaluation of the effectiveness of a program that experiences significant sample attrition must be interpreted with particular caution. Although such an assessment may produce interesting and important findings, particularly in the context of its potential impact in the real world, it says very little about how effective the service model would have been if it had been received more favorably by the intended recipients. In summary, the problem of sample attrition is a function of both the questions that are asked and how the findings are interpreted.

Ensuring Greater Quality Control

The importance of quality control is described earlier in this chapter as an essential feature of effective intervention. When addressed honestly, it represents a powerful strategy for enhancing the early childhood agenda. When thwarted by inadequate resources, professional inertia, or the fear of critical findings, it represents a serious threat to the field and to the children and families it is designed to serve.

In view of the extensive literature that has been accumulated based on descriptive and quasi-experimental research, the need for an open and honest commitment to true experimentation with randomization represents one of the most significant challenges facing early childhood policy makers, service providers, and program evaluators. In the final analysis, the future vitality of the field will depend on the extent to which well-designed experiments can be conducted in a nonthreatening atmosphere in an effort to promote continuous quality improvement based on continually expanding knowledge.

Defining and Achieving Cultural Competence

The development of all young children and the functioning of all families unfold within a distinctive cultural context. This fundamental concept, which is discussed in greater detail in Chapter 3, is reflected in the values and beliefs that shape parenting practices and the expectations that families (as well as societies) have for their children, beginning from the moment of birth (García Coll and Magnuson, 2000; Greenfield and Suzuki, 1998; Super and Harkness, 1986). The importance of examining the design and implementation of early childhood policies and practices through a cultural lens cannot be overstated.

All early childhood intervention initiatives, as described earlier in this chapter, are generally predicated on both a presumption of vulnerability (in the child or the family or both) and a belief that specific services can alter the child's daily experiences in a way that will increase the odds of a more favorable developmental outcome. Implicit in this model are two assumptions—first, that the caregiving environment needs modification and, second, that there is clear agreement between the family and the service program on the desired outcomes. In both cases, the potential for biased, ethnocentric value judgments on the part of the service provider is high, and therefore the need to guard against inappropriate or intrusive interventions is real.

As described in Chapter 3, there is considerable variability in the cultural practices that characterize families with young children. This diversity is manifested in a wide variety of scripts that reflect routine approaches to daily childrearing tasks, in conjunction with significant differences in the kinds of emerging skills that caregivers value and nurture in young children. For example, the cultural practices of many ethnic minority families in the United States, including but not restricted to recent immigrants, differ substantially from those of white, middle-class families. Consequently, the children in such families may exhibit developmental patterns or specific skills that differ from those required to succeed in school. In such circumstances, it would be most inappropriate to label the child as developmentally delayed or disabled, even though he or she would be at greater risk of failing in school and could benefit from services designed to enhance school readiness.

Differences in parental behaviors are also vulnerable to being judged as inappropriate or misclassified as abnormal. For example, different cultural beliefs and practices related to leaving young children unsupervised, or different patterns of discipline in association with disagreement about the criteria for defining maltreatment, can result in highly sensitive challenges for a child welfare system (Korbin, 1994; Rose and Meezan, 1996). Families from different cultures also have different beliefs and understanding about developmental disabilities and mental health problems, which may influence their reactions to diagnoses, adaptation to the challenges of caring for a child with special needs, and preferences among service delivery options (Bernheimer et al., 1990; Coates and Vietze, 1996; Lynch and Hanson, 1998; Seligman and Darling, 1997).

Recognizing the critical importance of cultural differences, as described in Chapter 3, each of the diverse service streams that constitute the early childhood intervention landscape endorses the central importance of cultural competence as a cornerstone of state-of-the-art practice. Consequently, an increasing number and variety of resources to provide guidance in this area have proliferated in recent years. Most of the available material, however, is conceptual rather than empirical (Johnson-Powell, 1997; Lewis, 2000; Lynch and Hanson, 1998), Thus, despite widespread consensus about its importance, the underlying science of cultural competence remains to be developed.

Identifying and Responding to the Special Needs of Distinctive Subgroups

Notwithstanding the common knowledge base that transcends the compartmentalized world of early childhood intervention, specific population subgroups confront unique challenges that require specialized expertise. For children, the presence of a biologically based disability, such as cerebral palsy or a sensory loss, requires an intervention strategy that incorporates knowledge about both normative child development and adaptation to a specific physical impairment. For mothers, the diagnosis of depression or a substance abuse problem adds an enormous burden to the normative stresses of parenting, and necessitates services that go beyond the provision of simple advice and support. And for families that confront severe economic hardship and ongoing domestic violence, the needs of their young children extend beyond the addition of educational enrichment activities. The overarching challenge for both policy makers and service providers is to integrate specialized services (when they are required) in a comprehensive framework that addresses the generic needs of all children and families, while recognizing the importance of individual differences and the necessity of cultural competence in an increasingly pluralistic society.

Another dimension of special needs requiring sensitive attention is the extent to which early childhood interventions might be beneficial for some but have unintended negative consequences for others. From the perspective of the family, programs that focus explicitly on parent training may send a message of presumed incompetence, which might undermine a mother's or father's self-confidence and contribute inadvertently to less effective performance. Similarly, parenting interventions that respond to cultural differences in a dismissive or pejorative manner are likely to precipitate significant conflict or be rejected as unacceptable. Related to these concerns, some observers have cautioned that the provision of formally organized support services may sometimes interfere with the natural development of the informal social networks needed by all families (Affleck et al., 1989). Indeed, one study found that professionally directed support groups may actually serve as additional stressors for some mothers (Krauss et al., 1993).

Some services may also have the unintended consequence of limiting child opportunities. For example, inappropriate interventions may cause some parents to interact with their child in an unnatural, therapeutic manner rather than through a natural and comfortable parent-child relationship. From the perspective of the child, a tightly structured intervention that is delivered in a highly prescriptive style may interfere with the normal adaptive and self-righting mechanisms that are inherent in the developmental process. In a comparable fashion, isolation from normative settings for a child with a disability results in a distorted social world that provides limited opportunities for healthy adaptation.

Inevitable tensions between the generic and idiosyncratic characteristics and needs of children and families create a complex agenda for the early childhood field. All children, with or without biological or environmental vulnerabilities, do best when they are reared in a nurturing environment that responds to their individuality and invests in their well-being. All families, regardless of their material resources, depend on informal social supports and varying levels of professional service. Thus, despite the challenges of special needs, the general principles of development apply to all children and families across the broad array of early childhood service systems.

Influencing and Assessing the Impacts of Postintervention Environments

The demands of policy makers for evidence of long-term impacts as a result of investments in early childhood programs have put service providers and program evaluators in a difficult bind. Central to this dilemma is the widely endorsed assertion that effective early intervention services do not serve as inoculations that confer a lifetime of immunity against the adverse effects of later experiences. Indeed, no intervention prior to school entry can ever be powerful enough to fully buffer a vulnerable child from the negative effects of attending a demoralizing school or living in a dangerous neighborhood.

The extensive documentation of IQ fade-out, particularly for children who live in impoverished environments and receive a mediocre public education, was described earlier. Nevertheless, the few studies that have followed early childhood program graduates through the school years and into adult life have demonstrated variable patterns of so-called sleeper effects in such areas as high school graduation, welfare dependence, income, and criminal behavior (Lally et al., 1988; Schweinhart et al., 1993). The need for more longitudinal data to further elucidate this phenomenon is clear, but follow-up studies must pay greater attention to the continuing influence of the child's environment throughout the life span.

The key challenge facing early childhood intervention professionals is the need to establish the standard of proof that must be met in order to endorse a program as effective. The immediate and short-term benefits for both families and taxpayers are real, and their value should not be diminished. Moreover, the medium-term benefits of reduced grade retention and special education referrals can be quite large economically and could justify the initial costs of early intervention, even in the absence of longer-term impacts.

Strengthening the Service Infrastructure

Services to promote the health and well-being of all young children, as well as early intervention efforts for those who are developmentally vulnerable, cover a diverse and highly fragmented array of policies, programs, and funding sources. This fragmentation has been the object of considerable criticism for decades. The extensive knowledge base presented in this report provides a powerful tool to guide the design of a more rational and efficient infrastructure for early childhood services that incorporates the multiple streams that have evolved independently over the years.

Beyond the general challenges of excessive service fragmentation and redundancy, the limited availability of mental health assistance for children under age 6 represents a massive gap in the current early childhood infrastructure (Knitzer, 2000). This shortcoming is particularly problematic in view of the high prevalence of emotional and behavioral problems in young children and the inextricable interrelation among cognitive, social, and emotional development, as elaborated in Chapters 5 and 6.

Two striking examples illustrate the magnitude of this problem. First, the federal mandate to provide family-centered services for infants and toddlers with developmental disabilities or delays, under the provisions of Part C of the Individuals with Disabilities Education Act, focuses primarily on cognitive, language, and motor impairments and does not accord a comparable entitlement to services for children whose difficulties lie in the domains of emotional and social development. In a similar fashion, multiple federal programs address the problem of child maltreatment, and all states require mandatory reporting of suspected child abuse or neglect, yet large numbers of maltreated young children are managed in child welfare systems that have limited professional expertise in normative child development, developmental disabilities, and early childhood mental health. Both the failure to incorporate state-of-the-art mental health expertise into policies and programs designed to address the needs of children with disabilities and the absence of sophisticated developmental services for young children who have been maltreated are dramatic examples of the significant gap between current knowledge and practice.

Assessing Costs and Making Choices Among Early Childhood Investments

The early era of early childhood intervention in the United States focused relatively little attention on the question of cost. Whether the target population was dealing with the stresses of poverty or the challenges of developmental disability, public funds were appropriated on the basis of assumed need and the return on investment was rarely quantified.

Beginning in the 1980s and continuing to the present, all health and human services have been faced with increasing demands for cost-effectiveness and demonstrated cost-benefit. This shift has been embedded in a changing political climate characterized by reductions in taxes and appropriations for government social programs, devolution of authority from the federal to state and local levels, and an increasing reliance on market solutions to address health and human services needs. In this context, early childhood intervention programs face a less forgiving environment that demands evidence of both measurable impacts and more efficient service delivery. Although much of the impetus for greater accountability has been stereotyped as a lack of commitment to the well-being of vulnerable children, it is important to note that the rigorous assessment of costs and benefits is the best way to ensure that finite resources are used in the best interests of children and families. It is essential, however, to also recognize that the distribution of benefits matters. For example, savings to a school budget do not necessarily accrue to families and children in need. Thus, although public financial gains are generally desirable, a policy that resulted in the same net benefits, but proportionally more for the children and relatively less for the general taxpayer, might be preferred.

The costs of early childhood services vary considerably. Averages per child range (in 1994 dollars) from Missouri Parents As Teachers (less than $1,000 per year) to the Avance Family Support and Education program

($1,600 per year for 1 or 2 years), Even Start Family Literacy Programs ($2,660 for 1 year), Child and Family Resource Programs ($3,220 per year for 5 years), Head Start Family Service Centers ($3,500 per year for 3 years), Head Start ($4,000 per year for 1 or 2 years), New Chance ($8,300 per year for 1.5 years), the Comprehensive Child Development Program ($8,600 per year for 5 years), and the Infant Health and Development Program ($10,000 per year for three years) (St. Pierre et al., 1995b). With such a wide discrepancy in costs, both annually and as a function of the number of years of program enrollment, the demand for evidence of intervention impacts is compelling and the need for more data on cost-effectiveness is clear.

In their efforts to develop model early childhood programs that can have significant and long-lasting impacts, interventionists have periodically designed and evaluated elaborate service models with costs per child that have exceeded $8,000 to $10,000 per year. Yet legislators and service providers typically have budgets that are too small to offer such programs to more than a small fraction of the children who could profit from them. Early intervention researchers generally ask "What works?" and "How does it work?" Budget-constrained policy makers and practitioners typically seek the most cost-effective programs that serve the largest possible number of needy children.

How significant an impact must an intervention have to be worthwhile? Is a cheaper-by-half, scaled-back version of a proven program likely to provide at least half the benefits? If several interventions show documented benefits but a decision maker cannot fund them all, how should he or she choose among the alternatives? Is the $4.66 billion the United States spent on Head Start programs in 1999 too much or too little? These are some of the difficult policy questions that arise.

Cost-effectiveness and cost-benefit frameworks (Gramlich, 1990; Levin, 1983) are useful though imperfect means of addressing all of these issues. Each begins with a systematic accounting of the full costs of an intervention program. Dollar expenditures on staff salaries and benefits generally make up the bulk of such costs. However, a complete cost accounting must include subtler expenditures, such as the value of the time volunteers spend helping out with the program and the cost of the needed classrooms or other facilities. Thus, volunteer time is not free, since it could have been used productively for some other purpose; facilities are not free, because scaling up a program to provide services for tens of thousands of children often requires major expenditures to rent or build facilities.

The benefits of early childhood programs are often difficult to quantify with a monetary value. Their accurate assessment requires a precise comparison of developmental outcomes for children who received program services and otherwise similar children who did not. As described in Chapter 4, randomized experimental designs often provide the strongest basis for estimating program impacts. But the measurement of child development is not always straightforward, and the assignment of a dollar value to a given outcome is a complex challenge. The most commonly measured dependent variable in the intervention literature is IQ. This report argues that important domains of child development and well-being also include emotional health and social behavior, and a full cost-benefit perspective underscores the importance of a broad conception of child outcomes. For example, IQ gains may benefit society by increasing the productivity of the nation's workforce. However, as shown by data from the High/Scope Perry Preschool Program, the societal value of improvements in children's mental health and reductions in criminal activity can easily exceed the value of IQ-based productivity gains.

Reactions to the assignment of dollar values to impacts on children's development often range from skepticism to moral indignation. Advocates often ask how one can assign a dollar value to the lives that are saved by child care safety regulations, or to a boost in self-esteem for a child who avoids the stigma of assignment to a special education program. In contrast to the questions asked of cost-benefit analyses, some investigators conduct cost-effectiveness studies to avoid the problem of benefit valuation by simply comparing the relative costs of programs designed to meet similar goals (Barnett, 2000).

In view of their systematic attempt to account for the dollar value of all important program benefits, cost-benefit studies are more complex and ambitious than cost-effectiveness approaches. Program benefits, such as reduced use of special education services or decreased grade repetition, can be assigned specific dollar values based on what school systems spend to provide special and regular education services. However, these valuations of school-related benefits are likely to be conservative, in the sense that they omit the value to children and their families of avoiding stigmatizing education classifications and tracks.

Quantifying the benefits of early childhood intervention programs for such long-term outcomes as criminal behavior and adult career success is exceedingly more difficult, since it requires the maintenance of contact with intervention and control group participants over a very long period of time. When the complete accounting of such benefits is not possible, a cost-benefit analysis evaluates all possible costs and benefits and then makes prudent judgments about whether the missing data would be likely to push the computed difference between benefits and costs in a positive or negative direction.

Table 13-1 summarizes results from a cost-benefit analysis of the High/Scope Perry Preschool Program (Schweinhart et al., 1993). Random assignment of children to intervention and control groups, the systematic follow-

TABLE 13-1 Costs and Benefits of the High/
Scope Perry Preschool Program

Total cost per child	$12,356
Total benefits per child	$70,786
K-12 expenditures saved	6,872
Higher adult earnings	14,498
Crime saving	49,044
Other	372

NOTE: Adapted from Schweinhart et al. (1993:Table 43).
Data are in 1992 dollars and discounted at 3 percent.

up of both groups through age 27, and a careful accounting of both costs
and benefits make this program a good example to illustrate the cost-
benefit approach. On the minus side, the study sample was small (117
children in all were interviewed at age 27) and located in a single Midwestern city, which suggests a need for replication before much is made of the
specific benefit estimates emerging from the study.

Since program impacts on IQ test scores were no longer found by the
time the children reached age 8, this study illustrates the potential value of
an early childhood intervention that produces long-term impacts in important social domains despite the apparent transient nature of its short-term
cognitive effects. Details on procedures for the cost and benefit accounting
method are provided by Schweinhart and his colleagues (1993).

Despite the value of the economic analyses that have been conducted
on the Perry Preschool Program, several features of the intervention make it
difficult to generalize from the findings. One remarkable factor is its high
cost ($12,356 per child in 1992 dollars and $14,683 in 1998 dollars for a 1-
to 2-year program), which is much higher than that of the typical Head
Start program ($5,021 per child in 1998). This reflects its greater intensity
of services compared with most early education programs, which makes it
all but impossible to generalize to less intensive interventions.

A second, and perhaps even more remarkable factor, is the size and
nature of the reported benefits. At age 27, the full complement of measured
benefits totaled $70,786, far in excess of the $12,356 costs of the program.
Thus, despite the IQ fade-out by third grade, the answer to the question of
whether the resources expended on the program were socially profitable is
a resounding "yes." Specifically, although the IQ impacts were short-lived,
children who participated in the intervention spent significantly less time in
special education programs and were less likely to repeat a grade, differences that saved their schools some $6,872 when averaged across all chil-
dren served. As large as these savings may seem, they are still not consid-

ered sufficient by some policy makers to outweigh program costs. Twice as large (some $14,498 per child) as the education benefits, however, were the higher earnings enjoyed by program participants in their young adult years.

Beyond the savings linked to education costs and employment earnings, the greatest impact in the Perry Preschool benefit-cost calculus was the computed value of the favorable differences in crime victim and incarceration costs for program participants relative to the control group. In fact, the costs to the criminal justice system and the costs of crime victimization are so large that the striking intervention-control differences in rates of criminal activity translated into a $49,044 program benefit per individual served.

Relatively few of the total benefits were reaped by the children enrolled in the Perry Preschool program. In fact, of the $70,786 total benefits, only $8,815 accrued to the participating children, mostly in the form of higher earnings in their early adult years. The $49,044 crime-related benefits constitute savings to taxpayers and potential crime victims, as did a nearly $7,000 savings from lower enrollment in special education programs. Thus, while a complete cost/benefit accounting considers all sources of benefits, it is important to identify to what extent the participants themselves are receiving the benefits.

The long-term analyses of the High/Scope Perry Preschool Program clearly demonstrate that a very intensive early intervention program can produce benefits far in excess of its costs. Despite the value of such a study, however, it does not begin to address a larger set of questions that are crucial for policy makers and practitioners. For example, do less expensive, less intensive programs also produce more benefits than costs? If resources are limited, is it better to offer high-quality programs to fewer children or more affordable programs to a larger number? Neither a single study nor a collection of evaluations of other high-cost, intensive studies can begin to answer these important questions.

The only way to address this complex and critically important issue is to evaluate a range of high- and low-intensity programs. Such evaluations may well suggest that there are smaller but still positive benefits for smaller programs. Welfare-to-work experiments in the 1980s resulted in precisely that conclusion (Gueron and Pauly, 1991). Very expensive (e.g., $10,000 per participant), intensive programs produced more benefits than costs, but so too did less expensive (e.g., $1,000 per participant) training-based programs, as well as extremely modest investments (e.g., $100 per participant) in job-search programs. Thus, cost-benefit information from a wide range of potential programs can help policy makers analyze trade-offs between intensity and coverage in the context of highly constrained budgets.

Regrettably, the number of early intervention services for which cost and benefit data are available is exceedingly small and confined largely to highly intensive programs. Consequently, it is difficult to provide economically guided answers to pressing questions about the optimal level of social investment that should be made in a wide range of early childhood efforts, such as Head Start, nutrition programs, and parenting education. Similarly, it is not possible to set safety and group size standards for child care settings based on reliable knowledge of their costs and benefits. The answers to these and many other important policy questions await further study.

CONCLUSIONS

Early childhood interventions are provided under the auspices of a wide variety of policies and programs. These include high-prevalence services, such as child care and early childhood education, as well as targeted interventions for a range of vulnerabilities, including economic hardship, childhood disabilities, parental substance abuse, and child maltreatment, among others. State-of-the-art early childhood programs are guided by a rich knowledge base that reflects a mixture of developmental theory, empirical research, and professional experience. A critical examination of this knowledge reveals considerable agreement on theoretical concepts, both replicable patterns and inconsistencies in the empirical data, and substantial gaps in potentially important areas of investigation.

The research literature on the efficacy and effectiveness of early intervention programs encompasses thousands of peer-reviewed papers, monographs, edited volumes, and project reports. Despite continuing debate about the nature of the underlying science and its methodological rigor, there is considerable agreement across all service streams about desired child outcomes, and about important family-based and community-based factors that influence child health and development. Generally speaking, well-designed early interventions that are child-focused produce immediate gains on standardized developmental measures, most commonly IQ scores. These findings have been replicated in multiple studies of children living in a variety of adverse circumstances and those with a wide range of diagnosed disabilities, although the largest benefits are typically found in model demonstration projects that generally incur high costs per child.

For children at risk because of low socioeconomic status, the short-term benefits of higher IQ scores typically fade out during the middle childhood years, but persistent intervention-control group differences have been documented, favoring those who received early services, in later academic achievement, retention in grade, and referral for special education. Long-term follow-up data on low-income children are more limited but provide some evidence of intervention-control differences in high school graduation, employment, dependence on public assistance, and involvement in the criminal justice system. Comparable longitudinal data on children with disabilities are not available.

Complementary but distinct from child-focused interventions, a variety of early childhood services are delivered through family-focused models, many of which are home-based. Research on model programs reveals that well-designed services with explicitly defined goals can be effective in changing parenting practices and influencing parent-child interactions. For families of children with cognitive, language, or sensory impairments, enhanced parental competencies linked to greater understanding of the child's special needs are important mediators of improved child outcomes. The measurable effects of parent-focused interventions on standardized child development scores in economically disadvantaged families, however, are less conclusive, and there is little empirical documentation that nonspecific, general family support models for high-risk families, which typically are less expensive to deliver, have significant impacts on either parent behavior or assessed child performance.

In the final analysis, there is considerable evidence to support the notion that model programs that deliver carefully designed interventions with well-defined goals can affect both parenting behavior and the developmental trajectories of children whose life course is threatened by socioeconomic disadvantage, family disruption, or diagnosed disability. Programs that combine child-focused educational activities with explicit attention to parent-child interaction patterns and relationship building appear to have the greatest impacts. In contrast, services that are supported by more modest budgets and based on generic support, often without a clear delineation of intervention strategies matched directly to measurable objectives, appear to be less effective for families facing significant risk.

The general question of whether early childhood programs can make a difference has been asked and answered in the affirmative innumerable times. This generic query is no longer worthy of further investigation. The central research priority for the early childhood field is to address more important sets of questions about how different types of interventions influence specific outcomes for children and families who face differential opportunities and vulnerabilities. To this end, program evaluators must assess the distinctive needs that must be met, the soundness of the intervention strategy, its acceptability to the intended recipients, the quality of its implementation, and the extent to which less intensive, broader-based programs can be developed that are both beneficial and cost-effective.

Programs with only transitory impacts on children's IQ scores may still be socially profitable investments. The measurement of specific program effects on children must go beyond traditional cognitive evaluations (such as IQ) and include greater focus on a broad range of functional capacities, particularly in the social and emotional domains. Middle- and long-term follow-up studies also must pay greater attention to the assessment of subsequent and continuing environmental influences on development after the intervention has been completed.

Although sometimes hard to quantify, program benefits and costs provide vital information for budget-constrained policy makers and practitioners. Nevertheless, there currently are few systematic data on the costs and benefits of intensive early childhood interventions, and almost none on the less intensive, real-world services that are more likely to be implemented on a large scale. Practitioners and policy makers need careful evaluations of a broad portfolio of intervention programs, including both modest and intensive models, as programs with the largest impacts on children are not always the most practical to implement. Although not all decisions about allocating resources for early childhood programs need be based solely on considerations of financial costs and benefits, the need for better economic data is clear.

The current agenda for early childhood policy and service delivery in the United States is embedded in four objectives:

- Full access to programs whose effectiveness has been demonstrated must be ensured for all eligible children and families.
- A culture of ongoing experimentation must be established to promote the design, implementation, and evaluation of alternative approaches for those circumstances in which existing interventions are found to have minimal impact.
- A strong commitment to rigorous quality control must be established and sustained, in order to ensure that all available resources are used in the most effective and efficient manner.
- It is essential that all early childhood policies and programs be designed and implemented within a culturally competent context and in a manner that respects the importance of individual differences among children and families.

A fundamental challenge facing the nation is to find an appropriate balance between long-term investment in human capital development and the moral responsibility to ensure that the quality of life for young children does not fall below a minimum level of decency. Stated simply, certain services are deemed worthy of support because they generate significant long-term dividends. Other programs are essential not because they result in later financial benefits but because they reflect society's commitment to those who are most vulnerable and who cannot help themselves.

IV   Knowledge into
Action

14

Conclusions and Recommendations

wo profound changes over the past several decades have coincided to produce a dramatically altered landscape for early childhood policy, service delivery, and childrearing in the United States. First, an explosion of research in the neurobiological, behavioral, and social sciences has led to major advances in understanding the conditions that influence whether children get off to a promising or a worrisome start in life. These scientific gains have generated a much deeper appreciation of: (1) the importance of early life experiences, as well as the inseparable and highly interactive influences of genetics and environment on the development of the brain and the unfolding of human behavior; (2) the central role of early relationships as a source of either support and adaptation or risk and dysfunction; (3) the powerful capabilities, complex emotions, and essential social skills that develop during the earliest months and years of life; and (4) the capacity to increase the odds of favorable developmental outcomes through planned interventions.

Second, the capacity to use this knowledge constructively has been constrained by a number of dramatic transformations in the social and economic circumstances under which families with young children are living in the United States. Among the most significant are: (1) marked changes in the nature, schedule, and amount of work engaged in by parents of young children and greater difficulty balancing workplace and family responsibilities for parents at all income levels; (2) continuing high levels of economic hardship among families with young children, despite overall increases in maternal education, increased rates of parent employment, and a strong economy; (3) increasing cultural diversity and the persistence of significant racial and ethnic disparities in health and developmental outcomes; (4) growing numbers of young children spending considerable time in child care settings of highly variable quality, starting in infancy; and (5) continuing high levels of serious family problems and adverse community conditions that are detrimental for children. While any given child may be affected by only one or two of these changes, their cumulative impact across the 24 million infants, toddlers, and preschoolers who are now growing up in the United States warrants our dedicated attention and most thoughtful responses.

This convergence of advancing knowledge and changing circumstances calls for a fundamental reexamination of the nation's responses to the needs of young children and their families, many of which were formulated several decades ago and revised only incrementally since then. It demands that scientists, policy makers, business and community leaders, practitioners, and parents work together to identify and sustain policies that are effective, generate new strategies to replace those that are not achieving their objectives, and consider new approaches to address new goals as needed. It is the strong conviction of this committee that the nation has not capitalized sufficiently on the knowledge that has been gained from nearly half a century of considerable public investment in research on children from birth to age 5. In many respects, we have barely begun to use existing science and our growing research capabilities to help children and families negotiate the changing demands and possibilities of life in the 21st century.

The fundamental issues addressed by this report concern the relation between early life experiences and early development. Although there have been long-standing debates about how much the early years really matter in the larger scheme of lifelong development, the committee is unequivocal in its conclusion: what happens during the first months and years of life matters a lot. It does not matter because all early damage is irreversible, because missed opportunities can never be made up later, or because the early years provide an indelible blueprint for adult outcomes: early damage may be reversible, some missed opportunities can be made up later, and adult outcomes do not proceed inexorably from early experiences. Rather, the early years of life matter because early damage—whether caused by prenatal injuries or personal rejection—can seriously compromise children's life prospects. Compensating for missed opportunities, such as the failure to detect early difficulties or the lack of exposure to environments rich in language, often requires extensive intervention, if not heroic efforts, later in life. Early pathways, though far from indelible, establish either a sturdy or fragile stage on which subsequent development is constructed.

This chapter presents the committee's conclusions and recommendations. They are designed to stimulate fresh thinking and promote constructive public dialogue and action about the most important issues facing the nation's youngest children and their families. They address two complementary agendas. The first is rooted in contemporary concerns about promoting human capital development in a highly competitive and rapidly changing world. It asks: How can society use knowledge about early child development to maximize the nation's human capital and ensure the ongoing vitality of its democratic institutions? The second is focused on the present and asks: How can the nation use knowledge to nurture, protect, and ensure the health and well-being of all young children as an important objective in its own right, regardless of whether measurable returns can be documented in the future? The first agenda speaks to society's economic, political, and social interests. The second speaks to its ethical and moral values. The committee is clear in our responsibility to speak to both.

POLICY AND PRACTICE

State-of-the-art knowledge about early childhood development is multidimensional and cross-disciplinary. It extends from painstaking efforts to understand the evolving circuitry and biochemistry of the immature brain to large-scale investigations of how family characteristics, neighborhood influences, and cultural values affect the well-being of children as they grow up. It includes studies of infants, toddlers, and preschoolers with a broad range of typical and atypical behavioral patterns, as well as young children with diagnosed developmental disabilities. It is derived from a variety of quantitative and qualitative research methods that have been used to understand the process of development as it unfolds, as well as from evaluations of efforts to alter its course.

Drawing on its extensive review of this highly diverse knowledge base, the committee identified four overarching themes that have guided scientific inquiry and have important implications for the design and implementation of the nation's early childhood policies: (1) all children are born wired for feelings and ready to learn, (2) early environments matter and nurturing relationships are essential, (3) society is changing and the needs of young children are not being addressed, and (4) interactions among early childhood science, policy, and practice are problematic and demand dramatic rethinking. These four themes provide a framework for our conclusions and recommendations to guide policy and practice. The chapter then addresses promising directions for research and evaluation and the challenges of informing the public about the early childhood years, with a particular focus on speaking to the aspirations and concerns of parents of young children.

All Children Are Born Wired for Feelings and Ready to Learn

From the time of conception to the first day of kindergarten, development proceeds at a pace exceeding that of any subsequent stage of life. Efforts to understand this process have revealed the myriad and remarkable accomplishment of the early childhood period, as well as the serious problems that confront some young children and their families long before school entry. A fundamental paradox exists and is unavoidable: development in the early years is both highly robust and highly vulnerable. The committee's review of research on the achievements and vulnerabilities that characterize the earliest years of life has led to the following conclusions:

• From birth to age 5, children rapidly develop foundational capabilities on which subsequent development builds. In addition to their remarkable linguistic and cognitive gains, they exhibit dramatic progress in their emotional, social, regulatory, and moral capacities. All of these critical dimensions of early development are intertwined, and each requires focused attention.

The early childhood years have value not only as a preparation time for the later accomplishments in school and beyond that have galvanized public attention, but they also have value in their own right as a time of extraordinary growth and change. The developmental tasks of this period range from the mastery of essential building blocks for learning and the motivation to succeed in school, to the ability to get along with other children, to make friends, and become engaged in a social group, as well as the capacity to manage powerful emotions. Although the study of child development has traditionally sorted such accomplishments into discrete functional categories (e.g., cognitive, linguistic, social), in practice they are inseparable beginning in the earliest years of life. Acknowledging and acting on this fundamental principle is critical to the success of a wide array of initiatives in child health, mental health, early education, and early intervention.

• Striking disparities in what children know and can do are evident well before they enter kindergarten. These differences are strongly associated with social and economic circumstances, and they are predictive of subsequent academic performance. Redressing these disparities is critical, both for children whose life opportunities are at stake and for a society whose goals demand that children be prepared to begin school, achieve academic success, and ultimately sustain economic independence and engage constructively with others as adult citizens.

School entry is a critical transition point at which individual differences in what young children know and can do begin to be predictive of longer-term patterns of learning and achievement. Marked inequalities in children's early learning opportunities are therefore a cause for serious concern. In this context, although there has been a proliferation of pre-kindergarten and early intervention initiatives designed to promote school readiness, access to these programs is highly uneven across the early childhood population in the United States.

• Early child development can be seriously compromised by social, regulatory, and emotional impairments. The causes of such impairments are multiple but often revolve around disturbances in close relationships. Indeed, young children are capable of deep and lasting sadness, grief, and disorganization in response to trauma, loss, and early personal rejection. Given the substantial short- and long-term risks that accompany early mental health impairments, the incapacity of many early childhood programs to address these concerns and the severe shortage of early childhood professionals with mental health expertise are urgent problems.

The mental health of young children has been a relatively neglected topic within the domains of both scientific inquiry and early childhood intervention. Yet debilitating levels of anxiety and emergent conduct disorders can be seen in the early years and may have enduring effects on how children view themselves and how they are accepted by others over time. Despite little demonstration of efficacy, extensive pharmacotherapy is being used to treat preschoolers with behavior problems. This is of concern for many reasons, not the least of which is the difficulty in these early years of differentiating children with serious emotional disorders from those who are simply immature or are experiencing transient delays in emotional control. Regardless of the severity of their difficulties, however, children with social or emotional impairments warrant our deepest concern, not only for who they might become as adolescents and adults, but because of their fundamental unhappiness and its consequences for their experiences as young children.

Recommendations

To support the early learning and social-emotional development of young children, as well as to address the serious mental health needs that can arise during the early years of life, three complementary recommendations require urgent attention.

Recommendation 1 — Resources on a par with those focused on literacy and numerical skills should be devoted to translating the knowledge base on young children's emotional, regulatory, and social development into effective strategies for fostering: (1) the development of curiosity, self-direction, and persistence in learning situations; (2) the ability to cooperate, demonstrate caring, and resolve conflict with peers; and (3) the capacity to experience the enhanced motivation associated with feeling competent and loved. Such strategies and their widespread diffusion into the early childhood field must encompass young children both with and without special needs. Successful action on this recommendation will require the long-term, collaborative investment of government, professional organizations, private philanthropy, and voluntary associations.

Recommendation 2 — School readiness initiatives should be judged not only on the basis of their effectiveness in improving the performance of the children whom they reach, but also on the extent to which they make progress in reducing the significant disparities that are observed at school entry in the skills of young children with differing backgrounds.

Recommendation 3 — Substantial new investments should be made to address the nation's seriously inadequate capacity for addressing young children's mental health needs. Expanded opportunities for professional training, as recently called for by the Surgeon General, and incentives for individuals with pertinent expertise to work in settings with young children are essential first steps toward more effective screening, early detection, treatment, and ultimate prevention of serious childhood mental health problems.

Early Environments Matter and Nurturing Relationships Are Essential

The scientific evidence—ranging from behavioral genetics and neuroscience to policy analysis and intervention research—on the significant developmental impacts of early experiences, caregiving relationships, and environmental threats is incontrovertible. Virtually every aspect of early human development, from the brain's evolving circuitry to the child's capacity for empathy, is affected by the environments and experiences that are encountered in a cumulative fashion, beginning early in the prenatal period and extending throughout the early childhood years. The science of early development is also clear about the specific importance of parenting and of regular caregiving relationships more generally. The question today is not whether early experience matters, but rather how early experiences shape individual development and contribute to children's continued movement along positive pathways. Within this context, the committee's synthesis of the pertinent scientific literature has led to the following conclusions:

• The long-standing debate about the importance of nature *versus* nurture, considered as independent influences, is overly simplistic and scientifically obsolete. Scientists have shifted their focus to take account of the fact that genetic and environmental influences work together in dynamic ways over the course of development. At any time, both are sources of human potential and growth as well as risk and dysfunction. Both genetically determined characteristics and those that are highly affected by experience are open to intervention. The most important questions now concern how environments influence the expression of genes and how genetic makeup, combined with children's previous experiences, affects their ongoing interactions with their environments during the early years and beyond.

The range of human possibilities is exceedingly broad. At the moment of birth, each baby is neither a preformed individual whose destiny is set, nor a blank slate whose individuality can be shaped entirely by external forces. Children clearly differ in their genetic endowment from the time of conception. Some actively seek out experiences and some are more inhibited. Some cry frequently and others are better able to soothe themselves. Some are more predictable and easy to read while others are less easily understood. Biology, however, is modified by life experience. Depending on the caregiving they receive and the environments they encounter, shy children can become sociable, fearful children can become secure explorers of their surroundings, and highly exuberant children can develop considerable self-control. Each child's individual capacities are both limited and broadened by his or her genetic makeup and life circumstances. Both operate together in influencing the probability of any given outcome.

• Parents and other regular caregivers in children's lives are "active ingredients" of environmental influence during the early childhood period. Children grow and thrive in the context of close and dependable relationships that provide love and nurturance, security, responsive interaction, and encouragement for exploration. Without at least one such relationship, development is disrupted and the consequences can be severe and long-lasting. If provided or restored, however, a sensitive caregiving relationship can foster remarkable recovery.

Young children establish and can benefit greatly from a variety of close relationships. Yet those adults who are most consistently available and committed to the child's well-being play a special role in promoting competence and adaptation that cannot be replaced by individuals who are present less consistently or whose emotional commitment is not unconditional. Young children who do not have a relationship with at least one emotionally invested, predictably available caregiver—even in the presence of adequate physical care and cognitive stimulation—display an array of developmental deficits that may endure over time. Some children develop intense emotional ties to parents and other caregivers who are unresponsive, rejecting, highly erratic, or frankly abusive. These relationships can also be a

source of serious childhood impairments, ranging from problems with focused attention and problem solving to difficulty in forming healthy relationships, failure to thrive, and a variety of serious psychiatric disorders.
The remarkable recovery that many such children demonstrate, once they
receive responsive and consistent caregiving, provides some of the strongest
evidence of the power of these earliest relationships. Indeed, the earlier that
children experience supportive and stable caregiving environments, the more
likely it will be that they will exhibit healthy development later.

   • Children's early development depends on the health and well-being
of their parents. Yet the daily experiences of a significant number of young
children are burdened by untreated mental health problems in their families, recurrent exposure to family violence, and the psychological fallout
from living in a demoralized and violent neighborhood. Circumstances
characterized by multiple, interrelated, and cumulative risk factors impose
particularly heavy developmental burdens during early childhood and are
the most likely to incur substantial costs to both the individual and society
in the future.
   Extensive research has documented the adverse impacts on young children of parental mental illness (particularly maternal depression), substance abuse, and recurrent violence. The prevalence of such problems is
high, the extent to which they are overlooked is problematic, and the
relatively limited availability of specialized expertise to address them reflects an urgent unmet need. Although these conditions are more common
among families living in poverty, they are found in all social classes. Moreover, significant dysfunctions frequently cluster together—i.e., maternal
depression and substance abuse often go hand in hand; family and community violence may often affect the same child. These youngsters and their
parents are among the most vulnerable members of society, and they require a level of professional expertise that is neither routinely considered in
the staffing of conventional early childhood programs nor necessarily available in many high-risk neighborhoods. The short-term financial costs of
the professional resources needed to confront these problems are high.
The long-term financial and social costs of ignoring serious family disadvantage or frank pathology, however, are much higher and ultimately
contribute to policy failures in other domains, such as education reform,
welfare reform, economic and workforce development, and violence prevention and crime control.

   • The time is long overdue for society to recognize the significance of
out-of-home relationships for young children, to esteem those who care for
them when their parents are not available, and to compensate them adequately as a means of supporting stability and quality in those relation-

ships for all children, regardless of their family's income and irrespective of their developmental needs.

The importance of primary caregiving relationships both within the family and in child care settings during the early childhood years has been documented extensively. For parents and child care providers alike, the experience of caring for a young child is deeply affected by the context in which it is conducted. As both the science of early childhood development and the prevalence of nonparental care have expanded dramatically over the past few decades, the failure to use available knowledge to influence the quality of the nation's child care is increasingly difficult to understand or to justify. Strategies that are used to recruit and retain talented elementary schoolteachers are no less important for children before they enter school. There is, in particular, an urgent need to upgrade the qualifications and compensation of child care providers.

- Early experiences clearly affect the development of the brain. Yet the recent focus on "zero to three" as a critical or particularly sensitive period is highly problematic, not because this isn't an important period for the developing brain, but simply because the disproportionate attention being given to the period from birth to 3 years begins too late and ends too soon.

The mechanisms of neurodevelopment are designed specifically to recruit and incorporate a broad spectrum of experience into the developing architecture of the brain. Animal studies make this abundantly clear, and there is no reason to expect that humans, so wonderfully capable of learning and adaptation, are any less sensitive to the effects of experience on brain development. Yet despite a small number of examples, we know remarkably little about the role of experience and the existence (or lack thereof) of time-limited sensitive periods during which specific experiences are obligatory for normal human brain development.. The evidence to either support or refute claims about critical or sensitive periods in humans simply does not exist. It does appear, however, that development of the neural systems supporting cognitive, social, and emotional competencies remains open to experience at least through adolescence. In fact, the brain's ongoing plasticity enables it to continually resculpt and reshape itself in response to new environmental demands well into adulthood. It is important to emphasize that these findings do not in any way diminish the importance of the early years. They simply remind us of the continuing importance of the years that follow.

- Abundant evidence from the behavioral and the neurobiological sciences has documented a wide range of environmental threats to the developing central nervous system. These include poor nutrition, specific infections, environmental toxins, and drug exposures, beginning early in the prenatal period, as well as chronic stress stemming from abuse or neglect throughout the early childhood years and beyond.

Decades of research on the early development of the brain convey a powerful and sobering message about its susceptibility to harmful influences. This leads us to be deeply concerned about the well-being of young children who suffer from extreme deprivation, inadequate nutrition, neurotoxic exposures, or other insults that can cause significant (although sometimes subtle) brain damage during the prenatal or early childhood years. Children who are born with auditory, visual, or motor impairments that interfere with the environmental input that their brains receive and children whose caregiving is seriously disrupted in their early years are also highly vulnerable. The greatest dangers arise from the combined and cumulative effects of multiple hazards. What remains to be understood with greater precision are the threshold levels below which adverse environmental effects do not occur, how and why multiple insults operate together to produce additive and sometimes multiplicative effects and, at the other end of the spectrum, how attempts to enhance children's development affect the developing brain. These questions will be best addressed through sustained scientific collaboration between child development researchers and neuroscientists.

Recommendations

To recognize and support the vital significance of the relationships that young children must have with their regular caregivers (parents as well as others) and to prevent the problems that arise from harmful early environments, the committee makes three recommendations that will require substantial shifts in national priorities.

Recommendation 4 — Decision makers at all levels of government, as well as leaders from the business community, should ensure that both public and private policies provide parents with viable choices about how to allocate responsibility for child care during the early years of their children's lives. During infancy, there is a pressing need to strike a better balance between options that support parents to care for their infants at home and those that provide affordable, quality child care that enables them to work or go to school. This calls for expanding coverage of the Family and Medical Leave Act to all working parents, pursuing the complex issue of income protection, and lengthening the exemption period before states require parents of infants to work as part of welfare reform. Throughout the early childhood years, policies must accommodate parents' considerable needs for flexibility and support as they raise young children and enhance their opportunities to choose from among a range of child care settings that offer the stable, sensitive, and linguistically rich caregiving that fosters positive early childhood development.

Recommendation 5 — Environmental protection, reproductive health services, and early intervention efforts should be substantially expanded to reduce documented risks that arise from harmful prenatal and early postnatal neurotoxic exposures, as well as from seriously disrupted early relationships due to chronic mental health problems, substance abuse, and violence in families. The magnitude of these initiatives should be comparable to the attention and resources that have been dedicated to crime prevention, smoking cessation, and the reduction of teen pregnancy. They will require the participation of multiple societal sectors (e.g., private, public, and philanthropic) and the development of multiple strategies.

Recommendation 6 — The major funding sources for child care and early childhood education should set aside a dedicated portion of funds to support initiatives that jointly improve the qualifications and increase the compensation and benefits routinely provided to children's nonparental caregivers. These initiatives can be built on the successful experience of the U.S. Department of Defense.

Society Is Changing and the Needs of Young Children Are Not Being Addressed

Developmental science points toward the importance of protecting the multiple environments in which young children live and acknowledging the complexity and significance of the work involved in rearing children both at home and in child care settings. Yet profound social and economic transformations are making it exceedingly difficult for parents to strike a healthy balance between spending time with their children, securing their economic needs, and protecting them from the many risks beyond the home that may have an adverse impact on their health and development. On the basis of its assessment of how the broader contexts within which children develop affect their well-being, the committee drew the following conclusions:

• Changing parental work patterns are transforming family life. Growing numbers of young children are being raised by working parents whose earnings are inadequate to lift their families out of poverty, whose work entails long and nonstandard hours, and whose economic needs require an early return to work after the birth of a baby. For mothers dependent on public assistance, paid employment and the associated reliance on nonmaternal child care are now mandated rather than a matter of choice. The consequences of this changing context of parental employment for young children are likely to hinge on how it affects the parenting they receive and the quality of the caregiving they experience when they are not with their parents.

Dramatic changes in what it means to be a working parent with young children, combined with changes in family structure, are having pervasive impacts on how the current generation of children is being raised. More young children than ever before are growing up with single parents who are their family's sole breadwinner or in two-parent families in which both parents work. The consequence of this dramatic, uncontrolled, natural experiment is a large and growing population of young children who must be cared for by someone other than their parents for a large part of each working day, starting in the first few months of life. In short, the care of infants and young children has been fundamentally reapportioned away from time with parents to extensive hours in nonparental child care settings. For many young children, the effects of maternal employment, in particular, appear to be positive. For others, including some young children of mothers participating in welfare reform, the effects appear to be neutral, although critical opportunities for early intervention are being missed. For yet others, particularly those in early and extensive child care that is of substandard quality, understimulating, and occasionally unsafe, there are serious concerns.

• The developmental effects of child care depend on its safety, the opportunities it provides for nurturing and stable relationships, and its provision of linguistically and cognitively rich environments. Yet the child care that is available in the United States today is highly fragmented and characterized by marked variation in quality, ranging from rich, growth-promoting experiences to unstimulating, highly unstable, and sometimes dangerous settings. The burden of poor quality and limited choice rests most heavily on low-income, working families whose financial resources are too high to qualify for subsidies yet too low to afford higher quality care.

A baseline standard of quality in the nation's child care settings is not being met at a time when historic numbers of infants, toddlers, and preschoolers are spending a considerable amount of time in these settings. Notwithstanding substantial increases in federal and state funding for child care in recent years, public expenditures have done little to restructure the inadequate system that existed a decade ago, when the National Research Council last conducted a major review of child care research and called for sweeping policy actions to improve the quality of care in the United States (National Research Council, 1990). Over the intervening years, additional research has confirmed the role of quality care in promoting the health and development of young children. The persistence of substandard quality in the nation's child care arrangements and continuing inequalities in access to quality care thus remains baffling and indefensible. Although some states and localities have taken exemplary steps to upgrade child care quality, significant efforts remain sporadic and uncoordinated.

• Young children are the poorest members of society and are more likely to be poor today than they were 25 years ago. Growing up in poverty greatly increases the probability that a child will be exposed to environments and experiences that impose significant burdens on his or her well-being, thereby shifting the odds toward more adverse developmental outcomes. Poverty during the early childhood period may be more damaging than poverty experienced at later ages, particularly with respect to eventual academic attainment. The dual risk of poverty experienced simultaneously in the family and in the surrounding neighborhood, which affects minority children to a much greater extent than other children, increases young children's vulnerability to adverse consequences.

Decades of broad-based economic policies and specific antipoverty initiatives have failed to ensure an adequate income for all families with young children in the United States, including many that are headed by full-time workers. For many children, persistent poverty has become a fact of life, despite a strong economy and much greater work effort by their parents. Work in the absence of sufficient income for a family to escape poverty may do little to facilitate more beneficial child outcomes, especially in the early years of life. This is the emerging message from today's welfare reform experiments. In light of the negative consequences for young children who experience persistent economic hardship, it is imperative that we develop more effective strategies to promote economic security, as well as acquire a better understanding of those aspects of being poor that are most damaging in order to direct interventions at these potential levers of change. The most suggestive evidence points to specific aspects of parenting and the home environment, namely severe punitiveness, reduced monitoring, increased parental psychological distress, and less support for early learning.

Recommendations

The challenges that arise at the juxtaposition of work, income, and the care of children reflect some of the most complex problems of contemporary society. Rather than offer recommendations for specific actions, many of which have been made before and gone unheeded, the committee wishes to underscore the compelling need for a focused, integrative, and comprehensive reassessment of the nation's child care and income support policies.

Recommendation 7 — The President should establish a joint federal-state-local task force charged with reviewing the entire portfolio of public investments in child care and early education. Its goal should be to develop a blueprint for locally responsive systems of early care and education for the coming decade that will ensure the following priorities: (1) that young children's needs are met through sustained relationships with qualified caregivers, (2) that the special needs of children with developmental disabilities or chronic health conditions are addressed, and (3) that the settings in which children spend their time are safe, stimulating, and compatible with the values and priorities of their families.

Recommendation 8 — The President's Council of Economic Advisers and the Congress should assess the nation's tax, wage, and income support policies (e.g., the earned income tax credit, minimum wage laws, Temporary Assistance to Needy Families, in-kind supports, and child support policies) with regard to their adequacy in ensuring that no child who is supported by the equivalent of a full-time working adult lives in poverty, and that no family suffers from deep and persistent poverty, regardless of employment status. The product of this effort should be a set of policy alternatives that would move the nation toward achieving these fundamental goals.

Interactions Among Early Childhood Science, Policy, and Practice Are Problematic and Demand Dramatic Rethinking

Policies and programs aimed at improving the life chances of young children come in many varieties. Some are home based and others are delivered in centers. Some focus on children alone or in groups, and others work primarily with parents. A variety of services have been designed to address the needs of young children whose future prospects are threatened by socioeconomic disadvantages, family disruption, and diagnosed disabilities. They range from small-scale model programs, with theoretically guided goals and painstaking attention to implementation, to more generic programs that are implemented widely and often intended to meet a broad array of objectives. They all share a belief that early childhood development is susceptible to environmental influences and that wise public investments in young children can increase the odds of favorable developmental outcomes. The scientific evidence resoundingly supports these premises. Nevertheless, the committee's examination of the current obstacles to more constructive cross-fertilization among the domains of science, policy, and practice, has led to the following conclusions:

- The overarching question of whether we can intervene successfully in young children's lives has been answered in the affirmative and should be put to rest. However, interventions that work are rarely simple, inexpensive, or easy to implement. The critical agenda for early childhood intervention is to advance understanding of what it takes to improve the odds of positive outcomes for the nation's most vulnerable young children and to determine the most cost-effective strategies for achieving well-defined goals.

The environmental change required to alter a child's developmental trajectory is likely to vary for different children in different circumstances. The plasticity of human development works both ways—environments can be both enhancing and debilitating; child change can be for better or worse; and the gains produced by an effective intervention can be maintained by continuing support or lost by the subsequent influences of an impoverished or abusive environment. In the final analysis, all abilities and behaviors unfold within boundaries set by constitutional endowment, and all children (including those with developmental impairments) are primed biologically to seek positive adaptation. Thus, all effective interventions "work" by supporting those self-righting tendencies. Intervention programs are not panaceas—they simply shift the odds in favor of more desirable outcomes. Nevertheless, on both an individual and a population basis, such probabilistic changes can make a significant difference. This will occur, however, only if the crucial elements of successful strategies are identified and sustained as model demonstration programs are transformed into larger-scale implementation.

• The scientific knowledge base guiding early childhood policies and programs is seriously constrained by the relatively limited availability of systematic and rigorous evaluations of program implementation; gaps in the documentation of causal relations between specific interventions and specific outcomes and of the underlying mechanisms of change; and infrequent assessments of program costs and benefits.

Recommendations for policy and practice are ideally based on causal evidence. These include, for example, inferences about the effects of early experience on brain development and behavior, the effects of early behavior on later adolescent and adult functioning, and the impacts of specific interventions (such as enhanced child care and early education, home visiting programs, etc.) on child health and development. The committee's assessment suggests that researchers, policy makers, and practitioners often overestimate the scientific basis for such causal inferences, generally in the service of ensuring continued support for a given policy or practice that is presumed to be effective.

Under such circumstances, some observers have drawn sweeping conclusions from single experiments and have not engaged in a critical examination of the assumptions underlying causal inferences based on nonexperimental investigations. In this context, it is important to recognize that strong, generalizable, causal inferences about early childhood development are most often based on the critical evaluation of streams of related research rather than on the findings of single studies. Such research streams typically include designs with varied strengths and limitations, yet they provide important convergent evidence that can be assessed in light of the best available theory. Thus, although key policy decisions are often based on evidence that is suggestive rather than conclusive, reasonable inferences based on well-established knowledge and strong evaluation evidence can provide a solid basis for constructive decision making.

• Model early childhood programs that deliver carefully designed interventions with well-defined objectives and that include well-designed evaluations have been shown to influence the developmental trajectories of children whose life course is threatened by socioeconomic disadvantage, family disruption, and diagnosed disabilities. Programs that combine child-focused educational activities with explicit attention to parent-child interaction patterns and relationship building appear to have the greatest impacts. In contrast, services that are based on generic family support, often without a clear delineation of intervention strategies matched directly to measurable objectives, and that are funded by more modest budgets, appear to be less effective.

The ultimate answers to questions about program effectiveness are unlikely to be found solely in the particular service format or strategy that is deployed, such as a home visiting model, a comprehensive center-based program, an antipoverty initiative, or a substance abuse treatment or mental health service. Rather, the key to success is more likely to be found in the quality of program implementation, which frequently is related to the level of available resources. This directs attention to a host of important factors, such as: (1) the program's relevance, sensitivity to, and respect for the individual needs and cultural values of the children, families, and community it is designed to serve (which, in turn, affect recruitment and retention of the children and families it is designed to reach); (2) the program's intensity and duration; and (3) staff competence and the training support and compensation that are provided to them. It also is essential to acknowledge that the possibilities for change are not infinite, and that some programs may achieve only modest goals at considerable cost. In the final analysis, an intervention program is simply one of many influences on a child's health and development. In some circumstances, its impact can be considerable; in others, its potential effects may be overwhelmed by forces beyond its control.

• The elements of early intervention programs that enhance social and emotional development are just as important as the components that enhance linguistic and cognitive competence. Some of the strongest long-term impacts of successful interventions have been documented in the domains of social adjustment, such as reductions in criminal behavior.

The assessment of social-emotional development in the first five years of life is complex, time-consuming, and generally not part of the standard repertoire of outcomes that are measured in many evaluations of early childhood programs. Yet these realms of development contain some of the most telling indicators of the success or failure of an intervention. To the extent that the early childhood intervention community seeks to draw on emerging research on brain development to support its efforts, it is important to recognize that selected aspects of regulatory behaviors and social interaction have become an important focus in the neurosciences.

• The reconciliation of traditional early intervention programs, formats, and strategies—many of which emphasize the importance of active parent involvement and the delivery of services in the home setting—with the economic and social realities of contemporary family life is a pressing concern. Particularly urgent is the need to ensure access to these intervention programs for parents who are employed full-time, those who work nonstandard hours, and those who are making the transition from public assistance to work.

Recent social and economic changes present major challenges to conventional early childhood interventions and service models that were designed over 30 years ago, when mothers were more commonly at home full-time with their young children. Central to the philosophy of many of these programs is the importance of regularly scheduled home visits and extensive parent involvement in out-of-home settings and activities. These requirements are increasingly difficult for many parents to meet, particularly for those working in full-time low-wage jobs. At a minimum, this situation calls for a significant restructuring of program practices in order to enhance their compatibility with parents' work schedules. In a broader context, it calls for innovative approaches that reflect creative rethinking of the concept of family-centered services.

• Early childhood policies and practices are highly fragmented, with complex and confusing points of entry that are particularly problematic for underserved segments of the population and those with special needs. This lack of an integrative early childhood infrastructure makes it difficult to advance prevention-oriented initiatives for all children and to coordinate services for those with complex problems.

Conventional approaches to the promotion of child health and development begin with a call for universal access to comprehensive prenatal care for all pregnant women and a "medical home" to provide primary health care services for all children. To this end, efforts to expand Medicaid eligibility for prenatal care for low-income women and the current federal-state program to provide health insurance for low-income children (State Children's Health Insurance Program under Title XXI of the Social Security Act) are vital public initiatives. Beyond the matter of insurance coverage, the content of pediatric primary care is also receiving attention through new initiatives that underscore the time-intensive need for relationship building among health care providers, parents, children, and a range of professionals who provide developmental and social services through nonmedical programs.

Central to an effective strategy to protect and promote the healthy development of young children is the need to both understand the important role of the personal health care system and recognize its significant limitations. This is particularly salient with respect to two critical challenges. First, many of the well-documented risk factors that can impair early brain development are embedded in the experiences of poverty, malnutrition, illiteracy, violence, toxic exposures, and substance abuse and other risk-taking behaviors. These threats to child health and development call for a strengthened prevention agenda that extends beyond the capacity of individually oriented medical care and requires a more vigorous and creative public health approach. Second, much of the expertise needed to address the needs of children with significant developmental and behavioral impairments is located in separate programs that are provided under the administrative and financial auspices of a variety of agencies (e.g., education, social or human services, child welfare). When communication and coordination among multiple systems is good, the needs of children and families are served. When it is poor, resources are not used efficiently and important needs are not met adequately. Developmentally vulnerable children who live in highly stressed environments, particularly where there are concerns about possible abuse and neglect, warrant special concern.

• The growing racial, ethnic, linguistic, and cultural diversity of the early childhood population requires that all early childhood programs and medical services periodically reassess their appropriateness and effectiveness for the wide variety of families they are mandated to serve. Poor "take-up" and high rates of program attrition that are common to many early intervention programs, while not at all restricted to specific racial, ethnic, or linguistic groups, nonetheless raise serious questions about whether those who design, implement, and staff early childhood programs fully understand the meaning of cultural competence in the delivery of health and human services.

Traditional program formats and strategies (both for children who are labeled at risk and for those with diagnosed disabilities) need to be reconciled with the values and cultural practices of an increasingly diverse population. For many families, including both immigrant and native-born families with widely varying cultural and linguistic backgrounds, involvement in an early intervention program can be a complex challenge. The potential complications may include different perceptions of: (1) parenting roles and functions, (2) expectations of young children and beliefs about appropriate developmental goals, (3) views about needing and accepting "help" from nonfamily members, (4) fears about being judged unfavorably, and (5) barriers imposed by language. Although major strides have been made in adapting traditional service formats to the needs and beliefs of an increasingly diverse array of families, such as those achieved by Head Start, the design of interventions that are perceived as relevant, engaging, and needed by the full spectrum of targeted families remains a central challenge to the field. If this challenge is not addressed, rates of program nonacceptance and attrition are likely to remain high and program effectiveness will be compromised.

• The general political environment in which research questions are formulated and investigations are conducted has resulted in a highly problematic context for early childhood policy and practice. In many circumstances, the evaluation of intervention impacts is largely a high-stakes activity to determine whether policies and programs should receive continued funding, rather than a more constructive process of continuous knowledge generation and quality improvement.

In view of the fact that responsible early childhood policy and practice typically require sound judgment in the face of incomplete information, the risks associated with alternative courses of action must always be weighed in light of the uncertainty about the strength of the available evidence. When research is used both to confirm effectiveness (in order to sustain successful programs) and to identify ineffectiveness (in order to abandon failed strategies and inform the design of alternative approaches), the interests of children are well served. However, when the purpose of research is simply to mobilize data to secure support for a specific program (or to terminate it), independent of its merits, the interests of children are thwarted, the field fails to move forward, and society pays a high price. As with the treatment of disease, the management of developmental vulnerability in young children should be driven not by a question of whether successful intervention is a worthy goal, but by a determination to continuously harness science in an effort to enhance the capacity to promote human health and well-being.

- As the rapidly evolving science of early child development continues to grow, its complexity will increase and the distance between the working knowledge of service providers and the cutting edge of the science will be staggering.

The professional challenges that this raises for the early childhood field are formidable. They range from relatively straightforward issues, such as curriculum content, to more fundamental questions about professional identification, career pathways, cross-disciplinary collaboration, the potential indications for new disciplines, the need for a culturally diverse workforce, and the critical issue of professional compensation.

Recommendations

To enhance the capacity of early childhood programs to address serious threats to early development and to ensure that practitioners and policy makers can learn from previous efforts to intervene in the lives of young children, three recommendations demand attention:

Recommendation 9 — Agencies and foundations that support evaluation research in early childhood should follow the example set by the nation's successful approach to clinical investigation in the biomedical sciences. In this spirit, the goals of program-based research and the evaluation of services should be to document and ensure full implementation of effective interventions, and to use evidence of ineffectiveness to stimulate further experimentation and study.

Recommendation 10 — The time is long overdue for state and local decision makers to take bold actions to design and implement coordinated, functionally effective infrastructures to reduce the long-standing fragmentation of early childhood policies and programs. To this end, the committee urges two compelling first steps. First, require that all children who are referred to a protective services agency for evaluation of suspected abuse or neglect be automatically referred for a developmental-behavioral screening under Part C of the Individuals with Disabilities Education Act. Second, establish explicit and effective linkages among agencies that currently are charged with implementing the work requirements of welfare reform and those that oversee the provision of both early intervention programs and child and adult mental health services.

Recommendation 11 — A comprehensive analysis of the professional development challenges facing the early childhood field should be considered as a collaborative effort involving professional organizations and representatives from the wide array of training institutions that prepare individuals to work with young children and their families. The responsibility for convening such a broad-based working group or commission should be shared among the fields of education, health, and human services.

RESEARCH AND EVALUATION

Research has historically played a significant role in enhancing human development and preventing, ameliorating, and treating a range of conditions that can begin prenatally, at birth, or during the early years of life. To identify priorities among the many possible recommendations that could be made for promising future research, the committee was guided by three goals.

First, it is clear that the capacity to increase the odds of favorable birth outcomes and positive adaptation in the early childhood years would be strengthened considerably by the new knowledge that would be generated by enhanced collaboration among child development researchers, neuroscientists, and molecular geneticists. A creative combination of biological and psychosocial research efforts would increase the ability to unlock some of the enduring mysteries about how biogenetic and environmental factors interact in a reciprocal fashion to influence developmental pathways. To accomplish this, the great divide that currently exists among these groups of researchers must be closed through the support of novel collaborations.

Second, there is a pressing need to integrate basic research aimed at understanding developmental processes with intervention research that assesses efforts to influence developmental outcomes. At present, evidence from the basic sciences about factors that shift developmental trajectories toward adaptive or maladaptive outcomes is, at best, haphazardly translated into the design and evaluation of initiatives aimed at changing these trajectories. Similarly, those who study interventions lack systematic opportunities to feed their insights and questions back into the basic research enterprise. Comprehensive research programs that integrate efforts to understand development with efforts to change it are even more unusual. There are, however, some pioneering examples (e.g., Cowan and Cowan, in press; Dishion et al., 1992; Egeland et al., 2000; Olds et al., 1999) whose experiences can pave the way for greater efforts in the future.

Third, the entire early childhood evaluation enterprise warrants a thorough reassessment in order to maximize opportunities for valid causal inference and generalization, to assess what has been learned cumulatively across the full array of evaluation studies, and to establish a constructive environment for the discussion of ongoing research and its application to policy.

With these goals as a guide, the committee makes the following recommendations for a three-pronged agenda for research and evaluation.

Integrating Child Developmental Research,
Neuroscience, and Molecular Genetics

The committee recommends that funds be earmarked for collaborative projects involving researchers who investigate environmental influences on development and those who study the biological bases of behavior, in order to advance the understanding of:

• How experience is incorporated into the developing nervous system and how the boundaries are determined that differentiate deprivation from sufficiency and sufficiency from enrichment for different children who are reared in a wide variety of environments.

Notwithstanding the current fascination with the relation between early experience and early brain development, there is very little research on how early environments specifically affect the rapidly developing central nervous system of the young child. Moreover, there are only a handful of investigators who have the skills needed to assess the effects of early interventions designed both to promote positive developmental outcomes and to remediate developmental impairments (including early sensorimotor difficulties) on various indicators of neurologic functioning. This area of potential investigation offers one of the few available avenues for addressing questions about thresholds of experience below which damage may occur and above which development may be enhanced.

• How biological processes, including neurochemical and neuroendocrine factors, interact with environmental influences to affect the development of complex behaviors, including self-regulatory capacities, prosocial or antisocial tendencies, planning and sustained attention, and adaptive responses to stress.

There is growing agreement among both scientists and clinicians that the underlying roots of attention problems, learning difficulties, and conduct disorders can be found in the (currently) poorly understood interactions between biological vulnerabilities and environmental demands. Further research in this area will advance both the development of effective interventions for improving the lives of children with impairments and a greater understanding of behavioral development in young children who are relatively free of problems. Research that extends evidence from animal models to expand understanding of how detrimental early experiences affect the regulation of the fear-stress system in human infants and young children will be particularly important.

• The dynamics of gene-environment interactions that underlie the development of behavior and contribute to differential susceptibility to risk and capacity for resilience.

The growing appreciation of large individual differences in susceptibility to environmental risks has galvanized the interest of both behavioral scientists and geneticists, yet researchers trained in these two empirical traditions continue to work largely along parallel tracks. Collaborative endeavors between these two groups, including those that address the complex methodological challenges in this field, could more fruitfully explore such significant concerns as: (1) differential birth outcomes associated with exposure to prenatal hazards (e.g., malnutrition, infection, and drug exposure), (2) the emergence of adverse outcomes (ranging from conduct disorders to frank pathology) in some children but not others in response to stressful rearing conditions, and (3) individual differences in susceptibility to diseases that manifest themselves across the full spectrum of the developmental timeline.

• The mechanisms that underlie nonoptimal birth outcomes and developmental disabilities and their implications for developing specific intervention strategies to modify developmental trajectories.

The increasingly sophisticated tools of molecular genetics and neurobiology, combined with technologies that are enhancing the capacity to study a wide variety of behaviors in young children, offer the potential for important insights into the processes that lead to a range of developmental vulnerabilities and diagnosed disabilities. Furthermore, while substantial progress has been made in preventing infant deaths associated with low birthweight and prematurity, society is still relatively unprepared to address the learning and behavioral problems that many of these infants exhibit as they grow up.

Integrating the Basic Science of Human Development and the Applied Science of Early Childhood Intervention

In an effort to promote greater cross-fertilization between those who study the underlying science of early development and those who evaluate the efficacy of interventions, the committee recommends that high priority be assigned to the following lines of inquiry:

• Research on early pathways toward psychopathology, which brings together those who study social-emotional development from a variety of disciplines (e.g., infant mental health, developmental psychology, social work, genetics, neuroscience, pediatrics, and psychiatry) and those involved in the design and implementation of both preventive and therapeutic interventions.

Several important research programs are investigating precursors to later antisocial behavior and anxiety-related pathology among constellations of temperamental and genetic vulnerability, dysfunctional parenting, and stressful or disorganized early environments that are found in the preschool years. Many of these empirical associations are now sufficiently consistent to warrant a solid investment in programmatic longitudinal studies designed to: (1) elucidate pathways toward psychopathology and identify factors that leave some children at continuing risk while steering others toward adaptive outcomes, (2) distinguish early clinical patterns that are indicative of serious emergent disorders from those that reflect transient concerns, and (3) support efforts to translate the findings from such research into (initially) small-scale interventions in a range of settings. To this end, the development of interventions geared to preschool classrooms offers a particularly promising avenue for advancing the early detection and prevention of problems that become apparent when children first encounter peer groups, with their associated demands for compliance with group norms.

• Research that integrates investigations focused on how early biological insults, (e.g., iron deficiency anemia, lead ingestion) and adverse environmental conditions (e.g., chronic stress) interfere with healthy prenatal and postnatal development, with efforts to design both preventive and ameliorative interventions for women and children who are exposed to such threats, as well as for children with identified disabilities.

A central objective of such integrative research is the exploration of interactions among biological vulnerability, environmental risk, and effective interventions. Previous investigations of this type have stimulated the development of a number of beneficial policies and programs, such as the Women, Infants, and Children (WIC) nutrition support program to prevent iron deficiency anemia and state initiatives to eliminate lead in gas and house paint to prevent lead intoxication. The important issues that such research could address include: (1) the timing and duration of effects, for both exposures and interventions; (2) the capacity for recovery and what it takes to produce improved outcomes; (3) factors that contribute to individual differences in outcomes; and (4) pathways from diverse deleterious experiences to common neurobehavioral outcomes.

• Studies that elucidate the causal pathways through which impoverished family resources contribute to adverse outcomes for individual children and persistent disparities across groups of children in learning skills and other developmental outcomes.

The committee reached strong agreement that there is little scientific merit in additional research that simply reconfirms the association between poverty and poor developmental outcomes. Furthermore, new evidence from studies of welfare reform underscores the urgent need for a new generation of research aimed at understanding: (1) the modifiable mechanisms through which financial hardship and economic insecurity affect parenting behaviors, the emotional climate of the home, and parent mental health which, in turn, affect children's well-being; (2) the levels of earned income and features of work that are associated with improved outcomes for children and the processes that account for observed relations among income, work, and child development; and (3) differing patterns of association and causality between children's circumstances and their well-being for children and families at varying initial levels of risk as defined by socioeconomic conditions, parent and child well-being, (health and developmental status), neighborhood conditions, and cultural factors.

• Experimental investigations of the developmental effects of variations in child care quality, extending from center-based early intervention programs, which have been the focus of previous program evaluations, through the broader range of child care and early education programs available, which have rarely been assessed with experimental designs.

Although there is firm, experimental evidence that high-quality, comprehensive, center-based early intervention programs can shift the odds in favor of more positive short- and long-term developmental outcomes for young children, and thereby produce a handsome social return on their investments, we lack comparable causal evidence on the developmental consequences of more typical child care arrangements, only some of which are center-based. Given the unlikely possibility that sufficient investments will ever be made to ensure access for all low-income children to programs that approach the magnitude and scope of the High/Scope Perry Preschool or Abecedarian projects, for example, policy makers need credible information about the potential impacts of lesser investments in program quality.

• New research and secondary data analyses that integrate studies of parenting with evaluations of parenting interventions in order to advance understanding of what it takes to change parenting practices and what magnitude of change is required to produce positive (and enduring) changes in child developmental outcomes in a wide range of circumstances, both inside and outside the home.

The inconsistent and uneven evaluation literature on parenting interventions is a serious deterrent to sound policy making at a time when many governors and state legislators are proposing greater investments in such early childhood initiatives. At this stage in the maturation of the field, there is little justification for additional correlational studies of home visiting or parent education programs. Alternatively, there is a compelling need for rigorous evaluations that examine causal links between parenting interventions and specific parent (or parenting) outcomes and that assess mediated pathways from treatment effects on the parent to developmental impacts on the child. At the same time, there are some very promising examples of parenting interventions that have been guided by basic research on parent influences and behavior change. These studies are contributing to growing understanding of the relative plasticity of parenting and the dimensions that matter most for children growing up in different circumstances. The challenge is to extend these models of theory-based, causal assessments of parenting programs to broader scale interventions.

• Research that draws on the significant theoretical work and practical guidelines that have been developed regarding culturally competent practice, in order to refine this construct empirically and assess the benefits that are gained from its incorporation into training models, policy development, service strategies, and program evaluations.

The growing ethnic, racial, and linguistic diversity of the early childhood population in the United States confronts service providers (who are a relatively homogenous population) with the complex task of considering when to tailor their efforts to specific populations of children and families and when to treat all families similarly. Currently, however, there is little empirical research to inform this pressing issue. Studies that integrate qualitative and quantitative methods are especially well suited to address the fundamental questions in this area.

• Efforts to undertake the laborious, but vitally needed, task of improving the available tools for measuring important but generally neglected early developmental outcomes (i.e., before school entry) for use in both basic and evaluation research. Leading candidates for this work include measures of the multiple components of self-regulation, emotional development, the capacity to make friends and engage with others as a contributing member of a group, language use (as distinct from static measures of vocabulary), and executive functions, such as working memory.

Notwithstanding the continuing emphasis on standardized cognitive evaluation and the persistent popularity of IQ scores in the policy arena, a lesson from the early intervention literature is that these assessments may not be very sensitive to the behaviorally meaningful effects of a program. The developmental sciences offer a richer array of assessment options. In the absence of dedicated attention to this agenda, multiple opportunities for detecting important intervention effects will continue to be missed.

Several challenges are central to this work. First, there is an urgent need to adapt instruments that are already available for use in intervention studies. Second, a balance of attention needs to be given to matters related to internal and external validity. Third, it is essential that this work not only ensure that validation samples include children from diverse cultural backgrounds, but also that it explicitly consider how competencies are most appropriately assessed in different cultural groups and how each instrument functions as part of a constellation of outcome measures for children with different backgrounds. Fourth, the development of instruments that could contribute to the integration of research on typically and atypically developing children would be a significant advance for developmental science. Finally, the compelling need and considerable costs of such an undertaking underscore the importance of public-sector leadership.

Improving Evaluations of Early Childhood Interventions

In an effort to improve the nation's capacity to learn more from evaluations of early childhood interventions, the committee recommends that:

• Much greater attention be paid to the challenges of program imple
mentation, using both qualitative and quantitative research methods, as an integral component of all early childhood evaluation research. To this end, it is essential that funding for evaluations of intervention services build in support for the time-consuming and ongoing assessment of the range of factors that are tied to effective implementation.

Inattention to implementation issues can undermine the utility of program evaluations aimed at causal questions and seriously compromise the interpretation of study findings. These issues include concerns about (1) program take-up and differential engagement by different targeted populations, (2) goodness of fit between program objectives and strategies and the needs and values of the families who are being served, (3) how the broader community responds to the intervention, (4) the skill and stability of program staff, and (5) the nature of the transactions that occur between the staff delivering the intervention and the individuals receiving it. Implementation is also a moving target that can change, sometimes dramatically, over the course of an intervention, making it a more complex and challenging endeavor than is commonly acknowledged.

• Funding agencies adopt higher standards and demand rigorous and appropriate study designs that: (1) draw explicit links between the theory guiding the program and the assessment of program effects, (2) maximize opportunities for making causal connections between intervention and outcomes through the use of experimental designs whenever feasible and well-designed quasi-experimental studies when necessary, (3) add to the field's understanding of the mechanisms involved in successful change efforts, and (4) assess the cost-effectiveness of alternative courses of action.

The development of effective early intervention strategies hinges on the validity of the reasoning that underlies the program's goals and design, the adequacy and fidelity of its implementation, and the availability of reliable information about the extent to which the program meets its objectives given its costs. Too often, these elements are poorly conceptualized or seriously compromised as a result of tight budgets, inadequate expertise, a rush to evaluate, or other related pressures. Funding agencies can play an instrumental role in upgrading the quality of the early childhood evaluation enterprise by addressing these concerns in both the selection of their grant recipients and the monitoring of funded projects. A high priority should be placed on research programs that move from efficacy trials (which test an intervention under optimal conditions) to effectiveness studies (which test the intervention under more typical conditions, as when the program is conducted on a larger scale) to dissemination studies (which examine the degree to which the program is conducted with fidelity to the model, once it has been exported to new communities and administered as a service rather than as an experimental intervention) (see Olds et al., 1999).

• The National Institutes of Health, in conjunction with appropriate programmatic agencies and private foundations, convene regular forums to synthesize evaluation research evidence across programs and strategies that share similar developmental aims.

There is an urgent need for more rigorous synthesis of streams of related intervention research across the multiple domains of early childhood services in order to investigate causal questions and assess the generalizability of findings. Consensus conferences convened by the National Institutes of Health provide a highly regarded mechanism for evaluating available scientific information and assessing its practical implications. These meetings afford a vehicle for moving beyond the piecemeal presentation of evidence from diverse bodies of literature and for ensuring the unbiased synthesis of findings that can inform broader discussions of effective strategies, in contrast to "up or down" appraisals of individual programs. Among the topics that such conferences could address are: (1) the relative costs and benefits of early interventions that are directed primarily at parents (and only indirectly at children) in comparison to those that provide services directly to children, or combine both approaches in a two-generation strategy; (2) the importance of timing, duration, and intensity of services, in addition to the qualifications, training, and supervision of staff, as significant determinants of their effectiveness; and (3) the issues discussed above regarding program implementation.

• The universe of programs that typically are assessed with regard to their impacts on early childhood development be expanded beyond the traditional child- and family-focused models to encompass broad-based economic and community interventions as well.

Despite growing awareness of the vulnerabilities and opportunities that characterize the early childhood years, several promising social and economic interventions and their evaluations have failed to include early childhood outcomes within their assessment protocols. Evaluations of the Moving to Opportunity neighborhood experiment and a number of state-designed welfare-to-work experiments are examples of such lost opportunities. These and other interventions that have not been designed explicitly to enhance child well-being may nevertheless have significant impacts on children. The committee therefore urges those who fund and design evaluations of broad-based social interventions, ranging from economic development strategies to housing and transportation initiatives, to consider the value of including assessments of early (and later) childhood outcomes.

THE CHALLENGE OF EDUCATING THE PUBLIC

New scientific information relevant to the health and development of children is always of interest to the general public. Parents of very young children are particularly eager for authoritative guidance, and this insatiable thirst provides a highly receptive environment for both responsible education and irresponsible manipulation. Within this context, research-based knowledge can be both informative and useful, but the reality of childrearing is always more of an art than a science.

Helping the public to understand the science of early childhood development is not an easy task. This challenge can be facilitated by differentiating among established knowledge, reasonable hypotheses, and unwarranted assertions. Established knowledge (e.g., the important influence of the infant-caregiver relationship on early cognitive and emotional development) is determined by strict rules of evidence and evolves continuously. Reasonable but untested hypotheses (e.g., repeated exposure to violence alters neural circuits in the developing brain that control an infant's reaction to threat) make up a large proportion of the knowledge base that guides responsible policy, service delivery, and parenting practices at any point in time, but they may be confirmed or disproved by subsequent investigation. Unwarranted assertions in the name of science (e.g., access to expensive educational toys will boost infant intelligence) distort or misrepresent knowledge, undermine its credibility, and are most insidious when put forth by individuals with professional credentials.

In a curiously parallel fashion, successful parenting, effective service delivery, and informed policy making may all very well be defined as the ability to make reasonable judgments and avoid irresponsible practices in the face of incomplete knowledge. Ultimately, each must reconcile the neverending quest for more information with a comfortable level of tolerance for the unavoidable ambiguity and essential mystery of human devel-

opment. In this context, an educated public would be better informed
about early childhood development by a clear understanding of state-of-
the-art concepts and expectations than by the rote memorization of age-
specific milestones and highly prescriptive advice. To this end, the committee presents the following scientific conclusions:

• The development of the brain begins before birth, continues throughout life, and is influenced by both genetics (i.e., what one is born with) and
experience (i.e., the kind of environment in which one lives).

• All behavior and development reflect brain function, but currently
there are very few scientific data that link specific experiences at specific
times with specific effects on the developing central nervous system. Moreover, more is known about the adverse impacts of deprivation than the
beneficial effects of enrichment, and most of the knowledge about brain
development comes from studies of adults and animals other than humans.

• The astonishing developmental achievements of the earliest years
occur naturally when parents and other caregivers talk, read, and play with
young children and respond sensitively to their cues. There are no special
programs or materials that are guaranteed to accelerate early learning during infancy.

• Nurturing, stable, and consistent relationships are the key to healthy
growth, development, and learning, and there are many ways to be a successful parent. The best enrichment comes from loving interactions with
people who provide a rich variety of opportunities for exploration and
discovery.

• The early years of life are an important time of active development,
foundation building, and clear periods of reorganization. There is, however, no sharp break at age 3 (or 5), and there is no scientific reason to
believe that the behavioral consequences of negative early experiences cannot be ameliorated by interventions initiated in later childhood, or that
positive early experiences provide permanent protection against later adversity.

• There are many variations along the road to competence, and a wide
range of individual differences among normally developing children can
present quite formidable challenges to parents and other caregivers along
the way. Notwithstanding the inevitable bumps in the road, the course of
human development, like that of all living organisms, moves naturally in
the direction of positive adaptation.

• The developing brain is dependent on the inputs of a variety of early
sensory, perceptual, and motor experiences (e.g., sound, binocular vision,
movement through space) that are easily met, unless a child is born with an
auditory, visual, or motor deficit that interferes with the expected input.

The early detection and remediation of such problems are essential components of primary health care.

• Efforts to protect early brain development are best embedded in an overall strategy of general health promotion and disease prevention. This includes attention to the importance of adequate nutrition (beginning during the prenatal period), the avoidance of harmful exposures (e.g., drugs, viruses, and environmental toxins), and protection from the stresses of chronic understimulation or significant maltreatment (i.e., abuse or neglect).

• There is considerable variability among childrearing environments that promote healthy development, much of which is embedded in different values and cultural practices that are passed on from one generation to the next and are continually transformed by each generation based on the times in which it lives.

• Well-described deviations that exist in all cultures (e.g., extreme and persistent poverty, serious parental psychopathology, family violence) can be extremely damaging to all children. Specific threats to development can originate from within the child or the environment, but significant vulnerability results less from a single source and more from the cumulative burden of multiple risk factors. Within this context, the boundaries among normative variations, transient maturational differences, and persistent disabilities are often blurred and difficult to define in the early childhood period. The combined impact of both biological and environmental risk presents the greatest threat.

• The early detection of problems and the prompt provision of an appropriate intervention can improve developmental outcomes (i.e., shift the odds) for both children living in high-risk environments and children with biologically based disabilities. However, not all interventions are effective, when they do work they are rarely panaceas, and (unlike immunizations followed by an occasional booster) they do not confer a lifetime of protection.

In summary, the well-being and "well-becoming" of young children are dependent on two essential conditions. First is the need for stable and loving relationships with a limited number of adults who provide responsive and reciprocal interaction, protection from harm, encouragement for exploration and learning, and transmission of cultural values. Second is the need for a safe and predictable environment that provides a range of growth-promoting experiences to promote cognitive, linguistic, social, emotional, and moral development. The majority of children in the United States today enjoy the benefits of both. A significant number do not.

CONCLUDING THOUGHTS

As this report moved to completion, it became increasingly clear to the members of the committee that the science of early childhood development has been viewed through highly personalized and sharply politicized lenses. In many respects, this is an area in which personal experience allows everyone to claim some level of expertise. Moreover, as a public issue, questions about the care and protection of children confront many of the basic values that have defined this country from its founding—personal responsibility, individual self-reliance, and restrained government involvement in people's lives. In a highly pluralistic society that is experiencing dramatic economic and social change, however, the development of children must be viewed as a matter of intense concern for both their parents and for the nation as a whole. In this context, and based on the evidence gleaned from a rich and rapidly growing science base, we feel an urgent need to call for a new national dialogue focused on rethinking the meaning of both shared responsibility for children and strategic investment in their future.

The time has come to stop blaming parents, communities, business, and government—and to shape a shared agenda to ensure both a rewarding childhood and a promising future for all children. Central to this agenda is the importance of matching needs and capabilities. Families, for example, are the best vehicle for providing loving and caring relationships and for creating safe and nurturing environments that promote healthy physical, cognitive, linguistic, social, emotional, and moral development. Communities are ideally situated to provide a wide range of supports for families through formal voluntary organizations and informal social networks. Businesses have the opportunity to support family well-being through creating positive work environments, offering flexible work schedules, and providing important financial benefits, such as family health insurance and child care. Local, state, and federal governments have substantial opportunities to influence the quality of family life and the availability of resources to support child needs through such diverse mechanisms as tax policies to alleviate economic hardship (e.g., earned income and child care tax credits), minimum wage laws to boost the incomes of low-wage workers, policies to support working parents and promote the health and development of their children (e.g., child care standards and subsidies), policies to support parent choice regarding employment (e.g., paid family leave), and funding for early intervention programs, among others. No single locus of responsibility can address all the needs of young children and their families. Effective policies clearly require aggregate responsibility.

Finally, there is a compelling need for more constructive dialogue between those who support massive public investments in early childhood services and those who question their cost and ask whether they really make a difference. Both perspectives have merit. Advocates of earlier and more intervention have an obligation to measure their impacts and costs. Skeptics, in turn, must acknowledge the massive scientific evidence that early childhood development is influenced by the environments in which children live. Continued "winner takes all" conflict between advocates and skeptics serves only to fuel a siege mentality in the early childhood community that undermines critical self-evaluation in the service of short-sighted self-preservation. In the final analysis, a constructive approach to early childhood policy would mobilize the best available knowledge (and promote its continued growth) in order to move beyond simple questions about whether environments and early experiences make a difference. The ultimate challenge for the nation is to answer questions about how to enhance the quality of those environments and experiences in an effort to promote the health and development of young children.

The charge to this committee was to blend the knowledge and insights of a broad range of disciplines to generate an integrated science of early childhood development. The charge to society is to blend the skepticism of a scientist, the passion of an advocate, the pragmatism of a policy maker, the creativity of a practitioner, and the devotion of a parent—and to use existing knowledge to ensure both a decent quality of life for all of our children and a promising future for the nation.

References

Abbott, S.
  1992   Holding on and pushing away: Comparative perspectives on an Eastern Kentucky child-rearing practice. *Ethos* 1:33-65.
Abel, E.L.
  1995   An update on incidence of FAS: FAS is not an equal opportunity birth defect. *Neurotoxicology and Teratology* 17(4):437-443.
Aber, J.L.
  1994   Poverty, violence, and child development: Untangling family and community level effects. Pp. 229-272 in *Threats to Optimal Development: Integrating Biological, Psychological, and Social Risk Factors: The Minnesota Symposia on Child Psychology*, Volume 27. C.A. Nelson, ed. Hillsdale, NJ: Lawrence Erlbaum Associates, Publishers.
Aber, J.L., N.G. Bennett, D.C. Conley, and J. Li
  1997   The effects of poverty on child health and development. *Annual Review of Public Health* 18:463-483.
Achenbach, T.M., S.H. McConaughy, and C.T. Howell
  1987   Child/adolescent behavioral and emotional problems: Implications of cross-informant correlations for situational specificity. *Psychological Bulletin* 101:213-232.
ACYF/NIMH Collaborative Mental Health Research Initiative
  2000   Mental Health Within Head Start: Head Start-University Partnerships. [Online]. Available: http://www2.acf.dhhs.gov/programs/hsb/core/dox/mhhs.html [Accessed June 25, 2000].
Administration on Children Youth and Families
  1998   *Head Start Program Performance Measures: Second Progress Report.* Washington, DC: U.S. Department of Health and Human Services.
  2000   *Head Start Program Performance Measures: Longitudinal Findings From the FACES Study.* Washington, DC: U.S. Department of Health and Human Services.

Affleck, G., H. Tennen, J. Rowe, B. Roscher, and L. Walker
  1989   Effects of formal support on mothers' adaptation to the hospital-to-home transi-
          tion of high-risk infants: The benefits and costs of helping. *Child Development*
          60(2):488-501.
Ainslie, R.C., and C.W. Anderson
  1984   Daycare children's relationships to their mothers and caregivers: An inquiry into
          the conditions for the development of attachment. In *The Child and the Day Care
          Setting: Qualitative Variations and Development.* R.C. Ainslie, ed. New York:
          Praeger.
Ainsworth, M.D.S.
  1967   *Infancy in Uganda: Infant Care and the Growth of Love.* Baltimore, MD: Johns
          Hopkins University Press.
  1973   The development of infant-mother attachment. Pp. 1-94 in *Review of Child Devel-
          opment Research*, Volume 3. B.M. Caldwell and H.N. Ricciuti, eds. Chicago, IL:
          University of Chicago Press.
Ainsworth, M.D.S., and S.M. Bell
  1970   Attachment, exploration, and separation: Illustrated by the behavior of one-year-
          olds in a strange situation. *Child Development* 41(1):49-67.
Ainsworth, M.D.S., M.C. Blehar, E. Waters, and S. Wall
  1978   *Patterns of Attachment.* Hillsdale, NJ: Erlbaum.
Alanese, A., G. Hamill, J. Jones, D.H. Skuse, D.R. Matthews, and R. Stanhope
  1994   Reversibility of physiological growth hormone secretion in children with psychoso-
          cial dwarfism. *Clinical Endocrinology* 40(5):687-692.
Albano, A.M., B.F. Chorpita, and D.H. Barlow
  1996   Childhood anxiety disorders. Pp. 196-241 in *Child Psychopathology.* E.J. Mash
          and R.A. Barkley, eds. New York: The Guilford Press.
Alessandri, S.M.
  1992   Effects of maternal work status in single-parent families on children's perception of
          self and family and school achievement. *Journal of Experimental Child Psychology*
          54:417-433.
Allen, M.C., P.K. Donohue, and A.E. Dusman
  1993   The limit of viability—Neonatal outcome of infants born at 22 to 25 weeks' gesta-
          tion [see comments]. *New England Journal of Medicine* 329(22):1597-1601.
Als, H.
  1997   Earliest intervention for preterm infants in the Newborn Intensive Care Unit. Pp.
          47-76 in *The Effectiveness of Early Intervention.* M.J. Guralnick, ed. Baltimore,
          MD: Paul H. Brookes Publishing Co., Inc.
Alwin, D.F.
  1984   Trends in parental socialization values: Detroit, 1958-1983. *American Journal of
          Sociology* 90:359-382.
Amato, P.R.
  1993   Children's adjustment to divorce: Theories, hypotheses, and empirical support.
          Journal of Marriage and the Family 55:23-38.
Amato, P.R., and B. Keith
  1991   Parental divorce and the well-being of children: A meta-analysis. *Psychological
          Bulletin* 110:26-46.
Amato, P.R., and F. Rivera
  1999   Paternal involvement and children's behavior problems. *Journal of Marriage and
          the Family* 61:375-384.
American Academy of Pediatrics Task Force on Infant Positioning and SIDS
  1992   Positioning and SIDS. *Pediatrics* 89:1120-1126.

American Medical Association
1994   *AMA Guidelines for Adolescent Preventive Services (GAPS): Recommendations and Rationale*. Baltimore, MD: Williams & Wilkins.
American Psychiatric Association
1994   *Diagnostic and Statistical Manual of Mental Disorders (DSM-IV)*, Fourth Edition. Washington, DC: American Psychiatric Association.
American Public Health Association and American Academy of Pediatrics Collaborative Project
1992   *Caring for Our Children—National Health and Safety Performance Standards: Guidelines for Out-of-Home Child Care Programs*. Washington, DC: American Public Health Association.
Ames, E.W.
1997   *The Development of Romanian Orphanage Children Adopted to Canada: Final Report to the National Welfare Grants Program: Human Resources Development Canada*. Burnaby, British Columbia: Simon Fraser University.
Anders, T.F.
1975   *Maturation of Sleep Patterns in the Newborn Infant*. New York: Spectrum.
1979   Night waking in infants during the first year of life. *Pediatrics* 63:860-864.
1982   Biological rhythms in development. *Psychosomatic Medicine* 44(1):61-72.
Anders, T.F., L.F. Halpern, and J. Hua
1992   Sleep through the night: A developmental perspective. *Pediatrics* 90:554-560.
Anderson, D.R., J. Bryant, A. Wilder, A.M. Crawley, A. Santomero, and M.E. Williams
2000   Researching Blue's Clues: Viewing behavior and impact. *Media Psychology* 2:179-194.
Anderson, D.R., A.C. Huston, K. Schmitt, D. Linebarger, and J.C. Wright
forth-   Early childhood television and adolescent behavior. *Monographs of the Society for*
coming *Research in Child Development*.
Anderson, E.R., S.M. Greene, E.M. Hetherington, and W.G. Clingenpeel
1999   The dynamics of parental remarriage: Adolescent parent and sibling influences. In *Coping With Divorce, Single Parenting, and Remarriage: A Risk and Resiliency Perspective*. E.M. Hetherington, ed. Hillsdale, NJ: Lawrence Erlbaum.
Anderson, V.
1998   Assessing executive functions in children: Biological, psychological, and developmental considerations. *Neuropsychological Rehabilitation* 8(3):319-349.
Andersson, B.
1989   Effects of public day care: A longitudinal study. *Child Development* 60:857-866.
Andrews, S.R., J.B. Blumenthal, D.L. Johnson, A.J. Kahn, C.J. Ferguson, T.M. Lasater, P.E. Malone, and D.B. Wallace
1982   The skills of mothering: A study of Parent Child Development Centers (New Orleans, Birmingham, Houston). *Monographs of the Society for Research in Child Development* (Serial No. 198) 47(6).
Annie E. Casey Foundation
2000   *Kids Count Data Book, 2000: State Profiles of Child Well-Being*. Baltimore, MD: The Annie E. Casey Foundation.
Anthony, E.J., and B.J. Cohler, eds.
1987   *The Invulnerable Child*. New York: The Guilford Press.
Arcus, D., S. Gardner, and C. Anderson
1992   Infant reactivity, maternal style, and the development of inhibited and uninhibited behavioral profiles. Presentation in the Temperament and Environment symposium conducted at the Biennial Meeting of the International Society for Infant Studies, Miami, Florida.

Arnold, D.
   1997   Co-occurrence of externalizing behavior problems and emergent academic difficul-
           ties in young high-risk boys: A preliminary evaluation of patterns and mechanisms.
           Journal of Applied Developmental Psychology 18:317-330.
Asendorpf, J.B.
   1989   Shyness as a final common pathway for two different kinds of inhibition. *Journal
           of Personality and Social Psychology* 57:481-492.
Asher, S.R.
   1985   An evolving paradigm in social skills training research with children. Pp. 157-174
           in *Children's Peer Relations: Issues in Assessment and Intervention*. B.H. Schneider,
           K.H. Rubin, and J.E. Ledingham, eds. New York: Springer-Verlag.
Asher, S.R., J.G. Parker, and D.L. Walker
   1996   Distinguishing friendship from acceptance: Implications for intervention and as-
           sessment. Pp. 366-405 in *The Company They Keep: Friendship in Childhood and
           Adolescence*. W.F. Bukowski, A.F. Newcomb, and W.W. Hartup, eds. New York:
           Cambridge University Press.
Asher, S.R., A.J. Rose, and S.W. Gabriel
   2000   Peer rejection in everyday life. In *Interpersonal Rejection*. M. Leary, ed. New
           York: Oxford University Press.
Astington, J.W.
   1993   *The Child's Discovery of the Mind*. Cambridge, MA: Harvard University Press.
Atkinson, J.
   1964   *An Introduction to Motivation*. Princeton, NJ: Van Nostrand.
Atkinson, L., V.C. Chisholm, B. Scott, S. Goldberg, B.E. Vaughn, J. Blackwell, S. Dickens,
and F. Tam
   1999   Maternal sensitivity, child functional level, and attachment in Down syndrome.
           Monographs of the Society for Research in Child Development 64(3):45-66.
Au, K.H., and J.M. Mason
   1981   Social organizational factors in learning to read: The balance of rights hypothesis.
           Reading Research Quarterly 17:115-152.
Aukett, M.A., Y.A. Parks, P.H. Scott, and B.A. Wharton
   1986   Treatment with iron increases weight gain and psychomotor development. *Ar-
           chives of Disease in Childhood* 61:849-857.
Avis, J., and P.L. Harris
   1991   Belief-desire reasoning among Baka children: Evidence for a universal conception
           of mind. *Child Development* 62(3):460-467.
Axelrod, J., and T.D. Reisine
   1984   Stress hormones: Their interaction and regulation. *Science* 224:452-459.
Azmitia, M.
   1988   Peer interaction and problem solving: When are two heads better than one? *Child
           Development* 59:87-96.
Azure, S.L.
   1996   *Child-Staff Ratios and Group Size Requirements in Child Care Licensing: A Com-
           parison of 1989 and 1996*. Boston, MA: The Center for Career Development in
           Early Care and Education, Wheelock College.
Bachevalier, J.
   1992   Cortical versus limbic immaturity: Relationship to infantile amnesia. *Minnesota
           Symposia on Child Psychology: Developmental Neuroscience* 24:129-153.

Bachevalier, J., C. Hagger, and M. Mishkin
1991   Functional maturation of the occipitotemporal pathway in infant rhesus monkeys. Pp. 231-240 in *Alfred Benzon Symposium No. 31: Brain Work and Mental Activity.* N.A. Lassen, D.H. Ingvar, M.E. Raichle, and L. Friberg, eds. Copenhagen, Denmark: Munksgaard.

Bachevalier, J., M. Brickson, and C. Hagger
1993   Limbic-dependent recognition memory in monkeys develops early in infancy. *NeuroReport* 4:77-80.

Bailey, D.J.
1997   Evaluating the effectiveness of curriculum alternatives for infants and preschoolers at high risk. Pp. 227-247 in *The Effectiveness of Early Intervention.* M.J. Guralnick, ed. Baltimore, MD: Paul H. Brookes Publishing Co., Inc.

Baillargeon, R., L. Kotovsky, and A. Needham
1995   The acquisition of physical knowledge in infancy. Pgs. 79-116 in *Causal Cognition: A Multidisciplinary Debate,* D. Sperber, D. Premack, and A.J. Premack, eds. New York: Clarendon Press/Oxford University Press.

Baker, A.J.L., C.S. Piotrkowski, and J. Brooks-Gunn
1999   The Home Instruction Program for Preschool Youngsters (HIPPY). *The Future of Children: Home Visiting: Recent Program Evaluations* 9(1):116-133.

Baldwin, A.L., J. Kalhorn, and F.H. Breese, eds.
1945   Patterns of parent behavior. *Psychological Monographs* 58(3):1-85.

Baldwin, D.A., and L.J. Moses
1996   The ontogeny of social information-processing. *Child Development* 67:1915-1939.

Barclay, J.R.
1966   Sociometric choices and teacher ratings as predictors of school dropout. *Journal of Consulting and Clinical Psychology* 53:500-505.

Barkley, R.A.
1996   Critical issues in research on attention. Pp. 45-56 in *Attention, Memory, and Executive Function.* G.R. Lyon and N. Krasnegor, eds. Baltimore, MD: Paul H. Brookes Publishing Co., Inc.

Barnard, K.E.
1997   Influencing parent-child interactions for children at risk. Pp. 249-268 in *The Effectiveness of Early Intervention.* M.J. Guralnick, ed. Baltimore, MD: Paul H. Brookes Publishing Co., Inc.

1998   Developing, implementing, documenting interventions with parents and young children. *Zero to Three [Special Issue: Opening the Black Box: Understanding How Early Intervention Programs Work]* 18:23-29.

Barnard, K.E., and J.F. Kelly
1990   Assessment of parent-child interaction. Pp. 278-302 in *Handbook of Early Childhood Intervention.* J.P. Shonkoff and S.J. Meisels, eds. New York: Cambridge University Press.

Barnard, K.E., G.S. Magyary, C.L. Booth, S.K. Mitchell, and S. Spieker
1988   Prevention of parenting alterations for women with low social support. *Psychiatry* 51:248-253.

Barnas, M.V., and E.M. Cummings
1994   Caregiver stability and toddlers' attachment-related behavior towards caregivers in day care. *Infant Behavior and Development* 17:141-147.

Barnes, H.V., B.D. Goodson, and J.I. Layzer
1995   *Review of Research on Supportive Interventions for Children and Families.* Cambridge, MA: Abt Associates.

Barnett, W.S.
   1995   Long-term effects of early childhood programs on cognitive and school outcomes. *The Future of Children* 5(3):25-50.
   2000   Economics of early childhood intervention. Pp. 589-612 in *Handbook of Early Childhood Intervention*, Second Edition. J.P. Shonkoff and S.J. Meisels, eds. New York: Cambridge University Press.
Barnett, W.S., and C.M. Escobar
   1990   Economic costs and benefits of early intervention. Pp. 560-582 in *Handbook of Early Childhood Intervention*. J.P. Shonkoff and S.J. Meisels, eds. New York: Cambridge University Press.
Baron, I.S., and G.A. Gioia
   1998   Neuropsychology of infants and young children. In *Neuropsychology. Human Brain Function: Assessment and Rehabilitation*. G. Goldstein, P.D. Nussbaum, and S.R. Bees, eds. New York: Plenum Press.
Baron-Cohen, S.
   1995   *Mindblindness: An Essay on Autism and Theory of Mind*. Cambridge, MA: MIT Press.
Barr, R.G.
   1990   The early crying paradox: A modest proposal. *Human Nature* 1(4):355-389.
   1993   Normality: A clinically useless concept in the case of infant crying and colic. *Developmental and Behavioral Pediatrics* 14(4):264-269.
Barr, R.G., R. Bakeman, M. Konner, and L. Adamson
   1987   Crying in !Kung infants: Distress signals in a responsive context. *American Journal of Diseases of Children* 141:386.
Barr, R.G., A. Rotmans, J. Yaremko, D. Leduc, and T.E. Francoer
   1992   The crying of infants with colic: A controlled empirical description. *Pediatrics* 90(1):14-21.
Barr, R.G., S. Chen, B. Hopkins, and T. Westra
   1996   Crying patterns in preterm infants. *Developmental Medicine and Child Neurology* 38(4):345-355.
Barrett, K.C., C. Zahn-Waxler, and P.M. Cole
   1993   Avoiders vs. amenders: Implications for the investigation of guilt and shame during toddlerhood. *Cognition and Emotion* 7:481-505.
Barry, J., and L.M. Paxon
   1971   Infancy and early childhood: Cross-cultural codes 2. *Ethnology* 10:466-508.
Barton, M.L., and D. Robins
   2000   Regulatory disorders. Pp. 311-325 in *Handbook of Infant Mental Health*, Second Edition. C.H. Zeanah, ed. New York: The Guilford Press.
Bartsch, K., and H.M. Wellman
   1995   *Children Talk About the Mind*. New York: Oxford University Press.
Bates, E.
   1990   Language about me and you: Pronomial reference and the emerging concept of self. Pp. 165-182 in *The Self in Transition: Infancy to Childhood*. D. Cicchetti and M. Beeghly, eds. Chicago, IL: University of Chicago Press.
Bates, E., and K. Roe
   in   Language development in children with unilateral brain injury. In *Handbook of*
   press *Developmental Cognitive Neuroscience*. C.A. Nelson and M. Luciana, eds. Cambridge, MA: MIT Press.
Bates, J.E., D. Marvinney, T. Kelly, K.A. Dodge, D.S. Bennett, and G.S. Pettit
   1994   Child care history and kindergarten adjustment. *Developmental Psychology* 30:690-700.

Bauer, P.J., and S.S. Wewerka
  1995   One- to two-year-olds' recall of events: The more expressed, the more impressed. *Journal of Experimental Child Psychology. Special Issue: Early Memory* 59(3):475-496.

Bauman, P., and F.E. Dougherty
  1983   Drug addicted mothers' parenting and their children's development. *International Journal of the Addictions* 18:291-302.

Baumrind, D.
  1967   Child care practices anteceding three patterns of preschool behavior. *Genetic Psychology Monographs* 75:43-88.
  1971   Current patterns of parental authority. *Developmental Psychology* 4(1, Pt. 2).
  1973   The development of instrumental competence through socialization. Pp. 3-46 in *Minnesota Symposium on Child Psychology* 7. A.D. Pick, ed. Minneapolis, MN: University of Minnesota Press.
  1993   The average expectable environment is not good enough: A response to Scarr. *Child Development* 64:1299-1317.

Baydar, N., and J. Brooks-Gunn
  1991   Effects of maternal employment and child care arrangements on preschoolers' cognitive and behavioral outcomes: Evidence from the children of the National Logitudinal Survey of Youth. *Developmental Psychology* 27:932-945.

Baydar, N., J. Brooks-Gunn, and F.F. Furstenberg Jr.
  1993   Early warning signs of functional illiteracy: Predictors in childhood and adolescence. *Child Development* 64(3):815-829.

Beals, D.E., J.M. De Temple, and D.K. Dickinson
  1994   Talking and listening that support early literacy development of children from low-income families. Pp. 19-40 in *Bridges to Literacy: Children, Families, and Schools.* D.K. Dickinson, ed. Cambridge, MA: Blackwell Publishers, Inc.

Beaudry, M., R. Dufour, and S. Marcoux
  1995   Relation between infant feeding and infections during the first six months of life. *The Journal of Pediatrics* 126(2):191-197.

Becker, G.S.
  1981   *A Treatise on the Family.* Cambridge, MA: Harvard University Press.

Becker, G.S., and H.G. Lewis
  1973   On the interaction between the quantity and quality of children. *Journal of Political Economy,* March/April, Pt. II:S279-S288.

Becker, G.S., and N. Tomes
  1986   Human capital and the rise and fall of families. *Journal of Labor Economics* 4(3):S1-S39.

Beckwith, L., and S.E. Cohen
  1989   Maternal responsiveness with preterm infants and later competency. *New Directions for Child Development* 43:75-87.

Beckwith, L., and A.H. Parmelee
  1986   EEG patterns of preterm infants, home environment, and later IQ. *Child Development* 57:777-789.

Beckwith, L., and C. Rodning
  1992   Evaluating effects of intervention with parents of preterm infants. Pp. 389-410 in *The Psychological Development of Low Birthweight Children.* S.L. Friedman and M.D. Sigman, eds. Norwood, NJ: Ablex Publishing Corporation.

Bedore, L., and L. Leonard
  1998   Specific language impairment and grammatical morphology: A discriminant function analysis. *Journal of Speech, Language, and Hearing Research* 41:1185-1192.

Beeghly, M., and D. Cicchetti
    1994   Child maltreatment, attachment, and the self-system: Emergence of an internal
            state lexicon in toddlers at high social risk. *Development and Psychopathology*
            6:5-30.
    1997   Talking about self and other: Emergence of an internal state lexicon in young
            children with Down Syndrome. *Development and Psychopathology* 9(4):729-748.
Bell, M.A., and N.A. Fox
    1992   The relations between frontal brain electrical activity and cognitive development
            during infancy. *Child Development* 63:1142-1163.
    1994   Brain development over the first year of life: Relations between electroencephalo-
            graphic frequency and coherence and cognitive and affective behaviors. Pp. 314-
            345 in *Human Behavior and the Developing Brain*. G. Dawson and K.W. Fischer,
            eds. New York: Guilford Press.
Bell, R.Q.
    1968   A reinterpretation of the direction of effects in studies of socialization. *Psychologi-
            cal Review* 75:81-95.
    1974   Contributions of human infants to caregiving and social interaction. Pp. 1-19 in
            The Effect of the Infant on Its Caregiver. M. Lewis and L. Rosenblum, eds. New
            York: Wiley.
Bell, R.Q., and M. Chapman
    1986   Child effects in studies using experimental or brief longitudinal approaches to so-
            cialization. *Developmental Psychology* 22:595-603.
Bellugi, U., S. Marks, A. Bihrle, and H. Sabo
    1988   Dissociation between language and cognitive functions in Williams syndrome. Pp.
            177-189 in *Language Development in Exceptional Circumstances*. D. Bishop and
            K. Mogford, eds. New York, NY: Churchill Livingstone.
Belsky, J.
    1984   The determinants of parenting: A process model. *Child Development* 55(1):83-96.
    1997   Theory testing, effect-size evaluation, and differential susceptibility to rearing influ-
            ence: The case of mothering and attachment. *Child Development* 64:598-600.
    1999   Interactional and contextual determinants of attachment security. Pp. 249-264 in
            Handbook of Attachment: Theory, Research, and Clinical Applications. J. Cassidy
            and P.R. Shaver, eds. New York: Guilford.
Belsky, J., and J. Cassidy
    1994   Attachment: Theory and evidence. Pp. 373-402 in *Development Through Life*. M.
            Rutter and D. Hay, eds. Oxford, UK: Blackwell.
Belsky, J., and D. Eggebeen
    1991   Early and extensive maternal employment and young children's socioemotional
            development: Children of the National Longitudinal Survey of Youth. *Journal of
            Marriage and the Family* 53:1083-1110.
Belsky, J., and R. Isabella
    1988   Maternal, infant, and social-contextual determinants of attachment security. Pp.
            41-94 in *Clinical Implications of Attachment*. J. Belsky and T. Nezworski, eds.
            Hillsdale, NJ: Erlbaum.
Belsky, J., C. Hertzog, and M. Rovine
    1986   Causal analyses of multiple determinants of parenting: Empirical and methodologi-
            cal advances. Pp. 153-202 in *Advances in Developmental Psychology*, Volume 4.
            M.E. Lamb, A.L. Brown, and B. Rogoff, eds. Hillsdale, NJ: Lawrence Erlbaum
            Associates, Publishers.

Belsky, J., S.B. Campbell, J.F. Cohn, and G. Moore
  1996a Instability of infant-parent attachment security. *Developmental Psychology* 32:921-924.
Belsky, J., B. Spritz, and K. Crnic
  1996b Infant attachment security and affective-cognitive information processing at age 3. *Psychological Science* 7:111-114.
Belsky, J., S. Woodworth, and K. Crnic
  1996c Trouble in the second year: Three questions about family interaction. *Child Development* 67:556-578.
Benasich, A.A., J. Brooks-Gunn, and B.C. Clewell
  1992 How do mothers benefit from early intervention programs? *Journal of Applied Developmental Psychology* 13:311-362.
Bennett, A.J., K.P. Lesch, A. Heils, J. Long, J. Lorenz, S.E. Shoaf, M. Champoux, S.J. Suomi, M. Linnoila, and J.D. Higley
  1998 Serotonin transporter gene variation, strain, and early rearing environment affect CSF 5-HIAA concentrations in rhesus monkeys (Macaca mulatta). *American Journal of Primatology.*
Bennett, N.G., J. Li, Y. Song, and K. Yang
  1999 *Young Children in Poverty: A Statistical Update.* June 1999 Edition. New York: National Center for Children in Poverty, Columbia University Mailman School of Public Health.
Benoit, T.C., L.J. Jocelyn, D.M. Moddeman, and J.E. Embree
  1996 Romanian adoption: The Manitoba experience. *Archives of Pediatric and Adolescent Medicine* 150:1278-1282.
Benton, A.
  1991 Prefrontal injury and behavior in children. *Developmental Neuropsychology* 7(3):275-281.
Berk, H.J., and M.L. Berk
  1982 A survey of day care centers and their services for handicapped children. *Child Care Quarterly* 11:211-214.
Berko, J.
  1958 The child's learning of English morphology. *Word* 14:150-177.
Berlin, L., and J. Cassidy
  1999 Relations among relationships: Contributions from attachment theory and research. Pp. 688-712 in *Handbook of Attachment: Theory, Research, and Clinical Applications.* J. Cassidy and P.R. Shaver, eds. New York: Guilford.
Berlin, L.J., C.R. O'Neal, and J. Brooks-Gunn
  1998 Understanding the processes in early intervention programs: The interaction of program and participants. *Zero to Three [Special Issue: Opening the Black Box: Understanding How Early Intervention Programs Work]* 18:4-15.
Bernal, J.F.
  1973 Night waking in infants during the first 14 months. *Developmental Medicine in Child Neurology* 15:760-769.
Bernal, M.E., and G.P. Knight
  1993 *Ethnic Identity: Formation and Transmission Among Hispanics and Other Minorities.* Albany, NY: State University of New York Press.
Bernard, J.A.
  1991 *Cultural Competence Training Handbook.* Ventura County, CA: Ventura County Medical Health Care Agency.

Bernheimer, L.P., R. Gallimore, and T.S. Weisner
  1990   Ecocultural theory as a context for the Individual Family Service Plan. *Journal of Early Intervention* 14(3):219-233.
Bernstein, V., R.J. Jeremy, and J. Marcus
  1986   Mother-infant interaction in multiproblem families: Finding those at risk. *Journal of the American Academy of Child and Adolescent Psychiatry* 25:632-640.
Berrey, E.C., and M.C. Lennon
  1998   Teen parent program evaluations yield no simple answers. *The Forum: Research Forum on Children, Families, and the New Federalism* 1(4):1-4.
Berry, J.W.
  1995   Preface. Pp. x-xv in *Handbook of Cross-Cultural Psychology*, Volume 1: Theory and Method, Second Edition. J.W. Berry, Y.H. Poortinga, and J. Pandey, eds. Needham Heights, MA: Allyn and Bacon.
Beswick, R.C., R. Warner, and J. Warkany
  1949   Congenital anomalies following maternal Rubella. *American Journal of Diseases in Children* 78:334-348.
Bhavnagri, N., and R.D. Parke
  1991   Parents as direct facilitators of children's peer relationships: Effects of age of child and sex of parent. *Journal of Social and Personal Relationships* 8:423-440.
Birch, E.E., D.G. Birch, D.R. Hoffman, and R. Uauy
  1992   Dietary essential fatty acid supply and visual acuity development. *Investigative Ophthalmology and Visual Science* 33(11):3242-3253.
Biringen, Z., R.N. Emde, J.J. Campos, and M.I. Appelbaum
  1995   Affective reorganization in the infant, the mother, and the dyad: The role of upright locomotion and its timing. *Child Development* 66:499-514.
Bishop, D., T. North, and C. Donlan
  1996   Nonword repetition as a behavioural marker for inherited languge impairment: Evidence from a twin study. *Journal of Child Psychology and Psychiatry* 37:391-403.
Black, J.E., and W.T. Greenough
  1986   Induction of pattern in neural structure by experience: Implications for cognitive development. Pp. 1-50 in *Advances in Developmental Psychology*, Volume 4. M.E. Lamb, A.L. Brown, and B. Rogoff, eds. Hillsdale, NJ: Lawrence Erlbaum Associates, Inc.
  1998   Developmental approaches to the memory process. Pp. 55-88 in *Neurobiology of Learning and Memory*. J. Martinez and R. Kesner, eds. New York: Academic Press.
Black, J.E., K.R. Isaacs, B.J. Anderson, A.A. Alcantara, and W.T. Greenough
  1990   Learning causes synaptogenesis, while motor activity causes angiogenesis, in cerebellar cortex of adult rats. *Proceedings of the National Academy of Sciences* 87:5568-5572.
Black, J.E., T.A. Jones, C.A. Nelson, and W.T. Greenough
  1998   Neuronal plasticity and the developing brain. Pp. 31-53 in *Handbook of Child and Adolescent Psychiatry*, Volume 6: Basic Psychiatric Science and Treatment. N.E. Alessi, J.T. Coyle, S.I. Harrison, and S. Eth, eds. New York: John Wiley & Sons.
Blau, D.M.
  1997   The production of quality in child care centers. *The Journal of Human Resources* 32(2):354-387.
  1999   The effect of income on child development. *The Review of Economics and Statistics* 81(2):261-276.

2000 The production of quality in child care centers: Another look. *Applied Developmental Science.*

Blau, D.M., and A.P. Hagy
1998 The demand for quality in child care. *Journal of Political Economy* 106(1):104-146.

Blazer, D.G., R.C. Kessler, K.A. McGonagle, and M.S. Swartz
1994 The prevalence and distribution of major depression in a national community sample: The National Comorbidity Survey. *American Journal of Psychiatry* 151(7):979-986.

Blumberg, C., and A. Porter
1983 Analyzing quasiexperiments: Some implications of assuming continuous growth models. *Journal of Experimental Education* 51:150-159.

Bohman, M.
1996 Predisposition to criminality: Swedish adoption studies in retrospect. Pp. 99-114 in *Genetics of Criminal and Antisocial Behavior (Ciba Foundation Symposium 194).* G.R. Bock and J.A. Goode, eds. Chichester, UK: Wiley.

Böhner, J.
1990 Early acquisition of song in the zebra finch, Taeniopygia guttata. *Animal Behavior* 39:369-374.

Bond, L.A., and B.E. Compas, eds.
1989 *Primary Prevention and Promotion in the Schools.* Newbury Park, CA: Sage.

Bonthius, D.J., and J.R. West
1990 Alcohol-induced neuronal loss in developing rats: Increased brain damage with binge exposure. *Alcoholism: Clinical and Experimental Research* 14:107-118.

Booth, C.L., and J.F. Kelly
1998 Child care characteristics of infants with and without special needs: Comparisons and concerns. *Early Childhood Research Quarterly* 13:603-622.
1999 Child care and employment in relation to infants' disabilities and risk factors. *American Journal on Mental Retardation* 104:117-130.

Booth, C.L., S.K. Mitchell, K.E. Barnard, and S. Spieker
1989 Development of maternal social skills in multiproblem families: Effects on the mother-child relationship. *Developmental Psychology* 25:403-412.

Booth, C.L., L. Rose-Krasnor, and K.H. Rubin
1991 Relating preschoolers' social competence and their mother's parenting behaviors to early attachment security and high-risk status. *Journal of Social and Personal Relationships* 8:363-382.

Borduin, C.M., and Henggeler
1981 Social class, experimental setting and task characteristics as determinants of mother-child interactions. *Developmental Psychology* 17:209-214.

Borkowski, J.G., and J.E. Burke
1996 Theories, models, and measurements of executive functioning: An information processing perspective. Pp. 235-261 in *Attention, Memory, and Executive Function.* G.R. Lyon and N. Krasnegor, eds. Baltimore, MD: Paul H. Brookes Publishing Co., Inc.

Borkowski, J., S.L. Ramey, and M. Bristol Powers, eds.
in *Parenting and the Child's World: Influences on Academic, Intellectual and*
press *Socioemotional Development.* Hillsdale, NJ: Lawrence Erlbaum.

Bornstein, M.H.
1989 Sensitive periods in development: Structural characteristics and causal interpretations. *Psychological Bulletin* 105(2):179-197.

Bos, H., A.C. Huston, R. Granger, G.J. Duncan, T. Brock, and V.C. McLoyd
    1999   *New Hope for People With Low Incomes: Two-Year Results of a Program to Reduce Poverty and Reform Welfare.* San Francisco, CA: Manpower Demonstration Research Corporation.
Bouchard, T., D. Lykken, M. McGue, N. Segan, and A. Tellegen
    1990   Sources of human psychological differences: The Minnesota study of twins reared apart. *Science* 250:223-228.
Bowe, F.G.
    1995   Population estimates: Birth-to-5 children with disabilities. *The Journal of Special Education* 20:461-471.
Bowlby, J.
    1969   *Attachment and Loss,* Volume 1 (Attachment). New York: Basic Books.
    1973   *Attachment and Loss,* Volume 2 (Separation). New York: Basic Books.
Boyce, W.T.
    1996   The dilemma of developmental and behavioral diagnosis. Pp. 94-95 in *Rudolph's Pediatrics,* 20th Edition. A.M. Rudolph, J.I.E. Hoffman, and C.D. Rudolph, eds. Stamford, CT: Appleton & Lange.
Boyce, W.T., E. Frank, P.S. Jensen, R.C. Kessler, C.A. Nelson, L. Steinberg, and The MacArthur Foundation Research Network on Psychopathology and Development
    1998   Social context in developmental psychopathology: Recommendations for future research from the MacArthur Network on Psychopathology and Development. *Development and Psychopathology* 10:143-164.
Boykin, A.W., and F.D. Toms
    1985   Black child socialization: A conceptual framework. Pp. 33-51 in *Black Children: Social, Educational, and Parental Environments.* H. McAdoo and J. McAdoo, eds. Newbury Park, CA: Sage Publications, Inc.
Bradley, R.H.
    1985   The HOME Inventory: Rationale and research. *Recent Research in Developmental Psychopathology* 4:191-201.
    1995   Environment and parenting. Pp. 235-261 in *Handbook of Parenting.* M.H. Bornstein, ed. Mahwah, NJ: Lawrence Erlbaum Associates.
Bradley, R.H., and B.M. Caldwell
    1980   The relation of home environment, cognitive competence, and IQ among males and females. *Child Development* 51(4):1140-1148.
    1984   The HOME inventory and family demographics. *Developmental Psychology* 20:315-320.
Bradley, R.H., B.M. Caldwell, and S.L. Rock
    1988   Home environment and school performance: A ten-year follow-up and examination of three models of environmental action. *Child Development* 59:852-867.
Bradley, R.H., B.M. Caldwell, S.L. Rock, C.T. Ramey, K.E. Barnard, C. Gray, M.A. Hammong, S. Mitchell, A.W. Gottfried, L. Siegel, and D.L. Johnson
    1989   Home environment and cognitive development in the first 3 years of life: A collaborative study involving six sites and three ethnic groups in North America. *Developmental Psychology* 25(2):217-235.
Bradley, R.H., L. Whiteside, D.J. Mundform, P.H. Casey, K.J. Kelleher, and S.K. Pope
    1994   Early indications of resilience and their relation to experiences in the home environments of low birthweight. *Child Development* 65:346-360.
Brandon, P.D.
    sub-   Child care utilization among working mothers raising children with disabilities.
    mitted *Journal of Family and Economic Issues.*

Brasel, K.E., and S.P. Quigley
  1977   Influence of certain language and communication environments in early childhood on the development of language in deaf individuals. *Journal of Speech and Hearing Research* 20(1):95 107.
Braungart, J.M., and C.A. Stifter
  1991   Regulation of negative reactivity during the Strange Situation: Temperament and attachment in 12-month-old infants. *Infant Behavior and Development* 14:349-364.
Brayfield, A.A., S.G. Deich, and S.L. Hofferth
  1995   *Caring for Children in Low-Income Families. A Substudy of the National Child Care Survey, 1990.* Washington, DC: Urban Institute Press.
Brazelton, T.B.
  1986   Issues for working parents. *American Journal of Orthopsychiatry* 56:14-25.
  1992   *Touchpoints: The Essential Reference to Your Child's Emotional and Behavioral Development.* Reading, MA: Addison-Wesley Publishing Company.
Brazelton, T.B., B. Koslowski, and M. Main
  1974   The origins of reciprocity: The early mother-infant interaction. Pp. 49-76 in *The Effect of the Infant on Its Caregiver.* M. Lewis and L. Rosenblum, eds. New York: John Wiley & Sons.
Brazy, J.E., C.O. Eckerman, J.M. Oehler, R.F. Goldstein, and A.M. O'Rand
  1991   Nursery Neurobiologic Risk Score: Important factor in predicting outcome in very low birth weight infants. *The Journal of Pediatrics* 118:783-792.
Breslau, N., D. Salkever, and K.D. Staruch
  1982   Women's labor force activity and responsibilities for disabled dependents: A study of families with disabled children. *Journal of Health and Social Behavior* 23(2).
Breslau, N., N. Klein, and L. Allen
  1988   Very low birthweight: Behavioral sequelae at nine years of age. *Journal of the American Academy of Child and Adolescent Psychiatry* 27(5):605-612.
Bretherton, I., and K.A. Munholland
  1999   Internal working models in attachment relationships: A construct revisited. Pp. 89-111 in *Handbook of Attachment: Theory, Research, and Clinical Applications.* J. Cassidy and P.R. Shaver, eds. New York: Guilford.
Bretherton, I., S. McNew, and M. Beeghly
  1981   Early person knowledge as expressed in gestural and verbal communication: When do infants acquire a "theory of mind". Pp. 333-373 in *Infant Social Cognition.* M.E. Lamb and L.R. Sherrod, eds. Hillsdale, NJ: Lawrence Erlbaum.
Bretherton, I., J. Fritz, C. Zahn-Waxler, and D. Ridgeway
  1986   Learning to talk about emotions: A functionalist perspective. *Child Development* 55:529-548.
Briggs, J.L.
  1991   Expecting the unexpected: Canadian Inuit training for an experimental lifestyle. *Ethos* 19:259-287.
  1992   Mazes of meaning: How a child and a culture create each other. *New Directions for Child Development: Interpretive Approaches to Children's Socialization* 58:25-50.
Brim, O.G., Jr., and J. Kagan
  1980   *Constancy and Change in Human Development.* Cambridge, MA: Harvard University Press.
Broberg, A.G., H. Wessels, M.E. Lamb, and C.P. Hwang
  1997   Effects of day care on the development of cognitive abilities in 8-year olds: A longitudinal study. *Developmental Psychology* 33(1):62-69.

Brody, D.J., J.L. Pirkle, R.A. Kramer, K.M. Flegal, T.D. Matte, E.W Gunter., and D.C. Paschal
    1994   Blood lead levels in the US population: Phase 1 of the Third National Health and Nutrition Examination Survey (NHANES III, 1988 to 1991). *Journal of the American Medical Association* 272:277-283.

Brody, G.H., and D.L. Flor
    1997   Maternal psychological functioning, family processes, and child adjustment in rural, single-parent, African-American families. *Developmental Psychology* 33:1000-1011.

Bronfenbrenner, U.
    1979   *The Ecology of Human Development*. Cambridge, MA: Harvard University Press.
    1986   Ecology of the family as a context for human development: Research perspectives. *Developmental Psychology* 22(6):723-741.

Bronfenbrenner, U., and S.J. Ceci
    1994   Nature-nurture reconceptualized in developmental perspective: A bioecological model. *Psychological Review* 101(4):568-586.

Bronson, G.W.
    1971   Fear of the unfamiliar in human infants. Pp. 59-71 in *The Origin of Human Social Relations*. H.R. Schaffer, ed. London: Academic Press.

Bronson, M.B.
    2000   *Self-Regulation in Early Childhood: Nature and Nurture*. New York: Guilford Press.

Brooks-Gunn, J., and G.J. Duncan
    1997   The effects of poverty on children and youth. *The Future of Children* 7(2):55-71.

Brooks-Gunn, J., and M. Lewis
    1983   Screening and diagnosing handicapped infants. *Topics in Early Childhood Special Education* 3(1):14-28.

Brooks-Gunn, J., and M. Weinraub
    1983   Origins of infant intelligence testing. Pp. 25-66 in *Origins of Intelligence: Infancy and Early Childhood*. M. Lewis, ed. New York: John Wiley.

Brooks-Gunn, J., G. Guo, and F.F. Furstenberg Jr.
    1993   Who drops out of and who continues beyond high school?: A 20-year follow-up of black urban youth. *Journal of Research on Adolescence* 3(3):271-294.

Brooks-Gunn, J., C.M. McCarton, P.H. Casey, M.C. McCormick, C.R. Bauer, J.C. Bernbaum, J. Tyson, M. Swanson, F.C. Bennett, D.T. Scott, J. Tonascia, and C. Meinert
    1994   Early intervention in low-birth-weight premature infants: Results through age 5 years from the Infant Health and Development Program. *Journal of the American Medical Association* 272(16):1257-1262.

Brooks-Gunn, J., B. Brown, G.J. Duncan, and K.A. Moore
    1995   Child development in the context of family and community resources: An agenda for national data collection. Pp. 27-97 in *Integrating Federal Statistics on Children: Report of a Workshop*. National Research Council and Institute of Medicine. Washington, DC: National Academy Press.

Brooks-Gunn, J., L.J. Berlin, and A.S. Fuligni
    2000   Early childhood intervention programs: What about the family? Pp. 549-587 in *Handbook of Early Childhood Intervention*, Second Edition. J.P. Shonkoff and S.J. Meisels, eds. New York: Cambridge University Press.

Brown, E. and C. Brownell
    1990   Individual differences in toddlers' interaction styles. Paper presented at the International Conference on Infant Studies, Montreal, Canada.

Brown, J.R., and J. Dunn
1996 Continuities in emotional understanding from 3 to 6 years. *Child Development* 67:789-802.

Brown, J.R., N. Donelan-McCall, and J. Dunn
1996 Why talk about mental states? The significance of children's conversations with friends, siblings and mothers. *Child Development* 67:836-849.

Brown, R.
1958 *Words and Things*. New York, NY: The Free Press.
1973 *A First Language*. Cambridge, MA: Harvard University Press.

Brownell, C.A.
1988 Combinatorial skills: Converging developments over the second year. *Child Development* 59(3):675-685.

Brownell, C.A., and M. Carriger
1990 Changes in cooperation and self-other differentiation during the second year. *Child Development* 61:1164-1174.

Bruce, M.L., D.T. Takeuchi, and P.J. Leaf
1991 Poverty and psychiatric status: Longitudinal evidence from the New Haven Epidemiologic Catchment Area Study. *Archives of General Psychiatry* 48(5):470-474.

Bruder, M.B.
1997 The effectiveness of specific educational/developmental curricula for children with established disabilities. Pp. 523-548 in *The Effectiveness of Early Intervention*. M.J. Guralnick, ed. Baltimore, MD: Paul H. Brookes Publishing Co., Inc.

Bruer, J.T.
1999 *The Myth of the First Three Years*. New York: The Free Press.

Bryant, D.M., and K. Maxwell
1997 The effectiveness of early intervention for disadvantaged children. Pp. 23-46 in *The Effectiveness of Early Intervention*. M.J. Guralnick, ed. Baltimore, MD: Paul H. Brookes Publishing Co., Inc.

Bryant, D.M., M.R. Burchinal, L. Lau, and J.J. Sparling
1994 Family and classroom correlates of Head Start children's developmental outcomes. *Early Childhood Research Quarterly* 9:289-304.

Bryk, A., and H. Weisberg
1977 Use of the nonequivalent control group design and when subjects are growing. *Psychological Bulletin* 84:950-962.

Bugenthal, D.B.
1992 Affective and cognitive processes within threat-oriented family systems. Pp. 219-248 in *Parental Belief Systems: The Psychological Consequences for Children*. I.E. Sigel, A.V. McGillicuddy-DeLisi, and J.J. Goodnow, eds. Hillsdale, NJ: Erlbaum.

Buhrmester, D.
1992 The developmental course of sibling and peer relationships. Pp. 19-40 in *Children's Sibling Relationships*. F. Boer and J. Dunn, eds. Hillsdale, NJ: Lawrence Erlbaum.

Buka, S., and I. Birdthistle
1997 Children's exposure to violence: Extending the research frontier. *The Chicago Project News* 3(1).

Buka, S., T. Stichick, I. Birdthistle, and F. Earls
sub- The epidemiology of witnessing community violence in childhood and adolescence.
mitted *American Journal of Orthopsychiatry*.

Bullock, M., and P. Lutkenhaus
1988 The development of volitional behavior in the toddler years. *Child Development* 59:664-674.
1990 Who am I? Self-understanding in toddlers. *Merrill-Palmer Quarterly* 36:217-238.

Burchinal, M.R., D.M. Bryant, M.W. Lee, and C.T. Ramey
    1992   Early day care, infant-mother attachment, and maternal responsiveness in the
            infant's first year. *Early Childhood Research Quarterly* 7:383-396.
Burchinal, M.R., S. Ramey, M.K. Reid, and J. Jaccard
    1995   Early child care experiences and their association with family and child characteris-
            tics during middle childhood. *Early Childhood Research Quarterly* 10:33-61.
Burchinal, M.R., J.E. Roberts, L.A. Nabors, and D.M. Bryant
    1996   Quality of center child care and infant cognitive and language development. *Child
            Development* 67:606-620.
Burchinal, M.R., F.A. Campbell, D.M. Bryant, B.H. Wasik, and C.T. Ramey
    1997   Early intervention and mediating processes in cognitive performance of children of
            low-income African American families. *Child Development* 68(5):935-954.
Burton, R.V., and J.W.M. Whiting
    1961   The absent father and cross-sex identity. *Merrill-Palmer Quarterly* 7:85-95.
Busch-Rossnagel, D. Knauf-Jensen, and F. DesRosiers
    1995   Mothers and others: The role of the socializing environment in the development of
            mastery motivation. Pp. 117-146 in *Mastery Motivation: Origins, Conceptual-
            izations, and Applications: Advances in Applied Developmental Psychology*, Vol-
            ume 12. R. MacTurk and G. Morgan, eds. Norwood, NJ: Ablex Publishing
            Corporation.
Buss, K.A., and H.H. Goldsmith
    1998   Fear and anger regulation in infancy: Effects on the temporal dynamics of affective
            expression. *Child Development* 69:359-374.
Cabrera, N., C.S. Tamis-LeMonda, R.H. Bradley, S. Hofferth, and M.E. Lamb
    2000   Fatherhood in the twenty-first century. *Child Development* 71(1):127-136.
Cadoret, R.J., W.R. Yates, E. Troughton, G. Woodworth, and M.A. Stewart
    1995a   Adoption study demonstrating two genetic pathways to drug abuse. *Archives of
            General Psychiatry* 52:42-52.
    1995b   Genetic-environmental interaction in the genesis of aggressivity and conduct disor-
            ders. *Archives of General Psychiatry* 52:916-924.
Cadoret, R.J., G. Winokur, D. Langbehn, E. Troughton, W.R. Yates, and M.A. Stewart
    1996   Depression spectrum disease, I: The role of gene-environment interaction. *Ameri-
            can Journal of Psychiatry* 153(7):892-899.
Cain, G., and H. Watts
    1972   Problems in making policy inferences from the Coleman Report. *American Socio-
            logical Review* 35(2):228-252.
Cain, K.M., and C.S. Dweck
    1995   The relation between motivational patterns and achievement cognitions through-
            out the elementary school years. *Merrill-Palmer Quarterly* 41:25-52.
Cairns, R.B.
    1998   The making of developmental psychology. Pp. 25-105 in *The Handbook of Child
            Psychology*, Fifth Edition, Volume 1. W. Damon, ed. New York: Wiley.
Caldji, C., B. Tannenbaum, S. Sharma, D. Francis, P.M. Plotsky, and M.J. Meaney
    1998   Maternal care during infancy regulates the development of neural systems mediat-
            ing the expression of fearfulness in the rat. *Proceedings of the National Academy
            of Sciences of the United States of America* 95(9):5335-5340.
Caldwell, B., and R.H. Bradley
    1984   *Home Observation for Measurement of the Environment.* Little Rock, AR: Center
            for Research on Teaching and Learning, University of Arkansas at Little Rock.

Calkins, S., and M.C. Johnson
  1998 Toddler regulation of distress to frustrating events: Temperamental and maternal correlates. *Infant Behavior and Development* 21:379-395.
Calkins, S.D., N.A. Fox, and T.R. Marshall
  1996 Behavioral and physiological antecedents of inhibition in infancy. *Child Development* 67:523-540.
Calvert, S.L.
  1999 *Children's Journeys Through the Information Age.* Boston, MA: McGraw Hill.
Campbell, D., and A. Erlebacher
  1970 How regression artifacts in quasiexperimental evaluations can mistakenly make compensatory education look harmful. Pp. 185-210 in *Compensatory Education: A National Debate*, Volume 3: The Disadvantaged Child. J. Helmuth, ed. New York: Brunner/Mazel.
Campbell, F.A., and C.T. Ramey
  1994 Effects of early intervention on intellectual and academic achievement: A follow-up study of children from low-income families. *Child Development* 65:684-698.
  1995 Cognitive and school outcomes for high risk African-American students at middle adolescence. Positive effects of early intervention. *American Educational Research Journal* 32:734-772.
Campbell, N.D., J.C. Appelbaum, K. Martinson, and E. Martin
  2000 *Be All That We Can Be: Lessons From the Military for Improving Our Nation's Child Care System.* Washington, DC: National Women's Law Center.
Campbell, S.B.
  1991 Longitudinal studies of active and aggressive preschoolers: Individual differences in early behavior and outcome. Pp. 57-90 in *Rochester Symposium on Developmental Psychopatholgy*. D. Cicchetti and S.L. Toth, eds. Hillsdale, NJ: Lawrence Erlbaum Associates, Publishers.
  1997 Behavior problems in preschool children. *Advances in Clinical Child Psychology* 19:1-26.
Campbell, S.B., and L.J. Ewing
  1990 Follow-up of hard-to-manage preschoolers: Adjustment at age 9 and predictors of continuing symptoms. *Journal of Child Psychology and Psychiatry and Allied Disciplines* 31(6):871-889.
Campbell, S.B., A.M. Breaux, L.J. Ewing, and E.K. Szumowski
  1986a Correlates and predictors of hyperactivity and aggression: A longitudinal study of parent-referred problem preschoolers. *Journal of Abnormal Child Psychology* 14(2):217-234.
Campbell, S.B., A.M. Breaux, L.J. Ewing, E.K. Szumowski, and E.W. Pierce
  1986b Parent-identified problem preschoolers: Mother-child interaction during play at intake and 1-year follow-up. *Journal of Abnormal Child Psychology* 14(3):425-440.
Campbell, S.B., J.F. Cohn, and T. Meyers
  1995 Depression in first-time mothers: Mother-infant interaction and depression chronicity. *Developmental Psychology* 31(3):349-357.
Campos, J.J., B.I. Bertenthal, and R. Kermoian
  1992a Early experience and emotional development: The emergence of wariness of heights. *Psychological Science* 3(1):61-64.
Campos, J.J., R. Kermoian, and M.R. Zumbahlen
  1992b Socioemotional transformations in the family system following infant crawling onset. *New Directions for Child Development: Emotion and Its Regulation in Early Development* 55:35-40.

Cantor, D., J. Kerwin, Levin K., S. Heltemes, and D. Becher
  1995   *The Impact of the Family and Medical Leave Act: A Survey of Employers.*
         Rockville, MD: Westat.
Capizzano, J., G. Adams, and F. Sonenstein
  2000   Child Care Arrangements for Children Under Five: Variation Across States. *New Federalism: National Survey of America's Families*, Series B (No. B-7). Washington, DC: The Urban Institute.
Capps, L., M. Sigman, and P. Mundy
  1994   Attachment security in children with autism. *Development and Psychopathology* 6:249-261.
Carey, S.
  1978   The child as word learner. Pp. 264-293 in *Linguistic Theory and Psychological Reality*. M. Halle, J. Bresnan, and G. Miller, eds. Cambridge, MA: MIT Press.
  1985   *Conceptual Change in Childhood.* Cambridge, MA: MIT Press.
Carlson, E.A., D. Jacobvitz, and L.A. Sroufe
  1995   A developmental investigation of inattentiveness and hyperactivity. *Child Development* 66:37-54.
Carmichael, L., ed.
  1946   *Manual of Child Psychology.* New York: J. Wiley & Sons, Inc.
Carnegie Task Force on Meeting the Needs of Young Children
  1994   *Starting Points: Meeting the Needs of Our Youngest Children.* New York: Carnegie Corporation of New York.
Carson, J., and R.D. Parke
  1996   Reciprocal negative affect in parent-child interactions and children's peer competency. *Child Development* 67:2217-2226.
Case, R.
  1992   The role of the frontal lobes in the regulation of cognitive development. *Brain and Cognition* 20:51-73.
Case, R., and S. Griffin
  1990   Child cognitive development: The role of central conceptual structures in the development of scientific and social thought. Pp. 193-230 in *Developmental Psychology: Cognitive, Perceptuo-Motor and Neuropsychological Perspectives.* C.A. Hauert, ed. Amsterdam, The Netherlands: Elsevier.
Casey, B.J., J.D. Cohen, P. Jezzard, R. Turner, D.C. Noll, R.J. Trainor, J. Gied, D. Kaysen, L. Hertz-Pannier, and J.L. Rappoport
  1995   Activation of prefrontal cortex in children during a nonspatial working memory task with functional MRI. *Neuroimaging* 2:221-229.
Caspi, A., and T.E. Moffitt
  1995   The continuity of maladaptive behavior: From description to understanding in the study of antisocial behavior. Pp. 472-511 in *Developmental Psychopathology*, Volume 2: Risk, Disorder, and Adaptation. D. Cicchetti and D.L. Cohen, eds. New York: John Wiley & Sons, Inc.
Caspi, A., B. Henry, R. McGee, T. Moffitt, and P. Silva
  1995   Temperamental origins of child and adolescent behavior problems: From ages three to fifteen. *Child Development* 66:887-895.
Cassidy, J.
  1988   Child-mother attachment and the self in six-year-olds. *Child Development* 59:121-134.
  1994   Emotion regulation: Influences of attachment relationships. *Monographs of the Society for Research in Child Development* (2/3, Serial No. 240) 59:228-249.

1995 Attachment and generalized anxiety disorder. Pp. 343-370 in *Rochester Symposium on Developmental Psychopathology*, Volume 6: Emotion, Cognition, and Representation. D. Cicchetti and S.L. Toth, eds. Rochester, NY: University of Rochester Press.

1999 The nature of the child's ties. Pp. 3-20 in *Handbook of Attachment: Theory, Research, and Clinical Applications.* J. Cassidy and P.R. Shaver, eds. New York: The Guilford Press.

Cassidy, J., and L.J. Berlin
1994 The insecure/ambivalent pattern of attachment: Theory and research. *Child Development* 65:971-991.

Cassidy, J., R.D. Parke, L. Butkovsky, and J.M. Braungart
1992 Family-peer connections: The roles of emotional expressiveness within the family and children's understanding of emotions. *Child Development* 63(3):603-618.

Cassidy, J., S. Kirsh, K.L. Scolton, and R.D. Parke
1996 Attachment and representations of peer relationships. *Developmental Psychology* 32:892-904.

Casto, G., and M.A. Mastropieri
1986 The efficacy of early intervention programs: A meta-analysis. *Exceptional Children* 52(5):417-424.

Caudill, W., and D.W. Plath
1966 Who sleeps by whom? Parent-child involvement in urban Japanese families. *Psychiatry* 29:344-366.

Caughy, M.O., J. DiPietro, and D.M. Strobino
1994 Day-care participation as a protective factor in the development of low-income children. *Child Development* 65 (Special Issue: Children and Poverty):457-471.

Chabris, C.F.
1999 Prelude or requiem for the "Mozart effect"? *Nature* 400:826-827.

Champoux, M., S.M. Coe, S.M. Schanberg, C.M. Kuhn, and S.J. Suomi
1989 Hormonal effects of early rearing conditions in the infant rhesus monkey. *American Journal of Primatology* 19:111-117.

Champoux, M., E. Byrne, R. DeLizio, and S.J. Suomi
1992 Motherless mothers revisited: Rhesus maternal behavior and rearing history. *Primates* 33(2):251-255.

Chandler, L.K., R.C. Lubeck, and S.A. Fowler
1992 Generalization and maintenance of preschool children's social skills: A critical review and analysis. *Journal of Applied Behavior Analysis* 25:415-428.

Chang, A., and R. Teramoto
1987 Children with special needs in private day care centers. *Child and Youth Care Quarterly* 16:60-67.

Chapieski, M.L., and K.D. Evankovich
1997 Behavioral effects of prematurity. *Seminars in Perinatology* 21:221-239.

Chase-Lansdale, P.L., and J. Brooks-Gunn, eds.
1995 *Escape From Poverty: What Makes a Difference for Children?* New York: Cambridge University Press.

Chase-Lansdale, P.L., F.L. Mott, J. Brooks-Gunn, and D.A. Phillips
1991 Children of the National Longitudinal Survey of Youth: A unique research opportunity. *Developmental Psychology* 27:918-931.

Chen, C., S. Lee, and H. Stevenson
1996 Long-term prediction of academic achievement of American, Chinese, and Japanese adolescents. *Journal of Educational Psychology* 88:750-759.

Cherkes-Julkowski, M.
    1998   Learning disability, attention-deficit disorder, and language impairment as out-
            comes of prematurity: A longitudinal descriptive study. *Journal of Learning Dis-
            abilities* 31:294-306.
Cherlin, A.
    1999   Going to extremes: Family structure, children's well-being, and social science. *De-
            mography* 36:421-428.
Cherlin, A.J., F.F. Frank Jr., P.L. Chase-Lansdale, K.E. Kiernan, P.K. Robins, D.R. Morrison,
and J.O. Teitler
    1991   Longitudinal studies of effects of divorce on children in Great Britain and the
            United States. *Science* 252:1386-1389.
Children's Defense Fund
    1994   The national incidence and prevalence of child abuse and neglect: 1988. Pp. 5-29
            in *Wasting America's Future: The Children's Defense Fund's Report on the Costs
            of Child Poverty*. Boston, MA: Beacon Press.
Chin-Quee, D.S., and S. Scarr
    1994   Lack of early child care effects on school-age children's social competence and
            academic achievement. *Early Development and Parenting* 3:103-112.
Chisholm, K.
    1998   A three year follow-up of attachment and indiscriminate friendliness in children
            adopted from Romanian orphanages. *Child Development* 69(4):1092-1106.
Chomsky, N.
    1965   *Aspects of the Theory of Syntax*. Cambridge, MA: MIT Press.
Christian, M.K., F.J. Morrison, and H.J. Bachman
    in   Schooling and cognitive development. In *Environmental Effects on Cognitive Abili-
    press   ties*. R.J. Sternberg and R.L. Grigorenko, eds. Mahwah, NJ: Lawrence Erlbaum
            Associates.
Chugani, H.T.
    1994   Development of regional brain glucose metabolism in relation to behavior and
            plasticity. Pp. 153-175 in *Human Behavior and the Developing Brain*. G. Dawson
            and K.W. Fischer, eds. New York: Guilford Press.
Chugani, H.T., and M.E. Phelps
    1986   Maturational changes in cerebral function in infants determined by [18]FDG
            positron emisson tomography. *Science* 231:840-843.
Chugani, H.T., M.E. Phelps, and J.C. Mazziota
    1987   Positron emission tomography study of human brain functional development. *An-
            nals of Neurology* 22(4):487-497.
Cicchetti, D.
    1990   The organization and coherence of socioemotional, cognitive, and representational
            development: Illustrations through a developmental psychopathology perspective
            on Down syndrome and child maltreatment. Pp. 259-366 in *Socioemotional De-
            velopment: Nebraska Symposium on Motivation*, Volume 36. R.A. Thompson, ed.
            Lincoln, NE: University of Nebraska Press.
    1994   Integrating developmental risk factors: Perspectives from developmental psychopa-
            thology. Pp. 285-325 in *Threats to Optimal Development: Integrating Biological,
            Psychological, and Social Risk Factors: The Minnesota Symposia on Child Psychol-
            ogy*, Volume 27. C.A. Nelson, ed. Hillsdale, NJ: Lawrence Erlbaum Associates,
            Publishers.
Cicchetti, D., and M. Beeghly
    1990   *The Self in Transition: Infancy to Childhood*. Chicago, IL.: University of Chicago
            Press.

Cicchetti, D., and V. Carlson, eds.
   1989   *Child Maltreatment: Theory and Research on the Causes and Consequences of Child Abuse and Neglect.* New York: Cambridge University Press.
Cicchetti, D., and D.J. Cohen
   1995   Perspectives on developmental psychopathology. Pp. 3-20 in *Developmental Psychopathology*, Volume 1: Theory and Methods. D. Cicchetti and D.J. Cohen, eds. New York: John Wiley & Sons.
Cicchetti, D., and M. Lynch
   1995   Failures in the expectable environment and their impact on individual development: The case of child maltreatment. Pp. 32-71 in *Developmental Psychopathology*, Volume 2: Risk, Disorder, and Adaptation. D. Cicchetti and D.J. Cohen, eds. New York: John Wiley & Sons.
Cicchetti, D., and K. Schneider-Rosen
   1986   An organizational approach to childhood depression. Pp. 71-134 in *Depression in Young People: Clinical and Developmental Perspectives.* M. Rutter, C.E. Izard, and P. Read, eds. New York: The Guilford Press.
Cicchetti, D., and S.L. Toth
   1995   Developmental psychopathology and disorders of affect. Pp. 369-420 in *Developmental Psychopathology*, Volume 2. D. Cicchetti and D.J. Cohen, eds. New York: Wiley.
   1998   Perspectives on research and practice in developmental psychopathology. Pp. 479-583 in *The Handbook of Child Psychology*, Volume 4: Child Psychology in Practice, Fifth Edition. W. Damon, ed. New York: Wiley.
   2000   Child maltreatment in the early years of life. Pp. 255-294 in *WAIMH Handbook of Infant Mental Health*, Volume 4: Infant Mental Health in Groups at High Risk. J.D. Osofsky and H.E. Fitzgerald, eds. New York: John Wiley & Sons, Inc.
Cicchetti, D., and S. Wagner
   1990   Alternative assessment strategies for the evaluation of infants and toddlers: An organizational perspective. Pp. 246-277 in *Handbook of Early Childhood Intervention.* J.P. Shonkoff and S.J. Meisels, eds. New York: Cambridge University Press.
Cillessen, A.H., H.W. van IJzendoorn, C.F. van Lieshout, and W.W. Hartup
   1992   Heterogenity among peer-rejected boys: Subtypes and stabilities. *Child Development* 63:893-905.
Clark, R., J. Shibley Hyde, M.J. Essex, and M.H. Klein
   1997   Length of maternity leave and quality of mother-infant interactions. *Child Development* 68(2):364-383.
Clarke-Stewart, K.A.
   1979   Evaluating parental effects on child development. Pp. 471-491 in L. Shulman, Ed., *Review of Research in Education,* Vol. 6. Itasca, IL: F.E. Peacock.
Clarke-Stewart, K.A., L.P. Vanderstoep, and G.A. Killian
   1979   Analysis and replication of mother-child relations at two years of age. *Child Development* 50:777-793.
Clayton, D.F.
   in   Neural basis of avian song learning and perception. In *Brain Mechanisms of Perception, Learning, and Memory.* J. Bolhuis, ed. Oxford, UK: Oxford University Press.
   press
Clinton, H.R.
   1996   *It Takes a Village and Other Lessons Children Teach Us.* New York: Simon & Schuster Books.

Coates, D.L., and P.M. Vietze
    1996   Cultural considerations in assessment, diagnosis, and intervention. Pp. 243-256 in
            Manual of Diagnosis and Professional Practice in Mental Retardation. J.W.
            Jacobson and J.A. Mulick, eds. Washington, DC: American Psychological Asso-
            ciation.
Cochran, W.
    1965   The planning of observational studies of human populations (with discussion).
            Journal of the Royal Statistical Society A(128):234-255.
Cocking, R.R.
    1994   Ecologically valid frameworks of development: Accounting for continuities and
            discontinuities across contexts. Pp. 393-409 in *Cross-Cultural Roots of Minority
            Child Development*. P.M. Greenfield and R.R. Cocking, eds. Hillsdale, NJ:
            Lawrence Erlbaum Associates, Inc.
Coelen, C., F. Glantz, and D. Calore
    1979   *Day Care Centers in the U.S.: A National Profile, 1976-1977*. Cambridge, MA:
            Abt Associates.
Cohen, J.
    1988   *Statistical Power Analysis for the Behavioral Sciences*, Second Edition. Hillsdale,
            NJ: Erlbaum.
Cohen, S., and T.A. Wills
    1985   Stress, social support, and the buffering hypothesis. *Psychological Bulletin*
            98(2):310-357.
Cohn, J.F., R. Matais, E.Z. Tronick, D. Connell, and K. Lyons-Ruth
    1986   Face-to-face interactions of depressed mothers and their infants. *New Directions
            for Child Development: Maternal Depression and Child Disturbance* 34:31-46.
Cohn, J.F., S.B. Campbell, and S. Ross
    1991   Infant response in the still-face paradigm at 6 months predicts avoidant and secure
            attachment at 12 months. *Development and Psychopathology* 3:367-376.
Coie, J.D., and K.A. Dodge
    1983   Continuities and changes in children's social status: A five-year longitudinal study.
            Merrill-Palmer Quarterly 29:261-281.
Coie, J.D., J.E. Lochman, R. Terry, and C. Hyman
    1992   Predicting early adolescent disorder from childhood aggression and peer rejection.
            Journal of Consulting and Clinical Psychology 60(5):783-792.
Coie, J., R. Terry, K. Lenox, and J. Lochman
    1995   Childhood peer rejection and aggression as predictors of stable patterns of adoles-
            cent disorder. *Development and Psychopathology* 7(4):697-713.
Coiro, M.J., N. Zill, and B. Bloom
    1994   Health of Our Nation's Children. *Vital Health and Statistics Series*, 10(191).
            Hyattsville, MD: U.S. Department of Health and Human Services, Public Health
            Service.
Cole, M., and J.S. Bruner
    1971   Cultural differences and inferences about psychological processes. *American Psy-
            chologist* 26:867-876.
Cole, P.M., M.K. Michel, and L.O. Teti
    1994   The development of emotion regulation and dysregulation: A clinical perspective.
            Monographs of the Society for Research in Child Development (Serial No. 240)
            59:73-102.
Coleman, A.
    1985   *Utopia on Trial*. London, UK: H. Shipman.

Coley, R.L., and P.L. Chase-Lansdale
  1999   Stability and change in paternal involvement among urban African American fathers. *Journal of Family Psychology* 13(3):1-20.
Collins, W.A., and B. Laursen
  1999   *Minnesota Symposia on Child Psychology: Relationships As Developmental Contexts* 30. Mahwah, NJ: Erlbaum.
Collins, W.A., E.E. Maccoby, L. Steinberg, E.M. Hetherington, and M.H. Bornstein
  2000   Contemporary research on parenting: The case for nature *and* nurture. *American Psychologist* 55(2):218.
Colten, M.E.
  1980   A comparison of heroin addicted and non-addicted mothers: Their attitudes, beliefs and parenting experiences. *Services Research Report: Heroin-Addicted Parents and Their Children.* National Institute on Drug Abuse, U.S. Department of Health and Human Services (Pub. No. 81-1028). Washington, DC: U.S. Government Printing Office.
Commission on Family and Medical Leave
  1996   *A Workable Balance: Report to Congress on Family and Medical Leave Policies.* Washington, DC: U.S. Department of Labor, Women's Bureau.
Conger, R.D., and G.H. Elder Jr.
  1994   *Families in Troubled Times: Adapting to Change in Rural America.* Hawthorne, NY: Aldine de Gruyter.
Conger, R.D., K.J. Conger, G.H. Elder Jr., F.O. Lorenz, R.L. Simons, and L.B. Whitbeck
  1992   A family process model of economic hardship and adjustment of early adolescent boys. *Child Development* 63:526-541.
Conger, R.D., X. Ge, G.H. Elder Jr., F.O. Lorenz, and R.L. Simons
  1994   Economic stress, coercive family process and developmental problems of adolescents. *Child Development* 65(2):541-561.
Connor, P.D., and A.P. Streissguth
  1996   Effects of prenatal exposure to alcohol across the life span. *Alcohol Health and Research World* 20(3):170-174.
Consumer Product Safety Commission
  1999   *Safety Hazards in Child Care Settings.* Washington, DC: U.S. Consumer Product Safety Commission.
Cook, T.D.
  1990   *The Generalization of Causal Connections: Multiple Theories in Search of Clear Practice. Keynote Address.* Research Methodology: Strengthening Causal Interpretations of Non-Experimental Data. Conference Proceedings. Washington, DC: U.S. Department of Health and Human Services.
  1993   A quasi-sampling theory of the generalization of causal relationships. *New Directions for Program Evaluation* 57:39-81.
Cook, T.D., and D.T. Campbell, eds.
  1979   *Quasi-Experimentation: Design and Analysis Issues for Field Settings.* Boston, MA: Houghton Mifflin.
Cook, T.D., J.-R. Kim, W.-S. Chan, and R. Settersten
  1998   How do neighborhoods matter? In *Managing to Make It: Urban Families in High Risk Neighborhoods.* F.F. Furstenberg Jr., T.D. Cook, J. Eccles, G.H. Elder Jr., and A.J. Sameroff, eds. Chicago, IL: University of Chicago Press.
Cooke, B., C.D. Hegstrom, L.S. Villeneuve, and S.M. Breedlove
  1998   Sexual differentiation of the vertebrate brain: Principles and mechanisms. *Frontiers in Neuroendocrinology* 19(4):323-362.

Cooksey, E.C.
    1997   Consequences of young mothers' marital histories for children's cognitive develop-
            ment. *Journal of Marriage and the Family* 59(2):245-261.
Coons, S., and C. Guilleminault
    1982   Development of sleep-wake patterns and non-rapid eye movement sleep stages dur-
            ing the first 6 months of life in normal infants. *Pediatrics* 69:793-798.
Cooper, H., and L.V. Hedges, eds.
    1994   *The Handbook of Research Synthesis.* New York: Russell Sage Foundation.
Coplan, J.D., L.A. Rosenblum, and J.M. Gorman
    1995   Primate models of anxiety: Longitudinal perspectives. *Pediatric Clinics of North
            America* 18:727-743.
Coplan, J.D., M.W. Andrews, L.A. Rosenblum, M.J. Owens, S. Friedman, J.M. Gorman, and
C.B. Nemeroff
    1996   Persistent elevations of cerebrospinal fluid concentrations of corticotropin-releas-
            ing factor in adult nonhuman primates exposed to early-life stressors: Implications
            for the pathophysiology of mood and anxiety disorders. *Proceedings of the Na-
            tional Academy of Sciences* 93(4):1619-1623.
Coplan, R.J., K.H. Rubin, N.A. Fox, and S.D. Calkins
    1994   Being alone, playing alone, and acting alone: Distinguishing among reticence and
            passive- and active-solitude in young children. *Child Development* 65:129-138.
Corsaro, W.A. and P.J. Miller
    1992   *New Directions for Child Development: Interpretive Approaches to Children's So-
            cialization,* Issue 58. San Francisco, CA: Jossey-Bass.
Cost, Quality, and Outcomes Study Team
    1995   *Cost, Quality, and Child Outcomes in Child Care Centers, Public Report,* Second
            Edition. Denver, CO: Economics Department, University of Colorado at Denver.
Coulton, C.C.
    1996   Effects of neighborhoods in large families on families and children: Implications for
            services. Pp. 87-120 in *Children and Their Families in Big Cities: Strategies for
            Service Reform.* A.J. Kahn and S.B. Kamerman, eds. New York: Cross-National
            Studies Program, Columbia University School of Social Work.
Cowan, C.P., and P.A. Cowan
    1992   *When Partners Become Parents.* New York: Basic Books.
Cowan, C.P., P.A. Cowan, G. Heming, and N.B. Miller
    1991   Becoming a family: Marriage, parenting, and child development. Pp. 79-109 in
            Family Transitions. P.A. Cowan and E.M. Hetherington, eds. Hillsdale, NJ:
            Erlbaum.
Cowan, P.A., and C.P. Cowan
    2000   What intervention design reveals about how parents affect their children's aca-
            demic achievement and behavior problems. In J.G. Borkowski, S. Ramey, and M.
            Bristol-Power, Eds., *Parenting and the Child's World: Influences on Intellectual,
            Academic, and Social-Emotional Development.* Mahwah, NJ: Erlbaum.
Cowan, P.A., D.R. Powell, and C.P. Cowan
    1998   Parenting interventions: A family systems perspective. Pp. 3-72 in *Handbook of
            Child Psychology,* Volume 4: Child Psychology in Practice, Fifth Edition. W.
            Damon, I.E. Sigel, and K.A. Renninger, eds. New York: John Wiley & Sons, Inc.
Cowen, E.L., A. Pedersen, H. Babigian, L.D. Izzo, and M.A. Trost
    1973   Long-term follow-up of early detected vulnerable children. *Journal of Consulting
            and Clinical Psychology* 41:438-446.
Cragg, B.G.
    1975   The development of synapses in the visual system of the cat. *Journal of Compara-
            tive Neurology* 160:147-166.

Craig, H.K., and J.A. Washington
1993   Access behaviors of children with specific language impairment. *Journal of Speech and Hearing Research* 36:322-337.
Crick, N.R., and K.A. Dodge
1994   A review and reformulation of social information-processing mechanisms in children's social adjustment. *Psychological Bulletin* 115:74-101.
Crittenden, P.M.
1983   The effect of mandatory protective daycare on mutual attachment in maltreating mother-infant dyads. *Child Abuse and Neglect* 7:297-300.
1988   Relationships at risk. Pp. 136-174 in *Clinical Implications of Attachment*. J. Belsky and T. Nezworski, eds. Hillsdale, NJ: Erlbaum.
Crnic, K.A., M.T. Greenberg, A.S. Ragozin, N.M. Robinson, and R.B. Basham
1983   Social interaction and developmental competence of preterm and full-term infants during the first year of life. *Child Development* 54:1199-1210.
Crockenberg, S.
1981   Infant irritability, mother responsiveness, and social support influences on the security of infant-mother attachment. *Child Development* 52:857-865.
1987   Support for adolescent mothers during the postnatal period: Theory and practice. Pp. 3-24 in *Research on Support for Parents and Infants in the Postnatal Period*. C.F.Z. Boukydis, ed. Norwood, NJ: Ablex Publishing Corp.
Crockenberg, S., and C. Litman
1990   Autonomy as competence in 2-year olds: Maternal correlates of child defiance, compliance, and self-assertion. *Developmental Psychology* 26:961-971.
Cross, T.L., B.J. Bazron, K.W. Dennis, and M.R. Isaacs
1989   *Towards a Culturally Competent System of Care (Monograph)*. Washington, DC: CASSP Technical Assistance Center.
Cummings, E.M.
1987   Coping with background anger in early childhood. *Child Development* 58:976-984.
Cummings, E.M., and P.T. Davies
1994a   *Children and Marital Conflict: The Impact of Family Dispute and Resolution*. New York: Guilford Press.
1994b   Maternal depression and child development. *Journal of Child Psychology and Psychiatry* 35(1):73-112.
1999   Depressed parents and family functioning: Interpersonal effects and children's functioning and development. Pp. 299-327 in *Advances in Interpersonal Approaches: The Interactional Nature of Depression*. T. Joiner and J.C. Coyne, eds. Washington, DC: American Psychological Association.
Cummings, E.M., and A.W. O'Reilly
1997   Fathers in family context: Effects of marital quality on child adjustment. Pp. 49-65 in *The Role of the Father in Child Development*, Third Edition. M.E. Lamb, ed. New York: Wiley.
Cummings, E.M., R.J. Iannotti, and C. Zahn-Waxler
1989   Aggression between peers in early childhood: Individual continuity and developmental change. *Child Development* 60(4):887-895.
Cunningham, A., and K. Stanovich
1997   Early reading acquisition and its relation to reading experience and ability 10 years later. *Developmental Psychology* 33:934-945.
Currie, J.
2000   Early Childhood Intervention Programs: What Do We Know? Working Paper from the Children's Roundtable. The Brookings Institution, Washington, D.C.

Currie, J., and D. Thomas
  1995   Does Head Start make a difference? *The American Economic Review* 85:341-364.
Curtiss, S.
  1977   *Genie: A Psycholinguistic Study of a Modern-Day "Wild Child"*. New York: Academy Press.
Dale, P.S., E. Simonoff, D.V.M. Bishop, T.C. Eley, B. Oliver, T.S. Price, S. Purcell, J. Stevenson, and R. Plomin
  1998   Genetic influence on language delay in two-year-old children. *Nature Neuroscience* 1(4):324-328.
Damon, W., ed.
  1998   *Handbook of Child Psychology*, 5th Edition. New York: John Wiley & Sons, Inc.
Danziger, S., M. Corcoran, S. Danziger, C. Heflin, A. Kalil, J. Levine, D. Rosen, K. Seefeldt, K. Siefert, and R. Tolman
  in   *Barriers to the Employment of Welfare Recipients*. In *Prosperity for All? The*
  press *Economic Boom and African Americans*. R. Cherry and W.M. Rodgers, III, eds. New York: Russell Sage Foundation.
Darling, N., and L. Steinberg
  1993   Parenting style as context: An integrative model. *Psychological Bulletin* 113:487-496.
Davidson, R.J.
  1992   Emotion and affective style: Hemispheric substrates. *Psychological Science* 3:39-43.
  1994   Temperament, affective style, and frontal lobe assymetry. Pp. 518-536 in *Human Behavior and the Developing Brain*. G. Dawson and K. Fischer, eds. New York: Guilford.
Davidson, R.J., P. Ekman, C. Saron, J. Senulis, and W.V. Friesen
  1990   Emotional expression and brain physiology I: Approach/withdrawal and cerebral asymmetry. *Journal of Personality and Social Psychology* 58:330-341.
Davies, P.T., and E.M. Cummings
  1994   Marital conflict and child adjustment: An emotional security hypothesis. *Psychological Bulletin* 116(3):387-411.
Dawson, D.A.
  1991   Family Structure and Children's Health: United States, 1988. *Vital Health and Statistics Series*, 10(178). Hyattsville, MD: U.S. Department of Health and Human Services, Public Health Service.
Dawson, G., and S. Ashman
  in   On the origins of a vulnerability to depression: The influence of the early social
  press environment on the development of psychobiological systems related to risk for affective disorder. *The Effects of Adversity on Neurobehavioral Development: Minnesota Symposia on Child Psychology*, Volume 31. C.A. Nelson, ed. Hillsdale, NJ: Lawrence Erlbaum Associates, Publishers.
Dawson, G., H. Panagiotides, L. Grofer Klinger, and D. Hill
  1992   The role of frontal lobe functioning in the development of infant self-regulatory behavior. *Brain and Cognition* 20:152-175.
Dawson, G., D. Hessl, and K. Frey
  1994   Social influences on early developing biological and behavioral systems related to risk for affective disorder. *Development and Psychopathology* 6:759-779.
De Bellis, M.D., and F. Putnam
  1994   The psychobiology of childhood maltreatment. Pp. 663-678 in *Child and Adolescent Psychiatric Clinics of North America: Child Abuse 3*. S. Kaplan and D. Pelcovitz, eds. Philadelphia, PA: W.B. Saunders.

De Bellis, M.D., M.S. Keshavan, D.B. Clark, B.J. Caseey, J.B. Giedd, A.M. Boring, K. Frustaci, and N.D. Ryan
1999a Developmental traumatology, Part 2: Brain development. *Biological Psychiatry* 45:1271-1284.

De Bellis, M.D., A.S. Baum, B. Birmaher, M.S. Keshavan, C.H. Eccard, A.M. Boring, F.J. Jenkins, and N.D. Ryan
1999b Developmental traumatology, Part 1: Biological stress systems. *Biological Psychiatry* 9:1259-1270.

de Haan, M., and C.A. Nelson
1997 Recognition of the mother's face by 6-month-old infants: A neurobehavioral study. *Child Development* 68:187-210.
1999 Brain activity differentiates face and object processing in 6-month-old infants. *Developmental Psychology* 35:1113-1121.

de Haan, M., P.J. Bauer, M.K. Georgieff, and C.A. Nelson
2000 Explicit memory in low-risk infants aged 19 months born between 27 and 42 weeks of gestation. *Developmental Medicine and Child Neurology* 42(5):304-312.

de Houwer, A.
1995 Bilingual language acquisition. Pp. 219-250 in *The Handbook of Child Language*. P. Fletcher and B. MacWhinney, eds. Oxford, UK: Blackwell Publishers.

de Regnier, R.A., C.A. Nelson, K. Thomas, S. Wewerka, and M.K. Georgieff
in press Neurophysiologic evaluation of auditory recognition memory in healthy newborn infants and infants of diabetic mothers. *Journal of Pediatrics*.

De Temple, J.M., and C.E. Snow
1992 Styles of parent-child book reading as related to mothers' views of literacy and children's literacy outcomes. Paper presented at biennial Conference on Human Development, Atlanta, GA, April 1992.

de Ungria, M., R. Rao, J.D. Wobken, M. Luciana, C.A. Nelson, and M.K. Georgieff
2000 Perinatal iron deficiency decreases cytochrome c oxidase (Cy + Ox) activity in selected regions of neonatal rat brain. *Pediatric Research* 48:169-176.

De Wolff, M.S., and M.H. van IJzendoorn
1997 Sensitivity and attachment: A meta-analysis on parental antecedents of infant attachment. *Child Development* 68:571-591.

Deater-Deckard, K., R. Pinkerton, and S. Scarr
1996 Child care quality and children's behavioral adjustment: A four-year longitudinal study. *Journal of Child Psychology and Psychiatry* 37:937-948.

Decarie, T.G.
1969 A study of the mental and emotional development of the thalidomide child. Pp. 167-187 in *Determinants of Infant Behavior*, Volume 4. B.M. Foss, ed. London, UK: Methuen.

Deci, E., and R. Ryan
1985 *Intrinsic Motication and Self-Determination in Human Behavior*. New York: Plenum.

deMaeyer, E., and M. Adiels-Tegman
1985 The prevalence of anaemia in the world. *World Health Statistics Quarterly* 38:302-316.

DeMulder, E.K., and M. Radke-Yarrow
1991 Attachment with affectively ill and well mothers: Concurrent behavioral correlates. *Development and Psychopathology* 3:227-242.

Denckla, M.B.
1989 Executive function: The overlap zone between Attention Deficit Hyperactivity Disorder and learning disabilities. *International Pediatrics* 4:155-160.

1996   A theory and model of executive function: A neuropsychological perspective. Pp. 263-278 in *Attention, Memory, and Executive Function*. G.R. Lyon and N. Krasnegor, eds. Baltimore, MD: Paul H. Brookes Publishing Co., Inc.

Denenberg, V.H.
1999   Commentary: Is maternal stimulation the mediator of the handling effects in infancy? *Developmental Psychobiology* 34(1):1-3.

Denham, S.A.
1998   *Emotional Development in Young Children.* New York: The Guilford Press.

Denham, S.A., D. Zoller, and E.A. Couchoud
1994   Socialization of preschoolers' emotion understanding. *Developmental Psychology* 30:928-936.

Denham, S.A., J. Mitchell-Copeland, K. Strandberg, S. Auerbach, and K. Blair
1997   Parental contributions to preschoolers' emotional competence: Direct and indirect effects. *Motivation and Emotion* 27:65-86.

Dennis, W.
1973   *Children of the Creche.* New York: Appleton-Century-Crofts.

Desai, S., P. Chase-Lansdale, and R.T. Michael
1989   Mother or market? Effects of maternal employment on the intellectual ability of 4-year-old children. *Demography* 26:545-561.

Dexter, E.R., S.E. LeVine, and P.M. Velasco
1998   Maternal schooling and health-related language and literacy skills in rural Mexico. *Comparative Education Review* 42(2):139-162.

Diamond, A.
1988   Differences between adult and infant cognition: Is the crucial variable presence or absence of language? Pp. 337-370 in *Thought Without Language*. L. Weiskrantz, ed. New York: Oxford University Press.
1990   The development and neural bases of memory functions, as indexed by the A-not-B and delayed response tasks, in human infants and infant monkeys. *Annals of the New York Academy of Sciences* 608:267-317.
1991   Frontal lobe involvement in cognitive changes during the first year of life. Pp. 127-180 in *Brain Maturation and Cognitive Development: Comparative and Cross-Cultural Perspectives*. K.R. Gibson and A.C. Petersen, eds. New York: Aldine De Gruyter.
1996   Evidence for the importance of dopamine for prefrontal cortex functions early in life. *Philosophical Transactions of the Royal Society (London)* 351:1483-1494.

Diamond, A., and B. Doar
1989   The performance of human infants on a measure of frontal cortex function, the delayed response task. *Developmental Psychobiology* 22:271-294.

Diamond, A., and P.S. Goldman-Rakic
1989   Comparison of human infants and rhesus monkeys on Piaget's A-not-B task: Evidence for dependence on dorsolateral prefrontal cortex. *Experimental Brain Research* 74:24-40.

Diamond, A., and C. Taylor
1996   Development of an aspect of executive control: Development of the abilities to remember what I said and to "do as I say, not as I do." *Developmental Psychobiology* 29:315-334.

Diamond, A., S. Zola-Morgan, and L.R. Squire
1989   Successful performance by monkeys with lesions of the hippocampal formation on A-not-B and object retrieval, two tasks that mark developmental changes in human infants. *Behavioral Neuroscience* 103:526-537.

Diamond, A., J.F. Werker, and C. Lalonde
  1994 Toward understanding commonalities in the development of object search, detour navigation, categorization, and speech perception. Pp. 380-426 in *Human Behavior and the Developing Brain*. G. Dawson and K.W. Fischer, eds. New York: Guilford.
Dickerson, J.W.T.
  1981 Nutrition, brain growth and development. Pp. 110-130 in *Maturation and Development: Biological and Psychological Perspectives*. K.J. Connolly and H.F.R. Prechtl, eds. Suffolk, England: The Lavenham Press.
Dickstein, S., R. Seifer, L.C. Hayden, M. Schiller, A.J. Sameroff, G. Keitner, I. Miller, S. Rasmussen, M. Matzko, and K.D. Magee
  1998a Levels of family assessment: II. Impact of maternal psychopathology on family functioning. *Journal of Family Psychology* 12(1):23-40.
Dickstein, S., R. Seifer, K.D. Magee, E. Mirsky, and M.M. Lynch
  1998b Timing of maternal depression, family functioning, and infant development: A prospective view. Paper presented at the Biennial Meeting of the Marce Society, June 1998, Iowa City, Iowa.
Diener, C.I., and C.S. Dweck
  1978 An analysis of learned helplessness: Continuous changes in performance, strategy, and achievement cognitions following failure. *Journal of Personality and Social Psychology* 36:451-462.
  1980 An analysis of learned helplessness: II. The processing of success. *Journal of Personality and Social Psychology* 39:940-952.
DiLalla, L.F., and M.W. Watson
  1988 Differentiation of fantasy and reality: Preschoolers' reactions to disruptions in their play. *Developmental Psychology* 24:286-291.
Dishion, T.J., and R.J. McMahon
  1998 Parental monitoring and the prevention of child and adolescent problem behavior: A conceptual and empirical formulation. *Clinical Child and Family Psychology Review* 1(1):61-75.
Dishion, T.J., G.R. Patterson, and K.A. Kavanagh
  1992 An experimental test of the coercion model: Linking theory, measurement and intervention. Pp. 253-282 in *Preventing Antisocial Behavior: Intervention From Birth Through Adolescence*. J. McCord and R.E. Tremblay, eds. New York: The Guilford Press.
Dobbing, J., and J.L. Smart
  1974 Vulnerability of developing brain and behavior. *British Medical Bulletin* 30:164-168.
Dodge, K.A.
  1990 Nature versus nurture in child conduct disorder: It is time to ask a different question. *Developmental Psychology* 26(5):698-701.
Dodge, K.A., and C.M. Frame
  1982 Social cognitive biases and deficits in aggressive boys. *Child Development* 53:620-635.
Dodge, K.A., G.S. Pettit, C.L. McClaskey, and M.M. Brown
  1986 Social competence in children. *Monographs of the Society for Research in Child Development* 51(2):1-85.
Dodge, K.A., J.E. Bates, and G.S. Pettit
  1990 Mechanisms in the cycle of violence. *Science* 250:1678-1683.
Dollaghan, C., and T. Campbell
  1998 Nonword repetition and child language impairment. *Journal of Speech, Language, and Hearing Research* 41:1136-1146.

Dommergues, M.P., B. Archambeaud, Y. Ducot, Y. Gerval, C. Hiard, C. Rossignol, and G. Tchernia
    1989   Iron deficiency and psychomotor development scores: A longitudinal study be-
            tween ages 10 months and 4 years. *Archives Francaises de Pediatrie* 46:487-490.
Donovan, W.L., and L.A. Leavitt
    1978   Early cognitive development and its relation to maternal physiologic and behav-
            ioral responsiveness. *Child Development* 49:1251-1254.
Dougherty, T.M., and M.M. Haith
    1997   Infant expectations and reaction time as predictors of childhood speed of process-
            ing and IQ. *Developmental Psychology* 33(1):146-155.
Douglas, V.I.
    1980   Higher mental processes in hyperactive children: Implications for training. Pp. 65-
            91 in *Treatment of Hyperactive and Learning Disordered Children: Current Re-
            search*. R.M. Knights and D.J. Bakker, eds. Baltimore, MD: University Park
            Press.
Downey, G., and J.C. Coyne
    1990   Children of depressed parents: An integrative review. *Psychological Bulletin*
            108(1):50-76.
Dozier, M., K.E. Albus, E. Higley, and A.B. Nutter
    in   Intervention services for foster and adoptive parents: Targeting three critical needs.
    press(a) *Infant Mental Health Journal*.
Dozier, M., K.E. Albus, K.C. Stovall, and B.C. Bates
    in   Foster infants' attachment quality: The role of foster mother state of mind. *Child
    press(b) Development*.
Duimstra, D., C. Johnson, C. Kutsch, B. Wang, M. Zentner, S. Kellerman, and T. Welty
    1993   A fetal alcohol syndrome surveillance pilot project in American Indian communi-
            ties in the Northern Plains. *Public Health Reports* 108:225-229.
Duncan, G.J.
    1988   The volatility of family income over the life course. Pp. 317-358 in *Life-Span
            Development and Behavior*. P.B. Baltes, D. Featherman, and R.M. Lerner, eds.
            Hillsdale, NJ: Lawrence Erlbaum Associates, Publishers.
Duncan, G.J., and J. Brooks-Gunn, eds.
    1997   *Consequences of Growing Up Poor*. New York: Russell Sage Foundation.
Duncan, G.J., and S. Raudenbush
    1999   *Neighborhoods and Adolescent Development: How Can We Determine the Links?*
            Evanston, IL: Joint Center for Poverty Research.
    in   Getting context right in studies of child development. In *The Well-Being of Chil-
    press   dren and Families: Research and Data Needs*. A. Thornton, ed. Ann Arbor, MI:
            University of Michigan Press.
Duncan, G.J., and W. Rodgers
    1998   Longitudinal aspects of childhood poverty. *Journal of Marriage and the Family*
            50:1007-1021.
Duncan, G.J., J. Brooks-Gunn, and P.K. Klebanov
    1994   Economic deprivation and early childhood development. *Child Development*
            65(2):296-318.
Duncan, G.J., R. Dunifon, M. Ward Doran, and W.J. Yeung
    1998a   How different ARE welfare and working families? And do those differences matter
            for children's achievement? Prepared for the Joint Center for Poverty Research
            conference "Family Process and Child Development in Low-Income Families", May
            7-8, 1998, Chicago, IL.

Duncan, G.J., W.J. Yeung, J. Brooks-Gunn, and J. Smith
  1998b How much does childhood poverty affect the life chances of children? *American Sociological Review* 63(3):406-423.
Duncan, G.J., K. Magnuson, and J. Ludwig
  2000 The endogeneity problem in developmental studies. Working paper. Institute for Policy Research, Northwestern University.
Dunn, J.
  1987 The beginnings of moral understanding: Development in the second year. Pp. 91-112 in *The Emergence of Mortality in Young Children*. J. Kagan and S. Lamb, eds. Chicago, IL: University of Chicago Press.
  1988 *The Beginnings of Social Understanding*. Cambridge, MA: Harvard University Press.
  1993 *Young Children's Close Relationships*. Newbury Park, CA: Sage.
  1994 Changing minds and changing relationships. Pp. 297-310 in *Children's Early Understanding of Mind*. C. Lewis and P. Mitchell, eds. Hove, UK: Erlbaum.
Dunn, J., and C. Kendrick
  1982 *Siblings: Love, Envy, and Understanding*. Cambridge, MA: Harvard University Press.
Dunn, J., and P. Munn
  1987 Development of justification in disputes with mother and sibling. *Developmental Psychology* 23:791-798.
Dunn, J., J. Brown, and L. Beardsall
  1991 Family talk about feeling states and children's later understanding of others' emotions. *Developmental Psychology* 27:448-455.
Dunn, J., J.R. Brown, and M. Maguire
  1995 The development of children's moral sensibility: Individual differences and emotion understanding. *Developmental Psychology* 31:649-659.
Dunn, L.
  1993 Proximal and distal features of the day care quality and children's development. *Early Childhood Research Quarterly* 8:167-192.
Dunst, C.J.
  1985 Rethinking early intervention. *Analysis and Intervention in Developmental Disabilities* 5(1-2):165-201.
Duvanel, C.B., C.L. Fawer, J. Cotting, P. Hohlfeld, and J.M. Matthieu
  1999 Long-term effects of neonatal hypoglycemia on brain growth and psychomotor development in small-for-gestational-age preterm infants [see comments]. *The Journal of Pediatrics* 134:492-498.
Duyme, M., A.-C. Dumaret, and S. Tomkiewicz
  1999 How can we boost IQs of "dull children"?: A late adoption study. *Proceedings of the National Academy of Sciences* 96(15):8790-8794.
Dweck, C.S.
  1991 Self-theories and goals: Their role in motivation, personality, and development. Pp. 199-235 in *Nebraska Symposium on Motivation, 1990*, Volume 36. R. Dienstbier, ed. Lincoln, NE: University of Nebraska Press.
Earls, F., and S. Buka
  2000 Measurement of community characteristics. Pp. 309-326 in *Handbook of Early Childhood Intervention*. S.J. Meisels and J.P. Shonkoff, eds. Massachusetts: Cambridge University Press.
East, P.L.
  1991 The parent-child relationships of withdrawn, aggressive, and sociable children: Child and parent perspectives. *Merrill-Palmer Quarterly* 37:425-444.

Easterbrooks, M.A., and W.A. Goldberg
   1990   Security of toddler-parent attachment: Relation to children's sociopersonality func-
           tioning during kindergarten. Pp. 221-244 in *Attachment in the Preschool Years*.
           M.T. Greenberg, D. Cicchetti, and E.M. Cummings, eds. Chicago, IL: University
           of Chicago Press.
Ebrahim, S.H., E.T. Luman, R.L. Floyd, C.C. Murphy, E.M. Bennett, and C.A. Boyle
   1998   Alcohol consumption by pregnant women in the United States during 1988-1995.
           Obstetrics and Gynecology 92:187-192.
Eckerman, C.O.
   1979   The human infant in social interaction. Pp. 163-178 in *The Analysis of Social
           Interactions: Methods, Issues, and Illustrations*. R.B. Cairns, ed. Hillsdale, NJ:
           Erlbaum.
Edin, K., and L. Lein
   1997   *Making Ends Meet: How Single Mothers Survive Welfare and Low Wage Work*.
           New York: Russell Sage Foundation.
Egeland, B., and M. Hiester
   1995   The long-term consequences of infant day-care and mother-infant attachment.
           Child Development 66:474-485.
Egeland, B., M. Kalkoske, N. Gottesman, and M.F. Erickson
   1990   Preschool behavior problems: Stability and factors accounting for change. *Journal
           of Child Psychology and Psychiatry and Allied Disciplines* 31(6):891-909.
Egeland, B., E. Carlson, and L.A. Sroufe
   1993   Resilience as process. *Development and Psychopathology* 5:517-528.
Egeland, B., N.S. Weinfield, M. Bosquet, and V.K. Cheng
   2000   Remembering, repeating, and working through lessons from attachment-based in-
           terventions. Pp. 35-90 in *WAIMH Handbook of Infant Mental Health*, Volume
           Four: Infant mental health in groups at high risk. J.D. Osofsky and H.E. Fitzgerald,
           eds. New York: John Wiley & Sons, Inc.
Ehrle, J., K. Tout, and G. Adams
   2000   Who's caring for our youngest children? Child care patterns for infants and tod-
           dlers. *New Federalism: National Survey of America's Families Series*. Washington,
           DC: The Urban Institute.
Eisenberg, A.R.
   1986   Teasing: Verbal play in two Mexicano homes. Pp. 182-198 in *Language Socializa-
           tion Across Cultures*. B.B. Schieffelin and E. Ochs, eds. New York: Cambridge
           University Press.
Eisenberg, N., and B. Murphy
   1995   Parenting and children's moral development. Pp. 227-257 in *Handbook of
           Parenting*, Volume 4: Applied and practical parenting. M.H. Bornstein, ed.
           Mahwah, NJ: Erlbaum.
Eisenstadt, T.H., S. Eyberg, C.B. McNeil, K. Newcomb, and B. Funderburk
   1993   Parent-child interaction therapy with behavior problem children: Relative effective-
           ness of two stages and overall treatment outcome. *Journal of Clinical Child Psy-
           chology* 22(1):42-51.
Elbert, T., C. Pantev, C. Weinbruch, B. Rockstroh, and E. Taub
   1995   Increased cortical representation of the fingers of the left hand in string players.
           Science 270:305-307.
Elder G.H., Jr.
   1979   Historical change in life patterns and personality. Pp. 117-159 in *Life-Span Devel-
           opment and Behavior*, Volume 2. P.B. Baltes and O.G. Brim Jr., eds. New York:
           Academic Press.

1991   Family transitions, cycles, and social change. Pp. 31-58 in *Family Transitions: Advances in Family Research*, Volume 2. P.A. Cowan and E.M. Hetherington, eds. Hillsdale, NJ: Erlbaum.

Elder, G.H., Jr., and R.D. Conger
2000   *Children of the Land.* Chicago, IL: University of Chicago Press.

Elder, G.H., Jr., J.K. Liker, and C.E. Cross
1984   Parent-child behavior in the Great Depression: Life course and intergenerational influences. Pp. 109-158 in *Life-Span Development and Behavior*, Volume 6. P.B. Baltes and O.G. Brim Jr., eds. Orlando, FL: Academic Press, Inc.

Elder, G.H., Jr., T.V. Nguyen, and A. Caspi
1985   Linking family hardship to children's lives. *Child Development* 56:361-375.

Elligson, R., and J. Peters
1980   Development of EEG and daytime sleep patterns in normal full-term infants during the first three months of life. *Electroencephalography and Clinical Neurophysiology* 49:112-124.

Elliot, M.R., E.L. Pederson, and S. Mogan
1997   Early infant crying: Child and family followup at 3 years. *Canadian Journal of Nursing Research* 29(2):47-67.

Ellis, S., and M. Gauvain
1992   Social and cultural influences on children's collaborative interactions. Pp. 155-180 in *Children's Development Within Social Context*. L.T. Winegar and J. Valsiner, eds. Hillsdale, NJ: Lawrence Erlbaum.

Elman, J.L., E. Bates, M.H. Johnson, A. Karmiloff-Smith, D. Parisi, and K. Plunkett
1996   *Rethinking Innateness: A Connectionist Perspective on Development.* Cambridge, MA: MIT Press.

Emde, R.N.
1980   Emotional availability: A reciprocal reward system for infants and parents with implications for prevention of psychosocial disorders. Pp. 87-115 in *Parent-Infant Relationships*. P.M. Taylor, ed. Orlando, FL: Grune and Stratton.
1987   The infant's relationship experience: developmental and affective aspects. Pp. 33-51 in *Relationship Disturbances in Early Childhood*. A.J. Sameroff and R.N. Emde, eds. New York: Basic.
1990   Mobilizing fundamental modes of development—An essay on empathic availability and therapeutic action. *Journal of the American Psychoanalytic Association* 38(4):881-913.
1998   Early emotional development: New modes of thinking for research and intervention. Pp. 29-45 in *New Perspectives in Early Emotional Development*. J.G. Warhol, ed. New Brunswick, NJ: Johnson & Johnson Pediatric Institute.

Emde, R.N., and H.K. Buchsbaum
1990   "Didn't you hear my Mommy?": Autonomy *with* connectedness in moral self emergence. Pp. 35-60 in *The Self in Transition: Infancy to Childhood*. D. Cicchetti and M. Beeghly, eds. Chicago, IL: University of Chicago Press.

Emde, R.N., and M.A. Easterbrooks
1985   Assessing emotional availability in early development. Pp. 79-101 in *Early Identification of Children at Risk: An International Perspective*. W.K. Frankenburg, R.N. Emde, and J.W. Sullivan, eds. New York: Plenum.

Emde, R.N., and J. Robinson
2000   Guiding principles for a theory of early intervention: A development-psychoanalytic perspective. Pp. 160-178 in *Handbook of Early Childhood Intervention*, Second Edition. J.P. Shonkoff and S.J. Meisels, eds. New York: Cambridge University Press.

Emde, R.N., T.J. Gaensbauer, and R.J. Harmon
1976   *Emotional Expressions in Infancy: A Biobehavioral Study*. New York: International University Press.

Emde, R.N., W.F. Johnson, and M.A. Easterbrooks
1987   The do's and don'ts of early moral development: Psychoanalytic tradition and current research. Pp. 245-276 in *The Emergence of Morality in Young Children*. J. Kagan and S. Lamb, eds. Chicago, IL: University of Chicago Press.

Emde, R.N., R.D. Bingham, and R.J. Harmon
1993   Classification and the diagnostic process in infancy. Pp. 225-235 in *Handbook of Infant Mental Health*. C.H. Zeanah, ed. New York: The Guilford Press.

Emmerich, W.
1977   Structure and development of personal-social behaviors in economically disadvantaged preschool children. *Genetic Psychology Monographs* 95:191-245.

Engfer, A., S. Walper, and M. Rutter
1994   Individual characteristics as a force in development. Pp. 79-111 in *Development Through Life: A Handbook for Clinicians*. M. Rutter and D.F. Hay, eds. Oxford, UK: Blackwell Scientific.

Engle, B.T.
1985   Stress in a noun! No, a verb! No, an adjective. Pp. 3-12 in *Stress and Coping*, Volume 1. T. Field, P. McCabe, and N. Sneiderman, eds. Hillsdale, NJ: Erlbaum.

Entwisle, D.R., and N.M. Astone
1994   Some practical guidelines for measuring youth's race/ethnicity and socioeconomic status. *Child Development* 65:1521-1540.

Entwisle, D.R., and D.P. Baker
1983   Gender and young children's expectations for performance in arithmetic. *Developmental Psychology* 19:200-209.

Erikson, E.
1950   *Childhood and Society*. New York: W.W. Norton & Co., Inc.

Erikson, K.M., D.J. Pinero, J.R. Connor, and J.L. Beard
1997   Regional brain iron, ferritin and transferrin concentrations during iron deficiency and iron repletion in developing rats. *The Journal of Nutrition* 127(10):2030-2038.

Erickson, M., and B. Egeland
1996   Child neglect. Pp. 4-20 in *The APSAC Handbook on Child Maltreatment*. J. Briere and L. Berliner, eds. Thousand Oaks, CA: Sage Publications, Inc.

Erickson, M.F., L.A. Sroufe, and B. Egeland
1985   The relationship between quality of attachment and behaviour problems in preschool in a high-risk sample. *Monographs of the Society for Research in Child Development* (1/2, Serial No. 209) 50:147-166.

Eriksson, P.S., E. Perfilieva, T. Bjork-Eriksson, A.M. Alborn, C. Nordborg, D.A. Peterson, and F.H. Gage
1998   Neurogenesis in the adult human hippocampus. *Nature Medicine* 4(11):1313-1317.

Escalona, S.K.
1982   Babies at double hazard: Early development of infants at biologic and social risk. *Pediatrics* 70(5):670-676.

Eslinger, P.J.
1996   Conceptualizing, describing, and measuring components of executive function: A summary. Pp. 367-395 in *Attention, Memory, and Executive Function*. G.R. Lyon and N. Krasnegor, eds. Baltimore, MD: Paul H. Brookes Publishing Co., Inc.

Eslinger, P.J., and L.M. Grattan
1991 Perspectives on the developmental consequences of early frontal lobe damage: Introduction. *Developmental Neuropsychology* 7(3):257-260.

Fabes, R.A., N. Eisenberg, S. Jones, M. Smith, I. Guthrie, R. Poulin, S. Shepard, and J. Friedman
1999 Regulation, emotionality, and preschoolers' socially competent peer interactions. *Child Development* 70(2):432-442.

Faden, V.B., B.I. Graubard, and M. Dufour
1997 The relationship of drinking and birth outcome in a U.S. national sample of expectant mothers. *Pediatric and Perinatal Epidemiology* 11(2):167-180.

Fagan, J.F.
1984 The relationship of novelty preferences during infancy to later intelligence and later recognition memory. *Intelligence* 8(4):339-346.

Fagot, B.
1973 Influence of teacher behavior in the preschool. *Developmental Psychology* 9:198-206.

Farnham-Diggory, S., and B. Ramsey
1971 Play persistence: Some effects of interruption, social reinforcement, and defective toys. *Developmental Psychology* 4:297-298.

Farran, D.C.
1990 Effects of intervention with disadvantaged and disabled children: A decade review. Pp. 501-539 in *Handbook of Early Childhood Intervention.* J.P. Shonkoff and S.J. Meisels, eds. New York: Cambridge University Press.

2000 Another decade of intervention for children who are low income or disabled: What do we do now? Pp. 510-548 in *Handbook of Early Childhood Intervention,* Second Edition. J.P. Shonkoff and S.J. Meisels, eds. New York: Cambridge University Press.

Farran, D.C., and C.T. Ramey
1977 Infant day care and attachment behaviors toward mothers and teachers. *Child Development* 48:1112-1116.

Farver, J.A.M.
1993 Cultural differences in scaffolding pretend play: A comparison of American and Mexican mother-child and sibling-child pairs. Pp. 349-366 in *Parent-Child Play: Descriptions and Implications.* K. MacDonald, ed. New York: State University of New York.

Farver, J.A.M., and W. Branstetter
1994 Preschoolers' prosocial responses to their peers' distress. *Developmental Psychology* 30:334-341.

Farver, J.A.M., and S. Wimbarti
1995 Indonesian children's play with their mothers and older siblings. *Child Development* 66:1495-1503.

Farver, J.A.M., Y.K. Kim, and Y. Lee
1995 Cultural differences in Korean- and Anglo-American preschoolers' social interaction and play behaviors. *Child Development* 66:1088-1099.

Fay, W.H.
1988 Infantile autism. Pp. 190-202 in *Language Development in Exceptional Circumstances.* D. Bishop and K. Mogford, eds. New York: Churchill Livingstone.

Feagans, L.V., J. Fendt, and D.C. Farran
1995 The effects of day care intervention on teachers' ratings of the elementary school discourse skills in disadvantaged children. *International Journal of Behavioral Development* 18:243-261.

Federman, M., T.I. Garner, K. Short, W.B. Cutter, J. Kiely, D. Levine, D. McDough, and M. McMillen
  1996   What does it mean to be poor in America? *Monthly Labor Review* 119(5):3-17.
Fein, G.G., and K.A. Clarke-Stewart
  1973   *Day Care in Context.* New York: John Wiley and Sons.
Feinman, S., ed.
  1992   *Social Referencing and the Social Construction of Reality in Infancy.* New York: Plenum.
Feldman, H.M.
  1994   Language development after early unilateral brain injury: A replication study. Pp. 75-90 in *Constraints on Language Acquisition: Studies of Atypical Children.* H. Tager-Flusberg, ed. Hillsdale, NJ: Erlbaum Associates.
Feldman, H.M., M.S. Scher, and S.S. Kemp
  1990   Neurodevelopmental outcome of children with evidence of periventricular leukomalacia on late MRI. *Pediatric Neurology* 6:296-302.
Feldman, R., C.W. Greenbaum, and N. Yirmiya
  1999   Mother-infant affect synchrony as an antecedent of the emergence of self-control. *Developmental Psychology* 35:223-231.
Fernald, A., and H. Morikawa
  1993   Common themes and cultural variation in Japanese and American mothers' speech to infants. *Child Development* 64:637-656.
Fernald, A., T. Taeschner, J. Dunn, M. Papoušek, and B. deBoysson-Bardies
  1989   A cross-language study of prosodic modifications in mothers' and fathers' speech to preverbal infants. *Journal of Child Language* 16(3):477-501.
Fey, M.E., H.W. Catts, and L.S. Larrivee
  1995   Preparing preschoolers for the academic and social challenges of school. Pp. 3-37 in *Language Intervention: Preschool Through the Elementary Years.* D.H. Abbott, M.E. Fey, J. Windsor, and S.F. Warren, eds. Baltimore, MD: Paul H. Brookes Publishing Co., Inc.
Field, T.
  1979   Interaction patterns of high-risk and normal infants. In *Infants Born At Risk.* T. Field, A. Sostek, S. Goldberg, and H.H. Shuman, eds. New York: Spectrum Publications.
  1991   Quality infant day care and grade school behavior and performance. *Child Development* 62:863-870.
  1995   Psychologically depressed parents. Pp. 85-99 in *Handbook of Parenting,* Volume 4: Applied and Practical Parenting. M.H. Bornstein, ed. Mahwah, NJ: Lawrence Erlbaum Associates, Publishers.
Field, T., S. Widmayer, R. Greenberg, and S. Stoller
  1982   Effects of parent training on teenage mothers and their infants. *Pediatrics* 69:703-707.
Field, T., S.M. Schanberg, F. Scafidi, C.R. Bauer, N. Vega-Lahr, R. Garcia, J. Nystrom, and C.M. Kuhn
  1986   Tactile/kinesthetic stimulation effects on preterm neonates. *Pediatrics* 77:654-658.
Fiese, B.H., A.J. Sameroff, H.D. Grotevant, F.S. Wamboldt, S. Dickstein, D. Fravel, K. Marjinsky, D. Gorall, J. Piper, M. St. Andre, R. Seifer, and M. Schiller
  1999   The stories that families tell: Narrative coherence, narrative interaction, and relationship beliefs. *Monographs of the Society for Research in Child Developmen* 64(2):1-162.

Finkelstein, J.W.
    1971   Behavioral state, sleep stage and growth hormone levels in human infants. *Journal of Clinical Endocrinology* 32:368-371.
Finnie, V., and A. Russell
    1988   Preschool children's social status and their mothers' behavior and knowledge in the supervisory role. *Developmental Psychology* 24:789-801.
Fischer, J., and B. Eheart
    1991   Family day care: A theoretical basis for improving quality. *Early Childhood Research Quarterly* 6:549-563.
Fisher, L., E.W. Ames, K. Chisholm, and L. Savoie
    1997   Problems reported by parents of Romanian orphans adopted to British Columbia. *International Journal of Behavioral Development* 20:67-82.
Fisher, R.
    1918   The causes of human variability. *Eugenics Review* 10:213-220.
Flavell, J.H., X.-D. Zhang, and H. Zou
    1983   A comparison between the development of the appearance-reality distinction in the People's Republic of China and the United States. *Cognitive Psychology* 15(4):459-466.
Flavell, J.H., E.R. Flavell, F.L. Green, and L.J. Moses
    1990   Young children's understanding of fact beliefs versus value beliefs. *Child Development* 61(4):915-928.
Flavell, J.J., and P.H. Miller
    1998   Social cognition. Pp. 851-898 in *Handbook of Child Psychology*, Volume 2: Cognition, perception, and language, Fifth Edition. W. Damon, ed. New York: Wiley.
Forbes, J.A.
    1969   Rubella: Historical aspects. *American Journal of Diseases in Children* 118:5-11.
Forehand, R., K.C. Wells, R.J. McMahon, D.L. Griest, and T. Rogers
    1982   Teaching parents to modify child behavior problems: An examination of some follow-up data. *Journal of Pediatric Psychology* 6:313-322.
Forgatch, M.S.
    1991   The clinical science vortex: A developing theory of antisocial behavior. Pp. 291-315 in *The Development and Treatment of Childhood Aggression*. D.J. Pepler and K.H. Rubin, eds. Hillsdale, NJ: Erlbaum.
Forgatch, M.S., and D.S. DeGarmo
    1999   Parenting through change: An effective prevention program for single mothers. *Journal of Consulting and Clinical Psychology* 67:711-724.
Fowler, A., R. Gelman, and L.R. Gleitman
    1994   The course of language learning in children with Down syndrome: Longitudinal and language level comparisons with young normally developing children. Pp. 91-140 in *Constraints on Language Acquisition Studies of Atypical Children*. H. Tager-Flusberg, ed. Hillsdale, NJ: Earlbaum Associates.
Fox, N.A.
    1985   Behavioral and autonomic antecedents of attachment in high-risk infants. Pp. 389-414 in *The Psychobiology of Attachment and Separation*. M. Reite and T. Field, eds. Orlando, FL: Academic Press.
    1994   *Monographs of the Society for Research in Child Development*, "The Development of Emotion Regulation: Biological and Behavioral Considerations" (Serial No. 240) 59.

Fox, N.A., and S.D. Calkins
    1993   Pathways to aggression and social withdrawal: Interactions among temperament, attachment and regulation. Pp. 81-100 in *Social Withdrawal, Inhibition and Shyness in Childhood*. K.H. Rubin and J. Asendorpf, eds. Hillsdale, NJ: Erlbaum.
Fox, N.A., and R.J. Davidson
    1987   Electroencephalogram asymmetry in response to the approach of a stranger and maternal separation. *Developmental Psychology* 23:233-240.
Fox, N.A., K.H. Rubin, S.D. Calkins, T.R. Marshall, R.J. Coplan, S.W. Porges, J. Long, and S. Stewart
    1995   Frontal activation asymmetry and social competence at four years of age. *Child Development* 66:1770-1784.
Fox, N.A., L.A. Schmidt, S.D. Calkins, K.H. Rubin, and R.J. Coplan
    1996   The role of frontal activation in the regulation and dysregulation of social behavior during the preschool years. *Development and Psychopathology* 8:89-102.
Fox, N.A., H.A. Henderson, K.H. Rubin, S.D. Calkins, and L.A. Schmidt
    in   Continuity and discontinuity of behavioral inhibition and exuberance: Psychophysi-
    press   ological and behavioral influences across the first four years of life. *Child Development*.
Fraiberg, S.
    1977   *Insights From the Blind: Comparative Studies of Blind and Sighted Infants*. New York: Basic Books.
Fraiberg, S., V. Shapiro, and D.S. Cherniss
    1980   Treatment Modalities. Pp. 49-77 in *Clinical Studies in Infant Mental Health: The First Year of Life*. S. Fraiberg, ed. New York: Basic Books, Inc., Publishers.
Francis, E.Z., C.A. Kimmel, and D.C. Rees
    1990   Workshop on the qualitative and quantitative comparability of human and animal developmental neurotoxicity: Summary and implications. *Neurotoxicity and Teratology* 12(3):285-292.
Frankel, K.A., and R.J. Harmon
    1996   Depressed mothers: They don't always look as bad as they feel. *Journal of the American Academy of Child and Adolescent Psychiatry* 35(3):289-298.
French, D.C.
    1988   Heterogenity of peer rejected boys: Aggressive and nonaggressive subtypes. *Child Development* 59:976-985.
Frey, K.S., and D.N. Ruble
    1990   Strategies for comparative evaluation: Maintaining a sense of competence across the lifespan. In *Competence Considered*. R. Sternberg and J. Kolligan, eds. New Haven, CT: Yale Press.
Frodi, A., L. Bridges, and W. Grolnick
    1985   Correlates of mastery-related behavior: A short-term longitudinal study of infants in their second year. *Child Development* 56:1291-1298.
Furstenberg Jr., F.F., T.D. Cook, J. Eccles, G.H. Elder Jr., and A.J. Sameroff
    1998   *Managing to Make It: Urban Families in High Risk Neighborhoods*. Chicago: University of Chicago Press.
Furstenberg Jr., F.F., T.D. Cook, J. Eccles, G.H. Elder Jr., and A.J. Sameroff
    1999   *Managing To Make It: Urban Families and Adolescent Success*. Chicago, IL: University of Chicago Press.
Gadian, D.G., M. Mishkin, and F. Vargha-Khadem
    1999   Early brain pathology and its relation to cognitive impairment: The role of quantitative magnetic resonance techniques. *Advances in Neurology* 81:307-315.

Gaensbauer, T.J., and K. Sands
  1979   Distorted affective communications in abused/neglected infants and their potential impact on caregivers. *Journal of the American Academy of Child Psychiatry* 18:238-250.
Galinsky, E., C. Howes, S. Kontos, and M. Shinn
  1994   *The Study of Children in Family Child Care and Relative Care.* New York: Families and Work Institute.
Gallimore, R., and C. Goldenberg
  1993   Activity settings of early literacy: Home and school factors in children's emergent literacy. Pp. 315-335 in *Contexts for Learning: Sociocultural Dynamics in Children's Development.* E. Forman, N. Minick, and C.A. Stone, eds. Oxford, UK: Oxford University Press.
Gallimore, R., J.W. Boggs, and C. Jordan
  1974   *Culture, Behavior, and Education: A Study of Hawaiian-Americans.* Beverly Hills, CA: Sage.
Galluzzo, D., C.C. Matheson, J. Moore, and C. Howes
  1990   Social orientation to adults and peers in infant day care. Pp. 183-192 in *Infant Day Care: The Current Debate.* N.A. Fox and F. Fien, eds. New York: Ablex.
Garbarino, J., and B. Ganzel
  2000   The human ecology of early risk. Pp. 76-93 in *Handbook of Early Childhood Intervention,* Second Edition. J.P. Shonkoff and S.J. Meisels, eds. New York: Cambridge University Press.
Garber, H.L.
  1988   *The Milwaukee Project: Preventing Mental Retardation in Children at Risk.* Washington, DC: American Association on Mental Retardation.
Garber, J., and K.A. Dodge, eds.
  1991   *The Development of Emotional Regulation and Dysregulation.* New York: Cambridge University Press.
Garber, J., N. Braafladt, and J. Zeman
  1991   The regulation of sad affect: An information-processing perspective. Pp. 208-240 in *The Development of Emotional Regulation and Dysregulation.* J. Garber and K.A. Dodge, eds. New York: Cambridge University Press.
García Coll, C.
  1990   Developmental outcome of minority infants: A process-oriented look into our beginnings. *Child Development* 61(2):270-289.
García Coll, C., and K. Magnuson
  2000   Cultural differences as sources of developmental vulnerabilities and resources. Pp. 94-114 in *Handbook of Early Childhood Intervention,* Second Edition. J.P. Shonkoff and S.J. Meisels, eds. New York: Cambridge University Press.
García Coll, C., J. Kagan, and J.S. Reznick
  1984   Behavioral inhibition in young children. *Child Development* 55:1005-1019.
García Coll, C., G. Lamberty, R. Jenkins, H.P. McAdoo, K. Crnic, B.H. Wasik, and H. Vazquez-Garcia
  1996   An integrative model for the study of developmental competencies in minority children. *Child Development* 67(5):1891-1914.
Garfinkel, I., S.S. McLanahan, and P.K. Robins, eds.
  1994   *Child Support and Child Wellbeing.* Washington, DC: The Urban Institute Press.
Garmezy, N.
  1983   Stressors of childhood. Pp. 43-84 in *Stress, Coping, and Development in Children.* N. Garmezy and M. Rutter, eds. New York: McGraw-Hill.

Garmezy, N., and M. Rutter
   1983   Stress, Coping, and Development in Children. New York: McGraw-Hill.
Garmezy, N., A.S. Masten, and A. Tellegen
   1984   The study of stress and competence in children: A building block for developmental
           psychopathology. Child Development 55(1):97-111.
Garrett, P., N. Ng'andu, and J. Ferron
   1994   Poverty experiences of young children and the equality of their home environ-
           ments. Child Development 65:331-345.
Garvey, C.
   1990   Play. Cambridge, MA: Harvard University Press.
Gathercole, S., and A. Baddeley
   1990   Phonological memory deficits in language disordered children: Is there a causal
           connection? Journal of Memory and Language 29:336-360.
Gaudin, J.
   1993   Child Neglect: A Guide for Intervention. Washington, DC: U.S. Department of
           Health and Human Services.
Gazmararian, J.A., S.A. James, and J.M. Lepowski
   1995   Depression and black and white women: The role of marriage and socioeconomic
           status. Annals of Epidemiology 5:455-463.
Ge, X., R.D. Conger, R.J. Cadoret, J.M. Neiderhiser, W.R. Yates, E. Troughton, and M.A.
Stewart
   1996   The developmental interface between nature and nurture: A mutual influence model
           of child antisocial behavior and parent behaviors. Developmental Psychology
           32(4):574-589.
Gecas, V.
   1979   The influence of social class on socialization. Pp. 365-404 in Contemporary Theo-
           ries About the Family, Volume 1. W.R. Burr, R. Hill, F.I. Nye, and I.L. Reiss, eds.
           New York: Free Press.
Gehart, M., and E.E. Maccoby
   1980   Sleep pattern development from 6 through 33 months. Journal of Pediatric Psy-
           chology 5(3):295-303.
Gekoski, M.J., C.K. Rovee-Collier, and V. Carulli-Rabinowitz
   1983   A longitudinal analysis of inhibition of infant distress: The origins of social expec-
           tations? Infant Behavior and Development 6:339-351.
Gelfand, D.M., and D.M. Teti
   1990   The effects of maternal depression on children. Clinical Psychology Review 10:329-
           353.
Gelfand, D.M., D.M. Teti, S.A. Seiner, and P.B. Jameson
   1996   Helping mothers fight depression: Evaluation of a home-based intervention pro-
           gram for depressed mothers and their infants. Journal of Clinical Child Psychology
           25(4):406-422.
Gelman, R.
   1998   Domain specificity in cognitive development: Universals and nonuniversals. Pp.
           557-579 in Advances in Psychological Science, Volume 2: Biological and Cognitive
           Aspects. M. Sabourin, F. Craik, and M. Robert, eds. Hove, UK: Psychology Press.
Gelman, R., and C.R. Gallistel
   1978   The Child's Understanding of Number. Cambridge, MA: Harvard University
           Press.
Gelman, S.A., and E.M. Markman
   1986   Categories and induction in young children. Cognition 23:183-209.

Gennetian, L.A., and C. Miller
    2000   *Reforming Welfare and Rewarding Work: Final Report on the Minnesota Family Investment Program.* New York: Manpower Demonstration and Research Corporation.
George, C., and M. Main
    1979   Social interactions of young abused children: Approach, avoidance, and aggression. *Child Development* 50(2):306-318.
Georgieff, M.K., and R. Rao
    1999   The role of nutrition in cognitive development. In *Handbook of Developmental Cognitive Neuroscience.* C.A. Nelson and M. Luciana, eds. Cambridge, MA: MIT Press.
Georgieff, M.K., J.S. Hoffman, G.R. Pereira, J. Bernbaum, and M. Hoffman-Williamson
    1985   Effect of neonatal caloric deprivation on head growth and 1-year developmental status in preterm infants. *The Journal of Pediatrics* 107:581-587.
Georgieff, M.K., M.M. Mills, L. Lindeke, S. Iverson, D.E. Johnson, and T.R. Thompson
    1989   Changes in nutritional management and outcome of very-low-birth-weight infants. *American Journal of Diseases in Children* 143:82-85.
Gertner, B.L., M.L. Rice, and P.A. Hadley
    1994   Influence of communicative competence on peer preferences in a preschool classroom. *Journal of Speech and Hearing Research* 37:913-923.
Gesell, A.L.
    1925   *The Mental Growth of the Pre-School Child.* New York: The Macmillan Company.
    1929   *Infancy and Human Growth.* New York: The Macmillan Company.
Gilkerson, L., and F. Stott
    2000   Parent-child relationships in early intervention with infants and toddlers with disabilities and their families. Pp. 457-471 in *Handbook of Infant Mental Health,* Second Edition. C.H. Zeanah, ed. New York: The Guilford Press.
Gilliam, W.S., and L.C. Mayes
    2000   Development assessment of infants and toddlers. Pp. 236-248 in *Handbook of Infant Mental Health,* Second Edition. C.H. Zeanah, ed. New York: The Guilford Press.
Ginsberg, H.P., A. Klein, and P. Starkey
    1998   The development of children's mathematical thinking: Connecting research with practice. Pp. 401-478 in *Handbook of Child Psychology,* Volume 4: Child Psychology in Practice, Fifth Edition. W. Damon, ed. New York: Wiley & Sons, Inc.
Glass, G., P. Peckham, and J. Sanders
    1972   Consequences of failure to meet assumptions underlying the analysis of variance and covariance. *Review of Educational Research* 42:237-288.
Gleitman, L.R.
    1986   Biological pre-programming for language learning. Pp. 120-151 in *The Brain, Cognition, and Education.* S.L. Friedman, K.A. Klivington, and R.W. Peterson, eds. Orlando, FL: Academic Press.
Gleitman, L.R., and E.L. Newport
    1995   The invention of language by children: Environmental and biological influences on the acquisition of language. Pp. 1-24 in *Language: An Invitation to Cognitive Science,* Second Edition. L.R. Gleitman and M. Liberman, eds. Cambridge, MA: MIT Press.
Gnepp, J., and C. Chilamkurti
    1988   Children's use of personality attributions to predict other people's emotional and behavioral reactions. *Child Development* 59:743-754.

Gnys, J.A., and W.G. Willis
   1991   Validation of executive function tasks with young children. *Developmental Neuropsychology* 7:487-501.
Gobbo, C., and M. Chi
   1986   How knowledge is structured and used by expert and novice children. *Cognitive Development* 1(3):221-237.
Gohlke, B.D., V.V. Khadilkar, D.H. Skuse, and R. Stanhope
   1998   Recognition of children with psychosocial short stature. *Journal of Pediatric Endocrinology and Metabolism* 11(4):509-517.
Gold, D., and D. Andres
   1978   Relations between maternal employment and development of nursery school children. *Canadian Journal of Behavioral Science* 10:116-129.
Goldberg, S.
   1990   Attachment in infants at risk: Theory, research, and practice. *Infants and Young Children* 2:11-20.
Goldberg, S., S. Brachfield, and B. Divitto
   1980   Feeding, fussing, and play: Parent-infant interaction in the first year as a function of prematurity and perinatal medical problems. In *High-Risk Infants and Children: Adult and Peer Interactions*. T. Field, S. Goldberg, D. Stern, and M. Sostek, eds. New York: Academic Press.
Goldberg, W.A., and M.A. Easterbrooks
   1988   Maternal employment when children are toddlers and kindergarteners. Pp. 121-154 in *Maternal Employment and Children's Development: Longitudinal Research*. A.E. Gottfried and A.W. Gottfried, eds. New York: Plenum Press.
Golden, C.J.
   1981   The Luria-Nebraska Children's Battery: Theory and formulation. Pp. 277-302 in *Neuropsychological Assessment and the School-Aged Child*. G.W. Hynd and J.E. Obrzut, eds. New York: Grune & Stratton.
Golden, M., and B. Birns
   1976   Social class and infant intelligence. Pp. 299-352 in *Origins of Intelligence*. M. Lewis, ed. New York: Plenum.
Goldenberg, C.L., L. Reese, and R. Gallimore
   1992   Effects of school literacy materials on Latino children's home experiences and early reading achievement. *American Journal of Education* 100:497-536.
Goldin-Meadow, S.
   1978   A study in human capacities. *Science* (200):649-651.
   1982   The resilience of recursion: A study of a communication system developed without a conventional language model. Pp. 51-77 in *Language Acquisition: The State of the Art*. E. Wanner and L.R. Gleitman, eds. New York: Cambridge University Press.
   1997   When gestures and words speak differently. *Current Directions in Psychological Science* 6(5):138-143.
Goldin-Meadow, S., and C. Mylander
   1998   Spontaneous sign systems created by deaf children in two cultures. *Nature* 391:279-281.
Goldin-Meadow, S., D. McNeill, and J. Singleton
   1996   Silence is liberating: Removing the handcuffs on grammatical expression in the manual modality. *Psychological Review* 103:34-55.
Goldman-Rakic, P.S.
   1987   Development of cortical circuitry and cognitive function. *Child Development* 58:601-622.

Goldsmith, H.H., and J.J. Campos
1982   Toward a theory of infant temperament. Pp. 161-193 in *The Development of Attachment and Affiliative Systems.* R.N. Emde and R.J. Harmon, eds. New York: Plenum.

Goldsmith, H.H., and I.I. Gottesman
1996   Heritable variability and variable heritability in developmental psychopathology. Pp. 5-43 in *Frontiers of Developmental Psychopathology.* M.F. Lenzenweger and J.J. Haugaard, eds. New York: Oxford University Press.

Goldsmith, H.H., A.H. Buss, R. Plomin, M.K. Rothbart, A. Thomas, S. Chess, R.A. Hinde, and R.B. McCall
1987   Roundtable: What is temperament? Four approaches. *Child Development* 58:505-529.

Gomby, D.S., M.B. Larner, C.S. Stevenson, E.M. Lewit, and R.E. Behrman
1995   Long-term outcomes of early childhood programs: Analysis and recommendations. *The Future of Children: Long-Term Outcomes of Early Childhood Programs* 5(3):6-24.

Gomby, D.S., P.L. Culross, and R.E. Behrman
1999   Home visiting: Recent program evaluations—Analysis and recommendations. *The Future of Children: Home Visiting: Recent Program Evaluations* 9(1):4-26.

Göncü, A.
1993   Development of intersubjectivity in the dyadic play of preschoolers. *Early Childhood Research Quarterly* 8:99-116.

Goodchilds, J.D., ed.
1991   *Psychological Perspectives on Human Diversity in America.* Washington, DC: American Psychological Association.

Goodlett, C.R., S.J. Kelly, and J.R. West
1987   Early postnatal alcohol exposure that produces high blood alcohol levels impairs development of spatial navigation learning. *Psychobiology* 15:64-74.

Goodman, G.S., R.E. Emery, and J.J. Haugaard
1998   Developmental psychology and law: Divorce, child maltreatment, foster care, and adoption. Pp. 775-874 in *Handbook of Child Psychology*, Volume 4: Child Psychology in Practice, Fifth Edition. W. Damon, I.E. Sigel, and K.A. Renninger, eds. New York: John Wiley & Sons, Inc.

Goodman, S.H., and I.H. Gotlib
1999   Risk for psychopathology in the children of depressed mothers: A developmental model for understanding mechanisms of transmission. *Psychological Review* 106(3):458-490.

Goodnow, J.J.
1987   Social aspects of planning. Pp. 179-201 in *Blueprints for Thinking: The Role of Planning in Cognitive Development.* S.L. Friedman, E.K. Scholnick, and R.R. Cocking, eds. New York: Cambridge University Press.

1996   Acceptable ignorance, negotiable disagreement: Alternative views of learning. Pp. 355-367 in *The Handbook of Education and Human Development: New Models of Learning, Teaching and Schooling.* D.R. Olson and N. Torrance, eds. Oxford, UK: Blackwell Publishers.

1997   Parenting and the transmission and internalization of values: From social-cultural perspectives to within-family analyses. Pp. 333-361 in *Parenting Strategies and Children's Internalization of Values: A Handbook of Contemporary Theory.* J.E. Grusec and L. Kuczynski, eds. New York: Wiley.

1998   Contexts of achievement. Pp. 105-129 in *Global Prospects for Education: Development, Culture, and Schooling*. S.G. Paris and H.M. Wellman, eds. Washington, DC: American Psychological Association.

Goodnow, J.J., and W.A. Collins
1990   *Development According to Parents: The Nature, Sources, and Consequences of Parents' Ideas*. Hillsdale, NJ: Erlbaum.

Goodnow, J.J., R. Knight, and J. Cashmore
1985   Adult social cognition: Implications of parent's ideas for approaches to development. Pp. 287-329 in *The Minnesota Symposia on Child Psychology*, Volume 18: Cognitive Perspectives and Behavioral Development. M. Perlmutter, ed. Hillsdale, NJ: Erlbaum.

Goodwyn, S.W., and L.P. Acredolo
1998   Encouraging symbolic gestures: A new perspective on the relationship between gesture and speech. Pp. 61-73 in *The Nature and Functions of Gesture in Children's Communications*. J.M. Iverson and S. Goldin-Meadow, eds. San Francisco: Jossey-Bass Publishers.

Goossens, F., and M. van IJzendoorn
1990   Quality of infants' attachment to professional caregivers: Relation to infant-parent attachment and day care characteristics. *Child Development* 61:550-567.

Gormally, S.M., and R.G. Barr
1997   Of clinical pies and clinical clues: Proposal for a clinical approach to complaints of early crying and colic. *Good Practice Guide* 3:137-153.

Gormley, W.T., J. Kagan, and N.E. Cohen
1995   *Options for Government and Business Roles in Early Care and Education: Targeted Entitlements and Universal Supports*. New Haven, Connecticut: Quality 2000, Yale University.

Gottfried, A.E., and A.W. Gottfried, eds.
1988   *Maternal Employment and Children's Development: Longitudinal Research*. New York: Plenum Press.

Gottfried, A.E., A.W. Gottfried, and K. Bathurst
1988   Maternal employment, family environment and children's development: Infancy through the school years. Pp. 11-58 in *Maternal Employment and Children's Development: Longitudinal Research*. A.E. Gottfried and A.W. Gottfried, eds. New York: Plenum Press.

Gottfried, A.W., ed.
1984   *Home Environment and Early Cognitive Development*. Orlando, FL: Academic Press.

Gottlieb, G.
1992   *Individual Development and Evolution: The Genesis of Novel Behavior*. New York: Oxford University Press.

Gottman, J.M., L.F. Katz, and C. Hooven
1997   *Meta-Emotion: How Families Communicate Emotionally*. Mahwah, NJ: Erlbaum.

Gould, E., A.J. Reeves, M.S. Graziano, and C.G. Gross
1999   Neurogenesis in the neocortex of adult primates. *Science* 286:548-552.

Graham, S., and K.R. Harris
1996   Addressing problems in attention, memory, and executive functioning: An example from self-regulated strategy development. Pp. 235-261 in *Attention, Memory, and Executive Function*. G.R. Lyon and N. Krasnegor, eds. Baltimore, MD: Paul H. Brookes Publishing Co., Inc.

Gralinski, J.H., and C.B. Kopp
1993   Everyday rules for behavior: Mothers' requests to young children. *Developmental Psychology* 29:573-584.

Gramlich, E.M.
1990   *A Guide to Benefit-Cost Analysis.* Englewood Cliffs, NJ: Prentice-Hall, Inc.

Green, J.A., G.E. Gustafson, J.R. Irwin, L.L. Kalinowski, and R.M. Wood
1995   Infant crying: Acoustics, perception, and communication. *Early Development and Parenting* 4:161-175.

Greenberger, E. and R. O'Neil
1991   Characteristics of fathers' and mothers' jobs: Implications for parenting and children's social development. Paper presented at the biennial meeting of the Society for Research in Child Development, Seattle, WA.

Greenfield, P.M.
1994   Independence and interdependence as developmental scripts: Implications for theory, research and practice. Pp. 1-40 in *Cross-Cultural Roots of Minority Child Development.* P.M. Greenfield and R.R. Cocking, eds. Hillsdale, NJ: Erlbaum.
1997   Culture as process: Empirical methods for cultural psychology. Pp. 301-346 in *Handbook of Cross-Cultural Psychology,* Volume 1: Theory and Method, Second Edition. J.W. Berry and Y.H. Poortinga, eds. Boston, MA: Allyn & Bacon, Inc.

Greenfield, P.M., and R.R. Cocking, eds.
1994   *Cross-Cultural Roots of Minority Child Development.* Hillsdale, NJ: Lawrence Erlbaum Associates, Publishers.

Greenfield, P.M., and L.K. Suzuki
1998   Culture and human development: Implications for parenting, education, pediatrics, and mental health. Pp. 1059-1109 in *Handbook of Child Psychology,* Volume 4: Child Psychology in Practice, 5th Edition. W. Damon, I.E. Sigel, and K.A. Renninger, eds. New York: John Wiley & Sons, Inc.

Greenfield, P.M., T.B. Brazelton, and C. Childs
1989   From birth to maturity in Zinacantan: Ontogenesis in cultural context. Pp. 177-216 in *Ethnographic Encounters in Southern Mesoamerica: Celebratory Essays in Honor of Evon Z. Vogt.* V. Bricker and G. Gossen, eds. Albany, NY: Institute of Mesoamerica, State University of New York.

Greenough, W.T.
1991   Experience as a component of normal development: Evolutionary considerations. *Developmental Psychology* 27:14-17.

Greenough, W.T., and J.E. Black
1992   Induction of brain structure by experience: Substrates for cognitive development. Pp. 155-200 in *Developmental Behavior Neuroscience,* Volume 24. M.R. Gunnar and C.A. Nelson, eds. Hillsdale, NJ: Erlbaum.

Greenspan, S.I.
1990   Comprehensive clinical approaches to infants and their families: Psychodynamic and developmental perspectives. Pp. 150-172 in *Handbook of Early Childhood Intervention.* J.P. Shonkoff and S.J. Meisels, eds. New York: Cambridge University Press.

Gregg, N.M.
1942   Congenital cataract following German Measles in the mother. *Transactions of the Ophthalmologic Society of Australia* 3:35-46.

Gresham, F.M., and D.L. MacMillan
1998   Early Intervention Project: Can its claims be substantiated and its effects replicated? *Journal of Autism and Developmental Disorders* 28:5-13.

Griffin, E.A., and F.J. Morrison
  1997   The unique contribution of home literacy environment to differences in early lit-
          eracy skills. *Early Child Development and Care* 127-128:233-243.
Grolnick, W., A. Frodi, and L. Bridges
  1984   Maternal control style and the mastery motivation of one-year-olds. *Infant Mental
          Health Journal* 5:72-82.
Grolnick, W.S., L.J. Bridges, and J.P. Connell
  1996   Emotion regulation in two-year-olds: Strategies and emotional expression in four
          contexts. *Child Development* 67:928-941.
Gross, R.T., D. Spiker, and C.W. Haynes, eds.
  1997   *Helping Low Birth Weight, Premature Babies: The Infant Health and Develop-
          ment Program.* Stanford, CA: Stanford University Press.
Groze, V., and D. Ileana
  1996   A follow-up study of adopted children from Romania. *Child and Adolescent Social
          Work Journal* 13:541-565.
Grubbs, P.R., and J.A. Niemeyer
  1999   Promoting reciprocal social interactions in inclusive classrooms for young children.
          Infants and Young Children 11:9-18.
Grusec, J.E., and J.J. Goodnow
  1994   The impact of parental discipline methods on the child's internalization of values:
          A reconceptualization of current points of view. *Developmental Psychology*
          30:4-19.
Grych, J., and F. Fincham
  1990   Marital conflict and children's adjustment: A cognitive-contextual framework. *Psy-
          chological Bulletin* 108:267-290.
Gueron, J.M., and E. Pauly
  1991   *From Welfare to Work.* New York: Russell Sage Foundation.
Gunnar, M.R.
  1980   Control, warning signals, and distress in infancy. *Developmental Psychology*
          16(4):281-289.
  in   Early adversity and the development of stress reactivity and regulation. In *The
  press   Effects of Adversity on Neurobehavioral Development: The Minnesota Symposia
          on Child Psychology*, Volume 31. C.A. Nelson, ed. Hillsdale, NJ: Lawrence
          Erlbaum Associates, Publishers.
Gunnar, M.R., C. Gonzales, C. Goodlin, and S. Levine
  1981   Behavioral and pituitary-adrenal responses during a prolonged separation period in
          infant Rhesus macaques. *Psychoneuroendocrinology* 6:65-75.
Gunnar, M.R., M. Larson, L. Hertsgaard, M. Harris, and L. Brodersen
  1992   The stressfulness of separation among 9-month-old infants: Effects of social con-
          text variables and infant temperament. *Child Development* 63:290-303.
Gunnar, M.R., L. Brodersen, M. Nachmias, K. Buss, and J. Rigatuso
  1996   Stress reactivity and attachment security. *Developmental Psychobiology* 29(3):191-
          204.
Gunnar, M.R., K. Tout, M. de Haan, S. Pierce, and K. Stansbury
  1997   Temperament, social competence, and adrenocortical activity in preschoolers. *De-
          velopmental Psychobiology* 31(1):65-85.
Gunnar-vonGnechten, M.R.
  1978   Changing a frightening toy into a pleasant toy by allowing the infant to control its
          actions. *Developmental Psychology* 14(2):157-162.
Guralnick, M.J.
  1976   The value of integrating handicapped and nonhandicapped preschool children.
          American Journal of Orthopsychiatry 46:236-245.

1988   Efficacy research in early childhood intervention programs. Pp. 75-88 in *Early Intervention for Infants and Children With Handicaps: An Empirical Base*. S.L. Odom and M.B. Karnes, eds. Baltimore, MD: Brookes.

1997   *The Effectiveness of Early Intervention*. Baltimore, MD: Paul H. Brookes Publishing Co., Inc.

1998   The effectiveness of early intervention for vulnerable children: A developmental perspective. *American Journal on Mental Retardation* 102:319-345.

1999   Family and child influences on the peer-related social competence on young children with developmental delays. *Mental Retardation and Developmental Disabilities Research Reviews* 5:21-29.

in   *Early Childhood Inclusion: Focus on Change*. Baltimore, MD: Paul H. Brookes
press Publishing Co., Inc.

Guralnick, M.J., and D.D. Bricker

1987   The effectiveness of early intervention for children with cognitive and general development delays. Pp. 579-610 in *The Effectiveness of Early Intervention for At-Risk and Handicapped Children*. M.J. Guralnick and F.C. Bennett, eds. Baltimore, MD: Brookes.

Guralnick, M.J., and B. Neville

1997   Designing early intervention programs to promote children's social competence. Pp. 579-610 in *The Effectiveness of Early Intervention*. M.J. Guralnick, ed. Baltimore, MD: Paul H. Brookes Publishing Co., Inc.

Guralnick, M.J., R. Connor, M. Hammond, J.M. Gottman, and K. Kinnish

1996   The peer relations of preschool children with communication disorders. *Child Development* 67:471-489.

Hack, M., and N. Breslau

1986   Very low birth weight infants: Effects of brain growth during infancy on intelligence quotient at 3 years of age. *Pediatrics* 77:196-202.

Hack, M., J.D. Horbar, M.H. Malloy, J.E. Tyson, E. Wright, and L. Wright

1991   Very low birth weight outcomes of the National Institute of Child Health and Human Development Neonatal Network [see comments]. *Pediatrics* 87(5):587-597.

Hadley, P.A., and C.M. Schuele

1998   Facilitating peer interaction: Socially relevant objectives for preschool language intervention. *American Journal of Speech-Language Pathology* 7:25-36.

Haith, M.M., and M. McCarty

1990   Stability of visual expectation at 3.0 months of age. *Developmental Psychology* 26:68-74.

Haith, M.M., C. Hazan, and G.S. Goodman

1988   Expectation and anticipation of dynamic visual events by 3.5-month-old babies. *Child Development* 59:467-479.

Hakuta, K.

1986   *Mirror of Language: The Debate on Bilingualism*. New York: Basic Books.

Hakuta, K., and D. D'Andrea

1992   Some properties of bilingual maintenance and loss in Mexican background high-school students. *Applied Linguistics* 13(1):72-99.

Halpern, R.

2000   Early intervention for low-income children and families. Pp. 785-841 in *Handbook of Early Childhood Intervention*, Second Edition. J.P. Shonkoff and S.J. Meisels, eds. New York: Cambridge University Press.

Hamilton, G.
    2000   Do Mandatory Welfare-to-Work Programs Affect the Well-Being of Children? A
            Synthesis of Child Research Conducted As Part of the National Evaluation of
            Welfare-to-Work Strategies. Washington, DC: U.S. Department of Health and
            Human Services, Administration for Children and Families and Office of the Secre-
            tary for Planning and Evaluation; and U.S. Department of Education, Office of the
            Under Secretary and Office of Vocational and Adult Education.

Hamilton, H., and D. Gordon
    1978   Teacher-child interactions in preschool and task persistence. *American Educa-
            tional Research Journal* 15:459-466.

Han, W., J. Waldfogel, and J. Brooks-Gunn
    2000   The effects of early maternal employment on later cognitive and behavioral out-
            comes. Unpublished manuscript. Columbia University School of Social Work.

Hannigan, J., R. Berman, and C. Zajac
    1993   Environmental enrichment and the behavioral effects of prenatal exposure to alco-
            hol in rats. *Neurotoxicology and Teratology* 15:261-266.

Harbin, G.L., R.A. McWilliams, and J.J. Gallagher
    2000   Services for young children with disabiilties and their families. Pp. 387-415 in
            Handbook of Early Childhood Intervention, Second Edition. J.P. Shonkoff and
            S.J. Meisels, eds. New York: Cambridge University Press.

Harden, B.J.
    1998   Building bridges for children: Addressing the consequences of exposure to drugs
            and to the child welfare system. Pp. 18-61 in *Substance Abuse, Family Violence,
            and Child Welfare: Bridging Perspectives*, Volume 10: Issues in children's and fami-
            lies' lives. R.L. Hampton, V. Senatore, and T.P. Gullotta, eds. Thousand Oaks,
            CA: Sage Publications, Inc.

Harkness, S., and C.M. Super
    1992   Parental ethnotheories in action. Pp. 373-391 in *Parental Belief Systems: The
            Psychological Consequences for Children*. I.E. Sigel, A.V. McGillicuddy-DeLisi,
            and J.J. Goodnow, eds. Hillsdale, NJ: Erlbaum.
    1996   *Parents' Cultural Belief Systems: Their Origins, Expressions, and Consequences*.
            New York: The Guilford Press.

Harlow, H.F., M.K. Harlow, and S.J. Suomi
    1971   From thought to therapy: Lessons from a primate laboratory. *American Scientist*
            59:538-549.

Harnish, J.D., K.A. Dodge, and E. Valente
    1995   Mother-child interaction quality as a partial mediator of the roles of maternal
            depressive symptomatology and socioeconomic status in the development of child
            behavior problems. *Child Development* 66(3):739-753.

Harper, L., and K. Huie
    1985   The effects of prior group experience, age, and famimliarity on quality and organi-
            zation of preschool social relationships. *Child Development* 56:704-717.

Harris, J.R.
    1995   Where is the child's environment? A group socialization theory of development.
            Psychological Review 102(3):458-489.
    1998   *The Nature Assumption: Why Children Turn Out the Way They Do*. New York:
            Free Press.

Harris, P.L.
    1993   Understanding emotion. Pp. 237-246 in *Handbook of Emotions*. M. Lewis and
            J.M. Haviland, eds. New York: Guilford.

Harris, P.L., G.R. Guz, M.S. Lipian, and Z. Man-Shu
  1985   Insight into the time-course of emotion among Western and Chinese children. *Child Development* 56:972-988.
Harris, S.R.
  1997   The effectiveness of early intervention for children with cerebral palsy and related motor disabilities. Pp. 327-348 in *The Effectiveness of Early Intervention.* M.J. Guralnick, ed. Baltimore, MD: Paul H. Brookes Publishing Co., Inc.
Harrison, A., F. Serafica, and H. McAdoo
  1984   Ethnic families of color. Pp. 329-365 in *Review of Child Development Research,* Volume 7: The family. R.D. Parke, ed. Chicago, IL: University of Chicago Press.
Harrison, A.O., M.N. Wilson, C.J. Pine, S.Q. Chan, and R. Buriel
  1990   Family ecologies of ethnic minority children. *Child Development* 61(2):347-362.
Hart, B., and T.R. Risley
  1995   *Meaningful Experiences in the Everyday Experiences of Young American Children.* Baltimore, MD: Paul H. Brookes Publishing Co., Inc.
Hart, C.H., G.W. Ladd, and B.R. Burleson
  1990   Children's expectations of the outcomes of social strategies: Relations with sociometric status and maternal disciplinary styles. *Child Development* 61:127-137.
Hart, C.H., D. DeWolf, P. Wozniak, and D.C. Burts
  1992   Maternal and paternal disciplinary styles: Relations with preschoolers' playground behavioral orientations and peer status. *Child Development* 63:879-892.
Hart, J., M.R. Gunnar, and D. Cicchetti
  1996   Altered neuroendocrine activity in maltreated children related to symptoms of depression. *Development and Psychopathology* 8(1):201-214.
Harter, S.
  1982   The perceived competence scale for children. *Child Development* 53:89-97.
Harter, S., and R. Pike
  1984   The Pictoral Perceived Competence Scale for Young Children. *Child Development* 55:1969-1982.
Hartmann, E.
  1995   Long-term effects of day care and maternal teaching on educational competence, independence and autonomy in young adulthood. Unpublished manuscript, University of Oslo, Oslo, Norway.
Hartup, W.W.
  1996   The company they keep: Friendships and their developmental significance. *Child Development* 67:1-13.
Hartup, W.W., and B. Laursen
  1993   Conflict and context in peer relations. Pp. 44-84 in *Children on Playgrounds: Research Perspectives and Applications.* C. Hart, ed. Albany, NY: State University of New York Press.
Hartup, W.W., and Z. Rubin, eds.
  1986   *Relationships and Development.* Hillsdale, NJ: Erlbaum.
Hartup, W.W., B. Laursen, M.A. Stewart, and A. Eastenson
  1988   Conflicts and the friendship relations of young children. *Child Development* 59:1590-1600.
Harvey, E.
  1999   Short-term and long-term effects of early parental employment on children of the national longitudinal survey of youth. *Developmental Psychology* 35(2):445-459.
Harwood, R.L.
  1992   The influence of culturally derived values on Anglo and Puerto Rican mothers' perceptions of attachment behavior. *Child Development* 63:822-839.

Harwood, R.L., J.G. Miller, and N.L. Irizarry
 1995 *Culture and Attachment: Perception of the Child in Context.* New York: The Guilford Press.
Haskins, R.
 1985 Public school aggression among children with varying day care experience. *Child Development* 56:689-703.
Hauser, R.M., B.V. Brown, and W.R. Prosser, eds.
 1997 *Indicators of Children's Well-Being.* New York: Russell Sage Foundation.
Hauser-Cram, P.
 1996 Mastery motivation in toddlers with developmental disabilities. *Child Development* 67:236-248.
Hauser-Cram, P., and J.P. Shonkoff
 1988 Rethinking the assessment of child focused outcomes. Pp. 73-94 in *Evaluating Family Programs.* H. Weiss and F. Jacobs, eds. New York: Aldine.
 1995 Mastery motivation: Implications for intervention. Pp. 257-272 in *Mastery Motivation: Origins, Conceptualizations, and Applications.* R. MacTurk and G. Morgan, eds. Norwood, NJ: Ablex Publishing Corporation.
Haveman, R., and B. Wolfe
 1984 Schooling and economic well-being: The role of nonmarket effects. *Journal of Human Resources* 19:377-407.
 1994 *Succeeding Generations: On the Effect of Investments in Children.* New York: Russell Sage Foundation.
Hawkins, J., and D. Lishner
 1987 Schooling and delinquency. Pp. 179-221 in *Handbook of Crime and Delinquency Prevention.* E.H. Johnson, ed. New York: The Guilford Press.
Hawkins, J.D., R.F. Catalano, and J.Y. Miller
 1992 Risk and protective factors for alcohol and other drug problems in adolescence and early adulthood: Implications for substance abuse prevention. *Psychological Bulletin* 112(1):64-105.
Hay, D.F., and H. Ross
 1982 The social nature of early conflict. *Child Development* 53:105-113.
Hay, D.F., J. Pederson, and A. Nash
 1982 Dyadic interaction in the first year of life. Pp. 11-40 in *Peer Relationships and Social Skills in Childhood.* K.H. Rubin and H.S. Ross, eds. New York: Springer-Verlag.
Hayghe, H.V.
 1997 Development in women's labor force participation. *Monthly Labor Review.* September 1997. Washington, DC: Bureau of Labor Statistics, U.S. Department of Labor.
Heath, S.B.
 1983 *Ways With Words: Language, Life, and Work in Communities and Classrooms.* Cambridge, UK: Cambridge University Press.
Heinicke, C.M.
 1993 Factors affecting the efficacy of early family intervention. Pp. 91-100 in *At-Risk Infants: Interventions, Families, and Research.* N.J. Anastasiow and S. Harel, eds. Baltimore, MD: Paul H. Brookes Publishing Co., Inc.

Heinicke, C.M., and V.A. Ponce
   1999   Relation-based early family intervention. Pp. 153-193 in *Rochester Symposium on Developmental Psychopathology*, Volume 9: Developmental Approaches to Prevention and Intervention. D. Cicchetti and S.L. Toth, eds. Rochester, NY: University of Rochester Press.
Heinicke, C.M., M. Goorsky, S. Moscov, K. Dudley, J. Gordon, and D. Guthrie
   1998   Partner support as a mediator of intervention outcome. *American Journal of Orthopsychiatry* 68(4):534-541.
Heinicke, C.M., N.R. Fineman, G. Ruth, S.L. Recchia, D. Guthrie, and C. Rodning
   1999   Relationship-based intervention with at-risk mothers: Outcome in the first year of life. *Infant Mental Health Journal* 20(4):349-374.
Helburn, S.W., ed.
   1995   *Cost, Quality, and Child Outcomes in Child Care Centers, Technical Report.* Denver, CO: Department of Economics, Center for Research in Economic and Social Policy, University of Colorado at Denver.
Helms, J.E.
   1990   *Black and White Racial Identity: Theory, Research and Practice.* Westport, CT: Greenwood Press.
Henderson, B.
   1984   Parents and exploration: The effect of context on individual differences in exploratory behavior. *Child Development* 55:1237-1245.
Hernandez-Reif, M., and T. Field
   2000   Preterm infants benefit from early interventions. Pp. 297-325 in *WAIMH Handbook of Infant Mental Health*, Volume Four: Infant Mental Health in Groups at High Risk. J.D. Osofsky and H.E. Fitzgerald, eds. New York: John Wiley & Sons, Inc.
Herrera, C., and J. Dunn
   1997   Early experiences with family conflict: Implications for arguments with a close friend. *Developmental Psychology* 33(5):869-881.
Hertsgaard, L., M.R. Gunnar, M.F. Erickson, and M. Nachmias
   1995   Adrenocortical responses to the Strange Situation in infants with disorganized/disoriented attachment relationships. *Child Development* 66(4):1100-1106.
Hess, R., and R. Hahn
   1974   Prediction of school failure and the Hess School Readiness Scale. *Psychology in the Schools* 11:134-136.
Hess, R., S. Holloway, W. Dickson, and G. Price
   1984   Maternal variables as predictors of children's school readiness and later achievement in vocabulary and mathematics in sixth grade. *Child Development* 55:1902-1912.
Hetherington, E.M., and M. Stanley-Hagan
   1999   The adjustment of children with divorced parents: A risk and resiliency perspective. *Journal of Child Psychology and Psychiatry* 40:129-140.
Hinshaw, S.P.
   1992   Externalizing behavior problems and academic underachievement in childhood and adolescence: Causal relationships and underlying mechanisms. *Psychological Bulletin* 111:127-154.
Hinshaw, S.P., and C.A. Anderson
   1996   Conduct and oppositional defiant disorders. Pp. 113-149 in *Child Psychopathology*, First Edition. E.J. Mash, ed. Alberta, Canada: Guilford.

Hinshaw, S.P., B.B. Lahey, and E.L. Hart
    1993   Issues of taxonomy and comorbidity in the development of conduct disorder. *Development and Psychopathology* 5:31-49.
Hirschfeld, L.A.
    1994   The child's representation of human groups. Pp. 133-185 in *The Psychology of Learning and Motivation: Advances in Research and Theory*, Volume 31. D.L. Medin, ed. San Diego, CA: Academic Press, Inc.
Hobcraft, J.N., J.W. McDonald, and S.O. Rutstein
    1984   Socio-economic factors in infant and child mortality: A cross-national comparison. *Population Studies* 38:193-223.
Hodges, J., and B. Tizard
    1989a   IQ and behavioural adjustment of ex-institutional adolescents. *Journal of Child Psychology and Psychiatry* 30:53-75.
    1989b   Social and family relationships of ex-institutional adolescents. *Journal of Child Psychology and Psychiatry* 30:77-97.
Hofferth, S.L.
    1995   Caring for children at the poverty line. *Children and Youth Services Review* 17:1031.
Hofferth, S.L. and D.D. Chaplin
    1998   State regulations: Effects on cost, quality, availability, and use of child care programs. Working paper. The Urban Institute, Washington, DC.
Hofferth, S.L., K.A. Shauman, R.R. Henke, and J. West
    1998   *Characteristics of Children's Early Care and Education Programs: Data From the 1995 National Household Education Survey*, NCES 98-128. Washington, DC: U.S. Department of Education, National Center for Education Statistics.
Hoff-Ginsberg, E.
    1991   Mother-child conversation in different social classes and communicative settings. *Child Development* 62:782-796.
    1997   *Language Development*. Pacific Grove, CA: Brooks/Cole Publishing Co.
Hoff-Ginsberg, E., and T. Tardif
    1995   Socioeconomic status and parenting. Pp. 161-187 in *Handbook of Parenting*, Volume 4. M.H. Bornstein, ed. Mahwah, NJ: Lawrence Erlbaum.
Hoffman, L.W.
    1979   Maternal employment: 1979. *American Psychologist* 34:859-865.
    1989   Effects of maternal employment in the two-parent family. *American Psychologist* 434:283-292.
Hoffman, L.W., L.M. Youngblade, R.L. Coley, A.S. Fuligni, and D.D. Kovacs
    1999   *Mothers at Work: Effects on Children's Well-Being*, Cambridge Studies in Social and Emotional Development. Cambridge, UK: Cambridge University Press.
Hoffman, M.L.
    1983   Affective and cognitive processes in moral internalization. Pp. 236-274 in *Social Cognition and Social Development*. E.T. Higgins, D.N. Ruble, and W.W. Hartup, eds. New York: Cambridge University Press.
    1988   Moral development. Pp. 497-548 in *Developmental Psychology: An Advanced Textbook*, Second Edition. M.H. Bornstein and M.E. Lamb, eds. Hillsdale, NJ: Erlbaum.
Hoffman-Plotkin, D., and C. Twentyman
    1984   A multimodal assessment of behavioral and cognitive deficits in abused and neglected preschoolers. *Child Development* 55:794-802.

Hoksbergen, R.A.C.
   1981   Adoption of foreign children in the Netherlands. *International Child Welfare Review* 49:28-37.
Holden, G.W.
   1983   Avoiding conflict: Mothers as tacticians in the supermarket. *Child Development* 54:233-240.
   1995   Parental attitudes towards childrearing. Pp. 359-392 in *Handbook of Parenting*, Volume 3. M.H. Bornstein, ed. Mahwah, NJ: Lawrence Erlbaum.
Holden, G.W., and P. Miller
   1999   Enduring and different: A meta-analysis of similarity in parents' child rearing. *Psychological Bulletin* 125:223-254.
Holden, G.W. and P.C. O'Dell
   1995   Just how stable is parental behavior?: Meta-analysis and reformulation. Unpublished manuscript, University of Texas at Austin.
Holland, P.
   1986   Statistics and causal inference. *Journal of the American Statistical Association* 81(396):945-960.
Holloway, S., and M. Reichart-Erickson
   1989   Child care quality, family structure, and maternal expectations: Relationship to preschool children's peer relations. *Journal of Applied Developmental Psychology* 10:281-298.
Holmberg, M.
   1980   The development of social interchange patterns from 12 to 42 months. *Child Development* 51:448-456.
Honig, A.S., and F.A. Oski
   1984   Solemnity: A clinical risk index for iron deficient infants. *Early Child Development and Care* 16:69-84.
Honzik, M.P.
   1983   Measuring mental abilities in infancy: The value and limitations. Pp. 67-106 in *Origins of Intelligence: Infancy and Early Childhood*. M. Lewis, ed. New York: John Wiley.
Hooven, C., L. Katz, and J. Gottman
   1994   The family as a meta-cognition culture. *Cognition and Emotion* 9:229-264.
Hoppenbrouwers, T., J.E. Hodgman, R.M. Harper, and M.B. Sternman
   1982   Temporal distribution of sleep states, somatic activity, and autnomic activity during the first half year of life. *Sleep* 5(2):131-144.
Horowitz, F.
   1999   Presidential Address for the Society for Research in Child Development. Albuquerque, NM, April, 1999.
Hotz, V.J. and M.R. Kilburn
   1992   Estimating the demand for child care and child care costs: Should we ignore families with non-working mothers? Unpublished manuscript, University of Chicago, Chicago, IL.
Howes, C.
   1983   Patterns of friendship. *Child Development* 54:1041-1053.
   1988a Peer interaction in young children. *Monographs of the Society for Research in Child Development* (Serial No. 217) 53(1).
   1988b Relations between early child care and schooling. *Developmental Psychology* 24:53-57.

1990   Can age of entry into child care and the quality of child care predict adjustment to kindergarten? *Developmental Psychology* 26:292-303.

1992   *The Collaborative Structure of Pretend.* Albany, NY: State University of New York Press.

1996   The earliest friendships. Pp. 66-86 in *The Company They Keep: Friendship in Childhood and Adolescence.* W.M. Bukowski, A.F. Newcomb, and W.W. Hartup, eds. Boston: Cambridge University Press.

1999   Attachment relationships in the context of multiple caregivers. Pp. 671-687 in *Handbook of Attachment: Theory, Research, and Clinical Applications.* J. Cassidy and P.R. Shaver, eds. New York: The Guilford Press.

2000   Social-emotional classroom climate in child care, child-teacher relationships and children's second grade peer relations. *Social Development* 9(2):191-205.

Howes, C., and C.E. Hamilton
1992   Children's relationships with caregivers: Mothers and child care teachers. *Child Development* 63:859-866.

1993   The changing experience of child care: Changes in teachers and in teacher-child relationships and children's social competence with peers. *Early Childhood Research Quarterly* 8:15-32.

Howes, C., and C.C. Matheson
1992   Sequences in the development of competent play with peers: Social and social-pretend play. *Developmental Psychology* 28:961-974.

Howes, C., and D. Norris
1997   Adding two school age children: Does it change quality in family child care? *Early Childhood Research Quarterly* 12:327-342.

Howes, C., and M. Olenick
1986   Family and child care influences on toddler compliance. *Child Development* 57:202-216.

Howes, C., and L. Phillipsen
1992   Gender and friendship: Relationships within peer groups of young children. *Social Development* 1:230-242.

Howes, C., and J.L. Rubenstein
1985   Determinants of toddler's experience in day care: Age of entry and quality of setting. *Child Care Quarterly* 14:140-151.

Howes, C., and O.A. Unger
1989   Play with peers in child care settings. Pp. 104-119 in *The Ecological Contexts of Children's Play.* M. Bloch and A. Pelligrini, eds. Norwood, NJ: Ablex.

Howes, C., C. Rodning, D. Galluzzo, and I. Myers
1988   Attachment and childcare: Relationships with mother and caregiver. *Early Childhood Research Quarterly* 3:403-416.

Howes, C., D.A. Phillips, and M. Whitebook
1992   Thresholds of quality: Implications for the social development of children in center-based child care. *Child Development* 63:449-460.

Howes, C., C.C. Matheson, and C.E. Hamilton
1994   Maternal, teacher, and child care correlates of children's relationships with peers. *Child Development* 65:253-263.

Howes, C., L. Sakai, M. Shinn, D.A. Phillips, E. Galinsky, and M. Whitebook
1995a   Race, social class, and maternal working conditions as influences on children's development. *Journal of Applied Developmental Psychology* 16:107-124.

Howes, C., E. Smith, and E. Galinsky
1995b   *The Florida Child Care Quality Improvement Study: Interim Report.* New York: Families and Work Institute.

Hughes, D., and L. Chen
  1997   When and what parents tell children about race: An examination of race-related socialization among African American families. *Applied Developmental Science* 1(4):200-214.
  1999   The nature of parents' race-related communications to children: A developmental perspective. Pp. 467-490 in *Child Psychology: A Handbook of Contemporary Issues*. L. Balter and C.S. Tamis-LeMonda, eds. Philadelphia, PA: Psychology Press/Taylor & Francis.
Hunziker, U.A., and R.G. Barr
  1986   Increased carrying reduces infant crying: A randomized controlled trial. *Pediatrics* 77(5):641-648.
Huppi, P.S., B. Schuknecht, C. Boesch, E. Bossi, J. Felblinger, C. Fusch, and N. Herschkowitz
  1996   Structural and neurobehavioral delay in postnatal brain development of preterm infants. *Pediatric Research* 39:895-901.
Hurtado, E.K., A.H. Claussen, and K.G. Scott
  1999   Early childhood anemia and mild/moderate mental retardation. *American Journal of Clinical Nutrition* 69:115-119.
Huston, A.C., ed.
  1991   *Children in Poverty: Child Development and Public Policy*. New York: Cambridge University Press.
Huston, A.C., and J.C. Wright
  1998   Mass media and children's development. Pp. 999-1058 in *Handbook of Child Psychology*, Volume 4: Child psychology in practice, Fifth Edition. W. Damon, I. Sigel, and K.A. Renninger, eds. New York: Wiley.
Huston, A.C., V.C. McLoyd, and C. García Coll
  1994   Children and poverty: Issues in comtemporary research. *Child Development* 65(2):275-282.
Huston, A.C., D.R. Anderson, J.C. Wright, D. Linebarger, and K.L. Schmitt
  in   Sesame Street viewers as adolescents: The recontact study. *G Is for Growing:*
  press   *Thirty Years of Research on Sesame Street*. S. Fisch and R. Truglio, eds. Mahwah, NJ: Erlbaum.
Huttenlocher, J., W. Haight, A. Bryk, M. Seltzer, and T. Lyons
  1991   Early vocabulary growth: Relation to language input and gender. *Developmental Psychology* 27(2):236-248.
Huttenlocher, P.R.
  1979   Synaptic density in human frontal cortex—Developmental changes and effects of aging. *Brain Research* 163:195-205.
Huttenlocher, P.R., and A.S. Dabholkar
  1997   Regional differences in synaptogenesis in human cerebral cortex. *The Journal of Comparative Neurology* 387(2):167-178.
Hymel, S., K.H. Rubin, L. Rowden, and L. LeMare
  1990   Children's peer relationships: Longitudinal predictions of internalizing and externalizing problems from middle to late childhood. *Child Development* 61:2004-2021.
Idjradinata, P., and E. Pollitt
  1993   Reversal of developmental delays in iron-deficient anaemic infants treated with iron. *Lancet* 341:1-4.
Ikonomov, O.C., A.G. Stoynev, and A.C. Shisheva
  1998   Integrative coordination of circadian mammalian diversity: neuronal networks and peripheral clocks. *Progress in Neurobiology* 54(1):87-97.

Immelmann, K.
   1969   Song development in the zebra finch and other estrilid finches. Pp. 61-74 in *Bird Vocalizations*. R.A. Hinde, ed. Cambridge, UK: Cambridge University Press.
Immelmann, K., and S.J. Suomi
   1982   Sensitive phases in development. Pp. 508-543 in *Behavioral Development: The Bielefeld Interdisciplinary Project*. K. Immelmann, G.W. Barlow, L. Petrinovich, and M.B. Main, eds. New York: Cambridge University Press.
Infant Health and Development Program
   1990   Enhancing the outcomes of low-birthweight, premature infants: A multisite, randomized trial. *Journal of the American Medical Association* 263(22):3035-3042.
Institute for Research on Poverty
   1976   *The Rural Income Maintenance Experiment*. Madison, WI: University of Wisconsin.
Institute of Medicine
   1996   *Fetal Alcohol Syndrome: Diagnosis, Epidemiology, Prevention, and Treatment*. Committee to Study Fetal Alcohol Syndrome. K. Stratton, C. Howe, F. Battaglia, eds. Division of Biobehavioral Sciences and Mental Disorders. Washington, DC: National Academy Press.
Isaacs, M.R.
   1986   *Developing Mental Health Programs for Minority Youth and Their Families*. Washington, DC: Georgetown University Child Development Center (CASSTP Technical Assistance Center).
Isaacs, M.R., and M.P. Benjamin
   1991   *Towards a Culturally Competent System of Care: Programs Which Utilize Culturally Competent Principles*. Washington, DC: Georgetown University Child Development Center.
Isabella, R.A.
   1995   The origins of infant-mother attachment: Maternal behavior and infant development. Pp. 57-82 in *Annals of Child Development*, Volume 10. R. Vasta, ed. London, UK: Jessica Kingsley Publishers, Ltd.
Ispa, J.
   1981   Social interactions among teachers, handicapped children, and nonhandicapped children in a mainstream preschool. *Journal of Applied Developmental Psychology* 1:231-250.
Izard, C.E.
   1991   *The Psychology of Emotions*. New York: Plenum Press.
Izard, C.E., S.W. Porges, R.F. Simons, O.M. Haynes, C. Hyde, M. Parisi, and B. Cohen
   1991   Infant cardiac activity: Developmental changes and relations with attachment. *Developmental Psychology* 27:432-439.
Jacobs, P., and S. McDermott
   1989   Family caregiver costs of chronically ill and handicapped children: Method and literature review. *Public Health Reports* 104(2):158-163.
Jacobson, J.L., S.W. Jacobson, R.J. Sokol, S.S. Martier, J.W. Ager Jr., and M.G. Kaplan-Estrin
   1993   Teratogenic effects of alcohol on infant development. *Alcoholism: Clinical and Experimental Research* 17(1):174-183.
Jacobson, J.L., S.W. Jacobson, R.J. Sokol, and J.W. Ager Jr.
   1998   Relation of maternal age and pattern of pregnancy drinking to functionally significant cognitive deficit in infancy. *Alcoholism: Clinical and Experimental Research* 22(2):345-351.

Jacobson, S.W.
1998   Specificity of neurobehavioral outcomes associated with prenatal alcohol exposure. *Alcoholism: Clinical and Experimental Research* 22(2):313-320.
Jacobson, S.W., and J.L. Jacobson
1999   What teratogenic insult can reveal about underlying components of cognitive and emotional function in infants and school-age children. *The Minnesota Symposia on Child Psychology*. C.A. Nelson, ed. Hillsdale, NJ: Lawrence Erlbaum Associates, Publishers.
Jacobson, S.W., J.L. Jacobson, and R.J. Sokol
1994   Effects of fetal alcohol exposure on infant reaction time. *Alcoholism: Clinical and Experimental Research* 18(5):1125-1132.
Jahoda, G., and B. Krewer
1997   History of cross-cultural and cultural psychology. Pp. 1-42 in *Handbook of Cross-Cultural Psychology*, Volume 1: Theory and Method, Second Edition. J.W. Berry and Y.H. Poortinga, eds. Boston, MA: Allyn & Bacon, Inc.
Jargowky, P.
1997   *Poverty and Place: Ghettos, Barrios, and the American City*. New York: Russell Sage Foundation.
Jarrett, R.L., and L.M. Burton
1999   Dynamic dimensions of family structure in low-income African American families: Emergent themes from qualitative research. *Journal of Comparative Family Studies* 30:177-187.
Jencks, C., and S.E. Mayer
1990   The social consequences of growing up in a poor neighborhood. Pp. 111-186 in *Inner-City Poverty in the United States*. Committee on National Urban Policy. L.E. Lynn and M.G.H. McGeary, eds. Commission on Behavioral and Social Sciences and Education, National Research Council. Washington, DC: National Academy Press.
Jencks, C., L. Perman, and L. Rainwater
1988   The social consequences of growing up in a poor neighborhood. *American Journal of Sociology* 93:1322-1357.
Johnson, C.J., J.H. Beitchman, A. Young, M. Escobar, L. Atkinson, B. Wilson, E.B. Brownlie, L. Douglas, N. Taback, I. Lam, and M. Wang
1999   Fourteen-year follow-up of children with and without speech/language impairments: Speech/language stability and outcomes. *Journal of Speech, Language, and Hearing Research* 42(3):744-760.
Johnson, D.L., and T. Walker
1991   A follow-up evaluation of the Houston Parent-Child Development Center: School performance. *Journal of Early Intervention* 15(3):226-236.
Johnson, E.O., T.C. Kamilaris, G.P. Chrousos, and P.W. Gold
1992   Mechanisms of stress: A dynamic overview of hormonal and behavioral homeostasis. *Neuroscience and Biobehavioral Reviews* 16:115-130.
Johnson, J., and E.L. Newport
1989   Critical period effects in second language learning: The influence of maturational state on the acquisition of English as a second language. *Cognitive Psychology* 21:60-99.
Johnson, M.H.
1998   The neural basis of cognitive development. Pp. 1-49 in *Handbook of Child Psychology*, Volume 2: Cognition, Perception, and Language, Fifth Edition. W. Damon, ed. New York: John Wiley.

Johnson, M.H., M.I. Posner, and M.K. Rothbart
  1991   Components of visual orienting in early infancy: Contingency learning, anticipatory looking, and disengaging. *Journal of Cognitive Neuroscience* 3(4):335-344.
Johnson, W.
  1998   Paternal involvement in fragile, African American families: Implications for clinical social work practice. *Smith College Studies in Social Work* 68(2):215-232.
Johnson-Powell, G.
  1997   The culturologic interview: Cultural, social, and linguistic issues in the assessment and treatment of children. Pp. 349-364 in *Transcultural Child Development: Psychological Assessment and Treatment*. G. Johnson-Powell and J. Yamamoto, eds. New York: Wiley.
Joint Committee on Health Policy of the World Health Organization and UNICEF
  1994   *Strategic Approach to Operationalizing Selected End-Decade Goals: Reduction of Iron Deficiency Anaemia*. Rep. No. JCHP30/95/4.5. Geneva, Switzerland: World Health Organization.
Jones, A.E., C. Ten Cate, and P.J.B. Slater
  1996   Early experience and plasticity of song in adult male zebra finches (Taeniopygia guttata). *Journal of Comparative Psychology* 110:354-369.
Jones, K.L., and D.W. Smith
  1973   Recognition of the Fetal Alcohol Syndrome in early infancy. *Lancet* 2:999-1001.
Kaestner, R., and H. Corman
  1995   The impact of child health and family inputs on child cognitive development. Cambridge, MA: National Bureau of Economic Research.
Kagan, J.
  1998a   *Three Seductive Ideas*. Cambridge, MA: Harvard University Press.
  1998b   Biology and the child. Pp. 177-235 in *Handbook of Child Psychology*, Volume 3: Social, Emotional, and Personality Development, Fifth Edition. W. Damon, ed. New York: Wiley.
Kagan, J., and N. Snidman
  1991   Infant predictors of inhibited and uninhibited profiles. *Psychological Science* 2:40-44.
Kagan, J., R. Kearsley, and P. Zelazo
  1978   *Infancy: Its Place in Human Development*. Cambridge, MA: Harvard University Press.
Kagan, J., J.S. Reznick, and N. Snidman
  1987   The physiology and psychology of behavioral inhibition in children. *Child Development* 58:1459-1473.
Kagan, J., N. Snidman, and D. Arcus
  1998   Childhood derivatives of high and low reactivity in infancy. *Child Development* 69:1483-1493.
Kagan, S.L.
  1993   *The Essential Functions of the Early Care and Education System: Rationale and Definitions*. New Haven, CT: Quality 2000, Yale University.
Kagan, S.L., and N.E. Cohen, eds.
  1996   *Reinventing Early Care and Education: A Vision for a Quality System*. San Francisco, CA: Jossey-Bass Publishers.
Kagan, S.L., and J.W. Newton
  1989   Public policy report. For-profit and nonprofit child care: Similarities and differences. *Young Children* 45(1):4-10.

Kaiser, A.P., and P.P. Hester
   1997   Prevention of conduct disorder through early intervention: A social-communicative
           perspective. *Behavioral Disorders* 22(3):117-130.
Kamerman, S.B.
   2000   Early childhood intervention policies: An international perspective. Pp. 613-629
           in *Handbook of Early Childhood Intervention*, Second Edition, J.P. Shonkoff and
           S.J. Meisels, eds. New York: Cambridge University Press.
Kamerman, S.B., and A.J. Kahn
   1995   *Starting Right: How America Neglects Its Youngest Children and What We Can
           Do About It.* New York: Oxford University Press.
Kamhi, A., H. Catts, D. Mauer, K. Apel, and B. Gentry
   1988   Phonological and spatial processing abilities in language- and reading-impaired
           children. *Journal of Speech and Hearing Disorders* 53:316-327.
Karofsky, P.S.
   1984   Infantile colic. *The Journal of Family Practice* 19(1):107-116.
Karoly, L.A., P.W. Greenwood, S.S. Everingham, J. Houbé, M.R. Kilburn, C.P. Rydell, M.
Sanders, and J. Chiesa
   1998   *Investing In Our Children: What We Know and Don't Know About the Costs and
           Benefits of Early Childhood Interventions.* Santa Monica, CA: RAND.
Kasarda, J.
   1993   Inner city concentrated poverty and neighborhood distress: 1970-1980. *Housing
           Policy Debate* 4:253-302.
Katz, L., J. Kling, and J. Liebman
   1999   Moving To Opportunity in Boston: Early Impacts of a Housing Mobility Program.
           Working paper. Industrial Relations Section, Princeton University.
Kaufman, J.
   1996   Child abuse. *Current Opinion in Psychiatry* 9:251-256.
Kaufman, J., and D.S. Charney
   1999   Neurobiological correlates of child abuse. *Biological Psychiatry* 45:1235-1236.
Kaufman, J., and J. Rosenbaum
   1992   The education and employment of low-income black youth in white suburbs. *Edu-
           cational Evaluation and Policy Analysis* 14:229-240.
Kazdin, A.E.
   1993   Treatment of conduct disorder: Progress and directions in psychotherapy research.
           Development and Psychopathology 5:277-310.
Keefe, M.R.
   1988   Irritable infant syndrome: Theoretical perspectives and practice implications. *Ad-
           vances in Nursing Science* 10(3):70-78.
Keefe, S.E.
   1992   Ethnic identity: The domain of perceptions of and attachment to ethnic groups and
           cultures. *Human Organization* 51(1):35-43.
Keefe, S.E., and A.E. Padilla
   1987   *Chicano Ethnicity.* Albuquerque, NM: University of New Mexico Press.
Kelly, J.F., and K.E. Barnard
   2000   Assessment of parent-child interaction: Implications for early intervention. Pp.
           258-289 in *Handbook of Early Childhood Intervention*, Second Edition. J.P.
           Shonkoff and S.J. Meisels, eds. New York: Cambridge University Press.
Kelly, J.F., and C.L. Booth
   1999   Child care for infants with special needs: Issues and applications. *Infants and
           Young Children* 12(1):26-33.

Kempe, R.S.
  1987   A developmental approach to the treatment of the abused child. Pp. 360-381 in
          The Battered Child, Fourth Edition. R.E. Helfer and R.S. Kempe, eds. Chicago,
          IL: University of Chicago Press.
Kerns, K.A.
  1996   Individual differences in friendship quality and their links to child-mother attach-
          ment. Pp. 137-157 in *The Company They Keep: Friendship in Childhood and
          Adolescence*. W.W. Bukowski, A.F. Newcomb, and W.W. Hartup, eds. New
          York: Cambridge University Press.
Kershaw, D., and J. Fair
  1976   *The New Jersey Income Maintenance Experiment*, Volume 1. New York: Aca-
          demic Press.
Kessen, W.
  1965   *The Child*. New York: Wiley & Sons.
  1991   Commentary: Dynamics of enculturation. Pp. 185-193 in *Cultural Approaches to
          Parenting*. M. Bornstein, ed. Hillsdale, NJ: Lawrence Erlbaum Associates.
Kessler, R.
  1982   A disaggregation of the relationship between socioeconomic status and psychologi-
          cal distress. *American Sociological Review* 47:752-764.
Kessler, R., and P.D. Cleary
  1980   Social class and psychological distress. *American Sociological Review* 45:463-478.
Kessler, R.C., K.A. McGonagle, S. Zhao, C.B. Nelson, M. Hughes, S. Eshleman, H. Wittchen,
and K. Kendler
  1994   Lifetime and 12-month prevalence of DSM-III-R psychiatric disorders in the United
          States: Results from the National Comorbidity Study. *Archives of General Psy-
          chiatry* 51(1):8-19.
Kim, U.
  1987   The parent-child relationship: The core of Korean collectivism. Paper presented at
          the meeting of the International Association for Cross-Cultural Psychology,
          Newcastle, Australia.
Kirsh, S.J., and J. Cassidy
  1997   Preschoolers' attention to and memory for attachment-relevant information. *Child
          Development* 68:1143-1153.
Kitzman, H., D.L. Olds, C.R. Henderson Jr., C. Hanks, R. Cole, R. Tatelbaum, K.M.
          McConnochie, K. Sidora, D. Luckey, D. Shaver, K. Engelhardt, D. James, and K.E.
          Barnard
  1997   Effect of prenatal and infancy home visitation by nurses on pregnancy outcomes,
          childhood injuries, and repeated childbearing. *Journal of the American Medical
          Association* 278(8):644-652.
Klebanov, P.K., J. Brooks-Gunn, and G.J. Duncan
  1994   Does neighborhood and family poverty affect mothers' parenting, mental health,
          and social support? *Journal of Marriage and the Family* 56(2):441-455.
Klebanov, P.K., J. Brooks-Gunn, R. Gordon, and P.L. Chase-Lansdale
  1997   The intersection of the neighborhood and home environment and its influence on
          young children. Pp. 79-118 in *Neighborhood Poverty: Context and Consequences
          for Children*. J. Brooks-Gunn, G.J. Duncan, and J.L. Aber, eds. New York: Russell
          Sage Foundation.
Klein, B.W., and P.L. Rones
  1989   A profile of the working poor. *Monthly Labor Review* 112:3-13.

Klein, N., and R. Sheehan
1987   Staff development: A key issue in meeting the needs of young handicapped children in day care settings. *Topics in Early Childhood Special Education* 7:13-27.

Klein, P.
1995   The needs of children. *Mothering* 74:39-45.

Klein, S.K., and I. Rapin
1988   Intermittent conductive hearing loss and language development. Pp. 96-109 in *Language Development in Exceptional Circumstances*. D. Bishop and K. Mogford, eds. New York: Churchill Livingstone.

Klerman, J. and A. Leibowitz
1998   The FMLA and the labor supply of new mothers: Evidence from the June CPS. Paper presented at the annual meeting of the Population Association of America, Chicago, IL, April 2, 1998.

Klerman, L.V.
1991   *Alive and Well? A Research and Policy Review of Health Programs for Poor Young Children.* New York: National Center for Children in Poverty.

Kliegl, R., J. Smith, J. Heckhausen, and P.B. Baltes
1987   Mnemonic training for the acquisition of skilled digit memory. *Cognition and Instruction* 4(4):203-223.

Klima, E., and U. Bellugi
1979   *The Signs of Language.* Cambridge, MA: Harvard University Press.

Klintsova, A.Y., J.T. Matthews, C.R. Goodlett, R.M.A. Napper, and W.T. Greenough
1997   Therapeutic motor training increases parallel fiber synapse number per Purkinje neuron in cerebellar cortex of rats given postnatal binge alcohol exposure: Preliminary report. *Alcoholism: Clinical and Experimental Research* 21(7):1257-1263.

Klintsova, A.Y., R.M. Cowell, R.A. Swain, R.M.A. Napper, C.R. Goodlett, and W.T. Greenough
1998   Therapeutic effects of complex motor training on motor performance deficits induced by neonatal binge-like alcohol exposure in rats: I. Behavioral results. *Brain Research* 800:48-61.

Knitzer, J.
2000   Early childhood mental health programs. Pp. 906-956 in *Handbook of Early Childhood Intervention*, Second Edition. J.P. Shonkoff and S.J. Meisels, eds. New York: Cambridge University Press.

Knudsen, E.I.
1999   Early Experience and Critical Periods. Pp. 637-654 in *Fundamental Neuroscience*. M.J. Zigmond, F.E. Bloom, S.C. Landis, J.L. Roberts, and L.R. Squire, eds. New York: Academic Press.

Kochanska, G.
1990   Maternal beliefs as long-term predictors of mother-child interaction and report. *Child Development* 61:1934-1943.
1991   Socialization and temperament in the development of guilt and conscience. *Child Development* 62:1379-1392.
1993   Toward a synthesis of parental socialization and child temperament in early development of conscience. *Child Development* 64:325-347.
1995   Children's temperament, mothers' discipline, and security of attachment: Multiple pathways to emerging internalization. *Child Development* 66:597-615.
1997   Multiple pathways to conscience for children with different temperaments: From toddlerhood to age 5. *Developmental Psychology* 33:228-240.

Kochanska, G., and R.A. Thompson
    1997   The emergence and development of conscience in toddlerhood and early childhood.
           Pp. 53-77 in *Parenting Strategies and Children's Internalization of Values: A Hand-
           book of Theoretical and Research Perspectives*. J.E. Grusec and L. Kuczynski, eds.
           New York: Wiley.
Kochanska, G., R. Casey, and A. Fukumoto
    1995   Toddlers' sensitivity to standard violations. *Child Development* 66:643-656.
Kochanska, G., K. Murray, T.Y. Jacques, A.L. Koenig, and K. Vandegeest
    1996   Inhibitory control in young children and its role in emerging internalization. *Child
           Development* 67:490-507.
Kochanska, G., K. Murray, and K.C. Coy
    1997   Inhibitory control as a contributory to conscience in childhood: From toddler to
           early school age. *Child Development* 68:263-277.
Kochanska, G., K. Murray, and E.T. Harlan
    2000   Effortful control in early childhood: Continuity and changes, antecedents, and im-
           plications for social development. *Developmental Psychology* 36(2):220-232.
Kohn, M.L.
    1959   Social class and the exercise of parental authority. *American Sociological Review*
           24:352-366.
    1963   Social class and the parent-child relationship: An interpretation. *American Journal
           of Sociology* 68:471-480.
    1969   *Class and Conformity: A Study in Values*. Homewood, IL: Dorsey Press.
    1976   Social class and parental values: Another confirmation of the relationship. *Ameri-
           can Sociological Review* 41:538-545.
Kohn, M.L., and C. Schooler
    1973   Occupational experience and psychological functioning: An assessment of recipro-
           cal effects. *American Sociological Review* 38:97-118.
Kolb, B., and I.Q. Whishaw
    1998   Brain plasticity and behavior. *Annual Review of Psychology* 49:43-64.
Kolko, D.J.
    1996   Child physical abuse. Pp. 21-50 in *The APSAC Handbook on Child Maltreatment*.
           J. Briere and L. Berliner, eds. Thousand Oaks, CA: Sage Publications, Inc.
Konner, M.
    1982   *The Tangled Wing: Biological Constraints on the Human Spirit*. New York: Holt,
           Rinehart and Winston.
Konner, M., and C. Worthman
    1980   Nursing frequency, gonadal function, and birth spacing among !Kung hunter-gath-
           erers. *Science* 207:788-791.
Kontos, S.
    1994   The ecology of family day care. *Early Childhood Research Quarterly* 9:87-110.
Kontos, S., and R. Fiene
    1987   Child care quality, compliance with regulations, and children's development. Pp.
           57-80 in *Quality in Child Care: What Does Research Tell Us?* D.A. Phillips, ed.
           Washington, DC: National Association for the Education of Young Children.
Kontos, S., H.C. Hsu, and L. Dunn
    1994   Children's cognitive and social competence in child care centers and family day
           care homes. *Journal of Applied Developmental Psychology* 15:87-111.
Kontos, S., C. Howes, M. Shinn, and E. Galinsky
    1995   *Quality in Family Child Care and Relative Care*. New York: Teachers College
           Press, Columbia University.

Koob, G.R.
  1992   The behavioral neuroendocrinology of corticotropin-releasing factor, growth hor-
         mone-releasing factor, somatostatin and gonadotropin-releasing hormone. Pp. 353-
         364 in *Neuroendocrinology*. C.B. Nemeroff, ed. Boca Raton, FL: CRC Press.
Kopp, C.B.
  1982   Antecedents of self-regulation: A developmental perspective. *Developmental Psy-
         chology* 18:199-214.
  1987   The growth of self-regulation: Caregivers and children. Pp. 34-55 in *Contempo-
         rary Topics in Developmental Psychology*. N. Eisenberg, ed. New York: Wiley.
  1989   Regulation of distress and negative emotions: A developmental view. *Developmen-
         tal Psychology* 25:343-354.
  1997   Young children: Emotion management, instrumental control, and plans. Pp. 103-
         124 in *The Developmental Psychology of Planning: Why, How, and When Do We
         Plan?* S.L. Friedman and E.K. Scholnick, eds. Mahwah, NJ: Lawrence Erlbaum
         Associates.
  2000   Self-regulation in children. In *International Encyclopedia of the Social and Behav-
         ioral Sciences*. J.J. Smelser and P.B. Baltes, eds. Oxford, UK: Elsevier.
Kopp, C.B., and N. Wyer
  1994   Self-regulation in normal and atypical development. Pp. 31-56 in *Disorders and
         Dysfunctions of the Self: Rochester Symposium on Developmental Psychopathol-
         ogy*, Volume 5. D. Cicchetti and S.L. Toth, eds. Rochester, NY: University of
         Rochester Press.
Korbin, J.E.
  1994   Sociocultural factors in child maltreatment. Pp. 182-223 in *Protecting Children
         From Abuse and Neglect: Foundations for a New Strategy*. G.B. Melton and F.D.
         Barry, eds. New York: The Guilford Press.
Korenman, S., and J.E. Miller
  1997   Effects of long-term poverty on physical health of children in the National Longitu-
         dinal Survey of Youth. Pp. 70-99 in *Consequences of Growing Up Poor*. G.J.
         Duncan and J. Brooks-Gunn, eds. New York: Russell Sage Foundation.
Kovacs, M.
  1989   Affective disorders in children and adolescents. *American Psychologist* 44:268-
         269.
Kraemer, H.C., A.E. Kazdin, D.R. Offord, R.C. Kessler, P.S. Jensen, and D.J. Kupfer
  1997   Coming to terms with the terms of risk. *Archives of General Psychiatry* 54(4):337-
         343.
Krauss, M., C. Upshur, J.P. Shonkoff, and P. Hauser-Cram
  1993   The impact of parent groups on mothers of infants with disabilities. *Journal of
         Early Intervention* 17:8-20.
Kuczynski, L.
  1993   Evolving metaphors of bidirectionality in socialization and parent-child relations.
         Paper presented at the annual meeting of the Canadian Psychological Association,
         Montreal, Canada.
Kuczynski, L., and G. Kochanska
  1990   Development of children's noncompliance strategies from toddlerhood to age 5.
         Developmental Psychology 26:398-408.
Kuczynski, L., G. Kochanska, M. Radke-Yarrow, and O. Girnius-Brown
  1987   A developmental interpretation of young children's noncompliance. *Developmen-
         tal Psychology* 23:799-806.

Kuczynski, L., S. Marshall, and K. Schell
   1997   Value socialization in a bidirectional context. Pp. 23-50 in *Parenting Strategies and Children's Internalization of Values: A Handbook of Theoretical and Research Perspectives*. J.E. Grusec and L. Kuczynski, eds. New York: Wiley.
Kupersmidt, J., and J.D. Coie
   1990   Preadolescent peer status, aggression, and school adjustment as predictors of externalizing problems in adolescence. *Child Development* 61:1350-1362.
Ladd, G.W., and C.H. Hart
   1992   Creating informal play opportunities: Are parents' and preschoolers' initiations related to children's competence wiith peers? *Developmental Psychology* 28:1179-1187.
Ladd, G.W., and J.M. Price
   1986   Promoting children's cognitive and social competence: The relation between parents' perceptions of task difficulty and children's perceived and actual competence. *Child Development* 57:446-460.
   1993   Playstyles of peer-accepted and peer-rejected children on the playground. Pp. 130-161 in *Children on Playgrounds: Research Perspectives and Applications. SUNY Series, Children's Play in Society*. C.H. Hart, ed. Albany, NY: State University of New York Press.
Ladd, G.W., S. Profilet, and C.H. Hart
   1992   Parent's management of children's peer relations: Facilitating and supervising children's activities in the peer culture. Pp. 215-254 in *Family-Peer Relationships: Modes of Linkage*. R.D. Parke and G.W. Ladd, eds. Hillsdale, NJ: Erlbaum.
LaFreniere, P.J., and F. Capuano
   1997   Preventive intervention as means of clarifying direction of effects in socialization: Anxious-withdrawn preschoolers case. *Development and Psychopathology* 9:551-564.
LaFreniere, P.J., and J.E. Dumas
   1992   A transactional analysis of early childhood anxiety and social withdrawal. *Development and Psychopathology* 4:385-402.
LaFreniere, P.J., and L.A. Sroufe
   1985   Profiles of peer competence in the preschool: Interrelations between measures, influence of social ecology, and relations to attachment history. *Developmental Psychology* 21:56-69.
LaFromboise, T.D., H.L.K. Coleman, and J. Gerton
   1993   Psychological impact of biculturalism: Evidence and theory. *Psychological Bulletin* 14(3):395-412.
Lahey, B.B., W.E. Pelham, M.A. Stein, J. Loney, C. Trapani, K. Nugent, H. Kipp, E. Schmidt, S. Lee, M. Cale, E. Gold, C.M. Hartung, E. Willcutt, and B. Baumann
   1998   Validity of DSM-IV attention-deficit/hyperactivity disorder for younger children. *Journal of the American Academy of Child and Adolescent Psychiatry* 37(7):695-702.
Lahey, B.B., T.L. Miller, R.A. Gordon, and A.W. Riley
   1999   Developmental epidemiology of the disruptive behavior disorders. Pp. 23-48 in *Handbook of Disruptive Behavior Disorders*. H.C. Quay and A.E. Hogan, eds. New York: Kluwer Academic/Plenum Publishers.
Laible, D.J., and R.A. Thompson
   1998   Attachment and emotional understanding in preschool children. *Developmental Psychology* 34(5):1038-1045.
   in   Mother-child discourse, attachment security, shared positive affect, and early con-
   press   science development. *Child Development*.

Lally, J.R., P.L. Mangione, and A.S. Honig
  1988   The Syracuse University Family Development Research Project: Long-range impact of an early intervention with low-income children and their families. Pp. 79-104 in *Parent Education As Early Childhood Intervention: Emerging Directions in Theory, Research, and Practice.* D.R. Powell, ed. Norwood, NJ: Albex.
Lamb, M.E.
  1998   Nonparental child care: Context, quality, correlates. Pp. 73-134 in *Handbook of Child Psychology,* Volume 4: Child Psychology in Practice, 5th Edition. W. Damon, I.E. Sigel, and K.A. Renninger, eds. New York: John Wiley & Sons, Inc.
  1999   *Parenting and Child Development in Nontraditional Families.* Mahwah, NJ: Erlbaum.
  in press   Research on father involvement: An historical overview. *Marriage and Family Review.*
Lamb, M.E., and C.M. Malkin
  1986   The development of social expectations in distress-relief sequences: A longitudinal study. *International Journal of Behavioral Development* 9:235-249.
Lamb, M.E., J.H. Pleck, E. Charnov, and J.A. Levine
  1985a   Paternal behavior in humans. *American Psychologist* 25:883-894.
Lamb, M.E., R.A. Thompson, W. Gardner, and E.L. Charnov
  1985b   *Infant-Mother Attachment.* Hillsdale, NJ: Erlbaum.
Lamb, M.E., C.P. Hwang, F.L. Bookstein, A.G. Broberg, G. Hult, and A. Frodi
  1988   Determinants of social competence in Swedish preschoolers. *Developmental Psychology* 24(1):58-70.
Lancaster, J.B., and C.S. Lancaster
  1987   The watershed: Change in parental investment and family formation strategies in the course of human evolution. Pp. 187-205 in *Parenting Across the Life Span: Biosocial Perspectives.* J.B. Lancaster, J. Altmann, A. Rossi, and L.R. Sherrod, eds. Hawthorne, NY: Aldine de Gruyter.
Landau, B., and L.R. Gleitman
  1985   *Language and Experience: Evidence From the Blind Child.* Cambridge, MA: Harvard University Press.
Landis, L.J.
  1992   Marital employment, and childcare status of mothers with infants and toddlers with disabilities. *Topics in Early Childhood Special Education* 12:496-507.
Landry, S.H., K.E. Smith, C.L. Miller-Loncar, and P.R. Swank
  1997   Predicting cognitive-language and social growth curves from early maternal behaviors in children at varying degrees of biological risk. *Developmental Psychology* 33(6):1040-1053.
Laosa, L.M.
  1980   Maternal teaching strategies in Chicano and Anglo-American families: The influence of culture and education on maternal behavior. *Child Development* 51:759-765.
  1983   School, occupation, culture and family. Pp. 79-135 in *Changing Families.* E. Sigel and L. Laosa, eds. New York: Plenum Press.
Larsen, J.M., and C.C. Robinson
  1989   Later effects of preschool on low-risk children. *Early Childhood Research Quarterly* 4:133-144.
Layzer, J.I., B.D. Goodson, and M. Moss
  1993   *Life in Preschool: Final Report,* Volume 1. Cambridge, MA: Abt Associates.
Lazar, I., and R. Darlington
  1982   Lasting effects of early education. *Monographs of the Society for Research in Child Development* (Serial No. 195) 47(2/3):1-151.

Lebra, T.S.
   1994   Mother and child in Japanese socialization: A Japan-U.S. comparison. Pp. 259-274
          in Cross-Cultural Roots of Minority Child Development. P.M. Greenfield and
          R.R. Cocking, eds. Hillsdale, NJ: Lawrence Erlbaum Associates, Publishers.
LeDoux, J.
   1996   The Emotional Brain. New York: Touchstone.
Leger, D.W.
   1992   Biological Foundations of Behavior: An Integrative Approach. New York: Harper
          Collins.
Lehtonen, L., T. Korhonen, and H. Korvenranta
   1994   Temperament and sleeping pattern in colicky infants during the first year of life.
          Journal of Developmental and Behavioral Pediatrics 15(6):416-420.
Lehtonen, L., S. Gormally, and R.G. Barr
   in   Clinical pies, etiology and outcome in infants presenting with early increased cry-
   press ing. In Crying As a Signal, a Sign, and a Symptom: Developmental and Clinical
          Aspects of Early Crying Behavior. R.G. Barr, B. Hopkins, and J. Green, eds.
          London: MacKeith Press.
Leif, N.R.
   1985   The drug user as parent. International Journal of the Addictions 20:63-97.
Lemery, K.S., and H.H. Goldsmith
   1999   Genetically informative designs for the study of behavioral development. Interna-
          tional Journal of Behavioral Development 23:293-317.
Lennon, M.C., J.L. Aber, and B.B. Blum
   1998   Program, Research, and Policy Implications of Evaluations of Teenage Parent
          Programs. New York: Research Forum on Children, Families, and the New
          Federalism.
Leonard, B., J. Brust, and J. Sapienza
   1992   Financial and time costs to parents of severely disabled children. Public Health
          Reports 107(3):302-311.
Leonard, L.
   1998   Children With Specific Language Impairment. Cambridge, MA: MIT Press.
Leonard, L., J. Eyer, L. Bedore, and B. Grela
   1997   Three accounts of the grammatical morpheme difficulties of English-speaking chil-
          dren with specific language impairment. Journal of Speech and Hearing Research
          40:741-753.
Leonard, R.
   1993   Mother-child disputes as arenas for fostering negotiation skills. Early Develop-
          ment and Parenting 2:157-167.
Lepper, M.
   1981   Intrinsic and extrinsic motivation in children: Detrimental effects of superfluous
          social controls. Pp. 155-214 in The Minnesota Symposia on Child Psychology:
          Aspects of the Development of Competence, Volume 14. A. Collins, ed. Hillsdale,
          NJ: Lawrence Erlbaum Associates.
Lepper, M.R., D. Greene, and R.E. Nisbett
   1973   Undermining children's intrinsic interest with extrinsic rewards: A test of the over-
          justification hypothesis. Journal of Personality and Social Psychology 28:129-137.
Lerner, R.M.
   1991   Changing organism-context relations as the basic process of development: A devel-
          opmental contextual perspective. Developmental Psychology 27:27-32.

Leslie, A.M., and S. Keeble
  1987   Do six-month-old infants perceive causality? *Cognition* 25(3):265-288.
Lesser, A.J.
  1985   Public programs for crippled children. Pp. 733-757 in *Issues in the Care of Children with Chronic Illness: A Sourcebook on Problems, Services, and Policies.* N. Hobbs and J.M. Perrin, eds. San Francisco, CA: Jossey-Bass Inc.
Lester, B.M., C.F.Z. Boukydis, and J.E. Twomey
  2000   Maternal substance abuse and child outcome. Pp. 161-175 in *Handbook of Infant Mental Health,* Second Edition. C.H. Zeanah, ed. New York: The Guilford Press.
LeVay, S., T.N. Wiesel, and D.H. Hubel
  1980   The development of ocular dominance columns in normal and visually deprived monkeys. *The Journal of Comparative Neurology* 191:1-51.
Levin, H.M.
  1983   *Cost-Effectiveness: A Primer.* Beverly Hills, CA: Sage.
Levin, H., K. Culhane, J. Hartmann, K. Evankovich, A. Mattson, H. Harward, G. Ringholz, Ewing-Cobbs, and J. Fletcher
  1991   Developmental changes in performance on tests of purported frontal lobe functioning. *Developmental Neuropsychology* 7:377-395.
Levine, R.A.
  1977   Child rearing as cultural adaptation. Pp. 15-27 in *Culture and Infancy: Variations in the Human Experience.* P.H. Leiderman, S. Tulkin, and A. Rosenfeld, eds. New York: Academic Press.
  1989   Cultural environments in child development. Pp. 349-378 in *Child Development Today and Tomorrow.* W. Damon, ed. San Francisco, CA: Jossey-Bass.
  1990   Infant environments in psychoanalysis: A cross-cultural view. Pp. 454-467 in *Cultural Psychology: Essays on Comparative Human Development.* J. Stigler, R.A. Shweder, and G. Herdt, eds. New York: Cambridge University Press.
Levine, R.A., S. Dixon, S. LeVine, A. Richman, P. Leiderman, C. Keefer, and T.B. Brazelton
  1994   *Child Care and Culture: Lessons From Africa.* New York: Cambridge University Press.
Levine, S., and E.B. Thoman
  1970   Maternal factors influencing subsequent adrenocortical activity in the offspring. Pp. 111-122 in *Postnatal Development of Phenotype.* S. Kazda and V.H. Denenberg, eds. Prague, Czechoslovakia: Academia.
Levine, S., and S.G. Wiener
  1988   Psychoendocrine aspects of mother-infant relationships in nonhuman primates. *Psychoneuroendocrinology* 13(1&2):143-154.
Levine-Coley, R.
  1998   Children's socialization experiences and functioning in single-mother households: The importance of fathers and other men. *Child Development* 69(1):219-230.
Lewis, M.L.
  1993   Self-conscious emotions: Embarrassment, pride, shame, and guilt. Pp. 563-573 in *Handbook of Emotions.* M. Lewis and J.M. Haviland, eds. New York: Guilford.
  2000   The cultural context of infant mental health: The development niche of infant-caregiver relationships. Pp. 91-107 in *Handbook of Infant Mental Health,* Second Edition. C.H. Zeanah, ed. New York: The Guilford Press.
Liaw, F., and J. Brooks-Gunn
  1993   Patterns of low-birth-weight children's cognitive development. *Developmental Psychology* 29(6):1024-1035.

Liaw, F., S.J. Meisels, and J. Brooks-Gunn
    1995   The effects of experience of early intervention on low birth weight, premature
            children: The Infant Health and Development Program. *Early Childhood Research
            Quarterly* 10:405-431.
Lieberman, A.F.
    1993   *The Emotional Life of the Toddler.* New York: Free Press.
Lieberman, A.F., and P. Van Horn
    1998   Attachment, trauma, and domestic violence. *Child Custody* 7:423-443.
Lieberman, A.F., D.R. Weston, and J.H. Pawl
    1991   Preventive intervention and outcome with anxiously attached dyads. *Child Devel-
            opment* 62(1):199-209.
Lieberman, A.F., R. Silverman, and J.H. Pawl
    2000   Infant-parent psychotherapy: Core concepts and current approaches. Pp. 472-484
            in *Handbook of Infant Mental Health*, Second Edition. C.H. Zeanah, ed. New
            York: The Guilford Press.
Light, R.J., J.D. Singer, and J.B. Willett
    1990   *By Design: Planning Research on Higher Education.* Cambridge, MA: Harvard
            University Press.
Lin, W., P.K. Robins, D. Card, K. Harknett, and S. Lui-Garr
    1998   *When Financial Incentives Encourage Work: Complete 18-Month Findings From
            the Self Sufficiency Project.* Ottowa, Canada: Social Research Demonstration
            Corporation.
Linver, M.R., J. Brooks-Gunn, and D. Kohen
    1999   Parenting behavior and emotional health as mediators of family poverty effects
            upon young low-birthweight children's cognitive ability. *Annals of the New York
            Academy of Sciences* 896:376-378.
Lipsey, M.W., and D.B. Wilson
    1993   The efficacy of psychological, education, and behavioral treatment. *American Psy-
            chologist* 48(12):1181-1209.
Litt, C.J.
    1981   Children's attachment to transitional objects: A study of two pediatric populations.
            American Journal of Orthopsychiatry 51:131-139.
Little, R.A., and L.H. Yau
    1998   Statistical techniques for analyzing data from prevention trials: Treatment of no-
            shows using Rubin's causal model. *Psychological Methods* 3(2):147-159.
Liu, D., J. Korio, B. Tannenbaum, C. Caldji, D. Francis, A. Freedman, S. Sharma, D. Pearson,
P.M. Plotsky, and M.J. Meaney
    1997   Maternal care, hippocampal glucocorticoid receptors, and hypothalamic-pituitary-
            adrenal responses to stress. *Science* 277:1659-1662.
Locurto, C.
    1991   Beyond IQ in preschool programs? *Intelligence* 15:295-312.
Loeber, R., and D. Hay
    1997   Key issues in the development of aggression and violence from childhood to early
            adulthood. *Annual Review of Psychology* 48:371-410.
Loeber, R., and M. Stouthamer-Loeber
    1987   Prediction. Pp. 325-392 in *Handbook of Juvenile Delinquency*. H. Quay, ed.
            New York: Wiley.
Loehlin, J.C., J.M. Horn, and L. Willerman
    1989   Modeling IQ change: Evidence from the Texas Adoption Project. *Child Develop-
            ment* 60:993-1004.

Looker, A.C., P. Dallman, M.D. Carroll, E.W. Gunter, and C.L. Johnson
  1997 Prevalence of iron deficiency in the United States. *Journal of the American Medical Association* 277:973-976.
Lovaas, O.I.
  1987 Behavioral treatment and normal educational and intellectual functioning in young autistic children. *Journal of Consulting and Clinical Psychology* 55:3-9.
Love, J.M., P.Z. Schochet, and A.L. Meckstroth
  1996 *Are They in Any Real Danger? What Research Does—and Doesn't—Tell Us About Child Care Quality and Children's Well-Being.* Princeton, NJ: Mathematica Policy Research, Inc.
Lowe, J., and L. Papile
  1990 Neurodevelopmental performance of very-low-birth-weight infants with mild periventricular, intraventricular hemorrhage: Outcome at 5 to 6 years of age. *American Journal of Diseases of Childhood* 144:1242-1245.
Lozoff, B., A.W. Wolf, and N.S. Davis
  1984 Cosleeping in urban families with young children in the United States. *Pediatrics* 74:171-182.
Lozoff, B., A.W. Wolf, J.J. Urrutia, and F.E. Viteri
  1985 Abnormal behavior and low developmental test scores in iron-deficient anemic infants. *Journal of Developmental and Behavioral Pediatrics* 6:69-75.
Lozoff, B., N.K. Klein, and K.M. Prabucki
  1986 Iron-deficient anemic infants at play. *Journal of Developmental and Behavioral Pediatrics* 7:152-158.
Lozoff, B., G.M. Brittenham, A.W. Wolf, D.K. McClish, P.M. Kuhnert, E. Jimenez, R. Jimenez, L.A. Mora, I. Gomez, and D. Krauskoph
  1987 Iron deficiency anemia and iron therapy: Effects on infant developmental test performance. *Pediatrics* 79:981-995.
Lozoff, B., E. Jimenez, and A.W. Wolf
  1991 Long-term developmental outcome of infants with iron deficiency. *New England Journal of Medicine* 325:687-694.
Lozoff, B., A.W. Wolf, and E. Jimenez
  1996 Effects of extended oral-iron therapy on infant developtmental test scores. *The Journal of Pediatrics* 129:382-389.
Lozoff, B., N.K. Klein, E.C. Nelson, D.K. McClish, M. Manuel, and M.E. Chacon
  1998 Behavior of infants with iron-deficiency anemia. *Child Development* 69(1):24-36.
Lozoff, B., E. Jimenez, J. Hagen, E. Mollen, and A.W. Wolf
  2000 Poorer behavioral and developmental outcome more than 10 years after treatment for iron deficiency in infancy. *Pediatrics* 105(4):E51.
Luciana, M., and C.A. Nelson
  1998 The functional emergence of prefrontally-guided working memory systems in four- to eight-year-old children. *Neuropsychologia* 36(3):273-293.
Luciana, M., L. Lindeke, M.K. Georgieff, M.M. Mills, and C.A. Nelson
  1999 Neurobehavioral evidence for working-memory deficits in school-aged children with histories of prematurity. *Developmental Medicine and Child Neurology* 41:521-533.
Ludwig, J., G.J. Duncan, and P. Hirschfield
  in   Urban poverty and juvenile crime: Evidence from a randomized housing-mobility
  press experiment. *Quarterly Journal of Economics.*
Luria, A.R.
  1966 *Higher Cortical Functions in Man.* New York: Basic Books.

Luster, T., and H. McAdoo
  1996   Family and child influences on educational attainment: A secondary analysis of the
         High/Scope Perry preschool data. *Developmental Psychology* 32:26-39.
Luster, T., K. Rhoades, and B. Haas
  1989   The relation between parental values and parenting behavior: A test of the Kohn
         Hypothesis. *Journal of Marriage and the Family* 51:139-147.
Lynch, E.W., and M.J. Hanson, eds.
  1998   *Developing Cross-Cultural Competence: A Guide for Working With Children and
         Their Families*, Second Edition. Baltimore, MD: Paul Brookes.
Lyon, G.R.
  1996   The need for conceptual and theoretical clarity in the study of attention, memory,
         and executive function. Pp. 3-9 in *Attention, Memory, and Executive Function*.
         G.R. Lyon and N. Krasnegor, eds. Baltimore, MD: Paul H. Brookes Publishing
         Co., Inc.
Lyons-Ruth, K., D.B. Connell, D. Zoll, and J. Stahl
  1987   Infants at social risk: Relations among infant maltreatment, maternal behavior, and
         infant attachment behavior. *Developmental Psychology* 23:223-232.
Lyons-Ruth, K., D.B. Connell, H.U. Grunebaum, and S. Botein
  1990   Infants at social risk: Maternal depression and family support services as mediators
         of infant development and security of attachment. *Child Development* 61:85-98.
Lyons-Ruth, K., B.M. Repacholi, S. McLeod, and E. Silva
  1991   Disorganized attachment behavior in infancy: Short-term stability, maternal and
         infant correlates, and risk-related subtypes. *Development and Psychopathology*
         3:377-396.
Lytton, H.
  1990   Child and parent effects in boys' conduct disorder: A reinterpretation. *Develop-
         mental Psychology* 26:683-697.
Maccoby, E.E.
  1980   *Social Development: Psychological Growth and the Parent-Child Relationship*.
         New York: Harcourt Brace Jovanovich, Inc.
  1983   Let's not overattribute to the attribution process: Comments on social cognition
         and behavior. Pp. 356-370 in *Social Cognition and Social Development*. E.T.
         Higgins, D.N. Ruble, and W.W. Hartup, eds. Cambridge, MA: Cambridge Uni-
         versity Press.
  1992   The role of parents in the socialization of children: An historical overview. *Devel-
         opmental Psychology* 28:1006-1017.
  1999   Parenting and the Child's World Conference: Multiple Influences on Intellectual
         and Social-Emotional Development. Presentation at the NICHD Conference on
         Parenting, Bethesda, MD, August 2-3.
  2000   Parenting and its effects on children: On reading and misreading behavior genetics.
         Annual Review of Psychology 51:1-27.
Maccoby, E.E., and J.A. Martin
  1983   Socialization in the context of the family: Parent-child interaction. Pp. 1-102 in
         Handbook of Child Psychology, Volume 4: Socialization, personality, and social
         development, Fourth Edition. P.H. Mussen and E.M. Hetherington, eds. New
         York: Wiley.
MacDonald, K., and R.D. Parke
  1984   Bridging the gap: Parent-child play interactions and peer interactive competence.
         Child Development 55:1265-1277.

MacTurk, R., and G. Morgan, eds.
1995 *Mastery Motivation: Origins, Conceptualizations, and Applications: Advances in Applied Developmental Psychology,* Volume 12. Norwood, NJ: Ablex Publishing Corporation.

Magee, E.M., and M.W. Pratt
1985 *1935-1985: 50 Years of U.S. Federal Support to Promote the Health of Mothers, Children, and Handicapped Children in America.* Vienna, VA: Information Sciences Research Institute.

Makino, S., P.W. Gold, and J. Schulkin
1994 Corticosterone effects on corticotropin-releasing hormone mRNA in the central nucleus of the amygdala and the parvocellular region of the paraventricular nucleus of the hypothalamus. *Brain Research* 640:105-112.

Malinosky-Rummell, R., and D.J. Hansen
1993 Long-term consequences of childhood physical abuse. *Psychological Bulletin* 114(1):68-79.

Mandler, J.M., and L. McDonough
1995 Long-term recall of event sequences in infancy. *Journal of Experimental Child Psychology. Special Issue. Early Memory* 59(3):457-474.

Mangelsdorf, S.C.
1992 Developmental changes in infant-stranger interaction. *Infant Behavior and Development* 15(2):191-208.

Mangelsdorf, S.C., M.R. Gunnar, R. Kestenbaum, S. Lang, and D. Andreas
1990 Infant proneness-to-distress temperament, maternal personality, and mother-infant attachment: Associations and goodness of fit. *Child Development* 61:820-831.

Manski, C.
1993 Identification of endogenous social effects: The reflection problem. *Review of Economic Studies* 60:531-542.

Marchman, V., B. Wulfeck, and S.E. Weismer
1999 Morphological productivity in children with normal language and SLI: A study of the English past tense. *Journal of Speech, Language, and Hearing Research* 42:206-219.

Markus, H., and S. Kitayama
1991 Culture and the self: Implications for cognition, emotion, and motivation. *Psychological Bulletin* 98(2):224-253.

Marler, P.
1990 Innate learning preferences: Signals for communication. *Developmental Psychobiology* 23:557-568.

Marschark, M.
1993 *Psychological Development of Deaf Children.* New York: Oxford University Press.

Mascolo, M.F., and S. Griffin, eds.
1998 *What Develops in Emotional Development?* New York: Plenum.

Mason, J.
1989 *The Cultural Competence Self-Assessment Questionnaire.* Portland, OR: Portland Research and Training Center for Children and Youth with Serious Emotional Handicaps and Their Families.

Mason, K.O., and K. Kuhlthau
1992 The perceived impact of child care costs on women's labor supply and fertility. *Demography* 29:523-543.

Masten, A.S.
  1994   Resilience in individual development: Successful adaptation despite risk and adver-
          sity. Pp. 3-25 in *Educational Resilience in Inner-City America: Challenges and
          Prospects*. M.C. Wang and E.W. Gordon, eds. Hillsdale, NJ: Lawrence Erlbaum
          Associates, Inc.
Matas, L., R.A. Arend, and L.A. Sroufe
  1978   Continuity of adaptation in the second year: The relationship between quality of
          attachment and later competence. *Child Development* 49:547-556.
Maughan, B., and M. Rutter
  1998   Continuities and discontinuities in antisocial behavior from childhood to adult life.
          Advances in Clinical Child Psychology 20:1-47.
Maxfield, M., and C. Widom
  1996   The cycle of violence: Revisited 6 years later. *Archives of Pediatric Adolescent
          Medicine* 150:390-395.
Mayberry, R.I.
  1992   The cognitive development of deaf children: Recent insights. Pp. 51-68 in *Hand-
          book of Neuropsychology*, Volume 7. S. Segalowitz and I. Rapin, eds. Amsterdam,
          The Netherlands: Elsevier.
Mayer, S.
  1997   *What Money Can't Buy: The Effects of Parental Income on Children's Outcomes*.
          Cambridge, MA: Harvard University Press.
Mayes, L.C.
  1995   Substance abuse and parenting. Pp. 101-125 in *Handbook of Parenting*, Volume
          4: Applied and Practical Parenting. M.H. Bornstein, ed. Mahwah, NJ: Lawrence
          Erlbaum Associates, Publishers.
McCall, R.B.
  1979   The development of intellectual functioning in infancy and the prediction of later
          I.Q. Pp. 707-741 in *Handbook of Infant Development*. J.D. Osofsky, ed. New
          York: Wiley.
McCall, R.B., and M.S. Carriger
  1993   A meta-analysis of infant habituation and recognition memory performance as
          predictors of later IQ. *Child Development* 64(1):57-79.
McCall, R.B., P.S. Hogarty, and N. Hurlburt
  1972   Transitions in infant sensorimotor development and the prediction of childhood
          IQ. *American Psychologist* 27(8):728-748.
McCartney, K.
  1984   The effect of quality of day care environment upon children's language develop-
          ment. *Developmental Psychology* 20:244-260.
McCartney, K., and R. Rosenthal
  2000   Effect size, practical importance, and social policy for children. *Child Develop-
          ment* 71(1):173-180.
McCarton, C.M., J. Brooks-Gunn, I.F. Wallace, C.R. Bauer, F.C. Bennett, J.C. Bernbaum,
R.S. Broyles, P.H. Casey, M.C. McCormick, D.T. Scott, J. Tyson, J. Tonascia, and C.L.
Meinert
  1997   Results at age 8 years of early intervention for low-birth-weight premature infants:
          The Infant Health and Development Program. *Journal of the American Medical
          Association* 277(2):126-132.
McClellan, R.P.
  1972   Optimizations and stochastic proximation techniques applied to supervised learn-
          ing. Unpublished doctoral dissertation, University of Arizona.

McCollum, J.A., and M.L. Hemmeter
   1997   Parent-child interaction intervention when children have disabilities. Pp. 549-576
          in *The Effectiveness of Early Intervention.* M.J. Guralnick, ed. Baltimore, MD:
          Paul H. Brookes Publishing Co., Inc.
McCune, L., B. Kalmanson, M.B. Fleck, B. Glazewski, and J. Sillari
   1990   An interdisciplinary model of infant assessment. Pp. 219-245 in *Handbook of
          Early Childhood Intervention.* J.P. Shonkoff and S.J. Meisels, eds. New York:
          Cambridge University Press.
McDonough, S.C.
   2000   Interaction guidance: An approach for difficult-to-engage families. Pp. 485-493 in
          Handbook of Infant Mental Health, Second Edition. C.H. Zeanah, ed. New York:
          The Guilford Press.
McEachin, J.J., T. Smith, and O.I. Lovaas
   1993   Long-term outcome for children with autism who received early intensive behav-
          ioral treatment. *American Journal on Mental Retardation* 97:359-372.
McGroder, S.M., M.J. Zaslow, K.A. Moore, and S.M. LeMenestrel
   2000   *Impacts on Young Children and Their Families Two Years After Enrollment: Find-
          ings From the Child Outcomes Study.* Washington, DC. U.S. Department of
          Health and Human Services, Administration for Children and Families and Office
          of the Secretary for Planning and Evaluation; and U.S. Department of Education,
          Office of the Under Secretary and Office of Vocational and Adult Education.
McKenna, J.J.
   1990   Evolution and sudden infant death syndrome: Part I: Infant responsivity to parental
          contact. *Human Nature* 1(2):145-177.
McKenna, J.J., and S. Mosko
   1990   Evolution and the sudden infant death syndrome: Part III: Infant arousal and par-
          ent-infant co-sleeping. *Human Nature* 1(3):291-330.
McKenna, J.J., E.B. Thoman, T.F. Anders, A. Sadeh, V.L. Schechtman, and S.F. Glotzbach
   1993   Infant-parent co-sleeping in an evolutionary perspective: Implications for under-
          standing infant sleep development and the sudden infant death syndrome. *Sleep*
          16(3):263-282.
McKenna, J.J., S. Mosko, C. Richard, S. Drummond, L. Hunt, M.B. Cetel, and J. Arpaia
   1994   Experimental studies of infant-parent co-sleeping mutual physiological and behav-
          ioral influences and their relevance to SIDS. *Early Human Development* 38:187-
          201.
McLanahan, S.
   1997   Parent absence or poverty: Which matters more? Pp. 35-48 in *Consequences of
          Growing Up Poor.* G.J. Duncan and J. Brooks-Gunn, eds. New York: Russell
          Sage Foundation.
McLanahan, S., and I. Garfinkel
   2000   The Fragile Families and Child Well-Being Study: Questions, Design, and a Few
          Preliminary Results. Working paper 00-07-FF, May. Bendheim Thoman Center
          for Research on Child Well-Being, Princeton University.
McLanahan, S., and G. Sandefur
   1994   *Growing Up With a Single Parent: What Hurts, What Helps.* Cambridge, MA:
          Harvard University Press.
McLean, L.K., and J.W. Cripe
   1997   The effectiveness of early intervention for children with communication disorders.
          Pp. 349-428 in *The Effectiveness of Early Intervention.* M.J. Guralnick, ed. Balti-
          more, MD: Paul H. Brookes Publishing Co., Inc.

McLeod, J.D., and R. Kessler
    1990   Socioeconomic status differences in vulnerability to undesirable life events. *Journal of Health and Social Behavior* 31:162-172.
McLeod, J.D., and M.J. Shanahan
    1993   Poverty, parenting, and children's mental health. *American Sociological Review* 58:351-366.
McLoyd, V.C.
    1989   Socialization and development in a changing economy: The effects of paternal job and income loss of children. *American Psychologist* 44:293-302.
    1990   The impact of economic hardship on black families and children: Psychological distress, parenting and socioeconomic development. *Child Development* 61(2):311-346.
    1997   The impact of poverty and low socioeconomic status on the socioemotional functioning of African-American children and adolescents: Mediating effects. Pp. 7-34 in *Social and Emotional Adjustment and Family Relations in Ethnic Minorities*. R. Taylor and M. Wang, eds. Mahwah, NJ: Lawrence Erlbaum Associates, Publishers.
    1998   Socioeconomic disadvantage and child development. *American Psychologist* 53:185-204.
McLoyd, V.C., and B. Lozoff
    2000   Racial and ethnic trends in children's behavior and development. In *America Becoming: Racial Trends and Their Consequences*. N.J. Smelser, W.J. Wilson, M.F. Mitchell, eds. Commission on Behavioral and Social Sciences and Education, National Research Council. Washington, DC: National Academy Press.
McLoyd, V.C., T.E. Jayaratne, R. Ceballo, and J. Borquez
    1994   Unemployment and work interruption among African American single mothers: Effects on parenting and adolescent socioemotional functioning. *Child Development* 65:562-589.
Mead, M.
    1931   The primitive child. In *A Handbook of Child Psychology*. C. Murchison, ed. Worcester, MA: Clark University Press.
Mead, M., and F.C. Macgregor
    1951   *Growth and Culture*. New York: Putnam.
Meaney, M.J., J. Diorio, D. Francis, J. Widdowson, P. La Plante, C. Caldui, S. Sharma, P.M. Plotsky, and J. Seckl
    1996   Early environmental regulation of forebrain glucocorticoid receptor gene expression: Implications for adrenocortical responses to stress. *Developmental Neuroscience* 18:49-72.
Meisels, S.J.
    1994   Designing meaningful measurements for early childhood. Pp. 205-225 in *Diversity in Early Childhood Education: A Call for More Inclusive Theory, Practice, and Policy*. B.L. Mallory and R.S. New, eds. New York: Teachers College Press.
    1996   Charting the continuum of assessment and intervention. Pp. 27-52 in *New Visions for the Developmental Assessment of Infants and Young Children*. S.J. Meisels and E. Fenichel, eds. Washington, DC: ZERO TO THREE: National Center for Infants, Toddlers, and Families.
Meisels, S.J., and S. Atkins-Burnett
    2000   The elements of early childhood assessment. Pp. 231-257 in *Handbook of Early Childhood Intervention*, Second Edition. J.P. Shonkoff and S.J. Meisels, eds. New York: Cambridge University Press.

Meisels, S.J., and J.P. Shonkoff
   2000   Early childhood intervention: A continuing evolution. Pp. 3-34 in *Handbook of Early Childhood Intervention*, Second Edition. J.P. Shonkoff and S.J. Meisels, eds. New York: Cambridge University Press.

Melhuish, E.C., A. Mooney, E. Hennesy, and S. Martin
   1992   Characteristics of child care in early childhood and child development in middle childhood. Paper presented at the European Conference on Developmental Psychology in Seville, Spain, September, 1992.

Meltzoff, A.N.
   1988   Infant imitation and memory: Nine-month-olds in immediate and deferred tests. *Child Development* 59(1):217-225.
   1995   Understanding the intentions of others: Re-enactment of intended acts by 18-month-old children. *Developmental Psychology* 31(5):838-850.

Meltzoff, A.N., and M.K. Moore
   1989   Imitation in newborn infants: Exploring the range of gestures imitated and the underlying mechanisms. *Developmental Psychology* 25(6):954-962.

Menaghan, E.G., and T.L. Parcel
   1995   Social sources of change in children's home environments: The effects of parental occupational experiences and family conditions. *Journal of Marriage and the Family* 57:69-84.

Ment, L.R.
   2000   Preserving plasticity: New directions in research for the developing brain. *Pediatrics in Review Neo Reviews* 1:E53-57.

Merzenich, M., W. Jenkins, P. Johnston, C. Schreiner, S. Miller, and P. Tallal
   1996   Temporal processing deficits of language-learning impaired children ameliorated by training. *Science* 271:77-81.

Meyers, M.K., H.E. Brady, and E.Y. Seto
   2000   *Expensive Children in Poor Families: The Intersection of Childhood Disabilities and Welfare*. San Francisco, CA: Public Policy Institute of California.

Michael, R.T.
   1972   *The Effect of Education on Efficiency in Consumption*. New York: Columbia University Press.

Mielke, H., S. Dugas, P.W. Mielke, K.S. Smith, S.L. Smith, and C.R. Gonzales
   1997   Associations between soil lead and childhood blood lead in urban New Orleans and rural Lafourche Parish of Louisiana. *Environmental Health Perspectives* 105:950-954.

Miller, A.R., and R.G. Barr
   1991   Infantile colic. *Pediatric Clinics of North America* 38(6):1407-1423.

Miller, C., V. Knox, P. Auspos, and J. Hunter-Manns
   1997   *Making Welfare Work and Work Pay: Implementation and 18 Month Impacts of the Minnesota Family Investment Program*. New York: Manpower Demonstration Research Corporation.

Miller, J.G.
   1997   Theoretical issues in cultural psychology. Pp. 85-128 in *Handbook of Cross-Cultural Psychology*, Volume 1: Theory and Method, Second Edition. J.W. Berry and Y.H. Poortinga, eds. Boston, MA: Allyn & Bacon, Inc.

Miller, J., and D. Davis
   1997   Poverty history, marital history, and quality of children's home environments. *Journal of Marriage and the Family* 59:996-1007.

Miller, P.J., and J.J. Goodnow
   1995   Cultural practices: Toward an integration of culture and development. *New Directions for Child Development* 67:5-16.

Miller, P.J.
  1994   Narrative practices: Their role in socialization and self-construction. Pp. 158-179 in *The Remembering Self: Construction and Accuracy in the Self-Narrative.* U. Neisser and R. Fivush, eds. Cambridge, MA: Cambridge University Press.
Miller, P.J., and L.L. Sperry
  1987   The socialization of anger and aggression. *Merrill-Palmer Quarterly* 33:1-31.
  1988   Early talk about the past: The origins of conversational stories of personal experience. *Journal of Child Language* 15:293-315.
Miller, P.J., R. Potts, H. Fung, L. Hoogstra, and J. Mintz
  1990   Narrative practices and the social construction of self in childhood. *American Ethnologist* 17:292-311.
Miller, P.J., H. Fung, and J. Mintz
  1996   Self-construction through narrative practices: A Chinese and American comparison of early socialization. *Ethos* 24:1-44.
Mirmiran, M., and S. Lunshof
  1996   Perinatal development of human circadian rhythms. *Progress in Brain Research* 111:217-226.
Mize, J., and G.W. Ladd
  1990   A cognitive-social learning approach to social skill training with low-status preschool children. *Developmental Psychology* 26:388-397.
Moffitt, T.E.
  1990   Juvenile delinquency and attention deficit disorder: Boys' developmental trajectories from age 3 to age 15. *Child Development* 61:893-910.
  1997   Adolescence-limited and life-course-persistent offending: A complementary pair of developmental theories. Pp. 11-54 in *Developmental Theories of Crime and Delinquency: Advances in Criminological Theory*, Volume 7. T.P. Thornberry, ed. New Brunswick, NJ: Transaction Publishers.
Mogford, K.
  1988   Language development in twins. Pp. 80-95 in *Language Development in Exceptional Circumstances.* D. Bishop and K. Mogford, eds. New York: Churchill Livingstone.
Moll, L.C., C. Amanti, D. Neff, and N. Gonzalez
  1992   Funds of knowledge for teaching: Using a qualitative approach to connect homes and classrooms. *Theory into Practice* 31(2):132-141.
Montgomery, J.
  1995   Sentence comprehension in children with specific language impairment. *Journal of Speech and Hearing Research* 38:187-199.
Moore, K.A., and A.K. Driscoll
  1997   Low-wage maternal employment and outcomes for children: A study. *The Future of Children* 7:122-127.
Moore, K.A., M. Zaslow, M.J. Coiro, S. Miller, and E. Magenheim
  1995   *The JOBS Evaluation: How Well Are They Faring? AFDC Families With Preschool-Aged Children in Atlanta at the Outset of the JOBS Evaluation.* New York: Manpower Demonstration Research Corporation.
Moore-Ede, M.C.
  1986   Physiology of the circadian timing system: Predictive versus reactive homeostasis. *American Journal of Physiology* 250:735-752.
Morelli, G.A., B. Rogoff, D. Oppenheim, and D. Goldsmith
  1992   Cultural variation in infants' sleeping arrangements: Questions of independence. *Developmental Psychology* 28(4):604-613.

Morford, J.P., and S. Goldin-Meadow
  1997   From here to there and now to then: The development of displaced reference in homesign and English. *Child Development* 68:420-435.
Morgan, B., and K. Gibson
  1991   Nutritional and environmental interactions in brain development. Pp. 91-106 in *Brain Maturation and Cognitive Development: Comparative and Cross-Cultural Perspectives*. K.R. Gibson and A.C. Petersen, eds. New York: Aldine De Gruyter.
Morgan, B.L.G., and M. Winick
  1985   Pathologic effects of malnutrition on the central nervous system. Pp. 161-206 in *Nutritional Pathology: Pathobiochemistry of Dietary Imbalances*. H. Sidransky, ed. New York: Dekker.
Morgan, G., and R.J. Harmon
  1984   Developmental transformations in mastery motivation. In *Continuities and Discontinuities in Development*. R.N. Emde and R.J. Harmon, eds. New York: Plenum Press.
Morgane, P., R. Austin-La France, J. Bronzino, J. Tonkiss, S. Diaz-Cintra, L. Cintra, T. Kemper, and J. Galler
  1993   Prenatal malnutrition and development of the brain. *Neuroscience and Biobehavioral Reviews* 17:91-128.
Morison, S.J., E.W. Ames, and K. Chisholm
  1995   The development of children adopted from Romanian orphanages. *Merrill-Palmer Quarterly* 41:411-430.
Morris, P., and C. Michalopoulos
  2000   *The Self-Sufficiency Project at 36 Months: Effects on Children of a Program That Increased Parental Employment and Income (Executive Summary)*. New York: Social Research and Demonstration Corporation.
Morrison, D., P. Mantzicopoulos, and E. Carte
  1989   Preacademic screening for learning and behavior problems. *Journal of the American Academy of Child and Adolescent Psychiatry* 28(1):101-106.
Morrison, F.J., E.M. Griffith, G. Williamson, and C.L. Hardway
  1995   The nature and sources of early literacy. Paper presented at the Biennial Meeting of the Society for Research in Child Development, Indianapolis, IN.
Morrison, F.J., E.M. Griffith, and D.M. Alberts
  1997   Nature-nurture in the classroom: Entrance age, school readiness, and learning in children. *Developmental Psychology* 33(2):254-262.
Morrison, F.J., J.A. Frazier, C.L. Hardway, E.M. Griffith, G.L. Williamson, and Y. Miyazaki
  1998   Early literacy: The nature and sources of individual differences.
The MTA Cooperative Group
  1999   Moderators and mediators of treatment response for children with attention-deficit/hyperactivity disorder: The Multimodal Treatment Study of Children with Attention-Deficit/Hyperactivity Disorder. *Archives of General Psychiatry* 56:1088-1096.
Mueller, E.
  1972   The maintenance of verbal exchanges between young children. *Child Development* 43:930-938.
Mueller, E., and J. Brenner
  1977   The origins of social skills and interaction among playgroup toddlers. *Child Development* 48:854-861.
Mueller, E., and N. Silverman
  1989   Peer relations in maltreated children. Pp. 529-578 in *Child Maltreatment: Theory and Research on the Causes and Consequences of Child Abuse and Neglect*. D. Cicchetti and V. Carlson, eds. New York: Cambridge University Press.

Murray, L., and P.J. Cooper
    1997   Editorial: Postpartum depression and child development. *Psychological Medicine* 27:253-260.
Myers, B., P. Jarvis, and G. Creasey
    1987   Infants' behaviors with their mothers and grandmothers. *Infant Behavior and Development* 10:245-259.
Nachmias, M., M.R. Gunnar, S. Mangelsdorf, R. Parritz, and K. Buss
    1996   Behavioral inhibition and stress reactivity: Moderating role of attachment security. *Child Development* 67:508-522.
National Association of State Boards of Education
    1991   *Caring Communities: Supporting Young Children and Families: The Report of the National Task Force on School Readiness.* T. Schultz and J. Lombardi, co-authors. Alexandria, VA: National Association of State Boards of Education.
National Center on Child Abuse and Neglect
    1997   *Child Maltreatment 1995: Reports From the States to the National Center on Child Abuse and Neglect.* Washington, DC: U.S. Department of Health and Human Services.
National Center for Health Statistics of the Centers for Disease Control
    1993   Advance Report of Final Natality Statistics, 1990. *Monthly Vital Statistics Report* 41(9):Supplement (February 25, 1993). Table 14.
    1999   Advance Report of Final Natality Statistics, 1997. Monthly Vital Statistics Report 47(18):(April 29, 1999). Table 46.
National Committee to Prevent Child Abuse
    1997   *Current Trends in Child Abuse Reporting and Fatalities: Results of the 1996 Annual 50 State Survey.* Chicago, IL: Author.
National Research Council
    1978   *Knowledge and Policy: The Uncertain Connection.*   Study Project on Social Research and Development, Volume 5. L.E. Lynn, Jr. ed. Assembly of Behavioral and Social Sciences. Washington, DC: National Academy of Sciences.
    1981   *Services for Children: An Agenda for Research.* Committee on Child Development Research and Public Policy, Assembly of Behavioral and Social Sciences. Washington, DC: National Academy Press.
    1982   *Making Policies for Children: A Study of the Federal Process.* Panel for the Study of the Policy Formation Process. C.D. Hayes, ed. Committee on Child Development Research and Public Policy, Assembly of Behavioral and Social Sciences. Washington, DC: National Academy Press.
    1990   *Who Cares for America's Children? Child Care Policy for the 1990s.* Panel on Child Care Policy. C.D. Hayes, J.L. Palmer, and M.J. Zaslow, eds. Committee on Child Development Research and Public Policy, Commission on Behavioral and Social Sciences and Education. Washington, DC: National Academy Press.
    1993   *Understanding Child Abuse and Neglect.* Panel on the Understanding and Control of Violent Behavior. A.J. Reiss, Jr., and J.A. Roth, eds. Commission on Behavioral and Social Sciences and Education. Washington, DC: National Academy Press.
    1998a   *Preventing Reading Difficulties in Young Children.* Committee on the Prevention of Reading Difficulties in Young Children, C.E. Snow, M.S. Burns, and P. Griffin, eds. Commission on Behavioral and Social Sciences and Education. Washington, DC: National Academy Press.
    1998b   *Starting Out Right: A Guide to Promoting Children's Reading Success.* Committee on the Prevention of Reading Difficulties in Young Children. M.S. Burns, P. Griffin, and C.E. Snow, eds. Commission on Behavioral and Social Sciences and Education. Washington, DC: National Academy Press.

2000   *Eager to Learn: Educating Our Preschoolers.* Committee on Early Childhood
        Pedagogy, Commission on Behavioral and Social Sciences and Education. Wash-
        ington, DC: National Academy Press.
National Research Council and Institute of Medicine
1995a   *Integrating Federal Statistics on Children: Report of a Workshop.* Committee on
        National Statistics and Board on Children and Families, Commission on Behavioral
        and Social Sciences and Education. Washington, DC: National Academy Press.
1995b   *Child Care for Low-Income Families: Summary of Two Workshops.* Steering
        Committee on Child Care Workshops. D.A. Phillips, ed. Board on Children and
        Families, Commission on Behavioral and Social Sciences and Education. Washing-
        ton, DC: National Academy Press.
1997   *Improving Schooling for Language-Minority Children: A Research Agenda.* Com-
        mittee on Developing a Research Agenda on the Education of Limited English
        Proficient and Bilingual Students. D. August and K. Hakuta, eds. Board on Chil-
        dren, Youth, and Families, Commission on Behavioral and Social Sciences and
        Education. Washington, DC: National Academy Press.
1998a   *From Generation to Generation: The Health and Well-Being of Children in Immi-
        grant Families.* Committee on the Health and Adjustment of Immigrant Children
        and Families. D.J. Hernandez and E. Charney, eds. Board on Children, Youth,
        and Families, Commission on Behavioral and Social Sciences and Education. Wash-
        ington, DC: National Academy Press.
1998b   *Educating Language-Minority Children.* Committee on Developing a Research
        Agenda on the Education of Limited English Proficient and Bilingual Students. D.
        August and K. Hakuta, eds., Board on Children, Youth, and Families. Commission
        on Behavioral and Social Sciences and Education. Washington, DC: National
        Academy Press.
2000   *Early Childhood Intervention: Views From the Field. Report of a Workshop.* Com-
        mittee on Integrating the Science of Early Childhood Development. J.P. Shonkoff,
        D.A. Phillips, and B. Keilty, eds. Board on Children, Youth, and Families, Com-
        mission on Behavioral and Social Sciences and Education. Washington, DC: Na-
        tional Academy Press.
Nelson, C.A.
1994   Neural correlates of recognition memory in the first postnatal year of life. Pp. 269-
        313 in *Human Behavior and the Developing Brain.* G. Dawson and K. Fischer,
        eds. New York: The Guilford Press.
1995   The ontogeny of human memory: A cognitive neuroscience perspective. *Develop-
        mental Psychology* 31:723-738.
1996   Electrophysiological correlates of early memory development. Pp. 95-131 in *Thir-
        teenth West Virginia University Conference on Life Span Developmental Psychol-
        ogy: Biological and Neuropsychological Mechanisms.* H.W. Reese and M.D.
        Franzen, eds. Mahwah, NJ: Lawrence Erlbaum.
1999   Neural plasticity and human development. *Current Directions in Psychological
        Science* 8:42-45.
Nelson, C.A., and F.E. Bloom
1997   Child development and neuroscience. *Child Development* 68:970-987.
Nelson, C.A., J. Lin, L.J. Carver, C.S. Monk, K.M. Thomas, and C.L. Truwit
2000   Functional neuroanatomy of spatial working memory in children. *Developmental
        Psychology* 36:109-116.
Nelson, K.
1993   Events, narratives, memory: What develops? Pp. 1-24 in *The Minnesota Symposia
        on Child Psychology: Memory and Affect in Development,* Volume 26. C.A.
        Nelson, ed. Hillsdale, NJ: Erlbaum.

1996   *Language in Cognitive Development: Emergence of the Mediated Mind.* New York: Cambridge University Press.

Nelson, K.E.

1977   Facilitating children's syntax acquisition. *Developmental Psychology* 13:101-107.

Neville, H.J., and D.L. Mills

1997   Epigenesis of language. *Mental Retardation and Developmental Disabilities Research Reviews* 3:1-11.

Neville, H.J., S.A. Coffey, D.S. Lawson, A. Fischer, K. Emmory, and U. Bellugi

1997   Neural systems mediating American Sign Language: Effects of sensory experience and age of acquisition. *Brain and Language* 57(3):285-308.

Neville, H.J., D. Bavelier, D. Corina, J. Rauschecker, A. Karni, A. Lalwani, A. Braun, V. Clark, P. Jezzard, and R. Turner

1998   Cerebral organization for language in deaf and hearing subjects: Biological constraints and effects of experience. *Proceedings of the National Academy of Sciences* 95:922-929.

Newcomb, A.F., and W.M. Bukowski

1983   Social impact and social preference as determinants of children's peer group status. *Developmental Psychology* 19:856-867.

1984   A longitudinal study of the utility of social preference and social impact sociometric classification schemes. *Child Development* 55:1434-1447.

Newport, E.L.

1991   Contrasting concepts of the critical period for language. Pp. 111-130 in *The Epigenesis of Mind: Essays on Biology and Cognition*. S. Carey and R. Gelman, eds. Hillsdale, NJ: Erlbaum Associates.

Newport, E.L., and R.P. Meier

1985   The acquisition of American Sign Language. Pp. 881-938 in *The Cross-Linguistic Study of Language Acquisition, Volume 1: The Data*. D.I. Slobin, ed. Hillsdale, NJ: Erlbaum Associates.

NICHD Early Child Care Research Network

1996   Characteristics of infant child care: Factors contributing to positive caregiving. *Early Childhood Research Quarterly* 11(3):269-306.

1997a   The effects of infant child care on infant-mother attachment security: Results of the NICHD Study of Early Child Care. *Child Development* 68:860-879.

1997b   Child care in the first year of life. *Merrill-Palmer Quarterly* 43(3):340-360.

1997c   Poverty and patterns of child care. Pp. 100-131 in *Consequences of Growing Up Poor*. J. Brooks-Gunn and G.J. Duncan, eds. New York: Russell Sage.

1997d   Mother-child interaction and cognitive outcomes associated with early child care: Results from the NICHD Study. Poster symposium presented at the Biennial Meeting of the Society for Research in Child Development, April, 1997, Washington, DC.

1998a   *Chronicity of Maternal Depressive Symptoms, Maternal Behavior, and Child Functioning at 36 Months: Results From the NICHD Study of Early Child Care.* Washington, DC: NICHD Early Child Care Research Network.

1998b   Relations between family predictors and child outcomes: Are they weaker for children in child care? *Developmental Psychology* 34(5):1119-1128.

1998c   Early child care and self-control, compliance and problem behavior at twenty-four and thirty-six months. *Child Development* 69(3):1145-1170.

1999a   Child care and mother-child interaction in the first three years of life. *Developmental Psychology* 35(6):1399-1413.

1999b   The roles of work and poverty in the lives of families with young children. Paper presented at the Biennial Meeting of the Society for Research in Child Development, April 1999, Albuquerque, NM.

1999c   Effect sizes from the NICHD Study of Early Child Care. Paper presented at the Biennial Meeting of the Society for Research in Child Development, April 1999, Albuquerque, NM.

2000   The relation of child care to cognitive and language development. *Child Development* 71(4):958-978.

in press(a)   The NICHD Study of Early Child Care: Contexts of development and developmental outcomes over the first seven years of life. In *Young Children's Education, Health, and Development: Profile and Synthesis Project Report.* J. Brooks-Gunn and L.J. Berlin, eds. Washington, DC: U.S. Department of Education.

in press(b)   Characteristics and quality of child care for toddlers and preschoolers. *Journal of Applied Developmental Science.*

in press(c)   Nonmaternal care and family factors in early development: An overview of the NICHD Study of Early Child Care. *Journal of Applied Developmental Psychology.*

submitted   Early child care and children's peer relationships at 24 and 36 months: The NICHD Study of Early Child Care. *Child Development.*

NIH Consensus Statement

1998   *Diagnosis and Treatment of Attention Deficit Hyperactivity Disorder (ADHD),* NIH Consensus Statement, November 16-18, 1998, 16(2).

Nokes, C., C. van den Bosch, and D. Bundy

1998   *The Effects of Iron Deficiency and Anemia on Mental and Motor Performance, Educational Achievement, and Behavior in Children.* Washington, DC: International Nutritional Anemia Consulting Group.

Nord, C.W., J. Lennon, B. Liu, and K. Chandler

1999   *Statistics in Brief: Home Literacy Activites and Signs of Children's Emerging Literacy, 1993 and 1999.* National Center for Education Statistics, NCES 2000-026. Washington, DC: U.S. Department of Education.

Nordin, J., S. Rolnick, E. Ehlinger, A. Nelson, T. Arneson, L. Cherney-Stafford, and J. Griffin

1998   Lead levels in high-risk and low-risk young children in the Minneapolis-St. Paul Metropolitan area. *Pediatrics* 101:72-76.

Nsamenang, A.B.

1992   *Human Development in Cultural Context: A Third World Perspective,* Volume 16 in the Cross-cultural Research and Methodology Series. Newbury Park, CA: Sage Publications.

Nugent, J.K.

1994   Cross-cultural studies of child development: Implications for clinicians. *Zero to Three* 15(2):3-8.

Oakes, L.M., and L.B. Cohen

1990   Infant perception of a causal event. *Cognitive Development* 5(2):193-207.

Ochs, E.

1986   From feelings to grammar: A Samoan case study. Pp. 251-272 in *Language Socialization Across Cultures.* B.B. Schieffelin and E. Ochs, eds. New York: Cambridge University Press.

1988   *Culture and Language Development: Language Acquisition and Language Socialization in a Samoan Village.* Cambridge, MA: Cambridge University Press.

1992   Indexicality and socialization. Pp. 287-308 in *Cultural Psychology.* J.W. Stigler, R.A. Shweder, and G. Herdt, eds. Cambridge, UK: Cambridge University Press.

Ochs, E., and B.B. Schieffelin

1984   Language acquisition and socialization: Three developmental stories and their implications. Pp. 276-332 in *Culture Theory: Essays on Mind, Self, and Emotion.* R. Schweder and R.A. LeVine, eds. New York: Cambridge University Press.

O'Connor, T.G., K. Deater-Deckard, D.W. Fulker, M. Rutter, and R. Plomin
    1998   Genotype-environment correlations in late childhood and early adolescence: Anti-
            social behavioral problems and coercive parenting. *Developmental Psychology*
            34:970-981.
O'Connor, T.G., D. Bredenkamp, M. Rutter, and The English and Romanian Adoptees (ERA)
Study Team
    1999   Attachment disturbances and disorders in children exposed to early severe depriva-
            tion. *Infant Mental Health Journal* 20(1):10-29.
O'Connor, T.G., M. Rutter, C. Beckett, L. Keaveney, J.M. Kreppner, and the English and
Romanian Adoptees (ERA) Study Team
    2000   The effects of global severe privation on cognitive competence: Extension and lon-
            gitudinal follow-up. *Child Development* 71:376-390.
Odom, S.L., S.R. McConnell, and L.K. Chandler
    1994   Acceptability and feasibilty of classroom-based social interaction interventions for
            young children with disabilities. *Exceptional Children* 60:226-236.
Oetting, J., and J. Horohov
    1997   Past tense marking by children with and without specific language impairment.
            Journal of Speech and Hearing Research 40:62-74.
Office of Inspector General
    1994   *Nationwide Review of Health and Safety Standards at Child Care Facilities.* Wash-
            ington, DC: U.S. Department of Health and Human Services.
Offord, D.R., R.J. Alder, and M.H. Boyle
    1986   Prevalence and sociodemographic correlates of conduct disorder. *The American
            Journal of Social Psychiatry* VI(4):272-278.
Offord, D.R., M.H. Boyle, P. Szatmari, N.I. Rae-Grant, P.S. Links, D.T. Cadman, J.A. Byles,
J.W. Crawford, H. Munroe Blum, C. Byrne, H. Thomas, and C.A. Woodward
    1987   Ontario Child Health Study: II. Six-month prevalence of disorder and rates of
            service utilization. *Archives of General Psychiatry* 44:832-836.
Ogbu, J.U.
    1994   From cultural differences to differences in cultural frame of reference. Pp. 365-391
            in *Cross-Cultural Roots of Minority Child Development.* P.M. Greenfield and
            R.R. Cocking, eds. Hillsdale, NJ: Erlbaum.
Ogden, C.
    1998   *Third National Health and Nutrition Examination Survey*, Unpublished Analyses.
            Atlanta, GA: Centers for Disease Controls.
Olds, D.L., and H. Kitzman
    1993   Review of research on home visiting for pregnant women and parents of young
            children. *The Future of Children* 3(3):53-92.
Olds, D.L., C.R. Henderson Jr., R. Tatelbaum, and R. Chamberlin
    1986   Improving the delivery of prenatal care and outcomes of pregnancy: A randomized
            trial of nurse home visitation. *Pediatrics* 77:16-28.
Olds, D.L., J.J. Eckenrode, C.R. Henderson Jr., H. Kitzman, J. Powers, R. Cole, K. Sidora, P.
Morris, L.M. Pettitt, and D. Luckey
    1997   Long-term effects of home vistiation on maternal life course and child abuse and
            neglect: Fifteen-year follow-up of a randomized trial. *Journal of the American
            Medical Association* 278(8):637-643.
Olds, D.L., C.R. Henderson Jr., H. Kitzman, J.J. Eckenrode, R. Cole, R. Tatelbaum, J.
Robinson, L.M. Pettitt, R. O'Brien, and P. Hill
    1998   Prenatal and infancy home visitation by nurses: A program of research. Pp. 79-130
            in *Advances in Infancy Research*, Volume 12. C. Rovee-Collier, L.P. Lipsitt, and
            H. Hayne, eds. Stamford, CT: Ablex Publishing Corporation.

Olds, D.L., C.R. Henderson Jr., H. Kitzman, J.J. Eckenrode, R.E. Cole, and R.C. Tatelbaum
  1999   Prenatal and infancy home visitation by nurses: Recent findings. *The Future of Children: Home Visiting: Recent Program Evaluations* 9(1):44-65.
Ollendick, T.H., M.D. Weist, M.G. Borden, and R.W. Greene
  1992   Sociometric status and academic, behavioral, and psychological adjustment: A five-year longitudinal study. *Journal of Consulting and Clinical Psychology* 60:80-87.
Olson, K., and L. Pavetti
  1996   *Personal and Family Challenges to the Successful Transition From Welfare to Work.* Washington, DC: The Urban Institute.
Olson, S.L., and B. Hoza
  1993   Preschool developmental antecedents of conduct problems in children beginning school. *Journal of Clinical Child Psychology* 22(1):60-67.
Olson, S., and K. Lifren
  1988   Concurrent and longitudinal correlates of preschool peer sociometrics: Comparing rating scale and nomination measures. *Journal of Applied Developmental Psychology* 9:409-420.
Olson, S.L., K. Bayles, and J.E. Bates
  1986   Mother-child interaction and children's speech progress: A longitudinal study of the first two years. *Merrill-Palmer Quarterly* 32(1):1-20.
Olweus, D.
  1991   Bully/victim problems among schoolchildren: Basic facts and effects of a school-based intervention program. Pp. 411-448 in *The Development and Treatment of Childhood Aggression.* D. Pepler and K.H. Rubin, eds. Hillsdale, NJ: Erlbaum.
  1993   Bullies on the playground: The role of victimization. Pp. 85-128 in *Children on Playgrounds.* C.H. Hart, ed. Albany, NY: SUNY Press.
Oosterwal, G.
  1994   *Community in Diversity.* Barrier Springs, MI: Andrews University Center for Intercultural Relations.
Oppenheim, D., A. Sagi, and M.E. Lamb
  1988   Infant-adult attachments on the kibbutz and their relation to socioemotional development 4 years later. *Developmental Psychology* 24:427-433.
Orlandi, M.A., ed.
  1992   *Cultural Competence for Evaluators.* Rockville, MD: Office of Substance Abuse Prevention.
Osofsky, J.D.
  1995   The effects of exposure to violence on young children. *American Psychologist* 50(9):782-788.
  1999   The impact of violence on children. *The Future of Children: Domestic Violence and Children* 9(3):33-49.
Osofsky, J.D., and H.E. Fitzgerald, eds.
  2000   *WAIMH Handbook of Infant Mental Health.* New York: John Wiley & Sons, Inc.
Palmer, F.B., B.K. Shapiro, R.C. Wachtel, M.C. Allen, J.E. Hiller, S.E. Harryman, B.S. Mosher, C.L. Meinert, and A.J. Capute
  1988   The effects of physical therapy on cerebral palsy. *New England Journal of Medicine* 318:803-808.
Palti, H., B. Pevsner, and B. Adler
  1983   Does anemia in infancy affect achievement on developmental and intelligence tests? *Human Biology* 55:189-194.

Palti, H., A. Meijer, and B. Adler
    1985   Learning achievement and behavior at school of anemic and non-anemic infants.
            Early Human Development 10:217-223.
Panksepp, J.
    1998   *Affective Neuroscience: The Foundations of Human and Animal Emotions.* New
            York: Oxford University Press.
Papile, L.A., G. Munsick-Bruno, and A. Schaefer
    1983   Relationship of cerebral intraventricular hemorrhage and early childhood neuro-
            logic handicaps. *The Journal of Pediatrics* 103:273-277.
Papoušek, M., and N. von Hofacker
    1998   Persistent crying in early infancy: A non-trivial condition of risk for the developing
            mother-infant relationship. *Child Care, Health, and Development* 24(5):395-424.
Parcel, T.L., and E.G. Menaghan
    1994   *Parents' Jobs and Children's Lives.* Hawthorne, NY: Aldine de Gruyter.
Park, K.A., and E. Waters
    1989   Security of attachment and preschool friendships. *Child Development* 60:1076-
            1081.
Park, S.Y., J. Belsky, S. Putnam, and K. Crnic
    1997   Infant emotionality, parenting, and 3-year inhibition: Exploring stability and law-
            ful discontinuity in a male sample. *Developmental Psychology* 33(2):218-227.
Parke, R.D.
    1996   *Fatherhood.* Cambridge, MA: Harvard University Press.
Parke, R.D., and R. Buriel
    1998   Socialization in the family: Ethnic and ecological perspectives. Pp. 463-552 in
            Handbook of Child Psychology, Volume 3: Social, Emotional, and Personality
            Development, Fifth Edition. W. Damon and N. Eisenberg, eds. New York: Wiley.
Parker, S., S. Greer, and B. Zuckerman
    1988   Double jeopardy: The impact of poverty on early childhood development. *Pediat-
            ric Clinics of North America* 35(6):1227-1240.
Parker, J.G., K.H. Rubin, J. Price, and M.E. DeRosier
    1995   Peer relationships, child development, and adjustment: A developmental psychopa-
            thology perspective. Pp. 96-161 in *Developmental Psychopathology,* Volume 2:
            Risk, Disorder and Adaptation. D. Cicchetti and D. Cohen, eds. New York:
            Wiley.
Parpal, M., and E.E. Maccoby
    1985   Maternal responsiveness and subsequent child compliance. *Child Development*
            56(5):1326-1334.
Parritz, R.H., S. Mangelsdorf, and M.R. Gunnar
    1992   Control, social referencing, and the infant's appraisal of threat. Pp. 209-228 in
            Social Referencing and the Social Construction of Reality in Infancy. S. Feinman,
            ed. New York: Plenum Press.
Pastor, D.L.
    1981   The quality of mother-infant attachment and its relationship to toddlers' initial
            sociability with peers. *Developmental Psychology* 17:326-335.
Patterson, G.R., and M.S. Forgatch
    1995   Predicting future clinical adjustment from treatment outcome and process vari-
            ables. *Psychological Assessment* 7:275-285.
Patterson, G.R., B.D. DeBaryshe, and E. Ramsey
    1989   A developmental perspective on antisocial behavior. *American Psychologist*
            44:329-335.

Patterson, G.R., J.B. Reid, and T.J. Dishion
1992   *Antisocial Boys.* Eugene, OR: Castalia.
Paul, R.
1991   Profiles of toddlers with slow expressive language development. *Topics in Language Disorders* 11:1-13.
Pearlin, L.I., and C. Schooler
1978   The structure of coping. *Journal of Health and Social Behavior* 19:2-21.
Peisner-Feinberg, E.S., and M.R. Burchinal
1997   Relationships between preschool children's child-care experiences and concurrent development: The cost-quality, and outcome study. *Merrill-Palmer Quarterly* 43(3):451-477.
Peisner-Feinberg, E.S., M.R. Burchinal, R.M. Clifford, M.L. Culkin, C. Howes, S.L. Kagan, N. Yazejian, P. Byler, J. Rustici, and J. Zelazo
2000   *The Children of the Cost, Quality, and Outcomes Study Go To School: Technical Report.* Chapel Hill, NC: Frank Porter Graham Child Development Center, University of North Carolina at Chapel Hill.
Pennington, B.F., L. Bennetto, O. McAleer, and R.J. Roberts
1996   Executive functions and working memory: Theoretical and measurement issues. Pp. 327-348 in *Attention, Memory, and Executive Function.* G.R. Lyon and N. Krasnegor, eds. Baltimore, MD: Paul H. Brookes Publishing Co., Inc.
Peterson, C.C., and M. Siegal
1999   Representing inner worlds: Theory of mind in autistic, deaf, and normal hearing children. *Psychological Science* 10(2):126-129.
Pettit, G.S., and J. Mize
1993   Substance and style: Understanding the ways in which parents teach children about social relationships. Pp. 118-151 in *Learning About Relationships.* S. Duck, ed. Newbury Park, CA: Sage.
Pettit, G.S., J.E. Bates, and K.A. Dodge
1997   Supportive parenting, ecological context, and children's adjustment: A seven-year longitudinal study. *Child Development* 68(5):908-923.
Phillips, D.A.
1984   The illusion of incompetence among academically competent children. *Child Development* 55:2000-2016.
1996   Reframing the quality issue. Pp. 43-64 in *Reinventing Early Care and Education.* S.L. Kagan and N.E. Cohen, eds. San Francisco, CA: Jossey-Bass.
Phillips, D.A., and C. Howes
1987   Indicators of quality in child care: Review of research. Pp. 1-20 in *Quality in Child Care: What Does Research Tell Us?* D.A. Phillips, ed. Washington, DC: National Association for the Education of Young Children.
Phillips, D.A., and D.J. Stipek
1993   Early formal schooling: Are we promoting achievement or anxiety? *Applied and Preventive Psychology: Current Scientific Perspectives* 2:141-150
Phillips, D.A., K. McCartney, and S. Scarr
1987a   Child care quality and children's social developoment. *Developmental Psychology* 23:537-543.
Phillips, D.A., K. McCartney, S. Scarr, and C. Howes
1987b   Selective review of infant day care research: A cause for concern? *Zero to Three* 7(3):18-21.
Phillips, D.A., C. Howes, and M. Whitebook
1991   Child care as an adult work environment. *Journal of Social Issues* 47:49-70.

1992   The social policy context of child care: Effects on quality. *American Journal of Community Psychology* 20:25-51.

Phillips, D.A., M. Voran, E. Kisker, C. Howes, and M. Whitebook
1994   Child care for children in poverty: Opportunity or inequity? *Child Development* 65:472-492.

Phillips, D.A., D. Mekos, S. Scarr, K. McCartney, and M. Abbott-Shim
in   Paths to quality in child care: Structural and contextual influences on classroom
press   environments.

Phillips, M., J. Brooks-Gunn, G.J. Duncan, P.K. Klebanov, and J. Crane
1998   Family background, parenting practices, and the Black-White test score gap. Pp. 103-144 in *The Black-White Test Score Gap*. C. Jencks and M. Phillips, eds. Washington, DC: Brookings Institution Press.

Phillipsen, L., M.R. Burchinal, C. Howes, and D. Cryer
1997   The prediction of process quality from structural features of child care. *Early Childhood Research Quarterly* 12:281-304.

Phinney, J.S.
1990   Ethnic identity in adolescence and adulthood: A review of research. *Psychological Bulletin* 108:499-514.

1996   When we talk about American ethnic groups, what do we mean? *American Psychologist* 51:918-927.

Piaget, J.
1932   *The Moral Judgment of the Child*. Glencoe, IL: Free Press.
1952   *The Origins of Intelligence in Children*. New York: International Universities Press.

Pianta, P.C., and S.L. Nimetz
1991   Relationship between children and teachers: Associations with classroom and home behavior. *Journal of Applied Developmental Psychology* 12:379-393.

Pianta, R.C., and B. Egeland
1990   Life stress and parenting outcomes in a disadvantaged sample: Results of the Mother-Child Interaction Project. *Journal of Clinical Child Psychology* 19(4):329-336.

Pianta, R.C., B. Egeland, and M.F. Erickson
1989   The antecedents of maltreatment: Results of the Mother-Child Interaction Research Project. Pp. 203-253 in *Child Maltreatment*. D. Cicchetti and V. Carlson, eds. New York: Cambridge University Press.

Pike, A., S. McGuire, E.M. Hetherington, D. Reiss, and R. Plomin
1996   Family environment and adolescent depressive symptoms and antisocial behavior: A multivariate genetic analysis. *Developmental Psychology* 32(4):590-603.

Pleck, E.H.
1997   Paternal involvement: Levels, sources, and consequences. Pp. 66-103 in *The Role of the Father in Child Development*, Third Edition. M.E. Lamb, ed. New York: Wiley.

Pleck, E.H., and J.H. Pleck
1997   Fatherhood ideals in the United States: Historical dimensions. Pp. 33-48 in *The Role of the Father in Child Development*, Third Edition. M.E. Lamb, ed. New York: Wiley.

Plomin, R., and M. Rutter
1998   Child development, molecular genetics, and what to do with genes once they are found. *Child Development* 69(4):1223-1242.

Plomin, R., and D. Daniels
1987   Why are children in the same family so different from each other? *Behavioral and Brain Sciences* 10(1):1-16.

Plomin, R., J.C. DeFries, G.E. McClearn, and M. Rutter
1997a   *Behavioral Genetics*, Third Edition. New York: W.H. Freeman and Company.
Plomin, R., D.W. Fulker, R. Corley, and J.C. DeFries
1997b   Nature, nurture, and cognitive development from 1 to 16 years: A parent-offspring adoption study. *Psychological Science* 8(6):442-447.
Plotsky, P.M., and M.J. Meaney
1993   Early, postnatal experience alters hypothalamic corticotropin-releasing factor (CRF) mRNA, median eminence CRF content and stress-induced release in adult rats. *Molecular Brain Research* 18:195-200.
Poortinga, Y.H.
1997   Towards convergence. Pp. 347-387 in *Handbook of Cross-Cultural Psychology*, Volume 1: Theory and Method, Second Edition. J.W. Berry and Y.H. Poortinga, eds. Boston, MA: Allyn & Bacon, Inc.
Porter, A.
1967   The effects of using fallible variables in the analysis of covariance. Unpublished doctoral dissertation, University of Wisconsin at Madison.
Portes, A.
1996   *The New Second Generation*. New York: Russell Sage Foundation.
Posner, M.I., M.K. Rothbart, and L. Thomas-Thrapp
1997   Functions of orienting in early infancy. Pp. 327-345 in *Attention and Orienting: Sensory and Motivational Processes*. P.J. Lang, R.F. Simons, and M. Balaban, eds. Mahwah, NJ: Lawrence Erlbaum Associates.
Posner, M.I., M.K. Rothbart, L. Thomas-Thrapp, and G. Gerardi
1998   The development of orienting to locations and objects. Pp. 269-288 in *Visual Attention: Vancouver Studies in Cognitive Science*, Volume 8. R.D. Wright, ed. New York: Oxford University Press.
Powell, C., and S. Grantham-McGregor
1989   Home visiting of varying frequency and child development. *Pediatrics* 84(1):157-164.
Presser, H.B.
2000   Nonstandard work schedules and marital instability. *Journal of Marriage and the Family* 62:93-110.
Presser, H.B., and A.G. Cox
1997   The work schedules of low-educated American women and welfare reform. *Monthly Labor Review* 120:25-34.
Price, D.A., G.C. Close, and B.A. Fielding
1983   Age of appearance of circadian rhythm in salivary cortisol values in infancy. *Archives of Disease in Childhood* 58:454-456.
Prizant, B.M., A.M. Wetherby, and J.E. Roberts
1993   Communication disorders in infants and toddlers. Pp. 260-279 in *Handbook of Infant Mental Health*. C.H. Zeanah, ed. New York: The Guilford Press.
Provence, S., and R.C. Lipton
1962   *Infants in Institutions*. New York: International Universities Press.
Pumariega, A.J., and T.L. Cross
1997   Cultural competence in child psychiatry. In *Handbook of Child and Adolescent Psychiatry*, Volume 4. J.D. Noshpitz, ed. New York: John Wiley and Sons.
Putallaz, M.
1987   Maternal behavior and children's sociometric status. *Child Development* 58:324-340.
Pynoos, R.S., and S. Eth
1985   Witnessing acts of personal violence. Pp. 17-43 in *Post-Traumatic Stress in Children*. S. Eth and R.S. Pynoos, eds. Washington, DC: American Psychiatric Press.

Pynoos, R.S., A.M. Steinberg, and R. Wraith
  1995   A developmental model of childhood traumatic stress. Pp. 72-95 in *Developmental Psychopathology*, Volume 2: Risk, Disorder, and Adaptation. D. Cicchetti and D.J. Cohen, eds. New York: John Wiley & Sons.
Pynoos, R.S., R.F. Ritzmann, A.M. Steinberg, A. Goenjian, and I. Prisecaru
  1996a   A behavioral animal model of posttraumatic stress disorder featuring repeated exposure to situational reminders. *Biological Psychiatry* 39(2):129-134.
Pynoos, R.S., A.M. Steinberg, and A. Goenjian
  1996b   Traumatic stress in childhood and adolescence: Recent developments and current controversies. Pp. 331-358 in *Traumatic Stress: The Effects of Overwhelming Experience on Mind, Body, and Society*. B.A. van der Kolk and A.C. McFarlane, eds. New York: The Guilford Press.
Queralt, M., and A.D. Witte
  1998   Influences on neighborhood supply of child care in Massachusetts. *Social Service Review* 72(1):17-47.
Quint, J., and B. Egeland
  1995   New Chance: Comprehensive services for disadvantaged young families. Pp. 91-133 in *Two Generation Programs for Families in Poverty: A New Intervention Strategy*. S. Smith, ed. Advances in Applied Developmental Psychology, Volume 9. Norwood, NJ: Ablex Publishing Corp.
Quint, J.C., J.M. Bos, and D.F. Polit
  1997   *New Chance: Final Report on a Comprehensive Program for Young Mothers in Poverty and Their Children*. New York: Manpower Demonstration Research Corporation.
Rabinovich, B.A., J.T. Suwalsky, and F.A. Pedersen
  1986   The effects of maternal employment on infants: A pretest-postest design. *Journal of Genetic Psychology* 147(2):283-285.
Raden, A.
  1999   *Universal Prekindergarten in Georgia: A Case Study of Georgia's Lottery-Funded Pre-K Program*, Foundation for Child Development, Working Paper Series. New York: Foundation for Child Development.
Radziszewka, B., J.L. Richardson, C.W. Dent, and B.R. Flay
  1996   Parenting style and adolescent depressive symptoms, smoking, and academic achievement: Ethnic, gender, and class differences. *Journal of Behavioral Medicine* 19:289-305.
Raiha, H., L. Lehtonen, and H. Korvenranta
  1995   Family context of infantile colic. *Infant Mental Health Journal* 16(3):206-217.
Raikes, H.
  1993   Relationship duration in infant care: Time with a high ability teacher and infant-teacher attachment. *Early Childhood Research Quarterly* 8:309-325.
Ramey, C.T., and F.A. Campbell
  1984   Preventive education for high-risk children: Cognitive consequences of the Carolina Abecedarian Project. *American Journal of Mental Deficiency* 88:515-523.
Ramey, C.T., and S.L. Ramey
  1998   Early intervention and early experience. *American Psychologist* 58:109-120.
  1999   *Right From Birth: Building Your Child's Foundation for Life Birth to 18 Months*. New York: Goddard Press.
Ramey, C.T., D.M. Bryant, B.H. Wasik, J.J. Sparling, K.H. Fendt, and L.M. LaVange
  1992   Infant Health and Development Program for low birth weight, premature infants: Program elements, family participation, and child intelligence. *Pediatrics* 89(3):454-465.

Ramon y Cajal, S.
  1989   *Recollections of My Life.* Cambridge, MA: The MIT Press. Originally published in 1917 as *Recuerdos de mi Vida,* Madrid: Moya. Translated into English and published in 1937 as *Recollections of My Life* by E.H. Craigie and J. Cano, Philadelphia, PA: American Philosophical Society.

Rasmussen, T., and B. Milner
  1977   The role of early left brain injury in determining lateralization of cerebral speech functions. *Annals of the New York Academy of Sciences* 299:355-369.

Rauscher, F.H., G.L. Shaw, and K.N. Ky
  1993   Music and spatial task performance. *Nature* 365:611.

Rautava, P., L. Lehtonen, H. Helenius, and M. Silanpaa
  1995   Infantile colic: Child and family three years later. *Pediatrics* 96(1):43-47.

Reese, E., C.A. Haden, and R. Fivush
  1993   Mother-child conversations about the past: Relationships of style and memory over time. *Cognitive Development* 8:403-430.

Reiss, D.
  1997   Mechanisms linking genetic and social influences in adolescent development: Beginning a collaborative search. *Current Directions in Psychological Science* 6(4):100-105.

Repacholi, B.M., and A. Gopnik
  1997   Early reasoning about desires: Evidence from 14- and 18-month-olds. *Developmental Psychology* 33(1):12-21.

Rescorla, L.
  1989   The language development survey: A screening tool for delayed language in toddlers. *Journal of Speech and Hearing Research* 54:587-599.

Rescorla, L., and E. Schwartz
  1990   Outcomes of specific expressive delay (SELD). *Applied Psycholinguistics* 11:393-408.

Ribar, D.C.
  1992   Child care and the labor supply of married women. *Journal of Human Resources* 21(1):134-164.
  1995   A structural model of child care and the labor supply of married women. *Journal of Labor Economics* 13(3):558-597.

Rice, M.L.
  1998   Models of assessment: In search of a grammatical marker of language impairment in children. *American Speech-Language-Hearing Association Special Interest Division 1 Newsletter* 5(1):3-7.

Rice, M.L., and P.A. Hadley
  1995   Language outcomes of the language-focused curriculum. Pp. 155-169 in *Building a Language Focused Curriculum,* Volume 1: A Foundation for Lifelong Communication. M.L. Rice and K.A. Wilcox, eds. Baltimore, MD: Paul H. Brookes Publishing Co., Inc.

Rice, M.L., and K. Wexler
  1996   Toward tense as a clinical marker of specific language impairment in English-speaking children. *Journal of Speech and Hearing Research* 39:1239-1257.

Richardson, D.K., J.E. Gray, S.L. Gortmaker, D.A. Goldmann, D.M. Pursley, and M.C. McCormick
  1998   Declining severity adjusted mortality: Evidence of improving neonatal intensive care [see comments]. *Pediatrics* 102(4):893-899.

Richman, A., P. Miller, and R.A. LeVine
  1992   Cultural and educational variations in maternal responsiveness. *Developmental Psychology* 28:614-621.

Richmond, J.
  1967   Child development: A basic science for pediatrics. *Pediatrics* 39:649-658.
Richman, N., J. Stevenson, and P.J. Graham
  1982   *Preschool to School: A Behavioral Study.* London, UK: Academic Press.
Rider, M.E., and J.L. Mason
  1990   *Issues in Culturally Competent Service Delivery: An Annotated Bibliography.* Port-
          land, OR: Research and Training Center of Family Support and Children's Mental
          Health.
Riley, E.P., S.N. Mattson, E.R. Sowell, T.L. Jernigan, D.F. Sobel, and K.L. Jones
  1995   Abnormalities of the corpus callosum in children prenatally exposed to alcohol.
          Alcoholism: Clinical and Experimental Research 19:1198-1202.
Roberts, D.F., U.G. Foehr, V.J. Rideout, and M. Brodie
  1999   *Kids and Media at the New Millennium.* Menlo Park, CA: Kaiser Family Founda-
          tion.
Roberts, J.E., S. Rabinowitch, D.M. Bryant, and M.R. Burchinal
  1989   Language skills of children with different preschool experiences. *Journal of Speech
          and Hearing Research* 32(4):773-786.
Roberts, R.
  1989   *Developing Culturally Competent Programs for Children With Special Needs.*
          Washington, DC: Georgetown University Development Center.
Robertson, S.B., and S.E. Weismer
  1999   Effects of treatment on linguistic and social skills in toddlers with delayed language
          development. *Journal of Speech, Language, and Hearing Research* 42(5):1234-
          1248.
Robins, J.M., and S. Greenland
  1992   Identifiability and exchangeability for direct and indirect effects. *Epidemiology*
          3(2):143-155.
Robins, J.M., S. Greenland, and F.C. Hu
  1999   Estimation of the causal effect of a time-varying exposure on the marginal mean of
          a repeated binary outcome. *Journal of the American Statistical Association* 94:687-
          700.
Roditti, M.G.
  1995   Child daycare: A key building block of family support and family preservation
          programs. *Child Welfare* 74(6):1043-1068.
Rogers, S.J.
  1998   Empirically supported comprehensive treatments for young children with autism.
          Journal of Clinical Child Psychology 27:168-179.
Roggman, L.A., J.H. Langlois, L. Hubbs-Tait, and L.A. Riesner-Danner
  1994   Infant day-care, attachment, and the "file drawer problem." *Child Development*
          65(5):1429-1443.
Rogoff, B.
  1990   *Apprenticeship in Thinking: Cognitive Development in Social Context.* New York:
          Oxford.
Rogoff, B., and P. Chavajay
  1995   What's become of research on the cultural basis of cognitive development? *Ameri-
          can Psychologist* 50(10):859-877.
Rogoff, B., J. Mistry, A. Göncü, and C.E. Mosier
  1991   Cultural variation in the role relations of toddlers and their families. Pp. 173-183
          in *Cultural Approaches to Parenting.* M.H. Bornstein, ed. Hillsdale, NJ: Lawrence
          Erlbaum Associates, Publishers.

1993   *Monographs of the Society for Research in Child Development* , "Guided Participation in Cultural Activity by Toddlers and Caregivers" (Serial No. 236) 58(8).

Rogosch, F.A., D. Cicchetti, and J.L. Aber
1995   The role of child maltreatment in early deviations in cognitive and affective processing abilities and later peer relationship problems. *Development and Psychopathology* 7:591-610.

Rolls, E.T.
1992   Neurophysiology and functions of the primate amygdala. Pp. 141-165 in *The Amygdala: Neurobiological Aspects of Emotion, Memory, and Mental Dysfunction.* J.P. Aggleton, ed. New York: John Wiley & Sons.

Roncagliolo, M., M. Garrido, T. Walter, P. Peirano, and B. Lozoff
1998   Evidence of altered central nervous system development in infants with iron deficiency anemia at 6 mo: Delayed maturation of auditory brainstem responses. *The American Journal of Clinical Nutrition* 68(3):683-690.

Rose, S.A., J.F. Feldman, and I.F. Wallace
1992   Infant information processing in relation to six-year cognitive outcomes. *Child Development* 63(5):1126-1141.

Rose, S.J., and W. Meezan
1996   Variations in perceptions of child neglect. *Child Welfare* 75(2):139-160.

Rose, S.L., S.A. Rose, and J.F. Feldman
1989   Stability of behavior problems in very young children. *Development and Psychopathology* 1:5-19.

Rosen, J.B., M. Sitcoske, and J.R. Glowa
1996   Hyperexcitability: Exaggerated fear-potential startle produced by partial amygdala kindling. *Behavioral Neuroscience* 110(1):43-50.

Rosenbaum, J.
1991   Black pioneers - do their moves to the suburbs increase economic opportunity for mothers and children? *Housing Policy Debate* 2(4):1179-1213.

Rosenbaum, P.R.
1995   *Observation Studies.* New York: Springer-Verlag.

Rosenbaum, P., and D. Rubin
1983   The central role of the propensity score in observational studies for causal effects. *Biometrika* 17:41-55.

Rosenberg, M., and L.I. Pearlin
1978   Social class and self-esteem among children and adults. *American Journal of Sociology* 84:53-77.

Rosenblum, L.A., and M.W. Andrews
1994   Influences of environmental demand on maternal behavior and infant development. *Acta Paediatrica* Supplement 397:57-63.

Rosenblum, L.A., J.D. Coplan, S. Friedman, T. Bassoff, J.M. Gorman, and M.W. Andrews
1994   Adverse early experiences affect noradrenergic and serotonergic functioning in adult primates. *Biological Psychiatry* 35(4):221-227.

Rosenthal, M.K.
1994   *An Ecological Approach to the Study of Child Care: Family Day Care in Israel.* Hillsdale, NJ: Erlbaum.

Rosenthal, R., and D. Rubin
1982   Comparing effect sizes of independent studies. *Psychology Bulletin* 92:500-504.

Rosenzweig, M.R., and K.I. Wolpin
1994   Are there increasing returns to intergenerational production of human capital? Maternal schooling and child intellectual development. *Journal of Human Resources* 29:670-693.

Ross, H.S., C. Conant, J.A. Cheyne, and E. Alevizos
    1992   Relationships and alliances in the social interactions of kibbutz toddlers. *Social Development* 1:1-17.
Ross, G., S. Boatright, P.A. Auld, and R. Nass
    1996   Specific cognitive abilities in 2-year-old children with subependymal and mild intraventricular hemorrhage. *Brain Cognition* 32:1-13.
Rossi, A.
    1977   Biosocial perspectives on parenting. *Daedalus* 106:1-31.
Rossi, P.H.
    1998   *Feeding the Poor: Assessing Federal Food Aid.* Washington, DC: The AEI Press.
Rothbart, M.K., D. Derryberry, and M.I. Posner
    1994   A psychobiological approach to the development of temperament. Pp. 83-116 in *Temperament: Individual Differences at the Interface of Biology and Behavior.* J.E. Bates and T.D. Wachs, eds. Washington, DC: American Psychological Association.
Rothbart, M.K., and J.E. Bates
    1998   Temperament. Pp. 105-176 in *Handbook of Child Psychology*, Volume 3: Social, Emotional, and Personality Development, Fifth Edition. W. Damon, ed. New York: Wiley.
Rothbart, M.K., M.I. Posner, and A. Boylan
    1990   Regulatory mechanisms in infant development. Pp. 47-66 in *The Development of Attention: Research and Theory.* J.T. Enns, ed. Amsterdam, The Netherlands: Elsevier.
Rothbart, M.K., M.I. Posner, and J. Rosicky
    1994   Orienting in normal and pathological development. *Development and Psychopathology* 6:635-652.
Rothbart, M.K., M.I. Posner, and K.L. Hershey
    1995   Temperament, attention, and developmental psychopathology. Pp. 315-340 in *Developmental Psychopathology.* D. Cicchetti and D.J. Cohen, eds. New York: Wiley.
Rowe, D.C.
    1994   *The Limits of Family Influence: Genes, Experience, and Behavior.* New York: Guilford.
Rowe, D.C., and J.L. Rodgers
    1997   Poverty and behavior: Are environmental measures nature and nurture? *Developmental Review* 17:358-375.
Rowe, D.C., E.J. Wouldbrown, and B.L. Gulley
    1994   Peers and friends as nonshared environmental influences. Pp. 159-173 in *Separate Social Worlds of Siblings.* E.M. Hetherington, D. Reiss, and R. Plomin, eds. Hillsdale, NJ: Lawrence Erlbaum.
Roy, A.W., and C. Howe
    1990   Effects of cognitive conflict, socio-conflict and imitation on children's socio-legal thinking. *European Journal of Social Psychology* 20:241-252.
Roy, P., M. Rutter, and A. Pickles
    2000   Institutional care: Risk from family background or pattern of rearing? *Journal of Child Psychology and Psychiatry* 41:139-149.
Rubenstein, J., and C. Howes
    1983   Social-emotional development of toddlers in day care: Role of peers and of individual differences. *Advances in Early Education and Day Care* 3:13-45.
Rubenstein, J.L., F.A. Pedersen, and L.J. Yarrow
    1977   What happens when mothers are away: A comparison of mothers and substitute caregivers. *Developmental Psychology* 13:529-530.

Rubin, D.B.
   1976   Multivariate matching methods that are equal percent bias-reducing: Maximums on bias reduction for fixed sample sizes. *Biometrics* 32:121-132.
Rubin, K.H.
   1985   Socially withdrawn children: An "at risk" population? Pp. 125-139 in *Children's Peer Relations: Issues in Assessment and Intervention.* B. Schneider, K.H. Rubin, and J. Ledingham, eds. New York: Springer-Verlag.
Rubin, K.H., and L.R. Krasnor
   1986   Social-cognitive and social behavioral perspectives on problem solving. Pp. 1-68 in *The Minnesota Symposia on Child Psychology*, Volume 18: Cognitive Perspectives on Children's Social and Behavioral Development. M. Perlmutter, ed. Hillsdale, NJ: Erlbaum.
Rubin, K.H., and R.S.L. Mills
   1988   The many faces of social isolation in childhood. *Journal of Consulting and Clinical Psychology* 6:916-924.
   1990   Maternal beliefs about adaptive and maladaptive social behaviors in normal, aggressive, and withdrawn preschoolers. *Journal of Abnormal Child Psychology* 18:419-435.
Rubin, K.H., R.S.L. Mills, and L. Rose-Krasnor
   1989   Maternal beliefs and children's social competence. Pp. 313-331 in *Social Competence in Developmental Perspective.* B. Schneider, G. Attili, J. Nadel, and R. Weissberg, eds. Boston, MA: Kluwer Academic.
Rubin, K.H., D. Lynch, R. Coplan, L. Rose-Krasnor, and C.L. Booth
   1994   "Birds of a feather...": Behavioral concordances and preferential personal attraction in children. *Child Development* 65:1778-1785.
Rubin, K.H., S. Stewart, and X. Chen
   1995a Parents of aggressive and withdrawn children. Pp. 255-323 in *Handbook of Parenting*, Volume 1. M.H. Bornstein, ed. New York: Plenum Press.
Rubin, K.H., R.J. Coplan, N.A. Fox, and S. Calkins
   1995b Emotionality, emotion regulation, and preschoolers' social adaptation. *Development and Psychopathology* 7:49-62.
Rubin, K.H., P.D. Hastings, S.L. Stewart, H.A. Henderson, and X. Chen
   1997   The consistency and concomitants of inhibition: Some of the children, all of the time. *Child Development* 68:467-483.
Rubin, K.H., W. Bukowski, and J.G. Parker
   1998   Peer interactions, relationships, and groups. Pp. 619-700 in *Handbook of Child Psychology*, Volume 3: Social, Emotional, and Personality Development, Fifth Edition. W. Damon, ed. New York: John Wiley & Sons, Inc.
Ruhm, C.J.
   2000   Parental employment and child cognitive development. Unpublished manuscript. University of North Carolina at Greensboro.
Rumbaut, R.G.
   1994   The crucible within: Ethnic identity, self-esteem, and segmented assimilation among children of immigrants. *International Migration Review* 28:748-794.
Ruopp, R., J. Travers, F. Glantz, and C. Coelen
   1979   *Children at the Center.* Cambridge, MA: Abt Associates.
Rutter, M.
   1972   Maternal deprivation reconsidered. *Journal of Psychosomatic Research* 16:241-250.
   1981a Stress, coping and development: Some issues and some questions. *Journal of Child Psychology and Psychiatry* 22(4):323-356.

1981b *Maternal Deprivation Reassessed.* New York: Penguin Books.
1981c Stress, coping and development: Some issues and some questions. *Journal of Child Psychology and Psychiatry* 22(4):323-356.
1994   Beyond longitudinal data: Causes, consequences, changes and continuity. *Journal of Consulting and Clinical Psychology* 62:928-940.
1997   Nature-nurture integration: The example of antisocial behavior. *American Psychologist* 52:390-398.
2000   Resilience reconsidered: Conceptual considerations, empirical findings, and policy implications. Pp. 6551-682 in *Handbook of Early Childhood Intervention*, Second Edition. J.P. Shonkoff and S.J. Meisels, eds. New York: Cambridge University Press.
in   Psychosocial influences: Critiques, findings and research needs. *Development and*
press *Psychopathology.*
Rutter, M., and the English and Romanian Adoptees (ERA) Study Team
1998   Developmental catch-up, and deficit, following adoption after severe global early privation. *Journal of Child Psychology and Psychiatry* 39(4):465-476.
Rutter, M., and M. Rutter
1993   *Developing Minds: Challenge and Continuity Across the Life Span.* New York: Basic Books.
Rutter, M., and L.A. Sroufe
in   Developmental psychopathology: Concepts and challenges. *Development and Psy-*
press *chopathology.*
Rutter, M., J. Dunn, R. Plomin, E. Simonoff, A. Pickles, B. Maughan, J. Ormel, J. Meyer, and L.J. Eaves
1997   Integrating nature and nurture: Implications of person-environment correlations and interactions for developmental psychopathology. *Development and Psychopathology* 9:335-364.
Rutter, M., H. Giller, and A. Hagell
1998   *Antisocial Behavior by Young People.* New York: Cambridge University Press.
Rutter, M., J.L. Silberg, T.G. O'Connor, and E. Simonoff
1999a Genetics and child psychiatry: I. Advances in quantitative and molecular genetics. *Journal of Child Psychology and Psychiatry* 40:3-18.
1999b Genetics and child psychiatry: II. Empirical research findings. *Journal of Child Psychology and Psychiatry* 40:19-55.
Rutter, M., K. Thorpe, and J. Golding
2000   *Twins As a Natural Experiment to Study the Causes of Language Delay.* Report to the Mental Health Foundation, London, UK.
Rutter, M., A. Pickles, R. Murray, and L. Eaves
in   Testing hypotheses on specific environmental causal effects on behavior. *Psycho-*
press *logical Bulletin.*
Saarni, C.
1990   Emotional competence: How emotions and relationships become integrated. Pp. 115-182 in *Socioemotional Development: Nebraska Symposium on Motivation*, Volume 36. R.A. Thompson, ed. Lincoln, NE: University of Nebraska Press.
1999   *The Development of Emotional Competence.* New York: Guilford.
Saarni, C., D. Mumme, and J.J. Campos
1998   Emotional development: Action, communication, and understanding. Pp. 237-309 in *Handbook of Child Psychology*, Volume 3: Social, Emotional, and Personality Development, Fifth Edition. W. Damon, ed. New York: Wiley.

Saigal, S., P. Szatmari, P. Rosenbaum, D. Campbell, and S. King
  1991 Cognitive abilities and school performance of extremely low birth weight children and matched term control children at age 8 years: A regional study. *The Journal of Pediatrics* 118:751-760.
Salkind, N.J., and R. Haskins
  1982 Negative income tax: The impact on children from low-income families. *Journal of Family Issues* 92:500-504.
Sameroff, A.J.
  1989 Models of developmental regulation: The environtype. Pp. 41-68 in *The Emergence of a Discipline: Rochester Symposium on Developmental Psychopathology*, Volume 1. D. Cicchetti, ed. Hillsdale, NJ: Lawrence Erlbaum Associates, Inc.
Sameroff, A.J., and M.J. Chandler
  1975 Reproductive risk and the continuum of caretaking casualty. Pp. 187-244 in *Review of Child Development Research*, Volume 4. F.D. Horowitz, M. Hetherington, S. Scarr-Salapatek, and G. Sigel, eds. Chicago, IL: University of Chicago Press.
Sameroff, A.J., and R.N. Emde, eds.
  1989 *Relationships Disturbances in Early Childhood: A Developmental Approach.* New York: Basic Books.
Sameroff, A.J., and B.H. Fiese
  1990 Transactional regulation and early intervention. Pp. 119-149 in *Handbook of Early Childhood Intervention.* J.S. Meisels and J.P. Shonkoff, eds. New York: Cambridge University Press.
  2000 Transactional regulation: The development ecology of early intervention. Pp. 135-159 in *Handbook of Early Childhood Intervention*, Second Edition. J.P. Shonkoff and S.J. Meisels, eds. New York: Cambridge University Press.
Sameroff, A.J., R. Seifer, B. Barocas, M. Zax, and S. Greenspan
  1987 IQ Scores of 4-year old children: Social environmental risk factors. *Pediatrics* 79:343-350.
Sampson, P.D., F.L. Bookstein, H.M. Barr, and A.P. Streissguth
  1994 Prenatal alcohol exposure, birthweight, and measures of child size from birth to age 14 years. *American Journal of Public Health* 84(9):1421-1428.
Sampson, R.J.
  1992 Family management and child development: Insights from social disorganization theory. Pp. 63-93 in *Facts, Frameworks, and Forecasts: Advances in Criminological Theory*, Volume 3. J. McCord, ed. New Brunswick, NJ: Transaction Publishers.
Sampson, R.J., and W.B. Groves
  1989 Community structure and crime: Testing social disorganization theory. *American Journal of Sociology* 94:774-802.
Sampson, R.J., S.W. Raudenbush, and F. Earls
  1997 Neighborhoods and violent crime: A multilevel study of collective efficacy. *Science* 277:918-924.
Sancilio, M.F., J.M. Plumert, and W.W. Hartup
  1989 Friendship and aggressiveness as determinants of conflict outcomes in middle childhood. *Developmental Psychology* 25(5):812-819.
Sargent, J.D., M.J. Brown, J.L. Freeman, A. Bailey, D. Goodman, and D.H. Freeman
  1995 Childhood lead poisoning in Massachusetts's communities: Its association with sociodemographic and housing characteristics. *American Journal of Public Health* 85:528-534.
Saxe, G.B., S.R. Guberman, and M. Gearhart
  1987 Social processes in early number development. *Monographs of the Society for Research in Child Development* (Serial No. 216) 52(2).

Scarr, S.
    1992   Developmental theories for the 1990s: Development and individual differences.
            Child Development 63:1-19.
Scarr, S., and M. Eisenberg
    1993   Child care research: Issues, perspectives, and results. *Annual Review of Psychology*
            44:613-644.
Scarr, S., and R.A. Weinberg
    1976   IQ test performance of black children adopted by white families. *American Psy-
            chologist* 31:726-739.
Scarr, S., M. Eisenberg, and K. Deater-Deckard
    1994   Measurement of quality in child care centers. *Early Childhood Research Quarterly*
            9:131-151.
Schaffer, H.R.
    1966   The onset of fear of strangers and the incongruity hypothesis. *Journal of Child
            Psychological Psychiatry* 7:95-106.
Schectman, V., R.K. Harper, and R.M. Harper
    1994   Distribution of slow-wave EEG activity across the night in developing infants.
            Sleep 17:316-322.
Scheeringa, M.S., and C.H. Zeanah
    1995   Symptom expression and trauma variables in children under 48 months of age.
            Infant Mental Health Journal 16(4):259-270.
Scheeringa, M.S., C.H. Zeanah, M.J. Drell, and J.A. Larrieu
    1995   Two approaches to the diagnosis of posttraumatic stress disorder in infancy and
            early childhood. *Journal of the American Academy of Child and Adolescent Psy-
            chiatry* 34:191-200.
Schieffelin, B.B., and E. Ochs
    1986   *Language Socialization Across Cultures.* Cambridge, UK: Cambridge University
            Press.
Schiff, M., M. Duyme, A. Dumaret, and S. Tomkiewitz
    1982   How much could we boost scholastic achievment and IQ scores? A direct answer
            from a French adoption study. *Cognition* 12:165-196.
Schiff-Myers, N.
    1988   Hearing children of deaf parents. Pp. 47-61 in *Language Development in Excep-
            tional Circumstances.* D. Bishop and K. Mogford, eds. New York: Churchill
            Livingstone.
Schmidt, L.A., and N.A. Fox
    1994   Patterns of cortical electrophysiology and autonomic activity in adults' shyness and
            sociability. *Biological Psychology* 38:183-198.
Schmitt, K.L., D.R. Anderson, and P.A. Collins
    1999   Form and content: Looking at visual features of television. *Developmental Psy-
            chology* 35:1156-1167.
Schneider, M.L.
    1992a   The effect of mild stress during pregnancy on birthweight and neuromotor matura-
            tion in Rhesus monkey infants (Macaca mulatta). *Infant Behavior and Develop-
            ment* 15:389-403.
    1992b   Prenatal stress exposure alters postnatal behavioral expression under conditions of
            novelty challenge in Rhesus monkey infants. *Developmental Psychobiology*
            25(7):529-540.
Schneider, M.L., C.L. Coe, and G.R. Lubach
    1992   Endocrine activation mimics the adverse effects of prenatal stress on the neuromo-
            tor development of the infant primate. *Developmental Psychobiology* 25(6):427-
            439.

Schneider, M.L., A.S. Clarke, G.W. Kraemer, E.C. Roughton, G.R. Lubach, S. Rimm-Kaufman, D. Schmidt, and M. Ebert
1998   Prenatal stress alters brain biogenic amine levels in primates. *Development and Psychopathology* 10:427-440.

Schore, A.N.
1994   *Affect Regulation and the Origin of the Self: The Neurobiology of Emotional Development.* Hillsdale, NJ: Erlbaum.

Schulkin, J., B.S. McEwen, and P.S. Gold
1994   Allostasis, amygdala, and anticipatory angst. *Neuroscience and Behavioral Reviews* 18(3):385-396.

Schulman, K., H. Blank, and D. Ewen
1999   *Seeds of Success: State Prekindergarten Initiatives, 1998-1999.* Washington, DC: Children's Defense Fund.

Schwartz, J., R. Strickland, and G. Krolick
1974   Infant day care: Behavioral effects at preschool age. *Developmental Psychology* 4:502-506.

Schweinhart, L., H. Barnes, D. Weikart, W.S. Barnett, and A.S. Epstein
1993   Significant benefits: The High/Scope Perry Preschool study through age 27. *Monographs of the High/Scope Educational Research Foundation,* Number 10. Ypsilanti, MI: The High/Scope Press.

Seifer, R.
1995   Perils and pitfalls of high-risk research. *Developmental Psychology* 31(3):420-424.

Seifer, R., and S. Dickstein
2000   Parental mental illness and infant development. Pp. 145-160 in *Handbook of Infant Mental Health,* Second Edition. C.H. Zeanah, ed. New York: The Guilford Press.

Seifer, R., A.J. Sameroff, S. Dickstein, G. Keitner, I. Miller, S. Rasmussen, and L.C. Hayden
1996   Parental psychopathology, multiple contextual risks, and one-year outcomes in children. *Journal of Clinical Child Psychology* 25(4):423-435.

Seitz, V., and S. Provence
1990   Caregiver models of early intervention. Pp. 400-427 in *Handbook of Early Childhood Intervention,* First Edition. S.J. Meisels and J.P. Shonkoff, eds. New York: Cambridge University Press.

Seligman, M., and R.B. Darling
1997   *Ordinary Families, Special Children.* New York: Guilford Press.

Seltenheim, K., L. Ahnert, H. Rickert, and M.E. Lamb
1997   The formation of attachments between infants and care providers in German daycare centers. Poster presented to the American Psychological Society, Washington, DC, May 1997.

Selye, H.
1973   The evolution of the stress concept. *American Scientist* 61(6):692-699.
1975   Confusion and controversy in the stress field. *Journal of Human Stress* 1(2):37-44.

Serdula, M., D.F. Williamson, J.S. Kendrick, R.F. Anda, and T. Byers
1991   Trends in alcohol consumption by pregnant women: 1985 through 1988. *Journal of the American Medical Association* 265:876-879.

Shadish, W.R., T.D. Cook, and D.T. Campbell
in   *Experimental and Quasi-Experimental Designs for Generalized Causal Inference.*
press   Boston, MA: Houghton-Mifflin.

Shallice, T.
1982   Specific impairments of planning. Pp. 199-209 in *The Neuropsychology of Cognitive Function.* D.E. Broadbent and L. Weiskrantz, ed. London, UK: The Royal Society.

Shanahan, T., and F. Rodriguez-Brown
    1993   Project FLAME: The theory and structure of a family literacy program for the
            Latino community, University of Illinois at Chicago. Paper presented at the annual
            meeting of the American Educational Research Association, Atlanta, GA.
Shaw, D.S., K. Keenan, and J.I. Vondra
    1994   Developmental precursors of externalizing behavior: Ages 1 to 3. *Developmental
            Psychology* 30(3):355-364.
Shaw, D.S., E.B. Owens, J.I. Vondra, K. Keenan, and E.B. Winslow
    1996   Early risk factors and pathways in the development of early disruptive behavior
            problems. *Development and Psychopathology* 8:679-699.
Sher, P.K., and S.B. Brown
    1975   A longitudinal study of head growth in pre-term infants. II: Differentiation between
            "catch-up" head growth and early infantile hydrocephalus. *Developmental Medi-
            cine and Child Neurology* 17:711-718.
Shields, A.M., D. Cicchetti, and R.M. Ryan
    1994   The development of emotional and behavioral self-regulation and social compe-
            tence among maltreated school-age children. *Development and Psychopathology*
            6:57-75.
Shonkoff, J.P.
    1982   Biological and social factors contributing to mild mental retardation. Pp. 133-181
            in *Placing Children in Special Education: A Strategy for Equity*. Panel on Selection
            and Placement of Students in Programs for the Mentally Retarded. K. Heller, W.
            Holtzman, and S. Messick, eds., Committee on Child Development Research and
            Public Policy. Commission on Behavioral and Social Sciences and Education, Na-
            tional Research Council. Washington, DC: National Academy Press.
    1983   The limitations of normative assessments of high risk infants. *Topics in Early
            Childhood Special Education* 3(1):29-43.
    2000   Science, policy, and practice: Three cultures in search of a shared mission. *Child
            Development* 71:181-187.
Shonkoff, J.P., and P. Hauser-Cram
    1987   Early intervention for disabled infants and their families: A quantitative analysis.
            Pediatrics 80:650-658.
Shonkoff, J.P. and P. Marshall
    2000   The biology of developmental vulnerability. Pp. 35-53 in *Handbook of Early
            Childhood Intervention*, Second Edition, J.P. Shonkoff and S.J. Meisels, eds. New
            York: Cambridge University Press.
Shonkoff, J.P., and S.J. Meisels, eds.
    2000   *Handbook of Early Childhood Intervention*, Second Edition. New York: Cam-
            bridge University Press.
Shonkoff, J.P., P. Hauser-Cram, M. Krauss, and C. Upshur
    1992   Development of infants with disabilities and their families: Implications for theory
            and service delivery. *Monographs of the Society for Research in Child Develop-
            ment* (Serial No. 230) 57(6).
Shonkoff, J.P., J. Lippitt, and D. Cavanaugh
    2000   Early childhood policy: Implications for infant mental health. Pp. 503-518 in
            Handbook of Infant Mental Health, Second Edition. C.H. Zeanah, ed. New York:
            The Guilford Press.
Shweder, R.A., L.A. Jensen, and W.M. Goldstein
    1995   Who sleeps by whom revisited: A method for extracting the moral goods implicit in
            practice. *New Directions for Child Development: Cultural Practices As Contexts
            for Development* 67:21-39.

Shweder, R.A., J.J. Goodnow, G. Hatano, R.A. LeVine, H.R. Markus, and P. Miller
  1998   The cultural psychology of development: One mind, many mentalities. Pp. 865-937 in *Handbook of Child Psychology*, Volume 1: Theoretical Models of Human Development. W. Damon, ed. New York: John Wiley & Sons, Inc.
Siegel, G.L., and L.A. Loman
  1991   *Child Care and AFDC Recipients in Illinois: Patterns, Problems, and Needs.* Prepared for the Division of Family Support Services, Illinois Department of Public Aid. St. Louis, MO: Institute of Applied Research.
Sigel, I.E., A.V. McGillicuddy-DeLisi, and J.J. Goodnow, eds.
  1992   *Parental Belief Systems: The Psychological Consequences for Children*, Second Edition. Hillsdale, NJ: Lawrence Erlbaum Associates, Inc.
Singer, M.I., T.M. Anglin, L. Song, and L. Lunghofer
  1995   Adolescents' exposure to violence and associated symptoms of psychological trauma. *Journal of the American Medical Association* 273:477-482.
Skeels, H.M.
  1966   Adult Status of Children with Contrasting Early Life Experiences: A Follow-up Study. *Monographs of the Society for Research in Child Development*, Volume 31, No. 3. Chicago, IL: University of Chicago Press.
Skuse, D.H.
  1985   Non-organic faliure to thrive: A reappraisal. *Archives of the Diseases of Childhood* 60(2):173-178.
  1988   Extreme deprivation in early childhood. Pp. 29-46 in *Language Development in Exceptional Circumstances*. D. Bishop and K. Mogford, eds. New York: Churchill Livingstone.
Skuse, D.H., A. Albanese, R. Stanhope, J. Gilmour, and L. Voss
  1996   A new stress-related syndrome of growth failure and hyperphagia in childen associated with reversibility of growth-hormone insufficiency. *Lancet* 348(9024):353-358.
Slaby, R.G., and N.G. Guerra
  1988   Cognitive mediators of aggression in adolescent offenders: I. Assessment. *Developmental Psychology* 24(4):580-588.
Slikker, W., and L. Chang
  1998   *Handbook of Developmental Neurotoxicology.* San Diego, CA: Academic Press.
Slobin, D.I.
  1985   *The Crosslinguistic Study of Language Acquisition.* Hillsdale, NJ: Erlbaum Associates.
  1997   The universal, the typological, and the particular in acquisition. Pp. 1-39 in *The Crosslinguistic Study of Language Acquisition*, Volume 5: Expanding the Contexts. D.I. Slobin, ed. Mahwah, NJ: Lawrence Erlbaum Associates, Inc.
Slomkowski, C.L., and J. Dunn
  1992   Arguments and relationships within the family: Differences in young children's disputes with mother and sibling. *Developmental Psychology* 28:919-924.
Smiley, P.A., and C.S. Dweck
  1994   Individual differences in achievement goals among young children. *Child Development* 65:1723-1743.
Smith, B.J., and P. McKenna
  1994   Early intervention public policy: Past, present, and future. In *Meeting Early Intervention Challenges: Issues From Birth to Three*, Second Edition. L.J. Johnson, R.J. Gallagher, M.J. LaMontagne, J.B. Jordan, J.L. Gallagher, P.L. Hutinger, and M.B. Karnes, eds. Baltimore, MD: Paul H. Brookes Publishing Co., Inc.

Smith, J.R., J. Brooks-Gunn, and P.K. Klebanov
  1997   Consequences of living in poverty for young children's cognitive and verbal ability
          and early school achievement. Pp. 132-189 in *Consequences of Growing Up Poor*.
          G.J. Duncan and J. Brooks-Gunn, eds. New York: Russell Sage Foundation.
Smith, S.
  1998   The past decade's research on child care quality and children's development: What
          we are learning, Directions for the future. Paper prepared for a meeting on "Child
          Care in the New Policy Context," sponsored by the Office of the Assistant Secre-
          tary for Planning and Evaluation, U.S. Department of Health and Human Services,
          and held in Bethesda, MD on April 30-May 1, 1998.
Smith, T., P.A. Donahoe, and B.J. Davis
  2000   The UCLA treatment model. Pp. 29-48 in *Preschool Education Programs for
          Children With Autism*, Second Edition. S.L. Harris and J.S. Handleman, eds.
          Austin, TX: Pro-Ed.
Smolek, L., and M. Weinraub
  1979   Separation distress and representational development. Paper presented at the bien-
          nial meeting of the Society for Research in Child Development, San Francisco, CA,
          March 1979.
Snow, C.E.
  1993   Families as social contexts for literacy development. *New Directions for Child
          Development* 61:11-24.
Sorce, J.F., and R.N. Emde
  1981   Mother's presence is not enough: The effect of emotional availability on infant
          exploration. *Developmental Psychology* 17(6):737-745.
Sorce, J.F., R.N. Emde, J.J. Campos, and M.D. Klinnert
  1985   Maternal emotional signaling: Its effect on the visual cliff behavior of 1-year-olds.
          Developmental Psychology 21(1):195-200.
Sowell, E.R., T.L. Jernigan, S.N. Mattson, E.P. Riley, D.F. Sobel, and K.L. Jones
  1996   Abnormal development of the cerebellar vermis in children prenatally exposed to
          alcohol: Size reduction in lobules I-V. *Alcoholism: Clinical and Experimental
          Research* 20:31-34.
Spalter-Roth, R., B. Burr, H. Hartmann, and L. Shaw
  1995   *Welfare That Works: The Working Lives of AFDC Recipients*. Washington, DC:
          Institute for Women's Policy Research.
Spangler, G., and M. Schieche
  1994   The Role of Maternal Sensitivity and the Quality of Infant-Mother Attachment for
          Infant Biobehavioral Organization. Paper presented at the 9th International Con-
          ference on Infant Studies, Paris, France.
Spitz, R.A.
  1945   Hospitalism: An inquiry into the genesis of psychiatric conditions in early child-
          hood. *Psychoanalytic Study of the Child* 1:53-74.
Sroufe, L.A.
  1979   Socioemotional development. Pp. 462-515 in *Handbook of Infant Development*.
          J.D. Osofsky, ed. New York: John Wiley & Sons.
  1996   *Emotional Development*. New York: Cambridge University Press.
Sroufe, L.A., and B. Egeland
  1991   Illustrations of person-environment interaction from a longitudinal study. Pp. 68-
          84 in *Conceptualization and Measurement of Organism-Environment Interaction*.
          T.D. Wachs and R. Plomin, eds. Washington, DC: American Psychological Asso-
          ciation.

Sroufe, L.A., and J. Fleeson
1986   Attachment and the construction of relationships. Pp. 51-71 in *Relationships and Development*. W.W. Hartup and Z. Rubin, eds. Hillsdale, NJ: Erlbaum.
1988   The coherence of family relationships. Pp. 27-47 in *Relationships Within Families*. R.A. Hinde and J. Stevenson-Hinde, eds. Oxford, UK: Clarendon.
Sroufe, L.A., and E. Waters
1977   Attachment as an organizational construct. *Child Development* 48:1184-1189.
Sroufe, L.A., N. Fox, and V. Pancake
1983   Attachment and dependency in developmental perspective. *Child Development* 54:1615-1627.
Sroufe, L.A., B. Egeland, and T. Kreutzer
1990   The fate of early experience following developmental change: Longitudinal approaches to individual adaptation in childhood. *Child Development* 61:1363-1373.
Sroufe, L.A., E. Carlson, and S. Schulman
1993   Individuals in relationships: Development from infancy through adolescence. Pp. 315-342 in *Studying Lives Through Time: Personality and Development*. D.C. Funder, R.D. Parke, C. Tomlinson-Keasey, and K. Widaman, eds. Washington, DC: American Psychological Association.
Sroufe, L.A., E.A. Carlson, A.K. Levy, and B. Egeland
1999   Implications of attachment theory for developmental psychopathology. *Development and Psychopathology* 11:1-13.
St. James-Roberts, I., and T. Halil
1991   Infant crying patterns in the first year: Normal community and clinical findings. *Journal of Child Psychology and Psychiatry* 32(6):951-968.
St. James-Roberts, I., S. Conroy, and K. Wilsher
1995a   Clinical, developmental and social aspects of infant crying and colic. *Early Development and Parenting* 4(4):177-189.
St. James-Roberts, I., J. Hurry, J. Bowyer, and R.G. Barr
1995b   Supplementary carrying compared with advice to increase responsive parenting as interventions to prevent persistent infant crying. *Pediatrics* 95(3):381-388.
St. Pierre, R.G., and J.I. Layzer
1998   Improving the life chances of children in poverty: Assumptions and what we have learned. *SRCD Social Policy Report* 12(4):1-28.
St. Pierre, R.G., and J.P. Swartz
1995   The Even Start Family Literacy Program. Pp. 37-66 in *Advances in Applied Developmental Psychology*, Volume 9: Two Generation Programs for Families in Poverty: A New Intervention Strategy. S. Smith, ed. Norwood, NJ: Ablex Publishing Corporation.
St. Pierre, R.G., B.D. Goodson, J.I. Layzer, and L. Bernstein
1994   *National Impact Evaluation of the Comprehensive Child Development Program*. Cambridge, MA: Abt Associates.
St. Pierre, R., J.P. Swartz, B. Gamse, S. Murray, D. Deck, and P. Nickel
1995a   *National Evaluation of the Even Start Family Literacy Program. Final Report*. Washington, DC: U.S. Department of Education, Office of the Under Secretary.
St. Pierre, R.G., J.I. Layzer, and H.V. Barnes
1995b   Two-generation programs: Design, cost, and short-term effectiveness. *The Future of Children: Long-Term Outcomes of Early Childhood Programs* 5(3):76-93.
Stams, G.J.J.M., F. Juffer, M.H. van IJzendoorn, and R.A.C. Hoksbergen
in   Attachment-based intervention in adoptive families in infancy and children's devel-
press   opment at age seven: Two longitudinal studies. *British Journal of Developmental Psychology*.

Starkey, P., and A. Klein
    1992   Economic and cultural influences of early mathematical development. Pp. 440-443
            in *New Directions in Child and Family Research: Shaping Head Start in the 90s.*
            F.L. Parker, R. Robinson, S. Sombrano, C.S. Piotrkowski, J. Hagen, S. Randolph,
            and A. Baker, eds. New York: National Council of Jewish Women.
Starkey, P., E.S. Spelke, and R. Gelman
    1983   Detection of intermodal numerical correspondences by human infants. *Science*
            222(4620):179-181.
State Policy Documentation Project
    2000   Exemptions from State Work Requirements (as of October 1999). Updated June
            2000. Table created by the State Policy Documentation Project, a joint project of
            the Center for Law and Social Policy and the Center on Budget and Policy Priori-
            ties. Available at http://www.spdp.org.
Stein, N.L., and L.J. Levine
    1989   The causal organisation of emotional knowledge: A developmental study. *Cogni-
            tion and Emotion* 3:343-378.
    1990   Making sense out of emotion: The representation and use of goal-structured knowl-
            edge. Pp. 45-73 in *Psychological and Biological Approaches to Emotion.* N.L.
            Stein, B. Leventhal, and T. Trabasso, eds. Hillsdale, NJ: Erlbaum.
Steinberg, L., P. Blinde, and K. Chan
    1984   Dropping out among language minority youth. *Review of Educational Research*
            54:113-132.
Steiner, G.Y.
    1976   *The Children's Cause.* Washington, DC: The Brookings Institution.
Stern, D.
    1977   *The First Relationship: Infant and Mother.* Cambridge, MA: Harvard University
            Press.
    1985   *The Interpersonal World of the Infant.* New York: Basic Books.
Stevenson, H., and S.-Y. Lee
    1990   Contexts of achievementt: A study of American, Chinese, and Japanese children.
            Monographs of the Society for Research in Child Development (Serial No. 221)
            55(1-2):1-106.
Stevenson, H., and R. Newman
    1986   Long-term prediction of achievement and attitudes in mathematics and reading.
            Child Development 57:646-659.
Stevenson, H.W., T. Parker, A. Wilkinson, A. Hegion, and E. Fish
    1976   Longitudinal study of individual differences in cognitive development and scholas-
            tic achievement. *Journal of Educational Psychology* 68:377-400.
Stifter, C., and M. Bono
    1998   The effect of excessive infant crying on maternal self-perceptions and mother-infant
            attachment. *Child Care, Health and Development* 24(5):339-351.
Stifter, C.A., and J. Braungart
    1992   Infant colic: A transient condition with no apparent effects. *Journal of Applied
            Developmental Psychology* 13:447-462.
Stifter, C.A., C.M. Coulehan, and M. Fish
    1993   Linking employment to attachment: The mediating effects of maternal separation
            anxiety and interactive behavior. *Child Development* 64:1451-1460.
Stipek, D.J.
    1992   The child at school. Pp. 579-625 in *Developmental Psychology: An Advanced
            Textbook*, Third Edition. M.H. Bornstein and M.E. Lamb, eds. Hillsdale, NJ:
            Lawrence Erlbaum Associates, Inc.

1993   *Motivation to Learn: From Theory to Practice*, Third Edition. Boston, MA: Allyn and Bacon.

in   Pathways to constructive lives: The importance of early school success. In *Con-*
press   *structive and Destructive Behavior: Implications for Family, School, and Society.* A. Bohart and D. Stipek, eds. Washington, DC: American Psychological Association.

Stipek, D.J., and J. Greene
in   Achievement motivation in early childhood: Cause for concern or celebration? In
press   *Psychological Perspectives on Early Childhood Education: Reframing Dilemmas in Research and Practice.* S. Goldbeck, ed. Mahwah, NJ: Lawrence Erlbaum Associates, Publishers.

Stipek, D.J., and J. Hoffman
1980   Development of children's performance-related judgments. *Child Development* 5:92-94.

Stipek, D.J., and R. Ryan
1997   Economically disadvantaged preschoolers: Ready to learn but further to go. *Developmental Psychology* 33(4):711-723.

Stipek, D.J., and L. Tannatt
1984   Children's judgments of their own and their peers' academic competence. *Journal of Educational Psychology* 76:75-84.

Stipek, D.J., T. Roberts, and M. Sanborn
1984   Preschool-age children's performance expectations for themselves and another child as a function of the incentive value of success and the salience of past performance. *Child Development* 55:1983-1989.

Stipek, D.J., J.H. Gralinski, and C.B. Kopp
1990   Self-concept development in the toddler years. *Developmental Psychology* 26(6):972-977.

Stipek, D.J., R. Feiler, D. Daniels, and S. Milburn
1995   Effects of different instructional approaches on young children's achievement and motivation. *Child Development* 66:209-223.

Stipek, D.J., R. Feiler, P. Byler, R. Ryan, S. Milburn, and J. Salmon
1998   Good beginnings: What difference does the program make in preparing young children for school? *Journal of Applied Developmental Psychology* 19:41-66.

Stith, S., and A. Davis
1984   Employed mothers and family day care substitute caregivers. *Child Development* 55:1340-1348.

Stoneman, Z.
1993   The effects of attitude on preschool integration. Pp. 223-248 in *Integrating Young Children With Disabilities into Community Programs: Ecological Perspectives on Research and Implementation.* C.A. Peck, S.L. Odom, and D.D. Bricker, eds. Baltimore, MD: Paul H. Brookes Publishing Co., Inc.

in   Attitudes and beliefs of parents of typically developing children: Effects on early
press   childhood inclusion. In *Early Childhood Inclusion: Focus on Change.* M.J. Guralnick, ed. Baltimore, MD: Paul H. Brookes Publishing Co., Inc.

Stratakis, C.A., and G.P. Chrousos
1995   Neuroendocrinology and pathophysiology of the stress system. Pp. 1-18 in *Stress: Basic Mechanisms and Clinical Implications*, Annals of the New York Academy of Sciences Volume 771. G.P. Chrousos, R. McCarty, K. Pacak, G. Cizza, E. Sternberg, P.W. Gold, and R. Kvetnansky, eds. New York: New York Academy of Sciences.

Streissguth, A.P., H.M. Barr, J. Kogan, and F.L. Bookstein
    1996a *Understanding the Occurrence of Secondary Disabilities in Clients With Fetal Alcohol Syndrome (FAS) and Fetal Alcohol Effects (FAE).* Seattle, WA: University of Washington Publications.
Streissguth, A.P., F.L. Bookstein, and H.M. Barr
    1996b A dose-response study of the enduring effects of prenatal alcohol exposure: Birth to 14 years. Pp. 141-168 in *Alcohol, Pregnancy and the Developing Child.* L. Spohr and C. Steinhausen, eds. Cambridge, UK: Cambridge University Press.
Strupp, B.J., and D.A. Levitsky
    1995   Enduring cognitive effects of early malnutrition: A theoretical reappraisal. *Journal of Nutrition* 125:2221S-2232S.
Stuss, D.T.
    1992   Biological and psychological development of executive functions. *Brain and Cognition* 20:8-23.
Subramanian, K.
    1985   Reducing child abuse through respite center intervention. *Child Welfare* LXIV(5):501-509.
Suess, G.J., K.E. Grossmann, and L.A. Sroufe
    1992   Effects of infant attachment to mother and father on quality of adaptation in preschool: From dyadic to individual organization of self. *International Journal of Behavioral Development* 15:73-95.
Sugarman, S.
    1981   The cognitive basis of classification in very young children: An analysis of object-ordering trends. *Child Development* 52(4):1172-1178.
Sullivan, M.W., M. Lewis, and S.M. Alessandri
    1991   The interface between emotion and cognition. Pp. 241-261 in *Visions of Aesthetics, the Environment, and Development: The Legacy of Joachim F. Wohlwill.* R.M. Downs and L.S. Liben, eds. Hillsdale, NJ: Lawrence Erlbaum Associates, Inc.
Suomi, S.J.
    1991   Adolescent depression and depressive symptoms: Insights from longitudinal studies with Rhesus monkeys. *Journal of Youth and Adolescence* 20(2):273-287.
    1997   Early determinants of behaviour: Evidence from primate studies. *British Medical Bulletin* 53(1):170-184.
    2000   A biobehavioral perspective on developmental psychopathology: Excessive aggression and serotonergic dysfunction in monkeys. In *Handbook of Developmental Psychopathology*, Second Edition. A.J. Sameroff, M. Lewis, and S. Miller, eds. New York: Plenum Press.
Super, C.M., and S. Harkness
    1982   The infant's niche in rural Kenya and metropolitan America. Pp. 47-55 in *Cross-Cultural Research at Issue.* L.L. Adler, ed. New York: Academic Press.
    1986   The developmental niche: A conceptualization at the interface of child and culture. *International Journal of Behavioral Development* 9(4):545-569.
    1997   The cultural structuring of child development. Pp. 1-39 in *Handbook of Cross-Cultural Psychology*, Volume 2: Basic Processes and Human Development, Second Edition. J.W. Berry, P.R. Dasen, and T.S. Saraswathi, eds. Boston, MA: Allyn and Bacon.
Super, C.M., S. Harkness, N. van Tigen, E. van der Vlugt, J.M. Fintelman, and J. Dijkstra
    1996   The three R's of Dutch childrearing and the socialization of infant arousal. Pp. 447-466 in *Parents' Cultural Belief Systems.* S. Harkness and C.M. Super, eds. New York: Guilford Press.

Swayze, V.W., V.P. Johnson, J.W. Hanson, J. Piven, Y. Sato, J.N. Giedd, D. Mosnik, and N.C. Andreasen
  1997 Magnetic Resonance Imaging of brain anomalies in Fetal Alcohol Sydrome. *Pediatrics* 99:232-240.
Symons, D.K.
  1998 Post-partum employment patterns, family-based care arrangements, and the mother-infant relationship at age two. *Canadian Journal of Behavioural Science* 30(2):121-131.
Tager-Flusberg, H.
  1989 A psycholinguistic perspective on language development in the autistic child. Pp. 92 115 in *Autism: Nature, Diagnosis, and Treatment.* G. Dawson, ed. New York: Guilford Press.
  1994 Dissociations in form and function in the acquisition of language of autistic children. Pp. 175-194 in *Constraints on Language Acquisition: Studies of Atypical Children.* H. Tager-Flusberg, ed. Hillsdale, NJ: Erlbaum Associates.
Takahashi, K.
  1986 Examining the Strage-Situation procedure with Japanese mothers and 12-month-old infants. *Developmental Psychology* 22:265-270.
  1990 Are the key assumptions of the "Strange Situation" procedure universal? A view from Japanese research. *Human Development* 33:23-30.
Tallal, P., R. Ross, and S. Curtiss
  1989 Familiar aggregation in specific language impairment. *Journal of Speech and Hearing Disorders* 54:167-173.
Tallal, P., S. Miller, G. Bedi, G. Byma, X. Wang, S. Nagarajan, C. Schreiner, W. Jenkins, and M. Merzenich
  1996 Language comprehension in language-learning impaired children improved with acoustically modified speech. *Science* 271:81-84.
Tangney, J.P., and K.W. Fischer, eds.
  1995 *Self-Conscious Emotions.* New York: Guilford.
Taylor, L.B.
  1991 Neuropsychologic assessment of patients with encephalitis. Pp. 111-124 in *Chronic Encephalitis and Epilepsy: Rasmussen Syndrome.* F. Andermann, ed. Stoneham, MA: Butterworth-Heinemann.
Taylor, L., B. Zuckerman, V. Harik, and B. Groves
  1992 Exposure to violence among inner city parents and young children. *American Journal of the Diseases of Children* 146:487-494.
Teachman, J., G.J. Duncan, W.J. Yeung, and D. Levy
  under review   Covariance structure models for fixed and random effects.
Tesla, C., and J. Dunn
  1992 Getting along or getting your own way: The development of young children's use of argument in conflicts with mother and sibling. *Social Development* 1:107-121.
Teti, D.M.
  1999 Maternal Depression/Mental Health and Home Visiting. Presentation at the *Workshop on Revisiting Home Visiting,* sponsored by the Board on Children, Youth, and Families of the National Research Council and Institute of Medicine. March 8-9, 1999, Georgetown University Conference Center, Washington, DC.
Teti, D.M., J. Sakin, E. Kucera, K.M. Corns, and R. Das Eisen
  1996a And baby makes four: Predictors of attachment security among preschool-aged firstborns during the transition to siblinghood. *Child Development* 67:579-596.

Teti, D.M., M.A. O'Connell, and C.D. Reiner
1996b Parenting sensitivity, parental depression and child health: The mediational role of parental self-efficacy. *Early Development and Parenting* 5(4):237-250.

Thal, D., and E. Bates
1988 Language and gesture in late talkers. *Journal of Speech and Hearing Research* 31:115-123.

Thal, D., and S. Tobias
1992 Communicative gestures in children with delayed onset of oral expressive vocabulary. *Journal of Speech and Hearing Research* 35:1281-1289.

Thal, D., S. Tobias, and D. Morrison
1991 Language and gesture in late talkers: A one-year follow-up. *Journal of Speech and Hearing Research* 34:604-612.

Thatcher, R.W.
1991 Maturation of the human frontal lobes: Physiological evidence for staging. *Developmental Neuropsychology* 7(3):397-419.

Thomas, K.M., S.W. King, P.L. Franzen, T.F. Welsh, A.L. Berkowitz, D.C. Noll, V. Birmaher, and B.J. Casey
1999 A developmental functional MRI study of spatial working memory. *NeuroImage* 10(3):327-338.

Thompson, A., and D.R. McDowell
1994 Determinants of poverty among workers in metro and nonmetro areas of the South. *Review of Black Political Economy* 22:159-177.

Thompson, L.A., J.F. Fagan, and D.W. Fulker
1991 Longitudinal prediction of specific cognitive abilities from infant novelty preference. *Child Development* 62(3):530-538.

Thompson, R.A.
1989 Causal attributions and children's emotional understanding. Pp. 117-150 in *Children's Understanding of Emotion*. C. Saarni and P. Harris, eds. New York: Cambridge University Press.
1990 Emotion and self-regulation. Pp. 383-483 in *Socioemotional Development: Nebraska Symposium on Motivation*, Volume 36. R.A. Thompson, ed. Lincoln, NE: University of Nebraska Press.
1994 Emotion regulation: A theme in search of definition. *Monographs of the Society for Research in Child Development* (Serial No. 240) 59:25-52.
1997 Sensitivity and security: New lessons to ponder. *Child Development* 68:595-597.
1998a Empathy and its origins in early development. Pp. 144-157 in *Intersubjective Communication and Emotion in Early Ontogeny*. S. Braten, ed. Cambridge, UK: Cambridge University Press.
1998b Early sociopersonality development. Pp. 25-104 in *Handbook of Child Psychology*, Volume 3: Social, emotional, and personality development, Fifth Edition. W. Damon, ed. New York: Wiley.
1999a Early attachment and later development. Pp. 265-286 in *Handbook of Attachment: Theory, Research, and Clinical Applications*. J. Cassidy and P.R. Shaver, eds. New York: Guilford.
1999b The individual child: Temperament, emotion, self, and personality. Pp. 377-409 in *Developmental Psychology: An Advanced Textbook*, Fourth Edition. M.H. Bornstein and M.E. Lamb, eds. Mahwah, NJ: Lawrence Erlbaum Associates, Publishers.
in Sensitive periods in attachment? In *Critical Thinking About Critical Periods*. D.B. press(a) Bailey Jr., ed. Baltimore, MD: Paul H. Brookes Publishing Co., Inc.

in   Childhood anxiety disorders from the perspective of emotion regulation and
press(b) attachment. In *The Developmental Psychopathology of Anxiety*. M.W. Vasey and
         M.R. Dadds, eds. Oxford, UK: Oxford University Press.

Thompson, R.A., and S.D. Calkins
1996   The double-edged sword: Emotional regulation for children at risk. *Development and Psychopathology* 8:163-182.

Thompson, R.A., and J.M. Wyatt
1999   Current research on child maltreatment: Implications for educators. *Educational Psychology Review* 11(3):173-201.

Thompson, R.A., D. Cicchetti, M.E. Lamb, and C. Malkin
1985   Emotional responses of Down syndrome and normal infants in the Strange Situation: The organization of affective behavior in infants. *Developmental Psychology* 21(5):828-841.

Thompson, R.A., M.F. Flood, and L. Lundquist
1995   Emotional regulation: Its relations to attachment and developmental psychopathology. Pp. 261-299 in *Emotion, Cognition, and Representation: Rochester Symposium on Developmental Psychopathology*, Volume 6. D. Cicchetti and S.L. Toth, eds. Rochester, NY: University of Rochester Press.

Thompson, R.A., E.H. Christiansen, S. Jackson, J.M. Wyatt, R.A. Colman, R. Peterson, B.L. Wilcox, and C.W. Buckendahl
1999   Parent attitudes and discipline practices: Profiles and correlates in a nationally representative sample. *Child Maltreatment* 4:316-360.

Thornberry, T.P., and M.D. Krohn
1997   Peers, drug use, and delinquency. Pp. 218-233 in *Handbook of Antisocial Behavior*. D. Stoff, J. Breiling, and J.D. Maser, eds. New York: Wiley.

Timmer, S.G., J. Eccles, and K. O'Brien
1985   How children use time. Pp. 353-382 in *Time, Goods, and Well-Being*. F.T. Juster and F. Stafford, eds. Ann Arbor, MI: Institute for Social Research, University of Michigan Survery Research Center.

Tingley, E.C., J.B. Gleason, and N. Hooshyar
1994   Mothers' lexicon of internal state words in speech to children with Down syndrome and to nonhandicapped children at mealtime. *Journal of Communication Disorders* 27(2):135-155.

Tizard, B., and J. Hodges
1978   The effect of early institutional rearing on the development of eight-year-old children. *Journal of Child Psychology and Psychiatry* 19:99-118.

Tizard, B., and A. Joseph
1970   Cognitive development of young children in residential care: A study of children aged 24 months. *Journal of Child Psychology and Psychiatry* 11:177-186.

Tizard, B., and J. Rees
1974   A comparison of the effects of adoption, restoration to the natural mother, and continued institutionalization on the cognitive development of four-year-old children. *Child Development* 45:92-99.

Tomasello, M.
1996   Do apes ape? Pp. 319-346 in *Social Learning in Animals: The Roots of Culture*. J. Galef and C. Heyes, eds. New York: Academic Press.
2000   Culture and cognitive development. *Current Directions in Psychological Science* 9(2):37-40.

Tomasello, M., A.C. Kruger, and H.H. Ratner
1993   Cultural learning. *Behavioral and Brain Sciences* 16:495-511.

Tomasello, M., R. Strosberg, and N. Akhtar
  1996 Eighteen-month-old children learn words in non-ostensive contexts. *Journal of Child Language* 23(1):157-176.
Tomblin, J.B.
  1989 Familial concentration of developmental language impairment. *Journal of Speech and Hearing Disorders* 54:287-295.
Tomblin, J.B., N.L. Records, P. Buckwalter, X. Zhang, E. Smith, and M. O'Brien
  1997 Prevalence of specific language impairment in kindergarten children. *Journal of Speech, Language, and Hearing Research* 40:1245-1260.
Tout, K., M. de Haan, E. Kipp-Campbell, and M.R. Gunnar
  1998 Social behavior correlates of adrenocortical activity in daycare: Gender differences and time-of-day effects. *Child Development* 69(5):1247-1262.
Tranel, D., S.W. Anderson, and A. Benton
  1994 Development of the concept of 'executive function' and its relationship to the frontal lobes. Pp. 125-148 in *Handbook of Neuropsychology*, Volume 9. F. Boller and J. Grafman, eds. Amsterdam, The Netherlands: Elsevier.
Trauner, D., B. Wulfeck, P. Tallal, and J. Hesselink
  1995 *Neurologic and MRI Profiles of Language Impaired Children.* San Diego, CA: Center for Research in Language, University of California at San Diego.
Tresch Owen, M., and M.J. Cox
  1988 Maternal employment and the transition to parenthood. Pp. 85-119 in *Maternal Employment and Children's Development: Longitudinal Research.* A.E. Gottfried and A.W. Gottfried, eds. New York: Plenum Press.
Trevarthen, C., and P. Hubley
  1978 Secondary intersubjectivity: Confidence, confiding and acts of meaning in the first year. Pp. 183-229 in *Action, Gesture, and Symbol: The Emergence of Language.* A. Lock, ed. London, UK: Academic Press.
Trevathan, W.R., and J.J. McKenna
  1994 Evolutionary environments of human birth and infancy: Insights to apply to contemporary life. *Children's Environments* 11(2):88-104.
Triandis, H.C.
  1988 Collectivism vs. individualism: A reconceptualization of a basic concept in cross-cultural social psychology. Pp. 60-95 in *Cross-Cultural Studies of Personality, Attitudes and Cognition.* G.K. Verma and C. Bagley, eds. London, UK: Macmillan.
Trickett, P.K., J.L. Aber, V. Carlson, and D. Cicchetti
  1991 Relationship of socioeconomic status to the etiology and developmental sequelae of physical child abuse. *Developmental Psychology* 37:148-158.
Tronick, E.Z., and M.K. Weinberg
  1997 Depressed mothers and infants: Failure to form dyadic states of consciousness. Pp. 54-81 in *Postpartum Depression and Child Development.* L. Murray and P.J. Cooper, eds. New York: The Guilford Press.
Troy, M., and L.A. Sroufe
  1987 Victimization among preschoolers: Role of attachment relationship history. *Journal of the American Academy of Child and Adolescent Psychiatry* 26:166-172.
Turkheimer, E., and M. Waldron
  2000 Nonshared environment: A theorectical, methodological, and quantitative review. *Psychological Bulletin* 126(1):78-108.

Turnbull, A., V. Turbiville, and H.R. Turnbull
    2000   Evolution of family-professional relationships: Collective empowerment for the early 21st century. Pp. 1370-1420 in *Handbook of Early Childhood Intervention, Second Edition.* J.P. Shonkoff and S.J. Meisels, eds. New York: Cambridge University Press.

U.S. Bureau of the Census
    1982   Trends in child care arrangements of working mothers. *Current Population Reports* (P23-117) June 1982. Washington, DC: U.S. Government Printing Office.
    1987   Who's minding the kids? Child care arrangements: Winter 1984-85. *Current Population Reports* Series P-70, No. 9. Washington, DC: U.S. Government Printing Office.
    1995   *What Does It Cost to Mind Our Preschoolers?* (P70-52 and PPL-34) September 1995. Washington, DC: U.S. Department of Commerce.
    1996   *Who's Minding Our Preschoolers?* (P70-53 and PPL-34) March 1996. Washington, DC: U.S. Department of Commerce.
    1997   *Who's Minding Our Preschoolers? Fall 1994 (Update)* (P70-62 and PPL-81) November 1997. Washington, DC: U.S. Department of Commerce.
    1998   Households and Family Characteristics: March 1998 (Update). *Current Population Reports* (P2-215). Washington, DC: U.S. Department of Commerce.

U.S. Bureau of Labor Statistics
    1996   *Occupational Employment Statistics (OES) Program Survey.* Washington, DC: U.S. Department of Labor.
    1998   *Occupational Projections and Training Data.* Washington, DC: U.S. Department of Labor.

U.S. Council of Economic Advisers
    1997   *The First Three Years: Investments That Pay.* Washington, DC: U.S. Government Printing Office.

U.S. Department of Health and Human Services
    1983   *Overview of the Seattle-Denver Income Maintenance Experiment Final Report.* Office of Income Security Policy. Washington, DC: U.S. Government Printing Office.
    1995   *The JOBS Evaluation: How Well Are They Faring? AFDC Families With Preschool-Aged Children in Atlanta at the Outset of the JOBS Evaluation.* Washington, DC: U.S. Department of Health and Human Services.
    1999a   *Trends in the Well-Being of America's Children and Youth: 1999.* Washington, DC: U.S. Government Printing Office.
    1999b   *Mental Health: A Report of the Surgeon General.* Rockville, MD: U.S. Department of Health and Human Services, Substance Abuse and Mental Health Services Administration, Center for Mental Health Services, and National Institutes of Health, National Institute of Mental Health.
    1999c   *Blending Perspectives and Building Common Ground: A Report to Congress on Substance Abuse and Child Protection.* Washington, DC: U.S. Government Printing Office.
    1999d   *Access to Child Care for Low-Income Working Families.* Washington, DC: U.S. Department of Health and Human Services. [Online]. Available: http://www.acf.dhhs.gov/programs/ccb/reports/ccreport.htm [Accessed July 6, 2000].

U.S. General Accounting Office
    1990   *Early Childhood Programs: What Are the Costs of High Quality Programs?* Washington, DC: U.S. Government Printing Office.
    1995   *Welfare to Work: Child Care Assistance Limited; Welfare Reform May Expand Needs.* Washington, DC: U.S. Government Printing Office.

1999   *Child Care: How Do Military and Civilian Center Costs Compare?* Washington, DC: U.S. Government Printing Office.

van den Boom, D.C.
1994   The influence of temperament and mothering on attachment and exploration: An experimental manipulation of sensitive responsiveness among lower-class mothers with irritable infants. *Child Development* 65(5):1457-1477.
1995   Do first-year intervention effects endure? Follow-up during toddlerhood of a sample of Dutch irritable infants. *Child Development* 66:1798-1816.

van der Lely, H., and L. Stollwerck
1996   A grammatical specific language impairment in children: An autosomal dominant inheritance? *Brain and Language* 52:484-504.

van IJzendoorn, M.H., and A. Sagi
1999   Cross-cultural patterns of attachment: Universal and contextual dimensions. Pp. 713-734 in *Handbook of Attachment: Theory, Research, and Clinical Applications*. J. Cassidy and P.R. Shaver, eds. New York: The Guilford Press.

van IJzendoorn, M.H., S. Goldberg, P.M. Kroonenberg, and O. Frenkel
1992   The relative effects of maternal and child problems on the quality of attachment: A meta-analysis of attachment in clinical samples. *Child Development* 63:840-858.

van IJzendoorn, M.H., F. Juffer, and M.G.C. Duyvesteyn
1995   Breaking the intergenerational cycle of insecure attachment: A review of the effects of attachment-based interventions on maternal sensitivity and infant security. *Journal of Child Psychology and Psychiatry and Allied Disciplines* 36(2):225-248.

Vandell, D.L., and M.A. Corasaniti
1988   The relation between third graders' after-school care and social, academic, and emotional development. *Child Development* 59:868-875.
1990   Variations in early child care: Do they predict subsequent social, emotional, and cognitive differences. *Early Childhood Research Quarterly* 5:555-572.

Vandell, D.L., and J.K. Posner
1999   Conceptualization and measurement of children's after-school environments. Pp. 167-196 in *Measuring Environment Across the Life Span: Emerging Methods and Concepts*. S.L. Friedman and T.D. Wachs, eds. Washington, DC: American Psychological Association.

Vandell, D.L., and J. Ramanan
1992   Effects of early and recent maternal employment on children from low-income families. *Child Development* 63:938-949.

Vandell, D.L., and L. Shumow
1999   After-school child care programs. *The Future of Children: When School Is Out* 9(2):64-80.

Vandell, D.L., K.S. Wilson, and N.R. Buchanan
1980   Peer interaction in the first year of life: An examination of its structure, content, and sensitivity to toys. *Child Development* 51:481-488.

Vargha-Khadem, F., and M. Mishkin
1997   Speech and language outcome after hemispherectomy in childhood. Pp. 774-784 in *Paediatric Epilepsy Syndromes and Their Surgical Treatment*. I. Tuxhorn, H. Holthausen, and H.E. Boenigk, eds. Sydney, Australia: John Libbey and Company, Ltd. Medical Books.

Vargha-Khadem, F., and C.E. Polkey
1992   A review of cognitive outcome after hemidecortication in humans. Pp. 137-151 in *Recovery from Brain Damage: Reflections and Directions*. F.D. Rose and D.A. Johnson, eds. New York: Plenum Press.

Vargha-Khadem, F., E. Isaacs, S. van der Werf, S. Robb, and J. Wilson
1992   Development of intelligence and memory in children with hemiplegic cerebral palsy: The deleterious consequences of early seizures. *Brain* 115:315-329.

Vargha-Khadem, F., D.G. Gadian, K.E. Watkins, A. Connelly, W. Van Paesschen, and M. Mishkin
1997   Differential effects of early hippocampal pathology on episodic and semantic memory. *Science* 277:376-380.

Vasey, M.W.
1998   A transactional developmental perspective on childhood anxiety disorders. Unpublished manuscript, Department of Psychology, Ohio State University.

Vaughn, B.E., B. Egeland, L.A. Sroufe, and E. Waters
1979   Individual differences in infant-mother attachment at twelve and eighteen months: Stability and change in families under stress. *Child Development* 50:971-975.

Vaughn, B.E., C.B. Kopp, and J.B. Krakow
1984   The emergence and consolidation of self-control from eighteen to thirty months of age: Normative trends and individual difference. *Child Development* 55:990-1004.

Verhulst, F., M. Althaus, and H.J.M. Versluis-Den Bieman
1990   Problem behavior in international adoptees: I. An epidemiological study. *Journal of the American Academy of Child and Adolescent Psychiatry* 1:94-103.

Verhulst, R., M. Althaus, and H.J.M. Versluis-Den Bieman
1992   Damaging backgrounds: Later adjustment of international adoptees. *Journal of the American Academy of Child and Adolescent Psychiatry* 3:518-524.

Verschueren, K., A. Marcoen, and V. Schoefs
1996   The internal working model of the self, attachment, and competence in five-year-olds. *Child Development* 67:2493-2511.

Vietze, P.M., and B.J. Anderson
1980   Styles of parent-child interaction. Pp. 255-283 in *Psycho-Social Influences in Retarded Performance*. M. Begab, H.C. Haywood, and H. Garber, eds. Baltimore, MD: University Park Press.

Vogt, L.A., C. Jordan, and R.G. Tharp
1987   Explaining school failure, producing school success: Two cases. *Anthropology and Education Quarterly* 18:276-286.

Volling, B., and L. Feagans
1995   Infant day care and children's social competence. *Infant Behavior and Development* 18:177-188.

Vondra, J.I., and D. Barnett
1999   *Monographs for the Society for Research in Child Development: Atypical Patterns of Attachment in Infancy and Early Childhood Among Children at Developmental Risk* (Serial no. 258)64(3).

Vygotsky, L.S.
1978   *Mind in Society: The Development of Higher Psychological Processes*. Cambridge, MA: Harvard University Press.

Wachs, T.D., and G. Gruen
1982   *Early Experience and Human Development*. New York: Plenum.

Waddington, C.H.
1966   *Principles of Development and Differentiation*. New York: Macmillan.

Wadsworth, M.E.J.
1976   Delinquency, pulse rates and early emotional deprivation. *British Journal of Criminology* 16(3):245-255.

Wahlsten, D.
1990   Insensitivity of the analysis of variance to heredity-environment interaction. *Behavioral and Brain Sciences* 13:109-161.

Wahlsten, D., and G. Gottlieb
  1997   The invalid separation of effects of nature and nurture: Lessons from animal ex-
          perimentation. Pp. 163-192 in *Intelligence, Heredity, and Environment*. R.J.
          Sternberg and E.L. Grigorenko, eds. New York: Cambridge University Press.
Waldfogel, J.
  1998   *The Future of Child Protection: How to Break the Cycle of Abuse and Neglect*.
          Cambridge, MA: Harvard University Press.
  1999a   The impact of the Family and Medical Leave Act. *Journal of Policy Analysis and
          Management* 18(2):281-309.
  1999b   Family leave coverage in the 1990s. *Monthly Labor Review* 122(10):13-21.
Waldfogel, J., W. Han, and J. Brooks-Gunn
  2000   Early maternal employment and child outcomes: A longitudinal analysis of children
          from the NLSY. Unpublished manuscript. Columbia University School of Social
          Work, New York.
Walker, T., and D. Johnson
  1988   A follow-up evaluation of the Houston Parent-Child Development Center: Intelli-
          gence test results. *Journal of Genetic Psychology* 149(3):377-381.
Walker, T., G. Rodriguez, D. Johnson, and C. Cortez
  1995   AVANCE Parent-Child Education Program. Pp. 67-90 in *Two Generation Pro-
          grams for Families in Poverty: A New Intervention Strategy*. S. Smith and I. Sigel,
          eds. Norwood, NJ: Ablex.
Walter, T., J. Kovalskys, and A. Stekel
  1983   Effect of mild iron deficiency on infant mental development scores. *The Journal of
          Pediatrics* 102:519-522.
Walter, T., I. De Andraca, P. Chadud, and C.G. Perales
  1989   Iron deficiency anemia: Adverse effects on infant psychomotor development. *Pedi-
          atrics* 84:7-17.
Walter, T., I. De Andraca, M. Castillo, F. Rivera, and C. Cobo
  1990   Cognitive effect at 5 years of age in infants who were anemic at 12 months: A
          longitudinal study. *Pediatric Research* 28:295 (abstract).
Warfield, M.E., and P. Hauser-Cram
  1996   Child care needs, arrangement, and satisfaction of mothers of children with devel-
          opmental disabilities. *Mental Retardation* 34:294-302.
Warren, S.F., P.J. Yoder, G.E. Gazdag, K. Kim, and H.A. Jones
  1993   Facilitating prelinguistic communication skills in young children with developmen-
          tal delay. *Journal of Speech and Hearing Research* 36:83-97.
Warren, S.L., L. Huston, B. Egeland, and L.A. Sroufe
  1997   Child and adolescent anxiety disorders and early attachment. *Journal of the Ameri-
          can Academy of Child and Adolescent Psychiatry* 36(5):637-644.
Wasik, B.H., C.T. Ramey, D.M. Bryant, and J.J. Sparling
  1990   A longitudinal study of two early intervention strategies: Project CARE. *Child
          Development* 61(6):1682-1696.
Waters, E.
  1978   The reliability and stability of individual differences in infant-mother attachment.
          Child Development 49:483-494.
Waters, E., L. Matas, and L.A. Sroufe
  1975   Infants' reactions to an approaching stranger: Description, validation, and func-
          tional significance of wariness. *Child Development* 46:348-356.
Waters, E., K. Kondo-Ikemura, G. Posada, and J.E. Richters
  1991   Learning to love: Mechanisms and milestones. Pp. 217-255 in *Minnesota Sympo-
          sia on Child Psychology: Self Processes and Development*, Volume 23. M.R.
          Gunnar and L.A. Sroufe, eds. Hillsdale, NJ: Erlbaum.

Waters, M.C.
1997   Immigrant families at risk: Factors that undermine chances for success. Pp. 79-90 in *Immigration and the Family: Research and Policy on U.S. Immigrants.* A. Booth, A.C. Crouter, and N. Landale, eds. Mahwah, NJ: Lawrence Erlbaum Associates.

Watson, J.B.
1928   *Psychological Care of Infant and Child.* New York: W.W. Norton.

Watson, J.E., R.S. Kirby, K.J. Kelleher, and R.H. Bradley
1996   Effects of poverty on home environment: An analysis of three-year outcome data for low birth weight premature infants. *Journal of Pediatric Psychology* 21:419-431.

Waxman, S.R.
1999   The dubbing ceremony revisited: Object naming and categorization in infancy and early childhood. Pp. 233-284 in *Folkbiology.* D.L. Medin and S. Atran, eds. Cambridge, MA: The MIT Press/Bradford Books.

Webster-Stratton, C.
1990   Long-term follow-up of families with young conduct problem children: From preschool to grade school. *Journal of Clinical Child Psychology* 19(2):144-149.
1992   Individually administered videotape parent training: "Who benefits?". *Cognitive Therapy and Research* 16(1):31-52.

Webster-Stratton, C., T. Hollinsworth, and M. Kolpacoff
1989   The long-term effectiveness and clinical significance of three cost-effective training programs for families with conduct-problem children. *Journal of Consulting and Clinical Psychology* 57(4):550-553.

Weikart, D.P., and L.J. Schweinhart
1992   High/Scope Preschool Program outcomes. Pp. 67-86 in *Preventing Antisocial Behavior: Interventions From Birth Through Adolescence.* J. McCord and R.E. Tremblay, eds. New York: The Guilford Press.

Weikart, D.P., J.T. Bond, and J.T. McNeil
1978   *The Ypsilanti Perry Preschool Project: Preschool Years and Longitudinal Results Through Fourth Grade.* Ypsilanti, MI: High/Scope Press.

Weinberg, J., C.K. Kim, and W. Yu
1995   Early handling can attenuate adverse effects of fetal ethanol exposure. *Alcohol* 12(4):317-327.

Weinberg, J., A.N. Taylor, and C. Gianoulakis
1996   Fetal ethanol exposure: Hypothalamic-pituitary-adrenal and ß-endorphin responses to repeated stress. *Alcoholism: Clinical and Experimental Research* 20(1):122-131.

Weinberg, M.K., and E.Z. Tronick
1998   The impact of maternal psychiatric illness on infant development. *Journal of Clinical Psychiatry* 59 (Supplement 2):53-61.

Weismer, S.E., J. Murray-Branch, and J. Miller
1994   A prospective longitudinal study of lanugage development in late talkers. *Journal of Speech and Hearing Research* 52:484-504.

Weisner, T.
1999   Comments prepared for the Committee on Integrating the Science of Early Childhood Development, July 1999. University of California at Los Angeles.

Weisner, T., and R. Gallimore
1977   My brother's keeper: Child and sibling caretaking. *Current Anthropology* 18(2):169-190.

Weisner, T., R. Gallimore, and C. Jordan
  1989   Unpackaging cultural effects on classroom learning: Native Hawaiian peer assis-
         tance and child-generated activity. *Anthropology and Education Quarterly*
         19(4):327-353.
Weiss, C.H.
  1995   Nothing as practical as a good theory: Exploring theory-based evaluation for com-
         prehensive community initiatives for children and families. In *New Approaches to
         Evaluating Community Initiatives: Concepts, Methods, and Contexts*. J.P. Connell,
         A.C. Kubisch, L.B. Schorr, and C.H. Weiss, eds. Washington, DC: The Aspen
         Institute.
Weitzman, E.D., C.A. Czeisler, J.C. Zimmerman, and J.M. Ronda
  1979   The sleep-wake pattern of cortisol and growth hormone secretion during non-
         entrained (free-running) conditions in man. Paper presented at the Human Pitu-
         itary Hormones: Circadian and Episodic Variations conference in Brussels, Bel-
         gium.
Weller, D., C. Schnittjer, and B. Tuten
  1992   Predicting achievement in grades three through ten using the metropolitan reading
         test. *Journal of Research in Childhood Education* 6:121-129.
Wellman, H.M.
  1990   *The Child's Theory of Mind*. Cambridge, MA: MIT Press.
Wellman, H.M., P.L. Harris, M. Banerjee, and A. Sinclair
  1995   Early understanding of emotion: Evidence from natural language. *Cognition and
         Emotion* 9:117-149.
Welsh, M.C., and B.F. Pennington
  1988   Assessing frontal lobe functioning in children: Views from developmental psychol-
         ogy. *Developmental Neuropsychology* 4:199-230.
Welsh, M.C., B.F. Pennington, and D.B. Groisser
  1991   A normative-developmental study of executive function: A window on prefrontal
         function in children. *Developmental Neuropsychology* 7:131-149.
Wentzel, K.R., and S.R. Asher
  1995   The academic lives of neglected, rejected, popular, and controversial children. *Child
         Development* 66:754-763.
Werner, E.
  1995   Resilience in development. *Current Directions in Psychological Science* 4:81-84.
  2000   Protective factors and resilience. Pp. 115-132 in *Handbook of Early Childhood
         Intervention*, Second Edition. J.P. Shonkoff and S.J. Meisels, eds. New York:
         Cambridge University Press.
Werner, E., and R. Smith
  1982   *Vulnerable but Invincible: A Study of Resilient Children*. New York: McGraw-
         Hill.
Wertheimer, R.F.
  1999   *Working Poor Families With Children*. Washington, DC: Child Trends, Inc.
Wessel, M.A., J.C. Cobb, E.B. Jackson, G.S. Harris, and A.C. Detwiler
  1954   Paroxysmal fussing in infancy, sometimes called "colic". *Pediatrics* 14:421-434.
White, J.L., T.E. Moffitt, F. Earls, L. Robins, and P.A. Silva
  1990   How early can we tell?: Predictors of childhood conduct disorder and adolescent
         delinquency. *Criminology* 28(4):507-533.
White, R.
  1959   Motivation reconsidered: The concept of competence. *Psychological Review*
         66:297-333.

Whitebook, M., and D. Bellm
  1999   *Taking on Turnover: An Action Guide for Child Care Center Teachers and Direc-
          tors.* Washington, DC: Center for the Child Care Workforce.
Whitebook, M., C. Howes, and D.A. Phillips
  1990   *Who Cares? Child Care Teachers and the Quality of Care in America*, Final report
          of the National Child Care Staffing Study. Oakland, CA: Child Care Employee
          Project.
Whitebook, M., L. Sakai, and C. Howes
  1997   *NAEYC Accreditation As a Strategy for Improving Child Care Quality: An Assess-
          ment by the National Center for the Early Childhood Work Force.* Washington,
          DC: National Center for the Early Childhood Work Force.
Whitehurst, G., J. Fischel, D. Arnold, and C. Lonigan
  1992   Evaluating outcomes with children with expressive language delay. Pp. 277-313 in
          Causes and Effects in Communication and Language Intervention. S. Warren and
          J. Reichle, eds. Baltimore, MD: Paul H. Brookes Publishing Co., Inc.
Whitehurst, G., D.S. Arnold, J.N. Epstein, and A.L. Angell
  1994   A picture book reading intervention in day care and home for children from low-
          income families. *Developmental Psychology* 30(5):679-689.
Whiting, J.W.M.
  1954   The cross-cultural method. Pp. 523-531 in *Handbook of Social Psychology.* G.
          Lindzey, ed. Boston, MA: Addison-Wesley.
Whiting, J.W.M., and I.L. Child
  1953   *Child Training and Personality: A Cross-Cultural Study.* New York: Yale Univer-
          sity Press.
Whiting, J.W.M., and B.B. Whiting
  1960   Contributions of anthropology to the methods of studying child rearing. Pp. 918-
          944 in *Handbook of Research Methods in Childhood Development.* P.H. Mussen,
          ed. New York: John Wiley.
Wigfield, A., J. Eccles, K. Yoon, R. Harold, A. Arbreton, C. Freedman-Doan, and P.
Blumenfeld
  1997   Change in children's competence beliefs and subjective task values across the el-
          ementary school years: A 3-year study. *Journal of Educational Psychology* 89:451-
          469.
Wilcox, M.J., and L. Leonard
  1978   Experimental acquisition of wh- questions in language-disordered children. *Jour-
          nal of Speech and Hearing Research* 21:220-239.
Willett, J.
  1988   Questions and answers in the measurement of change. *Review of Research in
          Education* 15:345-422.
Wilson, W.J.
  1987   *The Truly Disadvantaged: The Inner City, the Underclass and the Public Policy.*
          Chicago, IL: University of Chicago.
Wilson, M.N.
  1986   The Black extended family: An analytical review. *Developmental Psychology*
          22:242-258.
  1989   Child development in the context of the Black extended family. *American Psy-
          chologist* 44:380-385.
Winick, M.
  1976   *Malnutrition and Brain Development.* New York: Oxford University Press.

Winick, M., and P. Rosso
    1969   Head circumference and cellular growth of the brain in normal and marasmic
            children. *The Journal of Pediatrics* 74:774-778.
Winnicott, D.W.
    1965   *The Maturational Process and the Facilitating Environment.* New York: Interna-
            tional Universities Press.
Wishart, J.G.
    1993   The development of learning difficulties in children with Down's syndrome. *Jour-
            nal of Intellectual Disability Research* 37:389-403.
Wolery, M.
    2000   Behavioral and educational approaches to early intervention. Pp. 179-203 in *Hand-
            book of Early Childhood Intervention*, Second Edition. J.P. Shonkoff and S.J.
            Meisels, eds. New York: Cambridge University Press.
Wolf, A.W., I. De Andraca, and B. Lozoff
    sub-   Maternal depression in three Latin American samples. *Social Psychiatry and Psy-*
    mitted *chiatric Epidemiology.*
Wolfe, B., and S. Hill
    1995   The effect of health on the work effort of single mothers. *Journal of Human
            Resources* 30:42-62.
Wood, D.
    1986   Aspects of teaching and learning. Pp. 191-212 in *Children of Social Worlds*. M.
            Richards and P. Light, eds. Cambridge, MA: Polity Press.
Wood, D., J.S. Bruner, and G. Ross
    1976   The role of tutoring in problem solving. *Journal of Child Psychology and Psychia-
            try and Allied Disciplines* 17(2):89-100.
Wright, J.C., M. Giammarino, and H.W. Parad
    1986   Social status in small groups: Individual-group similarity and the social "misfit".
            Journal of Personality and Social Psychology 50:523-536.
Wright, J.D., and S.R. Wright
    1976   Social class and parental values for children: A partial replication and extension of
            the Kohn thesis. *American Sociological Review* 41(3):527-537.
Wright, P., H.A. MacLeod, and M.J. Cooper
    1983   Waking at night: The effect of early feeding experience. *Child Care and Healthy
            Development* 9:309-319.
Wynn, K.
    1992   Addition and subtraction by human infants. *Nature* 358(6389):749-750.
Yarrow, L., G. Morgan, K. Jennings, R. Harmon, and J. Gaiter
    1982   Infants' persistence at tasks: Relationships to cognitive functioning and early expe-
            rience. *Infant Behavior and Development* 5:131-141.
Yeung, W.J., J.F. Sandberg, P. Davis-Kean, and S.L. Hofferth
    1998   Children's time with fathers in intact families. Paper presented at the annual meet-
            ing of the Population Association of America, April 1998.
Yoshikawa, H.
    1994   Prevention as cumulative protection: Effects of early family support and education
            on chronic delinquency and its risks. *Psychological Bulletin* 115:28-54.
    1995   Long-term effects of early childhood programs on social outcomes and delinquency.
            The Future of Children 5(3):51-75.
    1999   Welfare dynamics, support services, mothers' earnings, and child cognitive devel-
            opment: Implications for contemporary welfare reform. *Child Development*
            70:779-801.

Young, L.D., S.J. Suomi, H.F. Harlow, and W.T. McKinney
   1973   Early stress and later response to separation in rhesus monkeys. *American Journal of Psychiatry* 130(4):400-405.
Young, K.T., K.W. Marsland, and E. Zigler
   1997   The regulatory status of center-based infant and toddler child care. *American Journal of Orthopsychiatry* 67:535-544.
Zahn-Waxler, C., and G. Kochanska
   1990   The origins of guilt. Pp. 183-258 in *Socioemotional Development: Nebraska Symposium on Motivation*, Volume 36. R.A. Thompson, ed. Lincoln, NE: University of Nebraska Press.
Zahn-Waxler, C., and M. Radke-Yarrow
   1990   The origins of empathic concern. *Motivation and Emotion* 14:107-130.
Zahn-Waxler, C., M. Radke-Yarrow, and R.A. King
   1979   Child rearing and children's prosocial initiations towards victims of distress. *Child Development* 50:319-330.
Zahn-Waxler, C., A. Mayfield, M. Radke-Yarrow, D. McKnew, L. Cytryn, and Y. Davenport
   1988   A follow-up investigation of offspring of bipolar parents. *American Journal of Psychiatry* 145:506-509.
Zahn-Waxler, C., P.M. Cole, and K.C. Barrett
   1991   Guilt and empathy: Sex differences and implications for the development of depression. Pp. 243-272 in *The Development of Emotional Regulation and Dysregulation*. J. Garber and K.A. Dodge, eds. New York: Cambridge University Press.
Zahn-Waxler, C., M. Radke-Yarrow, E. Wagner, and M. Chapman
   1992   Development of concern for others. *Developmental Psychology* 28:126-136.
Zametkin, A.J., and M. Ernst
   1999   Problems in the management of Attention-Deficit-Hyperactivity Disorder. *The New England Journal of Medicine* 340(1):40-46.
Zaslow, M.
   1987   Sex differences in children's response to maternal employment. Unpublished manuscript, prepared for the Committee on Child Development Research and Public Policy, National Research Council, Washington, DC.
Zaslow, M.J., F.A. Pedersen, J.T.D. Suwalsky, R.L. Cain, and M. Fivel
   1985   The early resumption of employment by mothers: Implications for parent-infant interaction. *Journal of Applied Developmental Psychology* 6:1-16.
Zeanah, C.H., ed.
   2000   *Handbook of Infant Mental Health*, Second Edition. New York: The Guilford Press.
Zeanah, C.H., N.W. Boris, and J.A. Larrieu
   1997   Infant development and developmental risk: A review of the past 10 years. *Journal of the American Academy of Child and Adolescent Psychiatry* 36(2):165-178.
Zeanah, C.H., J.A. Larrieu, S.S. Heller, and J. Valliere
   2000   Infant-parent relationship assessment. Pp. 222-235 in *Handbook of Infant Mental Health*, Second Edition. C.H. Zeanah, ed. New York: The Guilford Press.
Zeitlin, M.
   1996   My child is my crown: Yoruba parental theories and practices in early childhood. Pp. 407-427 in *Parents' Cultural Belief Systems*. S. Harkness and C.M. Super, eds. New York: Guilford Press.
Zellman, G.I., and A.S. Johansen
   1998   *Examining the Implementation and Outcomes of the Military Child Care Act of 1989*. Santa Monica, CA: RAND National Defense Research Institute.

ZERO TO THREES's Diagnostic Classification Task Force
   1994   *Diagnostic Classification of Mental Health and Developmental Disorders of Infancy and Early Childhood.* S.I. Greenspan and S. Wieder, eds. Washington, DC: ZERO TO THREE: National Center for Infants, Toddlers and Families.
Zhou, M., and C.L. Bankston III
   1998   *Growing Up American: How Vietnamese Children Adapt to Life in the United States.* New York: Russell Sage Foundation.
Zigler, E., and P.K. Trickett
   1978   IQ, social competence, and the evaluation of early childhood intervention programs. *American Psychologist* 33(9):789-798.
Zigler, E., and J. Valentine, eds.
   1979   *Project Head Start: A Legacy of the War on Poverty.* New York: Free Press.
Zigler, E., S.L. Kagan, and N.W. Hall, eds.
   1996   *Children, Families, and Government: Preparing for the Twenty-First Century.* New York: Cambridge University Press.
Zito, J.M., D.J. Safer, S. dosReis, J.F. Gardner, M. Boles, and F. Lynch
   2000   Trends in the prescribing of psychotropic medications to preschoolers. *Journal of the American Medical Association* 283(8):1025-1030.

A Related Reports from the National Academies

America's Children: Health Insurance and Access to Care (1998)
Committee on Children, Health Insurance, and Access to Care
   America's Children is a comprehensive analysis of the relationship between health insurance and access to care. The book addresses three broad questions: How is children's health care currently financed? Does insurance equal access to care? How should the nation address the health needs of this vulnerable population?

Children of Immigrants: Health, Adjustment, and Public Assistance (1999)
Committee on the Health and Adjustment of Immigrant Children and Families
   This book presents detailed analyses of more than a dozen existing datasets that constitute a large share of the national system for monitoring the health and well-being of the U.S. population, focusing specifically on the circumstances, health, and development of children in immigrant families and the delivery of health and social services to these children and their families. The papers in this book helped inform the work of the Committee on Health and Adjustment of Immigrant Children and Families. The committee's final report is titled *From Generation to Generation: The Health and Well-Being of Children in Immigrant Families*.

Development During Middle Childhood: The Years from Six to Twelve
(1984)
Panel to Review the Status of Basic Research on School-Age Children,
Committee on Child Development Research and Public Policy
   This report reviews the research and examines the physical health and
cognitive development of 6- to 12-year-old children as well as their surroundings, including school and home environment, ecocultural setting,
and family and peer relationships. In addition, it makes recommendations
for expanding and improving research aimed at understanding the nature
and processes of development in the early school years.

Disability in America: Toward a National Agenda for Prevention (1991)
Committee on a National Agenda for the Prevention of Disabilities
   Disability in America presents a five-prong strategy for reducing the
incidence and prevalence of disability as well as its personal, social, and
economic consequences. Although the preferred goal is to avoid potentially
disabling conditions, the report focuses on the need to prevent or reverse
the progression that leads to disability and reduced quality of life in persons
with potentially disabling conditions.

Eager to Learn: Educating Our Preschoolers (2000)
Committee on Early Childhood Pedagogy
   This report focuses on educational programs provided outside of the
home for children aged 2-5 (e.g., Head Start, preschool, child care centers).
It emphasizes that care and education of children go hand in hand, and
cannot, and should not, be thought of as two separate entities. The committee makes recommendations for the professional development of teachers, the development of teaching materials that reflect research-based understandings of children's learning, the development of public policies that
support the provision of quality preschool experiences, efforts to make
more recent understanding of development in the preschool years common
public knowledge, and future research needs in these areas.

*Educating One and All: Students with Disabilities and Standards-Based
Reform* (1997)
Committee on Goals 2000 and the Inclusion of Students with Disabilities
   Educating One and All addresses how to reconcile common learning
for all students with education for the 10 percent of school-age children
who have disabilities and qualify for special education. The report discusses the history of special education, the recent reform movement, curricula, and assessment systems and makes recommendations concerning
standards-based reform and policies and practices to make reform consistent with the requirements of special education.

Emergency Medical Services for Children (1993)
Committee on Pediatric Emergency Medical Services

This report explores why emergency care for children—from infants through adolescents—must differ from that for adults. This comprehensive overview of emergency medical services for children describes what seriously ill or injured children generally experience in today's emergency medical services systems and provides a realistic plan of action for integrating them into emergency programs and into broader aspects of health care for children.

Fetal Alcohol Syndrome: Diagnosis, Epidemiology, Prevention, and Treatment (1996)
Committee to Study Fetal Alcohol Syndrome

This volume discusses fetal alcohol syndrome and other possibly alcohol-related effects from two broad perspectives: (1) diagnosis and surveillance and (2) prevention and treatment. The report examines fundamental concepts for setting diagnostic criteria in general, reviews and updates the diagnostic criteria for fetal alcohol syndrome and related conditions, explores research findings and problems associated with epidemiology and surveillance, and describes an integrated multidisciplinary approach to research on prevention and treatment.

From Generation to Generation: The Health and Well-Being of Children in Immigrant Families (1998)
Committee on the Health and Adjustment of Immigrant Children and Families

From Generation to Generation explores what is known about the development of children and youth from numerous countries of origin. Describing the status of immigrant children and youth as "severely understudied," the report both draws on and supplements existing research to characterize the current status and outlook of immigrant children. The report also makes recommendations for improved research and data collection designed to advance knowledge about these children and, as a result, their visibility in current policy debates.

Growing Up Tobacco Free: Preventing Nicotine Addiction in Children and Youths (1994)
Committee on Preventing Nicotine Addiction in Children and Youths

Growing Up Tobacco Free explains nicotine's effects and the process of addiction and documents the search for an effective approach to preventing the use of cigarettes, chewing and spitting tobacco, and snuff by children and youths. The report examines the results of recent initiatives to limit young people's access to tobacco and discusses approaches to controls or bans on tobacco sales, price sensitivity among adolescents, and arguments for and against taxation as a prevention strategy for tobacco use.

How People Learn: Brain, Mind, Experience, and School (1999)
Committee on Developments in the Science of Learning

How People Learn examines the evidence from many branches of science that has significantly added to the understanding of what it means to know—from the neural processes that occur during learning to the influence of culture on what people see and absorb—and that calls into question concepts and practices firmly entrenched in the current U.S. education system. This report addresses the implications of this evidence for what we teach, how we teach it, and how we assess what children learn.

Improving Schooling for Language-Minority Children: A Research Agenda (1997)
Committee on Developing a Research Agenda on the Education of Limited-English-Proficient and Bilingual Students

This comprehensive volume provides perspective on the history of bilingual education in the United States; summarizes research on development of a second language, literacy, and content knowledge; reviews evaluation studies; explores what is known about effective schools and classrooms for these children; examines research on the education of teachers of culturally and linguistically diverse students; critically reviews the system for the collection of education statistics as it relates to this student population; and recommends changes in the infrastructure that supports research on these students.

Improving Student Learning: A Strategic Plan for Education Research and Its Utilization (1999)
Committee on a Feasibility Study for a Strategic Education Research Program

Improving Student Learning offers a long-range proposal for meeting the challenges of educating the nation's children. The report presents a strategic education research program that focuses on four key questions: How can advances in research on learning be incorporated into educational practice? How can student motivation to achieve in school be increased? How can schools become organizations capable of continuous improvement? How can the use of research knowledge be increased in schools?

Learning from Experience: Evaluating Early Childhood Demonstration Programs (1982)
Panel on Outcome Measurement in Early Childhood Demonstration Programs

In response to a widely perceived need to review and reshape the evaluation of demonstration programs that offer educational, diagnostic, and other services to young children and their families, this report examines the objective of contemporary demonstration programs; appraises the measures currently available for assessing the achievement of those objectives, particularly in light of their relevance for public policy; and recommends new approaches to evaluation and outcome measurement.

Measuring Lead Exposure in Infants, Children, and Other Sensitive Populations (1993)
Committee on Measuring Lead in Critical Populations

Because of growing evidence of lead toxicity at lower concentrations, the U.S. Centers for Disease Control and Prevention lowered its lead-exposure guideline to 10 µg/dl lead in blood from 25 µg/dl. *Measuring Lead Exposure in Infants, Children, and Other Sensitive Populations* addresses the public health concern about the logistics and feasibility of lead screening in infants and children at such low concentrations. This report presents guidelines for U.S. Public Health Service activities and state and local programs in monitoring lead.

Nutrition During Lactation (1991)
Committee on Nutritional Status During Pregnancy and Lactation

Nutrition During Lactation presents relevant data and points out specific directions for needed research in understanding the relationship between the nutrition of healthy mothers and the outcomes of lactation.

Nutrition During Pregnancy: Part I: Weight Gain; Part II: Nutrient Supplements (1990)
Committee on Nutritional Status During Pregnancy and Lactation

Part I of *Nutrition During Pregnancy* explores the issue of weight gain during pregnancy, places this in the context of the health of the infant and the mother, and calls for revisions in recommended weight gains for pregnant women. The report also presents specific target ranges for weight gain during pregnancy and guidelines for proper measurement. Part II examines the adequacy of diet in meeting nutrient needs during pregnancy, recommends specific amounts of vitamin and mineral supplements for special circumstances, and presents recommendations for research.

Nutrition Services in Perinatal Care (1992)
Committee on Nutritional Status During Pregnancy and Lactation

This book focuses on nutrition services beginning in the preconception period and extending well beyond birth. It provides the rationale for recommended nutritional services; briefly describes the necessary elements of these services; and indicates the personnel, knowledge, skills, and specialized education or training that may be needed to deliver them.

Pesticides in the Diets of Infants and Children (1993)
Committee on Pesticides in the Diets of Infants and Children

Pesticides in the Diets of Infants and Children explores whether regulations controlling pesticide use adequately protect infants and children, who may differ from adults in susceptibility and in dietary exposures to pesticide residues. The report covers the issues of susceptibility, exposure, toxicity, and assessing risk.

Placing Children in Special Education: A Strategy for Equity (1982)
Panel on Selection and Placement of Students in Programs for the Mentally Retarded, Committee on Child Development Research and Public Policy

This report addresses the issue of the overrepresentation of minorities and males in special education classes. From a thorough analysis of the data, this report concludes that there is a disproportion of nonwhite minorities and males in special education classes, and specifically in classes for educable, mentally retarded children. *Placing Children in Special Education* looks at the potentially problematic conditions underlying disproportion and makes recommendations that address the validity of referral and assessment procedures and the quality of instruction received in all classrooms.

Prenatal Care: Reaching Mothers, Reaching Infants (1988)
Committee to Study Outreach for Prenatal Care

This report addresses the issue of why over one-fourth of all pregnant women in the United States do not begin prenatal care in the first 3 months of pregnancy, despite the existence of successful prenatal programs. *Prenatal Care* presents findings from a review of 30 prenatal care programs and analysis of surveys of mothers who did not seek prenatal care and offers specific recommendations for improving the nation's maternity system and increasing the use of prenatal care programs.

Preventing Low Birthweight (1985)
Committee to Study the Prevention of Low Birthweight

Despite declines in infant mortality, the rates of low-birthweight deliveries in the United States continue to be high. *Preventing Low Birthweight* defines the significance of the problems, presents data on risk factors and etiology, and reviews state and national trends in the incidence of low birthweight among various groups. This report also describes the preventive approaches found most desirable, considers their costs, and discusses research needs.

Preventing Reading Difficulties in Young Children (1998)
Committee on the Prevention of Reading Difficulties in Young Children

Preventing Reading Difficulties in Young Children examines factors that put children at risk of poor reading. It explores in detail how literacy can be fostered from birth through kindergarten and the primary grades, including evaluation of philosophies, systems, and materials commonly used to teach reading. The report makes recommendations that address the identification of groups of children at risk, effective instruction for the preschool and early grades, effective approaches to dialects and bilingualism, the importance of these findings for the professional development of teachers, and gaps that remain in the understanding of how children learn to read.

Prevention of Micronutrient Deficiencies: Tools for Policymakers and Public Health Workers (1998)
Committee on Micronutrient Deficiencies

This report examines key elements in the design and implementation of interventions designed to prevent micronutrient deficiencies. It also provides a conceptual framework that will allow funders to tailor programs to existing regional and country capabilities and to incorporate within these programs the capacity to address multiple prevention strategies and multiple micronutrient deficiencies. *Prevention of Micronutrient Deficiencies* also contains three background papers that address the prevention of deficiencies of iron, vitamin A, and iodine.

Reducing the Odds: Preventing Perinatal Transmission of HIV in the United States (1999)
Committee on Perinatal Transmission of HIV

The report evaluates the extent to which state efforts have been effective in reducing the transmission of HIV from pregnant mother to unborn child. *Reducing the Odds* recommends that HIV testing be a routine part of prenatal care and that health care providers notify women that this is part of the usual array of prenatal tests and that they have an opportunity to refuse the HIV test. This approach could help both reduce the number of pediatric AIDS cases and improve treatment for mothers with AIDS.

Risking the Future: Adolescent Sexuality, Pregnancy, and Childbearing (1987)
Panel on Adolescent Pregnancy and Childbearing
   Risking the Future reviews in detail the trends in and consequences of teenage sexual behavior and offers thoughtful insights on the issues of sexual initiation, contraception, pregnancy, abortion, adoption, and the well-being of adolescent families. The report provides a systematic assessment of the impact of various programmatic approaches, both preventive and ameliorative, in light of the growing scientific understanding of the topic.

Schools and Health: Our Nation's Investment (1997)
Committee on Comprehensive School Health Programs in Grades K-12
   This report reviews information on Comprehensive School Health Programs for children in grades K-12, explores the needs of today's students, and examines how those needs can be met through program design and development. *Schools and Health* also gives broad recommendations for the programs, with suggestions and guidelines for national, state, and local actions.

Starting Out Right: A Guide to Promoting Children's Reading Success (1999)
Committee on the Prevention of Reading Difficulties in Young Children
   Based on the extensive research synthesized in *Preventing Reading Difficulties in Young Children*, this book identifies the most important questions and explores the authoritative answers on the topic of how children can grow into readers. Included are 55 activities to do with children to help them become successful readers, a list of recommended children's books, and a guide to CD-ROMs and websites.

The Best Intentions: Unintended Pregnancy and the Well-Being of Children and Families (1995)
Committee on Unintended Pregnancy
   The Best Intentions offers frank discussion, synthesis of data, and policy recommendations on family planning issues and sheds light on the questions and controversies surrounding unintended pregnancy. The report considers the effectiveness of over 20 pregnancy prevention programs and offers specific recommendations to put the United States on a par with other developed nations in terms of contraceptive attitudes and policies. In addition, it summarizes the health and social consequences of unintended pregnancies for men, women, and the children they bear and examines the variety of reasons unintended pregnancies occur.

The Children's Vaccine Initiative: Achieving the Vision (1993)
Committee on the Children's Vaccine Initiative: Planning Alternative Strategies

This report contains information on the nature and status of vaccine development and production efforts in the United States and abroad and recommends ways to enhance participation in the International Children's Vaccine Initiative.

Understanding Child Abuse and Neglect (1993)
Panel on Research on Child Abuse and Neglect

Understanding Child Abuse and Neglect provides a comprehensive, integrated, child-oriented research agenda on child abuse and neglect. The report presents an overview of three major areas that impact child abuse and neglect research, namely, definitions and scope; etiology, consequences, treatment, and prevention; and infrastructure and ethics.

Violence in Families: Assessing Prevention and Treatment Programs (1998)
Committee on the Assessment of Family Violence Interventions

Violence in Families examines the successes and failures of family violence interventions used in three institutional sectors (social services, health, and law enforcement) to combat maltreatment of children, domestic violence, and abuse of the elderly. The report discusses how to measure program effectiveness and offers recommendations to guide services, programs, policy, and research on victim support and assistance, treatments and penalties for offenders, and law enforcement. Also included in *Violence in Families* is an analysis of more than 100 evaluation studies on the outcomes of different kinds of programs and services.

Who Cares for America's Children? (1990)
Panel on Child Care Policy

Who Cares for America's Children? explores the critical need for a more coherent policy on child care, offers recommendations for the actions needed to develop such a policy, evaluates the factors in child care that are most important to children's development, and examines ways of protecting children's physical well-being and fostering their development in child care settings.

WIC Nutrition Risk Criteria: A Scientific Assessment (1996)
Committee on Scientific Evaluation of WIC Nutrition Risk Criteria

This report reviews the scientific basis for nutrition risk criteria used to establish eligibility for participation in the U.S. Department of Agriculture's Special Supplemental Nutrition Program for Women, Infants, and Children (WIC). *WIC Nutrition Risk Criteria* also examines the specific segments of the WIC population at risk for each criterion, identifies gaps in the scientific knowledge base, formulates recommendations regarding appropriate criteria, and when applicable, recommends values for determining who is at risk for each criterion. In addition, the report makes recommendations for program action and research to strengthen the validity of nutrition risk criteria used in the WIC program.

Work and Family: Policies for a Changing Work Force (1991)
Panel on Employer Policies and Working Families

This report examines the changes in work and family structures that coincide with the dramatic increase in the number of dual-earner and single-adult families. It also discusses the effects of these changes on worker productivity and employer practices, and presents a wide range of approaches to easing the conflicts between work and family by exploring appropriate roles for business, labor, and government. Work and Family describes the advantages and disadvantages of being part of a working family and takes a critical look at the range of benefits provided, including existing and proposed employer programs for families.

B
Defining and
Estimating Causal
Effects

What is a causal effect? Many discussions of causal inference and research design neglect to confront this issue. However, a theory that has come to dominate modern thinking in statistics about cause begins with this fundamental question. Pioneered by Rubin (1976) and Rosenbaum and Rubin (1983) and elaborated by Holland (1986), this theory has come to be known as the Rubin-Rosenbaum-Holland (RRH) theory of causal inference, although its roots can be traced to much earlier work on experimentation (e.g., Fisher, 1918; Cochran, 1965). To describe this theory, the simplest case will suffice: we have a causal variable (the treatment) with two possible values (experimental and control). For clarity, let us consider a case in which a child will receive either the new experimental approach to day care (call it E) or the currently available approach (call it C) and the outcome will be a measure of self-regulation. If the child were to receive E, the child would experience the outcome under E. However, if the child were to receive C, that same child would experience the outcome under C. The causal effect of the experimental treatment (relative to the control) is defined by a comparison between how that child would fare under E versus C. For example, we might define this treatment effect for that child as

Treatment effect = (Outcome under E) minus (Outcome under C),

that is the difference between the outcome a child would receive if assigned to treatment E and the outcome that same child would receive if assigned to treatment C.[1] These are called potential outcomes. Children are viewed, then, as having potential outcomes, only some of which will ever be realized. Several conclusions follow from this definition.

First, the causal effect is defined uniquely for each child. The impact of the treatment can thus vary from child to child. Modern thinking about cause thus rejects the conventional assumption that a new treatment adds a constant effect for every child. This assumption, never realistic to scientists or practitioners, was historically made to simplify statistical analysis.

Second, the causal effect cannot be observed. If a given child is assigned to E, we will observe the outcome under E but not the outcome under C for that child. But if the child is assigned to C, we will observe the outcome under C but not the outcome under E. Holland (1986) refers to the fact that only one of two potential outcomes can be observed as the fundamental problem of causal inference.

Third, although a given child will ultimately receive only one treatment, say, treatment E, it must be reasonable at least to imagine a scenario in which that child could have received C. And similarly, even though another child received C, it must be reasonable to imagine a scenario in which that child had received E. If it is not possible to conceive of each child's response under each treatment, then it is not possible to define a causal effect. There must, then, be a road not taken that could have been taken, for each child. Thus, both the outcome under E and the outcome under C must exist in principle even if both cannot be observed in practice. Therefore, in current thinking about cause in statistical science, a fixed attribute of a child (say sex or ethnic background) cannot typically be a cause. We cannot realistically imagine how a girl would have responded if she had been a boy or how a black child would have responded if that child had been white. Epidemiologists referred to such attributes as fixed markers (Kraemer et al., 1997), unchangeable attributes that are statistically related to an outcome but do not cause the outcome.

This theory of causation provides new insights into why randomized experiments are valuable. It also provides a framework for how to think about the problem of causal inference when randomized experiments are not possible.

According to the RRH theory, the problem of causal inference is a problem of missing data. If both potential outcomes were observable, the causal effect could be directly calculated for each participant. But one of the potential outcomes is inevitably missing. If the data were missing completely at random, we could compute an unbiased estimate of the average

---

[1]The causal effect could also be defined as the ratio $Y_i(E)/Y_i(C)$, depending on the scale of Y, but we limit this discussion to causal effects as differences for simplicity.

causal effect for any subgroup. A randomized experiment ensures just that: that the missing datum is missing completely at random, ensuring unbiased estimation of the average treatment effect.

Suppose, by contrast, that E or C could be selected by each child's parents. Suppose further that more-advantaged parents tended to choose E while the less-advantaged parents tended to chose C. Then the potential outcomes would be nonrandomly missing. The outcome under E would come to be observed more often for advantaged than for disadvantaged children. Selection bias is thus a problem of nonrandomly missing data.

Even more insidiously, suppose that some parents had previous knowledge about how well their child is likely to fare under the new day care program. For example, one parent might know that, without the new program, her child will be cared for by the paternal grandmother, who is known to be a master teacher of young children. Thus, this parent decides not to participate in the new day care program, knowing that the child will probably do better without it. Other parents who know their families do not include talented teachers with time to care for their child choose the new program. Such information is rarely available to researchers, yet it produces nonrandomly missing data.

We view the probability of assignment to E to be the propensity to receive the experimental treatment or simply "the propensity score" (Rosenbaum and Rubin, 1983). Under random assignment to treatments, the propensity score is independent of the potential outcomes. In the hypothetical case above, by contrast, family advantage is related to both the propensity score and to the potential outcomes. This creates a correlation between the propensity and the potential outcomes. Now suppose that it is impossible to conduct a randomized experiment but it is possible to determine exactly how family circumstances translates into propensity—that is, how families get selected into the treatment. We could then implement a statistical procedure:

- For every possible participant, predict the propensity of being in the experimental group.
- Divide all sample members into subgroups having the same propensity.
- Within each subgroup, compute the mean difference between those in E and C as the average treatment effect for that group.[2]

---

[2]In a variant of this procedure devised by Robins, Greenland, and Hu (1999), sample weights are computed that are inversely proportional to the propensity of receiving the treatment actually received. Experimental and control groups are then compared with respect to their weighted means. This procedure minimizes the influence of persons with the strongest propensity to receive the treatment they received and eliminates bias in estimating treatment effects when the propensity is accurately predicted. The method has especially useful applications when the treatments are time-varying.

- Average these treatment effects across all subgroups to estimate the overall average treatment effect.

The resulting estimate will be an unbiased estimate of the average treatment effect. Every comparison between those in E and those in C involves subsets of children having identical propensities to experience E. Therefore, the potential outcomes of the children compared cannot be associated with their propensities, and the estimates of the treatment effect will be unbiased. This procedure also makes it easy to estimate separate treatment effects for each subgroup.

When children are matched on propensity scores, the validity of the causal estimate depends strongly on the investigator's knowledge of the factors that affect the propensity to experience E versus C. More specifically, if some unknown characteristic of the child predicts the propensity to be in E versus C, and if that characteristic also is associated with the potential outcomes, then the estimate of the treatment effect based on propensity score matching will be biased. The assumption that no such confounding variable exists is a strong assumption. It is the responsibility of the investigator to collect the relevant background data and to provide sound arguments based on theory and data analysis that the relevant predictors of propensity have been controlled. Even then, doubts will remain in the minds of some readers. In contrast, all possible predictors of propensity are controlled in a randomized experiment, including those that would have escaped the attention of the most thoughtful investigator. Rosenbaum (1995) describes procedures for examining the sensitivity of causal inferences to lack of knowledge about propensity when randomization is impossible.

Perhaps the most common strategy for approximating unbiased causal inference in nonexperimental settings is the use of statistical adjustments. In early childhood research, it is very common to use linear models (regression, analysis of variance, structural equation models) to adjust estimates of treatment impact for covariates related to the outcome. These covariates must be pretreatment characteristics of the child or the setting, and the aim is to include all confounders in the set of covariates controlled. By statistically "holding constant" the confounders in assessing treatment impact, one aims to approximate a randomized experiment. Under some assumptions, this strategy will work. In particular, if the propensity score (the probability of receiving treatment E) is a linear function of the covariates used in the model, then this adjustment strategy will provide an unbiased estimate of the treatment effect. Aside from the possible fragility of this assumption, this strategy is limited, in that only a relatively small set of covariates may be included in the model. In a propensity score matching procedure mentioned earlier, it is possible—and advisable—to use as many possible covariates as one can obtain in the analysis that predicts propensity.

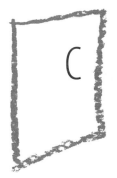

Technologies for Studying the Developing Human Brain

C

NEUROPSYCHOLOGICAL TOOLS

The strategy behind the use of neuropsychological tools is to generate a hypothesis about which area of the brain is involved in a particular behavior and then employ a behavioral test (or tests) to evaluate this hypothesis. Ideally one is able to dissociate one behavior from another (e.g., explicit from implicit memory) using a cluster of tasks or by applying such tasks to both normative and clinical populations.

In terms of elucidating brain-behavior relations in normative samples, neuropsychological tools are frequently adopted that have first been used in animal models or in clinical populations of humans. For example, if one is interested in the type of memory subserved by the medial temporal lobe (i.e., episodic memory), one might employ tasks that have been demonstrated in monkeys or in humans in whom the hippocampus has been lesioned through surgery or through injury to result in memory impairments.

The use of neuropsychological tools has received extensive study in the developing human. For example, Diamond has employed the Piagetian A-not-B task and its animal analogue, the delayed response task, to study the development of certain functions subserved by the prefrontal cortex (e.g., spatial working memory; see Diamond, 1990; Diamond and Doar, 1989; Diamond and Goldman-Rakic, 1989; Diamond et al., 1989). And Bachevalier (with respect to the monkey) and Nelson (with respect to the human) have utilized a set of tools (e.g., visual paired comparison; the "oddball" paradigm using event-related potentials) to study the development of explicit memory (see Bachevalier, 1992; Bachevalier et al., 1991, 1993; Nelson, C.A., 1994, 1995, 1996). Finally, Luciana and colleagues (e.g., Luciana and Nelson, 1998) have used an extensive battery of tasks to examine a range of cognitive behaviors.

The use of neuropsychological tools have several advantages over the other approaches discussed below: (a) they are completely noninvasive, (b) they can be used across the lifespan, (c) parallel studies can be conducted across species, and (d) they can provide insight into specific behaviors. The neuropsychological approach also has shortcomings: (a) these tools only indirectly couple brain structure and function (i.e., because no direct measures of the brain are taken) and thus may lack precision with regard to this relation; (b) when adopting such tools from the animal literature, it is important to consider whether both species are responding to the tasks the same way; (c) caution must be exercised when generalizing from clinical to normative samples; and (d) when used with the lesion method (i.e., the population under study has experienced a lesion to a particular part of the brain), it is important to be aware that the mapping of specific lesion to specific function may be less than one to one (i.e., a lesion in a particular area could affect the function of surrounding areas as well).

METABOLIC PROCEDURES

This class of tools depends on the ability to track various metabolic functions as they occur in real time. These include positron emission tomography and functional magnetic resonance imaging, each of which is described below.

Positron Emission Tomography

Positron emission tomography (PET) scanning typically involves the injection of a natural substance such as oxygen or glucose that has been made radioactive. In so doing one is able to track the metabolism of this substance by those regions of the brain calling for its use. Positrons are emitted as the radioactive substance decays, and these positrons can be measured using a positron detector (i.e., PET scanner). The detector, in turn, computes the point of origin of these positrons, and thus localizes in the brain (within centimeters of resolution) the source of neural activity.

A good example of this work comes from studies conducted by Chugani and his colleagues. Here a form of radioactive glucose (FDG) has been used in infants and children to infer the development of synapses (i.e., synapse formation requires energy and thus glucose can be used as an indirect marker for synaptogenesis; see Chugani, 1994; Chugani and Phelps, 1986;

Chugani et al., 1987). The participants in these studies are typically studied under resting conditions (sometimes under sedation); that is, no task is being performed.

A number of shortcomings with PET must be acknowledged. First, although the levels of radioactivity used in this work are relatively low, ethical constraints prevent samples of normally developing children from being evaluated; thus, currently all participants in this work require medical cause for doing the scan. Second, the spatial resolution of PET is typically confined to relatively large voxels (cubic centimeters of tissue), and thus it is difficult to pinpoint the locus of neural activity much beyond the centimeter range. Third, PET suffers from poor temporal resolution (i.e., on the order of minutes), and thus little useful information can be obtained about when brain activity is taking place. Finally, because a cyclotron is required to make the radioactive agents, PET studies are an expensive endeavor.

Functional Magnetic Resonance Imaging

Functional magnetic resonance imaging (fMRI) is a rapidly expanding technology that is increasingly finding a home in studies of development. The technique is based on the concept that deoxygenated hemoglobin is paramagnetic (paramagnetism refers to the ability of a normally nonmagnetic material to become magnetic) and thus can be detected using conventional magnetic resonance technology. When a particular part of the brain is called on to perform some task, that region receives increased blood flow and, as a by-product, increased oxygen. Increases and decreases in oxygen (generally on the order of 2 to 5 percent relative to background) are then monitored. By taking consecutive slices of the brain in various orientations, the MRI scanner is able to reconstruct where in the brain the greatest areas of activation occur.

Over the past 10 years, there have been hundreds of studies using fMRI in the adult human. Increasingly, however, developmental investigators have begun to utilize this technique with children. For example, Casey and colleagues (e.g., Casey et al., 1995; Thomas et al., 1999), as well as Nelson and colleagues (e.g., Nelson et al., 2000) have used fMRI to study the development of working memory in normally developing children as young as 6 years.

There are multiple advantages to fMRI. For example, it is completely noninvasive, does not require exposure to ionizing radiation, and can be performed in a relatively short period of time. Critically, the spatial resolution of fMRI is comparable to conventional MRI and thus can provide detailed anatomic images along the lines of a few millimeters. There are also a number of limitations that must be acknowledged. For example, participants must sit very still so as to keep motion artifacts to a minimum.

In addition, they must be able to tolerate a somewhat high (e.g., 90 dB) level of noise and a confining environment.

In summary, both PET and, in particular, fMRI lend themselves to the study of developing brain function. Unfortunately, neither PET nor fMRI provides much useful information about the chronometry of mental events.

D | Biographical Sketches

Jack P. Shonkoff (*Chair*) is dean of the Heller Graduate School and Samuel F. and Rose B. Gingold professor of human development at Brandeis University. He is an academic pediatrician whose work focuses on early childhood health and development and the interactions among research, policy, and practice. For the National Academies, he has served as chair of the Board on Children, Youth, and Families and as a member of the Panel on Child Care Policy, the Steering Group for the National Forum on the Future of Children and Families, the Committee on the Assessment of Family Violence Interventions, and the Roundtable on Head Start Research. He serves as a member of the scientific core group of the John D. and Catherine T. MacArthur Foundation and the James S. McDonnell Foundation Research Network on Early Experience and Brain Development and serves on the board of ZERO TO THREE. He was elected to the Institute of Medicine in 1999 and is a member of the American Pediatric Society. Other honors include a Kellogg national fellowship, a fellowship from the National Center for Clinical Infant Programs, and the distinguished contribution to child advocacy award from the Division of Child, Youth, and Family Services of the American Psychological Association. He has an M.D. from New York University School of Medicine.

Deborah L. Coates is professor of psychology at the City University of New York. Prior to assuming this position, she was director of the Institute for Healthier Babies of the March of Dimes Birth Defects Foundation and associate professor of psychology at Catholic University. Her research interests are the development of minority children and adolescents, mother-child interaction and its role in later school achievement, and the delivery of prenatal and postnatal health services to low-income and minority women and infants. She has received a number of research grants from the federal government and foundations, including the National Institute for Child Health and Human Development, the Public Health Service, the Rockefeller Foundation, and the Foundation for Child Development. She also serves on a number of national committees and acts as a consultant to various programs and projects focused on promoting the health and welfare of black children and families. She is a recipient of the American Psychological Association's minority achievement award for her work on clinical services to minority populations. She has a Ph.D. in psychology from Columbia University.

Greg Duncan is professor of education and social policy and faculty associate in the Institute for Policy Research at Northwestern University. He received a Ph.D. in economics from the University of Michigan in 1974 and has spent much of his career there working on the Panel Study of Income Dynamics data collection project. He is a member of National Institute of Child Health and Human Development's Family and Child Well-Being Research Network and the MacArthur Foundation Networks on Successful Pathways Through Middle Childhood and Family and the Economy. He directs the Northwestern University/University of Chicago Joint Center for Poverty Research.

Felton J. Earls is professor of psychiatry at the Harvard Medical School and director of the Project on Human Development in Chicago Neighborhoods at the Harvard University School of Public Health. He has published studies on behavioral problems in preschool children, risk factors for violence and HIV infection in adolescents and young adults, and international aspects of child and adolescent mental health. He was elected to the Institute of Medicine in 1995 and has served on several National Academies panels, including Understanding and Control of Violent Behavior and the 1998 Frontiers of Research on Children, Youth, and Families Symposium. He has an M.D. from Howard University.

Robert N. Emde is professor of psychiatry at the University of Colorado, adjunct professor of psychology at the University of Denver, and visiting professor at University College London. His research has focused on early socioemotional development and, most recently, on evaluating early childhood intervention programs. He has served as president of the Society for Research in Child Development and of the World Association for Infant Psychiatry and Allied Disciplines (now the World Association of Infant Mental Health). He has also served as editor of the *Monographs of the*

Society for Research in Child Development and associate editor of *Psychiatry* and the *Journal of the American Psychoanalytic Association.* He has an M.D. from Columbia University College of Physicians and Surgeons.

Yolanda Garcia is director of children's services in the Office of Education of Santa Clara County, California. Her office coordinates several government-funded programs, including Head Start, Parkway Child Development Center, and State Preschool, and she manages programs for approximately 3,300 children 2 to 5 years old. She has been recognized on both the state and national levels for developing innovative approaches to the challenging needs of children and families. She has M.A. degrees in social services administration with an emphasis in child welfare and public policy from the University of Chicago and in education administration from San Jose State University.

Susan Gelman is Frederick G. L. Huetwell professor of psychology at the University of Michigan, Ann Arbor. Her principal areas of research are cognitive development, language acquisition, and relationships between language and thought, and she is currently researching theory-based constructs underlying children's explanations in specific knowledge domains. In 1991 she received the distinguished scientific award from the American Psychological Association for early career contribution to psychology. She has also received a J.S. Guggenheim fellowship, the Boyd McCandless young scientist award from the American Psychological Association, and the American Psychological Foundation Robert L. Fantz award. She was elected a fellow of the American Psychological Society and is on the editorial board of several journals. She has a Ph.D. in psychology from Stanford University.

Susan J. Goldin-Meadow is professor in the Department of Psychology and has just served as chair of human development at the University of Chicago. Her research concerns language development in deaf children, and she has also done extensive work exploring the role that gesture plays in communication and thinking in hearing children. Her research has been continuously supported by the National Science Foundation, the National Institutes of Health, the Spencer Foundation, and the March of Dimes Birth Defects Foundation. She has been an associate editor of *Developmental Psychology* and on the editorial board of *Applied Psycholinguistics.* She is a member-at-large for the section on linguistics and language science of the American Association for the Advancement of Science and a member of the board of advisors of the Piaget Society and has served on review panels for the National Science Foundation and the National Institutes of Health. She is a fellow of the American Psychological Society and was recently the recipient of a John Simon Guggenheim fellowship and a James McKeen

Cattell fellowship, which she will use to write a book on gesture and the insights it yields about the mind. She has a Ph.D. in psychology from the University of Pennsylvania.

William T. Greenough directs the Center for Advanced Study and is Swanlund professor of psychology, psychiatry, and cell and structural biology at the University of Illinois, Urbana Champaign. He is also a member of the neuronal pattern analysis group in the university's Beckman Institute. His fields of professional interest include neural mechanisms of learning and memory, life-span developmental psychobiology, and molecular and cellular substrates of fragile X mental retardation syndrome. He was elected to the National Academy of Sciences in 1992. He has received the distinguished scientific contribution award from the American Psychological Association and the William James Fellow award from the American Psychological Society. He previously served on the National Academies committee that produced the report *How People Learn.* He has a Ph.D. in psychology from the University of California, Los Angeles.

Ruth T. Gross is professor emerita of pediatrics at Stanford University. At Stanford, where she was director of general pediatrics, she established a training program in adolescent medicine and directed the general pediatrics academic development training program. She was active in several research activities and was the national study director of the multisite clinical trial, the Infant Health and Development Program. In 1979 she was elected to the Institute of Medicine and is a member of numerous academic societies. She has served as a member of the IOM council as well as a member of the Mental Health and Behavior Board, the Board on Health Promotion and Disease Prevention, and the Board on Children, Youth, and Families. She has an M.D. from Columbia University College of Physicians and Surgeons.

Megan Gunnar is distinguished McKnight University professor in the Institute of Child Development at the University of Minnesota. She is on the editorial board of *Child Development* and *Developmental Psychobiology* and is also a board member of ZERO TO THREE: The National Center for Infants, Toddlers, and Families. She is the recipient of a National Institute of Mental Health research scientist development award. She has a Ph.D. in developmental psychology from Stanford University.

Michael Guralnick is director of the Center on Human Development and Disability at the University of Washington, Seattle, where he is also professor in the Departments of Psychology and Pediatrics. His areas of interest are developmental disabilities, early childhood mainstreaming, peer relations, and social and language development. He is a fellow of the American Association on Mental Retardation, a member of the Society for Research in Child Development, and a fellow of the American Psychological Association. He has a Ph.D. in psychology from Lehigh University.

Alicia F. Lieberman is professor of psychology in the Department of Psychiatry at the University of California, San Francisco. In addition, she is director of the Child Trauma Research Project and senior psychologist at the Infant-Parent Program, San Francisco General Hospital, and clinical consultant with the San Francisco Department of Human Services. Her major interests include toddler development, disorders of attachment, child-parent interventions with high-risk families, and the effects of early trauma in the first years of life. Her current research involves a treatment outcome study of child-parent psychotherapy with preschoolers who have witnessed domestic violence. As a bilingual, bicultural Latina, she has a special interest in cultural issues involving child development, childrearing, and child mental health. She is a member of the board of directors of ZERO TO THREE: The National Center for Infants, Toddlers, and Families and on the board of *Parents* magazine. She is the author of *The Emotional Life of the Toddler,* which has been translated to five languages. She was born in Paraguay and has a B.A. from the Hebrew University of Jerusalem and a Ph.D. in psychology from Johns Hopkins University.

Betsy Lozoff is professor of pediatrics in the Department of Pediatrics and Communicable Diseases at the Medical School and director of the Center for Human Growth and Development, both at the University of Michigan. Her research, conducted primarily in Third World countries, focuses on iron deficiency anemia and infant behavior, using epidemiological, ethnographic, neurophysiological, and intervention methods. She is also interested in health and development of children who grow up in poverty in the United States. Her recent research seeks to relate behavioral changes to the effects of iron deficiency on the developing brain. Her research support has come primarily from National Institutes of Health and several foundations. She has served on several National Institute for Child Health and Human Development and National Institutes of Health review panels, as well as on the executive council of the Society for Behavioral Pediatrics. She is a fellow of the American Academy of Pediatrics. She has an M.D. from Case Western Reserve University School of Medicine.

Nancy Geyelin Margie *(Research Assistant)* is research assistant at the Board on Children, Youth, and Families. Prior to joining the staff of the board, she was a researcher and fundraiser for the Heartland Alliance for Human Needs and Human Rights in Chicago, and performed research for a book on the history of the Fels family of Philadelphia titled *The Philadelphia Fels, 1880-1920: A Social Portrait.* She has a B.A. in history from Haverford College.

Ruth Massinga is chief executive officer of the Casey Family Program, a private foundation dedicated to the support of children in foster care and adoption settings and the creation of strategic alliances to sustain families in community-based service settings. She is also on the board of trustees for the Seattle Children's Home. She was formerly a caseworker at Harlem Hospital in New York, acting director of the Blundon Group Home for Children in Baton Rouge, Louisiana, director of Berkeley Children's Services, and executive director of the Social Services Administration in Baltimore. She is the immediate past chair and current member of the board of directors of the Family Resource Coalition and on the board of advisors of the National Center for Children in Poverty. She was also on the National Academies Panel on Child Care Policy. She has an M.S. in social services from Boston University.

Deborah A. Phillips *(Study Director)* is currently associate professor and chair of the Department of Psychology at Georgetown University. Prior to this she served as study director to the Committee on Integrating the Science of Early Childhood Development and as the first director of the Board on Children, Youth, and Families. She is a developmental psychologist who works in the field of early development, child care, and public policy. She is a coprincipal investigator on the National Institute of Child Health and Human Development Study of Early Child Care. She served on the Task Force on Meeting the Needs of Young Children of the Carnegie Corporation of New York, which produced the *Starting Points* report. She is a fellow of the American Psychological Association and the American Psychological Society. She has a Ph.D. in developmental psychology from Yale University.

Stephen Raudenbush is professor of research design and statistics in the Department of Counseling, Educational Psychology and Special Education at Michigan State University. He is scientific director of the Project on Human Development in Chicago Neighborhoods and is a member of the human development and aging study section of the National Institutes of Health. He is associate editor for several journals, including the *Journal of Education and Behavioral Statistics,* the *Journal of Educational Measurement,* and *Educational Evaluation and Policy Analysis.* He has an Ed.D. in policy analysis and evaluation research from Harvard University.

Ross Thompson is Carl A. Happold distinguished professor of psychology at the University of Nebraska. His research concerns sociopersonality development, early emotional growth, and developmental science and public policy. He is currently associate editor of *Child Development* (the flagship journal of the Society for Research in Child Development), edits a series of specialized volumes in developmental psychology for McGraw-Hill, and has served on several National Institutes of Health review committees. His books include *Preventing Child Maltreatment Through Social Support: A Critical Analysis, Early Brain Development and Public Policy*, and *The Postdivorce Family: Research and Policy Perspectives* (coedited with Paul Amato). He has a Ph.D. from the University of Michigan.

Charles A. Nelson (Liaison) is distinguished McKnight University professor of child psychology, pediatrics, and neuroscience at the University of Minnesota. His research interests lie in developmental cognitive neuroscience, with particular interests in brain and memory development and in neural plasticity. He chairs the MacArthur Foundation/McDonnell Foundation Research Network on Early Experience and Brain Development, and with Floyd Bloom has coauthored the book *Brain, Mind, and Behavior*. He has a Ph.D. in child development from the University of Kansas.

Index

A

Abecedarian Project, 76, 350, 351, 361, 363, 364, 407

Abuse, *see* Child abuse and neglect

Access barriers, 66, 254, 367-368, 400, 535

  see also "cultural competence" under Interventions

ADHD, *see "disorders" under* Attention

Adolescents, 125, 134, 135, 161-162, 249, 253, 259

  brain development, 6 185, 187, 201, 205, 397

  citizenship, 352

  friends and peers, 163, 176, 180

  nonparental child care, 312-313

  self-regulation, 94, 104, 115, 116, 118

  socioeconomic status, 277-278, 279, 290-291, 328, 329-330, 332, 335, 336

  teen pregnancy, 8, 226-227, 274, 355, 542

  urban low-income areas, 328, 329-330, 332, 335, 336

Adoption and foster care, 225, 233, 250-251, 257, 258-260, 364

  abused children, 250, 255, 257-259

  cognitive development, 42, 146

  genetics research, 41-44, 45-48, 250, 286

  IQ and, 45-46

  language learning, 134, 146

  see also Orphans and orphanages

African-Americans, 61, 65, 179, 269, 272, 281, 286

  nonparental child care, 306

  single-parent families, 283, 290-291

  sleeping practices, 61

  urban low-income areas, 329, 331, 344

AIDS, 541

Aid to Families with Dependent Children, 35

Alcohol abuse, 291

  maternal depression, 251

  prenatal exposure, 197, 198, 200-203

Aggressiveness, *see* Violence and aggressiveness

P

U

V

W